ORGANIZATIONS
A Micro/Macro Approach

The Scott, Foresman Series in Management and Organizations
James F. Veiga and John N. Yanouzas, Series Editors

The Scott, Foresman Series in Management and Organizations
Lyman W. Porter and Joseph W. McGuire, Editors

ORGANIZATIONS
A Micro/Macro Approach

Richard L. Daft
Texas A & M University

Richard M. Steers
University of Oregon

Scott, Foresman and Company
Glenview, Illinois
London, England

To Our Families:
Kathy, Danielle, and Amy and Sheila and Kathleen.

Acknowledgments
Acknowledgments for illustrations and other copyrighted materials in this book appear on the page with the copyrighted material or in the Acknowledgments section beginning on p. 617, which is an extension of the copyright page.

Library of Congress Cataloging-in-Publication Data

Daft, Richard L.
  Organizations: a micro/macro approach.

  Includes bibliographies and index.
  1. Organization. 2. Management. I. Steers, Richard M. II. Title.
HD31.D137 1986   658   85-27864
ISBN 0-673-18220-7

Kurt Lewin once observed that there is nothing so practical as a good theory. Lee Iacocca has said that to succeed you have to get out of your chair and do something. We agree with both of these observations. To learn about organizations and their management, it is essential that students have a firm grasp of the conceptual models and theories that explain how organizations work. However, action based on this understanding should, in our minds, characterize the study of organizations and management as well.

The primary aim of this book is to present practical theories, theories that work and translate into action. In doing so, we present a picture of organizations that is useful to both present and future managers. Important theoretical concepts are explained in simple and clear terms. Each chapter uses from three to six **Up Close** illustrations to show how the theories translate into action. Moreover, each chapter ends with a major case that students can use to apply the knowledge learned in the chapter. These add enough of the practical to a conceptual book to encourage the action-oriented problem solving that characterizes the management of organizations.

Still another aim of this book is to present both the *micro* and *macro* perspectives in the study of organizations. Most organizational behavior texts are concerned with the micro view, but we believe the macro perspective on organizations is equally valuable. Theories and applications for the organization as a whole have as much relevance for a student's preparation for management as do the theories and applications about people within organizations. This book was written for those combined courses and for instructors who choose a menu balanced between micro and macro organizational topics in the organizational behavior course.

In Part I, organizations are defined, and the important building blocks of individual, group, and management are integrated into the organizing framework for the book. Part II covers micro topics such as motivation, perception, individual differences, and group processes. Part III introduces macro topics such as organization design, technology, bureaucracy, and the external environment. Part IV integrates both the micro and macro levels of analysis, examining organizational processes such as leadership, conflict, communications, power, and organizational change. These topics are considered from both a micro and a macro perspective, an approach that affords a better understanding of the interaction of micro and macro variables in influencing organizational dynamics. A major feature is the equal emphasis given to micro and macro topics and the integration of these two perspectives to explain organizational processes.

The student will also learn what practicing managers can do to influence organizational dynamics to facilitate organizational effectiveness. From the first chapter, positive organizational outcomes are stressed. Emphasis on the practical—practical examples, lessons from real management situations—sets this book apart from others in the field.

As with any major project, this book was made possible by the coordinated efforts of many people. To begin with, we appreciate the detailed comments on the manuscript of Gib Akin, University of Virginia; Eileen A. Hogan, University of Virginia; Jeff Kaiser, Marquette University; Lyman Porter, University of California-Irvine; Timothy M. Stearns, University of Wisconsin-Madison; and Eric J. Walton, New York University. Their suggestions and ideas significantly improved the quality of the final text. In addition, John Nolan and Trisha Nealon of Scott, Foresman were most helpful in assisting in the developmental work on the manuscript and helping design and shape the finished product. Marisa L. L'Heureux's assistance is also appreciated.

We also wish to acknowledge and express our appreciation to Phyllis Washburn and Dorothy Wynkoop for their heroic assistance in typing this manuscript and in other ways preparing it for publication. We are truly grateful for their help.

Our appreciation also goes to Lyle Schoenfeldt, Department Head, and William Mobley, Dean of the College of Business at Texas A&M, and to James Reinmuth, Dean of the College of Business Administration at the University of Oregon. They provided resources and other support so important to this project. We also thank our many colleagues at Texas A&M and the University of Oregon for creating a positive intellectual climate that encouraged our personal development and motivated our writing.

And, finally, this book could not have been completed without the wonderful support and understanding of our wives and children. Book writing can be hard on families, but our wives and children responded with grace and generosity. We owe a very special debt of gratitude to Kathy, Danielle, and Amy and to Sheila and Kathleen, to whom this book is gratefully dedicated.

R.L.D.
R.M.S.

CONTENTS

P A R T III   Organizations: The Macro Perspective

PART IV Organizational Processes:
A Synthesis of Micro and Macro Perspectives

13 Leadership 402

14 Decision Making 436

15 Power and Politics 475

16 Intergroup Relations and Conflict 497

18 Innovation and Change 566

ORGANIZATIONS
A Micro/Macro Approach

PART

I

Overview: The Plan of the Book

Part I, Chapter 1, *Introduction to Organizations*, begins with the focus researchers and managers must take to understand organizations. Three levels of analysis are presented—the psychology of individuals, the composition and performance of work groups, and the structure and design of the organization as a whole. This section presents a model for organizational dynamics based on the building blocks of organizations. The role of management in making things work, problems facing management due to changes and challenges of the external environment, and methods of research for the field are given as basic to our study. The major demarcation in this research is between the individual and the organizational levels of analysis. These have come to be called the micro and macro perspectives, and they are the organizing framework for this book.

1 Introduction to Organizations

The year 1981 was the worst year in memory in the U.S. airline industry. The country was experiencing a deep recession, the air traffic controllers' strike occurred, and a series of airline price wars often meant flying passengers at a substantial loss. Industry-wide operating losses for the year were over $300 million. Laker's Skytrain went bankrupt, and Braniff was about to go bankrupt. At the same time, in a dingy suite of offices in Newark Airport's dilapidated old North Terminal, People Express received its operating license to begin business as one of the new discount airlines born out of deregulation.

Although one could hardly imagine a less opportune time to begin a new airline, People Express prospered. In fact, by any standard of comparison, People Express today is a success. The company started flying in April 1981 with three used Boeing 737s, traveling from Newark to Buffalo, Columbus, and Norfolk. By June 1982, People had seventeen planes flying to thirteen cities, 1200 employees, and was beginning to show a profit. By the end of 1985, after only four years of full operation, People Express was expected to have 4000 employees and be the ninth largest carrier in the U.S.

What caused the phenomenal success of People Express? Certainly one reason is Donald Burr, who co-founded the airline with a unique philosophy: "The whole purpose of creating this enterprise in the first place was to create an environment which would enable and empower employees to release their creative energies."[1] Burr believes that employees count more than anything else in a successful company, and People Express lives by that philosophy.

Consider Candee Brock. She says working for People has changed her life. She saw an ad announcing great opportunities as a customer-service manager. Despite a mob of 12,000 applicants, she was hired. Today Candee checks bags for passengers leaving the north terminal. When she is not checking baggage, Candee is team manager for fifty-four people in the accounting department. She works hard—ten to twelve hours a day, five or six days a week. Candee owns 8400 shares of People Express stock, trading recently at about $19 a share. She is twenty-five.

People Express's philosophy includes cross-utilization, which means that an employee spends time in some line function outside his or her primary area of responsibility. This heightens the company's competitive edge and improves productivity. Bob McAdoo, the managing officer for finance, frequently serves *drinks aboard a flight. Every employee is required to own stock, and they all have a stake in the action. If they make People successful, they each can be worth several hundred thousand dollars by thirty years of age.*

"Most organizations frustrate people who really want to work," Burr says. "They control them, and watch them, and check up on them. Nobody trusts anybody, and you wind up with cops all over the place."[2] Managers at People Express work at developing cohesive work teams. Self management (an absence of supervisors) is the norm. Decision making is participative. Careful attention is paid to the selection of new employees: the "People Express type" is bright, educated, mature, articulate, and hard working.

A second reason for People's success is that the airline knew exactly what its goals were. To ensure that the company's objectives were not lost among the daily distractions of a rapidly growing business, the top management team met to write down the goals. The meeting was an intense debate. Burr wrote the goals on large sheets of paper and taped them to the walls. "They put their blood on those walls," he says. People Express's underlying principles crystallized into six precepts that guided employee recruitment and training, organization structure, and assignment of job duties. The six precepts are: 1) to promote service and commitment to growth of people; 2) to be the best provider of air transportation; 3) to maintain the highest quality management; 4) to be a role model for other airlines; 5) to maintain simplicity; and 6) to maximize profit. To attain these goals, the company placed primary emphasis on offering the lowest fares possible and convenient flight schedules.

To deliver on this strategy, People tore out the galleys to increase the number of seats from 90 to 118 on each of its second-hand 737s. The planes flew more hours per day—eleven hours on average, compared to seven for the industry. Ruthless cost cutting was critical. All tickets are sold on board the airplane (no ticket counters exist); the airline is not linked to the industry's computerized ticketing system. Customers make reservations by telephone directly to People. No hot meals are served and snacks must be purchased. Passengers are charged for checked luggage.

The unique action plan devised by People Express has paid off. Within two years of operation, the company achieved startling results:

- *Over 3 million passengers have chosen to fly People.*
- *Total costs per available seat-mile are the lowest in the industry (5.2 cents compared to a 9.4 cent industry average).*
- *Aircraft productivity has surpassed the industry average by 50%.*
- *Employee productivity is 145% above industry average.*
- *Return on revenues is 15.3% above industry average, second only to Southwest Airlines.*

The managers at People Express did something right, yet success did not come easily.

The first crisis occurred early in 1982 when Gerry Gitner, a co-founder and president, resigned. He clashed with Burr over the philosophy of the company.

Gitner's resignation meant the loss of his skills as a scheduler and master strategist. Nevertheless, other managers took up the slack and the momentum resumed.

Another crisis occurred when Burr negotiated with Lufthansa, the West German airline, to buy seventeen airplanes. A Dallas bank that promised to lend the money backed out. The strike of air traffic controllers cut flights by 35 percent. The company was bleeding, and it decided on desperate strategy which was to bypass Newark on some flights directly to South Florida. The company squeezed enough money to stay alive, found another bank to finance the new airplanes, and finally closed the deal with Lufthansa.

The most recent problem hit in 1985. People Express lost money in the last quarter of 1984 and the first quarter of 1985. Two fare hikes in 1985 narrowed the fare gap with major competitors. The Airline Pilots Association is attempting to organize People's non-union pilots. The major airlines, now mostly in the black, are taking People's cheap fares head on. When competitors dropped prices, more passengers chose the full service airlines.

As People grows, maintaining its free-form atmosphere may become harder. The undeniable need for larger numbers of employees, combined with an increasingly complex operation, may require a new tighter structure. Costs increase closer to the major airlines. Burr recognizes this, and says 1985 may be the time to pull back and consolidate.

But the immediate problem should not obscure one fact: People Express is one of the most successful enterprises in the history of business. Don Burr expects to hit a billion dollars in a couple of years. And Candee Brock won't be surprised. She still marvels at the wonder of it all. "I wasn't really looking for a job," she says. "That ad just seemed to say, 'Candee, this might be for you.'"[3]

This book is about contemporary organizations like People Express. The success and the problems at People Express illustrate organizations in action. The study of contemporary organizations can help people understand why organizations succeed. The study of organizations can also explain why companies such as Braniff Airlines and Air Florida fail. The case of People Express provides a nice introduction to the study of organizations because it illustrates the major concepts to be described in this book. People Express was organized around its employees, and employees are the topics of chapters two through seven. These topics include individual differences, attitudes, motivation, job design, and group behavior. Understanding people like Candee Brock and knowing how to motivate them helped Burr build the most successful airline ever.

Managing a successful company has other concerns in addition to employee concerns. At People, management had to recognize both the demand and opportunities in the external environment. It had to organize people to handle the workflow. Top managers carefully delineated major goals, or precepts, that served to guide managers and employees. People Express was given a structure that enabled everyone to be a manager. These issues pertain to the organization as a whole, and to the relationship of the organization with the environment. The concepts of the environment, size, production workflow, goals, and organization structure are the topics of chapters eight through twelve.

Finally, there were several intangible factors that made People Express soar. The leadership provided by Donald Burr produced a unified philosophy as well as a successful strategy. Top managers made critical decisions and were willing to take risks. Power was shared throughout the organization. Employees found ways to work through their conflicts for the good of everyone. Communication was superb, and control was minimal. Innovation and creativity were commonplace. These issues pertain to the day-to-day operating dynamics and processes within the organization. These day-to-day operating dynamics are the topics to be covered in chapters thirteen through eighteen.

Again, this book is about companies like People Express. This book will describe concepts that apply to People Express and to other organizations, such as Westinghouse, the Bank of America, Dresser Industries, Toyota, and Miller Brewing Company. Throughout our discussion, we will draw heavily on actual corporate examples to help answer the questions most asked about organizations by the people in them. The study of organizations applies concepts to all organizations regardless of size, product or service, profitability, or environment.

WHAT ARE ORGANIZATIONS?

What are organizations and why is it important to study them? Everyone has an intuitive sense of an organization. All of us have had reason to interact with organization employees, consume organizational products and services, and work for an organization. We have also seen physical outcomes from organizations, such as skyscrapers, jet aircraft, the nuclear power plants, or the Grand Coulee Dam that clearly could not have been developed or constructed without enormous human, intellectual, and financial resources. Most of us assume that these outcomes are produced by people working together in some way, which is essentially correct.

Definition

Organizations that build buildings, provide medical services, educate students, harvest grain, and produce television shows all have certain features in common. When we look across these different entities, we can define an organization as follows. An organization is: 1) a social entity, which 2) is goal-directed, 3) has a deliberately structured activity system and 4) an identifiable boundary.[4] Each of the four elements in this definition are important to our understanding of organizations because in each step the organization is distinguished from other entities. Here is how:

Social Entity   The building block of the organization is the human being. To exist, an organization requires more than one person, and most organizations are composed of many people and groups. Employees interact in patterned ways to perform the essential functions of the organization. Don Burr of People Express understood the importance of employees and designed the organization to gain fully their cooperation and commitment.

Goal-directed   An organization exists for an explicit purpose. It is an instrument in the sense that it is designed to achieve a goal. Should an organization lose its purpose, it would decline and eventually cease to exist. People join organizations for different purposes, and the organization's goal may differ from individual employee goals. But there must be one or more major goals for the organization. At People, organizational goals were reflected in the six precepts that included commitment to people and the aim to be the best provider of air transportation.

Deliberately Structured Activity System   *Deliberately structured* means that organizational tasks are subdivided into separate departments and activities. Managers direct and coordinate the separate activities. The organization has a hierarchy of authority, with defined responsibility and decision-making authority. The subdivisions are designed to achieve efficiencies in the work process. The hierarchy may be somewhat loose and informal, as in the case of People Express, or it may be rigid and formal, as in the case of many military organizations. *Activity systems* means that organizations have a specific task. An organization uses knowledge, technology, people, and machines to transform inputs into the outputs that are the products of the organization. Individuals within the organization undertake directed activities that mesh together to accomplish the overall task, or fulfill the purpose of the organization.

Identifiable Boundary   An organization is able to distinguish which employees and organizational elements are inside and which are outside of itself. Membership is distinct. Members know they are part of the organization and are committed to the organization in exchange for money, common mission, or other return. If the organization's boundary becomes muted or unclear to people on either the inside or the outside, then the organization is in danger. Employees may no longer feel part of the organization or committed to it. When outsiders are unclear about the organization's purpose, they may not be able to identify what transactions are needed or how to conduct them. The organization must be identifiable as a distinct entity with a well-defined boundary. In our People Express example, we see that the company has well-defined boundaries.

Thinking About Organizations

The term "organizational sciences" has come into use in recent years to imply that diverse approaches are used to study organizations. The approaches are related by the focus on organizations and the behavior occurring within

EXHIBIT 1.1
A Basic Systems Model

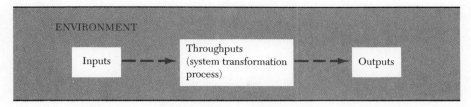

organizations.[5] Fields that study organizations include organizational psychology, organizational behavior, systems theory, management science, organization theory, and organizational sociology. These diverse perspectives can be confusing to the manager, yet the practitioner needs an overview of these subfields because solutions to practical problems may occur from more than one source. The fields are compatible; they simply view the organization from different angles. The organizational sciences in a broad perspective provides an important set of tools for thinking about organizations, three of which we will now discuss: systems approach, levels of analysis, and micro versus macro perspectives.

Systems Approach   We have already defined organizations as social systems made up of deliberately structured parts. A **system** is a set of interrelated elements that requires inputs, transforms them, and discharges outputs to the external environment, as illustrated in Exhibit 1.1. The idea of a system is important because it has to interact with the environment to survive, and subsystems must be coordinated into a coherent organizational whole.[6] One part of the organization must be designated to produce goods or services, another to maintain and repair the organization, and still others to span the boundary to the external environment for acquiring resources and customers. A management subsystem is typically required to direct and coordinate the other organizational parts.

The People Express example at the beginning of this chapter illustrated how subsystems fit together into an effective organization. The concern for employee welfare went hand-in-hand with a concern for markets and a concern for operating efficiency. If the company had focused exclusively on maintaining human resource satisfaction, and had neglected to assign subsystem components to develop route structure, customer satisfaction, or internal efficiency, the whole venture would have failed. Don Burr and other managers realized that all of these factors were interrelated. In order to succeed, management adopted a systems perspective in its approach to people and its approach to business.

Levels of Analysis   As social systems, organizations are composed of systems at different levels. To understand an organization or a specific problem, the focus of a researcher or the concern of a manager may concentrate on specific

EXHIBIT 1.2
Levels of Analysis in Organizations

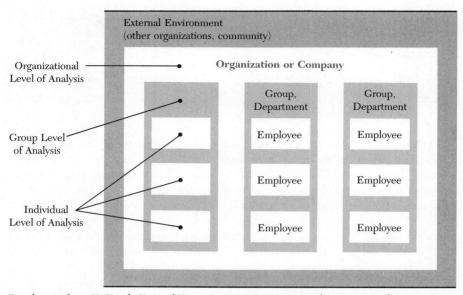

Based on Andrew H. Van de Ven and Diane L. Ferey, *Measuring and Assessing Performance* (New York: Wiley, 1980), p. 8.

levels of analysis. Organizational scientists generally think of three levels of analysis—the individual, the group or department, and the organization itself—as illustrated in Exhibit 1.2.

The three levels in Exhibit 1.2 are interrelated because lower-level units are the building blocks for higher units. Individuals make up the group or department, and groups make up the entire organization. The three levels influence one another, and all are important.

The entire organization can be so complex that researchers and managers cannot focus on all aspects of organizations at the same time. One level of analysis has to be chosen as the focus of research or as the responsibility of a manager. Indeed, entire fields of studies have grown up with a concern for individual versus organizational levels of analysis. Some researchers focus on the psychology of individuals, others on the makeup and performance of work groups, still others on the structure and design of the organization as a whole. All three levels are important to the understanding of organizations and will be covered in this book. The major demarcation in this research is between the individual and the organizational levels of analysis, which have come to be called *micro* and *macro perspectives.*

Micro and Macro Perspectives   The organizational sciences are often conceived as representing either a micro or macro perspective on organizations. The **micro perspective** generally focuses on problems and issues facing individuals and groups within organizations. The best-known approach to the micro perspective of organizations is the field of organizational behavior. **Organizational behavior** is concerned with individual motivation, learning, perception, job attitudes, and work group behavior. These are micro topics because they focus on the individual units of analysis that are the building blocks for the organization.

The **macro perspective** typically focuses on larger units of analysis, especially the organization itself. The field that best represents the macro perspective is organization theory. **Organization theory** is concerned with problems and issues such as the appropriate design for the entire organization, the relationship of the organization with the external environment, production technology, and the effects of organization size. The focus of the micro versus macro perspectives are illustrated in Exhibit 1.3.

The micro and macro perspectives are so important that they are the organizing framework for this book. The chapters in Part II pull together the micro issues, and the chapters in Part III bring together the macro issues on organizations. Throughout the micro and macro parts is an attempt to incorporate both perspectives into a comprehensive model for understanding organizational dynamics. Moreover, in Part IV the book goes a step further to outline a series of process issues that cut across both micro and macro perspectives and serve to integrate these concerns. For example, the topic of leadership is a micro concern when focused on the relationship between a supervisor and subordinates. It becomes a macro concern when a leader is responsible for the organization as a whole. Thus both micro and macro perspectives are included

EXHIBIT 1.3
Micro Versus Macro Perspectives on Organizations

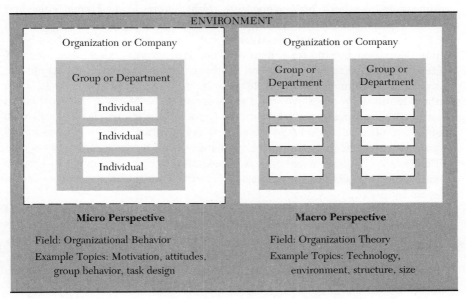

in the leadership chapter. Although most books adopt either the micro or macro perspective, both will be covered and stressed here. Both perspectives are needed to provide significant insights into why organizations behave as they do, and to help managers influence organizational outcomes.

A MODEL OF ORGANIZATIONAL DYNAMICS

At this point we would like to pull together the ideas concerning the definition of organizations, systems, levels of analysis, and micro and macro perspectives into a single conceptual framework for analyzing organizational dynamics. To do so, we draw upon earlier work by Leavitt, Nadler, and Tushman to present a formal model of organization.[7] To present this model, we will address the following topics: 1) What are the criteria for organizational success; 2) what should a model of organizational dynamics look like; and 3) what is the role of management in achieving organizational success? The answers to these three questions will set the stage upon which we will examine the subject of organizations and organizational behavior throughout the book.

Criteria for Organizational Success

Clearly, an important question that comes up in the study of organizations is how we distinguish between successful and unsuccessful organizations. As we saw with People Express, successful organizations have more opportunities to satisfy the needs and address the concerns of their various stakeholders (e.g., employees, stockholders, clients), while less successful organizations must focus more of their energies and resources simply on surviving. Like People, Laker Airways had a goal of cheap airfares, but due to its ineffectiveness and resulting failure both employees and clients were hurt. Hence, the first question to ask is what we mean by an effective organization.

The term **organizational effectiveness** has been used in a variety of contexts. Some people equate the term with profit or productivity, while others view it in terms of employee job satisfaction or quality of working life. If we accept the notion that organizations are systems with multiple levels of analysis, then either definition is too narrow and value-laden to be of much use. Instead, a more useful approach may be to follow the lead of Parsons and Etzioni, who define organizational success in terms of an organization's ability to acquire and efficiently utilize available resources to achieve their goals.[8] In many ways, the ultimate test of good management is the extent to which managers can achieve organizational objectives by successfully securing and utilizing resources from the environment.

As we apply the concept of organizational effectiveness to the study of organizations, it is useful to think of effectiveness as existing on the three levels of analysis of individual, work group, and organization. Organizational effectiveness will vary according to the level of focus.

For example, when we focus on criteria of success on an *organizational* level, we'll need to ask:

- Has the organization attained its overall goals?
- Has the organization made use of its resources efficiently?
- Has the organization successfully adapted to its environment?

On the other hand, when we focus on a *group* level of analysis, different questions about effectiveness emerge:

- Are the various work teams productive?
- Is group cohesiveness ("team spirit") strong among group members?
- Are intergroup relations harmonious?

Finally, on an *individual* level of analysis, other questions emerge:

- Are individual employees performing according to expectations?
- Are employees deriving personal satisfaction and growth from the job?
- Are employee goals being met?

Answers to questions like these can tell us at least on a general level whether the organization under study is effective. For People Express, the answer to most of these questions is in the affirmative.

The Model

Now that we understand facets of organizational success, we can outline the model itself. Organizational dynamics can be modeled in many ways. Our approach highlights the basic building blocks that comprise an organization in a dynamic environment.

Building Blocks of Organizations   At least six building blocks, or components, of organizations can be identified. These include the following:

1. **Individuals and Groups.** People who comprise an organization have abilities, skills, and motivations. How do differences in perception, learning abilities, and motivation affect job performance and, ultimately, organizational effectiveness? How do we evaluate and reward employees to insure equity and continued performance? Managers interested in developing and maintaining an effective work force must answer these questions. A related building block is work groups, including such issues as group cohesiveness, group norms, status systems, and role processes. Work group characteristics influence individual employees, and individuals influence group performance. Individuals and groups represent a critical element in the success of a company like People Express.
2. **Tasks and Technology.** A task is the job of an individual employee, and technology represents the overall knowledge base, techniques, and machinery used by the organization as a whole. The manner in which tasks are performed and in which technology is used have a marked impact on organizational functioning. At People Express many of the employees perform an array of jobs, in contrast to the job specialization common to larger and more established airlines. Job design significantly affects not only

overall efficiency and effectiveness, but also individual job attitudes and behavior.

3. **Organization Design.** Organizational design asks questions that focus on how managers put together the basic building blocks of an organization. That is, how do we structure an organization so it effectively coordinates employee behavior with technological requirements to facilitate organizational performance? How do we accommodate increased automation? Is there a "best way" to design an organization? The answers to these questions help create an entity that can successfully pursue individual and corporate objectives at the same time.

4. **Management.** Management is the building block that is responsible for directing and coordinating other parts of the organization. Management provides organizational direction by setting goals and defining strategy. Management helps interpret the external environment and monitors whether the organization is effective. Management hires employees and is concerned for their motivation and satisfaction. Management also is responsible for organization design, coordination between departments, and the resolution of conflicts. Managers are responsible for making the organizational system work.

5. **Organizational Processes.** Flowing through any organization is a series of organizational processes. In one sense, organizational processes represent the oil that makes the entire system run smoothly. Leadership, decision making, power and politics, conflict, communication and control, and change and innovation are such processes. They bring the organization to life, determining the way in which the organization functions. For example, organizational design represents a static structure that often appears on the organization chart. Organizational processes represent the dynamics of people interacting with one another to accomplish their tasks. Often the most challenging and difficult aspect of managing an organization is managing organizational processes.

6. **External Environment.** The final component in the study of organizations is the external environment in which the organization functions. Organizations are systems, and they must obtain resources from the environment and provide outputs to the environment. Organizations must adapt to the larger environment if they are to prosper and achieve their goals. People Express met this environmental challenge by providing a service that was desired by the environment at that time.

Putting It All Together: The Organizational Dynamics Model   If we now consider the six building blocks of organizations with reference to both the systems approach and the micro and macro perspectives, we can present a model for organizational dynamics.[9] In this model, as illustrated in Exhibit 1.4, inputs are seen as factors that enter the organization from the external environment. Inputs include capital, new technologies, raw materials and employees. Outputs, on the other hand, are indicators of organizational effectiveness at all three levels of analysis, as we discussed above. That is, is the

EXHIBIT 1.4
A Model of Organizational Dynamics

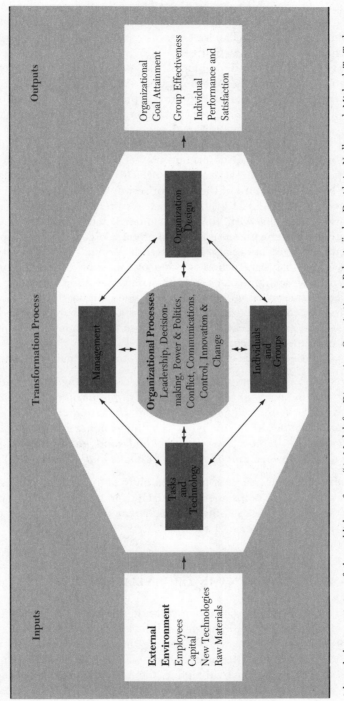

Inputs

External Environment
Employees
Capital
New Technologies
Raw Materials

Transformation Process

Management

Organizational Processes
Leadership, Decision-making, Power & Politics, Conflict, Communications, Control, Innovation & Change

Tasks and Technology

Individuals and Groups

Organization Design

Outputs

Organizational Goal Attainment
Group Effectiveness
Individual Performance and Satisfaction

organization functioning well? Is it attaining overall goals (selling a product? providing a service?) and successfully adapting to the environment? Is it developing productive, collaborative work groups? Is it facilitating individual performance and job satisfaction?

In between inputs and outputs is the organization. In this sense, the organization is actually a transformation system. Organizations transform energy, resources, and information into outputs. As shown in Exhibit 1.4, the process of transformation requires interaction between management, individuals and work groups, organization design, and tasks and technology. The interplay among these four factors are organizational processes (leadership, decision making, etc.) that determine how effectively inputs are transformed into outputs for the external environment. This interplay also determines the ultimate success or failure of the enterprise.

The model in Exhibit 1.4 illustrates the systems perspective because the organization interacts with the environment, and components within the organization interact with one another to produce organizational outputs. Micro and macro perspectives are also illustrated. Individuals and tasks represent the micro level of analysis. Technology and organization design are macro concerns. Organizational processes and the managerial components are concerned with the integration of micro and macro phenomena. Indeed, the primary responsibility of an organization's management is to coordinate and integrate diverse factors and processes. Their purpose is to maintain a unified, goal-directed entity—the successful organization.

In commenting on this challenge, Nadler and Tushman observed:

Understanding one individual's behavior is challenging in and of itself, understanding a group that's made up of different individuals and comprehending the many relationships among those individuals is even more complex. Imagine, then, the mind-boggling complexity of a large organization made up of thousands of individuals and hundreds of groups with myriad relationships among these individuals and groups.[10]

The organizational sciences provide a body of knowledge that is crucial to managers because it helps them understand and control organizations. The organizational sciences also study management directly, and they can tell us how to translate concepts into action.

ROLE OF MANAGEMENT IN ORGANIZATIONS

Given our model and approach to organizations, a useful next step is to look at the role managers play in organizational dynamics. When we see a successful company like People Express, we assume that management found the right configuration of factors in the model of organizational dynamics. To understand the role of managers, we will define the term *management*, and we will examine variations in managerial activities.

What Is Management?

Around the turn of the century, Mary Parker Follett defined management as the "art of getting things done through people."[11] That is, managers coordinate and oversee the work of others to accomplish ends not attainable by the individual alone. Today our definition has broadened—management is generally defined as the process of planning, organizing, directing, and controlling the activities of employees in combination with other organizational resources to accomplish stated organizational objectives.[12] In a broad sense, then, the task of management is to facilitate organizational effectiveness. Management exists in virtually all organizations seeking to achieve goals, whether in the public or private sector and whether in a socialist or a capitalist economy. Virtually all organizations have some type of management.

What Do Managers Do?

The second question often raised about managers is: what *activities* do managers typically perform at work in organizations? According to our definition, managers are involved in planning, organizing, directing, and controlling. A recent survey of 600 managers in a large electronic manufacturing organization provided more detailed insight into managerial activities. The managers responded to questions that described their activities, and the results suggested nine major types of activities.[13] These activities are summarized in Exhibit 1.5. The basic activities of planning, controlling, supervising, and coordinating are part of the reported activities. Managers also are involved in monitoring performance indicators, helping develop and produce primary products and services, customer relationships, external contacts, and providing technical expertise and advice to other members of the organization through consulting activities.

Do Managers Differ?

All managers are not the same in terms of the work they perform. Each manager may be involved with the activities detailed in Exhibit 1.5, but the amount of time and importance of each activity may vary from manager to manager. The two most important influences on managerial activities are the level in the organizational hierarchy and the type of department for which the manager is responsible.

Management Level For convenience, we can distinguish between three general levels of management: executive, middle, and first-line. Executive managers are at the top of the hierarchy and are responsible for the entire organization. Middle managers work at the middle of the hierarchy, are responsible for major departments, and may supervise other lower-level managers. First-line managers supervise rank-and-file employees and carry out day-to-day activities within departments.

EXHIBIT 1.5
Management Activities

Long-range planning
Engaging in planning, strategy development, and decision making for major divisions and functions. This includes determining the annual performance objectives of major divisions and functions, developing major plan revisions, revising the structure of one or more divisions, giving guidance in planning, determining international business potential, and consulting on corporate-wide problems.

Controlling
Having responsibility for controlling the allocation of human, financial, and material resources through activities such as assignment of supervisory responsibility, expense controls, performance goals, and budgets. Also included are employee relations responsibilities, establishing parameters to guide the planning of functional units, developing operational policies and procedures under which managers are expected to perform, and allocating and scheduling resources to assure that they will be available when needed.

Monitoring performance indicators
Being concerned with monitoring key business indicators, such as total new income, five-year return on equity, total assets that have been acquired, net income as a percent of sales, optimum return on investments of the organization, debt-equity ratio, and market conditions and indicators.

Supervising
Planning, organizing, and controlling the work of subordinates, including face-to-face contact with subordinates on an almost daily basis. The concerns covered by this factor revolve around getting work done efficiently through the effective utilization of employees. Activities include analyzing subordinates' strengths/weaknesses and training needs, reviewing their work methods for possible increases in productivity, providing them complete instructions when giving assignments, and scheduling their work so it flows evenly and steadily.

Coordinating
Coordinating the efforts of others over whom managers exercise no direct control. These activities include working in close association with individuals from other units, sharing information required by other units, coordinating interdependent activities of different groups, handling conflicts or disagreements when necessary, and consulting many different people before making major decisions.

Customer relations/marketing
Being involved in providing, promoting, and selling products or services to external customers; negotiating with customers; identifying and developing new markets for products or services; monitoring sales volume and market conditions affecting the users of products or services; anticipating new or changed demands for products or services.

External contact
Interacting with individuals external to the organization other than customers. These activities involve first-level contact and negotiation with employees of suppliers, representatives of community organizations, and representatives of federal or state governments.

Consulting
Applying technical expertise to special problems, issues, questions, or policies, having an understanding of advanced principles, theories, and concepts in more than one required field, and being asked to apply highly advanced techniques and methods to issues and questions.

Products/services
Being involved in planning, scheduling, and monitoring the design, development, production, and delivery of products and services; tracking their progress, quality, and profitability.

SOURCE: Luis Gomez-Mejia, Joseph E. McCann, and Ronald C. Page, "The Structure of Managerial Behaviors and Rewards," *Industrial Relations* 24 (1985): 147–154. Used with permission.

Exhibit 1.6 shows differences in managerial activities by hierarchical level. Top managers rate high on such things as long-range planning, monitoring performance indicators, coordinating, and consulting. Lower-level managers, by contrast, rate very high on supervising, because their responsibility is to accomplish tasks through rank-and-file employees. Middle managers are rated about in the middle for all activities. These findings suggest that the skills required of managers change as they move up the hierarchy and acquire greater responsibility.

EXHIBIT 1.6
Importance of Activities by Management Level

Managerial Activities	Management Level		
	First-Line	Middle	Executive
Long-range planning	25	45	84
Products and services	33	50	58
Controlling	38	50	61
Monitoring business indicators	30	49	74
Supervising	65	50	33
Coordinating	31	52	70
Customer relations/marketing	27	49	69
External contact	38	45	57
Consulting	30	52	70

SOURCE: Luis Gomez-Mejia, Joseph E. McCann, and Ronald C. Page, "The Structure of Managerial Behaviors and Rewards," *Industrial Relations* 24 (1985): 147–154. Used with permission.

Departmental Function Activities also differ with respect to the type of department. Exhibit 1.7 illustrates differences for manufacturing, quality assurance, marketing, accounting, and personnel departments. Manufacturing department managers rate high on product, controlling, and supervising. Marketing managers, by comparison, are very low on planning, coordinating, and consulting, but are very high on customer relations and external contact. Accounting and personnel are both high on long-range planning and low on product. Accounting is also concerned with controlling and performance indicators, while personnel provides consulting expertise, coordination, and external contacts. Exhibit 1.7 illustrates a different emphasis and intensity for managerial activities by department. Managerial experience is often shaped by rotation through departments, which provides a well-rounded perspective as people move toward upper management.

Through day-to-day management processes, managers must accomplish the planning, supervising, consulting, and coordinating that is the core of their job. They must emphasize the right activities depending on their department and level. Sometimes mistakes are made, and the manager gets fired, which happened at Fairchild Republic.

UP CLOSE 1.1: Fairchild Industries

Charles Collis made a big mistake when he was president of Fairchild Republic, which is the airplane manufacturing division of Fairchild Industries. The division had won a contract to build the A-10 Thunderbolt II attack plane, and Collis got hot under the collar with a zealous Air Force analyst. He didn't want Air Force people telling him how to run his business. The analyst was offended and complained to his superiors. The negative relationship with the Air Force meant that Collis had to be removed from his position.

Doc Grossman was appointed to replace Collis, and his first priority was to reestablish rapport with the Air Force. Grossman also helped solve technical problems by personally flying to the test site. The A-10 lost power in sharp turns, and Grossman solved it by attaching a small sheet of metal to the right spot on each wing.

But while Grossman was concentrating on solving problems with the A-10, development of another airplane, the Peacemaker, got out of control. Grossman admits that he was so involved in the design of the A-10 that he didn't watch the market for other types of airplanes. The Peacemaker was not accepted by the Air Force. General Dynamics won the contract with the F-16, which ended up being one of the biggest defense contracts ever.[14] ■

In terms of required managerial activities, Collis made his mistake by not giving enough emphasis to customer relations, which is a primary responsibility for senior managers. His replacement, Grossman, excelled at customer relations and providing technical consulting to others. He was not as successful at long-range planning, however, and missed the mark on the new fighter.

EXHIBIT 1.7

Importance of Management Activities by Department

Management Activities	Department				
	Quality Assurance	Manufacturing	Marketing	Accounting	Personnel
Long-range planning	21	39	21	68	72
Products and services	66	70	52	19	20
Controlling	66	70	53	80	48
Monitoring business indicators	21	30	62	73	32
Supervising	51	65	50	40	44
Coordinating	42	38	22	51	71
Customer relations	25	31	93	39	22
External contact	34	31	61	42	67
Consulting	32	41	26	61	80

SOURCE: Luis Gomez-Mejia, Joseph E. McCann, and Ronald C. Page, "The Structure of Managerial Behaviors and Rewards," *Industrial Relations* 24 (1985): 147–154. Used with permission.

Managers constantly try to balance their time across all of these activities, and a fast pace is required to handle the multiple demands and voluminous information.

PROBLEMS FACING MANAGEMENT

In this section, we want to address the kinds of problems facing organizations and their managers in the future. Many discussions of management activities emphasize issues and problems within the organization that are resolved through supervision and coordination. What we can learn from the organizational sciences, however, is that management, especially top management, is responsible for the entire organization. The major problems facing the entire organization originate in the environment. Problems from the environment influence both organizational dynamics and organizational effectiveness.

Contemporary organizations are, in a very real sense, products of their environment, and the environment is dynamic, not static. Managers of work organizations must be alert to future changes as they relate to organizational adaptation and effectiveness. What major changes can we expect that will impact on organizations in the future? Several environmental trends can be identified: 1) socionormative changes; 2) demographic changes; 3) economic changes; and 4) technological changes.[15] The way managers address these changes and challenges will determine how successful organizations will be at surviving, growing, and developing in the next decades. As shown in Exhibit

EXHIBIT 1.8
Influence of Societal Changes on Employee Attitudes and Behavior

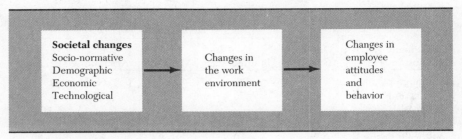

Adapted from R. T. Mowday, L.W. Porter, and R. M. Steers, *Employee-Organization Linkages: The Psychology of Commitment, Absenteeism, and Turnover* (New York: Academic Press, 1982).

1.8, changes in our society—such as changing work norms or changing technology—alter the work environment, affecting both employees' productivity and their job attitudes.

Socio-Normative Changes

Socio-normative changes include the work ethic, aspiration levels, attitudes toward authority, sex-role stereotypes, and trust in organizations and institutions. These changes can influence the work environment in at least three ways: 1) through the socialization process employees encounter; 2) through the normative beliefs other employees bring to the work place that can influence the individual; and 3) through the individual's general knowledge of what is happening in society, based on the media, communications, travel, and friends. In the next few years more people will want jobs and more people will want *good* jobs.[16] There will be an increasing emphasis on personal self-fulfillment and individual rights. Yankelovich, who has identified a "new breed" of employees, states, "[They will] feel that success is not enough to satisfy their yearnings for self-fulfillment. They are reaching out for something more and for something different . . . in effect, they demand full enjoyment as well as full employment."[17]

Demographic Changes

Second, changes are occurring in population *demographics*—in both the nature and composition of the labor force. Sizable changes in the educational level of the work force, the age level, the percentage of women and minorities entering managerial levels, and the percentage of dual-career or multiple wage earner households in the U.S. and Canada are of particular interest. Women and minorities will continue to press for equality in both personnel selection and promotion; and prevailing court decisions will consistently back up these demands. The percentage of families with only one (typically male) wage earner will decline from its current twenty-five percent of all households. Increased heterogeneity and diversity in the work force will result. Treating employees as though they were a single type or group will become increasingly difficult. As Yankelovich has suggested, "The work of managing diverse incentive packages poses an administrative and bureaucratic nightmare. Understandably, therefore, most managers choose to ignore the problem. Under the old value system they could do so with impunity; under the new value system they cannot. In the 1980s they will be obliged to face this new reality."[18]

Economic Changes

Third, *economic changes* can influence work life in at least two ways. Short-term changes in the economy can have rather marked effects on employee income level, experienced stress, absenteeism, and turnover. Brief economic downturns easily can create uncertainty, anxiety, and stress for employees. During such times, an employee's attachment to the organization may weaken. For instance, if few alternative jobs are available, absenteeism may increase as an escape mechanism, since turnover is less likely an option.

In the long term, major shifts in the economy can affect general levels of affluence and the amount of leisure time available. A downward turn in national economy creates difficulties for both managers and employees as they attempt to build a better work place. With less money available—and with many jobs eliminated or threatened—it is difficult to initiate the kind of changes that are necessary for an improved work experience for everyone involved.

Technological Changes

Fourth, change can be expected in the area of *technological innovation*. Technological change is evident in several ways. First, there has been a sharp increase in the amount of automated equipment used both in the office and in the plant. The introduction of advanced computers, electronic mail, and robots must of necessity change how we do our jobs—as well as *how many* people do those jobs and how such jobs are managed. In addition, increases in technological sophistication bring with them an increased need for technical experts or professionals to handle the software and hardware. This has clear implications for the personnel selection and placement process as well as the employee training and development function. In essence, employees will become technically obsolete more easily, and so efforts must be taken to countermand this threat.

But let's not forget that technological change, as well as changes in values, demographics, and the economy can have enormous positive benefits for employees and organizations. The trend toward automation and robotics means that boring, unsafe jobs can be taken over by machines. The goal of the organization sciences is to develop a higher quality of life for employees that will be partly attained through technological innovations. In the following **Up Close**, Craig Waters recalls his father's difficult and painful welding work. Think of what it was like to be a welder in the 1940s compared to today, when these tasks have been taken over by machines.

UP CLOSE 1.2:   New York Shipbuilding Corporation

I remember my father's body and I remember my father's stories. When I was young, my father, Jacob Waters, would come home each evening from the New York Shipbuilding Corp., in Camden, N.J., where he was a welder. He would peel off his work shirt and, occasionally, when he was changing for dinner, would remove his insulated undershirt as well. Then I would see the burns. At the time, the burns made no sense to me; half a dozen might run down his chest in what was nearly a straight line; three or four might be clustered in a circle on his stomach. Later, I understood: Hot slag from the welding iron burnt through his clothing and trickled down his chest, or, if it struck lower, bounced around in one confined area as he tried to free himself from the pain.

And my father told me stories. He told me about welding inside the gun turrets on battleships and cruisers during Work War II. It was summer, and the temperature outside was in the 90s, but the turrets were electrically heated to more than 200°F. to keep the metal at the proper temperature. Inside, his welding iron blazing, my father slaved in hell. He talked about working inside of tiny heated compartments in the bowels of atomic submarines where the metal was so hot he had to cover the four-foot by four-foot floor with layers of asbestos and lumber before he could sit, his legs folded up beneath him, to weld. When his knees began to hurt so badly that he could hardly walk, a doctor explained that the intense heat was burning off the fluid in his kneecaps.

Some of the spaces were so small that he couldn't wear a visor; dark glasses protected his eyes, but his face grew fiery with arc burn. Sometimes slag found its way around a lens, and a bit of molten metal would fall onto the surface of his eye and adhere to it until it was plucked off by the company doctor. Once, while he was welding on a yardarm, slag dropped into the top of his boot—his hands filled with equipment, his legs grasping the yardarm, my father was unable to do anything about it. The slag burnt a half-inch hole in the top of his foot.

But the worst job, my father said, was one requiring him to hang by his feet through a small hole in a metal plate and weld while hanging upside down, the red-hot iron inches from his face.

At New York Ship, my father had been burned and blinded and poisoned by what he did for a living. There were other jobs with other companies that yielded similar stories. The one that terrified me most had to do with an automobile-chassis line. When my father went to work for the Budd Co., in Philadelphia, he found that the welders who had been there for more than a short while screamed. The pace was so inhuman that, in order to relieve the incredible tension, they screamed for several hours each evening; the nightshift foreman told my father not to let it bother him. It was one of the few jobs my father ever quit.[19] ■

In recent years, robots have taken over the welding on assembly lines and have been designed to weld in the bottom of ships. Some people are concerned about whether robots will displace workers. While this is an important concern, robots can increase effectiveness for both the organization and for individual employees. Many jobs, such as the one performed by Craig Waters' father, should not be performed by people.

THE STUDY OF ORGANIZATIONS

The final issue to be addressed in this chapter is: How do we develop useful knowledge about organizations? Organizational scientists work hard to make discoveries and accumulate facts and ideas that explain how organizations work. In this way scientists can advance the practice of management. Equally important, managers themselves make discoveries and accumulate facts and ideas through trial and error experience within organizations. The scientific process and a manager's trial and error learning lead to the same end—useful knowledge about organizations. But the route is different. Organizational scientists use formal procedures while managers typically use intuitive learning.

The important point is that managers and scientists acquire new knowledge for the same reasons. One reason is *concern for performance*. If knowledge truly explains how organizations work, then it will ultimately help improve performance. Without both job performance and organizational effectiveness, the organization will not prosper, and may not even survive. A second reason is *concern for individual well being*. Organizations grow and prosper only when employees are allowed to grow and prosper. Many issues in addition to employee issues account for organizational performance, but employees, as at People Express, are the strong link in the process. For example, when we study employee motivation, we try to comprehend what underlies motivation and to learn lessons that can be passed to managers. Organization theory and behavior is meant to be used, not just appreciated. It is meant to be applied as well as understood.

Thus we see that the field of organizational science has the same goal of useful knowledge as practicing managers have. Managers and scientists share the concern for individual well being and the concern for performance. But we still haven't answered the question about how knowledge of organizations is developed. The answer is that virtually all research, whether formal or informal, is designed to develop or test theory.

What Is a Theory?

In simple terms, a **theory** is a description that explains the manner in which certain concepts or variables are interrelated. For scientists, this description is a formal set of statements based on our present knowledge of a given topic and our assumptions about the variables themselves that allow us to deduce logical propositions, or hypotheses, that can be tested in the field or laboratory.[20]

Managers have theories too. The theory reflects the manager's understanding of how the organization works, although it probably is not written down. A manager continuously tests and improves the theory through trial and error activities.

Why do we have theories in the study of organizations? Hamner and Organ suggest at least three reasons.[21] First, theories help us *organize* knowledge on a given subject into a pattern of relationships that lends meaning to a series of observed events. A theory provides a structure for understanding. For instance, rather than struggling with a lengthy list of factors that somehow relate to employee turnover, one theory of turnover might draw those factors together and suggest how they are related.

Second, theories help us *summarize* diverse findings so we can focus on major relationships and not get bogged down in details. A theory "permits us to handle large amounts of empirical data with relatively few propositions."[22]

Finally, theories *point the way* to future research efforts. They raise new questions and suggest answers. They have heuristic value—they help direct the researcher to differentiate between important and trivial questions for future research. Theories are useful both for the study and practice of management in organizations. Good theory is not just a formal, abstract, academic framework. It explains real behavior in real organizations. As Kurt Lewin said, "There is nothing so practical as a good theory."[23]

What Is a Good Theory?   Kaplan discusses in detail the criteria for evaluating the utility or soundness of a formal theory.[24] At least five such criteria can be mentioned:

- **Internal Consistency.** Are the ideas and relationships inherent in the theory free from contradiction? Are they logical?
- **External Consistency.** Are the relationships of a theory consistent with observations from real life?
- **Scientific Parsimony.** Does the theory contain only those concepts that are necessary to account for findings or to explain relationships? Simplicity is best unless added complexity furthers understanding or clarifies research findings.
- **Generalizability.** In order for a theory to have much utility, it must apply to a wide range of situations or organizations. A theory of employee motivation that applies only to one company does not help us understand motivational processes or apply such knowledge elsewhere.
- **Verification.** A good theory can be tested. Without an ability to operationalize the variables and subject a theory to field or laboratory testing, we cannot determine the theory's accuracy or utility.

To the extent that a theory satisfies these requirements, its usefulness to researchers and managers is enhanced. Although theory is what we strive for it is also a starting point. Researchers and managers design studies aimed at verifying and refining the theories themselves. In order to be valid, these studies proceed according to commonly accepted principles of scientific method.

The Scientific Method

Cohen and Nagel have suggested that there are four basic "ways of knowing."[25] Researchers and managers use all four of these techniques: tenacity, intuition, authority, and science. When managers form a theory (e.g., a happy worker is a productive worker) and continue to hold that belief out of habit or because they have not received contradictory information, they are using *tenacity*. They use *intuition* when they feel the answer is self-evident or when they have a hunch about how to solve a problem but can't really prove it. Managers use *authority* when they seek an answer to a problem from an expert or consultant who supposedly has experience in the area. The expert's theory is presumed to be better. Finally, *science* may be used when the researcher or manager is convinced that other methods allow for too much subjectivity or error in interpretation.

In contrast to tenacity, intuition, and authority, the scientific method of inquiry "aims at knowledge that is *objective* in the sense of being . . . independent of individual opinion or preference on the basis of data obtainable by suitable experiments or observations."[26] In other words, the scientific approach to problem solving sets some fairly rigorous standards in an attempt to substitute objectivity for subjectivity.

The scientific method in organizational studies consists of four stages: 1) observing real world facts; 2) formulating an explanation (theory) for such phenomena using the inductive process; 3) generating predications or hypotheses about the phenomena using the deductive process; and 4) verifying the predications or hypotheses by returning to real world facts gathered through systematic, controlled observation.[27] This process is shown in Exhibit 1.9. The scientific method is literally a continuing cycle. Real world facts are used to develop or refine theory which is then further tested with new facts.

When this rather abstract description of the steps of scientific inquiry is shown within the framework of an empirical study, the process becomes clearer.

The sequence of steps associated with a research study is shown in Exhibit 1.10. This is the formal, scientific approach that begins by first becoming aware of existing facts, and then posing clearly the research questions to be asked. To paraphrase Lewis Carroll, if you don't know where you're going, any road will take you there. Based on the research question, specific hypotheses can be defined. These hypotheses represent our best guesses about what we expect to find. We then select a study design that allows for a suitable testing of possible answers. Based on the study design we observe the phenomenon under study, analyze the data we collect, and draw relevant conclusions and implications. By following this formal sequence, the risks of being misguided by our own opinions or prejudices are minimized, and we arrive at useful answers to our original research questions.

It is important to remember that managers in organizations follow the same process, only in informal fashion. Empirical research is essentially question-

EXHIBIT 1.9
A Model Depicting the Scientific Method

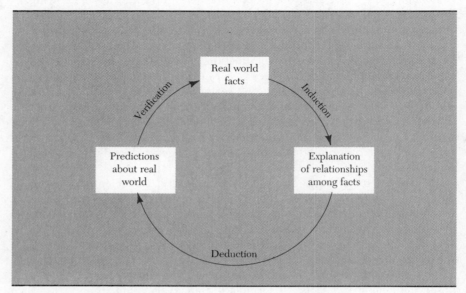

SOURCE: E. F. Stone, *Research Methods in Organizational Behavior* (Glenview, IL: Scott, Foresman and Company, 1978), p. 8.

experiment-conclusion. This process, repeated day after day, month after month in organizations helps managers learn more about their organizations. If managers are uncertain why market share is declining, or why turnover is high, they will develop questions about why these events occur. Then they will try an experiment, perhaps altering the product or gathering data through a survey about employee turnover. When the data reveal new market share quotations or survey results, conclusions will be drawn. This process occurs both formally and informally by both researchers and managers, and leads to the development of the knowledge base by which to understand and manage organizations.

Basic Research Designs

While a detailed discussion of the various research designs is beyond the scope of this chapter, we can identify five major research designs that are used to collect data in a study of organizations. First, **naturalistic observations** represent the most basic (least rigorous) method of research in organizations. Naturalistic observations are simply the conclusions we draw from observing events around us. Two forms of such observation can be identified: authoritative opinions and case studies.

EXHIBIT 1.10
A Model of the Empirical Research Process

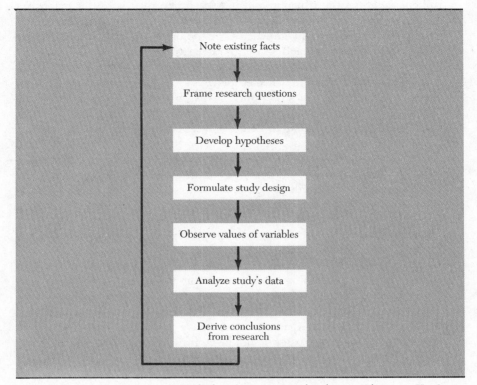

Note existing facts

Frame research questions

Develop hypotheses

Formulate study design

Observe values of variables

Analyze study's data

Derive conclusions
from research

SOURCE: E. F. Stone, *Research Methods in Organizational Behavior* (Glenview, IL: Scott, Foresman and Company, 1978), p. 17.

Authoritative opinions are the opinions of experts in the field. When Henry Fayol wrote his early works on management, for example, he was offering his advice as a former industrial manager. Based on his work experience and observations, Fayol and others have suggested that certain skills and ideas can be applied to a variety of organizations with relative ease. Other examples of authoritative opinions can be found in Barnard's *The Functions of the Executive*, Sloan's *My Years with General Motors*, and Townsend's *Up the Organization*. Throughout their works, these writers attempt to draw conclusions from their years of experience (informal question-experiment-conclusion) that can help other managers solve their problems.

The second form of naturalistic observation is the **case study.** During a case study, the investigator studies one situation in one organization in detail, especially examining the interpersonal dynamics between the members. Let's take the case of a middle manager who has burned out on the job; his performance seems to have reached a plateau. The case study would review the cast of characters in the situation and how each one related to this manager's problem. Moreover, it would review any actions taken to remedy the problem. Throughout, the study would emphasize what information managers could take from this real-life problem and apply to other situations.

Survey research is a second valuable option when managers wish to know something about the extent to which employees are satisfied with their jobs, are loyal to the organization, or experience stress on the job. In such cases, the managers (or the researchers) are interested mainly in considering survey responses to questions relating to such factors. Survey research applies to one moment in time and is not correlated with other events. Managers and researchers use survey data to assess the general feelings and attitudes of employees. Managers may make an annual attitude survey and track changes in attitudes over time. If attitudes begin to decline, management is alerted to the problem and can take corrective steps.

In a **field study,** the third type of basic research design, the researcher is interested in the relationship between a "predictor" variable (e.g., job satisfaction) and a subsequent "criterion" variable (e.g., employee turnover or performance). The researcher takes measures of each variable (satisfaction, perhaps through a questionnaire, and turnover, from company records) and compares them to determine the extent of correlation. No attempt is made to intervene in the system or to manipulate any of the variables, as is the case with experimental approaches. A manager may have a hypothesis that says that satisfaction is a primary indicator of employee turnover. After measuring both, the manager may find a moderate correlation between the two variables. But due to the moderate strength of the relationship, it is clear that other factors influence turnover as well, or the relationship would be much stronger. The manager concludes that, while efforts to improve job satisfaction may help solve the problem, other influences on turnover, such as salary level and supervisory style, must also be examined.

A **field experiment** is much like a field study with one important exception. Instead of simply measuring job satisfaction, the manager or researcher attempts to actually change satisfaction levels. In an experiment, we can try to manipulate the variables that are believed to cause the problem. Frequently this is done by dividing the sample of employees into two groups: an experimental group and a control group. We can then intervene and introduce a major change in the experimental groups. Perhaps we alter the compensation program or give their supervisors some human relations training. The control group receives no such treatment. After a period of time we compare turnover rates across the two groups. If we have identified the correct cause (that is, a true influence on turnover), turnover rates would be reduced in the experimental group but not in the control group. In other words, in a field experiment, as opposed to a field study, we intentionally manipulate one aspect of the work environment in the experimental group and compare the outcome with the untreated control group. Thus we can be relatively assured that the solution we have identified is in fact a true causal variable and is of use to management.

Up to this point, the research designs we have considered all make use of the actual work environment, the "field." In our last design, **laboratory experiments,** we employ the same level of rigor as in field experiments, and actually manipulate the causal variable, but we do so in an artificial environment instead of a real one. We might, for instance, wish to study the effects of different compensation programs (hourly rate versus piece-rate) on performance. To do this, we might ask two groups of business students to take part in a work exercise. Rather than using two real work groups, we are "simulating" a work situation. Each group would be "paid" differently. After the experiment, we would assess the kind of impact the two compensation plans had on student productivity.

Researchers or managers use all of these methods at various times to learn more about how organizations function. Knowledge of research methods helps the student of organizations understand and critically evaluate the theories and research findings discussed throughout this book. The selection of any specific research design will depend upon the amount of time managers have and the type of question to be answered. The important thing is to use the scientific method whenever feasible because it can provide answers that will inform organizational decisions. Consider the example of American Can.

UP CLOSE 1.3:   American Can Company

Flexible compensation packages are an important new device for satisfying employees. Flexible compensation allows each employee to receive a benefits package tailored to personal needs. An employee might substitute vacation time for additional medical insurance, or reduce disability insurance in order to increase retirement benefits. The vice president for human resources at American Can decided to explore if a flexible compensation system would be applicable to 9000 salaried employees. The new package raised many questions, such as whether the package would work and be acceptable to employees. American Can began by assigning a task force to gather all available information about similar programs at other companies and to design a potential program for use in-house.

After gathering information and designing a potential program the company decided on a two-stage test. The first stage involved gathering information from a hundred randomly selected employees in the Consumer Towel & Tissue Division. Based on these initial findings, certain options were modified or eliminated. The second stage was a trial implementation of the program in the Consumer Towel & Tissue Division. Employees in this division became the experimental group.

After receiving the benefits, questionnaires were distributed to employees in the experimental division and to the previously selected employees throughout the company who had not received the benefit plan. Both groups were asked to agree or disagree with the statement, "The overall value of the proposed benefits plan to me is greater than the present plan's overall value." In the randomly selected group, 66 percent agreed. In the group that actually received the new benefits package, 87 percent agreed with the statement. These findings indicate a genuine acceptance of the flexible benefits package, which was then extended to other parts of the company. [28] ▟▆

American Can used a combination of field experiment and field study. They gathered data from questionnaires but also compared data from an experimental group who received the plan to employees who did not receive it. This provided strong evidence that the plan would work and enabled the Human Resources vice-president to move ahead with further implementation. The scientific method works because it provides a logical way to ask questions that will produce objective answers.

PLAN OF THE BOOK

The plan of this book grows from the dynamic model of organizations presented back in Exhibit 1.4, the micro versus macro perspectives, and the theories and scientific knowledge from the organization sciences. The first stage begins in Part II with an examination of the *micro* aspects of organizational behavior. As we discussed, the micro perspective focuses on the individual as the unit of analysis. The chapters include individual differences among employees, employee perceptions in organizations, motivation, work design, job attitudes, work groups, performance appraisal, and reward systems. The primary focus in Part II is on individual and small groups and what can be learned to motivate and manage employees more effectively.

In Part III we focus on *macro* variables. The macro perspective focuses on the organization as the primary unit of analysis. Here the chapters are on organization design, technology, and the external environment. Within the macro perspective, however, the role of individuals and groups will be integrated into the discussion.

Finally, in Part IV, the emphasis shifts to an examination of key processes in organizations that include both micro and macro phenomena. These chapters look at leadership, communication, control, conflict, power, decision making, and innovation. In these chapters, both the individual and organizational level of analysis are considered. In this way we can integrate micro and macro perspectives to understand the full range of behavior in organizations.

Each chapter begins with a vignette or examples to illustrate the relevance of the topic to managers. Numerous **Up Close** sections, where an example is treated in depth, punctuate each chapter. Practical examples are also sprinkled throughout the text. Each chapter closes with a Case, as well as Key Words and Discussion Questions, to help you explore and apply the materials learned. In this way, we hope that you, the reader, will fully understand not only the topic at hand but the relationship between the micro and macro perspectives and how they apply to the practice of management.

KEY WORDS

authoritative opinion	micro perspective	scientific method
case study	naturalistic	staff manager
external consistency	observations	survey research
external environment	organization	system
field experiment	organization design	tasks
field study	organization theory	technological
inputs	organizational	innovation
internal consistency	behavior	technology
laboratory experiment	organizational	theory
line manager	effectiveness	transformation
macro perspective	organizational process	processes
management	outputs	work groups

DISCUSSION QUESTIONS

1. In analyzing People Express, what major factors can be identified that facilitated their success? What problems do you see on the horizon facing People Express?
2. What is an organization? What are the defining characteristics of an organization?
3. What is your definition of organizational effectiveness? How does your definition compare to the definition outlined in the book? How would you measure effectiveness in a particular organization?
4. Why is the concept of "level of analysis" useful in analyzing organizational dynamics and performance?
5. Critically evaluate the Nadler-Tushman model (Exhibit 1.4) of organizational dynamics. How can this model help us better understand organizations?
6. How can systems theory help us in diagnosing problems in a particular organization?
7. Define management in your own words. What is the relationship between management and organizations? How would you define *effective* management?
8. Evaluate the management activities in Exhibit 1.5. Are those activities consistent with your definition of management? What do you think should be added or deleted from the list?
9. Differentiate between organization theory and organizational behavior. What is the rationale for taking an integrative approach to the study of organizations?
10. From a scientific standpoint, which research method would yield the most useful results? From a managerial standpoint, which method of inquiry would yield the most useful results?

11. What do you consider to be the major problems facing organizations during the next five years? Next twenty years? What can managers do now to anticipate and cope with these problems?

NOTES

1. Lucien Rhodes, "That Daring Young Man and His Flying Machine," *Inc.*, January 1984, p. 44.
2. Rhodes, "That Daring Young Man . . . ," p. 44; William M. Carley, "People Express Flies Into Airlines' Big Time in Just 3 Years Aloft," *The Wall Street Journal*, March 30, 1984, p. 19.
3. Based on Rhodes, "That Daring Young Man . . . ," pp. 42–52; Carley, "People Express Flies Into Airlines' Big Time . . . ," pp. 1, 19; Howard Banks, "Now Everybody's Doing It," *Forbes*, May 6, 1985, pp. 32–33; "Growing Pains at People Express," *Business Week*, January 28, 1985, pp. 90–91; Wayne Beissert, "Rising Costs Shadow People Express Success," *USA Today*, April 15, 1985, p. 3b; P. Nolty, "A Champ of Cheap Airlines," *Fortune*, March 22, 1982, pp. 127–134; D. Whitestone, *People Express* (Cambridge, MA: Harvard Business School, Case #9-483-103).
4. Howard Aldrich, *Organizations and Environments* (Englewood Cliffs, NJ: Prentice-Hall, 1979), pp. 4–6; Arthur G. Bedeian, *Organizations: Theory and Analysis* (Hinsdale, IL: Dryden, 1980), p. 4; Richard L. Daft, *Organization Theory and Design* (St. Paul, MN: West, 1983), p. 8.
5. Thanks to Marty Gann for suggesting this perspective.
6. L. von Bertalanffy, "The History and Status of General Systems Theory," *Academy of Management Journal*, 15 (1972), pp. 407–426.
7. S. Nadler and M. Tushman, "A Model for Diagnosing Organizational Behavior," *Organizational Dynamics*, 9, 2 (1980), pp. 35–51.
8. For further details, see R. M. Steers, *Organizational Effectiveness: A Behavioral View* (Santa Monica, CA: Goodyear, 1977).
9. D. Nadler and M. Tushman, "A Model," pp. 35–51.
10. D. Nadler and M. Tushman, "A Model," p. 35.
11. Cited in R. M. Steers, G. R. Ungson, and R. T. Mowday, *Managing Effective Organizations: An Introduction* (Boston: Kent, 1985), p. 29.
12. R. M. Steers, G. R. Ungson, and R. T. Mowday, *Managing Effective Organizations*, p. 29.
13. Luis R. Gomez-Mejia, Joseph E. McCann, and Ronald C. Page, "The Structure of Managerial Behaviors and Rewards," *Industrial Relations*, 24 (1985), pp. 147–154; also see William Whitely, "Managerial Work Behavior: An Integration of Results from Two Major Approaches, *Academy of Management Journal*, 28 (1985), pp. 344–362.
14. Based on Joel Dreyfuss, "Handing Down the Old Hands' Wisdom," *Fortune*, June 13, 1983, pp. 97–104.
15. R. T. Mowday, L. W. Porter, and R. M. Steers, *Employee-Organization Linkages: The Psychology of Commitment, Absenteeism, and Turnover* (New York: Academic Press, 1982).
16. C. Kerr, "Industrialism with a New Face," in C. Kerr and J. Rostow (eds.), *Work in America: The Next Decade* (New York: Van Nostrand, 1979).
17. D. Yankelovich, "We Need New Motivational Tools," *Industry Week*, August 6, 1979, pp. 10–11.
18. D. Yankelovich, "We Need New Motivational Tools," pp. 21–22.
19. From Craig R. Waters, "There's a Robot in Your Future," *Inc.*, June 1982, p. 70. Used with permission.
20. R. Dubin, *Theory Building* (New York: The Free Press, 1976).
21. W. C. Hamner and D. Organ, *Organizational Behavior: An Applied Psychological Approach* (Dallas: BPI, 1978).
22. M. Shaw and P. Costanzo, *Theories of Social Psychology* (New York: McGraw-Hill, 1970).
23. From A. Marrow, *The Practical Theorist* (New York: Basic Books, 1969).

24. A. Kaplan, *The Conduct of Inquiry* (San Francisco: Chandler, 1964).

25. M. Cohen and E. Nagel, *An Introduction to Logic and Scientific Method* (New York: Harcourt, Brace & Co., 1934).

26. C. G. Hempel, *Aspects of Scientific Explanation* (New York: The Free Press, 1965), p. 141.

27. E. F. Stone, *Research Methods in Organizational Behavior* (Glenview, IL: Scott, Foresman, 1978).

28. Based on A. S. Schlachtmeyer and R. D. Bogart, "Employee-Choice Benefits—Can Employees Handle It?" *Compensation Review*, Third Quarter, 1979; and Don Hellriegel, John W. Slocum, Jr., and Richard W. Woodman, *Organizational Behavior* (St. Paul, MN: West, 1983), pp. 54–55.

PART

II

Individuals and Groups: The Micro Perspective

The *micro* perspective on the study of organizations focuses on individuals and small groups and what can be learned to motivate and manage employees more effectively. Part II begins with an examination of individual differences and behavior in Chapter 2, taken from the standpoint of personal traits, individual needs, and learning processes. Chapter 3 examines the related topics of individual perception and job attitudes that underlie employee behavior. Motivation and performance follow in Chapter 4, which concentrates on motivational processes and early and contemporary approaches to motivation in the work place. Following from this topic is performance appraisal and rewards in organizations, covered in Chapter 5. Job design, the subject of Chapter 6, is explored as it relates to on-the-job performance, work-related stress, and job redesign. The final micro chapter, Chapter 7, begins a bridge to the macro perspective with its treatment of work groups.

2 Individual Differences and Behavior

J erry Wilson, founder of Soloflex, has made millions by inventing and marketing a unique home weight-lifting machine. The Soloflex system is unique because it is a weight-lifting machine without the weights. Instead, it uses "weight straps" that stretch when the user pushes or pulls on one of the machine's bars. Wilson invented the machine in 1978 after seeing a need for home exercise equipment that didn't cost $10,000 and take up an entire room. "I became consumed with the project," Wilson notes.

Once he was convinced he had the right design for a marketable product, Wilson risked every possession he owned to create the company. Even his approach to marketing was unique. Instead of paying distributors, he put a toll-free number in his magazine ads and took orders himself at home. His "sales staff" consists of a large stock of $6.50 videotapes the company mails free to anyone who calls and requests one. Wilson found that this approach was much less expensive than sales representatives and gets into homes more easily. Clearly, Jerry Wilson represents an example of a modern-day entrepreneur, a person whose unique personal characteristics have driven him to success.[1]

What is it in Jerry Wilson's background that may explain his success? To begin with, Wilson manifests a strong achievement orientation. It is extremely important for him to succeed. He views his new company as an all-consuming commitment. It is important to him that the company succeed. In addition, stress seems to play a role in Wilson's success. He notes that stress can be used to one's advantage. For example, he risked his entire life savings to start Soloflex, a decision he constantly considered as he worked to build the company. Finally, Wilson exhibits a strong personal work ethic. That is, he feels each individual is responsible for his or her own accomplishments and must work hard to attain rewards. This combination of hard work, an achievement orientation, and a positive reaction to stress seems to explain to a large extent why Jerry Wilson is where he is today.

In this chapter, we begin by focusing on individual differences as they relate to behavior. In particular, we shall examine personal traits, individual motives and needs, and learning processes. Based on this assessment, we will expand our examination to the effects of environmental variables on behavior at work. As we explore this topic, think of the example of Jerry Wilson and the success that can be influenced by individual characteristics.

One of the first people to systematically study the behavior of individuals in group situations was Kurt Lewin.[2] *Lewin proposed that one of the most useful ways to examine individual behavior (B) was as a function of the interaction between a person (P) and his or her environment (E). Lewin suggested a formula for this relationship:* B=f (P, E). *This easy-to-remember equation forms the basis for much analytical study of employees at work. Simply, the formula reminds us that if we wish to understand employee behavior, it is essential to recognize that such behavior is determined by three factors: 1) individual differences among people; 2) the work environment; and 3) the interaction between people and the work environment. As such, this simple formula can help us considerably in the study of organizational behavior.*

RELEVANCE OF INDIVIDUAL DIFFERENCES FOR MANAGERS

Before examining individual differences in detail, let's consider briefly why managers need to understand the role of such differences in dynamics. The following points are relevant.

Managers need to know that all employees are not the same and do not react in the same way to similar situations. A knowledge of how employees differ can help the manager better understand his or her employees and act to facilitate (rather than inhibit) employee need satisfaction.

Employee abilities and traits are those individual characteristics that determine an employee's *capacity* to contribute to the organization, in contrast to motivation, which determines an employee's *will* to contribute. Understanding abilities and traits is important, since actual performance is a joint function of motivation and abilities and traits. Moreover, clearly recognizing the differences in employee traits allows managers to do a better job in matching people and jobs most suited to their individual talents and skills. This selection and placement process enhances the human resource function in organizations.

Learning is a prerequisite to most forms of behavior, both on the job and off. Managers, skilled craftspeople, and laborers must all learn certain skills that are necessary for good job performance. Hence, it is important to understand how learning takes place and how it influences behavior. Because most companies spend considerable sums on the process of training and development, their chances for success are enhanced when their managers understand the principles of learning that underly the process.

Just as personality and motivation are related, so too are learning and motivation. A knowledge of learning processes can improve our understanding of employee motivation at work. This connection is particularly evident in recent efforts to use behavior modification techniques in organizations.

A manager's awareness of the concept of employee needs has clear implications for employee selection and placement. Certain types of employees are likely to be more successful in sales positions, while others are likely to excel in staff positions, such as personnel administration. Understanding these differences can facilitate decisions concerning who is placed in which positions. Also, based on individual needs, employees respond differently to different rewards, and an awareness of needs differences can help the manager design appropriate reward systems. Finally, the recognition that employees pursue different needs helps the manager better understand why different employees behave as they do. For instance, an employee with a high need for achievement is likely to pursue task-related activities, while an employee with a high need for affiliation may pay more attention to developing social relationships on the job.

PERSONAL TRAITS AT WORK

Definition

A personal trait may be defined as a consistent predisposition or tendency to behave in a particular way.[3] In other words, if we observe someone who demonstrates empathy, social judgment, and insight in social situations, we say the person has *social sensitivity*. When a person seems overly assertive, dominant, and aloof, we may say the person has *ascendant tendencies*. In both cases, we are dealing with observed or measurable behaviors in predispositions to behave that can have an impact on the work place.

Some use the term *personality* instead of personal traits, but often the term personality is defined as a broader concept describing the individual's total self. Personal traits are used here to simply identify a series of individual dimensions along which we can differentiate employees in the work place. One way to see the importance of personal traits at work in organizations is a look at how a company such as Chase Manhattan Bank selects an executive.

UP CLOSE 2.1:   Chase Manhattan Bank

In the past, many corporations treated human resource planning and strategic planning as separate functions. Today, things are changing, as several American and Canadian organizations are realizing just how important the match is between the personal traits of managers and the basic mission of the company.[4]

When the trust manager of Chase Manhattan Bank retired, the bank decided the department, whose operations had been essentially stable, should change its focus to a more aggressive growth strategy. To do this, the bank took the unusual move of not looking inside for a veteran banker. For that matter, the bank didn't even look outside for a veteran banker. Instead, Chase hired a man whose primary experience has been with IBM. "We felt he had that strong IBM customer marketing orientation," explained Chase's executive vice-president for human resources.

Moreover, when Chase wanted to reorient its retail banking business from a low-margin operation, where the emphasis is on cost reduction, to a more expansionary enterprise offering broader consumer financial services, it hired a manager from a small overseas industrial firm. The new manager was seen as a real entrepreneur. The former head of retail banking, who was seen as a strong cost cutter, was transferred to another division where a lack of cost-cutting skills was a primary problem.

Matching managerial style with corporate objectives is no easy task, especially when objectives change. For example, the entrepreneurial type of manager who brought a product line from only 2 percent share of the market to 30 percent in three years may not be the right person to continue managing the product with equal effectiveness after it becomes a mature product with little growth potential. Instead of cost cutting and pushing productivity (the logical approach for a mature, cash-generating product), the entrepreneur may still push for innovation and risk-taking (the approach typically taken for new ventures).

Chase Manhattan Bank's strategy was to select managers based on a good fit between their personal characteristics and managerial style and desired divisional objectives. ▬

Measuring Personal Traits

In organizational situations, personal traits can be assessed in three principal ways: 1) inventories; 2) experimental procedures; and 3) independent ratings. The most popular of these techniques in industry is the self-report inventory. In this approach, individuals respond to a series of standardized questions on either a true-false format or a Likert-type scale (a scale where the respondent answers on a continuum from strongly agree to strongly disagree). The California Psychological Inventory, the Minnesota Multiphasic Personality Inventory, and the Personality Research Form are perhaps the most popular personality inventories. These inventories are structured to provide percentile scores on a variety of personal traits or characteristics (e.g., dogmatism, aggressiveness, cognitive complexity). A major benefit of such inventories is that a large number of traits can be measured with little time or effort.

A second way to measure traits is the use of experimental procedures. Here, individuals are placed in artificially created situations that attempt to simulate real life. Assessment centers are one application of this approach. Here a series of simulated management exercises such as role playing, in-basket techniques, or stress interviews are used to appraise personal characteristics.

The third technique, independent ratings, makes use of trained experts or peers to evaluate individuals on a set of predetermined traits. The most frequent use of independent ratings in industry are the recommendation forms many companies use for personnel selection and placement. All three techniques are subject to considerable measurement error, making their use in industry highly controversial.

Influence of Personal Traits on Work Behavior

Investigators of employee behavior at work have spent considerable time examining the role of personal traits in the work place. Trait theories of personality (those based on the study of personal traits) focus largely on the normal or healthy adult, in contrast to psychoanalytic theories, which focus largely on abnormal behavior. Second, trait theories identify several specific characteristics that describe people. Allport insisted that our understanding of individual behavior could progress only by breaking behavior patterns down into a series of elements (traits).[5] "The only thing you can do about a *total* personality is to send flowers to it," he once said.

In the study of people at work, we may discuss an employee's dependability, emotional stability, or cognitive complexity. When taken together, these traits form a large mosaic that gives us a "big-picture" insight into individuals. Finally, a third reason for the popularity of trait theories in the study of organizational behavior is that the traits are measurable and tend to remain relatively stable over time. This gives us tangible qualities to use for comparisons among employees.

One problem that does exist in studying personal traits is their sheer number. It has been estimated that there are over 17,000 traits to describe people.[6] Such a large number obviously makes it difficult to develop usable models of human behavior on the job. Fortunately, it is possible to cluster many of the more salient traits to develop building blocks to aid our analysis. Six of these clusters are: 1) cognitive complexity; 2) emotional stability; 3) dependability; 4) social sensitivity; 5) ascendant tendencies; and 6) interpersonal style.

Cognitive Style   This cluster of traits refers to the way people process and organize information and arrive at conclusions based on their observations of various situations. Three aspects of cognitive style are of particular importance for the study of people in organizations. The first of these is **dogmatism,** which refers to a particular cognitive style that is characterized by closed mindedness and inflexibility.[7] This trait is especially applicable to the managerial decision-making process. Dogmatic managers tend to reach decisions quickly, following only a limited search for information, and are highly confident about the accuracy of the resulting decisions.[8] Dogmatism can interfere with efficient performance of duties. One study found that highly dogmatic individuals report large discrepancies between how they actually spent their time on the job and how they would ideally spend their time. Apparently, their inflexibility and rigidity of cognitive style interferes with their handling of work-related problems.[9]

Individuals also vary in their **risk-taking propensity,** or their willingness to take risks in decision making. (Jerry Wilson of Soloflex has a high propensity for risk taking.) Research among managers indicates that high risk takers, like those high in dogmatism, tend to make decisions more quickly, limiting their search for relevant information, than do low risk takers.[10] Such differences are important for organizations, depending upon in what type of jobs high and low risk takers are placed. For example, a high risk-taking propensity is good for a sales representative who must act quickly to make a sale, but it could be financially disastrous for a bank loan officer.

The third trait, **cognitive complexity,** describes an individual's ability to acquire and sort through various pieces of information from the environment and organize them in a sensible way. Individuals with a high cognitive complexity tend to use more information—and to see the relationships between pieces of this information—than do individuals with low cognitive complexity. If a manager is assigned a particular problem, would he or she have the capacity to break the problem down into its various facets and understand how the facets relate to one another? A manager with low cognitive complexity tends to see only a few of the more salient aspects of the problem, while a manager with a higher cognitive complexity would understand more of the subtleties of the problem as they relate to each other and to the environment.

Research on cognitive complexity in organizations has focused on two important areas: leadership style and decision making. In the area of leadership, managers who rate high on cognitive complexity are better able to handle complex situations, such as rapid changes in the external environment. These managers also tend to use more resources and information when solving a problem and tend to be somewhat more considerate and consultative in their approach to managing subordinates.[11] In decision making, individuals with high cognitive complexity fairly consistently seek out more information for a decision, actually process or use more information, are better able to integrate discrepant information, consider a greater number of possible solutions to the problem, and employ more complex decision strategies than individuals with low cognitive complexity.[12]

Emotional Stability   This refers to a cluster of personal traits that relate to the emotional and mental well-being of individuals. The emotional stability cluster includes the positive traits of emotional balance and adjustment, as well as the negative traits of anxiety, defensiveness, depressive tendencies, and neuroticism. Studies have revealed that one of the more important emotional stability traits is **anxiety.**[13] Anxiety is a greater-than-normal uneasiness or concern about some uncertain or future event. Anxious individuals also can experience vague and uneasy feelings that are psychologically unpleasant—for no particular reason. Both types of anxiety interfere with responses to everyday life events. Individuals who are highly anxious consistently have problems in developing rewarding interpersonal relationships, generally have low aspirations on task performance, conform easily to group norms, alter their judgments and opinions when confronted by differing opinions, and are highly dependent on others for clues to acceptable behavior. Recent attempts in organizations to open communication and develop more interpersonal trust are often aimed at creating a work environment where employees experience less threat and anxiety and, as a result, become more productive members of the organization or work group.

Dependability   Individuals are also different with respect to their behavioral consistency and personal integrity. Individuals who are seen as self-reliant, consistent, and dependable are typically viewed by others as desirable colleagues or group members who will cooperate and work steadfastly toward group goals.[14] On the other hand, unconventional people are often thought to lack dependability and commitment to group goals. They are not respected and often are rejected by other group members. Individuals' perceptions of others are taken into account in hiring and promotion decisions (see Chapter 5).

Social Sensitivity   Another personal trait cluster centers around the extent to which individuals perceive and respond to the needs, emotions, and preferences of those around them. These traits include empathy, social judgment, and insight. Studies of organizations have consistently shown a relationship between these social skills and acceptance by group members, successful leadership attempts, amount of participation, and group performance effectiveness.[15] The lack of these skills is inversely related to friendliness and social interaction, as we might expect. Social sensitivity traits can have a significant effect on one's career.

Ascendant Tendencies   Finally, we should note that people vary considerably in the extent to which they are prominent, assertive, and domineering. An ascendant orientation reflects an individual's strong desire to stand apart from the group, to be different or unique in a superior way. People with ascendant tendencies are often self-assertive, creative, and popular. They frequently emerge as leaders and tend to be quite dissatisfied with the performance of *other* leaders.[16] We shall return to this problem in a later discussion of leadership processes in organizations (see Chapter 13).

Interpersonal Style   An important individual characteristic in the work place is **interpersonal style,** or the way in which people typically behave in group settings. Lee Iacocca, Chrysler's well-known president, had developed a reputation for both efficiency and sales prowess when he was last with Ford Motor Company in 1978. He was personally responsible for many of the company's major successes. However, as a result of a long-smouldering feud between Iacocca and Chairman Henry Ford, Iacocca was fired. Sources familiar with the discussions that preceded Iacocca's departure report that Iacocca said to Ford, "I've been with the company for thirty-two years. What did I do wrong?" Henry Ford reportedly replied, "I just don't like you."[17] Here, as the saying goes, one man's meat was another man's poison—in a clear-cut case of interpersonal style differences. Personal characteristics that fall into the interpersonal style cluster include the general tendency to trust (or not to trust) others, openness (or social distance), and one's orientation toward authority.

A great deal has been written about individual orientations toward authority. Early work by Adorno and his associates[18] found that this trait varies widely with people. An **authoritarian orientation** (or authoritarian personality) is characterized by several features, all reflecting the notion that it is right and proper for there to be clear status and power differences between people. A high authoritarian is typically demanding, directive, and controlling of subordinates; submissive and deferential to superiors; intellectually rigid; fearful of social change; highly judgmental and categorical in reactions to others; distrustful; and hostile in response to restraint. Nonauthoritarians, on the other hand, believe more firmly that status and power differences should be minimized, that social change can be constructive, and that people should be more accepting and less judgmental of those around them.

Overall, then, we can see how personal traits not only allow us to differentiate between individuals, but also how such traits can have important ramifications for employee behavior in organizations. Individuals behave in large part based on such traits, and it becomes important for managers to understand personal traits if they are to be efficient and effective in their jobs.

UP CLOSE 2.2:   Hisao Tsubouchi

Hisao Tsubouchi is a tough, autocratic boss who has earned a reputation for breaking unions, firing large numbers of employees, and instilling fear in subordinates.[19] *He does things his way. In doing so, Tsubouchi has established one of the world's largest fortunes. He owns 180 companies, with businesses ranging from movie theaters and hotels to a taxi service and a sake brewery. His holdings bring him $190 million in annual profits on sales of $3.3 billion.*

An example of how Tsubouchi works can be seen in his 1978 purchase of Sasebo Heavy Industries Company, one of Japan's largest shipbuilders. When Tsubouchi bought Sasebo, the company was $300 million in debt. Upon purchase, Tsubouchi immediately fired half of Sasebo's 6,628-member work force and cut the management staff from 460 to 39. Wages were sharply reduced, the lunch hour was cut in half and workers were pressured into working overtime without pay. Suppliers to the company were forced to accept price cuts as high as 20 percent or risk losing the shipyard's business.

Clearly, Tsubouchi has broken all the rules of Japanese consensus building, the prevalent form of Japanese management. His interpersonal style is highly unorthodox for the Japanese culture. Even so, after three years, Sasebo earned a $17 million profit.

Tsubouchi credits his success to his approach to life, in a sense, his personal traits. He leads a spartan life, works long hours, and attempts to be a "model manager." Unlike most Japanese managers, who try and foster loyalty toward the company, Tsubouchi has tried to create a personality cult. Employees are expected to call him "Owner Tsubouchi," and employees are clearly informed that bonuses come from the owner's own pocket. When workers at one shipyard doubled their productivity, he sent each worker $200 in bonus. He also sent $200 to each worker's wife to encourage her to see to it that her husband continued to work hard! This is a surprising way to award a worker's family a $400 bonus.

Clearly, Tsubouchi is a self-made leader who approaches management from a unique perspective, especially by Japanese standards. The personal traits Tsubouchi has developed play a major role in his interpersonal style, his definition of success, and his goals in life. ■

INDIVIDUAL MOTIVES AND NEEDS

Individual motives and needs are, in addition to personal traits, the second major way on-the-job behavior in organizations is influenced. A **need** is defined as a continuing or recurring fixation on a particular goal. Each need is generally believed to have two components: 1) a qualitative or directional component, which includes the object toward which the goal is directed; and 2) a quantitative or energetic component, which includes the strength or intensity of the need toward the object. Needs and motives often are viewed as a primary motivating force both on and off the job.

One of the most useful ways to conceptualize individual needs in the work place is to employ the **manifest needs theory,** developed by Murray.[20] This theory argues that individuals can be classified according to the strengths of their various needs. People possess a variety of needs at any one point in time, and these needs are major influences on behavior. Murray posited that individuals possess about two dozen needs, including the needs for achievement, affiliation, power, and so forth. These needs and their definitions are shown in Exhibit 2.1. Murray believed that these needs are mostly learned, rather than inherited, and that they are activated by cues from the external environment. For example, an employee with a high need for achievement can only be expected to pursue that need (i.e., to try to achieve something) when the environmental conditions are appropriate (e.g., when he is given a challenging task). Only then would the need become *manifest*. When the need was not cued, the need was said to be *latent*, or inactive.

Need for Achievement

Although the manifest needs model encompasses an entire set of needs, most research in organizations has focused on the three needs of achievement, affiliation, and power. These three needs seem to be particularly important for understanding people at work. We shall consider each of these needs as they relate to work settings. By far the most prominent need from the standpoint of organizational behavior is the **need for achievement** (also known as *n Ach* or *n Achievement*). Need for achievement is defined as "behavior toward competition with a standard of excellence."[21] High need for achievement is characterized by: a strong desire to assume personal responsibility for finding solutions to problems; a tendency to set moderately difficult achievement goals and take calculated risks; a strong desire for concrete feedback on task performance; and a single-minded preoccupation with task and task accomplishment. Low need for achievement, on the other hand, is typically characterized by a preference for low risk levels on tasks and for shared responsibility on tasks.

Need for achievement is important, not only for understanding human behavior in its own right, but also for understanding how people respond to the

EXHIBIT 2.1
Definitions of Murray's Manifest Needs

Need	Characteristics
Achievement	To overcome obstacles, to exercise power, to strive to do something difficult as well and as quickly as possible.
Affiliation	To form friendships and associations. To greet, join, and live with others. To co-operate and converse sociably with others. To love. To join groups.
Dominance	To influence or control others. To persuade, prohibit, dictate. To lead and direct. To restrain. To organize the behavior of a group.

SOURCE: From H. A. Murray (ed.), *Explorations in Personality*, 1938. New York: Oxford.

work environment. The concept has important implications for job design, for one example. Enriching an employee's job by providing greater amounts of variety, autonomy, and responsibility would probably enhance performance only for those employees who would be challenged by that enrichment—these would be high need achievers. Low need achievers, on the other hand, may be frustrated by the increased personal responsibility for task accomplishment and may perform poorly or even withdraw from the situation.

UP CLOSE 2.3   The Entrepreneurs

A characteristic trait of high need achievers is the strong desire to take risks and accomplish important goals. Young entrepreneurs are perhaps our best example. Frederick W. Smith, in his early thirties, founded the Federal Express Corporation to deliver packages that "absolutely, positively have to be there overnight." In only four years, the company grossed $600 million. Nolan K. Bushnell invented Pony, the first video game, at age twenty-nine. He then sold the company, Atari, to Warner Communications in 1976 for $28 million. Steven Jobs and Steven Wozniak, both in their early twenties, developed the first successful personal home computer in Wozniak's garage. After only six years, Apple Computer, Inc. had sales of $600 million and Jobs' and Wozniak's estimated net worth was $149 million each. (Their fortunes have changed somewhat since then.)

It is interesting that neither Europe nor Japan has a strong tradition of adventurous small-business entrepreneurs starting their own firms, and neither country has matched the U.S. record of success in this area. In Europe, financial backing for such ventures is quite difficult to secure; in Japan, ther country has matched the U.S. record of success in this area. In Europe, financial backing for such ventures is quite difficult to secure; in Japan, emphasis is on corporate development over the individual. Kenji Tamiya, president of Sony Corporation of America, notes, "Japanese society is more highly organized, and big organizations tend to avoid risk. Particularly in new fields like personal computers or video games, you must take risks and make decisions quickly. This gives the U.S. an advantage."[22]   ▰

Need for Affiliation

Need for affiliation *(n Aff)* may be defined as an "attraction to another organism in order to feel reassured from the other that the self is acceptable."[23] This does not mean being sociable or popular; instead, it is the need for human companionship and reassurance. Individuals with a high need for affiliation typically have: a strong desire for approval and reassurance from others; a tendency to conform to the wishes and norms of others when pressured by people whose friendship they value; and a sincere interest in the feelings of others. Such individuals tend to take jobs characterized by a high amount of interpersonal contact, like sales, teaching, counseling, and public relations.

How does need for affiliation affect employee behavior? Evidence suggests that individuals with a high need for affiliation have better attendance records than those with a low *n Aff.*[24] Some research suggests that high *n Aff* employees perform better in situations where personal support and approval is tied to performance. Support for this position comes from French, who found in a laboratory experiment that, while high *n Ach* individuals performed better when given *task-related* feedback, high *n Aff* individuals also performed better when given *supportive* feedback.[25] In addition, effort and performance for those high in *n Aff* can be enhanced under a cooperative work norm where pressure for increased output is exerted by one's friends only.[26] The implications for leadership or supervisory behavior are fairly clear. When supervisors can create a cooperative, supportive work environment in which positive feedback is tied to task performance, employees with a high need for affiliation are more productive. Working harder in such an environment leads to the kinds of need satisfaction desired by high *n Aff* individuals.

Need for Power

The third need that is important to understanding organizational behavior is an individual's need for power or dominance. Need for power is a desire to influence others and to control one's environment. Interest in the power motive dates from the early work of Adler, who believed that power was the major goal of all human activity.[27] Adler saw human development as a process by which people learn to exert control over the forces that have power over them. Hence, a person's ultimate satisfaction comes with his or her ability to have influence over the environment. While subsequent work suggests that power is not an all-consuming drive, it nevertheless is an important need in the study of organization.

McClelland argues that need for power can take two forms among managers: personal power and institutionalized power.[28] Employees with an orientation toward **personal power** strive for dominance almost for the sake of dominance. Personal conquest is very important to them. These people tend to reject institutional responsibilities. McClelland likens personal-power types to con- quistadores or feudal chieftains; they attempt to inspire their subordinates to heroic performance but want their subordinates to be responsible to their leader, not to the organization. The manager using **institutionalized power,** on the other hand, is more concerned with problems of the organization and what he or she can do to facilitate goal attainment. Institutionalized-power types are organization minded and feel personal responsibility for building up the organization; enjoy work and getting things done in an orderly fashion; seem quite willing to sacrifice some of their own self-interest for the welfare of the organization; have a strong sense of justice or equity; and are more mature (that is, they are less defensive and more willing to seek expert advice when necessary).

Individual Needs and Leadership Success

Based on the above description, what type of leader is most suited to the tasks of managing? A manager with a high need for achievement? Need for affiliation? Need for power? McClelland posits that the best manager is one who has a high need for power.[29] Managers who have a high need for achievement concentrate on personal accomplishments and improvement. They tend to be highly independent individuals who want to assume responsibility and credit for task accomplishment and who want short-term feedback on their performance. However, these same characteristics can be detrimental when the individual has to manage others. In complex organizations, managers cannot perform all the tasks necessary for success; teamwork is necessary. Feedback on the group's effort and performance is often vague and delayed. The need for power takes precedence because the managerial environment is not totally suitable to stimulate the need for achievement in managers.

Similar problems confront high *n Aff* managers. Affiliative managers have a strong need for group acceptance and can tend to be indecisive in decision making for fear of alienating one faction or another. A concern for maintaining good interpersonal relationships can result in their attention being focused on keeping subordinates happy rather than on work performance.

Finally, leaders with a high need for institutionalized power tend to supervise work groups that are both more productive and more satisfied than the groups of other managers. McClelland also found that managers with high personal power needs were less successful managers than those with a need for institutionalized power.

Power-oriented managers, when truly concerned about the organization as a whole, provide the structure, drive, and support necessary to facilitate goal-oriented group behavior. In this sense, they fit nicely into most definitions of managerial success.

UP CLOSE 2.4:   Lee Iacocca

One of the best-known managers in the U.S. today is Lee Iacocca, president of Chrysler Corporation. To many people, Iacocca embodies the ideal manager. He is an achievement-oriented "take charge" executive who makes skillful use of power to achieve institutional objectives. He is charismatic and an articulate spokesman for corporate America. One gets the impression that Lee Iacocca is not just devoted to Chrysler's success, he is also devoted to the success of the entire country.

Iacocca has many things going for him as a manager. When president of Ford Motor Company, he introduced the enormously successful Mustang, along with several other cars. At Chrysler, he is credited with literally saving the company and 600,000 jobs. He has a clear and visible record of performance. When asked the key to his success as a manager, Iacocca replies: "Boys, there ain't no free lunches in this country. And don't go spending your whole life commiserating that you got the raw deals. You've got to say, 'I think that if I keep working at this and want it bad enough I can have it.' It's called perserverance."[30]

Iacocca's approach to life and corporate management helps explain the widespread respect he has earned as an executive. It also helps explain the clout he wields in initiating and succeeding at projects others might shy away from. ■■

LEARNING

The third major type of individual difference focuses on the learning process. As we know, people learn at considerably different rates. They also choose to learn considerably different things. Learning is a foundation upon which one of the most popular theories of work motivation is based. Because of this and the implications this has for the work place, it is important to understand how and what individuals learn.

Nature of Learning

For our purposes, **learning** is defined as a relatively permanent change in behavior that occurs as a result of experience. Someone has learned something when he or she consistently exhibits a new behavior over time. Several aspects of this definition are noteworthy.[31] First, learning involves a change in attitude or behavior. The change does not necessarily have to be an improvement, however; one can learn bad habits or forming prejudices. In order for learning to occur, the change must be relatively permanent. Changes in behavior that result from fatigue or temporary adaptations to a unique situation would not normally be considered examples of learning.

In addition, learning typically involves some form of practice or experience. The change that results from physical maturation, for example, such as a baby developing the physical strength to walk, is in itself not considered learning. Practice or experience must be reinforced over time for learning to take place. When reinforcement does not follow practice or experience, the behavior would eventually diminish and disappear. Third, learning is an inferred process; it is not possible to directly observe learning. Instead, we must infer that learning took place from observing changes in overt behavior by individuals. How learning can have a profound impact on both organizations and society at large is seen in the teaching of the work ethic in Japan.

UP CLOSE 2.5:   The Japanese Work Ethic

What makes Japan such an economic success? How can a nation slightly smaller than Montana continue year after year to generate tremendous trade surpluses with the U.S.? One answer to these questions may lie in the personal characteristics of its people.[32]

A foreign visitor notices early that offices in Tokyo's high-rise business district are lit well into the night. Managers climbing the corporate ladder typically put in a day that begins in early morning and can last past midnight. Work on Saturdays and Sundays is common. And employees seldom take all the vacation time to which they are entitled. After work, it is expected that white-collar employees will entertain clients or have dinner and drinks with coworkers in the interests of company spirit and loyalty.

Many women with children have become what the Japanese call "education mothers." They are obsessed with pushing their children to excel in school so they can get into the best universities and, subsequently, get the best jobs. Japanese children go to school 5½ days a week, 240 days a year. By the time they graduate from high school, they have the equivalent of four more years of school than their U.S. counterparts. They score an average 11 points higher than American students on I.Q. tests.

The Japanese work ethic and demand for high standards of performance is developed early. Desirable personal traits are encouraged in the children who, in turn, become desirable employees. As Americans see their share of world and domestic markets shrinking, they are beginning to realize the economic—if not personal—consequences of a rigorous work ethic learned early. ■

Classical Conditioning in Learning

Three major theories of learning can be identified: 1) classical conditioning; 2) operant conditioning; and 3) cognitive learning theory. The first two models focus on the stimulus-response (S-R) connection as the basic unit of analysis in learning processes; each suggests alternative explanations about how these bonds are established. The third model, cognitive learning theory, represents a significant departure from the other two models.

Interest in learning processes dates from experiments of Pavlov at the turn of the century. Much of this early work, as well as much of today's research, results from laboratory experiments using animals. While these techniques help us understand the most basic forms of human learning, our study of organizations is best facilitated by examining more complex learning processes.

Pavlov's learning theory is known as classical conditioning. **Classical conditioning** focuses on the process in which bond is developed between a conditioned stimulus and a conditioned response through the repeated linking of a conditioned stimulus with an unconditioned stimulus. This process is shown in Exhibit 2.2.

Pavlov was interested in the question of whether animals could be trained to draw a causal relationship between previously unconnected factors. The experiment began with unlearned, or *unconditioned*, stimulus-response relationships. When a dog was presented with meat (unconditioned stimulus), the dog salivated (unconditioned response). No learning was taking place, since this relationship represented a natural physiological process. Next, Pavlov paired the unconditioned stimulus (meat) with a *conditioned* stimulus (the ringing of a bell). The ringing of the bell by itself would not be expected to elicit salivation. However, over time, a learned linkage developed for the dog between the bell and meat, ultimately resulting in a **stimulus-response (S-R) bond** between the conditioned stimulus (the bell) and the response (salivation), without the presence of the unconditioned stimulus (the meat). He concluded that learning had occurred, and that this learning resulted from conditioning the dogs to associate two normally unrelated objects, the bell and the salivation.

Even though classical conditioning can have applications to the work place (e.g., in the area of training and development), it has been criticized as explaining only a limited part of total human learning. Skinner argues that classical conditioning focuses on respondent, or reflexive, behaviors. It concentrates on explaining largely involuntary responses that result from stimuli.[33] More complex learning cannot be explained solely by classical conditioning. As an alternative explanation, Skinner argues that the operant conditioning model of learning is superior, particularly in organizational situations.

EXHIBIT 2.2
A Model of Classical Conditioning

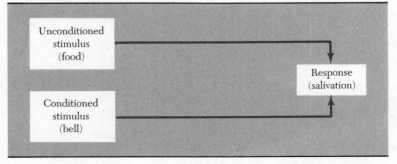

Operant Conditioning

Operant conditioning as a model of learning focuses on the effects of reinforcements or rewards on desired behaviors. One of the first psychologists to examine such processes was Watson, a contemporary of Pavlov, who posited that behavior was largely influenced by the rewards one received as a result of actions. This notion is summarized in Thorndike's *law of effect*, which states that, "of several responses made to the same situation, those which are accompanied or closely followed by satisfaction (reinforcement) . . . will be more likely to occur; those which are accompanied or closely followed by discomfort (punishment) . . . will be less likely to occur."[34] Thus, this law of effect argues that behavior leading to positive or pleasurable outcomes tends to be repeated, while behavior leading to negative outcomes or punishment tends to be avoided. In this manner, individuals learn appropriate, acceptable responses to their environment. For example, by repeatedly paying employees a bonus when they achieve a certain level of output, we would expect them to produce at the desired level.

The basic operant model of learning is presented in Exhibit 2.3. There are three important concepts of this model:

1. *Drive:* An internal state of disequilibrium; a felt need. A drive generally is believed to increase with the strength of deprivation. A drive or desire to learn must be present for learning to take place.
2. *Habit:* The experienced bond or connection between stimulus and response. For example, if a person learns over time that exercise feels good, a strong stimulus-response (exercise-good feelings) can develop. Habits determine the behaviors or courses of action we choose.
3. *Reinforcement or reward:* The feedback or consequences individuals receive as a result of action.

As can be seen in Exhibit 2.3, a stimulus activates an individual's motivation through its impact on drive and habit. The stronger the drive and habit (S-R bond), the stronger the motivation to behave in a certain way. Two things happen as a result of this behavior. First, the individual receives feedback that reduces the original drive. Second, the individual strengthens his or her belief in the veracity of the S-R bond to the extent that it proved successful. If one's response to a given stimulus satisfied a particular drive or need, the individual would come to believe more strongly in the appropriateness of the S-R connection and would respond in the same way under similar circumstances.

This process can be seen in attempts to impress upon chronically unemployed workers the importance of coming to work. A daily pay system instead of a weekly or monthly system is used. This is effective because the workers, who do not have a history of working, can more quickly see the relationship between coming to work and receiving pay. The S-R bond develops more rapidly because of the frequency of the reward or reinforcement.

Operant conditioning differs from classical conditioning in at least two ways. First, the two approaches differ in what is believed to cause changes in behavior. In classical conditioning, changes in behavior are believed to occur

EXHIBIT 2.3
A Model of Operant Conditioning

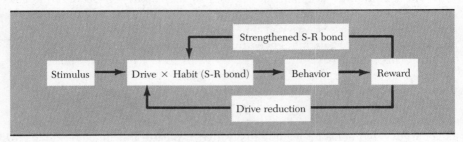

through changes in stimuli, that is, a change from an unconditioned stimulus to a conditioned stimulus. In operant conditioning, changes in behavior are thought to result from the consequences of previous behavior. When behavior has been rewarded, we would expect it to be repeated; when behavior has not been rewarded or has been punished, we would not expect it to be repeated. Second, the two approaches differ in the role and frequency of rewards. In classical conditioning, the unconditioned stimulus, acting as a type of reward, is administered during every trial. In operant conditioning, the reward results only when individuals choose the correct response. In operant conditioning, individuals must correctly operate on their environment before a reward is received. The response is instrumental in obtaining desired rewards.[35]

Cognition and Learning

The third model of learning is the **cognitive learning theory.** Without rejecting traditional stimulus-response approaches to the study of learning, cognitive theorists believe that much learning takes place outside of the S-R bond. Learning is viewed as a process that requires an individual's entire personality. The learning process is seen as being more complex than simple S-R connections.

Cognitive learning theorists believe that much learning results from simply thinking about a problem, from insight, and from piecing together known facts. The significant process in learning is the individual's acquisition of information (including abstract concepts and generalizations) rather than his or her specific responses.[36] The cognitive approach to understanding learning processes emphasizes an individual's reasoning and analytical, perceptual, and problem-solving abilities. This approach also emphasizes an individual's purposiveness and goal-orientation, assuming that the individual is motivated and desires to learn. The cognitive learning theory differs from the other two conditioning models, which rely exclusively on S-R bonds that develop over time within individuals.

Learning effectiveness is affected by five major factors, studies have shown. Classical or operant conditioning is for learning simple or repetitive tasks only, while complex learning of more sophisticated material requires the proper learning environment. These five influences on learning effectiveness are:

1. Research indicates that learning effectiveness is increased considerably when individuals have high *motivation* to learn. A student may work day and night to complete a term paper that is of interest to her. Yet she may postpone completing an uninteresting term paper until the last possible minute. When a student or employee is motivated to learn by his or her high need to know something, that person learns far more effectively.

2. Feedback on performance facilitates learning. A knowledge of results serves a gyroscopic function, showing individuals where they are correct or incorrect, furnishing them with the perspective to improve. Feedback also is an important positive reinforcer that can enhance an individual's desire to continue learning.

3. *Prior* learning can increase the ability to learn new materials or tasks by providing needed background or foundation materials. When the previous tasks and the present tasks exhibit similar stimulus-response connections, the beneficial effects for learning are greatest. For instance, most of the astronauts selected for the space program have years of experience flying airplanes. It is assumed that their prior experience and skills will facilitate their learning to fly spacecraft.

4. Another influence on learning effectiveness concerns whether the materials to be learned are presented in their entirety or in parts—*whole* versus *part* learning. When a task consists of several distinct and unrelated duties, part learning is more effective. Each task should be learned separately. When a task consists of several integrated and related parts (such as learning the components of a small machine), whole learning is best, because the major interrelationships between parts, as well as proper sequencing of parts, are not overlooked or underemphasized.

5. A final influence on learning highlights the advantages and disadvantages of *concentrated* as opposed to *distributed* training sessions. Distribution of practice, or short learning periods at set intervals, is more effective for learning motor skills than for learning verbal or cognitive skills. Distributed practice also seems to facilitate learning of very difficult, voluminous, or tedious material. Concentrated practice, however, appears to work well where insight is required for task completion. Apparently, concentrated effort over short durations provides a more successful approach to problem solving or complex decision making.[37]

UP CLOSE 2.6: Achievement Motivation Training

As we saw earlier in this chapter, high n Ach *managers tend to strive, and often succeed, in highly challenging jobs. If this motive can be developed through training programs, managerial performance can be enhanced. A good example of how learning processes work in organizations can be seen in their efforts to develop training techniques to instill the achievement motive in managers.*

McClelland has developed a unique approach to training with respect to achievement.[38] His behavioral approach to training consists of four steps. First, participants are taught how to think, talk, and act like a person with a high need for achievement. These activities are based on profiles of successful high n Ach managers, and they define "correct" behaviors. Next, participants are shown how to establish challenging (but realistic) work objectives for themselves. These behavioral objectives serve to guide goal-directed behavior. Third, participants are given considerable feedback about their behavior and their performance on the work objectives. And, finally, efforts are made to create an esprit de corps among the participants, and a support group is established to help foster and reinforce achievement-oriented behavior.

McClelland argues that these programs tend to be successful. With few exceptions, managers from various countries who completed these programs received more rapid promotions, earned more money, and expanded their businesses more quickly than did the control groups. It would follow that achievement motivation training can work for at least some groups. Perhaps more clearly, however, this example shows the value of training in work situations. ■

SUMMARY

In this chapter, we were introduced to the broad topic of individual differences as they relate to behavior in organizations. Three related topics were discussed: personal traits, individual needs, and learning processes.

A personal trait is defined as a relatively consistent predisposition to behave in a certain way. Six personal traits were covered: 1) cognitive complexity; 2) emotional stability; 3) dependability; 4) social sensitivity; 5) ascendant tendencies; and 6) interpersonal style. Personal traits are important for understanding organizational behavior because they have the potential to significantly influence how people respond to their work environment. Both a manager with a somewhat domineering, confronting interpersonal style and a manager with a more participative, consultative style may be successful, but each operates on his or her environment in a different manner.

Related to personal traits is the topic of individual need strengths. A need is a continuing or recurring fixation on a particular goal. Following Murray's manifest needs theory, we discussed the three related needs for achievement and entrepreneurial success. However, managerial success in major ongoing corporations requires not only an achievement orientation but also a need for institutionalized power.

Finally, we examined learning processes in organizations. Learning is a relatively permanent change in behavior that occurs as a result of experiences. Operant and classical conditioning form the basis for behavior modification techniques. Classical conditioning focuses on the process in which a bond is developed between a conditioned stimulus and a conditioned response through the repeated linking of a conditioned stimulus with an unconditioned stimulus. Thus, changes in behavior are thought to occur through changes in stimuli. In operant conditioning, changes in behavior are thought to result from the consequences of previous behaviors. When behavior is rewarded, it tends to be repeated; when behavior is not rewarded or is punished, it tends not to be repeated.

Finally, cognitive learning theory was introduced. Cognitive learning theory assumes that much learning takes place outside of the stimulus-response bond. That is, much learning occurs as a result of thinking and problem solving, or through the use of one's cognitive abilities.

KEY WORDS

anxiety	conditioned stimulus	need for power
ascendant tendencies	institutionalized power	operant conditioning
authoritarian orientation	interpersonal style	personal power
	law of effect	personal trait
classical conditioning	learning	reinforcement
cognitive complexity	manifest needs theory	reward
cognitive learning theory	need	risk-taking propensity
	need for achievement	social sensitivity
cognitive style	need for affiliation	S-R bond

DISCUSSION QUESTIONS

1. Why are personal traits important in organizations? Which personal traits do you consider most important? Why?
2. Explain how cognitive style affects managerial behavior on the job.
3. Using the various personal traits described in this chapter, how would you characterize the Japanese industrialist Hisao Tsubouchi?
4. How does the manifest needs theory operate? What use is the theory for understanding employee behavior at work?
5. How would you describe yourself according to the three needs discussed in this chapter?
6. How would you describe a successful manager following the manifest needs model? Would this description vary according to the organization (e.g., General Motors, McDonald's, Apple Computer, U.S. Navy)?
7. Describe the basic learning process. What are the three basic theories of learning and how do they differ? How are they similar?
8. Of the three models of learning, which do you feel is most useful for managers interested in developing an effective, highly motivated work force?

CASE 2.1:   Petersen Electronics

"Grow old along with me, the best is yet to be." When Robert Browning expressed this sentiment, he was not writing as a spokesman for business to promising young executives. Yet in the nineteenth century, while such poetry may have been out of place in business, the thought was very fitting.[39]

In fact, until quite recently corporations have been able to reward capable employees with increased responsibilities and opportunities. Based on our recently completed research into nine companies, however, the more prevalent corporate sentiment might be, "Stay young along with me, or gone you well may be."

We found a large number of managers who, in the judgment of their organization, have "plateaued." That is, there is little or no likelihood that they will be promoted or receive substantial increases in duties and responsibilities. These long-service employees are being regarded with growing concern because plateauing is taking place more markedly, and frequently earlier, than in years past. Further, executives feel that plateauing is frequently accompanied by noticeable declines in both motivation and quality of performance.

While plateauing, like aging, is inevitable, in years past it was a more gradual process. For the most part, those who sought advancement in their managerial careers had ample opportunity to get it, within broad limits of ability, while those who did not desire advancement (including competent indiviudals content with more modest levels of achievement and success) could be bypassed by colleagues still on the way up.

Today the situation has changed. Declining rates of corporate growth and an ever-increasing number of candidates have heightened the competition for managerial positions. The top of the pyramid is expanding much more slowly than the middle, and the managers who advanced rapidly during the growth boom of the 1960s are now at or just below the top. Their rate of career progress has necessarily slowed, and yet they are still many years from normal retirement and with many productive years to go. As these managers continue in their positions, the queue of younger, aggressive aspirants just below them is likely to grow longer, with spillover effects on opportunities and mobility rates throughout the organization.

This is precisely the dilemma confronting Benjamin Petersen, president and chairman of the board of Petersen Electronics.

Petersen founded the company in 1944, and it grew rapidly during the 1950s and 1960s, reaching sales of $200 million in 1968. Growth since then, though, has been uneven and at an average of less than 5 percent per year. However, 1974 was a good year, with sales and profits showing leaps of 12 percent and 18 percent respectively.

Despite the good year, Benjamin Petersen, now 61 years old, is concerned about the company as he nears retirement. His major problem involves George Briggs, 53, vice-president of marketing, and Thomas Evans, national sales manager, who is 34 years old and one of Briggs' four subordinates. Nor have the implications of the situation between Briggs and Evans been lost on Victor Perkins, 39, vice-president of personnel.

Petersen's View of the Predicament

"When we started, a handful of people worked very hard and very closely to build something bigger than any of us. One of these people was George Briggs. George has been with me from the start, as have almost all of my vice-presidents and many of my key department heads.

"For the first five years, I did almost all the inventing and engineering work. Tom Carroll ran the plant and George Briggs knocked on doors and sold dreams as well as products for the company.

"As the company grew, we added people, and Briggs slowly worked his way up the sales organization. Eight years ago, when our vice-president of marketing retired, I put George in the job. He has market research, product management, sales service, and the field sales force (reporting through a national sales manager) under him, and he has really done a first-rate job all around.

"About ten years ago we began bringing in more bright young engineers and MBAs and moved them along as fast as we could. Turnover has been high and we have had some friction between our young Turks and the old guard.

"When business slowed in the early seventies, we also had a lot of competition among the newcomers. Those who stayed have continued to move up, and a few are now in or ready for top jobs. One of the best of this group is Tom Evans. He started with us nine years ago in the sales service area. Later, he spent three years in product management.

"George Briggs got him to move from head of the sales service department to assistant product manager. After one year, George Briggs named him manager of the product management group, and two years later, when the national sales manager retired, George named Evans to the post.

"That move both surprised and pleased me. I felt that Evans would make a good sales manager despite the fact that he had had little direct sales experience. I was afraid, however, that George would not want someone in that job who hadn't had years of field experience.

"I was even more surprised, though, when six months later (a month ago) George told me he was afraid Evans wasn't working out, and asked if I might be able to find a spot for him in the corporate personnel department. While I'm sure our recent upturn in sales is not solely Evans' doing, he certainly seems to be one of the keys. Despite his inexperience, he seems to have the field sales organization behind him. He spends much of his time traveling with them, and from what I hear he has built a great team spirit.

"Despite this, George Briggs claims that he is in over his head and that it is just a matter of time before his inexperience gets him in trouble. I can't understand why George is so adamant. It's clearly not a personality clash, since they have always gotten along well in the past. In many ways, Briggs has been Evans' greatest booster until recently.

"Since George is going to need a replacement someday, I was hoping it would be Evans. If George doesn't retire before we have to move Evans again or lose him, I'd consider moving Evans to another area.

"When we were growing faster, I didn't worry about a new challenge opening up for our aggressive young managers—there were always new divisions, new lines —something to keep them stimulated and satisfied with their progress. Now I have less flexibility—my top people are several years from retirement. And yet I have some younger ones—like Evans, whom I would hate to lose—always pushing and expecting promotion.

"Evans is a good example of this; I could move him, but there are not that many *real* opportunities. He could go to personnel or engineering or even finance. Evans has the makings of a really fine general manager. But I'd hate to move him now. He really isn't ready for another shift—although he will be in a few years—and despite what George claims, I think he is stimulating team work and commitment in the sales organization as a result of his style.

"Finally, while I don't want to appear unduly critical of Briggs, I'm not sure he could get the job done in these competitive times without a bright young person like Evans to help him."

Briggs' Account of the Situation

"Before I say anything else, let me assure you there is nothing personal in my criticism of Evans.

"I like him. I have always liked him. I've done more for him than anyone else in the company. I've tried to coach him and bring him along just like a son.

"But the simple truth is that he's in way over his head and showing a side of his personality I've never seen before. I brought him along through sales service and product management and he was always eager to learn. While I couldn't give him a lot of help in those areas (frankly, there are aspects of them I don't yet fully understand), I still tried, and he paid attention and learned from others as well.

"The job of national sales manager, however, is a different story. In the other jobs Evans had—staff jobs—there was always time to consult, to consider, to get more data. In sales, however, all this participative stuff he uses takes too long. The national sales manager has to be able to make quick, intuitive decisions. What's more, like the captain of a ship, he has to inspire confidence in those below him. If the going gets rough, the only thing that keeps the sailors and junior officers from panicking is confidence in the skipper. I've been there and I know.

"Right now, with orders coming in strong, he can get away with all of his meetings and indecisiveness. The people in the field really like him and are trying to keep him out of trouble. In addition, I have been putting in 60 to 70 hours a week trying to do my job and also make sure he doesn't make any serious mistakes.

"I know he is feeling the pressure, too. Despite the fact that he has been his usual cheery self with others, when I call him in to question a decision he has made or is about to make, he gets very defensive. He was never that way with me before.

"I may have lost a little feel for what's going on in the field over the years, but I suspect I still know more about the customers and our sales people than Tom Evans will ever know. I've tried for the past seven months to get him to relax and let the old man help him, but it's no use. I'm convinced he's just not cut out for the job, and before we ruin him I want to transfer him somewhere else. He would probably make a fine personnel director someday. He's a very popular guy who seems genuinely interested in people and in helping them.

"I have talked with Ben Petersen about the move, and he has been stalling me. I understand his position. We have a lot of young comers like Evans in the company, and Ben has to worry about all of them. He told me that if anyone can bring Evans along I can, and he asked me to give it another try. I have, and things are getting worse.

"I hate to admit I made a mistake with Evans, but I plan on seeing Ben about this again tomorrow. We just can't keep putting it off. I'm sure he'll see it my way, and as soon as he approves the transfer, I'll have a heart-to-heart talk with Tom."

Evans' Side of the Story

"This has been a very hectic but rewarding period for me. I've never worked as hard in my life as I have during the last six months, but it's paying off. I'm learning more about sales each day, and more important, I'm building a first-rate sales team. My people are really enjoying the chance to share ideas and support each other.

"At first, particularly with our markets improving, it was hard to convince them to take time to meet with me and their subordinates. Gradually they have come to accept these sessions as an investment in teambuilding. According to them, we've come up with more good ideas and ways to help each other than ever before.

"Fortunately, I also have experience in product management and sales service. Someday I hope to bring representatives from this department and market research into the meetings with regional and branch people, but that will take time. This kind of direct coordination and interaction doesn't fit with the thinking of some of the old-timers. I ran into objections when I tried this while I was working in the other departments.

"But I'm certain that in a year or so I'll be able to show, by results, that we should have some direct contact across department levels.

"My boss, George Briggs, will be one of the ones I will have to convince. He comes from the old school and is slow to give up what he knows used to work well.

"George likes me, though, and has given me a tremendous amount of help in the past. I was amazed when he told me he was giving me this job. Frankly, I didn't think I was ready yet, but he assured me I could handle it. I've gotten a big promotion every few years and I really like that—being challenged to learn new skills and getting more responsibility. I guess I have a real future here, although George won't be retiring for some years and I've gone as high as I can go until then.

"George is a very demanding person, but extremely fair, and he is always trying to help. I only hope I can justify the confidence he has shown in me. He stuck his neck out by giving me this chance, and I'm going to do all I can to succeed.

"Recently we have had a few run-ins. George Briggs works harder than anyone else around here, and perhaps the pressure of the last few years is getting to him. I wish he'd take a vacation this year and get away for a month or more and just relax. He hasn't taken more than a week off in the nine years I've been here, and for the last two years he hasn't taken any vacation.

"I can see the strain is taking its toll. Recently he has been on my back for all kinds of little things. He always was a worrier, but lately he has been testing me on numerous small issues. He keeps throwing out suggestions or second-guessing me on things that I've spent weeks working on with the field people.

"I try to assure him I'll be all right, and to please help me where I need it with the finance and production people who've had a tough time keeping up with our sales organization. It has been rough lately, but I'm sure it will work out. Sooner or later George will accept the fact that while I will never be able to run things the way he did, I can still get the job done for him."

Perkins' Opinion

"I feel that George Briggs is threatened by Evans' seeming success with the field sales people. I don't think he realizes it, but he is probably jealous of the speed with which Tom has taken charge. In all likelihood, he didn't expect Tom to be able to handle the field people as well as he has, as fast as he has.

"When George put Tom on the job, I have a feeling that he was looking forward to having him need much more help and advice from the old skipper. Tom does need help and advice, but he is getting most of what George would offer from his own subordinates and his peers. As a result, he has created a real team spirit below and around him, but he has upset George in the process.

"George not only has trouble seeing Tom depend so much on his subordinates, I feel that he resents Tom's unwillingness to let him show him how he used to run the sales force.

"I may be wrong about this, of course. I am sure that George honestly believes that Tom's style will get him in trouble sooner or later. George is no doddering old fool who has to relive his past success in lower-level jobs. In the past, I'm told, he has shown real insight and interest in the big-picture aspects of the company.

"The trouble is he knows he was an outstanding sales manager, but I am not sure he has the same confidence in his ability as vice-president. I have seen this time and again, particularly in recent years. When a person begins to doubt his future, he sometimes drops back and begins to protect his past. With more competition from younger subordinates and the new methods that they often bring in, many of our experienced people find that doing their job the way they used to just isn't good enough anymore.

"Some reach out and seek new responsibilities to prove their worth. Others, however, return to the things they used to excel in and try to show that theirs is still the best way to do things. They don't even seem to realize that this puts them in direct competition with their subordinates.

"What do we do about this? I wish I knew! At lower levels, where you have more room to shift people around, you have more options. When the company is growing rapidly, the problem often takes care of itself.

"In this case, I am not sure what I will recommend if Ben Petersen asks my advice. Moving Tom to personnel at this time not only won't help me (I really don't have a spot for him), but it won't help Briggs or Evans either. Moving Evans now would be wasteful of the time and effort we've invested in his development. It may also reverse some important trends Tom has begun in team building within the sales force.

"If Briggs were seven or eight years older, we could wait it out. If the company were growing faster, we might be able to shift people. As things stand, however, I see only one approach as a possibility. And I'm not entirely sure it will work.

"I would recommend that we get busy refocusing Briggs' attention on the vice-president's job and get him to see that there is where he has to put his time and efforts. Perhaps the best thing would be to send him to one of the longer programs for senior executives. Don't forget he is a very bright and experienced person who still has a great deal to offer the company if we can figure out how to help him."

What Would You Suggest?

Petersen has agreed to talk with Briggs about Evans tomorrow afternoon. As he thinks about the situation, he wonders what he can do that would be best for the company and everyone concerned. Should he go along with Briggs' recommendation that Evans be transferred to personnel? Or would it be preferable to do as Perkins has suggested and send Briggs to an executive program? As you consider the various perspectives, why do you think the impasse came to be and what do you think could be done to resolve it?

CASE QUESTIONS

1. The situation involving George Briggs and Thomas Evans can be viewed as a result of individual differences. Using the concepts from this chapter, describe the ways in which these managers differ.
2. Considering the individual differences, how could this situation be resolved?

NOTES

1. "Soloflex Inventor: Audacity Made Him Rich," *Eugene Register–Guard*, May 6, 1984, p. 3E.
2. Kurt Lewin, *The Conceptual Representation and the Measurement of Psychological Forces* (Durham, NC: Duke University Press, 1938).
3. N. Brody, *Personality: Research and Theory* (New York: Academic Press, 1972).
4. "Wanted: A Manager to Fit Each Strategy." *Business Week*, February 25, 1980, pp. 166–173.
5. G. W. Allport, *Pattern and Growth in Personality* (New York: Holt, Rinehart & Winston, 1961).
6. G. W. Allport and H. Odbert, "Trait Names: A Psycho-lexical Study," *Psychological Monographs*, 47 (1936), p. 211.
7. M. Rokeach, *The Open and Closed Mind* (New York: Basic Books, 1960).

8. Ron Taylor and Marvin Dunnette, "Influence of Dogmatism, Risk-taking Propensity, and Intelligence on Decision-making Strategies for a Sample of Industrial Managers," *Journal of Applied Psychology,* 59 (1974), pp. 420–423.

9. J. Esposito and H. Richards, "Dogmatism and the Congruence between Self-reported Job Preference and Performance among School Superiors," *Journal of Applied Psychology,* 59 (1974), pp. 389–391.

10. Ron Taylor and Marvin Dunnette, "Influence of Dogmatism," pp. 420–423.

11. T. R. Mitchell, "Cognitive Complexity and Leadership Style," *Journal of Personality and Social Psychology,* 16 (1970), pp. 166–174.

12. H. Schroder, M. Driver, and S. Streufert, *Human Information Processing* (New York: Holt, Rinehart & Winston, 1967).

13. M. Shaw, *Group Dynamics: The Psychology of Small Group Behavior* (New York: McGraw-Hill, 1976), pp. 199–200.

14. F. Greer, *Small Group Effectiveness* (Philadelphia: Institute for Research in Human Relations, 1955).

15. M. Shaw, *Group Dynamics,* p. 194.

16. M. Shaw, *Group Dynamics,* pp. 195–196.

17. *London Daily Telegraph,* July 15, 1978.

18. T. Adorno, E. Frenkel-Brunswick, D. Levinson, and R. Sanford, *The Authoritarian Personality* (New York: Harper, 1950).

19. "A Japanese Boss Whose Consensus Is an Iron Fist," *Business Week,* November 19, 1984, pp. 176–178.

20. Henry Murray, *Explorations in Personality* (New York: Oxford University Press, 1938).

21. David McClelland, John Atkinson, R. A. Clark, and E. L. Lowell, *The Achievement Motive* (New York: Appleton-Century-Crofts, 1953).

22. "Striking It Rich," *Time,* February 15, 1982, pp. 38–45.

23. D. Birch and J. Veroff, *Motivation: A Study of Action* (Monterey, CA: Brooks/Cole, 1966), p. 65.

24. Richard M. Steers and Daniel N. Braunstein, "A Behaviorally-Based Measure of Manifest Needs in Work Settings," *Journal of Vocational Behavior,* 9 (1976), pp. 251–266.

25. E. French, "Effects of the Interaction of Motivation and Feedback on Task Performance," in J. W. Atkinson (ed.), *Motives in Fantasy, Action, and Society* (Princeton, NJ: Von Nostrand, 1958), pp. 400–408.

26. E. French, "Effects of the Interaction," pp. 400–408.

27. Alfred Adler, "Individual Psychology," translated by S. Langer, in C. Murchison (ed.), *Psychologies of 1930* (Worcester, MA: Clark University Press, 1930), pp. 398–399.

28. David McClelland, "Power Is the Great Motivator," *Harvard Business Review,* 54, 2 (1976): 100–110.

29. David McClelland, "Power," pp. 100–110.

30. "Behind the Wheels," *Newsweek,* October 8, 1984, pp. 50–71.

31. G. Kimble and N. Gormezy, *Principles of General Psychology* (New York: Ronald Press, 1963).

32. "Samurai Spirit Lives on in Japan's Economic Drive," *U.S. News & World Report,* November 19, 1984, pp. 47–48.

33. B. F. Skinner, "Operant Behavior," *American Psychologist,* 18 (1963), pp. 503–515.

34. E. L. Thorndike, *Animal Intelligence* (New York: Macmillan, 1911).

35. Fred Luthans, *Organizational Behavior* (New York: McGraw-Hill, 1977).

36. P. Zimbardo and F. Ruch, *Psychology and Life* (Glenview, IL: Scott, Foresman, 1979).

37. A. Filley, R. House, and S. Kerr, *Managerial Process and Organizational Behavior* (Glenview, IL: Scott, Foresman, 1975).

38. D. McClelland, "Toward a Theory of Motive Acquisition," *American Psychologist,* 20 (1965), pp. 321–333.

39. Reprinted by permission of the *Harvard Business Review,* "Case of the Plateaued Performer," by E. K. Warren, T. P. Ference, and James A. F. Stoner (January/February 1975). Copyright © 1975 by the President and Fellows of Harvard College; all rights reserved.

3 Perception and Attitudes

I n a classic study of managerial perceptions on the job, Dearborn and Simon asked twenty-three executives to read a detailed case study from a business policy course. After reading the case, each executive was asked to identify what he or she considered the most important problem facing the firm toward which a new incoming president should focus attention.

The results were enlightening: Five out of six executives in the marketing department identified sales as the foremost problem requiring immediate attention, while four out of five production managers saw operations and production problems as most pressing. People in public relations, industrial relations, and medicine identified human relations issues as the largest problem.

After reviewing the findings, the researchers concluded "that each executive will perceive those aspects of a situation that relate specifically to the activities and goals of his or her department."[1]

In this chapter, we focus on the related topics of perception and attitudes. As we see in the above example, a knowledge of perceptual processes in organizations is important, because so much of what we do at work is based on how we see, or perceive, certain situations and how we interpret or give meaning to these situations. In fact, the way we form our work-related attitudes (such as job satisfaction) is in large part influenced by our perceptions of surrounding events. A discussion of the nature and dynamics of perception and attitudes at work is important to our study of organizations in that it provides insight into employee behavior.

RELEVANCE OF PERCEPTIONS AND ATTITUDES FOR MANAGERS

A knowledge of employee perception and the perceptual process in organizations is important for managers in the following ways. First, people rationally behave based on how they see the environment, and views of the world differ considerably between individuals. A management directive to work harder may be seen by an aspiring young manager as an opportunity to move up in the organization. This same directive may be interpreted by a factory worker as an attempt by management to exploit the worker. It is important for managers to recognize that people perceive things differently and attempt to understand how perceptual processes work.

Perceptual processes can play a major role in the decisions managers make about employee selection, placement, and promotion. Managers are people, and people have subtle biases that affect their decisions. Managerial decisions are significant both for the individuals involved and for the organization. It is important for managers to understand as clearly as possible how their own biases are formed and how they affect their own attitudes and behavior within their organization.

Perception has a considerable role in the performance appraisal process. As will be seen later in this book, one of the most popular methods of evaluating employees is with the use of rating forms. These forms are subject to a wide variety of potential errors, many of which are due to poor or inaccurate perception. Understanding perceptual processes can help managers use more accurate appraisal systems which, in turn, help them more accurately tie rewards to behavior.

A good knowledge of perceptual processes can improve a manager's ability to communicate, orally or in writing, with employees. The notion of perceptual selectivity, discussed in this chapter, applies to how an individual screens out or allows in various messages from the environment. A knowledge of what gets attention can aid us in getting our message across to co-workers. Understanding the basic nature of perceptual processes also can help us better understand ourselves and our reactions to our surroundings. Any generalizations about a given occupational, national, or racial group, for example, are counterproductive and usually stem from inaccurate perceptual processes. These perceptions hardly serve to improve our capacity to manage.

Attitudes appear in every aspect of work life. They stem from perception. We have attitudes about most things that happen to us, as well as about most people we meet. Attitudes influence behavior. Much of how we behave at work is governed by how we feel about things. It follows that an awareness of attitudes can assist managers in understanding human behavior at work. Changes in employee behavior can be expected to the extent that managers can change employee attitudes. Poor attitudes on the job can cost money. Poor job attitudes can be reflected in subsequent poor performance, turnover, and absenteeism, all of which result in direct costs to the organization.

For reasons such as these, it is important that people who manage people understand both how perceptual processes and job attitudes operate within organizations.

PERCEPTION

We are constantly being subjected to stimuli or cues from the environment, all of which compete for our attention. In the work place, these stimuli include supervisors' instructions, coworker's comments, machine noises, people passing, and posted signs and notices. Individuals are faced continually with the problem of how to make sense out of so many variables in so many stimuli, how to organize and interpret the more relevant stimuli, and how to respond to them. The process by which this is done is perception.

Definition

Perception is the process by which a person screens, selects, organizes, and interprets stimuli so that they have meaning to that individual. It is a process one uses to make sense out of one's environment so he or she can make the appropriate behavioral responses. Perception does not necessarily lead to an *accurate* portrait of the environment, but rather to a *unique* portrait, influenced by the needs, desires, values, and disposition of the perceiver. As described by Krech, an individual's perception of a given situation:

> *is not, then, a photographic representation of the physical world; it is, rather, a partial personal construction in which certain objects, selected out by the individual for a major role, are perceived in an individual manner. Every perceiver is, as it were, to some degree a nonrepresentational artist, painting a picture of the world that expresses his individual view of reality.*[2]

Two important aspects of the perceptual process should be noted. First, the various objects that vie for our attention are *selected* or *screened* by individuals. This process is called **perceptual selectivity.** Certain of these objects catch our attention, while others do not. Once individuals notice a particular object, they attempt to make sense out of it by organizing or categorizing it according to their own unique frame of reference and their needs. This second process is termed **perceptual organization.** When individuals have attached meaning to an object, they are in a position to determine an appropriate response or reaction to it. For example, if we clearly recognize that the rock falling from the cliff above us may indeed cause us harm, we can quickly move out of the way to safety.

Perceptual Selectivity

Perceptual selectivity, as explained above, is the process by which individuals single out, or select, certain objects in the environment for attention. Without the ability to focus on one or a few stimuli instead of the hundreds of stimuli constantly surrounding us, we would be unable to process the relevant information necessary to initiate behavior. Perceptual selectivity works as follows (see Exhibit 3.1). An individual is first exposed to an object or stimulus—a loud noise, a new car, a tall building, another person, etc. As a result, the individual focuses attention on this one object or stimulus, as opposed to others, and concentrates his or her efforts on understanding or comprehending the stimulus. Once this has been achieved, the individual is more likely to retain an image of the object or stimulus in his or her memory. The object has become a focal point.

Perceptual selectivity is influenced by a variety of factors. These factors can originate from attributes of the object in question (its size, color, or novelty; motion against a static background) or from personal qualities, or traits, within the perceiver. These personal influences include response salience and response disposition. **Response salience** is a tendency to focus on objects that relate to our *immediate* needs or wants.[3] Certain at-the-moment conditions, such as hunger, fatigue, or anxiety, may affect what a person perceives. A person who is nervous may react intensely to a sudden loud noise, or a person who is fired may not be listening to every word her dinner companion is saying. Response salience in the work environment is easily identified. A worker who is hungry may be acutely sensitive to the number of minutes until the noon break. Employees negotiating a new contract may know to the penny the hourly wage of workers doing similar jobs across town. Managers with a high need to achieve may be sensitive to opportunities for work achievement, success, and promotion. Women or minorities may be more sensitive to condescending attitudes toward women or minorities.

Response disposition, on the other hand, is the tendency to recognize familiar objects more quickly than unfamiliar ones. The concept of response disposition incorporates the importance of past learning on what we perceive in the present. For instance, in an early study, Bruner and Postman presented a group of individuals with a set of playing cards with the colors and symbols reversed: hearts and diamonds were printed in black, and spades and clubs in red. Surprisingly, when subjects were presented with these cards for brief time periods, they consistently described the cards as they expected them to be (red hearts and diamonds, black spades and clubs) instead of how they really were. The individuals were predisposed to see things as they always had been.[4] Response is taken into account by corporate management, for example, when they decide not to introduce innovations (such as work redesign) at the same time wage negotiations are taking place. Management commonly feels that employees' preoccupation with wages will cause work redesign efforts to be ignored or rejected.

EXHIBIT 3.1
The Process of Perceptual Selectivity

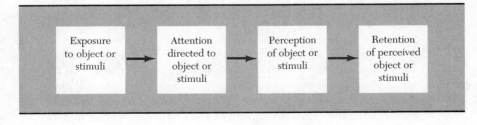

Social Perception in Organizations

Understanding how basic perceptual processes work lays the groundwork for an examination of how social perception in the work place affects life in organizations. Social perception consists of those processes by which we perceive other people. The study of social perception places particular emphasis on how we interpret other people, how we categorize them, and how we form impressions of them in the work place. Accurate perception of others has great significance. Whether employees as individuals accurately perceive a social situation at work (such as power relationships, status symbols, the attitudes of others) can make a major difference in organizational effectiveness on either the micro or macro level.

There are three basic influences on the way we perceive other people: 1) the characteristics of the person being perceived; 2) the characteristics of the particular situation; and 3) the characteristics of the perceiver (see Exhibit 3.2). When taken together, these three major influences are the dimensions of the environment in which we view other people. If perceptual accuracy is to be facilitated at work, it is important to understand the way in which these sets of influences interact.

Characteristics of the Person Perceived   The first influence on how people are perceived in social situations is their own personal characteristics. It is clear that a variety of *physical attributes* influence how we are seen by others. These attributes are many of the obvious demographic characteristics such as age, sex, race, height, and weight. But a less "given" example of the potency of physical appearance in influencing perception is seen in the clothing we wear. People dressed in business suits are generally thought to be professionals, while people dressed in work clothes are assumed to be blue-collar employees. The importance of these distinctions is that physical appearance, including clothing, influences how we respond to individuals.

In addition, what we say to others, as well as how we say it, can influence the impressions others form of us. Several aspects of *verbal communication* can be noted. First, the precision with which one uses language can influence impressions about cultural sophistication or education. An accent provides clues about a person's geographic background. The tone of voice provides clues about whether people are happy, angry, or sad. Finally, the topics about which people choose to converse provide clues about their background and motivations. Impressions can also be influenced by *nonverbal communication*, how people behave. For example, facial expressions often provide good clues in forming impressions of others. People who consistently smile are often thought to have positive attitudes.[5] A whole field of study has recently emerged in *body language*, or the way in which we express our inner feelings through physical actions; sitting up straight versus slumping; looking people straight in the eye versus looking away from them; crossing the arms instead of leaving them open. These forms of expressive behavior can let the perceiver know such things as how relaxed others are, how self-confident they are, or how open they are. Each has important implications for interpersonal behavior in organizations.

EXHIBIT 3.2
Primary Influences on Social Perceptions in Organizations

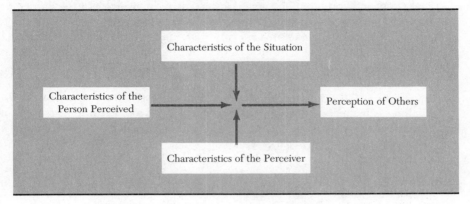

Finally, some characteristics are often ascribed before or at the beginning of an encounter, and these attributes can influence how we perceive others. These **ascribed attributes** include status and occupation. Status is ascribed to someone when we are told that he or she is an executive, holds the highest sales record, or has in some way achieved fame or wealth.[6] Occupation is ascribed when people are described as sales representatives, accountants, teamsters, or research scientists. In cases where status or occupation is ascribed, a perceiver may have a mental picture of a person before a firsthand encounter. In fact, a mental picture may even determine whether an encounter takes place.

Characteristics of the Situation A second influence on how we perceive others is the situation in which the perceptual process occurs. Considerable research has focused on the *social context* in which perception takes place.[7] Several conclusions relate these findings to organizational behavior. First, when people are given an opportunity to interact in a friendly and sociable work situation, they tend to see one another as similar to themselves. This environment is felt to be less threatening, allowing people to be more trusting and more willing to be open in their perceptions of others. Moreover, when members of a group or committee are congenial, they tend to be more accurate in assessing the work motives and goals of their colleagues, although they are less accurate in assessing personal (as opposed to work-related) goals. These findings imply that committees or work groups composed of adversaries may devote more time and energy to personal clashes at the expense of group goals.

An employee's *place in the organizational hierarchy* can also influence his or her perceptions. The classic study of managers by Dearborn and Simon at this chapter's opening, emphasizes this point. In addition to perceptual differences emerging horizontally across departments, perceptual differences can also be found vertically up or down the hierarchy. The most obvious difference appears between management and unions; management sees profits, production, and sales as vital areas of concern for the company, while unions place greater emphasis on wages, working conditions, and job security. Indeed, our views of managers and workers are clearly influenced by the group to which we belong.

Finally, our interpretation of events can also be influenced by the *location of the event*. Behaviors that may be appropriate at home may be inappropriate at the office. Acceptable customs vary internationally as well; for example, assertiveness is a desirable trait for a sales representative in the United States but is often seen as brash or coarse in Asian countries.

Characteristics of the Perceiver   Finally, characteristics unique to our own personalities can affect how we see others. Our *self-concept* represents a major influence on how we perceive others, and this influence is manifested in several ways.[8] Studies have shown that if we accept ourselves as we are, we broaden our view of others and are more likely to view people uncritically. Conversely, less self-accepting people often find faults in others. Moreover, our own personal characteristics influence the characteristics we are likely to see in others. For instance, people with authoritarian tendencies tend to view others in terms of power, while secure people tend to see others as warm rather than cold.

Our *cognitive structures* also influence how we view people.[9] People describe each other differently. Some often use physical characteristics like tall or short, while others tend to use central traits like deceitful, forceful, or meek. Other people have more complex cognitive structures and use multiple traits in their descriptions of others—a person may be described as being aggressive, honest, friendly, and hardworking. Ostensibly, the greater our cognitive complexity (in this sense, our ability to differentiate between people using multiple criteria), the more accurate our perception of others. Research in this area indicates that managers who exhibit high degrees of cognitive complexity are more effective. These individuals are able to form more accurate perceptions of the strengths and weaknesses of their subordinates, with the aim of capitalizing on their strengths while ignoring or working to overcome their limitations.

Finally, our own *previous experiences with others* often will influence the way in which we view their current behavior. When an employee has consistently received poor performance evaluations, there is a risk that an improvement in performance may go unnoticed due to the supervisors' preconceptions. Similarly, employees who begin their career with several successes develop a reputation as fast-track individuals and may continue to rise in the organization even after their performance has leveled off or even declined. Managers have an ongoing challenge in noticing changes in performance and tying rewards to these changes.

When taken together, these three sets of factors—characteristics of the person perceived, the situation, and the perceiver—jointly determine the impressions we form of others. With these impressions, we make conscious and unconscious decisions about how we behave toward people. Our behavior toward others, in turn, influences the way they regard us. Consequently, the importance of understanding the perceptual process, as well as factors that contribute to it, is apparent for managers. A better understanding of ourselves and careful attention to others can lead to more suitable behavior in the work place.

Barriers in Social Perception

In the perceptual process, it is not uncommon to see a series of systematic barriers emerge that serve to distort how we view and how we behave toward others. Of particular note here are several barriers found throughout interpersonal relations in organizations. These include stereotyping, halo effect, and selective perception.

Stereotyping A **stereotype** is a widely held generalization about a group of people. A stereotype assigns attributes to people solely on the basis of one or a few categories, such as their age, race, nationality, or occupation. Stereotypes often come into play when we meet new people, since we know very little about them at first. Based on a few prominent characteristics, we tend to ascribe a series of traits to them based upon the attributes of the category we have assigned them. For example, we may assume that an older person is old-fashioned or conservative. Or, professors may be viewed as absent-minded or idealistic.

Stereotypes are not necessarily dysfunctional, and in some situations they can be helpful. In unfamiliar social situations, we need general guidelines to assist us in interpreting our environment. Stereotypes provide us with simple and quick ways of reducing the ambiguity of our situations. They can protect us from making social mistakes. Even so, while stereotypes have certain positive effects for the perceiver, they more often have detrimental effects for the person being perceived.

UP CLOSE 3.1:   Union-Management Relations

In a classic study conducted by Mason Haire, photographs of two men were shown to a sample of 108 corporate industrial relations managers and 76 union leaders. Half the members in each group were told that picture 1 was a plant manager and picture 2 was a labor official. The other half of each group were given the same two photographs with the descriptions reversed.

The respondents were then asked to describe the people in both photographs using a standard list of adjectives. The results were illuminating. Regardless of which picture was identified as the "plant manager," the managers consistently described the person as more honest, dependable, and interpersonally competent than the "labor official." Union leaders responded in just the opposite manner.

In addition, the study found that managers were convinced that the "plant manager" was better able to appreciate labor's viewpoint than the "labor official" was capable of understanding management's viewpoint. Again, the reverse was found among union leaders.

Commenting on the results, an observer noted, "It is plain that unionists perceiving company officials in a stereotyped way are less efficient than would be desirable. Similarly, company executives who see all labor unions as identical are not showing good judgment or discrimination. To the extent that such stereotypes can be reduced, both managers and union leaders are in a better position to understand the other's point of view, to see the facts of a situation clearly, and to resolve differences with less stress, mistrust, and turmoil."[10]

Halo Effect   A **halo effect** is a tendency to allow knowledge of one trait to influence impressions of an individual's other traits. Halo effects, which can be either positive or negative, act as a screen inhibiting perceivers from actually seeing the trait they may be judging.[11] For example, in one study, army officers who were well liked were also judged as more intelligent than those who were disliked, despite equivalent intelligence test scores.[12] Moreover, a study by Asch found that when a stranger was described as warm, people also described him as wise, imaginative, popular, and humorous. No such descriptions were given of the same person when he was first described as being cold.[13]

Studies like these show how one attribute can color a person's impressions of other unrelated attributes of the same individual. This finding has important implications in the area of performance evaluation. Often, one positive attribute of an employee, like a consistent attendance record, can positively influence a supervisor's ratings of the employee's overall productivity or quality of work. Halo effects also affect the way employees view the organization. It has happened that one negative attitude has nullified many positive aspects of the work situation. For instance, a study examined employee attitudes in a company that was in receivership. The company paid relatively high salaries, provided excellent working conditions, and had above-average supervision. Even so, the insecurity brought about by the financial exigency of the company led to employees having a generalized negative attitude toward the company in all areas of evaluation.[14]

Selective Perception   Selective perception is the process by which we systematically screen out information we don't wish to hear, focusing instead on more salient information. Saliency in this case is a function of our own experiences, needs, and orientations. An example of selective perception in groups and organizations is provided by Miner.[15] Miner summarizes a series of experiments dealing with groups competing with one another on problem-solving exercises. Consistently, the groups tended to evaluate their own solutions as better than the solutions proposed by others. These findings resemble the **not-invented-here syndrome** found in many research organizations. Scientists with this "syndrome" tend to view ideas or products originating outside their organization or department as inferior, and they may judge other researchers as less competent and creative than themselves. Similar patterns of behavior appear in other occupational groupings as well.

Perception and Behavior: An Attributional Analysis

The study of perceptual processes has lead to the development of a useful model of human behavior known as attribution theory. This model is based on the premise that a major influence on behavior is people's interpretation of the events around them. One example: people who feel they have control over what happens to them may be more likely to accept responsibility for their actions than those who feel control of events is out of their hands. As such, **attribution theory** "concerns the process by which an individual interprets events as being caused by a particular part of a relatively stable environment."[16]

Attribution Theory   Attribution theory was developed primarily by Heider. Heider suggests that behavior is determined by a combination of internal forces (e.g., abilities or effort) and external forces (e.g., task difficulty or luck).[17] Following the cognitive approach of Lewin and Tolman, he emphasizes that *perceived* determinants, not the actual ones, really influence behavior. If employees perceive that their success is a function of their own abilities and efforts, they can be expected to behave differently than they would if they believed job success was due to chance alone.

Underlying attribution theory is the assumption that individuals are motivated to understand their environment and the causes of particular events. If they can understand the causes of events, they will then be in a better position to influence or control events. This process is shown in Exhibit 3.3. Attribution theory suggests that individuals will analyze a behavioral event, such as receiving a promotion, to determine its cause. The individual uses a cognitive interpretation process, and this may lead to the conclusion that the promotion resulted from the individual's own effort or, alternatively, from another cause, such as luck. Based on their cognitive interpretations of events, individuals revise the way they think (cognitive or casual structures). Then they make behavioral choices based on their revised cognitive structure, or their new way of thinking.

If our individual in question concludes that his performance does indeed lead to promotion, he goes on to make choices about his future behavior. He may decide to continue exerting high levels of effort in the hope that it will lead to further promotions. On the other hand, if our individual concludes that the promotion resulted from chance and was unrelated to performance, he may create a different cognitive structure and behave accordingly; he may find little reason to exert high levels of effort. Simply, the way we perceive and interpret events around us can significantly influence our future behaviors in job situations.

Locus of Control   The attributions we make are typically measured by the concept of **locus of control.**[18] An *internal* locus of control applies when employees feel they can influence their own outcomes and behavior through their abilities, skills, and effort. An *external* locus of control applies when employees feel that outcomes or behavior is largely beyond their own control. Research on attribution processes and locus of control has led to several interesting results. In a series of experiments it was consistently found that when individuals perceive a high internal locus of control and seem to have control over their own behavior, successful performance on previous tasks leads to increased expectations of success on future tasks.[19] Unsuccessful previous performance leads to reduced expectations for success on future tasks. As shown in Exhibit 3.4, success in one task for those with internal locus of control causes individuals to attribute the success to their own efforts, which augments their pride in accomplishment. This augmented pride in accomplishment, in turn, leads to increased expectations of success in future events. Failure on previous tasks for those with internal locus of control, in contrast, brings frustration, lack of confidence, and reduced future expectations. For those with an external locus of control, neither success nor failure on previous tasks influences subsequent expectations. This is because individuals feel that behavior and performance are largely influenced by other people or events. When performance is out of an individual's control, there is reason for neither great pride in accomplishment nor great disappointment in failure.

EXHIBIT 3.3
The Attribution Process

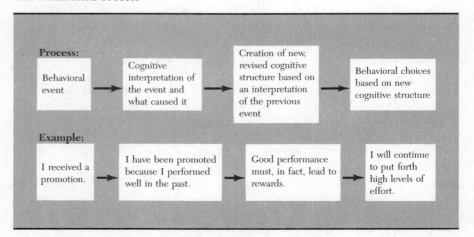

SOURCE: From *Organizational Behavior* by Abraham K. Korman, p. 273. Copyright © 1977 by Prentice-Hall, Inc. Adapted by permission of Prentice-Hall, Englewood Cliffs, New Jersey.

EXHIBIT 3.4

The Influence of the Locus of Control on Performance Expectations

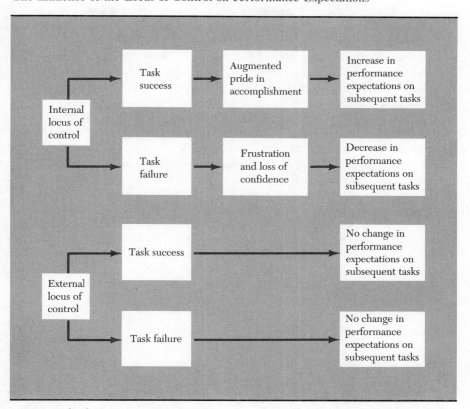

SOURCE: Richard M. Steers, *Introduction to Organizational Behavior* (Glenview, IL: Scott, Foresman and Company, 1984).

UP CLOSE 3.2:   VDTs in the Office

A major controversy has arisen over the use of video display terminals (VDTs) in the office that illustrates attribution processes at work. The problem focuses over the potential health threats, especially with respect to pregnancies, that may result from prolonged exposure to VDTs.[20]

"There have been a lot of miscarriages [in our department]; if there is a problem, we want to know," said one employee who works at a terminal at Southern Bell. She is not alone in her concern. In fact, a growing number of women who regularly operate VDTs are becoming increasingly concerned that working on VDTs can cause problems as serious as birth defects and miscarriages. Reports of these problems are emerging with alarming frequency. However, several medical studies of the problem have failed to turn up a

confirmed link between VDT use and the risk to pregnant women. "Every-body's found exactly the same thing," insists a radiation health specialist for Bell Labs. "There really isn't any problem."

Union responses to such conclusions differ markedly from those of manage-ment. "People who say there isn't really a radiation hazard are basing their claims on inconclusive data," claims a specialist with the Communications Workers of America. In fact, some unions are lobbying for legislation in several states that would require companies to transfer pregnant women to comparable jobs away from VDTs.

From the standpoint of attribution processes, the VDT debate is an interesting one. Unions claim (attribute) that potentially serious pregnancy-related health problems result from exposure to the VDTs. Citing member surveys and a lack of conclusive studies by management, they claim the problem is critical enough to warrant serious study and more attention. On the other hand, some managers point to the same data and suggest that there is no problem; the miscarriages and birth defects "must be" caused by something else. Hence, both sides differ considerably as to how they cognitively interpret the same event (health problems). Moreover, each side draws quite different conclusions and recommendations for action based on these cognitive interpre-tations. In the meantime, the problem—whatever the cause—goes unresolved for lack of consensus on a resolution strategy. ▄▄

WORK-RELATED ATTITUDES

Certainly one of the most widely discussed aspects of organizational life is the topic of work-related attitudes. We often hear references to how satisfied or dissatisfied employees are on the job. In addition, most managers have their own assumptions on how to improve job satisfaction. While the importance of job attitudes has been recognized for many years, it is only recently that serious study of the actual determinants of attitudes in organizational settings and their consequences for organizational well-being has begun. In this section, we will examine the role of work-related attitudes in behavior in organizations.

Definition of Attitudes

An **attitude** may be defined as a predisposition to respond in a favorable or unfavorable way to objects or persons in one's environment.[21] When we like or dislike something, we are, in effect, expressing our attitude toward the person or object. An attitude reflects our feelings toward other objects and individuals.

Several assumptions underlie this definition. To begin, an attitude is a hypothetical construct; while the consequences of an attitude may be observed, the attitude itself cannot. We only assume that attitudes exist inside people. Second, an attitude is a unidimensional variable. In all cases, an attitude can be measured along an evaluative continuum from very favorable to very unfavor-able. Finally, attitudes are believed to be related to subsequent behavior. Our definition of attitude implies that people behave based on how they feel.

A Model of Work-Related Attitudes

Some have suggested that the concept of attitude can be divided into three components: 1) a *cognitive* component, which deals with beliefs and ideas an individual has about a person or object; 2) an *affective* component, which deals with the individual's feelings toward the person or object; and 3) a *behavioral intention* component, which deals with the behavioral intentions an individual has toward the person or object as a result of affective responses.[22] Fishbein and Ajzen have added the assertion that the notion of attitudes is easier to understand if we separate these three components and define attitudes simply as affective responses, treating the cognitive and behavioral intentions components as antecedents and outcomes of the attitude themselves.[23] This is a more specific description of attitudes. Using the same three basic components of earlier models, this approach goes on to suggest how the components fit together; it is also helpful for measurement purposes (see Exhibit 3.5).

The Fishbein and Ajzen approach has four basic components: beliefs (cognitions), attitudes (affects), behavioral intentions, and actual behavior. *Beliefs* represent the information a person holds about an object. For instance, an employee may believe his or her job to be exciting or dull, dirty or clean, independent or dependent. These beliefs may or may not be based in fact. Regardless, beliefs are thought to be factual by the individual. These beliefs, then, influence the attitudes or affective responses, formed by employees. As Exhibit 3.5 shows, a person who believes his job is dull, dirty, and dependent may develop a negative attitude toward the job and be dissatisfied. His dissatisfaction may, in turn, lead him to choose undesirable forms of behavior —he may decide to seek another job or reduce his level of effort. A conscious decision to seek alternative employment is the *behavioral intention*. Finally, these behavioral intentions become translated into *actual job behavior* such as high turnover, absenteeism, and lower performance.

Influences on the Development of Attitudes

An important thing to note about the development of attitudes is that they are learned from environment and from prior experiences. At least four major influences on attitude learning can be identified. First, many of our general

EXHIBIT 3.5
Relationship Between Beliefs, Attitudes, and Behavior

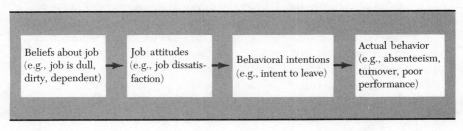

Beliefs about job (e.g., job is dull, dirty, dependent) → Job attitudes (e.g., job dissatisfaction) → Behavioral intentions (e.g., intent to leave) → Actual behavior (e.g., absenteeism, turnover, poor performance)

attitudes are learned as a result of *cultural influences*. Our attitudes toward allowing lower-level employees to have a major voice in the operations and decisions of a business firm are generally culturally based.[24] Second, attitudes are influenced by *group memberships*. One study demonstrated how managers and union members held different opinions of each other as a function of group membership.[25] Third, the *family* can influence attitudes. Many attitudes toward members of other races and economic classes are formed here.[26] Finally, *prior work experiences* influence our beliefs and attitudes about specific aspects of the job. For example, opinions about how much effort represents a fair day's work, what constitutes a fair day's pay, and how employees should be treated are usually influenced by an individual's prior experiences.

UP CLOSE 3.3:   Intel

A good example of how employee attitudes develop within an organization can be seen in recent events at Intel Corporation. Intel is a technology leader in the semiconductor industry. Since its founding, Intel has been an enormously successful company. During the 1970s, its annual growth rate averaged 60 percent per year. In the early 1980s, however, recession hit and corporate growth and profits plateaued. Profit margins fell to only 3 percent and corporate management took action to shore up the company. Salaries were cut across the board and more rigid management controls were imposed to achieve greater operating efficiency.

Unfortunately, the rationale for such changes was not adequately explained to employees who, in turn, experienced declining morale. As a result, several of Intel's key managers and designers left to work elsewhere. Those leaving included one of Intel's top scientists, the designer of the first successful microprocessor. "His leaving is a real indictment of Intel's ability to manage people," a former employee noted.

Although Intel clearly remains an industry leader in the semiconductor field, the negative work experiences and changes in culture at Intel did have the effect of worsening work attitudes, which have led to internal dissension and increased turnover.[27] ■

Do Attitude Surveys Make a Difference?

For a number of years, some organizations have taken annual attitude or morale surveys to assess the general level of satisfaction among employees. Two changes have been made in recent years that have emphasized the importance of attitude surveys. First, the surveys now focus on a wider range of organizational activities and provide more information to management about possible trouble spots; second, companies have begun to take attitude surveys more seriously and actually implement changes based on results.

For example, in a survey of more than 20,000 employees, General Electric found that over one-half of the respondents were dissatisfied with the information available, with recognition they received, and with opportunities for advancement. As a result, management instituted regular monthly meetings, brought in experts to answer questions, and initiated a newsletter. One year later, a follow-up survey found that the number of employees dissatisfied with the information available dropped from 50 percent to none, while the number dissatisfied with promotional opportunities fell from 50 percent to 20 percent. One Houston-based corporation, Geosource, found that its welders were extremely dissatisfied with pay levels, despite the competitive wage they were paid. In a survey feedback session, management discovered that employees were reading employment ads for welders offering "up to $7.84 per hour." When it was pointed out that no company hires at the maximum wage, most of the discontent subsided. A survey by American Can Company found employees concerned about a lack of career opportunities. As a result, the company initiated a job information center where employees could discuss their qualifications, ambitions, and training needs, and a weekly thirty-minute job seminar where senior executives would talk about career opportunities in their areas.[28]

Attitude surveys seem to be successful in two ways. First, they are successful when results are fed back to all employees, not just to top management. Second, successful programs are marked by a commitment from top management to initiate changes where needed. Quick action by management reassures employees that the company is concerned about creating a suitable work environment and that employees' opinions make a difference.

Job Satisfaction

Although a variety of work-related job attitudes can be discussed, from the standpoint of management it appears that attitudes relating to job satisfaction are particularly important. In fact, the notion of job satisfaction is one of the most widely studied variables in organizational behavior. **Job satisfaction** may be defined as "a pleasurable or positive emotional state resulting from the appraisal of one's job or job experience."[29] In other words, the employee has the perception that his or her job actually provides what he or she values in the work situation.

At least two important characteristics of the concept of job satisfaction follow from this definition. First, satisfaction is an emotional response to a job situation. We cannot observe satisfaction; we must infer its existence and quality either from an employee's behavior or verbal statements. Second, job satisfaction is perhaps best understood as a comparison. Several writers have pointed out that job satisfaction is a result of how much a person wants or expects from the job compared to how much he or she actually receives.[30] When expectations and reality match, job satisfaction can result. Expectations vary in both quality and intensity. Based on work experiences, people receive outcomes, or rewards, from the job. These outcomes include not only **extrinsic rewards,** such as pay and promotion, but also **intrinsic rewards,** such as satisfying co-worker relationships and meaningful work. To the extent that the outcomes an employee receives meet or exceed expectations, we can expect the employee to be satisfied with the job. When outcomes actually surpass expectations, we can expect employees to reevaluate their expectations and possibly raise them to meet available outcomes. However, when outcomes do not meet expectations, employees are dissatisfied and may seek alternative sources of satisfaction, either by changing jobs or by placing greater value on life outside of work.

Facets of Job Satisfaction   Investigators have argued that job satisfaction actually represents several related attitudes.[31] Because of this, when we speak of satisfaction, we must specify "satisfaction with what?" Five job dimensions are suggested to represent the most salient characteristics of a job about which people have affective responses. These five include:

• *Work itself.* The extent to which tasks performed by employees are interesting and provide opportunities for learning and for accepting responsibility.
• *Pay.* The amount of pay received, the perceived equity of the pay, and the method of payment.
• *Promotional opportunities.* The availability of realistic opportunities for advancement.
• *Supervision.* The technical and managerial abilities of supervisors, the extent to which supervisors demonstrate consideration for and interest in employees.
• *Co-workers.* The extent to which co-workers are friendly, technically competent, and supportive.

Additional facets of job satisfaction can be identified (satisfaction with company policies, fringe benefits), but these five dimensions are used most often in examining work-related attitudes.

Measuring Job Satisfaction   The most popular technique for measuring job satisfaction is the use of rating scales. **Rating scales** are direct verbal self-reports that are to measure job satisfaction. These instruments have been in use since the 1930s. One of the more well-known scales is the Minnesota Satisfaction Questionnaire, which uses a Likert-response format to generate satisfaction scores on twenty-six aspects, or scales.[32] Examples of MSQ questions are shown in Exhibit 3.6.

The MSQ and similar rating scales have several advantages for assessing job satisfaction. They are relatively short and simple and can be completed by large numbers of employees quickly. Because of the generalized wording of the various terms, rating scale questionnaires can be administered to a wide range of employees in various jobs. It is not necessary to alter the format for each job classification.

On the other hand, rating scales have at least two drawbacks. As with any self-report inventory, the scales assume that respondents are both willing to and capable of accurately describing their feelings. People can consciously or

EXHIBIT 3.6

Examples from the *Minnesota Satisfaction Questionnaire*

On my present job, this is how I feel about . . .	Not Satisfied	Only Slightly Satisfied	Satisfied	Very Satisfied	Extremely Satisfied
1. The change to be active much of the time	1	2	3	4	5
2. The variety in my work	1	2	3	4	5
3. The policies and practices toward employees of this company	1	2	3	4	5
4. The chance to be responsible for planning my work	1	2	3	4	5
5. The opportunities for advancement on this job	1	2	3	4	5

SOURCE: From *Minnesota Satisfaction Questionnaire* by the University of Minnesota Industrial Relations Center. Reprinted by permission.

unconsciously distort information that they feel is damaging and enhance information that they feel is beneficial. Employees who think their supervisors may see their questionnaire, for example, may report overly favorable job attitudes for fear of the consequences of reporting negative results. Rating scales also assume that questionnaire items mean the same thing to all people. There may, in fact, not be a common agreement of meaning across individuals. Despite their limitations, however, rating scales have proved to be useful in measuring job satisfaction in a variety of work environments.

Consequences of Job Satisfaction   The consequences of job satisfaction and dissatisfaction ask another important question. Research has consistently found satisfaction and employee *turnover* to be moderately related.[33] While most research suggests that several other factors influence turnover as well, job satisfaction is still a clear influence. Available evidence also outlines a moderate inverse relationship between satisfaction and employee *absenteeism*.[34]

One of the most controversial consequences of job satisfaction is its relationship to *job performance*. Three competing theories have been advanced: 1) satisfaction causes performance; 2) performance causes satisfaction; 3) rewards intervene between performance and satisfaction.[35] The first two theories can be rejected on theoretical grounds. That is, the fact that workers are satisfied does not mean they will necessarily produce more; it means only that they are satisfied. There is no compelling argument that performance necessarily causes satisfaction, particularly if performance goes unrewarded.

The third theory, which suggests that rewards mediate the performance-satisfaction relationship, receives considerable support. This model, shown in

Exhibit 3.7, was first suggested by Porter and Lawler.[36] As shown in the diagram, past performance of an employee leads to the receipt of rewards. These rewards can be both intrinsic (a feeling of personal accomplishment) and extrinsic (pay, promotion). The individual is satisfied to the extent that he or she perceives these rewards to be equitable (fair when compared to level of effort and to what other employees receive). The receipt of equitable rewards also tends to create strong performance-reward contingencies in the minds of employees, leading to future effort and performance. In short, performance is really not a consequence of satisfaction. Rather, the two variables by themselves are virtually unrelated. It is only when rewards and reward contingencies are considered together that a substantial relationship emerges.

Finally, influence of job satisfaction on *organizational effectiveness*, while admittedly indirect, is nonetheless important. One of the most popular indicators analysts and investigators use to assess organizational effectiveness is job satisfaction.[37] Job satisfaction does clearly affect organizational effectiveness by influencing turnover and absenteeism. Lawler notes that the cost of one turnover among lower-level jobs easily can surpass $2000, while the cost of one turnover among the managerial ranks can be five to ten times that amount.[38] From the standpoint of the effective functioning of the organization, managers have a responsibility to prevent turnover and absenteeism. Careful consideration of employee job attitudes and satisfaction can help facilitate this.

In summary, job satisfaction often leads to a variety of positive consequences, both from individual and organizational standpoints. It influences how an employee feels about the organization and contributes to his or her desire to maintain membership in it. Job satisfaction can influence significantly how people approach their jobs, their levels of effort and commitment, and their contributions to goal attainment in the work environment.

EXHIBIT 3.7
Relationship of Job Performance to Job Satisfaction

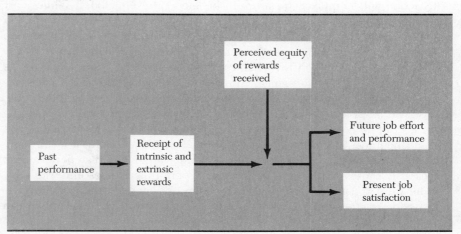

UP CLOSE 3.4: Ford's Louisville Assembly Plant

The Ford assembly plant in Louisville, Kentucky, gives a good example of the consequences of positive versus negative job attitudes. In the "bad old days," this assembly plant was described by workers as a "war zone," and the trucks and cars made there had the lowest quality rating of all U.S.-made vehicles. Today, the Ranger light trucks manufactured there—in the same plant by the same employees—receive Ford's highest quality scores. In fact, independent ratings suggest that the Ford Rangers built in this plant are the most defect-free vehicles built in the U.S. and easy rivals of Japanese competitors.[39]

What happened to turn things around? Ford invested considerable effort perfecting its Ranger light truck. The company's efforts included robots and other automated equipment, statistical controls, improved designs, a tougher inspection system, and tighter standards for vendors. But all of these changes are secondary to the effects of the change in plant "spirit" that happened when both labor and management realized they had a choice of either working together or perishing. In fact, the improvement in quality came along with a change in employee attitudes back in 1979—well before the other steps were implemented.

As one assembly-line worker recalls about the old days, "If something wasn't right, we'd let it go and hope the inspector caught it. We didn't care a lot." Indeed, labor-management relations were so poor that one industrial relations manager observed, "In one form or another this plant had everything wrong with it that had ever been written about the U.S. auto industry." The plant had been run by a succession of autocratic managers who, naturally enough, confronted intransigent labor leaders. The premises were filthy and littered with broken or discarded parts. Workers and supervisors often screamed at each other; forklift operators dropped or smashed their loads.

In 1979, several events occurred. The plant became a prime candidate for closure, and layoffs were beginning to occur. Simultaneously, and fortuitously, a new plant manager and a new labor union leader stepped in. Both felt that there must be a better way to run things.

Don Baker, 52, the new plant manager, met with the employees. His message was brief: "Saying to hell with the company is just like saying to hell with yourself. What do you want? Do you want to make a good product or do you want to shut down? We've got about six months left." Soon, small changes started happening. The workers had previously complained that they had nowhere to sit during meals. Picnic tables began appearing all over the plant. As workers began to accept responsibility for overall maintenance, the premises began to clean itself up. Other small improvements occurred; workers and managers began to talk to each other to solve problems. Before long, without any change in the basic production facility, these small steps (and the resulting improved attitudes) turned the plant around. By early 1980, auditors from Ford headquarters were giving the vehicles produced in Louisville high marks for quality.

*As morale and cooperation improved, union-management teams were estab-
lished to systematically work to improve efficiency and quality. Based on a new
sense of trust, the union did not resist when Ford introduced increased
automation into the factory in 1981. Ultimately, Ford's investment would
exceed $700 million. Vehicle output rose to 75 vehicles per hour, the second
highest rate of output of any auto factory in the U.S., and quality remained
high. Within two years, workers made over 700 proposals to improve quality
and operating efficiency as a new partnership in productivity was formed.*

*All of the antagonisms and suspicions of decades past have not disappeared,
but there is no doubt about the improvement in the atmosphere. Morale is up,
and unexpected absenteeism is down to 1 percent from 6 percent. Grievance
rates have been cut dramatically, and employee involvement groups continue to
expand. As one observer noted, "The Louisville Assembly Plant demonstrates
once again that U.S. industry has the potential to achieve huge improvements
in quality and productivity—but only, it appears, when circumstances force
labor and management to get together and work smarter."* ■

SUMMARY

In this chapter, we studied the related topics of perception and job attitudes.
Perception is the process by which people screen, select, organize, and
interpret stimuli so that they have meaning to the individual. It is, in essence,
the process of making sense out of one's environment.

Perceptual selectivity, a part of the perception process, incorporates how
people single out or select certain objects in the environment for attention. In
the process of perceptual selectivity, the related concepts of response salience
and response disposition emerge. Response salience is a tendency to focus on
objects that relate to our immediate needs or wants, while response disposition
is a tendency to recognize familiar objects more quickly than unfamiliar ones.

A model of social perception was presented; this model acknowledges the
importance of characteristics of both the perceiver and the perceived, as well as
characteristics of the situation, as they relate to perception of others. Three
barriers to accurate social perception were discussed. These include stereotyping, halo effect, and selective perception.

Attribution theory was examined as one mechanism by which people use
perceptual processes to explain their environments. Attribution theory is based
on the premise that a major influence on how we behave is the way we
interpret events around us. People attempt to understand their environment
and the causes of particular events in that environment. If they can understand
the causes of events, they should be in a better position to control or influence
many of those events.

Finally, work attitudes were examined. An attitude is defined as a predisposition to respond in a favorable or unfavorable way to objects or persons in one's
environment. A model of work attitudes suggested that beliefs about the job

influence job attitudes which, in turn, influence behavioral intentions and actual behavior.

Job satisfaction as an attitude can be divided into several categories, including satisfaction with the work itself, pay, promotional opportunities, supervision, and co-workers. It was also noted that job dissatisfaction can lead to several dysfunctional outcomes, including absenteeism, turnover, and poor job performance.

KEY WORDS

ascribed attribute	locus of control	rating scales
attitude	not-invented-here	response disposition
attribution theory	syndrome	response salience
extrinsic rewards	perception	selective perception
halo effect	perceptual	social perception
intrinsic rewards	organization	stereotype
job satisfaction	perceptual selectivity	

DISCUSSION QUESTIONS

1. What is the significance of Dearborn and Simon's experiment on selective perception? What can managers learn from this experiment?
2. What is perception? Describe the basic perceptual process.
3. Differentiate between perceptual organization and perceptual selectivity. How does perceptual selectivity operate?
4. What are the implications for the work place of response salience and response disposition?
5. What are the primary influences on social perception on the job? Among these various influences, which do you feel are the most important in determining social perception? Why?
6. What is body language? What role does it play in interpersonal relations?
7. In organizations, do you feel stereotyping or halo effects represents the more pronounced barrier to social perception? Explain.
8. Provide an example of attribution theory in operation drawing from your own personal experiences. How can attribution theory help you better understand this experience?
9. Do you consider yourself to have an internal or external locus of control? What are the implications of your self-assessment as you consider a managerial career?
10. Why is it important to understand job attitudes at work? What could Intel have learned that would have changed the outcome of their morale problem? Explain.
11. Why do you think some people assert that job attitudes are unimportant in organizations? In spite of the fact that we have emphasized the importance of job attitudes, can you see any rationale for this position? Why or why not?

CASE 3.1: L. J. Summers Company

Jon Reese couldn't think of a time in the history of L. J. Summers Company when there had been as many employee problems and as much anticompany sentiment among the workers as had emerged in the past few weeks. He knew that Mr. Summers would place the blame on him for the problems with the production workers because Jon was supposed to be helping Mr. Summers's son, Blaine, to become oriented to his new position. Blaine had only recently taken over as production manager of the company. (See Exhibit 1). He was unpopular with most of the workers, but the events of the past weeks had caused him to be resented even more. This resentment had increased to the point that several of the male workers had quit and all the women in the assembly department had refused to work.[40]

The programs that had caused the resentment among the workers were instituted by Blaine to reduce waste and lower production costs, but they had produced completely opposite results. Jon knew that on Monday morning he would have to explain to Mr. Summers why the workers had reacted as they did and that he would have to present a plan to resolve the employee problems, reduce waste, and decrease production costs.

Company History

L. J. Summers Company manufactured large sliding doors made of many narrow aluminum panels held together by thick rubber strips, which allowed the door to collapse as it was opened. Some of the doors were as high as eighteen feet and were used in buildings to section off large areas. The company had grown rapidly in its early years due mainly to the expansion of the building program of the firm's major customer, which accounted for nearly 90 percent of Summers' business.

When L. J. Summers began the business, his was the only firm that manufactured the large sliding doors. Recently, however, several other firms had begun to market similar doors. One firm in particular had been bidding to obtain business from Summers's major customer. Fearing that the competitor might be able to underbid his company, Mr. Summers began urging his assistant, Jon, to increase efficiency and cut production costs.

Conditions Before the Cost
Reduction Programs

A family-type atmosphere had existed at Summers before the cost reduction programs were instituted. There was little direct supervision of the workers from the front office, and no pressure was put on them to meet production standards. Several of the employees worked overtime regularly without supervision. The foremen and workers often played cards together during lunchtime, and company parties after work were common and popular. Mr. Summers was generally on friendly terms with all the employees, although he was known to get angry if something displeased him. He also participated freely in the daily operations of the company.

As Mr. Summers's assistant, Jon was responsible for seeing to it that the company achieved the goals established by Mr. Summers. He was considered hard working and persuasive by most of the employees and had a reputation of not giving in easily to employee complaints.

SOURCE: Reprinted by permission from *Organization and People*, Third Edition, by J. B. Ritchie and Paul R. Thompson. Copyright © 1984 by West Publishing Company. All rights reserved. Pages 358–362.

EXHIBIT 1
L. J. Summers Company Organizational Chart

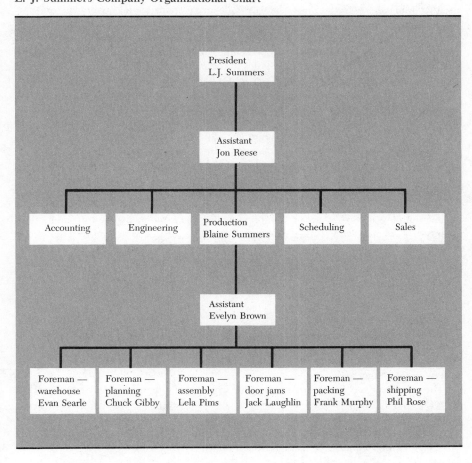

President
L.J. Summers

Assistant
Jon Reese

| Accounting | Engineering | Production
Blaine Summers | Scheduling | Sales |

Assistant
Evelyn Brown

| Foreman —
warehouse
Evan Searle | Foreman —
planning
Chuck Gibby | Foreman —
assembly
Lela Pims | Foreman —
door jams
Jack Laughlin | Foreman —
packing
Frank Murphy | Foreman —
shipping
Phil Rose |

Blaine Summers had only recently become the production manager of Summers. He was in his early twenties, married, and had a good build. Several of the workers commented that Blaine liked to show off his strength in front of others. He was known to be very meticulous about keeping the shop orderly and neat, even to the point of making sure that packing crates were stacked "his way." It was often commented among the other employees how Blaine seemed to be trying to impress his father. Many workers voiced the opinion that the only reason Blaine was production manager was that his father owned the company. They also resented his using company employees and materials to build a swing set for his children and to repair his camper.

Blaine, commenting to Jon one day that the major problem with production was the workers, added that people of such caliber as the Summers's employees did not understand how important cost reduction was and that they would rather sit around and talk all day than work. Blaine rarely spoke to the workers but left most of the reprimanding and firing up to his assistant, Evelyn Brown.

Summers employed about seventy people to perform the warehousing, assembly and door-jamb building, as well as the packing and shipping operations done on the doors.

Each operation was supervised by a foreman and crews that ranged from three men in warehousing to twenty-five women in the assembly department. The foremen were usually employees with the most seniority and were responsible for quality and on-time production output. Most of the foremen had good relationships with the workers.

The majority of the work done at Summers consisted of repetitive assembly tasks requiring very little skill or training; for example, in the pinning department the workers operated a punch press, which made holes in the panels. The job consisted of punching the hole and then inserting a metal pin into it. Workers commented that it was very tiring and boring to stand at the press during the whole shift without frequent breaks.

Wages at Summers were considered to be low for the area. The workers griped about the low pay but said that they tried to compensate by taking frequent breaks, working overtime, and "taking small items home at night." Most of the workers who worked overtime were in the door-jamb department, the operation requiring the most skill. Several of these workers either worked very little or slept during the overtime hours they reportedly worked.

The majority of the male employees were in their mid-twenties, about half of them were unmarried. There was a great turnover among the unmarried male workers. The female employees were either young and single or older married women. The twenty-five women who worked in production were all in the assembly department under Lela Pims.

The Cost Reduction
Programs

Shortly after Mr. Summers began stressing the need to reduce waste and increase production, Blaine called the foremen together and told them that they would be responsible for stricter discipline among the employees. Unless each foreman could reduce waste and improve production in his department, he would either be replaced or receive no pay increases.

The efforts of the foremen to make the workers eliminate wasteful activities and increase output brought immediate resistance and resentment. The employees' reactions were typified by the following comment: "What has gotten into Chuck lately? He's been chewing us out for the same old things we've always done. All he thinks about now is increasing production." Several of the foremen commented that they didn't like the front office making them the "bad guys" in the eyes of the workers. The workers didn't change their work habits as a result of the pressure put on them by the foremen, but a growing spirit of antagonism between the workers and the foremen was apparent.

After several weeks of no apparent improvement in production, Jon called a meeting with the workers to announce that the plant would go on a four-day, ten-hour-a-day work week in order to reduce operating costs. He stressed that the workers would enjoy having a three-day weekend. This was greeted with enthusiasm by some of the younger employees, but several of the older women complained that the schedule would be too tiring for them and that they would rather work five days a week. The proposal was voted on and passed by a two-to-one margin. Next Jon stated that there would be no more unsupervised overtime and that all overtime had to be approved in advance by Blaine. Overtime would be allowed only if some specific job had to be finished. Those who had been working overtime protested vigorously, saying that this would only result in lagging behind schedule, but Jon remained firm on this new rule.

Shortly after the meeting, several workers in the door-jamb department made plans to stage a work slowdown, so that the department would fall behind schedule and they would have to work overtime to catch up. One of the workers, who had previously been the hardest working in the department said, "We will tell them that we are working as fast as possible and that we just can't do as much as we used to in a five-day week. The only thing they could do would be to fire us, and they would never do that." Similar tactics were devised by workers in other departments. Some workers said that if they couldn't have overtime they would find a better paying job elsewhere.

Blaine, observing what was going on, told Jon, "They think I can't tell that they are staging a slowdown. Well, I simply won't approve any overtime, and after Jack's department gets way behind I'll let him have it for fouling up scheduling."

After a few weeks of continued slowdown, Blaine drew up a set of specific rules, which were posted on the company bulletin board early one Monday morning. (See Exhibit 2.) This brought immediate criticism from the workers. During the next week they deliberately continued to violate the posted rules. On Friday two of the male employees quit because they were penalized for arriving late to work and for "lounging around" during working hours. As they left they said they would be waiting for their foreman after work to get even with him for turning them in.

That same day the entire assembly department (all women) staged a work stoppage to protest an action taken against Myrtle King, an employee of the company since its beginning. The action resulted from a run-in she had with Lela Pims, foreman of the assembly department. Myrtle was about 60 years old and had been turned in by Lela for resting too much. She became furious, saying she couldn't work ten hours a day. Several of her friends had organized the work stoppage after Myrtle had been sent home without pay credit for the day. The stoppage was also inspired by some talk among the workers of forming a union. The women seemed to favor this idea more than the men.

When Blaine found out about the incident he tried joking with the women and in jest threatened to fire them if they did not begin working again. When he saw he was getting nowhere he returned to the front office. One of the workers commented, "He thinks he can send us home and push us around and then all he has to do is tell us to go back to work and we will. Well, this place can't operate without us."

Jon soon appeared and called Lela into his office and began talking with her. Later he persuaded the women to go back to work and told them that there would be a meeting with all the female employees on Monday morning.

Jon wondered what steps he should take to solve the problems at L. J. Summers Company. The efforts of management to increase efficiency and reduce production costs had definitely caused resentment among the workers. Even more disappointing was the fact that the company accountant had just announced that waste and costs had increased since the new programs had been instituted, and the company scheduler reported that Summers was further behind on shipments than ever before.

EXHIBIT 2
Production shop regulations

---

1. Anyone reporting late to work will lose one half hour's pay for each five minutes of lateness. The same applies to punching in after lunch.
2. No one is to leave the machine or post without the permission of the supervisor.
3. Anyone observed not working will be noted and if sufficient occurrences are counted the employee will be dismissed.

CASE QUESTIONS

1. Describe several perceptual processes and barriers that are contributing to the increasing hostility between management and labor at the L. J. Summers Company.
2. How might management better learn about the workers' dissatisfaction? What could management do to increase the workers' satisfaction?

NOTES

1. D. Dearborn and H.A. Simon, "Selective Perception: A Note on Departmental Identification of Executives," *Sociometry* 21 (1958), pp. 140–144.
2. D. Kretch, R. S. Crutchfield, and E. Ballachey, *Individual in Society* (New York: McGraw-Hill, 1962).
3. P. Secord and C. Backman, *Social Psychology* (New York: McGraw-Hill, 1964).
4. J. Bruner and L. Postman, "On the Perception of Incongruity: A Paradigm." *Journal of Personality*, 18 (1949), pp. 206–223.
5. P. Secord, "The Role of Facial Features in Interpersonal Perception," in R. R. Tagiuri and L. Petrullo (eds.), *Person Perception and Interpersonal Behavior* (Stanford, CA: Stanford University Press, 1958), pp. 300–315.
6. J. Thibaut and H. Riecker, "Authoritarianism, Status, and the Communication of Aggression," *Human Relations*, 8 (1955), pp. 96–120.
7. S. Zalkind and T. Costello, "Perception: Some Recent Research and Implications for Administration," *Administrative Science Quarterly*, 9 (1962), pp. 218–235.
8. S. Zalkind and T. Costello, "Perception," pp. 218–235.
9. William Scott and Terence R. Mitchell, *Organization Theory: A Structural and Behavioral Analysis* (Homewood, IL: Irwin, 1976).
10. Mason Haire, "Role Perception in Labor-Management Relations: An Experimental Approach," *Industrial and Labor Relations* 8 (1955), pp. 204–216.
11. S. Zalkind and T. Costello, "Perception," pp. 218–235.
12. S. Zalkind and T. Costello, "Perception," pp. 218–235.
13. S. Asch, "Forming Impressions of Personality," *Journal of Abnormal and Social Psychology*, 41 (1946), pp. 258–290.
14. B. Grove and W. Kerr, "Specific Evidence on Origin of Halo Effect in Measurement of Employee Morale," *Journal of Social Psychology*, 34 (1951), pp. 165–170.
15. John B. Miner, *The Management Process: Theory, Research, and Practice* (New York: Macmillan, 1973).
16. H. Kelley, "Attribution Theory in Social Psychology," in D. Levine (ed.), *Nebraska Symposium on Motivation* (Lincoln, NE: University of Nebraska, 1967), p. 193
17. Fritz Heider, *The Psychology of Interpersonal Relations* (New York: Wiley, 1958).
18. J. Rotter, "Generalized Expectancies for Internal vs. External Control of Reenforcement," *Psychological Monographs*, 80 (1966), pp. 1–28.
19. B. Weiner, *Achievement Motivation and Attribution Theory* (Morristown, NJ: General Learning Press, 1974).
20. "Pregnancy and VDT Workers: Pressure Leads to Quest for Hard Facts," *Business Week*, April 23, 1984, pp. 80–81.
21. G. Allport, "Attitudes," in C. Murchison (ed.), *Handbook of Social Psychology* (Worcester, MA: Clark University Press, 1935), pp. 798–884.
22. Harry Triandis, *Attitude and Attitude Change* (New York: Wiley, 1971).
23. Martin Fishbein and I. Ajzen, *Belief, Attitude, Intention and Behavior: An Introduction to Theory and Research* (Reading, MA: Addison-Wesley, 1975).
24. M. Rokeach, *The Nature of Human Values* (New York: The Free Press, 1973).

25. Mason Haire, "Role Perception," pp. 204–216.
26. S. Zalkind and T. Costello, "Perception," pp. 218–235.
27. "Why They're Jumping Ship at Intel," *Business Week*, February 14, 1983, pp. 107–108.
28. "A Productive Way to Vent Employee Gripes," *Business Week*, October 16, 1978, pp. 168–171.
29. Edwin A. Locke, "The Nature and Causes of Job Satisfaction," in M. D. Dunnette (ed.), *Handbook of Industrial and Organizational Psychology* (Chicago: Rand McNally, 1976), p. 1300.
30. Edwin A. Locke, "What is Job Satisfaction?" *Organizational Behavior and Human Performance*, 4 (1969), pp. 309–336; and Lyman W. Porter and Richard M. Steers, "Organizational, Work, and Personal Factors in Employee Turnover and Absenteeism," *Psychological Bulletin*, 80 (1973), pp. 151–176.
31. Patricia Smith, Lorne Kendall, and Charles Hulin, *The Measurement of Satisfaction in Work and Retirement* (Chicago: Rand McNally, 1969).
32. *The Minnesota Satisfaction Questionnaire* (Minneapolis: Industrial Relations Center, University of Minnesota, 1969).
33. Lyman W. Porter and Richard M. Steers, "Organizational, Work, and Personal Factors," pp. 151–176.
34. Richard M. Steers and Susan R. Rhodes, "Major Influences in Employee Attendance: A Process Model," *Journal of Applied Psychology*, 63 (1978), pp. 391–407.
35. Lyman W. Porter and Edward E. Lawler III, *Managerial Attitudes and Performance* (Homewood, IL: Irwin, 1968).
36. Lyman W. Porter and Edward E. Lawler III, *Managerial Attitudes and Performance*.
37. Richard M. Steers, *Organizational Effectiveness: A Behavioral View* (Santa Monica, CA: Goodyear, 1977).
38. Edward E. Lawler III, *Motivation in Work Organizations.* (Monterey, CA: Brooks/Cole, 1973).
39. Jeremy Main, "Ford's Drive for Quality," *Fortune*, April 18, 1983, pp. 62–70.
40. J. B. Ritchie and P. Thompson, *Organizations and People*, 2d ed. (St. Paul, MN: West, 1980), pp. 316–321.

4

Motivation and Performance

A *few days before Christmas, a railroad official telephoned the Chicago office of United Parcel Service to report that two UPS trailers on a flatcar had been inadvertently left on a siding in the middle of Illinois. The UPS regional manager in Chicago responded immediately. He ordered a high-speed diesel to transport the flatcar into Chicago (arriving ahead of the next regularly scheduled train) and then ordered two of UPS's fleet of Boeing 727s diverted to Chicago to pick up and deliver the contents of the trailers to their respective destinations in Florida and Louisiana in time for Christmas. Despite the extraordinary expense, the UPS manager who made the decision neither requested permission initially, nor did he inform corporate headquarters of the move until weeks later.*

"We applauded it when we heard about it," noted a corporate vice-president. "We give these guys complete authority to run their own operations and do their jobs. We push decision making down to the lowest possible levels." As a result of this policy, UPS also increases motivation to high levels. People like this manager work in an environment where they feel a keen sense of personal responsibility to perform and achieve. Employees are given a high level of autonomy and rewards are based on performance. Given this, it is not surprising that the manager went out of his way to achieve a high level of operating performance.[1]

In this chapter we explore the topic of employee motivation in work organizations. The topic of work motivation lies at the heart of any discussion of organizational effectiveness, since productivity and organizational goal attainment are influenced in no small way by the extent to which employees up and down the hierarchy are motivated to perform.

Several aspects of motivation will be examined. First, we will review basic motivational processes as they relate to human behavior. Next, early approaches to motivation are outlined, followed by a discussion of three rather different contemporary approaches: content theories, process theories, and reinforcement theories. Finally, two applications of motivation theories are discussed: goal setting and behavior modification. In all, we attempt here to present a balanced view of how motivational processes work in an organizational context.

RELEVANCE OF MOTIVATION FOR MANAGERS

The issue of employee motivation in organizations is clearly one of the most important topics for managers. One of the most persuasive arguments for studying motivation is based on three *behavioral requirements* organizations have of the people who work in them. First, people must be attracted to join the organization and remain with it. Second, people must dependably perform the tasks they were hired to do. Third, people must go beyond dependable role performance and engage in some form of creative, spontaneous, and innovative behavior at work. These three behavioral requirements deal squarely with the issue of motivation. Motivational techniques are valuable not only in encouraging employees to join and remain with an organization, but also in helping them perform in a dependable fashion and to think and take advantage of opportunities when they appear.

Motivational processes are pervasive in organizations. Motivation affects and is affected by innumerable factors in the work environment. An understanding of the way organizations function and survive requires knowledge of why people behave as they do in work situations.

With respect to the ever-tightening constraints placed on organizations by unions, government agencies, and foreign and domestic competition, companies must find way to improve their efficiency and effectiveness in the work place. Much of the slack organizations might have relied on in the past has diminished, requiring that all resources, including human resources, be utilized to their maximum capacity.

Considerable attention has been paid recently to developing employees as future resources—a type of talent bank—from which organizations can draw as they grow and develop. Examples of these efforts can be seen in the increase in management development programs, manpower planning, and job redesign. Motivation is the foundation upon which these resources are built.

From the individual's standpoint, motivation is a key to a productive life at work. And work consumes a sizable portion of our lives. If this time is to be meaningful and contribute toward the development of a healthy personality, the individual must be willing to devote effort toward task accomplishment. Motivation plays a central role in this.

In general, understanding motivational processes facilitates understanding organizational dynamics. Why do people behave as they do? What causes good or bad performance? Why is absenteeism or turnover high? The answers to questions such as these rest on understanding what motivates the employee.

Behavior modification, an application of learning theory, is gaining popularity among managers as a strategy for improving employee performance. An understanding of the mechanisms that underlie behavior modification allow managers to apply this technique toward the goals of organizational performance and effectiveness.

Finally, a major responsibility of managers is to evaluate and reward their subordinates. Reward practices rest on the principle of reinforcement. If managers are to maximize the impact of available (and often limited) rewards, familiarity with reinforcement techniques is essential.

BASIC MOTIVATIONAL PROCESSES

The term *motivation* is derived from the Latin *movere,* which means to move. For our study of employee motivation in work settings, a more comprehensive definition of the term is necessary: **motivation** is that which energizes, directs, and sustains human behavior. This definition emphasizes three distinct aspects of motivation. 1) Motivation represents an energetic force that *drives* people to behave in particular ways; 2) this drive is directed *toward* something; that is, motivation has strong goal orientation; and 3) motivation is perhaps best understood within a *systems* perspective; that is, to understand human motivation, it is necessary to examine the forces within individuals and their environments that provide them with feedback and reinforce their intensity and direction on the job.

Before examining contemporary theories of work motivation, it is useful to look at basic motivational processes. Most theories share basic assumptions about how behavior is energized, directed, and sustained over time. A general model of basic motivational processes is shown in Exhibit 4.1. There are four basic components of the process: 1) needs or expectations; 2) behavior; 3) goals; and 4) feedback.[2] At any given point in time, people are seen as having a constellation of needs, desires, and expectations. For instance, one employee may have a strong need for achievement, a desire for monetary gain, and an expectation that doing her job well will lead to rewards. When these needs, desires, and expectations are all present at once, that individual experiences a state of inner disequilibrium. Disequilibrium, in turn, may cause behavior that is motivated toward specific goals. The resulting behavior activates a series of cues (either within the individual or from the external environment) that feeds messages back to her concerning the impact of her behavior. This feedback may serve to reassure a person that the behavior is correct (that is, it satisfies her needs) or it may tell the individual that her present course of action is incorrect and should be changed.

Although this general model of motivation clearly does not take into account all of the different influences on human motivation, it illustrates the basic process. The model also emphasizes the cyclical nature of motivation, showing that individuals are in a continual state of disequilibrium, constantly striving to satisfy a variety of needs. Once one need has been met, another need emerges to prompt further action. In this way, individuals direct and redirect their energies as they attempt to adapt to their own changing needs and those of the world around them.

EXHIBIT 4.1
A Model of Basic Motivational Processes

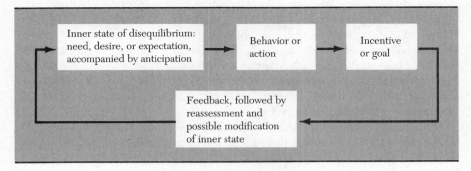

EARLY APPROACHES TO MOTIVATION

The development of managerial approaches to employee motivation has evolved through three relatively distinct stages: traditional; human relations; and human resources.[3]

Scientific Management

The industrial revolution of the late 1800s brought with it a reexamination of peoples' conception of the nature of work and the social relationships between individuals in various levels in organizations. A new philosophy of management emerged that was consistent with the prevailing managerial beliefs of the time. This philosophy has become known as the *traditional* model of management. It held that the average worker was basically lazy and was motivated almost entirely by money. Traditional management assumed that few workers wanted or could handle a high degree of autonomy or self-direction on their jobs. The best way to motivate employees based on these assumptions was to pay them using a piece-rate system, then redesign their jobs so the average worker could maximize his or her output. This job redesign, which was at the heart of the **scientific management** movement, was aimed not at enrichment but at increased job simplification and fractionation. The simpler the task, the greater the output. Far from seeing this approach as exploitative, the original advocates of scientific management (such as Frederick Taylor) thought it in the best interest of the workers, since workers' pay increased with output. They felt that, in exchange for increased income, employees would put up with fractionated and routinized jobs on the shop floor.

Human Relations

As the scientific management movement gained momentum, several problems began to emerge. First, it became increasingly apparent that factors other than money had motivating potential. Second, managers became aware that many employees were self-starters and did not need to be closely supervised and controlled. Finally, some managers attempted to use job simplification techniques without tying output to pay increases. This practice led to employee distrust of management, as wages fell behind productivity and as more workers were laid off because of increased efficiency. Workers reduced their effort, and drives for unionization began. Many managers learned the value of the human factor in maintaining long-term productivity. Emphasis on the human factor in employee performance, a movement that began around 1930, became known as the **human relations** movement.

The human relations movement changed the basic assumptions about the nature of people at work. Management now realized that people wanted to feel useful and important at work; they wanted to be recognized as individuals. These needs were seen to be as important as money. As a result, approaches to motivation took on a strong social emphasis. Attention shifted away from the scientific measurement of piece work toward a better understanding of the nature of interpersonal and group relations on the job. The Hawthorne studies were a forerunner in concluding that failure to treat employees as human beings was largely responsible for low morale, poor performance, high job turnover, absenteeism, and other problems.

To solve these problems, managers were told to make employees feel important and involved. Morale surveys became popular as an indicator of communication channels within organizations. Departmental meetings, company newspapers, and seminars on improving communications' effectiveness all appeared as an attempt to help employees feel they were involved and were important to the organization. Finally, supervisory training programs were initiated to train managers in group dynamics.

Within human relations, however, two aspects from the traditional theories of motivation continued. First, the basic goal of management remained employee compliance with managerial authority. Changed, however, were the strategies for accomplishing this. Second, within the human relations movement, almost no attention was given to changing the nature of the job itself. Instead, emphasis was placed on making employees more satisfied—and, it was hoped, more productive—primarily through the use of interpersonal strategies in the workplace.

Human Resources

The assumptions underlying the human relations model are an incomplete statement of human behavior at work, however. Contemporary models view motivation in more complex terms, assuming that many factors are capable of influencing behavior. Influential factors may include the nature of the incentive system, social influences, the nature of the job, supervisory style, employees' needs and values, and one's perceptions of the work situation. Newer models also assume that different employees want different rewards from their jobs, that many employees sincerely want to contribute, and that employees generally have the capacity to exercise a great deal of self-direction and self-control at work. In other words, contemporary managerial views of motivation focus on employees as potential *human resources*. It becomes management's responsibility to find ways to tap these resources to meet both the employees' and the organization's needs and goals.

Taking a human resources approach, several implications for management emerge. Attempts can be made to fit the person to the job, to integrate personal goals with the goals of the company, so individuals can reach their own goals while simultaneously contributing to corporate goals. Commissions paid to sales representatives is an example of this; both the individual and the company benefit from the sale.

Another result of the human resources approach is the use of participative decision techniques for organizational problem solving.[4]

UP CLOSE 4.1:   United Airlines

When Ed Carlson joined United Airlines in 1970 as CEO, the company was experiencing a $46 million loss for the year, its biggest loss in the company's forty-six-year history. The company was losing market share and had become top-heavy in management. Decisions were made at the top of a long vertical chain of command, and employees down in the ranks were discouraged from making suggestions.

Once Carlson assessed the problem, he immediately set to work on a series of remedies. One of his primary goals was to cut through the red tape he thought was strangling the organization so more individual initiative could show itself. He sought to be informed without being pivotal to the conduct of operations, to be exposed to different points of view without unleashing defensive reactions among his subordinates. Carlson felt that "authority is delegated upward." His approach reflected a basic philosophy that the chief executive officer of any organization has to respect and trust people.

Carlson also believed in "visible management." He felt that "employees of the company ought to see the man who's in charge." Among other things, visible management led to a direct, two-way exchange of information between Carlson and employees at all levels of the organization. According to Carlson, "Controlling employees to do a good job, at best, sets a minimum threshold of performance. Attainment about that threshold requires high morale and motivation."

Carlson's style reinforced this philosophy. His allocation of time, symbolic actions (e.g., informal chats with the baggage handlers), and near-obsessive concentration on details ultimately led to better service to the customer.

Through "visible management," decentralized decision making, and an emphasis on two-way communication, Ed Carlson was able to put the human resources approach to motivation and management into effect as United's chief executive officer.[5] ▪

CONTENT THEORIES OF MOTIVATION

At least three approaches to contemporary theories of motivation have been advanced. The first grouping of theories has been called **content theories,** because they emphasize what it is that is doing the motivating. The second grouping has been called **process theories,** because they focus on the dynamics of the motivation process. The third set of theories, **reinforcement theories,** focuses on the specific role of operant conditioning in motivated behavior. We will outline examples of all three theoretical approaches, then follow up with several specific applications of each model.

Need Hierarchy Theory

By far, the most popular content theory is Maslow's need hierarchy theory. Abraham Maslow was a clinical psychologist who, in the 1940s, began early developmental work on this theory with children with mental or emotional problems. He developed a model based on his observations of how the healthy personality evolves over time and how personality manifests itself in motivated behavior. Managers and organization analysts subsequently have popularized his work.

Need hierarchy theory consists of two basic premises. First, the theory asserts that people are motivated by a desire to simultaneously satisfy several types of specific needs. Second, it postulates that these needs are arranged in a hierarchical form and that people work their way through this hierarchy as their needs are satisfied. Maslow argues that there are two basic kinds of needs: deficiency needs and growth needs.[6] Deficiency needs must be satisfied if the individual is to be healthy and secure. The individual will only develop a healthy personality to the extent that these needs are met. Growth needs, on the other hand, relate to needs that help one develop and achieve one's potential. Maslow identifies five general motivating needs and arranges these needs in a hierarchy. In order of ascendance these are:

Deficiency Needs
1. *Physiological Needs.* The most basic needs, including the needs for food, water, and sex.
2. *Safety Needs.* The need to provide a safe and secure physical and emotional environment, one that is free from threats to continued existence.
3. *Belongingness Needs.* The desire to be accepted by one's peers, to have friendships, and to be loved.

Growth Needs
4. *Esteem Needs.* The desire to have a worthy self-image and to receive recognition, attention, and appreciation from others for one's contributions.
5. *Self-actualization Needs.* The need for self-fulfillment, the highest need category. The person is concerned with developing his or her full potential as an individual, becoming all that it is possible to become.

According to the theory, people move up the hierarchy by a process of *deprivation* and *gratification.* That is, when a particular need is unfulfilled, or a person is deprived, that need will dominate the individual's consciousness. A person concerned about physical safety will ignore other higher-order needs and devote all of his or her efforts to securing a safer environment. Once this need is gratified, it declines in importance and the next need up the hierarchy is activated (in this case, belongingness). The dynamic cycle of alternating deprivation, domination, gratification, and activation continues throughout the need levels until the individual reaches the self-actualization level of needs.

ERG Theory

A modification of Maslow's original theory has been proposed by Alderfer, who reformulated it largely in response to the failure of Maslow's five-level hierarchy to hold up to empirical validation. Alderfer's model is called **ERG Theory.** Instead of Maslow's five need levels, Alderfer recategorizes them into three more general need levels.[7]

1. *Existence Needs.* Needs necessary to sustain human existence, including both physiological and safety needs.
2. *Relatedness Needs.* Needs dealing with how people relate to their surrounding social environment, including the need for meaningful social and interpersonal relationships.
3. *Growth Needs.* Needs focusing on the development of human potential, including the needs for self-esteem and self-actualization.

EXHIBIT 4.2
Satisfaction-Progression, Frustration-Regression Components of ERG Theory

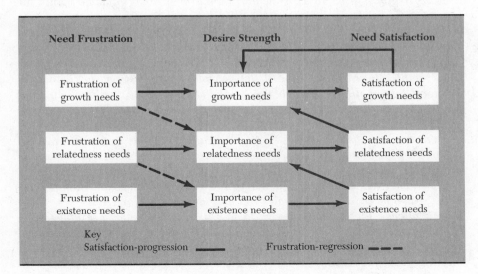

SOURCE: F. J. Landy and D. A. Trumbo, *Psychology of Work Behavior,* 2d ed. (Homewood, IL: Dorsey Press, 1980).

The ERG model and Maslow's need hierarchy are similar in positing that individuals move up the hierarchy one step at a time. ERG differs from Maslow, however, in two important regards. According to Maslow, individuals progress up the hierarchy as a result of the satisfaction of the lower-order needs. In contrast, Alderfer suggests that in addition to this satisfaction-progression process, there is also a frustration-regression process (see Exhibit 4.2). For example, when an individual is continually frustrated in his or her attempts to satisfy growth needs, relatedness needs will reemerge as a primary motivating force, and the individual is likely to redirect his or her efforts toward lower-level needs. A second difference is that Maslow has individuals focusing on one need at a time, while Alderfer suggests that more than one need may be operative or activated at the same time. Alderfer's model is less rigid, allowing for greater flexibility in describing human behavior in various situations.

UP CLOSE 4.2:   IBM

A basic premise of need theories is that people are motivated primarily by the needs that are most prominent at a given time. What happens, then, when a company changes its compensation system so that it fosters security needs instead of growth needs? During the past decade, there has been a shift in the U.S. away from having sales representatives on commission and toward paying them straight salary. The change was not so much an effort to improve productivity as it was to protect employees from the variability of business cycles. As one observer puts it, "Today's salesman was raised in an affluent society. A guy is used to a particular standard of living, and he wants the security of a fixed salary. He doesn't want to assume much risk."

Some view offering such security as "enlightened" management. They argue that salaries made for more professional marketing help reps avoid foot-in-the-door pressure tactics. Others, however, feel that putting sales representatives on straight salary (or salary with low commissions) destroys motivation to produce. Recent studies show that building too much protection into pay plans tends to favor the least productive salespeople and provides little stimulus to put forth maximum effort.

Consider the case of IBM.[8] In recent years, IBM has been lowering the commission content of its sales compensation program, causing discord among the top performers. One high performer spent several months cultivating a new customer to land a $2 million mainframe contract. His commission for this effort was a mere $2000. The sales rep no longer works for IBM.

A challenge for management is created when need levels are affected. A company must decide what kinds of employees it wants to attract, develop, and retain. By implementing a compensation system for its sales force aimed at meeting security but not growth needs, an organization may end up with security-minded sales reps, not achievement-oriented ones. The choice, to at least some degree, is up to the company. ■

PROCESS THEORIES OF MOTIVATION

The second approach to studying employee motivation focuses on understanding the basic motivational processes—*how* does motivation work? Two theories are particularly relevant here: equity theory and expectancy theory.

Equity Theory

Equity theory focuses on individuals' perceptions of how fairly they are being treated compared to others and the behavioral implications of their perceptions. It rests on two basic assumptions about human behavior.[9] First, equity theory assumes that individuals engage in a process of evaluating their social relationships much like they would evaluate economic transactions in the marketplace. Social relationships are an exchange process in which individuals make contributions or investments and expect certain outcomes in return. Second, equity theory assumes that people do not assess the equity of an exchange in a vacuum. Instead, they compare their own situation with others' to determine the relative balance. People determine whether an exchange is satisfactory by comparing what happens to themselves with what happens to others.

The Social Comparison Process   Social comparison processes involved in equity theory are typically based on the relationship between two variables: inputs and outcomes. *Inputs,* or investments, represent those things an individual contributes to an exchange. In a work situation, inputs can include previous work experience, education, and level of effort on the job. *Outcomes* are items that an individual receives from the exchange. Outcomes can include pay, fringe benefits, accrued status, seniority, and positive feedback from one's supervisor.

If an input or outcome is to be meaningful in assessing exchange relationships, two conditions must be met. First, the existence of an input or outcome must be recognized by one or both parties in the exchange. A major outcome of a particular job is irrelevant unless at least one of the parties involved considers it a major outcome. Second, an input or outcome must be seen as important and relevant, or have marginal utility, to the exchange. Unless both conditions —recognition and relevancy—are met, potential inputs or outcomes cannot be said to determine the degree of equity in the exchange relationship.

The way social comparison processes work is as follows. Individuals assign weights to the various inputs and outcomes based on their perceived importance. This is not to say that people are highly precise. Instead, they roughly differentiate between more important and less important inputs and outcomes. Intuitively, people arrive at a ratio of their outcomes to inputs *as compared to* the ratio of another individual's or group's outcomes to inputs. The other individual or groups may be people with whom we engage in direct exchanges; other individuals engaged in exchanges with a common third party; or persons in a previous or hypothetical work situation. The *referent other* becomes the point of comparison for people in determining how equitably treated they feel in the exchange.

Following the theory, a state of *equity* exists whenever the ratio of a person's outcomes *(O)* to inputs *(I)* is equal to the ratio of other's outcomes to inputs. A formula can be given, where *p* represents the ratio of the person and *o* represents the ratio of the referent other:

$$\frac{O_p}{I_p}=\frac{O_o}{I_o}$$

A state of *inequity* exists where these two ratios are unequal. This can occur when either part is advantaged or disadvantaged:

$$\frac{O_p}{I_p}<\frac{O_o}{I_o} \text{ or } \frac{O_p}{I_p}>\frac{O_o}{I_o}$$

Several aspects of this model of social exchange are worth emphasizing. First, the conditions necessary to produce a state of equity or inequity are based on a person's *perceptions* of inputs and outcomes. A person can incorporate what is actually a distorted view of the major factors involved in an exchange (e.g., thinking that co-workers were earning far more than they actually are), into his or her calculations of equity or inequity.

Second, inequity is a *relative* phenomenon. Inequity does not necessarily exist simply because a person has high inputs and low outcomes, as long as the comparison other also has a similar ratio. Employees may be fairly satisfied with a job demanding high effort and offering low rewards if their frame of reference has been a similar job elsewhere.

Third, it is important to note that inequity occurs when people are relatively underpaid or overpaid. Although the threshold for underpayment is lower than it is for overpayment, both theory and research suggest that people who experience overpayment sometimes are motivated to reduce the exchange imbalance by working harder.[10]

Results of Perceived Inequity   The major postulates of equity theory, as shown in Exhibit 4.3, are as follows: 1) perceived inequity (underpayment or overpayment) creates tension within individuals; 2) the tension is proportionate to the magnitude of the inequity; 3) the tension experienced by individuals motivates them to attempt to reduce it; and 4) the strength of the motivation or drive to reduce it is proportionate to the perceived inequity. Six methods of resolution are seen as most common for reducing perceived inequity:[11]

• *People may change their inputs.* Individuals may increase or decrease their inputs depending upon whether the inequity is advantageous or disadvantageous. For example, underpaid individuals may reduce their level of effort on the job or increase absenteeism, while overpaid individuals may increase effort on the job.

EXHIBIT 4.3
Motivational Implications of Perceived Inequity

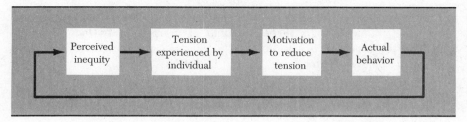

- *People may change their outcomes.* Similarly, people can increase or decrease outcomes received on the job. Union efforts to improve wages, hours, and working conditions without parallel increases in employee effort is an attempt to increase outcomes.
- *People may distort cognitively their inputs or outcomes.* People who feel inequitably treated may artificially increase the status outcomes attached to their job ("This is really an important job") or may feel they have decreased effort ("I really don't work that hard on this job"). By doing so, the input-outcome ratios become more favorable, and individuals may become more content about the situation.
- *People may leave the job.* People who feel inequitably treated may decide to leave the situation by transferring to another job or department or by quitting. In doing so, they apparently hope to find a more favorable balance of inputs to outcomes.
- *People may distort cognitively the inputs or outcomes of others.* In the face of perceived inequity, people may distort the input-outcome ratio of the referent. They may come to believe that the referent other actually works harder than they do, and thereby deserves greater rewards. Or, they may believe the referent other makes a lower salary and thereby reduce the other's outcomes.
- *People may change their objects of comparison.* Finally, people may decide that their referent other is not the most suitable point of comparison and may select another who will yield a more favorable balance in the social exchange process. If the other receives a salary increase or promotion while the person does not, he or she may decide that the other is on a different level in the organization hierarchy, and he or she should find another point of comparison.

Through mechanisms such as these, people attempt to cope with situations they believe are unfair. They aim their efforts at returning to a state of equity and reduced tension. Equity theory views individuals as existing in a constant state of flux, continually trying to understand their environment and to act in order to satisfy their more pressing needs, desires, and expectations. Equity theory describes a continual fight for fairness in the work situation.

UP CLOSE 4.3   Equitable Life

From a financial standpoint, the Equitable Life Assurance Company has performed admirably. Its revenues stand at more than $6 billion and its earnings continue to rise faster than the industry. Even so, the company thought it could do better.

Under the leadership of Coy G. Eklund, Equitable Life initiated a "More Profitable Growth (MPG)" program. Its goal was to curb rising operating expenses and thereby make the firm more profitable. As part of the program, Eklund fired 550 of the company's 15,000 employees. The terminations were primarily in headquarters and affected personnel from file clerks to senior vice presidents.[12]

The firings had a devastating impact on employee morale. They completely reversed a long-standing company policy of lifetime employment for employees with acceptable levels of performance. In fact, over the years, Equitable often bragged about this policy. Now the rules were changed, as Eklund stated, "A policy of lifetime employment has clearly become an inconsistent one as we have moved in recent years to meet competition. . . ."

Although Eklund claims that morale has not been affected by the cutbacks, a Business Week *survey of past and present employees found just the opposite. Said one employee, "The loyalty and dedication are gone. In the past, people always put out a little more than was expected of them, but not any more."*

While the layoffs themselves hurt morale, what really took its toll was the way in which they were done. Eklund simply told all departments to cut back the number of positions by 10 percent, thereby eliminating what he termed all "non-essential" jobs. Many employees felt that what ensued was a popularity contest in which quality of performance or even tenure became less important than the good graces of one's supervisor. Even Eklund admits that many of those fired were "highly capable and were skilled and excellent in their performance."

What this move has done at Equitable was call into question the company's commitment to equity towards its employees. Consistent with equity theory, the employees simply felt they were not being treated fairly. As a result, they decreased effort, performance fell, and turnover increased. A final irony may be that when many American firms have attempted to learn the secrets of successful Japanese management practices, they have seen one lesson cropping up again and again: there appear to be benefits in lifetime employment for suitably performing employees. ■

Expectancy/Valence Theory

The second process theory of employee motivation is **expectancy/valence theory.** This theory of work motivation dates from the early work of Lewin and Tolman during the 1930s and 1940s. These investigators argued that much of human behavior results from interaction between the characteristics of individuals (e.g., their personality traits, attitudes, needs, and values), and their perceived environment. This basic model was first applied to work settings by Georgopoulos, Mahoney, and Jones in their path-goal theory of motivation.[13] Expectancy/valence theory is known by many titles, including path-goal theory, instrumentality theory, valence-instrumentality-expectancy theory, and simply expectancy theory.

Following the model, people are thinking, reasoning individuals who make conscious choices about present and future behavior. People are not inherently motivated or unmotivated. Instead, motivational level depends on the particular work environment people find themselves in. They are motivated to the extent that this environment is compatible with their needs, goals, and expectations.

Determinants of Motivation   In expectancy theory, motivation is determined by a combination of expectancies and valences. An *expectancy* is a belief about the likelihood or probability that a particular behavioral act (such as working harder) will lead to a particular outcome (such as a pay raise). The degree of this belief can vary from 0, where an individual sees no chance that the behavior will lead to the outcome, to 1.0, where an individual is absolutely certain that the behavior will lead to the outcome. Of course, most expectancies fall somewhere in between these two extremes. *Valence* refers to the value an individual places on available outcomes or rewards. A valence can range from $+1.0$ to -1.0, depending upon whether the outcome is highly prized by the employee (money) or highly undesirable (getting fired).

Expectancies, in turn, can be divided into two types: 1) effort-performance (or $E \rightarrow P$) expectancies and 2) performance-outcome (or $P \rightarrow O$) expectancies.[14] An $E \rightarrow P$ expectancy is an individual's belief that effort will, in fact, lead to performance. For example, an employee may feel that working overtime will lead to a higher level of output. A performance-outcome expectancy (or $P \rightarrow O$ expectancy), on the other hand, is the belief that if a person performs well in a given situation, certain desired outcomes will follow. For instance, an employee may believe that a higher level of output will result in a pay raise.

Valence is the value individuals place on the available outcomes or rewards. If employees truly do not value the rewards offered by an organization, we do not expect them to be motivated to perform. The valence attached to certain outcomes can vary widely. Some employees do not want to be promoted into positions of increased responsibility and stress, while others welcome such opportunities. Up-or-out promotional policies in many large companies have had detrimental effects. On the other hand, some rewards, like money, it is safe to say, are consistently valued.

As shown in Exhibit 4.4, these three variables ($E \rightarrow P$ expectancies, $P \rightarrow O$ expectancies, and valences) influence an employee's motivational level in a multiplicative fashion. According to expectancy theory, employee motivation (not to be confused with actual performance) is a result of an employee's $E \rightarrow P$ expectancies *times* the $P \rightarrow O$ expectancies *times* the valences for the outcomes. A simple example illustrates how this process works. If a salesperson believes that the chances are good (say 8 out of 10, or .8) that increased effort in selling

EXHIBIT 4.4
A Model of Expectancy/Valence Theory of Motivation and Performance

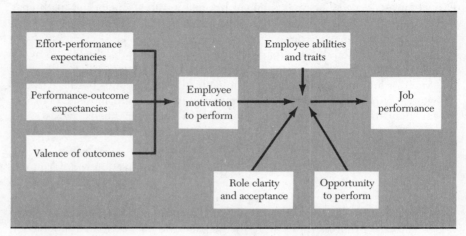

Adapted from L. W. Porter and E. E. Lawler, *Managerial Attitudes and Performance* (Homewood, IL: Irwin, 1968).

will lead to higher sales, we say the person has a high $E \rightarrow P$ expectancy. Moreover, if this individual also believes (again at a .8 level of probability) that sales increases would lead to a bonus or a pay raise, we say that he or she has a high $P \rightarrow O$ expectancy. Finally, let's assume the salesperson places a high value on this bonus or pay raise (say .9 on a scale from -1.0 to $+1.0$). When these three factors are combined in a multiplicative fashion (.8 $\times$.8 $\times$ .9 = .58), it becomes clear that the salesperson has a high motivational force. On the other hand, if expectancies were high (.8 and .8, respectively), but the salesperson genuinely had little desire for money (say a valence of .1 instead of .9), the motivational force would be considerably lower (.8 $\times$ .8 $\times$ .1 = .06). There-fore, for an employee to be highly motivated, all three factors must be high. In the absence of just one of the factors, we would not expect to see high employee motivation.

Determinants of Performance   Motivation and performance are not synony-mous. Motivation represents an employee's desire to perform, or level of effort, while performance is the extent to which an individual can successfully accomplish a task or achieve a goal. Performance as a concept includes not only the production of certain tangible units of output but also less tangible outputs. Some less tangible outputs may be effectively supervising others, thinking in a creative way, inventing a new product, resolving a conflict between others, or selling a good or service. In many ways, effective employee performance is the ultimate criterion by which managerial effectiveness should be evaluated.

As shown in Exhibit 4.4, performance is influenced by at least four factors. First, motivation is clearly a central influence. But in addition to motivation, at least three ingredients are involved: 1) abilities and traits; 2) role clarity and acceptance; and 3) opportunity to perform. The *abilities and traits* employees bring to the job largely determine their capacity to perform, as opposed to employee motivation, which is concerned with employees' will to perform. Abilities and traits are believed to be enduring and stable over time, although some changes in them are possible as a result of outside intervention, such as employee training.

Job performance can be influenced by employee abilities and traits in several ways. For example, it has been shown that managerial effectiveness is modestly related to intellectual capabilities such as verbal comprehension, inductive reasoning, and memory. Ghiselli suggested that these capabilities grow in importance as individuals move up the managerial hierarchy into increasingly responsible positions.[15]

However, being motivated to perform and having the requisite abilities still do not insure good job performance. In addition, employees must understand and accept the requirements of the job.[16] Providing employees with greater *role clarity* increases the amount of energy that is directed specifically toward work goals and decreases the amount of energy that is wasted on other activities. For instance, if supervisors know that they bear primary responsibility for reducing shop floor accidents, they will try to accomplish this goal. On the other hand, if roles are not clear, supervisors may take a "let the employee worry about it" attitude, with negative results.

Finally, an important influence on employee motivation is *opportunity to perform*.[17] If a salesperson is asked to sell a product nobody wants, such as buggy whips, or if a production manager is given an unrealistic deadline, the chances of successful job performance are low—even if the employee is motivated, has the requisite abilities, and has a clear picture of the task.

The inhibiting effects placed on the opportunity to perform can be seen in the problems managers face when asked to improve employee motivation without changing the compensation and reward system. Under such circumstances, it is not surprising that managers are unable to improve motivation substantially, because employees simply are not given any new opportunities to perform. Another example of the lack of opportunity to perform can be seen in assembly-line jobs where the pace of production is determined by machines. When technology controls production, improved motivation can do little to increase quantity of output, although it may influence quality of output in some instances.

These four primary influences on motivation suggest that successful job performance is indeed determined jointly by individuals and their environment, as suggested by Kurt Lewin. Individuals can contribute to job performance through their motivation to perform and the skills and abilities they bring to the work place. On the other hand, managers can contribute to job performance by insuring that reward systems encourage motivation and that job requirements are clear and precise. Moreover, managers can attempt to create work assignments in which employees have real opportunities to perform. In this way, the more control employees have over their performance environment, the greater the potential impact of their motivation on subsequent performance.

UP CLOSE 4.4:   Kroger's

A major tenet of expectancy/valance theory is that employees' effort and performance is heavily influenced by the beliefs they hold that their effort will lead to performance and performance will lead to valued rewards. The notion of equity, or what is a "fair" wage-effort bargain, is an important part of this. What happens when a company converts to a "two-tier" approach to compensation, in which employees hired after a certain date receive less money for the same job?[18]

Two-tier wage systems have become popular in recent years as a compromise strategy to keep wages down and prevent layoffs in the face of poor economic conditions while at the same time "protecting" more senior employees. A company in need of financial savings goes to its union and says, in effect, we will keep your wages at current levels in exchange for an agreement to pay new hires on the same job substantially less. The company benefits and current employees benefit. Subsequent hires clearly do not.

Kroger's, the major retail food chain, uses a two-tiered system. At some stores, retail clerks doing the same work are paid five different wage levels ranging from $6.34 per hour to $10.02 per hour, depending upon when they were hired. As one manager puts it, "This is the only way we've been able to stay alive in an industry where there is strong, organized competition." The manager points out that the system is not a problem for the company. "It's a constant communication thing to show employees that it's in their best interest" to allow lower paid jobs; otherwise, there would be no jobs at all.

The argument may be convincing but for the motivational effects such a system has on the newer, lower paid employees. From an expectancy theory standpoint, the lower paid employees would probably have the same beliefs, or expectancies, concerning their ability to do the job as the higher paid people. If they put forth the effort, they will succeed. However, if they do succeed, what happens? They are still paid substantially less than the person standing next to them. Should they be motivated to perform? Probably not. Should they be motivated to stay? Probably not, if they can find another job. The situation is clearly inequitable from the employee's standpoint. On top of it, knowing that one's senior colleagues "sold me out" cannot help one's feelings of unfair treatment. Hence, while such two-tiered compensation systems are probably born of necessity, they are clearly not designed to enhance employee motivation. ■

REINFORCEMENT THEORIES OF MOTIVATION

The third general approach to understanding employee motivation is reinforcement theory. Reinforcement theory is acognitive. **Acognitive theories** of motivation assert that it is possible to predict behavior without an understanding of internal thought processes. They stress instead the relationship between external stimuli and behavior and do not explore the effects of internal

mechanisms. People are seen as being largely reactive to environm
stimuli, making it unnecessary, according to this view, to examine in
processes. **Cognitive theories** of motivation, such as the process theorie
equity or expectancy theory, rest on the assumption that individuals ......
conscious decisions about their behavior, and that we must understand this
decision process in order to understand human behavior. Cognitive theories
emphasize the how and why of behavior by focusing on internal mechanisms.
Individuals are seen as active organisms in their environment. They are
proactive as well as reactive to environmental forces. While these two basic
approaches to understanding human behavior are not incompatible, they do
represent distinct differences in emphasis and assumptions about the nature of
people.

Types of Reinforcement

A central aspect of reinforcement theory and behavior modification is the
concept of reinforcement. This concept dates from Thorndike's law of effect
which, as discussed in Chapter 2, states that behavior that is positively
reinforced tends to be repeated, while behavior that is not reinforced tends not
to be repeated. Hence, **reinforcement** can be defined as anything that causes a
certain behavior to be repeated or inhibited. From a managerial standpoint,
several strategies for behavioral change are available to facilitate learning in
organizational settings. Four basic types can be identified: 1) positive reinforcement; 2) avoidance learning or negative reinforcement; 3) extinction; and 4)
punishment.[19] Each type plays a different role in how and how much learning
occurs.

Positive Reinforcement Positive reinforcement occurs when we present
someone with an attractive outcome following a desired behavior. As Skinner
noted, "a positive reinforcer is a stimulus which, when added to a situation,
strengthens the probability of an operant response." [20] A simple example of
positive reinforcement is praise—a supervisor may praise an employee for
being consistently punctual in attendance. This process is shown in Exhibit 4.5.
The behavior-praise pattern is designed to encourage subordinates to be on
time in the future in the hope of receiving additional praise from the
supervisor.

According to the theory, in order for a positive reinforcement to effectively
elicit the repetition of desired behavior, several conditions must be met. First,
the employee must value praise, the reinforcer itself. Second, the reinforcer
must be strongly tied to the desired behavior. It is important to keep in mind
that desired behavior represents behavior defined by the supervisor, not the
employee. Finally, there must be ample opportunity for the reinforcer to be
administered. If the praise is tied to certain behavior that seldom occurs, such
as getting to work well before starting time, then individuals will seldom
receive praise and will probably not associate this behavior with a reward. It is
important that the performance-reward contingencies be set so that they are

relatively easily attainable by employees. In other words, the praise must go to someone who values it for his or her regular on-time (not occasionally early) arrival at work.

Avoidance Learning   The second approach to reinforcement is avoidance learning, or negative reinforcement. Avoidance learning occurs when we seek to avoid an unpleasant situation or outcome by following a desired behavior.

Employees learn to avoid unpleasant situations by behaving in certain ways. If an employee correctly performs a task, or is continually prompt in coming to work, as shown in Exhibit 4.5, the supervisor may refrain from harassing, reprimanding, or otherwise embarrassing the employee. Presumably, the employee would learn that engaging in correct behavior diminishes admonishing from the supervisor. In order to avoid this unpleasantness, the employee would continue to behave as desired by the supervisor.

Extinction   The concept of extinction posits that undesired behavior will decrease or cease as a result of a lack of positive reinforcement for it. That is, if the perpetually tardy employee consistently fails to receive praise and is not recommended for a pay raise, he or she may realize, albeit subtly, that being late is not leading to desired outcomes and may try being on time for work for a change.

Punishment   The final approach to behavioral change that managers and supervisors use is punishment. Punishment is the administration of unpleasant or adverse outcomes to employees in response to their undesired behavior. When a supervisor publicly reprimands or harasses an employee who is habitually tardy (see Exhibit 4.5) punishment is occuring. Presumably, the employee would refrain from being tardy in the future in order to avoid such an undesirable outcome. The use of punishment is indeed one of the most controversial issues of reinforcement theory.

Positive reinforcement and avoidance learning focus on bringing about the desired response from the employee. With positive reinforcement the employee behaves in order to gain desired rewards, while with avoidance learning the employee behaves in order to avoid undesired outcomes. In both cases, however, the behavior the supervisor wants is enhanced. In contrast, extinction and punishment focus on supervisory attempts to reduce the incidence of undesired behavior. That is, extinction and punishment are typically used to get someone to stop doing something. It does not necessarily follow that the individuals who cease undesired behavior then begin acting in the most desired manner. For managers, questions arise about which strategy of behavioral change is most effective. Advocates of behavior modification answer that positive reinforcement combined with extinction is the best way to bring about desired behavior. Several reasons back up this focus on the positive approach to reinforcement. First, positive reinforcement does more than inhibit or eliminate undesired behavior, it can provide some information to the individual about how or in which direction to change. Negative reinforcement does not do

EXHIBIT 4.5

Strategies for Behavioral Change

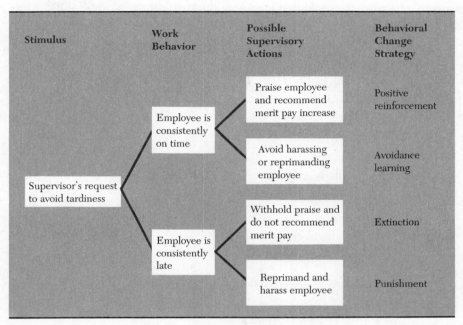

SOURCE: R. M. Steers, *Introduction to Organizational Behavior*, 2d ed. (Glenview, IL: Scott, Foresman and Company, 1984), p. 197.

this. Also punishment can cause the individual to become alienated from the work situation, and the chances for useful change become limited. Similarly, avoidance learning tends to emphasize the negative; that is, people are taught to stay clear of certain behaviors, like tardiness, for fear of the repercussions. In contrast, it is felt that combining positive reinforcement with the use of extinction has the least undesirable side effects and allows individuals to receive the rewards they desire. A positive approach to reinforcement is believed by some to be the most effective tool management has to effect favorable changes in the work situation.

Schedules of Reinforcement

It has been argued that the speed with which learning occurs and also how lasting its effects will be is determined by the timing of reinforcement.[21] With this in mind, understanding **schedules of reinforcement** is essential to managers if they are to know how to choose rewards that will have maximum influence on employee on-the-job behavior.

Although there are a variety of ways rewards can be administered, most approaches can be categorized into two groups: continuous and partial reinforcement schedules. A *continuous reinforcement schedule* rewards desired behavior every time it occurs. For example, a manager could praise (or pay) employees every time they perform properly. Given the time and resource constraints most managers work under, this is difficult or impossible. Most managerial reward strategies operate on a partial schedule. A *partial reinforcement schedule* rewards desired behavior at specific intervals—not every time it is exhibited. Compared to continuous schedules, partial reinforcement schedules often lead to slower learning but stronger retention. Thus learning is generally more permanent.

Four types of partial reinforcement schedules can be identified: 1) fixed interval; 2) fixed ratio; 3) variable interval; 4) variable ratio. These are detailed in Exhibit 4.6.

Fixed Interval Schedule   This schedule rewards individuals for their performance at prespecified intervals. As a result, if employees perform even minimally, they are paid. This approach generally does not promote high or sustained levels of performance, since employees know that marginal performance usually leads to the same level of rewards as high performance. There is little incentive for high effort and performance. Also, when rewards are withheld or suspended, extinction of desired behavior occurs quickly. Many work redesign efforts in organizations have been prompted by recognition of the need for strategies of motivation other than pay on fixed interval schedules.

Fixed Ratio Schedule   In the fixed ratio schedule, the reward is administered to individuals only upon the completion of a given number of desired responses. Thus rewards are tied to performance in a ratio of rewards to results. For every so many results, employees receive a reward. A common example of the fixed ratio schedule is a piece-rate pay system, in which employees are paid for each unit of output they produce. Performance rapidly reaches high levels under this system. However, on the negative side, performance declines sharply when the reward is no longer offered (as with fixed interval schedules).

Variable Interval Schedule   Both variable interval and variable ratio reinforcement are administered at random times that cannot be predicted by employees. Under a variable interval schedule, rewards are administered at intervals of time that are based on an average. For example, an employee may know that on the average his or her performance is evaluated and rewarded about once a month; he or she may not know when this event will occur, only that it will occur sometime during the month. Under this schedule, effort and performance are generally high and fairly stable over time.

Variable Ratio Schedule   Finally, the variable ratio schedule is one in which rewards are administered only after an employee has performed the desired behavior a number of times. The number of performances needed to elicit a reward changes from the administration of one reward to the next but averages over time to a certain ratio of number of performances to rewards. For example, a manager may determine that a salesperson will receive a bonus for every

EXHIBIT 4.6
Schedules of Partial Reinforcement

Schedule of Reinforcement	Nature of Reinforcement	Effects on Behavior When Applied	Effects on Behavior When Perceived	Example
Fixed interval	Reward on fixed time basis	Leads to average and irregular performance	Quick extinction of behavior	Weekly paycheck
Fixed ratio	Reward consistently tied to output	Leads quickly to very high and stable performance	Quick extinction of behavior	Piece-rate pay system
Variable interval	Reward given at variable intervals around some average time	Leads to moderately high and stable performance	Slow extinction of behavior	Monthly performance appraisal and reward at random times each month
Variable ratio	Reward given at variable output levels around some average output	Leads to very high performance	Slow extinction of behavior	Sales bonus tied to selling X accounts, but X constantly changes around some mean

SOURCE: R. M. Steers, *Introduction to Organizational Behavior*, 2d ed. (Glenview, IL: Scott, Foresman, 1984), p. 199.

fifteen new accounts sold. However, instead of administering the bonus every fifteenth sale, the manager varies the number of sales that are necessary for the bonus; perhaps ten sales are required for the first bonus and twenty are required for the second. On the average, however, the 15:1 ratio prevails. Like the variable interval, the variable ratio schedule typically leads to high and stable performance. Moreover, under this condition, extinction of desired behavior is slow compared to other methods.

Which of these four schedules of reinforcement is most effective? In general, the performance-contingent (or ratio) reward schedules lead to better performance than the time-contingent (or interval) schedules, regardless of whether each schedule is fixed or variable. We will see why when we examine reward systems in the next chapter.

APPLICATIONS OF MOTIVATION THEORIES

We have explored a variety of practical applications of the various models of employee motivation throughout this chapter. In view of their popularity in work organizations, two additional applications should be explained. These are goal-setting techniques and behavior modification. Goal setting as a technique of motivation is based on cognitive theory, while behavior modification is based on reinforcement principles. As such, the two applications that follow each represent a primary example of putting a major theory of motivation to work.

Goal-Setting Techniques

Goal-setting techniques in organizations often appear in some form of management-by-objectives program. **Management by objectives (MBO)** is a process in which employees of complex organizations, working in conjunction with one another, identify common goals and coordinate their efforts toward achieving them.[22] It is a future-oriented technique, focusing attention and effort on "where are we going" instead of "where have we been." MBO does help managers provide greater structure, clarity, and focus in otherwise ambiguous situations.

Task-Goal Attributes and Behavior   In the design of MBO or goal-setting programs, it is important to recognize how variations on task goals, as well as other factors, can influence goal-setting success. For our purposes, a *task-goal attribute* may be defined as a characteristic or dimension of an employee's task goals.[23] It is possible to identify four relatively distinct task-goal attributes that facilitate task performance in a goal-setting environment: 1) goal specificity; 2) goal difficulty; 3) participation in goal-setting; and 4) feedback. The relationship of these to employee performance is summarized in Exhibit 4.7.

EXHIBIT 4.7
Major Influences on Goal-Setting and Performance

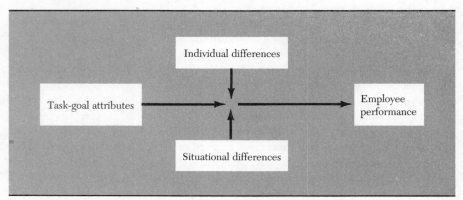

First, it has been found that *goal specificity* is consistently related to increased performance. When employees are given specific goals, they almost always perform at higher levels than when they are simply told to do their best or are given no instructions at all. The more specific the goals, the higher the performance.[24] Increasing goal specificity on a task reduces role ambiguity and reduces the search for acceptable modes of behavior. The employee has a very clear idea of what is expected. In addition, increasing the *difficulty* of employees' goals often increases the perceived challenge of the task and increases the amount of effort the employee expends for goal attainment. This is particularly true for employees with high achievement needs (see Chapter 2). More difficult goals tend to lead to increased effort and performance, at least to the point such goals are still seen as feasible. However, there are exceptions to this trend. Difficult goals may lose their motivating potential when they are not properly reinforced. Past failures on previous goals may negate the effects of setting difficult future goals. Goals apparently must not be set on a level at which they are seldom, if ever, achieved. Under these conditions, employees may simply give up and reduce their effort.

Participative decision making has long been valued as a means not only of increasing organizational efficiency and effectiveness but also of increasing employee involvement and job satisfaction. Unfortunately, available evidence suggests that, while more *participation* in goal-setting may increase job satisfaction and attendance, it has only mixed effects on job performance. While participation does not seem to detract from performance, it appears that the act of setting goals (goal specificity) is a more powerful tool in influencing performance.[25] Finally, another influence on goal-setting effectiveness is the extent to which employees are given *feedback* on task-oriented behavior. Feedback serves at least two functions: first, it acts as a directive, keeping a goal-directed behavior on target, and second, it serves as an incentive, stimulating employees to greater effort. When available evidence is considered, it becomes clear that no simple feedback-performance relationship exists. While feedback is obviously important in facilitating performance for some people, other factors, such individuals' needs, appear to moderate the relationship.

Individual and Situational Differences   We discovered that several aspects of the goal-setting environment (task-goal attributes) influence the extent to which goals are actually achieved. We also found that, in some cases, there is no direct relationship between these task-goal attributes and subsequent performance. Instead, two major moderators of the task-goal attribute-performance relationship can be identified, as seen in Exhibit 4.7. First, several *individual differences* can be identified. In particular, employees' need for achievement can moderate the extent to which attributes influence performance. For instance, it has been found that high need achievers perform better when given high levels of feedback and very specific goals, while low need achievers perform better when allowed to participate in goal setting.[26] These findings are consistent with the achievement motive theory. Other evidence suggests that goal-setting techniques, particularly goal specificity, are more effective with less educated employees rather than highly educated individuals.[27]

In addition, several *situational differences* must be taken into account. Variations in reward systems (zero-sum games vs. non-zero sum games), past history of goal successes, technology (independent vs. interdependent), and the nature of the product (quantity vs. quality) all can influence performance under goal-setting conditions. Supervising behavior is an additional factor. We might expect that attempts to allow employees greater participation in goal setting would be facilitated by a considerate leadership style, rather than by a task-oriented one. Under a considerate leadership style, employees feel that their supervisor has a sincere interest in their opinions and inputs.[28] In summary, then, the notion of goal setting is complex. For the successful implementation of goal-setting techniques in organizations, managers must pay attention not only to the attributes of task goals but also to employees' characteristics and various situational characteristics.

UP CLOSE 4.5:   Word Processing Center

Does goal setting really work? If so, which aspects of goal setting have the most influence on employee behavior? To answer this question, Latham and Yukl have carried out a series of studies relating aspects of goal-setting programs to employee performance. One study focused on typists.[29] Forty-one typists from the word processing center of a major corporation were assigned to two groups. In the first group, the supervisor assigned productivity goals, while the second group of typists and their supervisors participatively set the goals. Goals were established each week, and the previous week's performance was used in setting goals for the next week. Performance was measured by an index of the weighted sum of the number of lines typed each week divided by the number of hours worked. The weights were determined based upon the difficulty level of the material typed.

The results came out as predicted. After ten weeks, both groups had significantly higher performance rates than they did before the experiment. Productivity increased 18 percent in the participative group and 15 percent in the assigned group. Therefore, while level of goal difficulty and goal specificity (whether or not goals were set at all) were both found to be important influences on performance, participation in setting goals did not prove to be a major influence. Instead; the basic utility of goal-setting processes in facilitating employee performance was clearly established.   ■

Behavior Modification

The second application of motivation theory to be discussed is **behavior modification.** Behavior modification is the use of operant conditioning principles to shape human behavior to conform to desired standards defined by superiors. Behavior modification has been applied in a wide variety of organizations in recent years. Positive results occur in most cases. For example, at Emery Air Freight, the implementation of some behavior modification purportedly led to a cut in operating costs of $2 million during its first three years of operation. The 3M Company estimated that the technique saved them $3.5 million in one year alone. In the accounting department of Collins Foods International, behavior modification led to a reduction in the error rate in accounts payable from 8 percent to 0.2 percent.[30] These and other examples stimulate interest in the technique as a management tool to improve performance and effectiveness of operations.

Behavior modification as a management technique rests on three ideas. First, advocates of the process believe that individuals are basically passive and reactive (instead of proactive). They respond to stimuli in their environment rather than assuming personal responsibility in initiating behavior. This assertion is in direct contrast to cognitive theories of motivation (such as expectancy theory), which hold that individuals make conscious decisions about their present and future behaviors and take an active role in shaping their environment. In addition, behavior modification focuses on behavior itself—on observable, measurable behaviors instead of nonobservable needs, attitudes, goals, or motivational levels. In contrast, cognitive theories (including goal-setting techniques) focus on both observable and unobservable factors as they relate to motivation. Finally, behavior modification stresses that permanent change can be brought about only as a result of reinforcement. Behaviors that are positively reinforced will be repeated (learned) while behaviors not so reinforced will diminish.

Stages in a Behavior Modification Program Systematic application of a well-thought-out behavior modification program is critical to success. These programs typically go through five phases, as shown in Exhibit 4.8.

1. Management defines and clearly specifies the behavioral aspects of acceptable performance. Management clearly designates what constitutes acceptable behavior in objective, measurable terms. Examples of *behavioral criteria* are good attendance, promptness in arriving for work, and completeing tasks on schedule.
2. Once behavioral criteria have been specified, a *performance audit* is done. Because management is concerned about the extent to which employees are successfully meeting behavioral criteria, the audit is aimed at pinpointing trouble spots where desired behaviors are not being carried out. For instance, a review of departmental records may reveal a particular department in which absenteeism is unusually high. Action can then be taken to focus on this problem area.
3. *Specific behavioral goals* are set for each employee. Failure to specify concrete behavioral goals is a primary reason for the failure of many behavior modification programs. Examples of goals are to decrease absenteeism or meet production schedules. The goals should be both acceptable to employees and reasonably achievable.
4. Employees are asked to *keep a record* of their own work. This record provides them with continuous feedback about the extent to which they are meeting their respective goals.

EXHIBIT 4.8
Stages in Implementing Behavior Modification

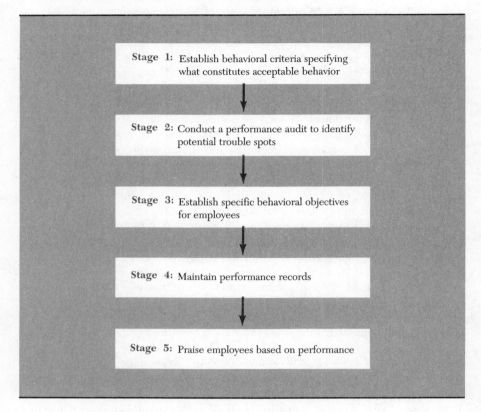

5. Finally, supervisors examine the employees' records, as well as other
   available performance indicators, and *praise* the positive aspects of their
   work performance. This praise is designed to strengthen the performance
   the supervisor wants (positive reinforcement). Withholding praise for less
   than adequate performance or performance below established goals supposedly causes employees to change inappropriate behavior (extinction). It is
   this fifth step in the program that advocates of behavior modification suggest
   differentiates it from many other motivational strategies and techniques.

UP CLOSE 4.6:   Emery Air Freight

*One of the best-known examples of a successful application of behavior
modification in industry is that of Emery Air Freight. Under the direction of
Edward J. Feeney, Emery selected behavior modification as the answer to the
persistent problems of inefficiency and low productivity. In an air freight firm,
rapid processing of parcels is critical to corporate profitability.*[31]

The company began the process with a performance audit, which attempted to identify the kind of job behaviors that had the greatest impact on profit and the extent to which these behaviors were appearing. One area of special concern was the use of containers. Emery loses money if shipping containers are not fully loaded when shipped. One goal was to make sure that empty container space was minimized. Before the program was implemented, workers reported that they believed they were filling the containers about 90 percent of the time. However, the performance audit revealed that the containers were shipping full only about 45 percent of the time. In other words, over half of the containers were shipped unfilled.

By using feedback (in the form of self-report checklists provided to each worker) and positive reinforcement (praise), the percentage of full containers rose swiftly from 45 percent to 95 percent. Cost reductions for the first year alone exceeded $500,000, and reductions rose to $2 million during the first three years. In other words, when workers were given consistent feedback and were kept informed of their performance, their output increased rapidly. As a result of this initial success, similar programs were initiated at Emery, including the setting of performance standards for handling customer problems on the telephone and for accurately estimating the container sizes needed for shipment of lightweight packages. Again, positive results were found.

However, although the use of praise as a reinforcer proved at first to be a successful and inexpensive reinforcer, its effects diminished over time—it became repetitious. As a result, Emery had to seek other reinforcers. These included invitations to business luncheons, formal recognition such as a public letter or a letter home, being given a more enjoyable task after completing a less desirable one, delegating responsibility and decision making, and allowing special time off from the job. The use of verbal praise alone did not appear to have sustained effects, and managers sought fresh reinforcers to keep the program going. ▪

SUMMARY

This chapter has focused on motivational processes in organizations. Motivation is defined as that which energizes, directs, and sustains behavior. As such, motivation is a dynamic variable in organizational behavior. Several early approaches to motivation were reviewed, including scientific management and the human relations model. These approaches largely have been replaced by the human resources approach, which takes into account the multifaceted nature of individuals and their needs in the work place.

Three general theoretical approaches to motivation were discussed. These are content theories, process theories, and reinforcement theories. Content theories focus on those factors that tend to motivate. A primary example is Maslow's need hierarchy model. Process theories attempt to model the dynamics of the motivational process. They attempt to discover how motivation works. In this regard, we reviewed equity theory and expectancy/valence theory. Both models examine how individual goals, needs, and expectations interact with organizational experiences to determine behavior. As such, they are cognitive theories; they examine the thought processes we go through in our work lives.

The third general model reviewed is the reinforcement approach. Reinforcement models are acognitive; that is, they do not deal with cognitions. Instead, emphasis is placed upon shaping desired behavior through the reinforcement process. Positive reinforcement is particularly important.

Finally, two motivational techniques popular in contemporary organizations were reviewed. These are goal-setting and behavior modification. While each has rather different theoretical roots, the implications for management are not significantly different.

KEY WORDS

acognitive theories	fixed interval schedule	punishment
avoidance learning	fixed rate schedule	reinforcement
behavior modification	goal setting	reinforcement theories
cognitive theories	gratification	schedules of
content theories	growth needs	reinforcement
deficiency needs	human relations	scientific management
deprivation	management by	self-actualization
ERG theory	objectives	task-goal specificity
equity theory	motivation	variable interval
expectancy/valence	need hierarchy theory	schedule
theory	performance audit	variable ratio schedule
extinction	process theories	

DISCUSSION QUESTIONS

1. Describe the behavioral requirements of organizations. How can managers help meet these requirements through a knowledge of motivational techniques?
2. How have managerial approaches to motivation evolved over the years? What do you feel are the next logical steps in this evolution?
3. Evaluate the strengths and weaknesses of the need hierarchy model of motivation from a managerial standpoint. Does the ERG theory represent an improvement? Why or why not?
4. With reference to the IBM example on compensation and security needs (**Up Close 4.2**), how would you approach the subject of commissions for sales representatives?
5. What lessons can managers learn from equity theory? What limitations does equity theory have from a managerial standpoint?
6. Why do you feel expectancy/valence theory has received widespread attention? What lessons does the theory suggest for managers?

7. If you were a manager at Kroger's (**Up Close 4.4**), how would you resolve the motivational problem resulting from the two-tiered compensation system while at the same time keeping labor costs competitive?
8. Compare and contrast reinforcement theory and expectancy/valence theory. What are the relative benefits of each from a managerial standpoint? Explain.
9. Do you believe it is easier to motivate managers or workers? Why?
10. Compare and contrast goal setting and behavior modification as two techniques to motivate employees. Which would you choose as a manager? Why?

CASE 4.1:   General Motors Assembly Division

The General Motors Assembly Division is a tough, no-nonsense outfit charged with the responsibility "of being able to meet foreign competition." GMAD" adopted 'get tough' tactics to cope with increased worker absenteeism and boost productivity." According to *Business Week*, the new division was set up in 1965 to tighten and revamp assembly operations. "The need for GMAD's belt-tightening role was underscored during the late 1960s when GM's profit margin dropped from 10 percent to 7 percent."[32]

At Lordstown, efficiency became the watchword. At 60 cars an hour, the pace of work had not been exactly leisurely, but after GMAD came in the number of cars produced almost doubled. Making one car a minute had been no picnic, especially on a constantly moving line. Assembly work fits the worker to the pace of the machine. Each work station is no more than 6 to 8 feet long. For example, within a minute on the line, a worker in the trim department had to walk about 20 feet to a conveyor belt transporting parts to the line, pick up a front seat weighing 30 pounds, carry it back to his work station, place the seat on the chassis, and put in four bolts to fasten it down by first hand-starting the bolts and then using an air gun to tighten them according to standard. It was steady work when the line moved at 60 cars an hour. When it increased to more than 100 cars an hour, the number of operations on this job were not reduced and the pace became almost maddening. In 36 seconds the worker had to perform at least eight different operations, including walking, lifting, hauling, lifting the carpet, bending to fasten the bolts by hand, fastening them by air gun, replacing the carpet, and putting a sticker on the hood. Sometimes the bolts fail to fit into the holes; the gun refuses to function at the required torque; the seats are defective or the threads are bare on the bolt. But the line does not stop. Under these circumstances the workers often find themselves "in the hole," which means that they have fallen behind the line.

"You really have to run like hell to catch up, if you're gonna do the whole job right," one operator named Jerry told me when I interviewed him in the summer of 1972. "They had the wrong-sized bolt on the job for a whole year. A lot of times we just miss a bolt to keep us with the line."

In all plants workers try to make the work a little easier for themselves. At Lordstown, as in other automobile plants, there are many methods for making the work tolerable. Despite the already accelerated pace, workers still attempt to use the traditional relief mechanism of "doubling up." This method consists of two workers deciding that they will learn each other's operation. One worker performs both jobs while the other worker is spelled. At Lordstown, a half-hour "on" and a half-hour "off" is fairly normal pattern. The worker who is on is obliged to do both jobs by superhuman effort. But workers would rather race to keep up with the line than work steadily—in anticipation of a half-hour off to read, lie down, go to the toilet, or roam the plant to talk to a buddy. Not all jobs lend themselves to this arrangement, especially those where a specific part like a front seat must be placed on all models; here the work is time consuming, and full of hassles. But there are many operations where doubling up is feasible, particularly light jobs which have few different movements. Fastening seat belts and putting on windshield wipers are examples.

"The only chance to keep from goin' nuts," said one worker, "is to double up on the job. It's the only way to survive in the plant. . . ."

The company claims that doubling up reduces quality. The method engenders a tendency for workers to miss operations, especially when they fall behind, according to one general foreman. Some workers believe that the company blames workers for doubling up as an excuse to explain its own quality control failures. There is a widespread feeling among the line workers that the doubling-up "issue" has more to do with the company's program of harrassment than with the problem of quality control.

The tenure of the previous management at the Chevrolet division of GM was characterized by a plethora of shop floor agreements between foremen and line workers on work rules. These agreements were not written down, but were passed from worker to worker as part of the lore of the job. As in many workplaces, a new line supervisor meant that these deals had to be "renegotiated."

When GMAD took over at Lordstown, management imposed new, universally applicable rules which, in fact, were applied selectively. On Mondays, "when there are not many people on the line," the company tolerates lateness. On Tuesdays, when young workers come back from their long weekends, "they throw you out the door" for the rest of the shift for coming in fifteen minutes or a half-hour late. "When the company gets a bug up its ass to improve quality, they come down on you for every little mistake. But then things start goin' good on the cars, so they start to work on other areas. Then you are not allowed to lay down—not allowed to read on the job; no talkin' (you can't talk anyway the noise is so terrific); no doubling up."

Efficiency meant imposing on workers the absolute power of management to control production. GMAD instituted a policy of compulsory overtime at the time of the model changeover. The "normal" shift became ten hours a day and there were no exceptions to the rule. Absenteeism and lateness became the objects of veritable holy crusades for the new management. Nurses refused to grant permission for workers to go home sick. The company began to consider a worker a voluntary quit if he stayed off for three days and failed to bring a doctor's note certifying his illness. Doctors were actually sent to workers' homes to check up on "phony" illnesses in an effort to curb absenteeism.

The average hourly rate for production line workers was $4.56 an hour in mid-1972. In addition, annual cost of living increases geared to the consumer price index had been incorporated into the contract. Gross base weekly earnings for ten hours a day were more than $195. With overtime, some workers had made more than $13,000 a year. Besides, GM workers have among the best pension, health insurance, and unemployment benefits programs in American industry. Certainly, there is no job in the Warren area whose terms compare with high wages and benefits enjoyed by the GM workers. Equally significant, GM is among the few places in the area still hiring a large number of employees. The steel mills, electrical plants, and retail trades offer lower wages to unskilled workers and less steady employment to low-seniority people. For some, General Motors is "big mother." Many workers echo the sentiment of Joe, a forty-five-year-old assembly line worker who said that GM offered better wages and working conditions than he had ever enjoyed in his life—"I don't know how anybody who works for a living can do better than GM." Compared to the steel mill where he did heavy dirty jobs, GM was "not near as hard."

Of course Joe has had differences with company policies. The job was "too confining." He didn't like to do the same thing every day. He objected to the company harassment of the men and had actually voted for a strike to correct some of the injustices in the plant. But, like many others, Joe had "married the job" because he didn't know where else he could get a retirement plan which would give him substantial benefits after thirty years of service, full hospital benefits, and real job security.

GMAD likes workers like Joe too. They know Joe isn't going anywhere. They believe him when he says he is sick, and, if he misses installing parts on a car he can "chalk it up." In such cases, he simply tells the foreman about the missing operation and the "repairmen will take care of it."

Yet high wages and substantial fringe benefits have not been sufficient to allay discontent among the young people working on the line. If other area employers paid wages competitive with GM wages, GM would have serious difficulty attracting a labor force. The wages are a tremendous initial attraction for workers and explain why many are reluctant to leave the shop. But even the substantial unemployment in the Warren and Youngstown areas has not succeeded in tempering the spirit of rebellion among young workers or preventing the persistence of turnover among them. The promise of high earnings has not reduced the absentee rate in the plant. One young worker, married with a child, earned a gross income of $10,900 in 1971, a year when overtime was offered regularly to employees. This was a gross pay at least $2,000 below his possible earnings. He had taken at least one day off a week and refused several offers of Saturday work.

GM acknowledges that absenteeism, particularly on Mondays and Fridays, constitutes its most distressing discipline problem. Workers report line shutdown "for as much as a half hour" on Mondays because there are simply not enough people to perform the operations. But many young people are prepared to sacrifice higher earnings for a respite from the hassles of assembly line work, even for one day.

At Lordstown and other plants where youth constitute either a majority or significant minority of the work force there is concrete evidence that the inducements to hard work have weakened. Older workers in the plant as well as a minority of the youth admit that they have never seen this kind of money in their lives. But the young people are seeking something more from their labor than high wages, pensions, and job security. At Lordstown, they are looking for "a chance to use my brain" and a job "where my high school education counts for something." Even though workers resent the demanding pace of the line, no line job takes more than a half-hour to learn. Most workers achieve sufficient speed in their operation to keep up with the line in about a half a shift. The minute rationalization of assembly line operations to a few simple movements has been perfected by GMAD. One operator whose job was to put two clips on a hose all day long said, "I never think about my job. In fact, I try to do everything I can to forget it. If I concentrated on thinking about it, I'd go crazy. The trouble is I have to look at what I'm doing or else I'd mess up every time." This worker spent some of his time figuring out ways to get off the line, especially ways to take days off. "I always try to get doctor's slips to take three days if I can." Another worker reported provoking a foreman to give him a disciplinary layoff (DLO) just to avoid the monotony of his tasks.

The drama of Lordstown is the conflict between the old goals of decent income and job security, which have lost their force but are by no means dead, and the new needs voiced by young people for more than mindless labor. The company and the union represent the promise that the old needs can be met on a scale never before imagined for many of the people on the line. The youth are saying that these benefits are not enough.

The picture is complicated by the fact that not all young people share the same attitudes. Even though the overwhelming majority of workers in the shop are between twenty and thirty years old, they are not all cut from the same cloth. The most disaffected group in the plant are the youth who were raised in the Warren-Youngstown area. Their fathers and mothers were industrial workers, or at least had been part of an urban environment for most of their lives. Since the area has had a long industrial tradition (it lies in the heart of the Ohio valley), high wages and traditional union protections and benefits are part of the taken-for-granted world of a generation brought up in the shadows of the steel mills and rubber factories. These workers share the same upbringing, went to the same schools, frequented the same neighborhood social centers, and speak the same symbolic languages. When they came to General Motors, they brought with them a set of unspoken expectations about their work and their future. Many were high school graduates; a smaller, but significant number were attending college. Although it cannot be denied that the "good money" paid by GM was an important inducement for these young people to choose to work there, few of them considered steady work and good wages sufficient to satisfy a life's ambition.

CASE QUESTIONS

1. This case elaborates the problems GM has in employee motivation. Explain which behavioral requirements of organization are being well attended by GM and which are not.
2. Use need theory and expectancy theory to explain the motivation problems at GM.

NOTES

1. "Behind the UPS Mystique: Puritanism and Productivity," *Business Week,* June 6, 1983, pp. 66–70.
2. Marvin Dunnette and W. Kirchner, *Psychology Applied to Industry* (New York: Appleton-Century-Crofts, 1965).
3. Raymond Miles, Lyman Porter, and J. A. Croft "Leadership Attitudes Among Public Health Officials," *American Journal of Public Health,* 56 (1966), pp. 1990–2005.
4. Victor Vroom and Phillip Yelton, *Leadership and Decision Making* (Pittsburgh: University of Pittsburgh Press, 1973).
5. R. T. Pascale and A. G. Athos, *The Art of Japanese Management* (New York: Simon and Schuster, 1981), pp. 156–167.
6. Abraham Maslow, *Toward a Pshychology of Being* (New York: Van Nostrand, 1968); and Abraham Maslow, *Motivation and Personality* (New York: Harper, 1954).
7. Clayton Alderfer, "A New Theory of Human Needs," *Organizational Behavior and Human Performance,* 4 (1969), pp. 142–175.
8. J. A. Byrne, "Motivating Willy Loman," *Forbes,* January 30, 1984, p.91.
9. Stacy Adams, "Injustice in Social Exchange," in L. Berkowitz (ed.) *Advances in Experimental Social Psychology,* 2 (New York: Academic Press, 1965); and Karl E. Weick, "The Concept of Equity in the Perception of Pay," *Administrative Science Quarterly,* 11 (1966), pp. 414–439.

10. Richard T. Mowday, "Equity Theory Predictions of Behavior in Organizations," in R. M. Steers and L. W. Porter (eds.) *Motivation and Work Behavior*, Third Edition (New York: McGraw-Hill, 1983), pp. 91–112.

11. Stacy Adams, "Injustice in Social Exchange."

12. "Why Equitable Life Looks Good but Feels Bad," *Business Week*, March 26, 1979, pp. 80–81.

13. B. S. Gorgopoulos, G. M. Mahoney, and N. Jones, "A Path-Goal Approach to Productivity," *Journal of Applied Psychology*, 41 (1957), pp. 345–353.

14. Lyman W. Porter and Edward E. Lawler III, *Managerial Attitudes and Performance* (Homewood, IL: Irwin, 1968).

15. Edwin Ghiselle, *Explorations in Managerial Talent* (Santa Monica, CA: Goodyear, 1966).

16. Lyman W. Porter and Edward E. Lawler III. *Managerial Attitudes and Performance.*

17. John Campbell and Robert Pritchard, "Motivation Theory in Industrial and Organizational Psychology," in M. D. Dunnette (ed.) *Handbook of Industrial and Organizational Psychology* (Chicago: Rand McNally, 1976), pp. 63–130.

18. "The Double Standard That's Setting Worker Against Worker," *Business Week*, April 8, 1985, pp. 70–71.

19. H. Rachlin, *Modern Behaviorism* (San Francisco: W. H. Freeman, 1970).

20. B. F. Skinner, *Science and Human Behavior* (New York: Macmillan, 1953), p. 73.

21. T. Costello and S. Zalkind, *Psychology in Administration: A Research Orientation* (Englewood Cliffs, NJ: Prentice-Hall, 1963).

22. Richard M. Steers and Lyman W. Porter, "The Role of Task-Goal Attributes in Employee Performance," *Psychological Bulletin*, 81 (1974), pp. 434–451.

23. Richard M. Steers and Lyman W. Porter, "The Role of Task-Goal Attitudes."

24. Edwin A. Locke, "The Motivational Effects of Knowledge of Results: Knowledge or Goal-Setting?" *Journal of Applied Psychology*, 51 (1967), pp. 324–329.

25. L.C. Lawrence and P.C. Smith, "Group Decision and Employee Participation," *Journal of Applied Psychology*, 39 (1955), pp. 334–337.

26. Richard M. Steers, "Task-Goal Attributes, *n* Achievement, and Supervisory Performance," *Organizational Behavior and Human Performance*, 13 (1975), pp. 392–403.

27. Gary P. Latham and Gary Yuhl, "A Review of Research on the Application of Goal-Setting in Organizations," *Academy of Management Journal*, 18 (1975), pp. 824–845.

28. Richard M. Steers and Lyman W. Porter, "The Role of Task-Goal Attributes."

29. Gary P. Latham and Gary Yuhl, "Effects of Assigned and Participative Goal-Setting on Performance and Job Satisfaction," *Journal of Applied Psychology*, 61 (1976), pp. 166–171.

30. "Productivity Gains from a Pat on the Back," *Business Week*, January 23, 1978, pp. 56–62.

31. W. C. Hamner and E.P. Hamner, "Behavior Modification on the Bottom Line," *Organizational Dynamics*, 4 (1976), pp. 8–21.

32. Stanley Aronowitz, *False Promises* (New York: McGraw-Hill, 1973). Used with permission.

5 Performance Appraisal and Rewards

I n 1981, International Telephone and Telegraph (ITT) had an average return on stockholders' equity of 11 percent, an annual growth rate in earnings per share of 3.5 percent, and a change in the price of its common stock of −12 percent. During the same time, the comparable figures for the Raytheon Corporation were 20.7 percent, 24.1 percent, and +147 percent. Even so, ITT's president was paid $1,150,000 (including a $133,000 pay raise), and Raytheon's chief executive officer received $635,000.

Texaco's CEO earned approximately $1 million in 1981 (including bonuses), the third highest income in the industry, although "among large oil companies Texaco's performance has in the last decade been lousy."[1]

During the recent acquisition battle between Bendix, Martin Marietta, and United Technologies, the Bendix Board of Directors voted themselves and their president major severance pay packages (amounting to $4 million for the president alone) in case their company lost the acquisition battle.

What do these examples have in common? Each represents a real-life example of top corporate executives being rewarded based on criteria that are not related to corporate performance and accountability. In the first example, CEO income appears to be more a function of the size of the organization than of actual performance. The second example suggests that CEO income is inversely related to corporate performance. The third case is an example of the establishment of a major protective cushion (i.e., reward) to be paid in the event of failure, not success. In all three cases, the existence of a clearly specified performance appraisal system and clear pay-performance contingencies would probably have led to better corporate results and a more equitable reward system.[2]

One of the more pressing problems managers face is how to evaluate and reward the performance of their employees. When employee efforts fall short of acceptable standards, managers have a responsibility to devise mechanisms to improve performance. But how does a manager assess the quality of a subordinate's work? In most work organizations, evaluation is done through a formal performance appraisal system. In a study by Locher and Teel, ninety percent of the organizations contacted had some form of performance appraisal system.[3]

Since performance appraisals and subsequent reward systems are proven important for employee development and organizational strength, we will *examine various aspects of each. First, the focus will be on general characteristics of appraisal systems, including their associated problems. Specific appraisal techniques will be detailed. The purpose of reward systems in organizations will be considered next, followed by a discussion of various incentive plans. To conclude, several new developments in reward systems will be presented as they relate to contemporary work organizations. We will be able to note a close relationship throughout this chapter between appraisal and reward systems and employee motivation, which we discussed in the previous chapter.*

RELEVANCE OF PERFORMANCE APPRAISAL AND REWARDS FOR MANAGERS

Why is an understanding of both performance appraisal systems and corporate reward practices important for managers? Several reasons can be identified. Performance evaluations provide one means of systematically evaluating employees across various performance dimensions to insure that organizations are getting what they pay for. In addition, performance appraisals can provide valuable feedback to employees and managers. They may help identify promotable people as well as people with room for improvement. Reward systems can represent a powerful motivational force in organizations, as long as the systems are fair and tied to performance. An understanding of reward systems helps managers select the system best suited to the needs and goals of the organization.

FUNCTIONS OF PERFORMANCE APPRAISAL SYSTEMS

The specific reasons why organizations use performance appraisals range from improving employee output to developing the employees themselves. A recent survey designed to determine the uses for appraisals in 216 organizations documented a diversity in usage.[4] As shown in Exhibit 5.1, compensation and performance improvement were most prominent.

In view of this information, it is possible to identify some major functions of performance appraisal systems. To begin with, performance appraisals provide feedback to employees about quantity and quality of job performance. Performance appraisals can also be *self-development indicators*. One way individuals learn about their strengths and weaknesses on the job is through other people. In addition, appraisals may form the basis of *organizational reward systems*, particularly merit-based compensation plans. Performance appraisals serve personnel-related functions as well. Performance appraisals are useful in making *personnel decisions*, such as those relating to promotions, transfers, and terminations. In addition, appraisal systems help the organization evaluate the

EXHIBIT 5.1
Primary Uses of Performance Appraisals

Use	Percent
Compensation	71.3
Performance improvement	55.2
Feedback	29.3
Promotion	25.1
Documentation	10.7
Training	8.7
Transfer	7.9
Manpower planning	6.2
Discharge	2.3
Research	1.4
Layoff	0.3

effectiveness of its *selection and placement decisions.* If newly hired employees seem to be consistently performing well after a six-month period, for example, personnel managers can be assured that they are achieving a good fit between people and job requirements. Alternatively, poor performance may be due to inadequate employee *training and development.* Appraisal systems highlight areas for which training programs may be developed or improved to the benefit of employee performance.

Since performance appraisals serve a variety of important functions in organizations, the selection of methods of evaluation that maximize the accuracy and fairness of the appraisal are critical. Many fair and accurate methods of performance appraisal exist. The job for the manager is to select the technique or combination of techniques that best serves the particular needs and constraints of the organization.

METHODS OF PERFORMANCE APPRAISAL

While countless variations on the most popular performance evaluation techniques can be found, the basic methods themselves provide a good summary of how the performance process is commonly used in organizations. The six main techniques are: 1) graphic rating scales; 2) critical incident technique; 3) behaviorally anchored rating scales; 4) behavioral observation scale; 5) management by objectives; and 6) assessment centers.

Graphic Rating Scales

The most popular method of evaluation used in organizations today is the **graphic rating scale.** Locher and Teel found that 57 percent of the organizations they surveyed used rating scales.[5] This method appears in many formats, but in a typical one the rater is presented with a printed form that contains both the employee's name and several evaluation dimensions (quantity of work, quality of work, knowledge of job). The supervisor is asked to evaluate the employee by assigning a number, or rating, on each of the dimensions. Exhibit 5.2 in an example of the graphic rating scale for a real company.

Assuming that evaluator biases can be minimized, it is possible to compare employees in terms of who received the best and poorest ratings. It is also possible to examine the relative strengths and weaknesses of a single employee by comparing scores on the various dimensions. One of the most serious drawbacks of this technique, however, is its openness to rating errors. It is possible to rate most everyone in the middle of the scale or, conversely, at one end of the scale. In order to control this, some companies have assigned required percentage distributions to the various scale points. Supervisors may be allowed to rate only 10 percent of their people outstanding and must rate 10 percent unsatisfactory, perhaps assigning 20 percent, 40 percent, and 20 percent to the remaining middle categories. By doing this, a distribution is forced within each department. The limitations of this technique are obvious; a large group of outstanding performers may be penalized or a large group of poor performers may be rewarded.

Critical Incidents

In the **critical incident** approach to performance evaluation, managers record incidents in each subordinate's behavior that lead to either a notable success or a notable failure on some aspect of the job. Managers keep either a daily or weekly log of these incidents under predesignated categories (planning, decision making, interpersonal relations, report writing). A final evaluation consists of a series of descriptive paragraphs highlighting various aspects of an employee's performance on the job.

This method is useful in appraisal interviews because it provides points, or specific incidents, around which managers and subordinates can discuss performance. Good qualitative data are generated. However, since no quantitative data emerge, it can be difficult to use this technique for promotion or salary decisions. The overbalance of qualitative output here has led some companies to combine the critical incident technique with one of the quantitative techniques, such as rating scales.

An example of a critical evaluation form is shown in Exhibit 5.3. This form is used by the same company that uses the graphic rating scale shown in Exhibit 5.2.

Behaviorally Anchored Rating Scales

The **behaviorally anchored rating scale,** or BARS, is another popular system. It requires considerable work prior to evaluation but, if the work is carefully done, can lead to highly accurate ratings with high inter-rater reliability. Specifically, the BARS technique begins by selecting a job that can be described in observable behaviors. Managers and personnel specialists then identify these behaviors as they relate to superior or inferior performance.

An example of a BARS scale is shown in Exhibit 5.4, where the BARS technique is applied to the job of custodian. As shown, as one moves from high performance to low performance, the performance descriptions, or behavioral

EXHIBIT 5.2

Example of Graphic Rating Scale for Company X

Name:_____   Date:_____

Classification:_____   Department:_____

1 - Outstanding   2 - Excellent   3 - Good   4 - Adequate   5 - Inadequate

Factor	Overall Performance On		Evaluation			

1. **Job Technology** ☐

   A. Safety Effectiveness

       Attitude 1 2 3 4 5

       Performance 1 2 3 4 5

       Influence on others 1 2 3 4 5

       *Development of program for others 1 2 3 4 5

   B. Job Knowledge—Technical and/or Specialized ....

       1 2 3 4 5

2. **Human Relations** ☐

   A. Ability to Communicate 1 2 3 4 5

   B. Results Achieved Through Others 1 2 3 4 5

3. **Conceptualizing** ☐

   A. Originality 1 2 3 4 5

   B. Ability to Use New Methods-Ideas-Technology ... 1 2 3 4 5

4. **Self-Motivation** ☐

   A. Acceptance and Use of Responsibility 1 2 3 4 5

   B. Initiative 1 2 3 4 5

5. ***Supv./Mgr. Duties** ☐

   A. Supervision and Development of People 1 2 3 4 5

   B. Ability to Plan - Organize Work 1 2 3 4 5

   C. Decision-Making and Judgment 1 2 3 4 5

6. **Over-All Evaluation** 1 2 3 4 5

(*Evaluate only those with supervisory responsibilities)

Comments: _____

_____

_____

_____

_____

Prepared by: _____

EXHIBIT 5.3

Example of Critical Incident Evaluation for Company X

The following performance areas are designed to assist you in preparing this appraisal and in discussing an individual's performance with him. It is suggested that areas of performance that you feel are significantly good or poor be documented below with specific examples or actions. The points listed are suggested as typical and are by no means all-inclusive. Examples related to these points may be viewed from either a positive or negative standpoint.

1. Performance on Technology of the Job

    A. Safety Effectiveness — possible considerations:
        1. Sets an excellent safety example for others in the department by words and action.
        2. Trains his people well in safety areas.
        3. Gains the cooperation and participation of his people in safety.
        4. Insists that safety be designed into procedure and processes.
        5. Is instrumental in initiating departmental safety program.
        6. Accepts safety as a fundamental job responsibility.

Item   Related Examples

    B. Job Knowledge — Technical and/or Specialized — possible considerations:
        1. Shows exceptional knowledge in methods, materials, and techniques; and applies in a resourceful and practical manner.
        2. Stays abreast of development in field and applies to job.
        3. "Keeps up" on latest material in his special field.
        4. Participates in professional or technical organizations pertinent to his activities.

Item   Related Examples

2. Performance on Human Relations

    A. Ability to Communicate — possible considerations:
        1. Gives logical, clear-cut, understandable instructions on complex problems.
        2. Uses clear and direct language in written and oral reporting.
        3. Organizes presentations in logical order and in order of importance.
        4. Provides supervisor and subordinates with pertinent and adequate information.
        5. Tailors communications approach to group or individual.
        6. Keeps informed on how subordinates think and feel about things.

Item   Related Examples

    B. Results Achieved Through Others — possible considerations:
        1. Develops enthusiasm in others that gets the job done.
        2. Has respect and confidence of others.
        3. Recognizes and credits skills of others.
        4. Coordinates well with other involved groups to get the job done.

Item   Related Examples

3. Performance on Conceptualizing

    A. Originality — possible considerations:
        1. Originates new approaches to problems.
        2. Improvises effectively in developing unique solutions to unforeseen changes and problems.
        3. Has ability to think abstractly or theoretically and relate to the concrete.
        4. Has ability to innovate for needed improvement.

Item   Related Examples

    B. Ability to Use New Methods — Ideas — Technology — possible considerations:
        1. Searches out best sources of information, I.E., associates, specialists, and literature.
        2. Relates to and adapts newest technology available.
        3. Creates a climate conducive to innovation and improvements.

Item   Related Examples

EXHIBIT 5.4

Example of a Behaviorally Anchored Rating Scale for a Custodian's Job

---

Directions: Put an X over the circled number that indicates the person's performance concerning PEOPLE.

PEOPLE

Ability to get along with other people, such as co-workers, professors, secretaries, and students.

HIGH PERFORMANCE	⑦	BEHAVIORAL EXAMPLES:
Gets along very well with other people, such as co-workers, professors, secretaries, and students.	⑥	Works and communicates well with building deputy.
		Knows professors, secretaries, and graduate students by name.

AVERAGE PERFORMANCE	⑤	Asks co-workers if they need help.
Is courteous to others and helps co-workers only after finishing his or her own work.	④	If a trash can must be emptied while people are talking in office, custodian enters quietly and does not interrupt conversation.
	③	Knocks before entering office.

LOW PERFORMANCE	②	Tries to avoid contact with others.
Avoids or is unpleasant to others.		Uses foul language around others.
	①	Refuses to help others.

SOURCE: D. Ilgen and J. Barnes-Farrell, *Performance Planning and Evaluation* (Chicago: SRA, 1984), p. 14.

---

anchors, change. Often six to ten scales are used to describe performance on the job. Exhibit 5.4 evaluates the custodian's ability to get along with people. Other scales could relate to cleanliness, promptness, or attendance. Once these scales are determined, managers have only to check the category that describes what they observe on the job, and the employee's rating is established.

The BARS approach exhibits several advantages over other techniques. Many of the sources of error (central tendency, leniency, halo—which are discussed ahead on pages 135–136) should be significantly reduced with BARS, since raters consider verbal descriptions of specific behaviors instead of general categories of behaviors like those used in graphic rating scales. The technique focuses on job-related behavior and does not consider less relevant issues like an employee's personality. Also, the performance appraisal interview places emphasis on actual behaviors, not on the person; hence, employees may be less defensive in the review process. Finally, BARS can aid in employee training and development by identifying those performance domains needing most attention.

On the negative side, however, considerable time and effort in designing the forms is required before the rating. Because a separate BARS is required for each job, it is only cost efficient on common jobs. Finally, since the technique relies on observable behavior, it has little application to many jobs where much of the work is intellectual and behavior is not readily observable, such as the job of a research scientist.

Behavioral Observation Scales

The **behavioral observation scale** (BOS) is similar to BARS in that both focus on identifying observable behaviors as they relate to performance. A major difference in BOS, however, is the task facing the evaluator. Typically, the evaluator is asked to rate each behavior on a scale from 1 to 5 to indicate the frequency with which employees exhibit that behavior. Evaluation of an employee's performance on a particular dimension is derived by summing the frequency ratings for the behaviors in each dimension.

An example of this technique is shown in Exhibit 5.5, which is a form designed to evaluate a manager's ability to overcome resistance to change. The rater has simply to circle the appropriate numbers describing observed behaviors and get the summary rating by adding the results.

This technique is easier to construct than the BARS technique and makes the evaluator's job somewhat simpler. Even so, this is a relatively new technique that is only now receiving some support in industry.

EXHIBIT 5.5
An Example of a Behavioral Observation Scale

Overcoming resistance to change

1. Describes the details of the change to subordinates.
   Almost never   1   2   3   4   5   Almost always

2. Explains why the change is necessary.
   Almost never   1   2   3   4   5   Almost always

3. Discusses how the change will affect the employee.
   Almost never   1   2   3   4   5   Almost always

4. Listens to the employee's concerns.
   Almost never   1   2   3   4   5   Almost always

5. Asks the employee for help in making the change work.
   Almost never   1   2   3   4   5   Almost always

6. If necessary, specifies the date for a follow-up meeting to respond to the employee's concerns.
   Almost never   1   2   3   4   5   Almost always

Total = _____

Below adequate	Adequate	Full	Excellent	Superior
6–10	11–15	16–20	21–25	26–30

SOURCE: G. Latham and K. Wexley, *Increasing Productivity Through Performance Appraisal* (Reading, Mass.: Addison-Wesley, 1981).

Management by Objectives

We explained MBO in Chapter 4 in terms of its broader context in the goal-setting theory of motivation. Management by objectives incorporates an organization-wide motivation, performance, and control system, but here we will focus on its narrower role in the evaluation process.

Under MBO, employees or groups work with their supervisor to establish goals and objectives for the coming year. These goals are stated in clear language and relate to tasks that are within the domain of the employee. An example of these goals for a salesperson is shown in Exhibit 5.6. Following a specific period of time (usually one year) employee's performances are compared to their goals to determine the extent to which the goals have been met.

A number of advantages of MBO can be identified. Most notably, "the assumed benefits include better planning, improved motivation because of knowledge of results, improving commitment through participation, and improving supervisory skills in such areas as listening, counseling, and evaluating."[6]

However, on the negative side, MBO has been criticized because it emphasizes quantitative goals at the expense of qualitative goals and often creates too much paperwork. It is difficult to compare performance levels among employees, since most employees are responsible for different goals. Finally, in order to succeed, MBO must have constant attention and support from management; it does not run itself. In the absence of this support, the technique loses legitimacy and often becomes discredited.

Assessment Centers

A relatively new method of evaluation that is gaining in popularity is the **assessment center.** Assessment centers are unique among appraisal techniques

EXHIBIT 5.6

An Example of an MBO Evaluation Report for a Salesperson

	Objectives Set	Period Objective	Accomplishments	Variance
1.	Number of sales calls	100	104	104%
2.	Number of new customers contacted	20	18	90
3.	Number of wholesalers stocking new product 117	30	30	100
4.	Sales of product 12	10,000	9750	92.5
5.	Sales of product 17	17,000	18,700	110
6.	Customer complaints/service call	35	11	66.6
7.	Number of sales correspondence courses successfully completed	4	2	50
8.	Number of sales reports in home office within 1 day of end of month	12	10	80

SOURCE: William Glueck, *Personnel: A Diagnostic Approach*, rev. ed. (Dallas: BPI, 1978); p. 307.

EXHIBIT 5.7
Example of Assessment Center

DAY 1

Orientation Meeting

Management Game—"Conglomerate." Forming different types of conglomerates is the goal with four-man teams of participants bartering companies to achieve their planned result. Teams set their own acquisition objectives and must plan and organize to meet them.

Background Interview—A 1½ hour interview conducted by an assessor.

Group Discussion—"Management Problems." Four short cases calling for various forms of management judgment are presented to groups of four participants. In one hour the group, acting as consultants, must resolve the cases and submit its recommendation in writing.

Individual Fact-Finding and Decision-Making Exercise—"The Research Budget." The participant is told that he has just taken over a division manager. He is given a brief description of an incident in which his predecessor has recently turned down a request for funds to continue a research project. The research director is appealing for a reversal of the decision. The participant is given 15 minutes to ask questions to dig out the facts in the case. Following this fact-finding period, he must present his decision orally with supporting reasoning and defend it under challenge.

DAY 2

In-Basket Exercise—"Section Manager's In-Basket." The contents of a section manager's in-basket are simulated. The participant is instructed to go through the contents, solving problems, answering questions, delegating, organizing, scheduling and planning, just as he might do if he were promoted suddenly to the position. An assessor reviews the contents of the completed in-basket and conducts a one-hour interview with the participant to gain further information.

Assigned Role Leaderless Group Discussion—"Compensation Committee." The Compensation Committee is meeting to allocate $8,000 in discretionary salary increases among six supervisory and managerial employees. Each member of the committee (participants) represents a department of the company and is instructed to "do the best he can" for the employee from his department.

Analysis, Presentation and Group Discussion: "The Pretzel Factory." This financial analysis problem has the participant role-play a consultant called in to advise Carl Flowers of the C. F. Pretzel Company on two problems: what to do about a division of the company that has continually lost money, and whether the corporation should expand. Participants are given data on the company and are asked to recommend appropriate courses of action. They make their recommendation in a seven-minute presentation after which they are formed into a group to come up with a single set of recommendations.

Final Announcements

DAYS 3 and 4

Assessors meet to share their observations on each participant and to arrive at summary evaluations relative to each dimension sought and overall potential and training needs.

SOURCE: William C. Byham, "The Assessment Center as an Aid in Management Development," *Training and Development Journal*, December 1971, pp. 10–19.

---

because they focus more on evaluating an employee's long-range potential to an organization instead of his or her performance over the past year. They are also unique in that they are used almost exclusively among managerial personnel.

A typical assessment center consists of a series of standardized evaluations of behavior based on multiple inputs.[7] Over a two- or three-day period (usually away from the job) trained observers make judgments on managers' behavior as a result of specially developed exercises. These exercises may consist of in-basket exercises, role playing, and case analyses, as well as personal interviews and psychological tests. An example of an assessment center program is shown in Exhibit 5.7.

Results from assessment center programs appear promising, and the technique is showing potential for identifying future managerial talent. Even so, some problems with the technique have been cropping up.[8] In particular, due to the highly stressful environment created in assessment centers, many otherwise good managers simply may not be performing up to their potential. And the results of a poor evaluation in an assessment center may be far-reaching; individuals may receive a "loser" image that will follow them for a long time. Finally, there is some question concerning exactly how valid and realiable assessment centers really are in predicting future managerial success, or whether predicting success itself might not be too tricky a project. While some initial successes have been noted, more research is needed to evaluate the true potential for the technique.

Comparison of Appraisal Techniques

From an administrative viewpoint, questions often come up about which appraisal technique or set of techniques is best for a given situation. Although there is no simple answer to this question, we can consider the various strengths and weaknesses of each technique. Exhibit 5.8 makes this comparison.

As we might expect, the easiest and least expensive techniques are also the least accurate. They are also the least useful for purposes of personnel decisions and employee development. Once again, it appears that managers and organizations get what they pay for. If performance appraisals represent an important aspect of organizational life, clearly the more sophisticated—and the more time-consuming—techniques offer more useful information. If, on the other hand, it is necessary to evaluate employees quickly and with few resources at hand, techniques like the graphic rating scale may be more appropriate. Managers must make cost-benefit decisions about the price (in time and money) they can pay for a performance appraisal program.

PROBLEMS WITH PERFORMANCE APPRAISAL SYSTEMS

A variety of problems can pose a threat to the utility of performance appraisal systems. Many of these problems deal with the related issues of validity and reliability. **Validity** is the extent to which an instrument actually measures what it intends to measure; **reliability** is the extent to which the instrument consistently yields the same results each time it is used. Ideally, a good performance appraisal system exhibits high levels of both validity and reliability. If a system is not valid and reliable, its utility and even its legality are questionable.

We can identify at least five rather common sources of error, or problems, found in performance appraisal systems that jeopardize validity and reliability. These include: 1) central tendency error; 2) strictness or leniency error; 3) halo effect; 4) recency error; and 5) personal biases.

Central Tendency Error

Oftentimes, supervisors rate most of their employees within a narrow range.[9] Regardless of how people actually perform, the rater fails to distinguish significantly between group members, lumping everyone together in an average or above average category. This is called central tendency error and is shown in Exhibit 5.8. In short, **central tendency error** is the failure to recognize both very good and very poor performances among a work group.

EXHIBIT 5.8
Major Strengths and Weaknesses of Appraisal Techniques

	Ratings	Critical Incidents	BARS	BOS	MBO	Assessment Centers
Meaningful dimensions	Sometimes	Sometimes	Usually	Usually	Usually	Usually
Amount of time required	Low	Medium	High	Medium	High	High
Developmental costs	Low	Low	High	Medium	Medium	High
Potential for rating errors	High	Medium	Low	Low	Low	Low
Acceptability to subordinates	Low	Medium	High	High	High	High
Acceptability to superiors	Low	Medium	High	High	High	High
Usefulness for allocating rewards	Poor	Fair	Good	Good	Good	Fair
Usefulness for employee counseling	Poor	Fair	Good	Good	Good	Good
Usefulness for identifying promotion potential	Poor	Fair	Fair	Fair	Fair	Good

Strictness or Leniency Error

A related problem in evaluations occurs when a supervisor is overly strict or overly lenient in evaluations, as shown in Exhibit 5.9. In college classrooms, we hear of professors who are "tough graders" or "easy A's." Similar situations exist in the work place, where some supervisors see most subordinates as not measuring up to their high standards, while others see most subordinates as deserving of a high rating. Similar to central tendency error, **strictness and leniency error** fails to adequately distinguish between good and bad performers, instead relegating almost everyone to the same or related categories on the rating scale.

Halo Effect

The error of **halo effect** occurs when a rater assigns the same rating to each factor being evaluated for an individual. An employee rated "above average" on quantity of performance may also be rated "above average" on quality of performance, interpersonal competence, attendance, or readiness for promotion. The rater fails to separate strong points from weak, apparently not differentiating across presumably distinct categories of behavior on the job.

An example of the halo effect in operation can be seen in a description of performance appraisal systems in General Motors.[10] A former GM executive claims that so much emphasis was placed on cost cutting in the company that other important areas of managerial accountability went almost unnoticed in evaluations. GM's Tarrytown, New York, assembly division once had the dubious distinction of producing the poorest quality cars of all General Motors' twenty-two U.S. plants. During this time, some cars were so poorly built that dealers refused to accept them. Even so, the plant had the lowest manufacturing costs in the company. As a result, the plant manager at Tarrytown received one of the largest bonuses of all the assembly divisions—while building the worst cars! Clearly, the manager's evaluation concerning costs overshadowed considerations of product quality or customer satisfaction. (Note: Tarrytown no longer has this reputation. Recent work redesign efforts have dramatically improved product quality.)

Recency Error

Evaluators often focus on an employee's most recent behavior in the evaluation process. That is, in an annual evaluation, a supervisor may give undue emphasis to performance during the past two or three months and ignore performance levels prior to this. This practice, if known to employees, can lead to uneven performance—a situation where employees float for the initial months of the evaluation period and then overexert themselves in the last few months prior to evaluation. On the other hand, a recency error can be unfair to employees who may be having an ill-timed temporary slump.

EXHIBIT 5.9
Examples of Rating Errors

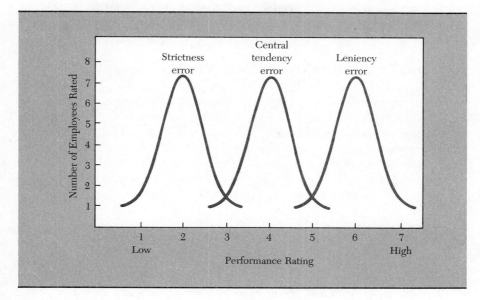

Personal Biases

Finally, several studies have confirmed that supervisors may allow their own personal biases to influence their appraisals.[11] Biases include simply like or dislike for someone, as well as racial, ethnic, sexual, and age-related prejudices. Personal biases can interfere with the fairness and accuracy of an evaluation, thereby leading to inequity. And from inequity sometimes comes litigation.

REDUCING ERRORS IN PERFORMANCE APPRAISAL SYSTEMS

A number of ideas to minimize the effects of biases and errors in performance appraisal have been advanced.[12] When errors are reduced, more accurate information is available for personnel decisions and employee development. Methods for reducing error include the following.

First, each dimension or factor on a performance appraisal should represent a single job activity instead of a group of job activities. Terms like "average" encourage errors, since different evaluators react differently to them. Moreover, raters need to observe subordinates on a regular basis throughout the evaluation period. It is even helpful if the rater takes notes for future reference. To the extent possible, the number of persons one rater must evaluate ought to be reasonably limited. When one person must evaluate many subordinates, it becomes difficult to discriminate. The fatigue of rating increases with the number of ratees.

Also, the dimensions used are best when clearly stated, meaningful, and relevant to good job performance. Finally, raters should be trained so they can recognize various sources of error and understand the rationale underlying the evaluation process.

REWARD SYSTEMS IN ORGANIZATIONS

After the organization has conducted a systematic performance appraisal, the next step is to consider how to tie rewards to the outcomes of the appraisal. Behavioral research consistently demonstrates that *performance levels are highest when rewards are contingent upon performance.* So, in this section, we will examine four aspects of reward systems in organizations: 1) functions of reward systems; 2) bases for reward distribution; 3) types of rewards; and 4) money and motivation.

Functions of Rewards

Among the uses of rewards in an organization are the following:

- *Increasing Performance.* Rewards can be used to motivate performance. According to expectancy theory, employees would be expected to increase their effort and performance when they felt that rewards were contingent upon good performance. Reward systems serve a basic motivational function.[13]
- *Reducing Turnover and Absenteeism.* Reward systems have also been shown to influence an employee's decision to come to work or to remain with the organization.[14]
- *Enhancing Organizational Commitment.* Reward systems in no small way influence commitment to the organization, primarily through the exchange process.[15]
- *Improving Job Satisfaction.* Job satisfaction has been shown to be related to rewards. Lawler has summarized available evidence on satisfaction as follows: a) satisfaction with a reward is a function of both how much is received and how much the individual feels should be received; b) satisfaction is influenced by comparisons with what happens to others; c) people differ with respect to the rewards they value; and d) some extrinsic rewards are satisfying because they lead to other rewards.[16]
- *Facilitating Occupational and Organizational Choice.* The selection of an occupation by an individual, as well as the decision to join a particular organization within that field, is influenced by the rewards that are thought to be available in the occupation or organization.

Hence, reward systems in organizations can have far-reaching consequences for both individual satisfaction and organizational effectiveness.

Unfortunately, cases can be cited in which good performance has been redefined or facts distorted to further unethical practice or inhibit creativity. Consider, for example, the Greyhound Bus Company driver who was suspended for ten days without pay for breaking a company rule against using a CB radio on his bus. The bus driver had used the radio to alert police that his bus, with thirty-two passengers on board, was being hijacked by an armed man. The police arrested the hijacker, and the bus driver was suspended for breaking company rules.[17]

Further evidence of good performance being punished can be seen in a series of examples where U.S. government bureaucracies punished whistle blowers in their own agencies. Ernest Fitzgerald was a civilian employee in the U.S. Air Force in charge of cost controls. In 1968, in the course of carrying out his job, he discovered and reported to the Joint Congressional Economic Committee that the Air Force was incurring a $2.5 billion cost overrun on the C-5A transport plane. Shortly after this whistle blowing, the Air Force laid off Fitzgerald in an "economy move."[18]

Or, consider the case of Oscar Hoffman, a government inspector of pipe welds on combat ships being built for the U.S. Navy. In the course of his inspections he discovered many defects in welds, which he reported to his superiors. Hoffman's superiors ignored the reports and threatened him with reprimand if he persisted in reporting the defects. When he filed a grievance against this threat, Hoffman was reprimanded and transferred from Seattle to Tacoma. Soon after his transfer, the Navy laid him off (in 1970) because his services were "no longer needed." Ironically, a series of accidents involving faulty welds have occurred on many of the ships identified by Hoffman. What has since happened to Hoffman? Although his superior has been promoted, Hoffman has been unable to secure another job as a government inspector.[19]

Numerous other examples could be cited. The point here is that in at least two major government bureaucracies, effective means have been found to stifle or eliminate those who take their jobs too seriously. One can just imagine the effects of these layoffs on other employees who are equally concerned with facilitating effectiveness of operations in their organizations.

Basis for Reward Distribution

Inequity in the distribution of available rewards is common in many contemporary work organizations. One sometimes sees little correlation between those who perform well and those who receive the greatest rewards. At the extreme, it is hard to understand how one company could pay its president over $1 million per year (as many large corporations do), while it pays its secretaries less than $10,000.

How do organizations actually decide on the distribution of available rewards? At least four mechanisms can be identified. In more cases than we may choose to admit, rewards go to those with the greatest *power*. In many of the corporations whose presidents earn seven-figure incomes, we find that these same people are major shareholders in the company. Often an important or high-performing manager's threat to resign leads to a salary increase.

A second basis for reward distribution is *equality*. Here, all individuals within one job classification receive the same rewards. Many labor union contracts establish and standardize pay rates with no reference to performance level. These systems do recognize seniority, however.

The basis for the social welfare reward system in this country is *need*. In large part, the greater the need, the greater the level of support. It is not uncommon to see layoff situations in business firms where need is taken into account; an employee who is the sole support of a family is the last laid off.

A fourth basis upon which organizations allocate rewards is **distributive justice.** Under this system, employees receive (at least a portion of) their rewards as a function of their level of contribution. The greater the contribution, the greater the rewards. This mechanism is most prominent in merit-based incentive programs where pay and perhaps bonuses are determined by levels of individual performance.

UP CLOSE 5.1:   Comparable Worth

Of the four bases for reward distribution, probably the most widely used is power. That is, executives often receive exhorbitant salaries because of their position and clout in the organizations. Similarly, many predominantly male union members receive fairly high wages because of the power of their unions. Many junior managers receive fairly good starting salaries because their relative scarcity in the marketplace gives them bargaining power upon entry into the corporation. And many corporate staff executives (lawyers, controllers, etc.) have clout because of the uniqueness and value of their expertise to the organization.[20]

A large segment of the labor force that does not have significant clout—and coincidently is often significantly underpaid—is the mainly female clerical and administrative staffs. Clerical workers, for example, are notoriously underpaid and because supply and demand (market forces) may dictate this.

Enter comparable worth. In many states, labor group and women's groups are pressing legislation that would mandate that salary levels be determined not by the labor market but by how comparable (in terms of difficulty or skill level) one job is with another. Hence, a job evaluation may determine that a clerk typist (a predominantly female job) is roughly comparable in skill level to a drill press operator (a predominantly male job). As such, the legislation would require that both job incumbents earn approximately the same salary. The argument underlying this is based on the concept of distributive justice. The legislative efforts can be seen as an effort to shift power distributions so that the distributive justice system works.

Proponents of comparable worth argue that the system represents a more equitable approach to salary administration and is a way to reduce systematic discrimination against women. Opponents argue that comparable worth ignores the realities of the labor market and that it will lead to significant increase in labor costs. In either case—and whoever wins—the concept is not likely to eliminate feelings of inequity in the work place. If one group makes progress up the salary ladder, another feels unfairly treated. Whatever its merits, comparable worth is clearly a win-lose situation for the various working groups in organizations. ■

Extrinsic and Intrinsic Rewards

The types of rewards employees can receive in exchange for their contribution of time and effort are classified into extrinsic and intrinsic rewards. **Extrinsic rewards** are those rewards external to the work itself. They are administered by someone else, or externally. Examples of extrinsic rewards include wages and salary, fringe benefits, promotions, and recognition and praise from others. On the other hand, **intrinsic rewards** are those rewards that are related directly to performing the job. They are often described as self-administered rewards since doing in the task itself leads to their receipt. Examples of intrinsic rewards include feelings of task accomplishments, autonomy, and personal growth on the job.

Money and Motivation

Is money is a primary motivator? Opsahl and Dunnette suggest that money serves several functions in work settings. These include: 1) money as a goal or incentive; 2) money as a source of satisfaction; 3) money as an instrument for gaining other desired outcomes; 4) money as a standard of comparison for determining relative standing or worth; and 5) money as a conditional reinforcer where its receipt is contingent upon a certain level of performance.[21]

Even so, the effectiveness of pay as a motivator varies considerably. At times there seems to be almost a direct relationship between pay and effort, while at other times no such relationship is found. Why? Lawler suggests that certain conditions must be present in order for pay to act as a strong motivator.[22] These are when: 1) Trust level between managers and subordinates is high; 2) individual performance can be accurately measured; 3) pay rewards to high performers are substantially higher than those to poor performers; and 4) few perceived negative consequences of good performance exist. Under conditions such as these, a climate is created in which employees can believe that significant performance-reward contingencies truly exist. Under this perception—and assuming the reward is valued—we would expect performance to be increased.

INCENTIVE PLANS

We turn now to an examination of various employee incentive programs organizations use. Managers have choices among alternative plans and must make decisions about which plan is most effective for their particular organization and work force. Incentive systems in organizations are usually divided into two categories, based on whether the unit of analysis—and the recipient of the reward—is the individual or the group (or organization).

Individual Incentive Plans

Each individual incentive plan assumes that the most effective method of motivating employee performance is by tying rewards to individual initiative and effort. These plans include:

- *Merit-based Compensation Plan.* When a major portion of employee salary is determined by performance level, individuals have increased control over their output. In most organizations using these plans, all employees receive a base (cost-of-living) pay raise, and merit pay is added to this as a function of rated performance on the job.
- *Piece-rate Plan.* On many blue-collar production jobs, employees are paid according to each unit of output they produce. The most common variation on this plan happens when employees are guaranteed an hourly rate for performing at a minimum level of output (the standard). Production over and above the standard is then rewarded based on pay for each unit of output.
- *Bonus Plans.* A variety of bonus plans can be found in organizations, particularly among upper managers in private firms (not public organizations). Under a bonus plan, individuals receive an additional payment that is usually a percentage of a given figure. Senior auto sales executives, for example, receive a bonus based on car sales volume above certain levels.
- *Commissions.* Sales personnel typically receive commissions—part or all of their salary is tied to their level of sales.

While individual incentive systems in many cases leads to improved performance, some reservations have been noted. In particular, these programs can encourage unproductive competitive behavior. For instance, department store salespeople on commission may fight over customers. Second, unions typically resist these plans, preferring compensation to be based on seniority or job classification. Third, where quality control systems are lax, individual incentives such as piece rates may lead employees to sacrifice quality by maximizing units of output. Finally, in order for these programs to be successful, an atmosphere of trust and cooperation between employees and managers is necessary. In order to overcome some of these shortcomings, many organizations have turned to group or organizational incentive plans.

Group and Organizational Incentive Plans

Several incentive systems can be identified in which employees as a group benefit from improved performance, reduced costs, or increased profits. Three of the major plans are:

1. *Profit-sharing plans.* Basically, profit-sharing plans pay company employees a certain percentage of profits each year. At least 100,000 corporations currently have these plans.[23] The overall rationale is that by contributing to company profitability, all employees benefit.
2. *Employee Stock Option Plans.* This plan, known as ESOP, is designed to give employees of public companies some ownership in the organization. Typically, a block of stock is set aside each year for distribution to employees based on tenure, performance level, or salary. Employees usually pay for the stocks at reduced rates. ESOPs are probably more useful in developing commitments among employees and reducing turnover than in improving performance.
3. *Company Incentive Plans.* A variety of organization-wide incentive plans are currently in use. Two of the most publicized plans are the Lincoln Electric Plan and the Scanlon Plan. These plans typically reward employees based on cost savings or production increases that have been achieved during the past year or quarter.[24]

Guidelines for Effective Incentive Plans

Whichever incentive program is selected, a good fit between the plan and the particular organization and work force is essential. Mathis and Jackson note five guidelines for effective incentive programs.[25] First, they point out that the plan should be tied as closely as possible to performance. This point was noted earlier.

Second, the incentive programs should allow for individual differences if possible. A good plan recognizes that different people want different outcomes from a job. Cafeteria-style plans, discussed later, do this.

Third, incentive programs should reflect the type of work that is done and the structure of the organization. This simply means that the program should be tailored to the particular needs, goals, and structures of a given organization. Individual incentive programs, for example, would probably be less successful among unionized personnel than would group programs.

Fourth, the incentive program should be consistent with the climate and constraints of the organization. When trust levels are low, for example, it may take considerable effort to get any program to work. In an industry already characterized by high levels of efficiency, basing an incentive system on a desire for greater efficiency may have little effect, since employees may see the task as nearly impossible.

Finally, incentive programs should be carefully monitored over time to insure that they are being fairly administered and that they accurately reflect current technological and organizational conditions. For instance, offering an incentive to sales clerks to sell out older merchandise may be more valuable to a department store than offering an incentive to sell current fashion items, which can "sell themselves."

Responsibility falls on managers to consider the unique situation and needs of their own organization. With this understanding, a program can be developed and implemented that will facilitate goal-oriented performance and maximize employee satisfaction.

UP CLOSE 5.2:   Crown Zellerbach

Worker productivity has long been an issue in the forest product industry. In the light of reduced demand for lumber and increased imports (primarily from Canada), profitability and survival are critically dependent on a company's ability to cut and mill lumber at low costs.[26]

In an effort to enhance productivity and preserve jobs, Crown Zellerbach and its union agreed to experiment with a pay-for-performance system among its loggers. This system was an application of basic motivational concepts.

Under the plan, the incentive to be more productive was that pay depends entirely on how much wood a crew produces each day, measured in units of 100 cubic feet. In addition, the union agreed to eliminate up to twenty-five job classifications that pigeonholed workers into specific tasks. Both sides predicted that eliminating these classifications would make the crews more productive.

In return, Crown Zellerbach agreed to give union members greater input into the design of their jobs. Joint union-management committees are to decide how many crews to form and which job function to include in each crew. The company decides where to log, but the committees decide how to organize the work. Since workers are paid based on how much they can produce, they are hopefully motivated to develop the most efficient harvesting plan. It has been estimated that workers earn about $3 an hour more than they did under the previous plan. ■

NEW DEVELOPMENTS IN REWARD SYSTEMS

Over the past ten years· organizations have become increasingly willing to experiment with different methods of compensation and reward systems. This development is part of a "quality-of-working-life" movement, representing one aspect of managerial efforts to improve the work situation to the benefit of both individuals and organizations. At least five fairly recent developments in reward systems can be identified, as Exhibit 5.10 summarizes.

Cafeteria-Style Fringe Benefits

A typical fringe-benefit package provides the same benefits, and the same amount of benefits, to all employees, largely ignoring individual differences or preferences. Studies by Lawler indicate that different employees prefer variations in the benefits they receive.[27] For instance, young unmarried men

EXHIBIT 5.10

Summary of Alternative Pay Practices

	Major advantages	Major disadvantages	Favorable situational factors
Cafeteria-style fringe benefits	Increased satisfaction with pay and benefits	Cost of administration	Well-educated heterogeneous work force
Lump-sum salary increases	Increased satisfaction with pay; greater visibility of pay increases	Cost of administration	Fair pay rates
Skills-based evaluation	More flexible and skilled work force; increased satisfaction	Cost of training and higher salaries	Employees who want to develop themselves; jobs that are interdependent
Open salary information	Increased satisfaction with pay; greater trust and motivation; better salary administration	Pressure to pay all employees the same; complaints about pay rates	Open climate, fair pay rates, pay based on performance
Participative pay decisions	Better pay decisions; increased satisfaction, motivation, and trust	Time consumed	Democratic management climate; work force that wants to participate and that is concerned about organizational goals

SOURCE: E. E. Lawler, "New Approaches to Pay: Innovations that Work," *Personnel*, September-October 1976.

and women often prefer more vacation time, while young married people often prefer to give up vacation time for higher pay. Older employees often want more retirement benefits, while younger employees prefer greater disposable income.

Using a cafeteria-style compensation program, employees are allowed some discretion in the determination of their package and can make trade-offs within certain limits. TRW and the Educational Testing Service are among the organizations now using cafeteria-style benefit programs. While certain problems of administration exist with the programs, their use can help increase need satisfaction among employees.

Lump-Sum Salary Increases

A second technique that has received some attention is to allow employees to decide how (that is, in what amounts) they wish to receive their yearly pay raise. Under the traditional program, pay raises are apportioned equally in each paycheck over the year. Under this plan, employees have this traditional option or they can choose to take the entire raise in one lump sum.

This plan allows employees greater discretion over their own financial matters. If an employee wants to use the entire pay raise for a vacation, it can be paid in a lump sum in June. If the employee quits before the end of the year, the unearned part of the pay raise is subtracted from the final paycheck. This plan increases the visibility of the reward to the employee. But as with the cafeteria-style plan, the administration costs of the lump-sum plan can be greater than those of the traditional method.

Skills-Based Evaluation

Compensation programs are typically tied to evaluations of the job itself. In these evaluations, jobs are first analyzed to assess their characteristics, then salary levels are assigned to each job based on factors such as job difficulty and scarcity in the labor market. In other words, pay levels are not set based on individual skills. This approach does not encourage employees to continue learning new skills on the job, since there is no reward for the learning. Job-based evaluation tends to keep everyone in their places and minimizes the possibility of inter-job transfers.

Under the skills-based evaluation program, employees are paid according to their skills level (that is, the number of jobs they can perform), regardless of the actual tasks they do perform. This approach has proven successful at Procter & Gamble and General Foods. Employees are encouraged to learn additional skills and are appropriately rewarded. The organization gains a better trained and more flexible work force. By the same token, training compensation costs are necessarily increased, so the program is appropriate only in some situations. The technique most often is part of a larger quality-of-working-life program where it is associated with job redesign efforts—such as those at Cadillac.

UP CLOSE 5.3:   Cadillac

The Cadillac engine plant in Livonia, Michigan, is one of nine General Motors plants that use the "pay for knowledge" team concept to make factory work less boring and more productive. The approach used at Cadillac differs radically from the practice in most union shops, where workers perform narrow functions. Instead, at Livonia production workers can learn all of the jobs in one section, giving management flexibility in making work assignments and covering for absenteeism.[28]

In exchange for their labor, workers are paid according to the skills they acquire, thereby providing an incentive to learn new jobs. Under the old system, there were forty-five job classifications, each with its own wage rate. Now there are just four. Under the old system, workers could advance only through seniority when an opening occurred. Now it is possible for everyone to rise to the top classification if they can master the work. The engines are still produced on an assembly line, but the employees now have varied routines and are allowed to participate more in decisions affecting how the work is done.

One year after implementing the new skills-based compensation program, several results emerged. The Livonia plant now uses less manpower per engine while producing higher-quality products. It hit its break-even point in one year instead of the projected two years. Moreover, the scrap rate has fallen by 50 percent, while worker suggestions saved Cadillac more than $1.2 million in the first year alone. The experiment has apparently paid off for both workers and company. ■

Open-Salary Information

Secrecy about pay rates seems to be the norm in work organinzation, particularly among managerial personnel. The rationale is simply privacy. Evidence compiled during the past decade, however, suggests that pay secrecy in organizations may have several negative side effects.

To begin with, it has been consistently found that, in an absence of actual knowledge, people have a tendency to overestimate the pay of co-workers and those above them in the hierarchy. As a result, much of the motivational potential of a differential reward system is eliminated. Even if an employee receives a relatively sizable salary increase, the individual may still feel that he or she is receiving less than is due. This problem was highlighted in a study by Lawler. In considering the effects of pay secrecy on motivation, Lawler noted:

> *Almost regardless of how well the individual manager was performing, he felt he was getting less than the average raise. This problem was particularly severe among high performers, since they believed that they were doing well yet received minimal reward. They did not believe that pay was in fact based upon merit. This was ironical, since their pay did reflect performance. . . . Thus, even though pay was tied to performance, these managers were not motivated because they could not see the connection.*[29]

Pay secrecy can also affect motivation because it eliminates feedback, which motivates performance.

When salary information is open, employees are generally provided with more recognition for satisfactory performance and are often more motivated to perform on subsequent tasks. It is easier to establish feelings of pay equity and trust in the salary administration system. On the other hand, publicizing pay rates and pay raises can cause jealousy among employees and create pressures on managers to reduce perceived inequities in the system. There is no correct answer to the question of whether pay rates should be secret or open. As is true for so many aspects of management, individual organizational situations are what best determine pay secrecy or pay openness.

Participative Pay Decisions

Recently several organizations have been experimenting with involving employees in pay raise decisions and policy. The results seem quite positive. By allowing employees to participate either in the design of the reward system or in actual pay raise decisions (perhaps through a committee), it is argued that decisions of higher quality are made based on greater information. Also, employees have greater reason to place confidence in the fairness of the decisions. On the negative side, this approach requires considerably more time for both the manager and for the participating subordinates. Costs must be weighed against the benefits to determine which approach is most suitable for the particular organization and its objectives.

UP CLOSE 5.4: Levi Strauss

In August, 1984, as they faced the prospect of laying off employees, managers at Levi Strauss decided to take a rather unusual step. Their layoffs were forced due to a decline in the market for jeans. However, management wanted to be as fair as possible in the decision process and felt coworkers could provide useful information.[30]

As a result, Levi Strauss asked about 2000 executive, sales, and other professional staff members to participate in its "Objective Judgement Quotient," the name given to the company's appraisal system. The ratings were to help supervisors identify job-loss candidates at Levi's San Francisco headquarters and in regional offices.

According to a company spokesman, "Most people who are laid off will clearly have not performed well enough to be retained. There will additionally be some hard decisions at the margin. . . ."

The peer evaluation system was to focus on quality, quantity, communication skills, and technical knowledge. Workers were to be evaluated by their supervisor and up to nine fellow employees named by the person under review. Hence, by attempting to secure increased input, the company had hoped to make more informed and equitable decisions in the face of an unpleasant situation. ■

Selecting an Appropriate Compensation System

In deciding which, if any, of the newer compensation approaches to implement, Lawler defines two principal issues: the management style of the organization, and the condition of the present-day system (see Exhibit 5.11). If the organization prefers a participative style, a different approach may be in order than if the organization has an authoritative or top-down style. Beyond this, the fairness of the present system should be evaluated. As noted in Exhibit 5.10, the majority of the newer techniques mandate fairness for success. While

EXHIBIT 5.11

Guide to Choosing Among the New Approaches to Pay Administration

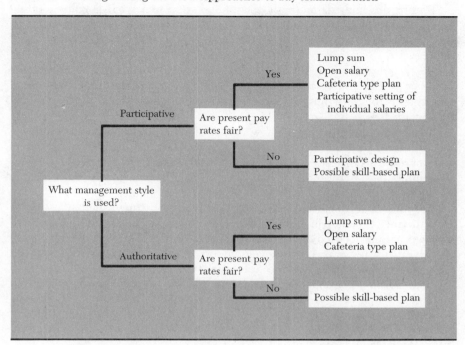

SOURCE: E.E. Lawler, "New Approaches to Pay: Innovations that Work," *Personnel*, September-October, 1976.

the diagram is meant to be illustrative, it does suggest some of the more relevant concerns when management is deciding on changes in compensation and reward systems.

It must be remembered that employee participation in pay decisions and benefit plans is a relatively new practice and in many cases still untested. Several of these procedures do hold considerable promise for improving the equity and fairness of pay decisions and pay practices. But managers should carefully consider the suitability of the techniques in their own unique work environments. Thus, the important role of management is to decide how (or if) the compensation should be modified. Whatever solution is chosen, it should be consistent with the larger purpose and goals of the organization and facilitate organizational objectives.

SUMMARY

This chapter examined performance appraisal and reward systems in organizations. Six functions of performance appraisals were identified, including: 1) feedback to employees; 2) self-develpment indicators for employees; 3) basis for reward distribution; 4) basis for personnel decisions; 5) information for future hires and placement decisions; 6) employee training and development.

Toward this end, six methods of appraisal were reviewed: 1) graphic rating scales; 2) critical incident techniques; 3) behaviorally anchored rating scales; 4) behavioral observation scales; 5) management by objectives; 6) assessment centers.

Next, a variety of measurement problems that can potentially reduce the accuracy or effectiveness of appraisals were discussed. These are the central tendency error, strictness or leniency error, halo effect, recency error, and personal biases.

Based on the discussion of how corporations typically evaluate employee performance, we examined the basis for reward distributions at work. Functions of reward systems were reviewed, as were the various means by which we determine pay systems. The issue of comparable worth was discussed to illustrate the controversy surrounding efforts at pay equity.

In addition, intrinsic and extrinsic rewards were distinguished. We considered the role of money in motivation and reviewed several incentive programs. These programs focused either on individual incentive plans or group incentive plans. Finally, several recent developments in incentive and reward systems were reviewed. These include cafeteria-style fringe benefits, skills-based evaluation, and participative pay decisions. The importance of tailoring a compensation system to the needs of the particular organization was emphasized throughout.

KEY WORDS

assessment center
behaviorial
    observation scale
behaviorally anchored
    rating scale
cafeteria-style fringe
    benefits
central tendency error
critical incident
    method
distributive justice
employee stock option
    plans

extrinsic rewards
graphic rating scale
halo effect
intrinsic rewards
leniency error
lump-sum salary
    increase
management by
    objectives
merit-pay
    compensation
open salary
    information

participative pay
    decisions
performance appraisal
piece-rate plan
profit-sharing plan
recency error
reliability
reward systems
skills-based evaluation
strictness error
validity

DISCUSSION QUESTIONS

1. What are the primary uses of performance appraisals in organizations?
2. Compare and contrast the various methods of performance appraisals in terms of validity and reliability and in terms of cost and ease of use. Which system do you prefer? Why?
3. In what ways is management by objectives different from the other evaluation methods? In what ways are assessment centers different?

4. Identify the major problems with performance appraisal systems. How can these problems be minimized?
5. What functions are served by reward systems in organizations? Explain.
6. Examine the various bases for reward distribution. In your answer, consider the topic of comparable worth as described in this chapter.
7. Does pay motivate? Explain and defend your answer.
8. Compare and contrast individual group incentive plans. Which do you feel would be most effective? Why?
9. Among the recent developments in reward systems, which do you feel have the most promise of success in organizations? Why?

CASE 5.1:   Derco United Corporation

"I just wonder how to make a Bonus Award Program really effective in this company," thought Jerry Barker, Assistant to the President of Derco United Corportion as he sat in his Menlo Park office late one afternoon in September 1975. "The concept of rewarding 'singular, outstanding achievements that significantly contribute to the success of the company' makes so much sense—but it is not at all easy to translate this concept into a program that will work here in this plant."

Barker, with a background in finance, had recently joined Derco upon completion of the MBA program at Stanford. A job prior to his graduate work had given Barker some exposure to the compensation area, and the President of Derco, Robert James, had asked him to take part in designing the Bonus Award program. Barker had been involved in the several top management discussions about the Program. In two days, he was to present a proposal that would capture the philosophy of top management and address the need for effective shop-floor implementation.

THE COMPANY

Derco United Corporation (DU) was a publicly held corporation with two divisions—nonunion Derco Engineering (the focus of this case) in Menlo Park, California, and unionized Derco Systems in Chicago. Corporate offices were with Derco Engineering in Menlo Park.

DU had been founded in 1950 to develop and manufacture highly technical equipment. By 1975, Derco Engineering products ranged from small, standardized devices manufactured in modest quantities (up to 5,000 per year) to large, one-of-a-kind pieces of gas-process equipment. These products comprised four main groups: military, industrial, advanced technology and gas-process. The Division marketed its products worldwide using its own marketing group and selected sales representatives. In 1975, approximately 20% of total sales were outside the United States, a slight drop from 1974. Sales under government contracts or subcontracts were approximately 40% of the 1975 total. The company had been facing strong competition at home and abroad.

The year 1974 had been a record breaker for DU. Corporate sales had reached $23 million, a 34% increase over 1973. Net income had doubled to $730,931 or 44¢ per share (Exhibit 1). Similar growth had occurred during the first two quarters of 1975.

EXHIBIT 1

Sales and Income before Taxes—Five-Year Summary ($000's)

	Derco Engineering	Derco Systems	Total
1974			
Sales	$17,672	$5,557	$123,229
Income before taxes	1,427	20	1,447
1973			
Sales	15,538	1,772	17,310
Income before taxes	565	(368)	197
1972			
Sales	14,233	476	14,709
Income before taxes	870	(68)	802
1971			
Sales	9,706	359	10,065
Income before taxes	638	(59)	579
1970			
Sales	7,298	34	7,332
Income before taxes	584	—	584

In September 1975, Derco Engineering employed 315 people. The Division actively sought skilled, well-educated workers and generally found them locally for all but the most specialized jobs. Turnover was low and wages good, relative to other local high-technology companies.

The Chicago-based Derco Systems Division was smaller (125 people). Its 100 production workers were members of the United Automobile, Aerospace and Agricultural Implement Workers of America (UAW). The Division had never experienced any work stoppage due to labor problems.

Derco United had four corporate officers and a seven-person Board of Directors (Exhibit 2). Robert James, 41, had been promoted from Vice-President to President in 1970; he had come to Derco in 1966 with a business-oriented education and with management experience in manufacturing. John Williams, 45, had joined Derco in 1974 as Corporate Vice-President and President of Derco Engineering; he had a background in engineering and had worked for a consulting firm. Kurt Shaeffer, 42, had held various management positions in another company before joining Derco in 1975 as a Corporate Vice-President and President of Derco Systems. Ben Burdoe, 41, had joined Derco in 1972 as Corporate Vice-President and Secretary-Treasurer, had had an accounting background, and had previously been the Controller of an electronics firm.

THE PRODUCT LINE AND PRODUCTION PROCESS

Derco Engineering's four product groups—military, industrial, advanced technology, and gas-process—fell along a spectrum with a wide range of product size, unit volume, worker skill, and process characteristics. A worker was assigned to a specific product group and, to a large extent, was identified with that group; nonetheless, the small size of the plant ensured some daily social contact among most of the workers. In general, Derco Engineering both designed and manufactured its products. Except for the gas-process line, most manufacturing was assembly work; fabrication of components was

EXHIBIT 2
Organizational Chart

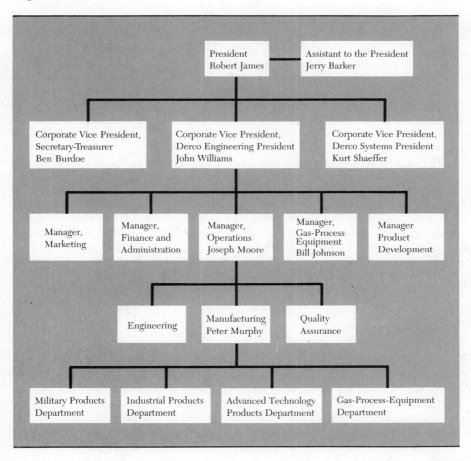

subcontracted. All manufacturing was supervised by Joseph Moore, Manager of Operations, who had been with the company since 1961.

The military products were small (about the size of a coffee mug) and standardized. The work consisted of routine, repetitive assembly operations performed at benches; the product was carried from one worker to the next. Unit volume numbered in the hundreds per month, and these products represented about 25% of the Division's business in 1975. Cost was the most significant competitive factor. This product group, while at the low end of Derco's skill and quality spectrum, had good growth potential and the workers derived a certain intra-divisional prestige from this fact.

The industrial products were larger (about the size of a portable TV), although still standardized. An individual unit was typically placed on a cart, and a group of workers were assigned to assemble each particular model. Worker skill levels were higher than in the military products department, reflecting the greater complexity of the assembly work. Unit volumes were 20 to 100 per month per model, and production was scheduled in batches. Industrial products, as a whole, represented about 45% of the Division's business. Both cost and quality were important, with the emphasis depending upon the individual model. New-product development was constant in a market environment in which the major portion of business in any one year might be in a market that had not existed three years before. The workers shared this sense of newness and quick pace.

The advanced technology products were large units (refrigerator-sized) for educational and research laboratories. In contrast to the military and industrial departments, a unit in this department remained in one spot during the one-month assembly period, and the group of skilled workers came to it. Typically, three units were in process at any one time. Output from this department was about 20% of the Division's business. Quality was paramount, not only for the customer but also for Derco, as the products typically could not be tested until they were complete. The market for these products was relatively stable, and the workers reflected this with a generally slower, more painstaking pace of work.

The gas-process products were huge (box-car-sized), one-of-a-kind pieces of equipment. Usually state-of-the-art, these projects ran in the million dollar range and took six months to a year to complete. The department had beeen formed in 1973; in 1975 it accounted for about 10% of the Division's business. While actual manufacturing work was under the direction of Joseph Moore, the gas-process line had a program manager, Bill Johnson, who coordinated each project from sales through engineering to manufacturing. On the shop floor, a core team (a lead person, two assembly technicians, and a welder) typically was appointed for each project and carried the primary responsibility for fabrication and assembly. This team, however, was supported by other workers and departments, and as many as 15 to 20 people often contributed to any one project.

COMPENSATION

Production workers were paid a straight hourly rate with no formal incentive or bonus pay system, although the Division President, from time to time and without publicity, presented an individual worker with a bonus check for an outstanding accomplishment.

In January 1971, DU had set up a formal Management Incentive Compensation Plan for key executives and employees. Payments were made when the Corporation or the Division met or exceeded annual financial goals; a payment represented a percentage of the individual's total standard compensation. Originally, about 20 people had been involved in this Plan.

In a series of meetings earlier in 1975, James, Williams, Shaeffer, and Burdoe had decided that this Plan had accumulated too many participants (some three times the original 20). In addition, they felt that the Plan did not provide the specific accountability they believed necessary in an incentive program appropriate to the company's size, and James had worked extremely hard to build a successful company and expected all other employees to contribute their utmost, too. He would like to find a way to reward those who do outstanding work: "In any organization, 5 to 10% of the people are typically truly outstanding. They make the organization go, and their contributions should be recognized." He suggested a small "Nobel Prize" type of program.

On Criteria

Williams wanted to reward "the extra measure of resourcefulness." Shaeffer sought "an unusual commitment" and "extraordinary on-the-job performance." James looked for "stand-alone-effort." All agreed that it is an important managerial skill to be able to identify such superior performance.

Burdoe felt that care should be taken to insure that performance selected for recognition was viewed as worthy of such attention by other employees as well as by management.

On Nomination and Decision

James felt that recommendations should come from an employee's immediate supervisor, or perhaps from one level above that. Williams and Shaeffer both felt the Division President should make the final decision on an award in his Division.

On the Amount of the Award

All felt that the award should be "significant," and should depend upon both the achievement and the recipient's salary. James suggested the $500 to $1,500 range as appropriate.

On Announcement and Presentation

James felt that an award should be publicized within the company to enhance the Program's power as a motivator and to increase the recognition given to the recipient. Williams suggested that the company newspaper would be the appropriate medium. Both liked the idea of a special presentation ceremony in the President's office.

Shaeffer expressed hesitation about surrounding an award with much publicity. He would prefer to post a brief notice on the department bulletin board and enclose the award check within the recipient's regular pay envelope.

On Administration

Williams and Shaeffer both felt that the Program should be administered separately by each Division, with each President determining the appropriate Pool of Bonus money to establish (an absolute $ amount? a percent of payroll? a percent of profits?), the recipients, and size of an award.

Burdoe would like to review the size of any Pool set up.

On Implementation

All agreed that the circulation of a clear statement of the Program would be sufficient, and that formal training of supervisors would not be necessary.

A BRIEF VISIT FROM THE PRESIDENT

As Barker sat at his desk late on that September afternoon, Robert James dropped in and voiced his expectations:

Jerry, I'm really looking forward to seeing your Program proposal on Wednesday. I'm proud of what we have been able to accomplish here at Derco, and I'm eager to build into our policies a means of really recognizing and rewarding the people who make the outstanding contributions that continue to spark our growth and success.

CASE QUESTIONS

1. What is the stated purpose of the bonus award program? Who is to be rewarded? How is the purpose translated into terms that are relevant for the work done in the different product groups?
2. Describe the four product groups. How should the differences in skill, type of production process, and varying emphasis on cost and quality be figured into the bonus program?
3. What are the differences between Derco Engineering and Derco Services? What are the potential problems and benefits in having the president of each division administer the program?
4. Design a plan that you feel will accomplish the organization's goals.

NOTES

1. C. Loomis, "The Madness of Executive Compensation," *Fortune*, December 15, 1980, pp. 42–43.
2. Gerardo R. Ungson and Richard M. Steers, "Motivation and Politics in Executive Compensation," *Academy of Management Review*, 9, 2 (1984), pp. 313–323.
3. Alan Locher and Kenneth Teel, "Performance Appraisal—A Survey of Current Practices," *Personnel Journal*, May, 1977.
4. Alan Locher and Kenneth Teel, "Performance Appraisal," pp. 245–247, 254.
5. Alan Locher and Kenneth Teel, "Performance Appraisal."
6. J. Gibson, J. Ivancevich, and J. Donnelly, *Organizations: Structure, Process and Behavior* (Dallas: BPI, 1979), p. 367.
7. D. Bray and J. Moss, "Personnel Selection," *Annual Review of Psychology* (Palo Alto, CA: Annual Reviews, 1972) pp. 545–576.
8. Richard Klinoski and W. J. Strickland, "Assessment Centers: Valid or Merely Prescient," *Personnel Psychology*, 30 (1977), pp. 353–361.
9. William Glueck, *Personnel: A Diagnostic Approach* (Dallas, Texas: BPI, 1978).
10. J. P. Wright, *On A Clear Day You Can See General Motors* (Grosse Point, MI: Wright Enterprises, 1979), pp. 251–252.
11. S. Jones, "Self and Interpersonal Evaluations," *Psychological Bulletin*, 80 (1973), pp. 185–199.
12. John Barnardin and C. S. Walter, "The Effects of Rater Training and Diary Keeping on Psychometric Error in Ratings," *Journal of Applied Psychology*, 61 (1977), pp. 64–69.
13. Lyman W. Porter and Edward E. Lawler III, *Managerial Attitudes and Performance*, (Homewood, IL: Irwin, 1968).
14. William Mobley, *Employee Turnover: Causes, Consequences, and Control* (Reading, MA: Addison-Wesley, 1982); and Richard M. Steers and Susan R. Rhodes, "Major Influences on Employee Attendance: A Process Model," *Journal of Applied Psychology*, 63 (1978), pp. 391–407.
15. Richard T. Mowday, Lyman W. Porter, and Richard M. Steers, *Employee-Organization Linkages: The Psychology of Commitment, Absenteeism, and Turnover* (New York: Academic Press, 1982).
16. Edward E. Lawler III, "New Approaches to Pay Administration," *Personnel*, 53, 5 (1976), pp. 11–23.
17. *Eugene Register-Guard*, July 15, 1980, p. 2A.
18. Robert Vaughn, *The Spoiled System* (New York: Charterhouse Books, 1975).
19. Robert Vaughn, *The Spoiled System*.
20. Daniel Seligman, "Pay Equity is a Bad Idea," *Fortune*, May 14, 1984, pp. 133–140.

21. R. L. Opsahl and M. D. Dunnette, "The Role of Financial Compensation in Industrial Motivation," *Psychological Bulletin*, 66 (1966), pp. 94–96.
22. Edward E. Lawler III, *Pay and Organizational Effectiveness* (New York: McGraw-Hill, 1971).
23. William Glueck, *Personnel*, pp. 441–471.
24. William Glueck, *Personnel*.
25. Robert Mathis and John Jackson, *Personnel*, Second Edition (St. Paul, MN: West, 1979).
26. "Loggers Tie Pay to Productivity," *Business Week*, November 29, 1982, p. 35.
27. Edward E. Lawler III, "New Approaches," Chapter 4.
28. "A Plant Where Teamwork is More Than Just Talk," *Business Week*, May 16, 1983, p. 108.
29. Edward E. Lawler III, *Pay and Organizational Effectiveness*, p. 174.
30. "Levi Workers to Rate Peers Before Layoffs," *Eugene Register-Guard*, August 5, 1984, p. 6F.

6 Job Design

T he computer revolution is changing the way people at all levels of the organization perform their work. In factories, workers are using (or being replaced by) robots and computer-controlled tools. Engineers are making greater use of computer-aided design systems, while secretaries are using word processors or electronic memory typewriters. Finally, the advent of the personal desktop computer has caused a fundamental revolution in the way managerial work is performed.

In 1983 only about 3 percent of managers had desktop computers; by 1990 it is estimated that 65 percent will have them. As Business Week predicted in 1983, "The advent of desktop computers and other information tools, linked together by advanced telecommunications networks that provide access to widely diverse sources of data, heralds a huge surge in productivity for approximately 10 million managers in the U.S."[1] This increased productivity can only be realized through a major change in the way managers do their work. The fundamental way in which managers carry out their work—job design—is changing and will continue to change. For this reason, managers need to understand job design in organizations as it relates to performance, job-related stress, and employee attitudes.

In this chapter, several aspects of job design are examined. First, work adjustment problems are explored to clarify why job design is important. Included in this section is a discussion of work-related stress. Next, early developments in job design are reviewed, followed by a contemporary model of job design. Finally, several additional methods of job design are discussed as they relate to people and productivity. Throughout the discussion, examples and applications are presented.

RELEVANCE OF JOB DESIGN FOR MANAGERS

This chapter focuses on the interaction between people and the tasks they perform. An awareness of this interaction and its consequences is important for the following reasons:

Individual characteristics and needs often conflict with organizational requirements. The nature of this conflict—as well as modes of resolution—must be clearly understood by managers interested in optimizing employee commitment and performance.

Work-related stress is a major cause of employee turnover and absenteeism, and it inhibits the effectiveness of organizations. Moreover, stress experienced by one employee can jeopardize the safety of others, as can be seen with air traffic controllers and machine operators. Reducing stress can improve an employee's contribution to an organization and increase his or her satisfaction with the job itself.

Prolonged stress has been shown to have negative physical and psychological effects on individuals and particularly on managers. Thus, employee health is also jeopardized.

Recent experiments in work redesign have improved job performance and attitudes and reduced stress. Work redesign represents an important tool in improving organizational effectiveness.

Work redesign experiments have become increasingly popular in recent years. Managers must understand why before they can decide whether to attempt similar programs in their own organizations. Before adopting work redesign techniques, they must also know the possible drawbacks, as well as ways of overcoming them.

PROBLEMS OF WORK ADJUSTMENT

A major problem facing managers and employees in organizations is the issue of work adjustment—that is, how employees adjust to the work situation and what managers can do to ease this adjustment. Failure to adjust to work represents a major problem in industry today. Between 80 and 90 percent of industrial accidents are estimated to be caused by personal factors.[2] High turnover and absenteeism, drug abuse, alcoholism, and sabotage are common in contemporary work organizations. To the extent that individuals are unable to adjust to work, they are likely to persist in behavior that is detrimental to themselves and the organization.

Reasons for Work Adjustment Problems

Five reasons have been proposed for adjustment failures:

1. Some people lack the initial motivation to work. They have a negative conception of work and choose to avoid it.
2. Some people experience severe anxiety when faced with demands for increased productivity. They simply cannot face the job.
3. Some individuals are openly hostile and aggressive, particulary toward authority figures like supervisors. They view work-place demands as hostile acts to be resisted.
4. Other people are characterized by severe dependency and feel helpless on the job. Such individuals consistently seek advice from others and often cannot show personal initiative on the job.
5. Finally, some individuals exhibit significant social naivete. They do not understand the needs and feelings of others and may not realize how their

behavior affects others. They simply don't know how to behave in social situations, so they often fail in social interactions.[3]

Several important points follow from this analysis. First, failure to adjust to a normal job or work schedule does not mean an individual is lazy or stupid. Deep psychological problems can keep people from making a normal adjustment. Second, only the first type above represents a motivational problem. Managers must look beyond motivation for answers to psychopathology at work. Third, the last type represents a form of personality disorder, or at least social immaturity.

The remaining three types—anxiety, aggression, and dependency—relate not only to personality, but to how the job affects that personality. Anxiety, aggression, and dependency, are inherent in stressful jobs. Hence, at least three reasons for failure to adjust to work relate to the extent to which the job is experienced as stressful and makes the individual want to withdraw. To the extent that jobs can be altered to reduce anxiety, aggression, and dependency, and hopefully increase motivation, both the individual and the organization will benefit.

Conflicts Between Individuals and Organizations

A second way to understand problems of work adjustment is to examine basic conflicts between what individuals and organizations want from each other. A model of person–organization relationships proposed by Chris Argyris, called the **basic incongruity thesis,** consists of three parts: what individuals want from organizations, what organizations want from individuals, and how these two potentially conflicting sets of desires are harmonized.[4]

The model begins by examining how healthy individuals change as they mature. As people grow to maturity, they develop in the following ways:

- From a state of passivity as infants to a state of increasing activity as adults.
- From a state of dependence on others to a state of relative independence.
- From having only a few ways of behaving to having many diverse ways of behaving.
- From having many shallow, casual, and erratic interests to having a few deep interests.
- From having a short time perspective (behavior is determined by present events) to having a longer time perspective (behavior is determined by a combination of past, present, and future events).
- From being in a subordinate position to being in a teaching or supervisory position (from child to parent or from trainee to manager).
- From having a poor understanding of themselves to having a greater understanding of and control over themselves as adults.

Although these changes differ from one person to another, the general tendencies from childhood to adulthood are fairly standard.

Next, the defining characteristics of traditional work organizations are examined. In the pursuit of efficiency and effectiveness, organizations increase task specialization, unity of command, and a rules orientation to turn out a standardized product with standardized people. This pursuit of standardization has several consequences:

- Individuals have little control over their work; control is often shifted to machines.
- Individuals are expected to be passive, dependent, and subordinate.
- Individuals are allowed only short-term horizons in their work.
- Individuals are given repetitive jobs that require minimal skills and abilities.
- Because of the preceding consequences, individuals are expected to produce under conditions that lead to psychological failure.

In short, many jobs today are structured in such a way that they conflict with the basic growth needs of a healthy personality. This conflict between personality and organization is represented in Exhibit 6.1. The magnitude of the conflict is a function of several factors. The strongest conflict can be expected when employees are very mature, organizations are highly struc-

EXHIBIT 6.1
Basic Conflict Between Employees and Organizations

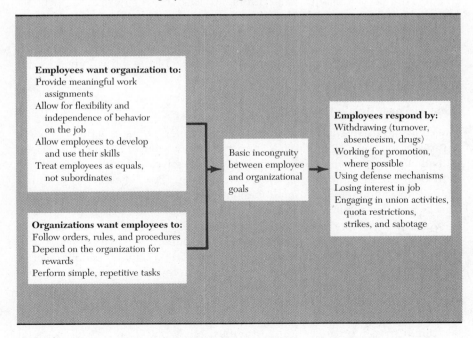

Employees want organization to:
Provide meaningful work assignments
Allow for flexibility and independence of behavior on the job
Allow employees to develop and use their skills
Treat employees as equals, not subordinates

Organizations want employees to:
Follow orders, rules, and procedures
Depend on the organization for rewards
Perform simple, repetitive tasks

Basic incongruity between employee and organizational goals

Employees respond by:
Withdrawing (turnover, absenteeism, drugs)
Working for promotion, where possible
Using defense mechanisms
Losing interest in job
Engaging in union activities, quota restrictions, strikes, and sabotage

SOURCE: R. M. Steers, *Introduction to Organizational Behavior*, 2d ed. (Glenview, IL: Scott, Foresman, 1984), p. 120.

tured, rules and procedures are formalized, and jobs are fragmented and mechanized. Hence, the strongest conflict should occur at the lower levels of the organization, among blue-collar and clerical workers. Manager tend to have jobs that are less mechanized and less subject to formalized rules.

When strong conflicts exist between what employees and organizations want from each other, employees are faced with difficult choices. They may choose to leave the organization or to work hard to climb the ladder into the upper echelons of management. They may defend their self-concepts and adapt through the use of defense mechanisms. Dissociating themselves psychologically from the organization (e.g., losing interest in their work or lowering their work standards) and concentrating instead on the material rewards available from the organization is another possible response. Or they may find allies in their fellow workers and adapt as a group through such activities as quota restrictions, unionizing efforts, strikes, and sabotage. Unfortunately, while such activities may help employees "get back" at the organization, they do not change the basic situation. One must recognize the powerful role personality plays in determining work behavior before one can implement meaningful change to improve the effectiveness or efficiency of operations.

WORK-RELATED STRESS

It is clear that work-adjustment problems can create internal conflicts for individuals, which often take the form of job stress and strain. Job-related stress has received considerable attention in recent years because of the harmful effects it can have on both the individual and the organization. Hence, an understanding of stress as it relates to the nature of the job is important for practicing managers.

What Is Work-Related Stress?

The concept of **stress** in organizational settings refers to the reaction of people to threatening environmental characteristics. Stress points to a poor fit between individuals and an environment in which excessive demands are made or individuals are ill equipped to handle the situation.[5] People under stress cannot respond to environmental stimuli without psychological or physiological damage, as revealed in chronic fatigue, tension, or high blood pressure.

Most workers experience stress at some time or other.[6] Almost any aspect of the work environment can produce stress, including excessive or inadequate noise, light, heat, responsibility, work, or supervision. Not all people react in the same way to stressful situations, even those in the same occupation. A high need achiever, for example, may thrive on a level of job-related tension that makes another individual question his or her ability to cope with the situation. In general, moderate levels of stress not only keep people alert to environmental stimuli (possible dangers, opportunities, etc.), but often provide a useful motivational function. Some experts argue that the most satisfying and productive work employees perform is carried out under moderate stress levels.

From a managerial perspective, it is useful to focus on two types of stress: frustration and anxiety. **Frustration** refers to an internal or external impediment to goal-oriented behavior. Examples include inability to make a sale, to keep pace with a machine, or even to get correct change from a coffee machine. **Anxiety** is the sense of being unable to deal with anticipated harm. It occurs when people lack appropriate responses or plans for coping with anticipated problems, and is characterized by a persistent apprehension about the future for reasons that may be unknown to the individual.

Problems Caused by Stress

Before we can discuss the consequences of work-related stress, we must distinguish between three levels of work-related stress: no stress, low job stress, and high job stress (see Exhibit 6.2). Associated with these variations in stress intensity are three categories of outcome: health problems, performance, and dysfunctional behavior.

Stress and Health Problems   High levels of stress are typically accompanied by severe anxiety and frustration, high blood pressure, and high cholesterol levels. These psychological and physiological changes impair health in several

EXHIBIT 6.2
Consequences of Work-Related Stress

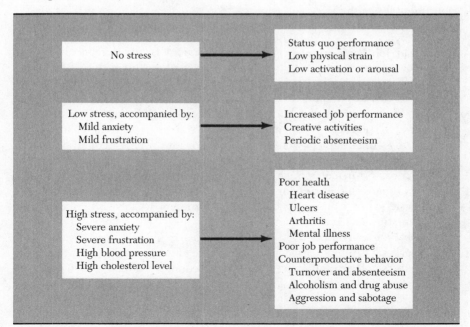

SOURCE: R. M. Steers, *Introduction to Organizational Behavior*, 2d ed. (Glenview, IL: Scott, Foresman and Company, 1984), p. 524.

ways. Most important, high stress clearly contributes to heart disease,[7] which kills well over half a million people every year. High job stress also contributes to a variety of other ailments, including peptic ulcers, arthritis, and several forms of mental illness.[8]

In a classic study of the mental health of automobile assembly-line workers, Kornhauser found that 40 percent had symptoms of mental health problems. His main findings may be summarized as follows:

- Employee job dissatisfaction, stress, and absenteeism were all related directly to the characteristics of the job. Dull, repetitious, unchallenging jobs were associated with the poorest mental health.

- Employee feelings of helplessness, withdrawal, alienation, and pessimism were widespread throughout the plant. Fifty percent of the assembly-line workers felt they had little influence over their futures, compared to only 17 percent of nonfactory workers.

- Employees with the poorest mental health also tended to be most passive in their nonwork activities; typically, they did not vote or take part in community affairs.[9]

In conclusion, Kornhauser noted: "Poor mental health occurs whenever conditions of work and life lead to continuing frustration by failing to offer means for perceived progress toward attainment of strongly desired goals which have become indispensable elements of the individual's self-esteem and dissatisfaction with life, often accompanied by anxieties, social alienation and withdrawal, a narrowing of goals and curtailing of aspirations—in short . . . poor mental health."[10]

Stress and Job Performance   While management is greatly concerned with the effects of stress on job performance, this relationship is not as simple as might be supposed. The stress–performance relationship resembles a curve much like that in Exhibit 6.3. At *very low or no stress* levels, individuals maintain their current levels of performance. They do not experience any stress-related physical strain and probably see no reason to change their performance, regardless of whether it is high or low.[11] Under conditions of *low to moderate stress*, people are often motivated sufficiently to improve their performance. For instance, many salespeople and managers perform best when they experience mild anxiety or frustration. Stress in modest amounts acts as a stimulus, as when a manager has a tough problem to solve. Similarly, mild stress can stimulate creative activities.

Finally, under conditions of *high job stress*, individual performance often drops markedly. Individuals focus considerable effort on attempts to reduce the severe stress, often employing a variety of counterproductive behaviors, as noted below. Little energy is left to devote to job performance, with obvious harmful results.

EXHIBIT 6.3
Relationship Between Stress and Job Performance

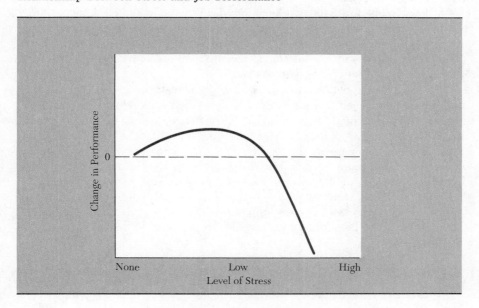

SOURCE: R. M. Steers, *Introduction to Organizational Behavior*, 2d ed. (Glenview, IL: Scott, Foresman, 1984), p. 526.

Stress and Dysfunctional Behavior   Several forms of dysfunctional behavior are known to result from prolonged stress, including a high number of resignations, absenteeism, alcoholism and drug abuse, and aggression and sabotage. Although temporary, resignations (turnover) and absenteeism represent convenient forms of withdrawal from a highly stressful job. Results of several studies have indicated a fairly consistent, if modest, relationship between stress and subsequent rates of turnover and absenteeism.[12] In fact, one survey found that while there has been a 22 percent rise over the last fifteen years in the amount of absenteeism attributable to purely physical diseases, during the same period absenteeism associated with psychological ills increased 152 percent for men and 302 percent for women.[13]

Stress has long been linked to alcoholism and drug abuse at all levels in the organizational hierarchy. These two forms of withdrawal offer a temporary respite from severe anxiety and frustration. Researchers who conducted one study for the Department of Health, Education, and Welfare reported, "Our interviews with blue-collar workers in heavy industry revealed a number who found it necessary to drink large quantities of alcohol during lunch to enable them to withstand the pressure or overwhelming boredom of their tasks."[14] A similar study by the New York Narcotics Addiction Control Commission revealed a surprising amount of drug abuse by young blue-collar workers, especially assembly-line employees and long-haul truckdrivers. A study of a UAW local involving 3400 workers found 15 percent addicted to heroin.[15] Although many companies have begun in-house rehabilitation programs, these forms of withdrawal continue to increase, presenting another serious problem for modern managers. One solution to this problem involves reducing the stress that is creating the need for withdrawal.

Finally, extreme frustration can also lead to aggression against other people and inanimate objects. Aggression occurs when individuals can find no legitimate outlets for their frustration. For instance, a busy secretary may be asked to type a stack of letters, only to be told later that the boss changed his mind and no longer needs the letters. The frustrated secretary may react by covert verbal abuse or an intentional slowdown on subsequent work. A more extreme example of aggression can be seen in the periodic reports in newspapers about workers who "go berserk" (usually after a reprimand or punishment) and attack fellow employees. Clearly, then, the consequences of high job stess can be serious and warrant the attention of managers.

UP CLOSE 6.1:   O'Hare International Airport

One of the most stressful jobs in contemporary society is that of the air traffic controller, the person who monitors and guides airplanes in takeoffs and landings. Nowhere is this stress more acute than at Chicago's O'Hare International Airport, the busiest airport in the world, called the "ulcer factory" by the controllers who work there. O'Hare Airport handles 1900 flights a day and has one takeoff or landing every twenty seconds during peak hours. Because of this pressure, controllers can work only ninety minutes at a stretch during peak hours, landing one plane every two minutes while simultaneously monitoring a half-dozen more.[16]

This pressure, combined with the ever-present fear of permitting a crash or collision (known with studied casualness as an "aluminum shower"), places controllers under tremendous stress on the job. Of the ninety-four controllers at O'Hare, only two have been there more than ten years; most don't reach five years. Two thirds have ulcers or ulcer symptoms. Most exhibit signs of prolonged stress: high blood pressure, arthritis, colitis, skin disorders, headaches, allergies, and upset stomachs. Some struggle with more severe problems, like alcoholism, depression, persistent nightmares, and acute anxiety. In one year alone, seven men had to be carried from the O'Hare control tower on stretchers, victims of acute hypertension. Since 1970 more than forty controllers have been permanently removed from their jobs for medical reasons.

Although the nature and extent of the problem are widely acknowledged, the prevailing work environment and Federal Aviation Administration (FAA) policies seem to conspire to prevent a workable solution. First, controllers contend that their supervisors and FAA policies place them in a no-win situation. Supervisors encourage controllers to overlook FAA regulations about spacing and prevent delays, but if a near-miss occurs, the controller is disciplined for not following regulations.

Second, the controllers complain of understaffing, computer malfunctions, inadequate training programs, unrealistic transfer policies, and nerve-wracking conditions that jeopardize their health and public safety. However, a lawsuit they filed against the FAA to remedy these conditions was dismissed on the grounds that the controllers had not pursued other avenues of redress.

Third, controllers who experience high stress are subject to a "Catch-22" transfer policy. Since O'Hare is understaffed, the FAA is reluctant to transfer healthy controllers to smaller, less stressful airports. Yet when controllers can no longer cope with the pressure at O'Hare, the FAA prefers to terminate them rather than transfer them to smaller, less stressful airports.

Finally, while the FAA maintains a staff of qualified flight physicians, controllers seldom visit them for fear that their stress-related disorders will be reported. Hence, the controller's only way out is through some physical ailment.

In August 1981 the U.S. air traffic controllers went on an illegal strike, insisting something be done to address the problem of job fatigue (and demanding more money). Within days President Reagan terminated about 12,000 striking controllers. After some confusion, replacements were hired and trained and flight schedules returned to normal. After about 18 months, however, the controllers began complaining of increased job-related stress and talking about forming another union. ■

EARLY DEVELOPMENTS IN JOB DESIGN

As noted above, many causes of work-related stress derive from the nature of the job. That is, aspects of the job can either foster or moderate stress. Thus, if managers understand the nature of jobs, they can take actions to reduce stress as well as to enhance job performance. We shall begin our discussion with a look back at the first so-called scientific approach to designing jobs.

Scientific Management

Efforts to design jobs efficiently date from the rise of the Industrial Revolution. As factories grew in size and sophistication, managers made greater efforts to fractionate, or break down, jobs so they could be performed more quickly and with less training cost and time. Companies would benefit because of increased efficiency and output, it was thought, while workers would benefit because the piece-rate compensation system tied monetary rewards directly to output.

Efforts to simplify job design reached their zenith in the assembly-line production techniques that became popular in the early 1900s. These efforts formed the basis for what became known as the *scientific management* movement,[17] and were characterized by the following:

- *Machine pacing.* The production rate was determined by the speed of the conveyor belt, not by the workers.
- *Task repetitiveness.* Tasks were performed over and over during a single work shift. On auto assembly lines, for example, typical *work cycles* (that is, times allowed for completion of an entire piece of work) ranged from thirty seconds to one and a half minutes. This means a worker performed the same task up to 500 times a day.
- *Low skill requirements.* Because of simplified task requirements, jobs could be easily learned and workers were easily replaced.
- *Task specialization.* Each job consisted of only a few operations. Final product assembly was often done elsewhere in the factory so workers seldom saw the complete product.
- *Limited social interaction.* Because of the speed of the assembly line, noise, and physical separation, it was difficult to develop meaningful social relationships on the job.
- *Tools and techniques specified.* Staff specialists (usually industrial engineers) selected the tools and techniques to be used by workers to maximize efficiency.

Although these techniques led to early successes on the shop floor, drawbacks also appeared that nullified many of the advances. First, job fractionation ignored human needs for growth and development. Frederick Taylor noted that "one of the very first requirements for a man who is fit to handle pig iron as a regular occupation is that he more nearly resembles in his mental makeup the ox than any other type."[18] This view of employees hardly encouraged efforts to improve the quality of working life.

It also became apparent in the early 1920s that job fractionation led to unauthorized breaks.[19] People did not like their jobs, and reacted by refusing to cooperate. Unionization efforts and sabotage also became more common during this period.

These problems led to rising concern for improving workers' attitudes in the 1930s. Behavioral scientists turned their attention to finding ways to make employees happier on their jobs. Human relations training came into vogue, as did company newspapers, employee awards, and company social events. However, the basic nature of the job remained unchanged and the problems persisted. It was not until the late 1950s that the concept of job enrichment emerged as a potential solution to poor performance and employee alienation.

Initial Efforts Toward Job Enrichment

The most significant early contributor to job redesign was Frederick Herzberg,[20] who discovered in a study of accountants and engineers that employees tended to describe satisfying experiences in terms of factors that were intrinsic to the job itself. These factors, which he called **motivators,** included variables like achievement, recognition, responsibility, advancement, and personal growth. The same employees described unsatisfying experiences, called **hygiene factors,** in terms of factors that surrounded but did not include the job activities themselves. Hygiene factors included salary, company policies, supervisory style, and co-worker relations.

As a result of this study, Herzberg argued against the human relations efforts that prevailed at the time. These efforts treated hygiene factors, while the roots of employee motivation lay in the job itself. The implication of this conclusion for managers was clear: *Employee motivation can be significantly enhanced through changes in the nature of the job.* Efforts to change or enrich the job include:

- *Control over resources.* Employees should have maximum control over the mechanisms of task performance.
- *Accountability.* Employees should be held accountable for their performance.
- *Feedback.* Supervisors should provide direct, clear, and frequent feedback.
- *Work pace.* Within limits, employees should set their own work pace.
- *Achievement opportunities.* Jobs should allow employees to experience a feeling of accomplishment.
- *Personal growth and development.* Employees should be able to learn new procedures on the job and to experience some personal growth.

Comparing this list with the earlier list of attributes of scientific management shows the significant difference in attitudes toward tasks in the work place. The philosophy underlying **job enrichment** takes a more optimistic view of the nature of workers and their needs, drives, and aspirations. It assumes that employees want to tackle problems at work and show their creativity. Thus, it assumes that money is not the only important motivator of good performance.

THE JOB CHARACTERISTICS MODEL

More recently, a new model of work redesign was proposed by Richard Hackman and Greg Oldham that takes into account more factors in the work place (such as individual differences).[21] Hackman and Oldham define **work redesign** as any activity that involves altering specific jobs (or interdependent systems of jobs) to increase both the quality of employees' work experience and their productivity. Work redesign is not a panacea for organizational problems, nor is it appropriate in all situations. Rather, work redesign represents a systematic technique that can help improve life at work in a number of situations.

The **job characteristics model** developed by Hackman and Oldham is shown in Exhibit 6.4.[22] Five core job dimensions influence three critical psychological states, which in turn influence several desired personal and work outcomes. The links between job dimensions, psychological states, and outcomes are moderated by employee growth need strength. We shall briefly review each aspect of the model.

EXHIBIT 6.4
The Job Characteristics Model of Work Motivation

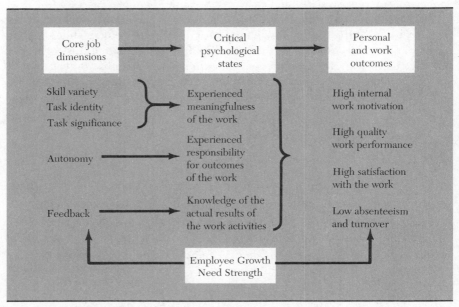

SOURCE: J. R. Hackman and G. R. Oldham, "Motivation Through the Design of Work: A Test of Theory," *Organizational Behavior and Human Performance* 16 (1976): 256.

Critical Psychological States

An employee's motivation and satisfaction are influenced by three **critical psychological states:**

- *Experienced meaningfulness of the work.* Employees must feel that the work is important and worthwhile.
- *Experienced responsibility for work outcomes.* Employees must feel responsible for the results of the work they perform.
- *Knowledge of results.* Employees must receive regular feedback concerning the quality of their performance.

Hackman explains: "The model postulates that internal rewards are obtained by an individual when he *learns* (knowledge of results) that he *personally* (experienced responsibility) has performed well on a task that he *cares about* (experienced meaningfulness).[23] The more these three conditions are met, the more satisfied individuals will feel when they perform well. These internal rewards act as incentives for individuals to continue to perform in order to obtain additional intrinsic rewards. When individuals fail to perform well, they do not receive positive reinforcement and may be motivated to try harder on subsequent tasks (see Chapter 4).

Core Job Dimensions

The five **core job dimensions** combine to determine motivational level. **Skill variety** is the degree to which a job requires a variety of activities that involve the use of several skills and talents. **Task identity** is the degree to which the job requires the completion of a whole and identifiable piece of work—that is, doing a job from beginning to end with a visible outcome. **Task significance** is the degree to which a job has a substantial impact on the lives or work of other people in the immediate organization or the external environment. **Autonomy** is the degree to which a job provides substantial independence and discretion in scheduling work and determining how to carry it out. The fifth dimension is *feedback*—the degree to which carrying out work activities required by the job gives individuals clear information about their performance.

The first three dimensions are believed to influence the experienced meaningfulness of work. Autonomy influences experienced responsibility for work outcomes, while feedback influences knowledge of results. Any work redesign effort should attempt to develop jobs that are high on all these core dimensions.

The core job dimensions are typically measured using a questionnaire developed by Hackman and Oldham.[24] This questionnaire permits the calculation of a **motivating potential score** (MPS) that reflects the extent to which employees see their jobs as motivating. According to the model, a high motivating potential score is only possible if a job is high on at least one of the three dimensions that influence experienced meaningfulness, high on autonomy, *and* high on feedback. The existence of these three dimensions creates the necessary work environment for all three critical psychological states. The MPS can be calculated as follows:

$$\text{Motivating potential score} = \left[\frac{\text{Skill variety} + \text{Task identify} + \text{Task significance}}{3}\right] \times \text{Autonomy} \times \text{Feedback}$$

As this formula indicates, a low score on any factor will reduce the MPS score to near zero.

Employee Growth Need Strength

Growth need strength represents a collection of higher-order needs (achievement, affiliation, and autonomy) that moderate the way employees react to the work environment. This influence emerges at two points in the model. First, employees with high growth need strength (GNS) are more likely to respond when their job has been enriched than those with low GNS because they are more sensitive to the enriched dimensions. Second, high GNS individuals tend to respond more favorably to the resulting psychological states than low GNS individuals because these states are more likely to satisfy the higher-order needs.

For example, a person who has a high need for achievement (high *n Ach*) can satisfy that need by successfully performing challenging tasks, while a person with a low *n Ach* may become frustrated or anxious. Clearly, individual differences must be considered when jobs are designed.

Several personal and work-related outcomes result from various combinations of psychological states and GNS. When people experience the positive states described above, they should exhibit high levels of motivation, performance, and job satisfaction, and low rates of turnover and absenteeism. While the psychological states are clearly not the only variables that affect these outcomes, they are a primary influence on job behavior.

Implications for Redesigning Work

The job characteristics model suggests five principles for enriching jobs and redesigning work. These principles illustrate how the model can be applied in real work environments, and may be summarized as follows:

1. To the extent possible, workloads should be divided into **natural work units:** pieces of work that logically fit together. For instance, a typist may be assigned all the typing responsibilities for a person or department, instead of sharing the work with other typists who never see completed projects. Forming natural work units allows employees to increase their ownership of the work and see its significance.
2. Similarly, jobs can be enlarged by *combining several related tasks* and thus increasing skill variety and task identity.
3. Jobs that are designed traditionally (e.g., assembly-line jobs) provide little or no contact with clients, whether inside or outside the organization. *Establishing client relationships* increases feedback because the ultimate user can respond to the quality of the product or service. Skill variety may also increase since the employee must develop the interpersonal skills needed to interact with clients. Finally, autonomy may increase as the employee must decide how to manage the relationship with the client.
4. The principle of **vertical loading** aims at closing the gap between the doing and controlling aspects of work. For example, employees are permitted to select their own work methods, inspect their own work, choose their hours of work, or participate in decisions affecting their job or organization. In this way, employee autonomy is often increased.
5. A fifth substantive work change occurs by *opening feedback channels.* Most employees receive supervisor-provided feedback about their job performance. However, work redesign also leads to job-provided feedback. When jobs have built-in feedback mechanisms (allowing employees to check their own work), employees are continually reminded of their performance without confronting the interpersonal problems inherent in supervisory feedback.[25]

UP CLOSE 6.2:   Traveler's Insurance

While enrichment principles may sound fine in theory, how do they work in actual practice? Hackman and associates provide one answer by describing Traveler's Insurance Company's effort to redesign the job of keypunch operators.[26] With core job dimensions described in the model, the job of keypunch operator prior to enrichment could be described as follows:

- *Skill variety. Only a single skill was needed: the ability to accurately punch data on cards.*
- *Task identity. Batches were assembled to provide an even work load but not whole, identifiable jobs.*
- *Task significance. While keypunching was necessary to provide service to company customers, individual operators were isolated by an assignment clerk and a supervisor from any knowledge of what the operation meant to the receiving department, let alone to the ultimate consumer.*
- *Autonomy. The operators had no freedom to arrange their daily tasks to meet schedules, to resolve problems with receiving departments, or even to correct information that was obviously wrong.*
- *Feedback. Once a batch was completed, the operators received no feedback on performance quality.*

The investigators, using the job characteristics model, made the following simple modifications in the work:

- *Natural work units. Instead of working on randomly assigning batches, each operator was assigned continuing responsibility for certain accounts.*
- *Task combination. Some planning and controlling functions were integrated with the main task of keypunching.*
- *Client relationships. Each operator was given several channels of direct contact with clients. Operators, not assignment clerks, could now examine documents for legibility and autonomy. When a problem arose, the operator contacted the client.*
- *Feedback. In addition to client feedback, the operators also received feedback from the job itself. For example, all incorrect cards were returned to operators for correction. Weekly computer printouts listing error rates and productivity were sent directly to the operators.*
- *Vertical loading. Operators were allowed to correct obvious errors on their own. They could also set their own schedules and plan their daily work.*

These changes had several consequences: (1) While the control group showed an increase in productivity of 8.1 percent during the trial period, the work redesign group showed an increase of 39.6 percent. (2) Prior to the study the experimental group had an error rate of 1.53 percent; following the intervention the rate fell to 0.99 percent. (3) During the study period, absenteeism in the experimental group declined 24.1 percent while it increased 29 percent in the control group. (4) While no attitude changes occurred in the control group, overall job satisfaction increased 16.5 percent in the experimental group after intervention. (5) Because of improved operator proficiency, fewer controls were necessary, reducing supervisory needs. (6) Since the operators took over many mundane supervisory responsibilities, supervisors were now able to devote more time to developing feedback systems, setting up work modules, overseeing the enrichment effort, and planning. That is, supervisors were now able to manage instead of dealing with day-to-day problems. While other change techniques could have been tried (e.g., behavior modification), it is doubtful that they would have led to such successful results in terms of both productivity and work attitudes. ■

ADDITIONAL APPROACHES TO JOB DESIGN

Related approaches to job design include quality control circles, four-day work weeks, flextime, job sharing, and job rotation. Each approach aims to modify the work experience in some way to make it more productive, satisfying, or both.

Quality Control Circles

An approach to work design that has received increased attention in recent years is the involvement of production workers in decisions concerning improvements in productivity and product quality through **quality control (QC) circles.** A QC circle consists of all employees who work closely on a particular job. The circle leader may be a worker or a supervisor. The group meets periodically, perhaps one hour a week, to discuss production problems and look for useful solutions. The idea behind QC circles is simple. As L. J. Hudspeth, vice-president for corporate productivity at Westinghouse, says, "They [shopfloor workers] know more about operations than you do."[27] That is, the employees themselves are best able to identify problems and suggest improvements, assuming, of course, that they have the necessary problem-solving skills or training, data, time, and financial support.

Rewards to employers for participating in quality circles vary. At Northrup, for example, members of the circle receive 10 percent of any dollar savings resulting from a suggestion. Usually, however, no monetary reward is used because the increased employee involvement and resulting pride are considered sufficient. In any case, the technique continues to gain in popularity.

Several successful examples of QC techniques can be identified. Employees at Northrup became concerned because the bits used to drill holes in titanium for F-5 fighter planes kept breaking. After investigating the problem, the group suggested that the drilling angle be changed and harder bits be used. The resulting change saved Northrup $70,000 in time. Similarly, Ford Motor

Company recently adopted a variation on the QC approach by giving workers forty-eight hours of special training at the two plants it was preparing to manufacture Ford Escorts and Mercury Lynxes. The training was intended to help workers spot start-up problems on the assembly line, saving Ford trouble later on. Early results suggest that the technique was successful, since the first cars were far more trouble-free than comparable new introductions. A third example of a QC effort in action can be seen in the dramatic turnaround at the GM plant in Tarrytown, New Jersey. In the early 1970s the plant was plagued by violence and absenteeism. Car quality was extremely poor, and each year employees filed about 3000 grievances. After the introduction of worker-management teams, car quality improved substantially and grievances fell to about forty a year. Irving Bluestone, a retired UAW vice-president, suggested the new spirit of cooperation may have prevented the big facility from closing.[28]

UP CLOSE 6.3:   Quasar Electronics

Before the Japanese firm Matsushita took over the Quasar Electronics TV factory from Motorola, Motorola experienced 150 defects per 100 sets.[29] After conversion to the new management style, Quasar reduced that rate to three or four defects per 100 sets using the same workers and the same quality control people. The only difference was the new approach to quality control by managers.

Several procedures instituted after conversion account for the change:

- *Scrubdown of new products. New products are carefully tested before they go into production to eliminate bugs. Previously much of this "scrubdown" was done during production to hold down production costs.*
- *Emphasis on quality. A TV set has three principal quality characteristics: picture quality, cabinet appeal, and reliability. Many U.S. television companies focus on the first two characteristics and ignore the third. In contrast, Quasar places higher emphasis on reliability with many more people working on inspection as the sets are assembled. As a result, typical color TV sets fail in service at a rate five times higher than Quasar TV sets.*
- *Components. Quasar carefully tests all components before putting them into the set, while most American companies do less testing. Quasar also pays more attention to quality and price in selecting vendors.*
- *Training. Training is emphasized at all levels. Top managers attend classes on production quality, and design engineers must work in operations prior to designing new products so they understand production problems. Most production workers are trained in quality control circles.*
- *Employee relations. Quasar emphasizes teamwork and worker responsibility for quality control. Line managers and workers both have greater input into decision making about products and, as a result, feel greater responsibility, accountability, and pride than their counterparts at other companies.*

Through the application of these simple techniques, Quasar Electronics found it could turn around a manufacturing plant in a short period of time and in the process improve both productivity and employee job satisfaction. ■

In summary, three principles account for the success of QC circles. First, to be successful, workers must be adequately trained in problem-solving techniques so they can analyze the problem. Second, workers must be assured that suggested changes will not lead to their being penalized in any way (e.g., through increased layoffs or increased job fractionation). Third, workers must feel that top management clearly and actively supports QC efforts. Without this support, it is difficult for QC circles to be taken seriously by employees.

Four-Day Workweek

The **4/40 workweek** (four days/forty hours) has emerged recently as a popular experiment in work redesign. Close to 2000 companies employing over 1 million people now use the 4/40 plan.[30] The major push came from companies that hoped to increase productivity and efficiency and workers who wanted more leisure time. The plan aims at accomplishing both without changing job technology.

A survey by the American Management Association of companies using the 4/40 plan showed that it increased production in 62 percent of the companies, increased efficiency in 66 percent, and boosted profits for 51 percent. Similarly, a Bureau of Labor Statistics study showed that companies that had installed the plan generally met their objectives, whether they were to reduce costs, improve efficiency, reduce absenteeism, or improve job satisfaction.[31] On the negative side, the AMA study revealed that 4/40 plans often presented problems for working mothers, as well as shipping and receiving problems, customer confusion about new hours, and occasionally cost increases. Clearly, an organization must consider the characteristics of the work force and whether its product or service performed lends itself to a four-day week before committing to the plan.

Olin Ski Company of Middletown, Connecticut, initiated the four-day workweek in 1972 to compete more effectively for skilled workers.[32] Employees work Monday through Thursday, ten hours a day. Since its introduction, employee response has been consistently positive. As one employee notes, "I love it. That was the reason I came to work here. I like my three-day weekends."[33]

After implementation of the plan at Olin, productivity initially dropped, but after several months it rose again and exceeded previous levels. Absenteeism declined slightly. After over a decade with the program, neither employees or managers want to return to the five-day workweek.

Flextime

Another change that has received increasing attention in recent years is **flextime,** which is currently being used in over 5000 firms of varying sizes. Flextime gives employees more latitude in determining their work schedules.

It differs from plans like the four-day workweek in that employees have some choice over starting and quitting time, although all must be present during certain daily core hours so necessary interpersonal and interdepartmental communcation can take place.

Sandoz-Wander of New Jersey introduced a flextime program with the following parameters:

Earliest starting time:	7:30 AM
Latest starting time:	9:30 AM
Earliest leaving time:	4:00 PM
Latest leaving time:	6:00 PM
Lunch period:	12:00–2:00 PM
Maximum lunch period:	2 hours
Minimum lunch period:	1 hour
Core hours (when everyone must be present):	9:30–12:00 noon 2:00–4:00 PM
Average workweek:	37.5 hours
Maximum workweek:	40 hours
Minimum workweek:	22.5 hours
Average workday:	7.5 hours
Maximum workday:	9.5 hours
Minimum workday:	4.5 hours[34]

Within these parameters, employees are free to select the working hours that best fit their own needs and desires. Following this plan does not alter the basic nature of the job, but allows employees some discretion as to when to perform. Results of a series of experiments reveal fairly consistent positive results. Both attitudes and behaviors (particularly in the form of reduced absenteeism and turnover) generally improve after implementation of flextime.[35]

Job Sharing

A technique for relieving job fatigue while accommodating the needs of part-time workers is **job sharing,** which involves two or more persons' jointly covering one job over a forty-hour week. For example, one manuscript typist may work in the morning and one in the afternoon. The typing gets done and both employees have ample time for outside activities. While job sharing does not change the basic nature of the work, it does allow an organization to tap previously unavailable labor markets.

Job Rotation

When an organization has a series of dull or routine jobs that cannot be combined or enriched, it may rotate workers from one job to another. The aim of **job rotation** is to minimize the boredom through changes in activities. The employee learns different jobs and the company develops a more flexible work force. However, job rotation does not solve the basic problem of unchallenging jobs and should be used only as a temporary or last-resort solution.

SUMMARY

In this chapter we considered job design and those work factors that make it an important issue. First, several problems of work adjustment were identified, including lack of motivation to work, severe anxiety, hostility and aggression, severe dependency, and social naivete. These reasons often create a situation in which individuals experience great difficulty in managing the demands of the workplace.

There sometimes is a basic conflict between what individuals want from organizations and what organizations want from individuals. Individuals look for opportunities for growth and development in the work place, while organizations are more concerned with compliance and conformity. The conflict that results creates one more source of stress for individuals.

Stress is defined in this chapter as the reaction of people to threatening environmental characteristics. Stress is a common feature in many work situations and has been found to be associated with a variety of dysfunctional consequences for both individuals and organizations. One way organizations attempt to reduce stress and increase performance and promote better job attitudes is through the redesign of work.

The scientific management movement was one of the earliest efforts at job design. Scientific management attempted to maximize human performance capabilities through studies of the interactions between workers and machines. Recent efforts in work design have aimed to look beyond individuals as human machines and instead focus on individuals as human resources. Contemporary efforts focus on how jobs can be designed so they maximize to the extent possible both performance and personal development.

One of the most popular contemporary models of work design is the job characteristics model. This model posits that core job dimensions in conjunction with the differing strengths of employees' needs for growth influence critical psychological states, which in turn influence personal and work outcomes.

In addition to job redesign, additional work-improvement techniques include quality control circles, four-day work weeks, flextime, job sharing, and job rotation. Each technique aims at reshaping the job so it is more conducive to satisfying, productive work.

KEY WORDS

anxiety	4/40 workweek	motivating potential
basic incongruity	growth need strength	score
thesis	hygiene factors	motivators
core job dimensions	job characteristics	natural work unit
critical psychological	model	quality control circle
states	job enrichment	stress
flextime	job rotation	vertical loading
frustration	job sharing	work redesign

DISCUSSION QUESTIONS

1. Why do people have trouble adjusting to work? What can managers do to ease the adjustment process?
2. Explain how the basic incongruity thesis works. How widespread is this problem? What can be done to reduce it?
3. How does stress arise on the job? What problems are caused by stress?
4. **Up Close** 6.1 reviews the problem of work-related stress at O'Hare International Airport. What recommendations would you make to reduce stress levels at the airport while maintaining efficient operations?
5. How can managers use the job characteristics model to improve work effectiveness and job satisfaction? Explain.
6. What problems do you see with the job characteristics model from a managerial standpoint?
7. Techniques such as quality control circles are simple and apparently effective. Why do you think comparatively few companies use the technique?
8. Compare the advantages and disadvantages of the four-day workweek and flextime from the employees' and management's standpoints. Which technique would you select?
9. How would you characterize the future of job redesign efforts in industry? Explain.

CASE 6.1:   Windelle Faculty Secretaries

At Uris Hall, two kinds of roles have been developed to provide direct clerical and secretarial support for faculty in the Graduate School of Business. Each floor has a number of faculty secretaries who are assigned to faculty members. These secretaries perform normal clerical support activities, including typing of correspondence, class materials, examinations, research proposals, manuscripts for articles, and so on. In addition, these individuals perform other routine clerical duties as appropriate. Secretaries do not, however, have any responsibilities concerning phone communications (or related communication) with faculty. Each floor also has a receptionist whose job is answering telephones when faculty are absent and taking messages for faculty, either over the phone or from visitors. The receptionist also may have secretarial responsibilities for a number of faculty members.[36]

PHYSICAL ARRANGEMENTS

Each of the major faculty floors (4–7) contains approximately twenty-six faculty offices all facing the outside of the building and situated around a core of cubicles. Each floor also has partitioned space allocated for clerical support and doctoral students (see Exhibit 1 for a typical floor diagram). There are at least four regular faculty secretaries per floor, usually at the ends of the floor, and one receptionist, in the small office directly opposite

EXHIBIT 1
Design of Faculty Floors

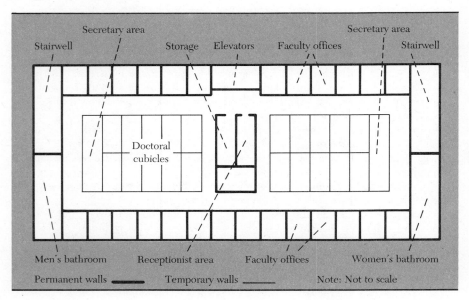

the elevator. Most of the remaining space is allocated to doctoral students as study cubicles. On some floors, however, some of the cubicle space has been utilized differently; it is allocated to extra clerical personnel, research projects, "chair secretaries" (who report to chair professors), and so on. The cubicles are all locked regularly to prevent theft.

REPORTING RELATIONSHIPS

Each secretary may be assigned to a number of faculty members. Secretaries may work for as few as three and as many as five faculty members at any time. Allocation of secretaries to faculty members is made on the basis of expected work load determined by various factors (previous faculty productivity, existence of other support in the form of funded research clerical staff, leave status, and the like). No formal procedures exist for secretaries to make decisions among the potentially conflicting demands of different faculty members other than the rule that class-related work takes priority over other types of work.

Although secretaries are assigned to work with faculty members, they do not formally report to faculty within the hierarchy. All faculty clerical personnel (with the exception of those on outside funding or chair secretaries) report directly to the manager of staff operations. (See Exhibit 2 for an organizational chart.) The manager of staff operations has direct supervisory authority over the secretaries and receptionists and makes determinations in areas such as hiring and firing, disciplinary activities, job assignments, promotion, and pay. Faculty who want to affect any of these areas with regard to the clerical personnel reporting to them must work through the manager.

WORKING ARRANGEMENTS

Over the years, a number of working arrangements have developed. The rule exists that the receptionist's desk must be covered at all times because of the heavy volume of phone calls coming for faculty members who frequently may be absent. Thus, whenever the receptionist needs to leave the desk (to take a break, to go to the bathroom, or to go to lunch), he or she must arrange with one of the other secretaries to cover the desk for that time. On most floors a rotation schedule has been developed so that secretaries share the coverage of the receptionist position on an equitable basis.

SYMPTOMS

The current system of job design and organization has been in place, with a few minor modifications, for a number of years. There are varying opinions on the effectiveness of the structure. Some feel that it works effectively, given limited resources of space, budget, and personnel. Others feel that the system is cumbersome and overly rigid. Secretaries and receptionists themselves express varying degrees of satisfaction with the structure. It should be noted, however, that turnover in these positions has been relatively high, and that on some floors the receptionist job in particular may have turned over as many as four or five times within a year. Additional data on the perceptions of job holders is in Exhibit 3, which summarizes responses to the *Job Diagnostic Survey* (Hackman and Oldham, 1975) for a nonrandom sample of employees in these jobs. Typical responses are given in Exhibit 4.

EXHIBIT 2
Organizational Structure for Clerical Support

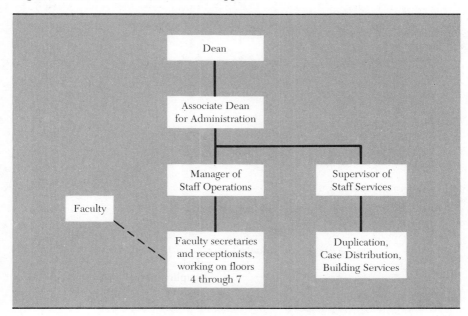

CONSTRAINTS ON REDESIGN

Any structural or technological redesign must be done within some general constraints. First, no additional secretaries can be hired. Assume approximately 3.5 faculty members to each secretary. Also assume that competing uses of space (research projects, doctoral cubicles) will continue unchanged; the proportion of space allocated to these activities should remain constant. However, changes can be made in any temporary partitions, including those in the doctoral cubicles. Changes can also be made in job assignments, reporting relationships, routines, responsibilities, and so on.

EXHIBIT 3
Job Diagnostic Survey Data*

Survey scales	Secretaries	Receptionists
Job dimensions		
Skill variety	2.3	1.0
Task identity	5.3	5.0
Task significance	2.7	3.7
Autonomy	3.8	1.0
Feedback from the job	4.7	2.0
Feedback from agents	4.1	2.0
Dealing with others	3.8	5.7
Experienced psychological states		
Meaningfulness of work	2.6	2.3
Responsibility for work	5.1	4.5
Knowledge of results	4.0	4.0
Affective responses to job		
General satisfaction	3.5	1.0
Internal work motivation	5.1	2.3
Specific satisfactions		
Pay satisfaction	2.8	1.0
Security satisfaction	5.5	2.5
Social satisfaction	5.4	1.3
Supervisory satisfaction	5.2	1.3
Growth satisfaction	2.9	1.0
Individual growth need strength	6.4	7.0
Motivating Potential Score (MPS)	61.32	6.5

*Based on a nonrandom sample of staff from different floors. Numbers in each job are not included to protect confidentiality.

SOURCE: J. Richard Hackman and Greg R. Oldham, "Development of the Job Diagnostic Survey," *Journal of Applied Psychology, 60,* pp. 159–170.

EXHIBIT 4

Means of Job Dimensions by Equal Employment Opportunity Commission (EEOC) Categories

Job dimension	EEOC job categories								
	Overall sample	Administrators	Professionals	Technicians	Protective services	Paraprofessionals	Office, clerical	Skilled craft	Maintenance, service
Skill variety	5.18	5.98	5.84	5.33	5.83	5.05	4.47	5.06	4.23
Task identity	3.09	5.42	5.30	5.18	4.58	5.11	4.89	5.15	5.12
Task significance	6.06	6.26	6.22	5.94	6.43	6.20	5.90	5.78	5.87
Autonomy	5.04	5.60	5.50	5.20	4.97	4.89	4.75	4.85	4.59
Feedback from job	5.12	5.39	5.25	5.22	4.92	4.83	5.13	5.14	4.92
Feedback from agents	4.01	4.58	4.31	3.80	4.07	4.02	3.90	3.68	3.70
Dealing with others	5.68	6.29	6.05	5.70	6.13	5.95	5.36	5.09	5.14
Experienced meaningfulness of work	5.68	6.08	5.86	5.69	5.95	5.46	5.47	5.50	5.36
Experienced responsibility for work	5.67	6.10	5.89	5.63	5.52	5.52	5.73	5.42	5.34
Knowledge of results	5.40	5.52	5.32	5.46	5.21	5.06	5.53	5.48	5.40
Internal work motivation	5.64	5.96	5.86	5.66	5.68	5.48	5.62	5.42	5.33
Motivating Potential Score (MPS)	140	178	167	149	137	129	124	133	115
N	3059	368	477	380	352	159	582	287	427

SOURCE: Work in the public sector. Washington, D.C. National Training and Development Service Technical Report, 1974.

CASE QUESTIONS

1. How do you interpret the results of the Job Diagnostic Survey data for secretaries? For receptionists?
2. The book presents five principles for redesigning work. Suggest how the work can be redesigned following these principles.
3. Where does growth need strength fit into the problem presented?

NOTES

1. "How Computers Remake the Manager's Job," *Business Week*, April 15, 1983, pp. 68–70.
2. S. A. Yolles, "Mental Health at Work," in A. McLean (ed.), *To Work Is Human: Mental Health and the Business Community* (New York: Macmillan, 1967).

3. W. S. Neff, *Work and Human Behavior* (New York: Atherton, 1968).
4. Chris Argyris, *Personality and Organization* (New York: Harper & Row, 1957).
5. John French, "Job Demands and Worker Health," paper presented at the 84th Annual Convention of the American Psychological Association (San Francisco: September 1976).
6. J. McGrath, "Stress and Behavior in Organizations," in M. D. Dunnette (ed.), *Handbook of Industrial and Organizational Psychology* (Chicago: Rand McNally, 1976), pp. 1351–1395.
7. Cary Cooper and Roy Payne, *Stress and Work* (London: Wiley, 1978).
8. M. Susser, "Causes of Peptic Ulcer: A Selective Epidemiologic Review," *Journal of Chronic Diseases*, 20 (1967); and S. Cobb, *The Frequency of Rheumatic Diseases* (Cambridge, MA: Harvard University Press, 1971).
9. A. Kornhauser, *Mental Health of the Industrial Worker*, (New York: Wiley, 1965).
10. A. Kornhauser, *Mental Health*, p. 225.
11. Dan Gowler and Karen Legge (eds.), *Managerial Stress*, (London: Wiley, 1975).
12. Lyman W. Porter and Richard M. Steers, "Organizational, Work, and Personal Factors in Employee Turnover and Absenteeism," *Psychological Bulletin*, 80 (1973): pp. 151–176.
13. J. D. Kearns, *Stress in Industry* (London: Priory Press, 1973).
14. Department of Health, Education, and Welfare, *Work in America* (Cambridge, MA: MIT Press, 1973), p. 85.
15. Special Action Office for Drug Abuse Prevention, Executive Office of the President, cited in Department of Health, Education and Welfare, *Work in America* (Cambridge, MA: MIT Press, 1973), p. 87.
16. D. Martindale, "Sweaty Palms in the Control Tower," *Psychology Today*, February 1977, pp. 71–73; and "The Constant Quest for Safety," *Time*, April 11, 1977.
17. Frederick Taylor, *The Principles of Scientific Management*, (New York: Harper & Row, 1911).
18. Frederick Taylor, *The Principles of Scientific Management*, p. 59.
19. H. M. Vernon, *On the Extent and Effects of Variety in Repetitive Work* (London: Industrial Fatigue Research Board, Report #26, Her Majesty's Stationary Office, 1924).
20. Frederick Herzberg, B. Mausner, and B. Snyderman, *The Motivation to Work* (New York: Wiley, 1959).
21. J. Richard Hackman and Greg Oldham, "Motivation Through the Design of Work: Test of a Theory," *Organizational Behavior and Human Performance*, 16 (1976), pp. 250–279.
22. J. Richard Hackman and Greg Oldham, "Motivation Through the Design of Work."
23. J. Richard Hackman, "Work Design," in J. R. Hackman and J. L. Suttle (eds.), *Improving Life at Work* (Santa Monica, CA: Goodyear, 1976), p. 129.
24. J. Richard Hackman and Greg Oldham, "Motivation Through the Design of Work."
25. J. Richard Hackman, "Work Design."
26. J. Richard Hackman, Gred Oldham, R. Janson, and K. Purdy, "A New Strategy for Job Enrichment," *California Management Review*, 17; (1975), pp. 57–71.
27. L. J. Hudspeth, quoted in *Newsweek*, September 8, 1980, p. 59.
28. L. J. Hudspeth, p. 59.
29. J. M. Juran, "Japanese and Western Quality—A Contrast," *Quality Progress*, December, 1978.
30. Paul Dickson, *The Future of the Workplace* (New York: Weybright and Talley, 1975).
31. Paul Dickson, *The Future of the Workplace*.
32. "Workers Love Four-Day Week," *Eugene Register-Guard*, July 22, 1984, p. 4C.
33. "Workers Love Four-Day Week."
34. Paul Dickson, *The Future of the Workplace*.
35. Robert Golembiewski and C. W. Proehl, "A Survey of the Empirical Literature on Flexible Workhours: Character and Consequences of a Major Innovation," *Academy of Management Review*, 3 (1978), pp. 837–855.
36. D. Nadler, M. Tushman, and N. Hatvany, *Managing Organizations: Readings and Cases* (Boston: Little, Brown, 1982), pp. 492–496.

7 Work Groups

T he attitudes and behavior of groups in work organizations
are not to be ignored. Consider the example of Anne
Burford, former administrator of the U.S. Environmental Protection Agency.
When Burford, in response to White House directives, steered the EPA toward
a less proactive stance on environmental protection, many of the civil servants
surrounding her were quick to object. Her response to their "insubordination"
was to crack down on those not on her "team." Career employees began leaking
damaging stories of mismanagement, political favors, and employee "hit lists"
to congressional committees and the media. In the end, the leaks helped lead to
the departure of Burford and a dozen political appointees. Burford had
committed one of the biggest mistakes in public management: she had taken a
political position strongly opposed by her subordinates and had challenged the
forces of the civil service. She lost.[1]

Research on group processes in organizations demonstrates that individual
behavior is highly influenced by co-workers in work groups. For instance,
many individuals choose to work in groups even though they earn less than they
would if they worked alone. Other individuals remain on undesirable jobs
because they work with friends, even though better jobs are available
elsewhere. Hackman and Morris concluded, "There is substantial agreement
among researchers and observers of small task groups that something important happens in group interaction which can affect performance outcomes.
There is little agreement about just what that "something" is—whether it is
more likely to enhance or depress group effectiveness, and how it can be
monitored, analyzed, and altered."[2]

To gain a clearer understanding of this "something," we must first consider
in detail what we mean by a group, how groups are formed, and how groups
differ. Then we must ask what managers can do to make work groups more
effective—the purpose of this chapter.

RELEVANCE OF WORK GROUPS FOR MANAGERS

We should study groups for several reasons. First, groups are a fact of
organizational life. They are the building blocks of organizations. A knowledge
of organizational behavior would be incomplete without a thorough understanding of basic group processes in the work place.

All organizations contain a variety of groups, each with different members and goals. A knowledge of the various types of groups helps managers recognize and deal with diversity of purpose. Moreover, knowing why people join groups (e.g., why some employees unionize while others do not) can be useful.

Groups structure themselves in many ways. In designing a work group or assigning employees to various tasks in work groups, managers need to know how group size influences behavior and attitudes, how managerial behavior influences the development of group norms and roles, and how these norms and roles constrain behavior.

Power relationships within and between groups can influence who does what for whom. Status relationships determine one's standing in a particular group or organization. Again, an understanding of these relationships can help managers understand and deal with interpersonal dynamics in group situations.

Group cohesiveness helps determine the level of group effort and performance. Managers need to know how they can use group cohesiveness, under what conditions cohesive groups will facilitate or hinder organizational goal attainment.

Managers need to know what group effectiveness is and how it can be promoted.

WORK GROUPS: AN INTRODUCTION

What Is a Group?

The literature on group dynamics contains many definitions of work groups. We might conceive of a group in terms of *perceptions*—if individuals see themselves as a group, then a group exists.[3] Or we can view a group in *structural* terms. For instance, McDavid and Harari define a group as "an organized system of two or more individuals who are interrelated so that the system performs some function, has a standard set of role relationships among its members, and has a set of norms that regulate the function of the group and each of its members."[4] Groups can also be defined in *motivational* terms as "a collection of individuals whose existence as a collection is rewarding to the individuals."[5] Finally, a group can be viewed with regard to *interpersonal interaction*, the degree to which members communicate and interact with one another over time."[6]

Building on these approaches to defining groups, we shall define a **group** as a collection of individuals who share a set of norms or standard of behavior, who generally have differentiated roles or parts to play, and who interact to pursue common goals. This definition leads us to focus on two major aspects of groups: group structure and group processes. We shall first examine how groups structure themselves for protection and task accomplishment. Then we shall discuss how they pursue effective task accomplishment.

Formal Versus Informal Groups

There are two primary types of groups: formal and informal. **Formal groups** are work units that are prescribed by an organization. Examples include sections of departments (like the accounts receivable section of the accounting department), committees, or special task forces. These groups are set up by management on a temporary or permanent basis to accomplish prescribed goals and activities.

Organizations also have many **informal groups.** These groups evolve in response to the individual and collective self-interest of its members, and are not the result of deliberate organizational design. People join informal groups because of common interests, social needs, or simply friendship. Informal groups typically develop their own norms and roles and establish unwritten rules for their members. Studies in social psychology have documented the important role of informal groups in facilitating or inhibiting performance and organizational effectiveness.[7]

An interesting aspect of group dynamics in organizations is the way informal groups work with or against formal groups. Both types of groups establish norms and roles, set goals and objectives, and demand loyalty from their members. When individuals are members of many groups—both formal and informal—they are faced with a wide array of potential conflicts that can affect their individual and collective behavior.

Origins of Group Membership

As noted above, individuals join groups for a variety of reasons.[8] In some cases they have a basic need for protection from external threats, real or imagined. These threats include the possibility of being intimidated or fired by the boss, the fear of being embarrassed in a new situation, or simply anxiety about being alone. Groups are a primary source of *security*. In addition, most individuals have relatively strong *social needs*. They need to interact with other people and develop meaningful relationships. Groups provide structured environments in which individuals can pursue such friendships.

Membership in groups can keep individuals develop *self-esteem*. People often take pride in being associated with prestigious groups, such as professors elected to membership in the National Academy of Sciences or salespersons who qualify for a "million dollar club" as a reward for sales performance.

Another reason people associate with groups is to pursue their own *economic self-interest*. Labor unions are a prime example of such a group, as are various professional and accrediting agencies, such as the American Bar Association. These organizations often attempt to limit the supply of tradespeople or professionals in order to maintain employment and salary levels.

Some groups are formed to pursue goals that are of *interest* to group members. Included here are bridge clubs, company-sponsored baseball teams, and literary clubs. By joining together, individuals can pursue group goals that are typically not feasible alone. And finally, many groups form simply as a result

of people being located in close *proximity* to one another. An example of this is
the social relationships that develop between members of a typing pool. Often
joining one group can satisfy several needs; for example, joining a company-
sponsored baseball team can satisfy social and esteem needs and help meet
group goals.

Understanding the Role of Groups in Organizations

A model for understanding the role of group processes in organizational
behavior is shown in Exhibit 7.1. Group structure is influenced by two primary
types of factors. The first, called **personal factors,** includes the attitudes and
abilities individuals bring to the work situation, as well as their individual
motives. Personality and other background factors can also be included here.
These variables were discussed earlier in this book. Simply put, the way groups
structure themselves is a function of their members' personal characteristics.

A second primary influence on group structure is the **situational factors** that
must be taken into account. Situational factors include the type of group under
consideration, the reasons people chose to join the group, the motives or
objectives of the group, and the stage of group development. Situational factors
set the conditions under which group structure develops.

The remainder of this chapter will focus on **group structure**—the way group
members organize themselves for task accomplishment. In subsequent chapters we shall discuss **group processes**—what groups actually do. Topics will
include communication, conflict, decision making, power and politics, and
leadership. According to the model, group processes are influenced by
personal factors, situational factors, and group structure. Finally, tangible
outcomes result from the existence of most groups, including individual
attitudes and individual and group performance.

WORK GROUP STRUCTURE

In this section we shall examine several variables that make one group different
from another: work group size, work group norms, role relationships, status
relationships, and group cohesiveness.

Work Group Size

Work groups come in many sizes. Classical management theorists wasted
considerable time and effort attempting to identify the ideal size for various
types of work groups. While there is no right number of people for most group
activities, research suggests what happens as group size increases. At least five
size-outcome relationships are relevant. These involve the relation of group
size to group interaction patterns, satisfaction, productivity, absenteeism, and
turnover.[9]

A series of classic studies begun by Bales and Borgatta examined variations in
group interaction patterns as a result of changes in group size.[10] Using a

EXHIBIT 7.1

A General Framework for Analyzing Groups in Organizations

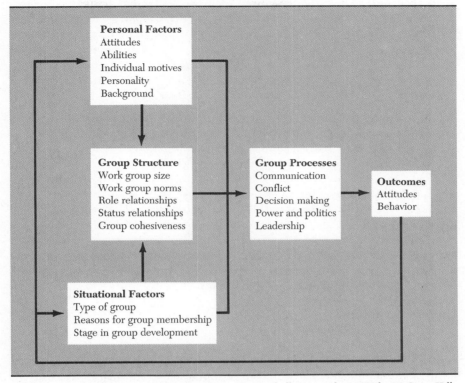

SOURCE: From *People in Organizations* by Terence R. Mitchell. Copyright ©1982 by McGraw-Hill, Inc. Reprinted by permission.

technique called *interaction process analysis,* which records who says what to whom, Bales and his colleagues found that smaller groups (two to four persons) typically exhibited greater tension, agreement, and opinion seeking, while larger groups (five to seven persons) showed more tension release and giving of suggestions and information. Harmony seemed crucial in smaller groups, and people had more time to develop their thoughts and opinions. On the other hand, individuals in larger groups seemed more direct because of the increased competition for time and attention.

Increases in work group size appear to be inversely related to *satisfaction,* although the relationship is not strong.[11] That is, people working in smaller work units or departments report higher levels of satisfaction than those in larger units. This finding is not surprising in view of the greater attention one receives in smaller groups and the greater importance one feels. No clear relationship has been found between group size and *productivity* unless the type of task being performed is taken into consideration.[12] Mitchell explains:

Think of a task where each new member adds a new independent amount of productivity (certain piece-rate jobs might fit here). If we add more people, we will add more productivity. . . . On the other hand, there are tasks where everyone works together and pools their resources. With each new person the added increment of new skills or knowledge decreases. After a while increases in size will fail to add much to the group except coordination and motivation problems. Large groups will perform less well than small groups. The relationship between group size and productivity will therefore depend on the type of task that needs to be done. [13]

Other studies have found that increases in work group size and *absenteeism* are moderately related among blue-collar workers, but unrelated for white-collar workers. [14] One explanation is that increased work group size leads to lower group cohesiveness, higher task specialization, and poorer communication. As a result, it becomes more difficult to satisfy higher-order needs on the job, and job attendance becomes less appealing. In view of the increased job autonomy and control of white-collar workers compared to blue-collar, this explanation is more relevant for the latter group. White-collar workers typically have more avenues for need satisfaction. Similar findings exist for employee *turnover*. Turnover rates are higher in larger groups. [15] Again, since larger groups make need satisfaction more difficult, there may be less reason for individuals to remain with the organization.

Work Group Norms

The concept of work group norms is a complex one that has been studied for several decades. In this section we shall highlight several essential aspects of norms and examine how they relate to people at work. We shall consider group norms' development, characteristics, pattern and intensity, and behavioral consequences.

A **norm** is a standard that is shared by group members and that regulates member behavior. McGrath notes that group norms include a frame of reference for viewing relevant objects in the environment, prescribed attitudes and behaviors toward those objects, feelings about the correctness of the attitudes and about violators of norms, and positive and negative sanctions by which acceptable behavior is rewarded and unacceptable behavior is punished by group members. [16] For example, in a typical classroom situation students develop a norm against speaking up in class too often. They believe that highly visible students improve their grades at the expense of others, and create a norm that will prevent this.

Development of Group Norms   Festinger has suggested two principal reasons why norms develop. [17] First, norms provide group members with an easy frame of reference for understanding the complicated world of work. They provide readily apparent cues to what is right and wrong. Union members are often cautioned not to cooperate with management, for example, because questionable motives are attributed to management. Second, norms standardize the action that is needed for the group to survive and reach its goals. When all members behave in a like manner (toward a supervisor, for example), group cohesiveness is enhanced and group goals are facilitated.

Characteristics of Group Norms   Hackman suggests that norms have five major characteristics.[18] First, they summarize and simplify the processes by which groups regularize member behavior. Second, they apply only to behavior, not to thoughts and feelings. Private acceptance of group norms is unnecessary, only public compliance.

Third, norms are generally developed only for behaviors that group members consider important. In addition, norms usually develop gradually, but the process can be quickened if members wish. For example, norms can be quickly developed if a threat to group integrity arises. Finally, not all norms apply to all members. Some norms apply only to initiates (like getting the coffee), while others are based on sex, race, or economic class.

Pattern and Intensity of Group Norms   A better appreciation of work group norms can be achieved by considering two factors that distinguish various norms—pattern and intensity. **Pattern** refers to behaviors that are acceptable or unacceptable, while **intensity** refers to the degree to which these behaviors are approved or disapproved. Pattern and intensity are incorporated into Jackson's Return Potential Model (RPM) of group norms.[19]

The RPM model has a variety of applications in organizational settings. One recent study used the model to measure the norms people have about co-workers' leaving the organization.[20] Using the RPM model allows us to examine a norm's pattern and intensity and thus better understanding how it affects behavior in work groups.

Effects of Norms on Behavior   Experiments carried out by Solomon Asch help explain the effects of group norms on individual behavior.[21] Asch created a laboratory situation in which a naive subject was placed in a room with several confederates. Each person was asked to compare the length of a line against three other lines. Confederates, who spoke first, had all been instructed to identify line C as the closest in length, even though line A was clearly the correct answer. In over one third of the trials, the naive subjects denied the evidence of their own senses and agreed with the answers given by the confederates. In other words, a large percentage of individuals chose to go along with the group rather than express a conflicting opinion, even though they knew their own answer was correct.

This basic principle can be seen in the work place in a variety of ways. For example, a group norm about a reasonable level of effort on a job can have a serious effect on performance, especially when groups are highly cohesive and exert strong pressures to conform. Group norms are a force managers must acknowledge when seeking to optimize motivation and performance at work.

UP CLOSE 7.1:   Pemex

A recent example of the power of group norms in human behavior comes from Pemex, Mexico's state-owned oil company. When Mexican President Miguel de la Madrid took office in 1983, he set as a primary goal a "moral revolution" of Mexican society. Petroleos Mexicanos (Pemex) was identified as a key to that goal. Pemex had a reputation for inefficiency and corruption, and to the extent de la Madrid could reduce such practices, an example might be set for other corporations. [22]

At the heart of the problem was the primary union at Pemex, the Mexican Oil Worker's Union. This was the largest and most powerful union in the country, and its members could generate 75 percent of Mexico's foreign exchange. Members of the union had enjoyed kickbacks and other benefits for decades. Clear norms existed concerning limited work output and rewards. For example, the union could award contracts covering 40 percent of the company's service and maintenance work to subcontractors. Union leaders channeled those contracts to their friends and relatives—and collected a 2 percent fee from the company for overseeing the contract awards.

Efforts to change such practices (a move to reduce the work force and increase performance standards) led to threats to "dry up the oil fields." Clearly, de la Madrid has had work cut out for him in the challenge to shift norms and work practices away from graft and inefficiency. ■

Role Processes

For groups to accomplish their goals and maintain their norms, they must differentiate between the activities of their members. One or more members assume leadership positions, others carry out the major work of the group, and still others serve as "go-fers." This specialization of activities is commonly referred to as **role differentiation.** More specifically, a **role** is an expected behavior pattern assigned or attributed to a particular position that defines individuals' responsibilities on behalf of the group.

The best way to understand the nature of roles is to examine a **role episode,** which demonstrates how a particular role is learned and acted upon. As can be seen in Exhibit 7.2, a role episode begins with group members' expectations about what a person should be doing in a particular position (Stage 1). These expectations are communicated to the individual (Stage 2), who then perceives them (Stage 3). Finally, the individual acts out the role-related behavior (Stage 4). In other words, Stages 1 and 2 deal with the *expected* role, while Stage 3 focuses on the *perceived* role and Stage 4 focuses on the *enacted* role.

For example, a group may decide that its newest member should get coffee for members during breaks. This role is then explained to the member, who becomes aware of his or her expected role and performs it.

Several characteristics of this role episode model should be noted. First, Stages 1 and 2 are initiated by the group and aimed at the individual, while

EXHIBIT 7.2
A Simplified Model of a Role Episode

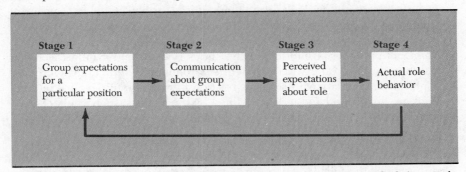

Stage 1	Stage 2	Stage 3	Stage 4
Group expectations for a particular position	Communication about group expectations	Perceived expectations about role	Actual role behavior

Adapted from D. Katz and R. Kahn, *The Social Psychology of Organizations*, 2d ed. (New York: Wiley, 1978).

Stages 3 and 4 represent of the individual's responses to the stimuli. In addition, Stages 1 and 3 represent cognitive and perceptual evaluations, while Stages 2 and 4 represent actual behaviors. The sum total of all the roles assigned to one individual is called the **role set.** A secretary, for example, may have a role set that includes typing, answering the phone, overseeing office budgets, and acting as a receptionist.

Status Systems

A fourth attribute of work groups is the existence of **status systems,** which differentiate individuals from each other based on some criteria. Parsons identifies five bases on which status differentiations are made: birth, personal characteristics, achievement, possessions, and formal authority.[23] For example, an employee may achieve high status because he is the boss's son (birth), the brightest or strongest member of the group (personal characteristics), the best performer (achievement), the richest or highest paid (possessions), or the foreman or supervisor (formal authority).

Status systems are typically found throughout organizations. Distinctions are made between blue-collar and white-collar employees, skilled tradespersons and unskilled workers, senior and junior employees, high achievers and low achievers, and popular and unpopular individuals. Scott suggests that status differentiation (and concomitant status symbols) serve four purposes in organizations:

1. *Motivation to perform.* We ascribe status to persons as rewards or incentives for performance and achievement. If high achievement is recognized as positive behavior by an organization, individuals are more willing to exert effort.
2. *Identification of rank.* Status and status symbols provide useful cues to acceptable behavior in new situations. In the military, for example, badges

of rank quickly tell members who has authority and who is to be obeyed. Similarly, in business, titles serve the same purpose.

3. *Dignification of individuals.* People are often ascribed status as a means of signifying respect that is due them. A clergyman's attire, for instance, identifies a representative of the church.

4. *Stabilization and continuity.* Finally, status systems and symbols facilitate stabilization in an otherwise turbulent environment by providing a force for continuity. Authority patterns, role relationships, and interpersonal interactions are all affected and indeed defined by the status system in effect. As a result, much ambiguity in the work situation is reduced.[24]

In organizations, status can be conferred on an individual in many ways. One of the most common is through the assignment and decoration of offices. John Dean provides the following account of status in the Nixon White House:

> *Everyone on the White House staff jockeyed for a position close to the President's ear, and even an unseasoned observer could sense minute changes in status. Success and failure could be seen in the size, decor, and location of offices. Anyone who moved into a smaller office was on the way down. If a carpenter, cabinetmaker, or wallpaper hanger was busy in someone's office, this was a sure sign he was on the rise. Every day, workmen crawled over the White House complex like ants. Movers busied themselves with the continuous shuffling of furniture from one office to another as people moved in, up, down, or out. We learned to read office changes as an index of the internal bureaucratic power struggles. The expense was irrelevant to Haldeman. . . . He once retorted when we discussed whether we should reveal such expense, "This place is a national monument, and I can't help it if the last three Presidents let it go to hell." Actually, the costs had less to do with the fitness of the White House than with the need of its occupants to see tangible evidence of their prestige.*[25]

One aspect of status systems in organizations that is worthy of note is **status incongruence.** This arises when a person is high on certain valued dimensions but low on others, or when a person's characteristics seem inappropriate for his or her job. Status incongruence exists when a college student takes a janitorial job during the summer, the president's son begins to work his way up through the organizational hierarchy (at an accelerated rate, needless to say), or a young fast-track manager is promoted to a level typically held by more senior managers.

Status incongruence can present a problem for everyone involved. Co-workers often feel hostility and jealousy toward an individual who has risen above his or her station, forcing them to acknowledge their own lack of success or achievement. There are two ways to avoid such conflict: an organization can select or promote only individuals whose characteristics are congruent with the job and work group, or it can attempt to change the values of the group.[26] Neither possibility is realistic and fair. Hence, organizations that reward high achievement (instead of seniority) must accept some conflict resulting from status incongruence.

Group Cohesiveness

The final aspect of groups to be discussed here is group cohesiveness. We have all come in contact with groups whose members feel a high degree of group spirit. In such groups, members are concerned about the welfare of other group members, as well as that of the group as a whole. **Group cohesiveness** may be defined as the extent to which individual members of a group are motivated to remain in the group. According to Shaw, "members of highly cohesive groups are more energetic in group activities, they are less likely to be absent from group meetings, they are happy when the group succeeds and sad when it fails, etc., whereas members of less cohesive groups are less concerned about the group's activities."[27]

Determinants of Group Cohesiveness   Cartwright and Zander developed a model to determine why people join groups and develop high group cohesiveness (see Exhibit 7.3).[28] At least four factors appear to influence the extent to which cohesiveness develops. A primary influence on group cohesiveness is individuals' motive bases, such as their needs for affiliation, recognition, and security. Second, groups have incentive properties, which include members' goals, programs, characteristics, styles of operation, prestige, and other significant properties. Common incentives support group cohesiveness. Third, members feel to varying degrees that group membership and involvement will help them achieve personal goals. Finally, members compare the cost-benefit ratio of membership and involvement in one group against alternative paths to goal attainment.

A variety of interesting implications follow from this formulation. For instance, Cartwright and Zander explain:

> If, for example, a person joins a group with the expectation of fulfilling certain personal needs, but these change while he is a member, the attractiveness of the group will decrease for him unless the group is able to fulfill the new needs equally well or better. It is possible, of course, for an individual's needs to be modified through experience in the group. Indeed, some groups deliberately attempt to change the needs of their members. Sometimes such groups "lure" members into joining by promising certain inducements, and then work on the members to develop other needs and interests that are considered more important to the group.[29]

The exact way these processes occur is not known, but managers must recognize their existence if they are to understand group dynamics in organizations.

Consequences of Group Cohesiveness   The second aspect of group cohesiveness that managers must understand is their consequences. As shown in Exhibit 7.3, several consequences can be identified. The first and most obvious is maintenance of membership. If the group is significantly more attractive than alternative groups, individuals are unlikely to voluntarily leave it and turnover rates should be low.

EXHIBIT 7.3
Determinants and Consequences of Group Cohesiveness

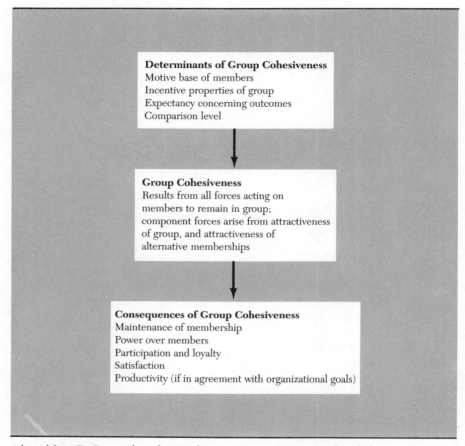

Determinants of Group Cohesiveness
Motive base of members
Incentive properties of group
Expectancy concerning outcomes
Comparison level

Group Cohesiveness
Results from all forces acting on
members to remain in group;
component forces arise from attractiveness
of group, and attractiveness of
alternative memberships

Consequences of Group Cohesiveness
Maintenance of membership
Power over members
Participation and loyalty
Satisfaction
Productivity (if in agreement with organizational goals)

Adapted from D. Cartwright and A. Zander, *Group Dynamics: Research and Theory*, 3d ed. (New York: Harper & Row, 1968), p. 92.

In addition, high group cohesiveness typically provides the group with considerable power over group members. This is because the power of a group over members depends on the benefits members expect to receive from the group compared to what they could receive through alternate means.[30] When members believe the group will advance their personal goals, they typically submit to its will.

Third, members of highly cohesive groups tend to participate more and be more loyal. Studies have shown that as cohesiveness increases, communication among members and participation in group activities also increase, while absenteeism declines. Moreover, members of highly cohesive groups tend to be more cooperative and friendly, and generally behave in ways designed to promote integration of members.

Fourth, members of highly cohesive groups generally report high levels of satisfaction. In fact, the concept of group cohesiveness almost demands that this be the case since it is unlikely that members would remain with a group with which they were dissatisfied.

No clear relationship exists between group cohesiveness and productivity. The extent to which cohesiveness and productivity are related is moderated by the extent to which group members accept organizational goals. When cohesiveness and acceptance of organizational goals are high, performance is usually high, as well. With low cohesiveness and high goal acceptance, performance is not quite so high, but still good. Performance suffers when cohesiveness is high and goal acceptance is low because group effort is directed away from organizational goals and toward goals valued by the group. Finally, when both cohesiveness and goal acceptance are low, effort is dissipated, leading to low productivity.

UP CLOSE 7.2:   Saab Scania

The effects of group cohesiveness on employee attitudes and performance can be seen in studies carried out at the Swedish company of Saab Scania. These studies, which focused largely on job redesign, suggest that job redesign can work miracles for organizations. However, often overlooked is the fact that the most successful results were achieved before *the jobs were technologically redesigned.*

In 1969, when the engine plant of Saab Scania (a truck manufacturer) initiated its Quality of Working Life experiments, phase one addressed itself to building highly cohesive, well-integrated work teams. In two experimental groups, employees were brought into the decision-making process and asked to help the company solve its productivity and morale problems. Technical help was given to group members when requested, but work groups were largely responsible for solving their own problems.

The results of phase one—before any technical redesign of jobs—were significant. Between 1969 and 1972, unplanned work stoppages dropped from 6 to 2 percent of total time, extra work and adjustment needed to correct omissions and errors in the finished products dropped by one third, and turnover dropped from an average of 55 to 20 percent per year. Clearly, allowing employees greater involvement in problem solving led to increased cohesiveness among group members and greater commitment to group goals, which were largely compatible with those of the organization. The second phase at Saab Scania, involving redesigning the assembly techniques themselves, has yet to produce such dramatic results.[31]

DETERMINANTS OF WORK GROUP EFFECTIVENESS

We are now in a position to examine the way work groups become effective (or ineffective). To do this, we shall make use of Hackman's model of work group effectiveness, shown in Exhibit 7.4.[32] The effectiveness of a work group is influenced by environmental factors, design factors, and task-related interpersonal processes, which in turn influence intermediate criteria. These intermediate criteria then combine with the nature of work technology to determine ultimate work group effectiveness.

What Is Work Group Effectiveness?

The first question to raise in analyzing work group effectiveness is what we mean by the concept itself. According to the model presented here, effectiveness is defined by three ultimate criteria:

1. *Productive output.* The productive output of the group must meet or exceed standards of quantity and quality as defined by the organization.
2. *Personal need satisfaction.* The experience of individuals in the group serves to satisfy personal needs. That is, groups are effective if they facilitate long-range individual growth and development.

EXHIBIT 7.4
Determinants of Work-Group Effectiveness

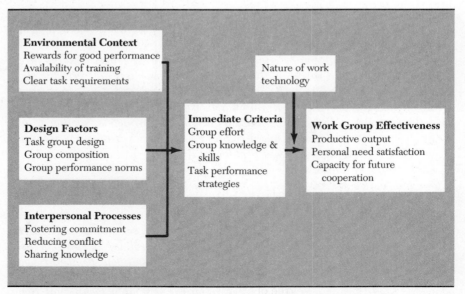

SOURCE: From *Managing Organizational Behavior* by David A. Nadler, J. Richard Hackman and Edward E. Lawler III. Copyright © 1979 by David A. Nadler, J. Richard Hackman and Edward E. Lawler III. Reprinted by permission of Little, Brown and Company.

3. *Capacity for future cooperation.* Finally, the social processes employed to complete the tasks should maintain or enhance the capacity of members to work together on subsequent tasks. If a group becomes divisive or destructive in completing its assigned tasks, its future productivity is in doubt. Hence, the effective work group avoids destructive social processes in its efforts to complete tasks.

Immediate Criteria for Work Group Effectiveness

The three intermediate criteria are as follows:

1. *Group effort.* The amount of effort group members exert toward task accomplishment.
2. *Group knowledge and skill.* The amount of knowledge and skills possessed by the group that are available for group effort and performance.
3. *Task performance strategies.* The extent to which the group's strategies for task performance (i.e., how it views and goes about solving the problem) are appropriate.

Clearly, while the relative importance of the intermediate criteria may vary with the task or situation, they significantly influence actual group performance. Without considerable effort, appropriate skills and knowledge, and a clear strategy for task completion, a work group can rarely be effective.

An important factor in determining the relative importance of each variable is the nature of work technology. The equipment and materials used in manufacture, the prescribed work procedures, and the layout of the work site can have a strong impact on the relative importance of the immediate criteria. For example, if jobs are highly routinized, individual skill or knowledge may be less important than simple effort. In a complex task such as research and development, however, effort alone will be of little help without concomitant skills and a specific performance strategy. Thus, while the relative importance of the three criteria may vary with the job technology, all should be considered in any effort to understand determinants of work group effectiveness in a particular situation.

Design Factors

The intermediate criteria of work group effectiveness are, in turn, influenced by three key design factors. First is the *design of the group task.* The way the group task is structured can have important ramifications for effectiveness. For example, if the task assigned does not challenge or motivate group members (see Chapter 6), there is little reason for group effort or commitment to follow. This is a major argument for the use of autonomous work groups.

The second important factor is the *composition of the group itself.* If the group is to exhibit a high degree of knowledge and skill, an immediate criteria, its members must be talented. A group of talented employees (however talent is defined) can significantly enhance ultimate performance.

Finally, *group norms,* discussed earlier in this chapter, must support the task performance strategies employed. Without the support of group norms, effort and subsequent performance can suffer tremendously. Taken together, these three factors facilitate or inhibit the intermediate criteria, which set the stage for task performance.

Fostering a Supportive Environment

The final part of the Hackman model of work group effectiveness emphasizes the need for a supportive work environment. Managers can foster such an environment in several ways. Suitable rewards for good performance and training programs can promote a performance orientation. Clarity of task requirements can also help. The point is that performance can be enhanced to the extent that management takes steps to eliminate obstacles from the performance environment.

In addition, management can enhance the group's interpersonal relationships. To the extent that conflict and hostility are reduced, employees should be more motivated to contribute. Solid interpersonal processes combined with positive work environment factors promote greater energy for task-related efforts.

In summary, a careful analysis of the work group effectiveness model should prove a useful exercise for those interested in truly understanding group processes and factors related to group effectiveness. In this way, the model can be of heuristic value as managers attempt to better understand organizational behavior.

UP CLOSE 7.3:   Ford Motor Company

At Ford Motor Company's Edison, New Jersey, plant, employees on the assembly line move back and forth between storage bins and the conveyor, picking up parts and installing them on freshly painted body shells that will soon become Ford Escorts and Mercury Lynxes. Each worker has about one minute for his or her task, which is highly repetitive and dull. One might expect to see the traditional foreman stalking up and down the line berating workers for omitting a bolt or failing to tighten a screw, but that doesn't happen very often.

Instead, most foremen chat with employees, solicit their input, and even encourage them to use recently installed buttons to stop the line if a defect prevents them from correctly doing their job. Indeed, this "stop concept" is one aspect of a worker participation program at Ford that has improved quality, reduced absenteeism, and lessened hostility between workers and management.

At the heart of this turnaround is Ford's Employee Involvement Program, which consists of thirteen problem-solving groups that meet once every two weeks to discuss production and quality problems. The "stop concept" resulted from one such meeting. Frequently an assembler stops the line (usually for less than a minute) so the supervisor and worker can identify the problem and decide how to resolve it. This puts pressure on the foreman, but also leads to fewer defects in the cars.

Commenting on the Employee Involvement Program, one supervisor admitted some initial difficulty accepting the fact that line workers might know more than he did. Now, he explains, "if an hourly guy brings something to me, I'll go and try it. It's surprising how much an employee can see that's wrong with a job."

What Ford has done is increase the responsibility felt by work groups to perform well. Such a move is designed to trigger the processes described above that can lead to improved group performance and attitudes. As a union official noted, "Ford has discovered that to build a good car, they've got to have harmony. Now, it's like we're all one family."[33] ■

SUMMARY

We have examined the nature and structure of work groups, which differ along such dimensions as size, norms, and roles. Despite these differences, managers can take several actions to encourage groups to be more effective. First, managers can educate themselves about the nature of groups and the functions groups perform for individuals. By understanding why individuals join groups, for example, managers can understand the motivational implications of group dynamics.

Managers should also be sensitive to group norms and the extent to which they facilitate or inhibit group and organizational performance. The potency of group norms has been clearly established. It has also been shown that company actions can increase the likelihood that norms will work to the benefit of the organization. Much of the thrust of current organizational development efforts is toward using process consultation techniques to develop group norms that are compatible with company goals.

The importance of group cohesiveness for group effectiveness was discussed. When highly cohesive groups are desirable, managers can promote their formation by showing employees how they can help each other by working together. However, group cohesiveness by itself does not guarantee increased group effectiveness. Instead, managers must show group members why they benefit from working toward organizational goals.

Finally, a model of work group effectiveness was presented to tie together the various influences as they bear on task performance. The model is designed not only to enhance understanding, but also to help in analyzing successes and failures in the task performance process.

KEY WORDS

formal group	intensity	role conflict
group cohesiveness	norm	role differentiation
group interaction	role	role episode
patterns	pattern	role overload
group processes	personal factors	role set
group structure	situational factors	status incongruence
informal groups	role ambiguity	status systems

DISCUSSION QUESTIONS

1. What functions do formal and informal groups serve in organizations?
2. Why is a knowledge of group interaction patterns useful for managers?
3. What is a group norm? How do norms influence individual behavior?
4. Describe how the return potential model works in a group setting.
5. **Up Close 7.2** described some norms at Pemex of Mexico. If you were the president, how would you change the norms to increase efficiency?
6. Give an example of a role episode. What is the importance of role processes from a managerial standpoint?
7. Is status incongruence a problem for contemporary organizations? Explain.
8. Discuss the behavioral implications of high and low group cohesiveness.
9. Describe Hackman's model of work group effectiveness. What are its implications for managers?

CASE 7.1: The Slade Company*

Ralph Porter, production manager of The Slade Company, was concerned by reports of dishonesty among some employees in the Plating Department. From reliable sources, he had learned that a few men were punching the time cards of a number of their workmates who had left early. Mr. Porter had only recently joined the Slade organization. He judged from the conversations with the previous production manager and other fellow managers that they were, in general, pleased with the overall performance of the Plating Department.

The Slade Company was a prosperous manufacturer of metal products designed for industrial application. Its manufacturing plant, located in central Michigan, employed nearly 500 workers, who were engaged in producing a large variety of clamps, inserts, knobs, and similar items. Orders for these products were usually large and on a recurrent basis. The volume of orders fluctuated in response to business conditions in the primary industries which the company served. At the time of this case, sales volume had been high for over a year. The bases upon which The Slade Company secured orders, in rank of importance, were quality, delivery, and reasonable price.

*All names have been disguised.

EXHIBIT 1   Manufacturing Organization

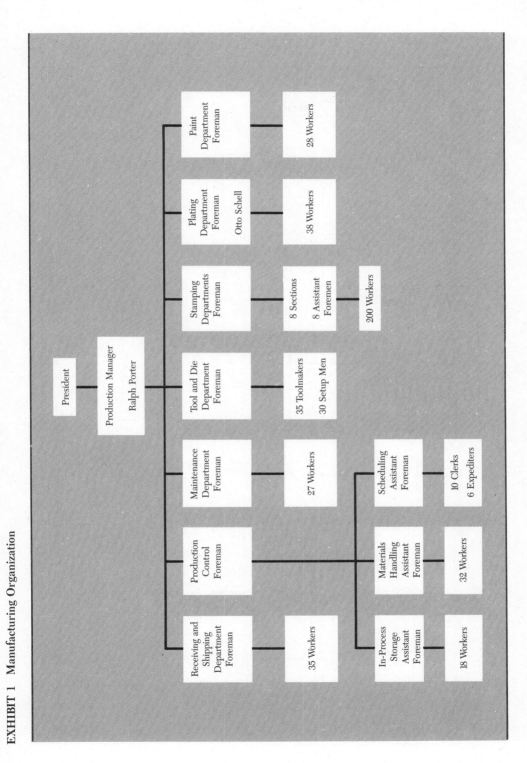

EXHIBIT 2
Plating Room Layout

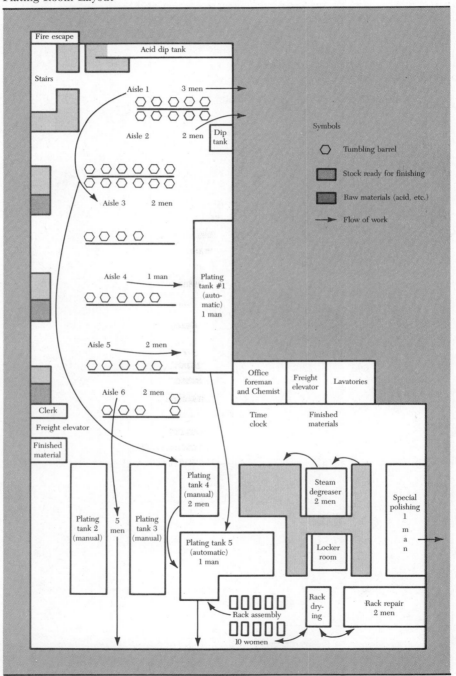

The organization of manufacturing operations at the Slade plant is shown in Exhibit 1. The departments listed there are, from left to right, approximately in the order in which material flowed through the plant. The diemaking and setup operations required the greatest degree of skill, supplied by highly paid, long-service craftsmen. The finishing departments, divided operationally and geographically between plating and painting, attracted less highly trained but relatively skilled workers, some of whom had been employed by the company for many years. The remaining operations were largely unskilled in nature and were characterized by relatively low pay and high turnover of personnel.

The plating room was the sole occupant of the top floor of the plant. Exhibit 2 shows the floor plan, the disposition of workers, and the flow of work throughout the department. Thirty-eight men and women worked in the department, plating or oxidizing the metal parts or preparing parts for the application of paint at another location in the plant. The department's work occurred in response to orders communicated by production schedules which were revised daily. Schedule revisions, caused by last-minute order increases or rush requests from customers, resulted in short-term volume fluctuations, particularly in the plating, painting, and shipping departments. Exhibit 3 outlines the activities of the various jobs, their interrelationships, and the type of work in which each specialized. Exhibit 4 rates the various types of jobs in terms of

EXHIBIT 3
Outline of Work Flow, Plating Room

Aisle 1: Worked closely with Aisle 3 in preparation of parts by barrel tumbling and acid dipping for high-quality plating in Tanks 4 and 5.* Also did a considerable quantity of highly specialized, high-quality acid-etching work not requiring further processing.

Aisle 2: Tumbled items of regular quality and design in preparation for painting. Less frequently, did oxidation dipping work of regular quality, but sometimes of special design, not requiring further processing.

Aisle 3: Worked closely with Aisle 1 on high-quality tumbling work for Tanks 4 and 5.

Aisles 4, 5: Produced regular tumbling work for Tank 1.

Aisle 6: Did high-quality tumbling work for special products plated in Tanks 2 and 3.

Tank 1: Worked on standard, automated plating of regular quality not further processed in plating room, and regular work further processed in Tank 5.

Tanks 2, 3: Produced special, high-quality plating work further plated in Tank 5.

Tank 4: Did special, high-quality plating work further plated in Tank 5.

Tank 5: Automated production of high and regular-quality, special- and regular-design plated parts sent directly to shipping.

Rack assembly: Placed parts to be plated in Tank 5 on racks.

Rack repair: Performed routine replacement and repair of racks used in Tank 5.

Polishing: Processed, by manual or semimanual methods, odd-lot special orders which were sent directly to shipping. Also, sorted and reclaimed parts rejected by inspectors in the shipping department.

Degreasing: Took incoming raw stock, processed it through caustic solution, and placed clean stock in storage ready for processing elsewhere in the plating room.

* Definition of terms: *High or regular quality:* The quality of finishes could broadly be distinguished by the thickness of plate and/or care in preparation. *Regular or special work:* The complexity of work depended on the routine or special character of design and finish specifications.

---

the technical skill, physical effort, discomfort, and training time associated with their performance.

Activities in the plating room were of three main types:

1. Acid dipping, in which parts were etched by being placed in baskets which were manually immersed and agitated in an acid solution.
2. Barrel tumbling, in which parts were roughened or smoothed by being loaded into machine-powered revolving drums containing abrasive, caustic, or corrosive solutions.
3. Plating—either manual, in which parts were loaded on racks and were immersed by hand through the plating sequence; or automatic, in which racks or baskets were manually loaded with parts, then carried by a conveyor system through the plating sequence.

Within these main divisions, there were a number of variables, such as cycle times, chemical formulas, abrasive mixtures, and so forth, which distinguished particular jobs as they have been categorized in Exhibit 3.

The work of the plating room was received in batch lots whose size averaged 1,000 pieces. The clerk moved each batch, which was accompanied by a routing slip, to its first operation. This routing slip indicated the operations to be performed and when each major operation on the batch was scheduled to be completed, so that the finished product could be shipped on time. From the accumulation of orders before him, each man was to organize his own work schedule so as to make optimal use of equipment, materials, and time. Upon completion of an order, each man moved the lot to its next work position or to the finished material location near the freight elevator.

The plating room was under the direct supervision of the foreman, Otto Schell, who worked a regular 8:00 A.M. to 5:00 P.M. day, five days a week. The foreman spent a good deal of his working time attending to maintenance and repair of equipment, procuring supplies, handling late schedule changes, and seeing that his people were at their proper work locations.

Working conditions in the plating room varied considerably. That part of the department containing the tumbling barrels and the plating machines was constantly awash, alternately with cold water, steaming acid, or caustic soda. Men working in this

EXHIBIT 4
Skill Indices by Job Group*

Jobs	Technical skill required	Physical effort required	Degree of discomfort involved	Degree of training required†
Aisle 1	1	1	1	1
Tanks 2–4	3	2	1	2
Aisles 2–6	5	1	1	5
Tank 5	1	5	7	2
Tank 1	8	5	5	7
Degreasing	9	3	7	10
Polishing	6	9	9	7
Rack assembly and repair	10	10	10	10

* Rated on scales of 1 (the greatest) to 10 (the least) in each category.
† The amount of experience required to assume complete responsibility for the job.

part of the room wore knee boots, long rubber aprons, and high-gauntlet rubber gloves. This uniform, consistent with the general atmosphere of the "wet" part of the room, was hot in the summer, cold in winter. In contrast, the remainder of the room was dry, was relatively odor-free, and provided reasonably stable temperature and humidity conditions for those who worked there.

The men and women employed in the plating room are listed in Exhibit 5. This exhibit provides a certain personal data on each department member, including a productivity-skill rating (based on subjective and objective appraisals of potential performance), as reported by the members of the department.

The pay scale implied by Exhibit 5 was low for the central Michigan area. The average starting wage for factory work in the community was about $1.25. However, working hours for the plating room were long (from 60 hours to a possible and frequently available 76 hours per week). The first 60 hours (the normal five-day week) were paid for on straight-time rates. Saturday work was paid for at time and one half; Sunday pay was calculated on a double-time basis.

As Exhibit 5 indicates, Philip Kirk, a worker in Aisle 2, provided the data for this case. After he had been a member of the department for several months, Kirk noted that certain members of the department tended to seek each other out during free time on and off the job. He then observed that these informal associations were enduring, built upon common activities and shared ideas about what was and what was not legitimate behavior in the department. His estimate of the pattern of these associations is diagrammed in Exhibit 6.

The Sarto group, so named because Tony Sarto was its most respected member and the one who acted as arbiter between the other members, was the largest in the department. The group, except for Louis Patrici, Al Bartolo, and Frank Bonzani (who spelled each other during break periods), invariably ate lunch together on the fire escape near Aisle 1. On those Saturdays and Sundays when overtime work was required, the Sarto group operated as a team, regardless of weekday work assignments, to get overtime work completed as quickly as possible. (Few department members not affiliated with either the Sarto or the Clark groups worked on weekends.) Off the job, Sarto group members often joined in parties or weekend trips. Sarto's summer camp was a frequent rendezvous.

Sarto's group was also the most cohesive one in the department in terms of its organized punch-in and punch-out system. Since the men were regularly scheduled to work from 7:00 A.M. to 7:00 P.M. weekdays, and since all supervision was removed at 5:00 P.M., it was possible almost every day to finish a "day's work" by 5:30 and leave the plant. What is more, if one man were to stay until 7:00 P.M., he could punch the time cards of a number of men and help them gain free time without pay loss. (This system operated on weekends also, at which times members of supervision were present, if at all, only for short periods.) In Sarto's group the duty of staying late rotated, so that no man did so more than once a week. In addition, the group members would punch a man in in the morning if he were unavoidably delayed. However, such a practice never occurred without prior notice from the man who expected to be late and never if the tardiness was expected to last beyond 8:00 A.M., the start of the day for the foreman.

Sarto explained the logic behind the system to Kirk:

> You know that our hourly pay rate is quite low, compared to other companies. What makes this the best place to work is the feeling of security you get. No one ever gets laid off in this department. With all the hours in the week, all the company ever has to do is shorten the work week when orders fall off. We have to tighten our belts, but we can all get along. When things are going well, as they are now, the company is only

EXHIBIT 5
Plating Room Personnel

Location	Name	Age	Marital status	Company seniority (years)	Department seniority (years)	Pay
Aisle 1	Tony Sarto	30	M	13	13	$1.50
	Pete Facelli	26	M	8	8	1.30
	Joe Lambi.	31	M	5	5	1.20
Aisle 2	Herman Schell. . .	48	S	26	26	1.45
	Philip Kirk	23	M	1	1	0.90
Aisle 3	Dom Pantaleoni . .	31	M	10	10	1.30
	Sal Maletta	32	M	12	12	1.30
Aisle 4	Bob Pearson	22	S	4	4	1.15
Aisle 5	Charlie Malone . .	44	M	22	8	1.25
	John Lacey	41	S	9	5	1.20
Aisle 6	Jim Martin	30	S	7	7	1.25
	Bill Mensch.	41	M	6	2	1.10
Tank 1	Henry LaForte. . .	38	M	14	6	1.25
Tanks 2, 3	Ralph Parker	25	S	7	7	1.20
	Ed Harding.	27	S	8	8	1.20
	George Flood . . .	22	S	5	5	1.15
	Harry Clark.	29	M	8	8	1.20
	Tom Bond.	25	S	6	6	1.20
Tank 4	Frank Bonzani . . .	27	M	9	9	1.25
	Al Bartolo	24	M	6	6	1.25
Tank 5	Louis Patrici	47	S	14	14	1.45
Rack assembly	10 women	30–40	9M, 1S	10 (av.)	10 (av.)	1.05
Rack	Will Partridge . . .	57	M	14	2	1.20
maintenance	Lloyd Swan	62	M	3	3	1.10
Degreasing	Dave Susi	45	S	1	1	1.05
	Mike Maher	41	M	4	4	1.05
Polishing	Russ Perkins	49	M	12	2	1.20
Foreman	Otto Schell	56	M	35	35	n.a.
Clerk	Bill Pierce.	32	M	10	4	1.15
Chemist	Frank Rutlage . . .	24	S	2	2	n.a.

* HS = High school, GS = Grade school.
† On a potential scale of 1 (top) to 10 (bottom), as evaluated by the men in the department.
‡Kirk was the source of data for this case and, as such, in a biased position to report accurately perceptions about himself.

interested in getting out the work. It doesn't help to get it out faster than it's really needed—so we go home a little early whenever we can. Of course, some guys abuse this sort of thing—like Herman—but others work even harder, and it averages out.

Whenever an extra order has to be pushed through, naturally I work until 7:00 P.M. So do a lot of the others. I believe that if I stay until my work is caught up and my equipment is in good shape, that's all the company wants of me. They leave us alone and expect us to produce—and we do.

Education*	Familial relationships	Productivity-skill rating†
HS	Louis Patrici, uncle; Pete Facelli, cousin	1
HS	Louis Patrici, uncle; Tony Sarto, cousin	2
2 yrs. HS		2
GS	Otto Schell, brother	8
College		—‡
1 yr. HS		2
3 yrs. HS		3
HS	Father in tool and die dept.	1
GS		7
1 yr. HS	Brother in paint dept.	7
HS		4
GS		4
HS		6
HS		4
HS		4
HS		5
HS		3
HS		4
HS		2
HS		3
2 Yrs. college	Tony Sarto, nephew; Pete Facelli, nephew	1
GS (av.)	6 with husbands in company	4 (av.)
GS		7
GS		7
HS		5
GS		6
HS		4
HS	Herman Schell, brother	3
HS		4
2 yrs. college		6

When Kirk asked Sarto if he would not rather work shorter hours at higher pay in a union shop (Slade employees were not organized), he just laughed and said: "It wouldn't come close to an even trade."

The members of Sarto's group were explicit about what constituted a fair day's work. Customarily, they cited Herman Schell, Kirk's work partner and the foreman's brother, as a man who consistently produced below that level. Kirk received an informal orientation from Herman during his first days on the job. As Herman put it:

EXHIBIT 6
Informal Groupings in the Plating Room

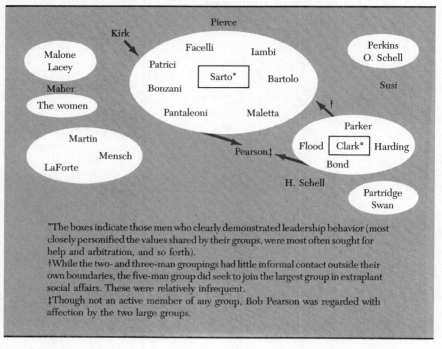

*The boxes indicate those men who clearly demonstrated leadership behavior (most closely personified the values shared by their groups, were most often sought for help and arbitration, and so forth).

†While the two- and three-man groupings had little informal contact outside their own boundaries, the five-man group did seek to join the largest group in extraplant social affairs. These were relatively infrequent.

‡Though not an active member of any group, Bob Pearson was regarded with affection by the two large groups.

I've worked at this job for a good many years, and I expect to stay here a good many more. You're just starting out, and you don't know which end is up yet. We spend a lot of time in here; and no matter how hard we work, the pile of work never goes down. There's always more to take its place. And I think you've found out by now that this isn't light work. You can wear yourself out fast if you're not smart. Look at Pearson up in Aisle 4. There's a kid who's just going to burn himself out. He won't last long. If he thinks he's going to get somewhere working like that, he's nuts. They'll give him all the work he can take. He makes it tough on everybody else and on himself, too.

Kirk reported further on his observations of the department.

As nearly as I could tell, two things seemed to determine whether or not Sarto's group or any others came in for weekend work on Saturday or Sunday. It seemed usually to be caused by rush orders that were received late in the week, although I suspect it was sometimes caused by the men having spent insufficient time on the job during the previous week.

Tony and his group couldn't understand Herman. While Herman arrived late, Tony was always half an hour early. If there was a push to get out an extra amount of work, almost everyone but Herman would work that much harder. Herman never worked overtime on weekends, while Tony's group and the men on the manual tanks almost always did. When the first exploratory time study of the department was made, no one in the aisles slowed down, except Herman, with the possible exception, to a lesser degree, of Charlie Malone. I did hear that the men in the dry end of the room slowed down so much you could hardly see them move; but we had little to do with them, anyway. While the men I knew best seemed to find a rather full life in their work, Herman never really got involved. No wonder they couldn't understand each other.

There was quite a different feeling about Bobby Pearson. Without the slightest doubt, Bob worked harder than anyone else in the room. Because of the tremendous variety of work produced, it was hard to make output comparisons, but I'm sure I wouldn't be far wrong in saying that Bob put out twice as much as Herman and 50 percent more than almost anyone else in the aisles. No one but Herman and a few old-timers at the dry end ever criticized Bobby for his efforts. Tony and his group seemed to feel a distant affection for Bob, but the only contact they or anyone else had with him consisted of brief greetings.

To the men in Tony's group the most severe penalty that could be inflicted on a man was exclusion. This they did to both Pearson and Herman. Pearson, however, was tolerated; Herman was not. Evidently, Herman felt his exclusion keenly, though he answered it with derision and aggression. Herman kept up a steady stream of stories concerning his attempts to gain acceptance outside the company. He wrote popular music which was always rejected by publishers. He attempted to join several social and athletic clubs, mostly without success. His favorite pastime was fishing. He told me that fishermen were friendly, and he enjoyed meeting new people whenever he went fishing. But he was particularly quick to explain that he preferred to keep his distance from the men in the department.

Tony's group emphasized more than just quantity in judging a man's work. Among them had grown a confidence that they could master and even improve upon any known finishing technique. Tony himself symbolized this skill. Before him, Tony's father had operated Aisle 1 and had trained Tony to take his place. Tony in his turn was training his cousin Pete. When a new finishing problem arose from a change in customer specifications, the foreman, the department chemist, or any of the men directly involved would come to Tony for help, and Tony would give it willingly. For example, when a part with a special plastic embossing was designed, Tony was the only one who could discover how to treat the metal without damaging the plastic. To a lesser degree, the other members of the group were also inventive about the problems which arose in their own sections.

Herman, for his part, talked incessantly about his feats in design and finish creations. As far as I could tell during the year I worked in the department, the objects of these stories were obsolete or of minor importance. What's more, I never saw any department member seek Herman's help.

Willingness to be of help was a trait Sarto's group prized. The most valued help of all was of a personal kind, though work help was also important. The members of Sarto's group were constantly lending and borrowing money, cars, clothing, and tools among themselves and, less frequently, with other members of the department. Their daily lunch bag procedure typified the "common property" feeling among them. Everyone's lunch was opened and added to a common pile, from which each member of the group chose his meal.

On the other hand, Herman refused to help others in any way. He never left his aisle to aid those near him who were in the midst of a rush of work or a machine failure, though this was customary throughout most of the department. I can distinctly recall the picture of Herman leaning on the hot and cold water faucets which were located directly above each tumbling barrel. He would stand gazing into the tumbling pieces for hours. To the passing, casual visitor, he looked busy; and as he told me, that's just what he wanted. He, of course, expected me to act this same way, and it was this enforced boredom that I found virtually intolerable.

More than this, Herman took no responsibility for breaking in his assigned helpers as they first entered the department, or thereafter. He had had four helpers in the space of little more than a year. Each had asked for a transfer to another department, publicly citing the work as cause, privately blaming Herman. Tony was the one who taught me the ropes when I first entered the department.

The men who congregated around Harry Clark tended to talk like and copy the behavior of the Sarto group, though they never approached the degree of inventive skill or the amount of helping activities that Tony's group did. They sought outside social contact with the Sarto group; and several times a year, the two groups went "on the town" together. Clark's group did maintain a high level of performance in the volume of work they turned out.

The remainder of the people in the department stayed pretty much to themselves or associated in pairs or triplets. None of these people were as inventive, as helpful, or as productive as Sarto's or Clark's groups, but most of them gave verbal support to the same values as those groups held.

The distinction between the two organized groups and the rest of the department was clearest in the punching-out routine. The women could not work past 3:00 P.M., so they were not involved. Malone and Lacey, Partridge and Swan, and Martin, La Forte, and Mensch arranged within their small groups for punch-outs, or they remained beyond 5:00 P.M. and slept or read when they finished their work. Perkins and Pierce went home when the foreman did. Herman Schell, Susi, and Maher had no punch-out organization to rely upon. Susi and Maher invariably stayed in the department until 7:00 P.M. Herman was reported to have established an arrangement with Partridge whereby the latter punched Herman out for a fee. Such a practice was unthinkable from the point of view of Sarto's group. It evidently did not occur often because Herman usually went to sleep behind piles of work when his brother left or, particularly during the fishing season, punched himself out early. He constantly railed against the dishonesty of other men in the department, yet urged me to punch him out on several "emergency occasions."

Just before I left The Slade Company to return to school after 14 months on the job, I had a casual conversation with Mr. Porter, the production manager, in which he asked me how I had enjoyed my experience with the organization. During the conversation, I learned that he knew of the punch-out system in the Plating Department. What's more, he told me, he was wondering if he ought to "blow the lid off the whole mess."

CASE QUESTIONS

1. Identify the various groups in this case. Describe the goals, motivations, and beliefs of each group.
2. What is the central problem in the case? What are subsidiary problems? Explain using text material.
3. As a manager, what actions would you initiate to solve the problem(s)? Explain.

NOTES

1. "It's Not Very Civil in the Civil Service," *U.S. News & World Report*, August 29, 1983, pp. 53–54.
2. J. Richard Hackman and C. G. Morris, "Group Interaction Process and Group Performance Effectiveness: A Review and Proposed Integration," in L. Berkowitz (ed.), *Advances in Experimental Social Psychology*, (New York: Academic Press, 1975), p. 49.

3. R. F. Bales, *Interaction Process Analysis: A Method for the Study of Small Groups* (Cambridge, MA: Addison-Wesley, 1950).

4. J. McDavid and M. Harari, *Social Psychology: Individuals, Groups, Societies* (New York: Harper & Row, 1968), p. 237.

5. B. M. Bass, *Leadership, Psychology and Organizational Behavior* (New York: Harper & Row, 1960), p. 39.

6. George Homans, *The Human Group* (New York: Harcourt, Brace, & World, 1950).

7. Marvin Shaw, *Group Dynamics: The Psychology of Small Group Behavior* (New York: McGraw-Hill, 1976).

8. C. Kemp, *Perspectives on Group Processes* (Boston: Houghton Mifflin, 1970).

9. Larry Cummings and Chris Berger, "Organization Structure: How Does It Influence Attitudes and Performance?" *Organizational Dynamics*, 5 (1976), pp. 34–49.

10. R. F. Bales and E. F. Borgatta, "Size of Group as a Factor in the Interaction Profile," in A. P. Hare, E. F. Borgatta, and R. F. Bales (eds.), *Small Groups* (New York: Knopf, 1956).

11. Lyman W. Porter and Edward E. Lawler III, "Properties of Organization Structure in Relation to Job Attitudes and Job Behavior," *Psychological Bulletin*, 64 (1965), pp. 23–51.

12. Larry Cummings and Chris Berger, "Organization Structure."

13. Terrence Mitchell, *People in Organizations* (New York: McGraw-Hill, 1978), p. 188.

14. Richard M. Steers and Susan R. Rhodes, "Major Influences on Employee Attendance: A Process Model," *Psychological Bulletin*, 63 (1978), pp. 391–407.

15. Lyman W. Porter and Richard M. Steers, "Organizational, Work, and Personal Factors in Employee Turnover and Absenteeism," *Psychological Bulletin*, 80 (1973), pp. 151–176.

16. Joseph McGrath, *Social Psychology: A Brief Introduction* (New York: Holt, Rinehart & Winston, 1964).

17. Leon Festinger, "Informal Social Communication," *Psychological Review*, 57 (1950), pp. 271–282.

18. J. Richard Hackman, "Work Design," in J. R. Hackman and J. L. Suttle (eds.), *Improving Life at Work* (Santa Monica, CA: Goodyear, 1976), pp. 96–162.

19. J. M. Jackson, "Structural Characteristics of Norms," in I. D. Steiner and M. Fishbein (eds.), *Current Studies in Social Psychology* (New York: Holt, Rinehart & Winston, 1965).

20. Daniel Spencer, *The Influence of Intrasubjective Normative Expectations on Turnover Intent*, Ph.D. dissertation (Eugene, OR: Graduate School of Management, University of Oregon, 1979).

21. Solomon Asch, "Studies of Independence and Conformity: A Minority of One Against a Unanimous Majority," *Psychological Monographs*, 20 (1955) p. 416.

22. "A Powerful Union Resists the Renovation of Pemex," *Business Week*, October 17, 1983, pp. 186–198.

23. Talcott Parsons, *Essays in Sociological Theory: Pure and Applied* (New York: Free Press of Glencoe, 1949).

24. William G. Scott, *Organization Theory* (Homewood, IL: Irwin, 1967).

25. John Dean, *Blind Ambition* (New York: Simon & Schuster, 1976).

26. Terrence Mitchell, *People in Organizations.*

27. Marvin Shaw, *Group Dynamics*, p. 197.

28. Dorwin Cartwright and Alvin Zander, *Group Dynamics: Research and Theory*, 3d ed. (New York: Harper and Row, 1968).

29. Dorwin Cartwright and Alvin Zander, *Group Dynamics*, p. 96.

30. J. W. Thibaut and H. H. Kelley, *The Social Psychology of Groups* (New York: Wiley, 1959).

31. Robert Katz and Daniel Kahn, *The Social Psychology of Organizations*, 2d ed. (New York: Wiley, 1978), pp. 722–728.

32. D. A. Nadler, J. R. Hackman, and E. E. Lawler, *Managing Organizational Behavior* (Boston: Little, Brown, 1979), Chapter 8.

33. "The Old Foreman Is on the Way Out, and the New One Will Be More Important," *Business Week*, April 25, 1983, pp. 74–75.

34. D. Nadler, M. Tushman, and N. Hatvany, *Managing Organizations: Readings and Cases* (Boston: Little, Brown, 1982), pp. 497–504.

Organizations: The Macro Perspective

T he previous six chapters described individuals and groups within organizations, called the *micro* perspective. Concepts were drawn from organizational behavior for managing people within the organization. Now we will turn to the organization itself as the focus of attention. The next five chapters describe concepts about the organization as a whole, called the *macro* perspective. The macro perspective begins in the next chapter with the basic considerations of size and bureaucracy. Subsequent chapters will cover organizational technology, the external environment, organizational goals and effectiveness, and structural design. These five chapters draw from organization theory to build on the micro concepts in the previous chapters, and the chapters provide concepts for managing the entire organization.

8 Organizations: Basic Considerations

I n 1982, investment bankers and Wall Street analysts argued
that Brunswick Corporation was not healthy and should get
out of its traditional recreation business. This assessment made chief executive
Jack S. Reichert mad, and he vowed to make Brunswick a success with its
current businesses. Reichert used shock therapy to pump life into the slow-
moving bureaucratic company. He eliminated four group executive positions.
He merged four product lines—Mercury and Mariner Outboard Motors,
MerCruiser Stern Drives, and Quicksilver Boating Parts—under one management to save $5 million in overhead. He reduced corporate staff from 560 to 230
people and streamlined the hierarchy. Gone, too, are two corporate planes and
the executive dining room. A new climate has been imposed of "go ahead and
try it," to replace the previous overcautious executive decision making. All
employees are being compensated with Brunswick shares under a stock-
ownership plan. A rebate program has improved Brunswick's relations with
dealers. These moves are already bearing fruit. Mercury Marine's sales
increased 27% and earnings increased 300% in 1983. Brunswick's stock
tripled—from 9 to 28—by 1984.[1]

The purpose of this chapter is to introduce the macro perspective on
organizations and to discuss basic concepts and frameworks for understanding
organizations on the whole. Jack Reichert was concerned with the macro
perspective because he had to manage Brunswick Corporation as a complete
entity. The organizational behavior concepts covered in previous chapters are
important for management within organizations, but they are not directly
applicable to the management of an entire organization. In this chapter we will
define organizations again, explaining their basic dimensions from an organization theory perspective. We will also explore the concept of bureaucracy, as
well as the impact of large size on bureaucracy. We will close the chapter by
consolidating these ideas into a model of organizational differences with respect
to stage in the organizational life cycle. Following this chapter, the next four
chapters will describe other important aspects of the macro perspective on
organizations. Those chapters will cover the topics of organizational technology, the external environment, goals and effectiveness, and structural design.
The package of concepts in these chapters describe the perspective necessary
for the management of large organizations and provide the basis for organizational decisions like those Jack Reichert implemented at Brunswick.

RELEVANCE OF THE MACRO PERSPECTIVE FOR MANAGERS

As we described in Chapter 1, three levels of analyses can be used to describe organizations. The individual employee is the basic building block of organizations. The next level is the group, department or division, and the highest level of analyses is the organization itself. The organization is a collection of groups and departments that form the total organization.

Recall from Chapter 1 that organizations are defined as 1) social entities that are 2) goal-directed, 3) deliberately structured activity systems, with an 4) identifiable boundary.[2] Organization theory and the macro perspective are concerned with the entire organization system. Organization theory is concerned with the aggregate of people that make up the total organization and with differences across organizations.

This chapter introduces some basic concepts about the entire organization that can be used to explain, predict, and understand organizational form and activities. The study of organizations from the macro perspective provided by organization theory is important to managers for several reasons.

Organizations are a prominent feature on the social landscape. The world is made up of thousands of organizations, and thousands of new organizations are created every year. Organizations touch us every day. We are born in a hospital, are educated in a school, eat food raised on a corporate farm and sold through a supermarket chain, live and work in buildings assembled by a construction company, use identification provided from state agencies, use a telephone company and the post office for communication, join clubs such as the League of Women Voters or the Jaycees, acquire insurance from a financial institution, and spend about forty hours a week working in an organization of which we are a part.[3]

The macro approach is important as a way to understand organizations in the environment. Organization theory provides an appreciation and understanding of what happens in organizations and why. Knowledge of organizations provides information on how to deal with them, how to respond to them, how to pass laws to control them, and how to benefit from them.

Organizations exist in a variety of forms and have a number of purposes. Organizations are not all alike. Organizations vary enormously in size, ranging from a small, family-owned enterprise to a multinational conglomerate. Organizations exist for a variety of purposes, including for-profit versus not-for-profit, volunteer organizations, service organizations, and organizations designed to benefit owners or employees.

A great many problems can arise in organizations from the assumption that all organizations can be treated as similar.[4] An organization structure appropriate for a manufacturing firm will not be successful in a school system. The rules and policies appropriate to a federal government agency may not be appropriate for a municipal government. The internal management systems for a chain of restaurants may fail terribly if imposed on a bank. Understanding basic differences across organizations and the appropriate management responses to these differences is one of the major contributions organization theory makes to management.

Organizational performance ultimately rests with managers of organizations. Any number of factors can take away from an organization's performance. The factors causing performance are especially noticeable when organizations fail. Braniff Airways, Schlitz Brewing Company, International Harvester, and Air Florida experienced a range of difficulties and surprises, including abrupt changes in customer demand, government regulation, increased competitiveness, inefficient production, and difficulties with unions. Despite the variety of problems that hit organizations, the ultimate responsibility for interpreting and responding to these problems rests with management.

The specific events that influence the organization are called contingencies. **Contingency** means that one thing depends upon another thing—simply; "it depends." The appropriate organization technology, goals, or control system may be contingent upon organization size or the rate of change in the external environment. Adaptation to the external environment may be contingent upon the quality of a research department, or on competent management within the marketing department. Most concepts in organization theory pertain to contingencies. By understanding contingencies among organizational variables, managers can decide which strategies and structures are appropriate for each situation that arises. The goal of organization theory is to help managers understand the forces acting on the organization so they can answer the question, "What does it take for this organization to deal with different environments, technologies, or sizes?"

This is why organization theory—and the ensuing macro approach—is valuable. Organization theory is a way of thinking about organizations. The way of thinking about organizations is based upon patterns and regularities in organizational design and behavior. Concepts in organization theory provide a way to see and analyze organizations more accurately and deeply than one could otherwise. Organization theory helps managers define and understand basic issues that pertain to the organization as a whole. These concepts, often related to one another as contingency relationships, provide the basis for diagnosing and analyzing problems and responding to these problems with well-formulated solutions. Organization theory helps managers formulate a response to the contingencies they face. Jack Reichert knew how to solve the problems at Brunswick Corporation, by understanding contingency relationships and his organization as a whole.

DIMENSIONS OF ORGANIZATIONS

In this section we are going to define some basic dimensions that can be used to describe organizations. These characteristics are analogous to personality and physical characteristics of individuals, and they can be used to describe any organization.

Organizational dimensions fall into two categories—context and structure.[5] **Contextual dimensions** are basic organizational properties that are stable in the short run. They characterize the whole organization and its environment and represent important contingencies for organization design. Contextual dimensions are fundamental characteristics to which structural dimensions are tailored. **Structural dimensions** pertain to internal characteristics of organizations. They pertain to the structural design of organizations and can be influenced directly by management. Both contextual and structural dimensions are important to the evaluation and understanding of organizations.

Contextual Dimensions

Size is the magnitude of the organization. In organization theory, size is typically measured as the number of employees, because employees represent the magnitude of the social system. Other measures of size, such as total sales or amount of assets, also represent magnitude but along economic rather than social dimensions.

Organizational technology is the nature of the production process used in the organization. Technology includes the actions, knowledge, and machines used to change organizational inputs into organizational outputs.[6] Organizational technologies vary from simple, routine activities to highly sophisticated, continuous-process and robotic technologies.

The **environment** includes all elements outside the boundary of the organization. Important elements include competitors in the same industry, government, suppliers, the community, customers, and economic conditions. The environmental context can vary from a simple, stable environment to a multidimensional, rapidly changing environment.

Structural Dimensions

Formalization is the amount of written and formal documentation in the organization. Formal documentation includes written rules and procedures, job descriptions, regulations, and policy manuals.[7] Written documentation defines employee roles within the organization and prescribes employee behavior. Formalization is often measured by counting the amount of written documentation in policy and procedures manuals and job descriptions within the organization. Because rules and procedures provide direction and guidelines to employees, formalization represents impersonal control. When formalization is extensive, written documentation may become red tape and hinder organizational activities.

Complexity refers to the number of subparts within the organization. A complex organization has many parts that have to be interrelated and coordinated, while a simple organization may have only a few separate parts. Complexity is sometimes called differentiation, a term which refers to the extent of organizational subdivision. Complexity is typically measured along three dimensions—vertical, horizontal, and geographical.[8] **Vertical complexity** refers to the number of management levels in the hierarchy of authority. A complex organization may have ten or more levels from top to bottom, which makes communication and coordination up and down the hierarchy difficult. **Horizontal complexity** refers to the number of occupational specialties across the organization. This is measured as either the number of job titles or the number of departments that exist across the organization. **Geographical complexity** refers to the dispersion of organizational offices and personnel to multiple geographical locations. A geographically complex organization must expend additional effort to maintain communication and coordination among distant parts of the organization.

Span of control is the number of subordinates who report to a manager. The span of control in some parts of an organization can be very wide, with twenty, thirty or even forty employees. A narrow span of control would entail two or three employees reporting to a supervisor. A narrow span of control throughout the organization typically means a tall organization with more levels in the hierarchy. A narrow span of control exists because of requirements for close supervision or the personal involvement of supervisors. Close supervision is necessary when employees are not well trained or when job requirements are complex and rapidly changing.[9]

Centralization means that the authority to make decisions is at a high level in the organization. **Decentralization** means that decision authority has been delegated to middle or lower hierarchical levels. The extent of decentralization is a function of the preferences of top managers, along with other factors in the organization. Decisions made in organizations that can be decentralized include selection of goals and strategies, price of products, choice of suppliers, amount of money that can be spent on capital goods, or hiring and promotion of employees.

Professionalism is the level of education and training of employees. It is a way to measure the overall capability of personnel. Professionalism is considered high when employees require a long period of training to be job holders. Professionals in universities, engineering firms, research organizations, and hospitals require many years of university education and additional years of experience. Work on an assembly line or in a construction company usually requires no university education and only moderate job training and experience.

Personnel configuration refers to the deployment of people to the administrative, clerical, and professional staff components of the organization. Personnel configuration is measured by ratios. The **administrative ratio** is the percentage of employees devoted to top administration, and it represents the percentage of human resources allocated to administering the organization. The **clerical ratio** indicates the amount of secretarial and clerical support used to maintain formal, written documentation and communication within the organization. **Professional staff ratio** indicates the amount of specialized technical staff used in the organization. Professional staff include engineers and machine repair specialists. Sometimes an overall **indirect-to-direct ratio** of employees indicates organizational efficiency with respect to the percentage of employees engaged in direct production activities versus employees engaged in support activities.

Exhibit 8.1 summarizes the contextual and structural dimensions of organizations. These dimensions are concepts that describe organizations from a macro perspective. The characteristics of context and structure represent dimensions that can be analyzed to understand any organization. Although

EXHIBIT 8.1
Contextual and Structural Dimensions of Organizations

Contextual	Structural
1. Size	1. Formalization
2. Technology	2. Complexity
3. Environment	Vertical
	Horizontal
	Spatial
	3. Span of Control
	4. Centralization
	5. Professionalism
	6. Personnel Configuration
	Administrative ratio
	Clerical ratio
	Professional staff ratio
	Direct to indirect employees

perhaps taken for granted by employees, these characteristics reveal significant information about the overall organization. In the following example, we will see that Quad/Graphics differs significantly from the welfare office along these dimensions.

UP CLOSE 8.1: Quad/Graphics Inc. vs. The Newark Welfare Office

Quad/Graphics transforms rolls of paper into magazine pages on eleven sophisticated printing presses, each worth more than $3 million. Quad/Graphics is the darling of the industry because it is the tenth largest magazine-printing company and is only eleven years old. Q/G has extended its reach to include artistic development of in-house graphics and lithographic plate-finishing as well as research and development for new inks, better machinery, and computerized controls for printing presses. The 700 employees produced output worth well over $75 million in 1984.

The guiding philosophy of President Harry V. Quadracci is that all employees should be allowed individual initiative and responsibility. Indeed, for one day every May, the entire management team walks out, and rank and file workers take control of the presses. A single mistake can cost thousands of dollars. Managers and employees both are reminded that the workers have the ability to run things themselves. During the rest of the year, management delegates ruthlessly. Truck drivers were given the responsibility to obtain ICC permission for common-carrier status and to acquire back haul loads to finance expansion of the trucking fleet. Employees in engineering help decide when to hire new engineers and how many. Paperwork is kept to a minimum, with just enough documentation to let employees know benefits and technical regulations. Line employees are hired without requirements for education beyond high school, but they are given extensive training and guidance from supervisors. Employees are given all the responsibility they can handle, and several years may be required to learn the intricacies of the printing business.[10]

Compare this to the situation in the Newark, New Jersey, welfare office. One hundred thirty-five employees are trying to cope with new regulations resulting from Congress rewriting the laws concerning food stamp distribution. Workers say they can't keep track of the rules. One worker pointed to a four-inch stack of memos pertaining to recent rule changes. Employees don't have time to read the memos, much less learn the enormous number of rules and policies guiding the food stamp distribution systems. Applicants have to fill out four-page forms, and a single mistake can hold up food stamps for more than a month. With the recent recession, the number of applicants has been increasing. The federal government is increasing rules to reduce fraud so workers are caught in the middle. Most lower-level employees have been thrown into serving clients, and there is little support staff to handle typing and clerical activities. Top administration costs are relatively high in the welfare system, and more administrators are needed as the volume of paperwork increases.

The work in the welfare office is fairly routine and mechanical. Employees wait in line to talk to a food-stamp worker. Information is obtained and forms are completed. Most employees are middle-aged and need these jobs because their education and training are limited. Employees are frustrated and so are welfare applicants. Workers say they can hardly serve the poor because they can't unravel the red tape. People are so frustrated that fights break out occasionally. One employee commented, "We're lucky we don't have a riot."[11] ▪

Selected characteristics for Quad/Graphics and the Newark welfare office are illustrated in Exhibit 8.2. Quad/Graphics has a complex production technology and is medium sized. Formalization and centralization are both low. Professionalism is moderate to high, and Quad/Graphics has a fairly large technical support group to maintain machines and provide expertise. The welfare office, by contrast, is small but is part of a large government bureaucracy. Production technology is routine, and formalization and centralization are high. Professionalism is low, and staff support is moderate.

The difference between Quad/Graphics and the welfare office illustrates the variation that exists across organizations. This variation has implications for management style, goals, and organizational performance. In the next section, we will explore the implications of organization size in more detail, and in subsequent chapters we will explore the impact of other contextual dimensions.

ORGANIZATION SIZE AND THE BUREAUCRATIC MODEL

Since organizations are such a prominent and visible part of today's society, it's hard to believe that large organizations were hardly in existence just over 100 years ago. Managers did not have the skills or the administrative systems to run

EXHIBIT 8.2
Selected Organizational Dimensions
for Quad/Graphics versus the Newark Welfare Office

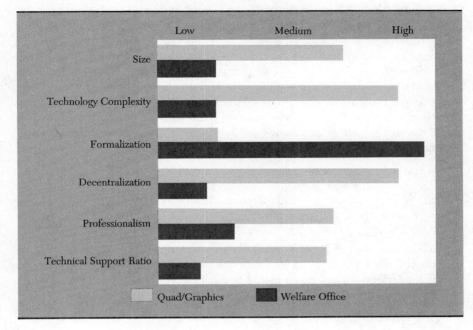

a large enterprise. Prior to 1850, organizations were family owned and did not need more than the most simple administrative structure. Railroads were one of the first industries to require organization. In the United States, railroads were increasing in size and there was a need to manage these larger organizations. The wisdom of the day was that long railroads were not efficient. The preferred size was a small railroad of about 50 miles in length. Daniel McCallum, general superintendent of the Erie Railroad, in 1855 noted:

> *A superintendent of a road fifty miles in length can give its business his personal attention . . . and any system however imperfect may under such circumstances prove comparatively successful. In the government of a road five hundred miles in length a very different state exists. Any system which may be applicable to the business . . . of a short road would be found entirely inadequate to the wants of a large one; and I am fully convinced that in the want of a system . . . properly adapted and vigilantly enforced, lies the true secret of their (the large road's) failure; and that this disparity of cost per mile in operating long and short roads, is not produced by a difference in length, but is in proportion to the perfection of the system adopted.*"[12]

Gradually, managers did learn to develop systems and structures for managing organizations of large size. Max Weber, studying organizations in

Europe, developed a framework to describe the administrative characteristics that made organizations rational and efficient. Weber studied government organizations that were growing larger to cope with the problems of governing large populations. The organization form Weber described was called **bureaucracy,** and the characteristics Weber defined were appropriate for most organizations of large size.

Weber's exposition of bureaucratic characteristics represented a fundamental perspective on what was required for an organization to act rationally, be efficient, and make the best use of scarce resources provided to it, while being large enough to meet the needs of its constituency. Weber's bureaucratic model was intended to describe positive features and represent a theoretical ideal toward which organizations could strive. The following characteristics basically summarize what Weber theorized would be an ideal bureaucracy.[13]

- *Activities are divided into a systematic division of labor.* The task, authority, and responsibility for each employee is clearly defined. The job holder works within a specific domain of responsibility, and other employees do not interfere with those responsibilities.

- *Employees are selected and promoted on the basis of technical competence.* Administrative job holders should be appointed rather than elected. Using competence to hire and promote people is more rational than using criteria such as friendship, or political and family ties. People should be qualified to do their specific tasks.

- *Positions follow the principle of hierarchy so that each position is controlled by one on a higher level.* The hierarchy of authority provides a basis of supervision and control to ensure activities are performed as needed by the organization.

- *Rules and regulations are developed to provide direction and guidelines to employees.* Rules and procedures are impersonal and enable organizational activities to be performed in a predictable, routine manner. Rules also provide continuity with the past, because many rules evolved to handle specific problems. Rules ensure equal treatment for employees and clients.

- *The organization keeps records of administrative decisions, activities, and rules.* Record keeping adds to the rationality of the organization because previous decisions can be evaluated, and rules and decisions are visible to everyone. Records also provide continuity over time, add to the organization's memory, and help educate and train new employees.

- *The property and affairs of the organization will not be appropriated by administrative officials.* Officials are paid a salary so they do not need to accept gifts or bribes. Individuals should not use the office to increase personal gain. Administrators should be objective and impersonal so that employees and clients are treated fairly.

Each of Weber's bureaucratic dimensions exist in today's large organizations. Organizations have rules, a division of labor, written records, and a hierarchy of authority. Employees are not allowed to take the property of the organization for themselves. These basic characteristics have become widely accepted as an appropriate way to organize.

When organizations do not follow the bureaucratic model, they may be inefficient for their own purposes and disruptive for society. There are classic reports of organizations in other countries in which the absence of rational bureaucracy sets back progress and inhibits production. In Mexico, a retired American lawyer had to pay a bribe of $500 to purchase a telephone. The lawyer then discovered the government technician also sold the number to another family as well. The nonbureaucratic practice of accepting bribes or making decisions for reasons other than rationality and efficiency can quickly become widespread. Mexican customs officials and police officials have a reputation for collecting pocket duties and fines to be cooperative with the public. Many highly placed employees have accumulated millions of dollars through graft and bribery.[14] These organizations are based on informality, absence of rules, and the appropriation of the office for a personal gain. By comparison, the bureaucratic form of organization seems efficient and serves the needs of society in a rational way.

IMPACT OF SIZE ON STRUCTURE

Weber's characteristics of bureaucracy suggest mechanisms to help administrators control organizations of large size. A clearly defined division of tasks among employees, rules and procedures to direct behavior, a hierarchy of authority so that everyone reports to a superior, the hiring of employees with technical skills compatible with job requirements, and written records and documentation all provide ways for managers to extend their reach. These characteristics provide regularity, standardization, and predictability for organizational activities. A railroad with bureaucratic characteristics can grow from a 50- to 500- or 1000-mile road. Bureaucratic characteristics provide impersonal means of control and regulation so that top managers do not have to personally supervise all organizational activities.

If having bureaucratic structural characteristics enables an organization to grow larger, then a positive relationship between organization size and bureaucratic characteristics should exist. The relationship between size and bureaucracy has probably been the most frequently studied relationship in organization theory.[15] Size relates to Weber's bureaucratic concepts as well as to the other structural and contextual dimensions defined earlier in this chapter. The bureaucratic model suggests that large organization size presents strong forces and pressures that lead to different structural characteristics than does small size. There have been rather consistent findings with respect to certain aspects of size and bureaucratic structure.

Large size is associated with greater complexity.[16] With respect to horizontal complexity, the number of job titles and departments is greater in large organizations. As organizations grow larger, their departmental structure changes. A process of subdivision takes place that produces a greater division of labor. As departments grow larger, they are harder to manage, so large departments are often subdivided into two or more departments, and these departments reflect greater specialization. Moreover, as the organization grows larger, managers encounter more problems of administrative control, so some new administrative departments are created to help manage the overall organization.[17] Large organizations often create special departments for planning and control that do not exist in small organizations. Large organizations also encounter greater diversity from the environment. The organization that is already large and complex experiences demands from the environment for even greater complexity in the departments required to provide goods and services.

Vertical complexity also increases, because, as more employees are hired and more departments are created, the lines of authority grow longer. New administrative levels often must be formed to keep the span of control from becoming too large. Thus a small organization may have only two or three levels of authority, but a large organization can easily have six levels of authority and may go as high as ten.

Geographical dispersion is also greater in large organizations. Often the entire physical plant and work force cannot be located in a single area, so the organization will be subdivided into various locations. Multiple locations also allow a large organization to serve its large and complex constituency more effectively.

The division of labor and hierarchy of authority envisioned by Weber thus is more prominent in large organizations. The division of labor is efficient because employees become highly specialized and competent at their tasks. The phenomenon of greater complexity in larger organizations has been found in practically every type of organization, including manufacturing firms, high schools, universities, and other types of business organizations.

Large organization size is associated with greater formalization.[18] Formalization represents policy manuals, rules, procedures, directives, job descriptions, and other written documentation. When organizations are large, they are more formalized and impersonal. Rules and directives help standardize behavior because exceptions, diversity and deviations occur when there are a large number of employees and departments. Rules and procedures provide impersonal means of control so that managers are not forced to deal with every issue on a personal basis. Managers can rely on standard ways of doing things. Huge organizations such as General Motors or the United States Army have hundreds of books of documents that prescribe rules and standard procedures for use throughout the organization. In the bureaucratic form of organization, rules and procedures take the place of personal surveillance, and their use enables the organization to increase in size.

Large organization size is associated with greater decentralization.[19] Decentralization refers to the delegation of authority and decision making responsibility downward from the top level of the organization. Decentralization is a necessary outcome of greater size. When the organization is large and complex, the number of decisions that can converge on top management is too great. Complexity and formalization both enable decentralization to occur. The greater division of labor means that domains of competence exist below top management, so decisions can be delegated to departments based upon expertise. Formalization provides rules and guidelines that provide direction to middle-level managers. Decentralized decision making occurs within the guidelines so that delegated decisions still fit the basic goals top managers have for the organization. Thus discretion at middle-management levels may increase with organization size. Through formalization, top managers maintain sufficient control so decisions can be made at a lower level without causing loss of efficiency or bad decision making.

Large organization size is associated with larger clerical and technical support staff ratios.[20] An increase in rules, procedures, records, and other written documentation means that a larger clerical, secretarial, and support staff is necessary to maintain and run the bureaucracy. More people are needed to process written communications, revise policy manuals, and keep files current. Thus the ratio of clerical employees to total employees tends to be greater in large organizations. The ratio of technical support staff is also larger. Technical support staff includes finance, engineering, personnel, and other staff specialists who provide expertise and advice for the organization. The ratio of staff specialists to total employees is greater in large organizations, primarily because of the increased division of labor. In a small, informal organization, managers may handle these staff matters on their own. But as the organization gets large, experts are hired to perform specialized duties.

The effect of higher clerical and support staff ratios in large organizations means that a smaller percentage of employees are engaged in line production activities. In a large manufacturing firm, this would mean that a smaller percentage of employees would work on the shop floor. In a large high-school district, a smaller percentage of employees would be assigned directly to teaching, while a larger percentage would provide support of various types. This relationship seems to imply that large organizations are less efficient, but that is not necessarily true. In large organizations, line employees can concentrate exclusively on production activities because responsibility for support activities are removed from them. In a small school district, for example, teachers may have to type their own tests, take attendance, counsel students, take tickets at football games, and teach courses in unfamiliar areas. In a large school district this would not happen. Teachers can teach exclusively in their own area of expertise, because there are more students who need that expertise. Clerical and technical support staff provide help for typing tests, taking attendance, and counseling students. The division of labor in large organizations means that fewer people do production work, but they can do it more efficiently.

Large organization size is associated with a smaller administrative ratio.[21] The administrative ratio applies to managers at the top of the organization who administer the organization as a whole. Administrative ratio has been studied in churches, hospitals, employment agencies, business firms, school systems, and voluntary organizations. The general pattern is that the ratio of top administrators is smaller in large organizations. This is because larger organizations experience administrative economies as they grow. Large organizations have a more refined division of labor, so that experts work in their own sphere of competence and need less direct supervision. We have said that rules and procedures act as impersonal means of supervision. Formalization is necessary in large organizations because it substitutes for top administrators. Top-level direction and control is through impersonal policies and procedures. The bureaucratic characteristics mean less personal supervision is required from the top in large organizations.

Two factors—complexity and the environment—can alter the relationship between size and a smaller administrative ratio. If the large organization is very complex, with a great number of departments and locations to be coordinated, more administrators are required. It sometimes happens that a large organization may have a larger administration ratio than a small organization, and the cause is not the size itself, but rather a more complex division of labor for top managers to coordinate. The other factor that can lead to a greater administrative ratio is the external environment. In one study of high school districts, a larger administrative ratio enabled administrators to work on obtaining additional resources and funding from the external environment, including winning approval for tax increases and obtaining specialized grants from state and federal governments.[22] Thus the administrative ratio will not *always* be smaller in large organizations, especially if top administrators have to coordinate a very complex structure or act as an interface with certain elements in the external environment. However, large size in general tends to lead to administrative economies of scale and a smaller administrative ratio.

UP CLOSE 8.2:   K mart Corporation

K mart Corporation was born in 1962 from the remnants of the failing S. S. Kresge chain of five-and-dime stores. K mart was to be something new—a discount retailer. The idea succeeded so well that K mart is now second in size to Sears Roebuck among non-food retailers. But times are changing. In the 1980s K mart is struggling to redesign itself for the future.

Discount retailers achieve their competitive edge through internal cost efficiency. Small, regional discounters such as Wal-Mart, Caldor, and Target are chipping away at K mart's share of the market. The smaller chains are more efficient than K mart because overhead costs are a smaller percentage of sales, as illustrated in Exhibit 8.3. Sears is the high cost operator in the industry but does not rely on the discount trade. Sears is so large that staff, support, and overhead costs are the highest in the industry. Sears' solution is to sell fashion goods at higher prices and to enter nonretail businesses. K mart, to stay in the discount business, needs to maintain efficiencies comparable to its smaller competitors.

K mart's overhead expense ratio was rising during the 1970s. The company had been adding 200 new stores a year to attain growth targets. Inflation was hard on K Mart. Costs for heating, cooling, salaries, and other overhead

EXHIBIT 8.3
Size and Overhead Ratio for K Mart Versus Other Retail Chains

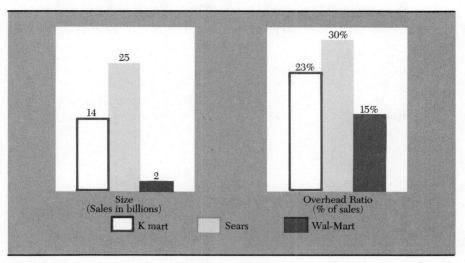

| | K mart | Sears | Wal-Mart |

Adapted from Jeremy Main, "K Mart's Plan to Be Born Again, Again," *Fortune*, September 21, 1981, pp. 74–85; and "How Sears Became a High Cost Operator," *Business Week*, February 16, 1981, pp. 52–57.

expenses went up as fast as the consumer price index, but fierce competition meant that prices could not be increased to keep pace. Profit margins became too thin.

K mart's redesign includes major steps to increase internal efficiency. Ten enormous distribution centers have been completed. The automated centers cut from two weeks to one week the time it takes to deliver merchandise after a store orders it. Faster delivery means smaller inventories. The centers also reduced by half the cost of labor needed to handle merchandise. K mart also has been building a system that will link all stores with a central computer. The K mart Information Network will handle inventories, orders, shipments, payrolls, accounting, and other operations. Other moves include trimming headquarter's staff by 9%, or about 270 people. Within the stores, marginal customer services such as layaway plans have been eliminated. Merchandise is unpacked and stamped in back rooms rather than in the aisles, which is more efficient.

To increase income, K mart is broadening its range of merchandise and including more fashion items. This strategy will place K mart in a niche between the regional discounters and Sears Roebuck. K mart has slowed the rate of expansion of new stores, and will try to make more money on existing stores by remodeling the buildings and stocking more fashionable merchandise.

Some successful chains control their managers rigidly, but K mart wants its managers to have special freedom. Store managers may refill inventories as they see fit, and they have the freedom to lower prices to be competitive in their communities. Top managers believe that decentralization is a special asset at K mart. A manager's incentive pay is based on store profits, so managers are motivated to seek the right balance between cutting prices and maintaining profit margins. [23] ■

K mart illustrates some of the problems of increasing size. Efficiency is paramount in the discount retail business, and smaller chains have an advantage because of lower overhead ratios. K mart is not a high-cost operator like Sears, but is struggling to maintain competitiveness with the smaller chains. K mart managers understand that a giant retail organization cannot be as price competitive as the small chains, so while it strives to improve efficiency, K mart is also trying to increase profit margins by introducing fashion items at higher prices.

Summary of Size-Structure Relationships

A summary of the relationship between size and organizational characteristics is in Exhibit 8.4. Large organization size is associated with greater complexity, decentralization, and formalization. Greater complexity occurs because of a greater division of labor and the need for more levels in the hierarchy. Decentralization occurs because top managers cannot handle all decisions in a large organization and specialized expertise facilitates decentralized decision making. Formalization provides an impersonal way to standardize and regularize behavior and activities in a large, diverse organization system.

Complexity, decentralization and formalization influence the personnel configuration of the organization. The standardization of behavior through formalization, and decentralizing decision making to lower levels, means that fewer demands are placed on the administrative component. Thus the ratio of administrators to total employment often is smaller in a large organization. On the other hand, the phenomenon of increasing complexity means the organization will require larger technical staff and clerical staff ratios. Complexity and the external environment may also add to the requirements for larger administrative components to help coordinate and integrate the diverse activities. Depending on the balance between complexity, decentralization, and formalization, the administrative ratio may decline as organizations increase in size. The clerical and technical support staff will tend to increase as the organization grows, so that the total ratio of employees in administrative, clerical, and technical support components is greater in large organizations.

Impact of Size on Employee Professionalism

The final aspect of bureaucracy that has been studied is its impact on employees, especially professionals. The general pattern is as follows: *Large organization size is associated with greater conflict between bureaucratic characteristics and professionals.* [24] Increasing size and bureaucracy means a

EXHIBIT 8.4
Relationships Among Size and Other Organization Dimensions

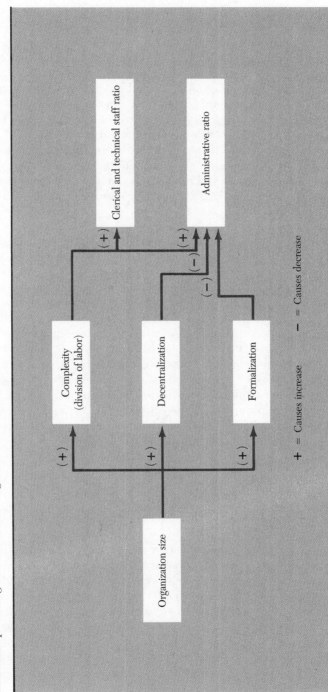

greater division of labor and more rules, both of which can cause conflicts between the organization and professional employees. A large corporation with a strong division of labor may employ a healthy staff of trained professionals —lawyers, engineers, or scientists. However, sometimes the division of labor goes too far and tasks are reduced to their smallest component and are routine and unchallenging. Routine tasks do not require professional skills. Moreover, formalization is designed to standardize and regulate behavior of members for greater control. Highly trained professionals, in contrast, have long periods of formal training and work experience. Professionals have extensive knowledge of their tasks and are able to work without close supervision.[25] Physicians, scientists, geologists, and other professionals are trained to internalize high standards of performance. Thus the mixing of professional norms and bureaucratic rules cause a conflict. Professionals do not need direction, yet the bureaucracy provides extensive direction for regulating behavior. Professionals in large organizations may resent the bureaucracy. They even may resign if the bureaucracy constrains them too tightly.

One solution is to distinguish between what Mintzberg called a machine bureaucracy and a professional bureaucracy.[26] A **machine bureaucracy** is designed as a mechanized system, with high formalization and specialization. Employees in the production core are low professional. In a **professional bureaucracy,** the production core is composed of professionals, as in hospitals, universities, and consulting firms. In a professional bureaucracy, the organization may be kept smaller, rules are fewer, and employees have more autonomy.

When professionals make up a small part of the organization, another solution to the bureaucracy-professional conflict is to create a separate department that has fewer rules and regulations. A research department, for example, can have fewer hierarchical levels, fewer rules, and a more collegial atmosphere than other departments in the organization. Because professionals have their own standards of performance and do not need as many rules to regulate behavior, it is wise not to overbureaucratize.

ARE BUREAUCRACIES BENEFICIAL?

Organization theory assumes that bureaucratic characteristics are necessary in large organizations. Rules, division of labor, and written records enable management to control the organization and gain the efficiencies of large size.

However, bureaucracies often receive strong criticism. Bureaucracies are regularly accused of having too many rules, too much paperwork, too many different tasks, and of being rigid and unadaptable in the face of a need for change. Perhaps the greatest criticism of bureaucracies concerns their impact on employees. Employees are treated in an impersonal manner. They feel constrained by rules and procedures. The loose, personal way of conducting affairs in small organizations is not possible when the organization is large. Technical competence and output is at the expense of than personal relationships.[27] Bureaucracies also can have negative impact on clients and others who deal with the organization. Employees can be so oriented toward following rules and regulations literally that client satisfaction becomes secondary. Employees develop what has been called the "bureaucratic personality," because rigid compliance with bureaucratic procedures is important in their minds.[28] The goal of compliance takes priority for them over client satisfaction. Employees are reluctant to break rules even if it would serve the good of the organization.

Thus the bureaucratic form of organization, which has advantages because it enables organizations to grow large and to be efficient, also has disadvantages because employees are treated impersonally and clients may be turned off by the bureaucratic personality of employees. The pros and cons of bureaucracy stem from tradeoffs between advantages and disadvantages of bureaucratic characteristics.

Tradeoffs   From a management perspective, the strength of bureaucracy is its ability to bring together a large number of people and tasks in a single organization and to coordinate and direct these tasks to achieve organizational goals. Bureaucratic structural characteristics provide a mechanism for control and coordination of a very large system. The tradeoff is that bureaucratic characteristics may be associated with slower response to external change and less innovation. Bureaucracy provides enough security for individuals so that sometimes they are more willing to take risks, but the network of rules and procedures slows down innovation in most cases. The usefulness of bureaucratic dimensions for standardizing, regulating, controlling, and directing a large number of diverse tasks is offset by less flexibility, less innovation, and a slower response to change.

From an employee's perspective, bureaucracies also represent a tradeoff. On the negative side, bureaucracy may stifle spontaneity, freedom, and discretion. Moreover, if jobs are divided into very small components, jobs are unchallenging and employees suffer job dissatisfaction and alienation. However, on the positive side, rules also benefit employees. Rules reduce uncertainty and protect employees from capricious behavior from superiors. With an absence of rules, employees do not know where they stand, do not have job tenure, and are not certain of the guidelines and directives that are appropriate to their tasks. Once again, the appropriateness of bureaucracy involves a tradeoff between employee freedom and employee security and certainty.[29]

Performance   The extent to which bureaucracy enables organizations to be efficient can be partly answered by measuring organizational performance. A study by John Child in England surveyed business corporations.[30] He measured bureaucratic characteristics and related bureaucracy to performance in both large and small corporations. He found that high performance was related to the fit between size and bureaucracy as illustrated in Exhibit 8.5. Very large corporations with many bureaucratic characteristics achieved a higher level of performance than large corporations with few bureaucratic characteristics. The bureaucratic characteristics help very large organizations attain the economies

EXHIBIT 8.5
Relationship Between Size, Bureaucracy, and Performance

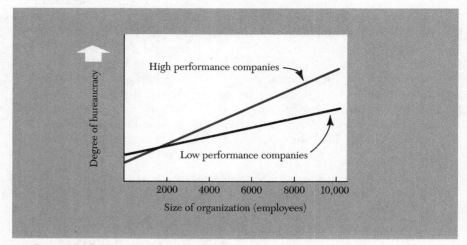

Based on John Child, "Managerial and Organizational Factors Associated with Company Performance—Part II. A Contingency Analysis," *Journal of Management Studies* 12 (1975): 12–27.

of scale and internal coordination needed for efficient performance. On the other hand, very small corporations tended to perform better if they were nonbureaucratic. For small companies, bureaucratic procedures were not needed because tasks could be personally supervised by managers. The high-performing small organizations tended to be less bureaucratic than low-performing small organizations. The general finding from this research, then, is that bureaucratic characteristics should fit organization size. Small organizations should be less bureaucratic and large organizations more bureaucratic.

In a study of not-for-profit school organizations, bureaucratic characteristics were related to performance factors associated with a good educational experience for students, including student-teacher ratio, teacher expertise, and the educational rating of school performance.[31] The findings indicated that a division of labor within the schools, a support staff sufficient to support educational activities, and an administrative component large enough to acquire resources all worked together to provide a better education for students. Thus the adoption of bureaucratic characteristics enabled larger school districts to provide an array of educational services and greater teacher expertise than was possible in small, nonbureaucratic districts.

The answer to whether bureaucracies promote high performance is a matter of "fit." Some bureaucracy is functional for organizations, especially as they grow large. However, overbureaucracy is dysfunctional. One place where a poor fit with bureaucracy has been demonstrated in recent years is the acquisition of small companies by giant bureaucratic corporations. Large companies that acquire a small firm may impose their bureaucratic characteristics on the small firm, which can cause many problems, as happened when Schlumberger acquired Fairchild.

UP CLOSE 8.3:   Fairchild Camera & Instrument Corporation

Fairchild Camera was a once-great semiconductor maker that gradually lost its competitive edge and couldn't seem to do anything right. Profits and market share dwindled. In 1979, Schlumberger, a huge and successful oil field service firm, took over Fairchild. Schlumberger executives expected to turn Fairchild around. They poured cash into Fairchild for new buildings and plants, and increased research and development spending. They also imposed the management style and administrative characteristics of Schlumberger onto Fairchild. The result? Fairchild is performing even worse than before. In 1983, sales plunged 20% and the company lost more than $100 million.

A major reason for the failure of Fairchild to turn around is that it is poorly suited to the management style and practices of its huge parent. Schlumberger executives thought Schlumberger's administrative structure was well suited to the world of semiconductors. But the new structure was an imposition and caused resentment at Fairchild. One executive, who now works at another semiconductor firm, said that the management style imposed on Fairchild simply would not work in an organization that required an entrepreneurial spirit. Schlumberger's approach was too slow for the semiconductor world. The rapidity of change in semiconductors was something Schlumberger could not handle. A six-month lead time for a semiconductor product is considered a long time. In oil services, a product might last twenty years. A former Fairchild division manager said that clearance for spending money could take six to nine months under Schlumberger procedures, instead of the three months required before the acquisition. A six-month delay in semiconductors puts a company too far behind. The rate of change is so fast in the field that 50% of all revenues should come from products developed within the previous three years. At Fairchild, the slower pace meant that half the revenues came from products developed over five years.

Bureaucratic procedures and slow adaptation were Schlumberger's way. Schlumberger has also failed to help Fairchild close the technological gap in metal-oxide semiconductors. They are important to semiconductor users, but Fairchild hasn't caught up with the industry. A number of professional employees have either left or been fired because of the turmoil at Fairchild. Although Fairchild was a big company, it was not previously laden with bureaucracy so it could compete in the electronics industry. The extensive administrative procedures designed for its larger parent did not fit Fairchild.[32] ■

In many companies managers are aware of the pressures of large size and the need for bureaucracy, but they do not overbureaucratize small companies or companies that need to change rapidly. Executives at Minnesota Mining & Manufacturing Company (3M) are keenly aware of the disadvantages of large size. They make a conscious effort to keep professional units small to maintain flexibility. If a division gets too large, top management breaks it into separate divisions that become independent companies and hence do not need as much bureaucracy. 3M is organized into many small, independent companies rather than as one large organization.[33] Of course not all companies have learned this lesson. When huge Tenneco took over Houston Oil & Minerals, the result was something of a disaster. As a freewheeling organization, the small, flexible Houston Oil had been successful in discovering oil deposits. Tenneco's rigid rules and procedures brought Houston Oil to a temporary halt.[34] Finding the right fit between size and bureaucracy is one of the major challenges facing executives in large companies.

ORGANIZATIONAL LIFE CYCLE

Another important concept for understanding organizational entities from a macro perspective is the life cycle. Organizations, like human beings, are born, grow older, and eventually die. Organization size and bureaucratic characteristics relate to the stage an organization is in its life cycle.

The life-cycle concept proposes that organizational structure and administrative systems follow a predictable pattern associated with major developmental stages in the life cycle. The developmental stages are sequential in nature and follow a natural progression that is not easily reversed. The stages involve changes in a range of organizational activities and overall structure. A number of authors have proposed models for life-cycle stages and the organizational characteristics typical of each stage. A summary model is described below and in Exhibit 8.6. This model is based on the work of Quinn and Cameron, and proposes four stages of birth, youth, midlife, and maturity.[35]

Birth Stage

The organization is born, and the emphasis is on survival. The founders typically are entrepreneurs who have created a production or marketing idea that is attractive in the market, and the founders devote energy to the technical activities of production and marketing. The organization is very informal and has few systems for planning, coordination, or formalization. Authority is centralized with the owner/entrepreneur, who has personal control over organizational activities. Management is concerned with creativity, survival, and acquiring resources from the environment rather than with management systems and organization structure. Apple Computer, Inc., was in this stage of development when it was created by Steven Jobs and Stephen Wozniak in

EXHIBIT 8.6

Stages of Development and Organizational Characteristics During the Life Cycle

	Birth Stage	Youth Stage	Midlife Stage	Maturity Stage
Bureaucracy	Nonbureau-cratic	Prebureau-cratic	Bureaucratic	Very Bureaucratic
Emphasis	Creativity, Survival	Growth, Innovation	Control, Efficiency	Renewal
Structure	One-person rule, informal, centralized, overlapping tasks	Collective, informal, centralized, some departments	Formal procedures and control systems, some decentralization, many departments	Extensive financial controls, decentralization, multiple staff and line departments
Management Style	Enterpreneurial	Sense of Mission	Delegation with control	Collaboration, team approach to offset bureaucracy
Transition to Next Stage	Leadership Crisis	Control Crisis	Red Tape Crisis	Turnaround Crisis

SOURCE: Adapted from Robert E. Quinn and Kim Cameron, "Organizational Life Cycles and Some Shifting Criteria of Effectiveness: Some Preliminary Evidence," *Management Science* 29 (1983): 33–51; and Larry E. Greiner, "Evolution and Revolution as Organizations Grow," *Harvard Business Review* 50 (July-August, 1972): 37–46.

Wozniak's parents' garage. Wozniak and Jobs sold personal belongings to raise money to build 200 Apple computers. New software companies like Microsoft and Software Publishing are in the birth stage today.

Youth Stage

The organization has survived, and is now succeeding in the marketplace. The organization is characterized by growth, innovation, and excitement. Members identify with the mission and purpose of the organization and spend long hours helping the organization succeed. Members feel part of a collective, and communication, structure, and control are mostly informal. Control is still relatively centralized and the organization is not yet large. Continued growth is a major goal. Apple Computer was in the youth stage during the years of rapid growth from 1978–81 when the major product line was established and over 2000 dealers signed on to sell Apple computers. Polaroid Corporation was in this stage during the 1950s because of the innovation, excitement, and rapid growth associated with instant photography.

Midlife Stage

The organization has continued to grow and is now quite large. An emphasis on control and internal efficiency replaces the previous emphasis on survival and growth. The organization adopts bureaucratic characteristics. Formal procedures and an explicit hierarchy of authority are imposed. The organization adds staff support groups and internal accounting and control systems. Flexibility and innovation are reduced. The organization may adopt new products, but through institutionalized procedures rather than from the creativity of a single individual. Primary emphasis is on developing and maintaining internal efficiency through the use of a stable structure, division of labor, role definition, and formal planning. Some authority is decentralized to managers below the top levels of the organization. Apple and Polaroid are both in the midlife stage of the life cycle at this time.

Maturity Stage

The mature organization is large and bureaucratic. Control systems, rules, policies, and a complex organization structure are in place. The organization is decentralized to the extent necessary for efficient decision making. The organization may become concerned with its role in the larger environment and seek new domains of activity, new products, or a new role in the community. Another concern of the mature organization is institutionalization as a prominent force in its environment. The organization may make special attempts to become more flexible and adaptable by the use of team procedures and further decentralization to encourage moderate growth and innovation. A dominant concern to an organization in this stage is stagnation. Mature organizations may experience some decline. Managers seek mechanisms for renewal, turnaround, and streamlining of what can become an overgrown bureaucracy. Companies such as Sears, Procter & Gamble, Westinghouse, John Deere, and General Motors are examples of large, mature organizations.

Crises of Transition

An important aspect of the life-cycle is that the four stages do not unfold in a logical, orderly fashion. Although life stages typically occur in the same sequence, some stages may lead or lag, such as when an organization acquires bureaucratic control mechanisms during the youth stage, or when an entrepreneur does not delegate authority until well into the midlife stage. The important point is that the transition from one stage to the next is difficult. Transitions are episodic and characterized by radical changes over a short period of time followed by periods of smooth development. The transition from one stage to another is not unlike transitions in the human life cycle. The change from childhood to adulthood is filled with emotional, stormy periods of stress and conflict. Organizational transitions are also filled with stress and conflict.

The crises associated with stages of development were defined by Greiner, who examined historical studies of organizations and found that certain issues or crises seemed to be associated with the transition to a new stage of development.[36] Three of the crises Greiner identified are leadership, control, and red-tape crises. A fourth crisis, turnaround, also occurs in many companies. These crises are illustrated in Exhibit 8.6 according to their typical time of occurrence during the organization's life cycle.

Leadership Crisis   The leadership crisis occurs after the organization starts to grow and experiences some success in the marketplace. The founders are entrepreneurs, who have technical and marketing skills, but they do not have skill or interest in dealing with management issues. Employees may become dissatisfied with centralized control and what appears to be arbitrary management. Growth will be restricted unless the organization solves this problem. This crisis often leads to the emergence of a strong leader who can carry the organization into the next stage of development. Employees identify with the leader and mission of the organization. This leader has skills to manage the growing organization, motivate employees, and provide direction to the production and marketing activities. At Apple Computer, the leadership crisis occurred early because neither Jobs nor Wozniak were top-flight managers. A. C. Markkula was brought in as a partner to run the company, while Jobs and Wozniak provided technical leadership and a sense of mission for employees.

Control Crisis   The control crisis occurs after the organization is approaching large size. Managers sense that the organization is going in several directions at once, and they cannot maintain personal control over all activities. Top managers experience a need for greater control, stability, and internal efficiency. The resolution to this crisis is the implementation of rules and procedures, accounting and control systems, and an expressed emphasis on internal efficiency. Policies, rules, and regulations are developed. Employees may resent the change in emphasis from the growth and excitement of the youth stage to the concern for control and efficiency in the maturity stage. Some people may leave. The resolution of the control crisis enables the organization to make the transition to a middle-aged, successful organization. John Sculley was hired from PepsiCo to bring discipline to Apple after several years of uncontrolled growth. He imposed cost controls, reduced overhead, and pushed for a balanced product line. The shock to Apple produced 25 percent turnover in the company's executive committee. Polaroid went through the same transition when Edwin Land retired in 1969 and Bill McCune imposed a painful management realignment to bring about internal discipline and cost efficiency.

Red-tape Crisis   After the organization adopts bureaucratic procedures, top managers at some point may feel that systems, procedures and controls are strangling middle-level managers. The organization may seem overregulated and overmanaged. Managers of major divisions and departments may want more authority over their operations. The red-tape crisis is resolved when managers shift away from formal control procedures as the exclusive means of internal control. When managers begin to stress horizontal relationships, mechanisms for flexibility, team building, and further decentralization, a cohesive culture is fostered within the organization. Bureaucratic procedures are still important, but they are not dominant. The emphasis is on personal relationships and team building that can complement and moderate bureaucratic characteristics. K Mart was coping with the red tape crises in **Up Close 8.2.** A more decentralized, flexible K Mart emerged.

Turnaround Crisis   After the organization reaches maturity, it may enter periods of temporary decline.[37] Outright failure is not likely, as the organization has become institutionalized to the external environment, but the organization may get out of step with the times. The organization stresses renewal and internal streamlining. Certain products may be eliminated and new products developed. Staff groups may be cut back and the bureaucracy may be reduced. New managers may be hired and consultants used to give the organization fresh energy. Top managers often are replaced during this crisis. The renewal crisis may happen every ten to twenty years, and the streamlining and renewal are gradually repeated. Brunswick Corporation—described at this chapter's opening—was a mature organization that went through the turnaround crisis. In recent years, large automobile companies such as Ford and General Motors have gone through the turnaround crisis as reflected in employee layoffs, shrinkage, and streamlining. Selective cutbacks combined with investment in new plants and equipment enabled Ford and GM to reestablish themselves as a strong force in the industry.

All organizations experience movement through the life cycle if they are to grow and be successful. A primary challenge of management is to recognize the management style and administrative structure needed to move into and through each stage of an organization's development. One example of an organization that has moved through the life cycle over the last thirty years is Kentucky Fried Chicken. The organization experienced difficulty and stress at certain points, but each time moved through the crisis to a new stage of development and success.

UP CLOSE 8.4:   Kentucky Fried Chicken

"Finger-lickin' good." "Secret formula of 11 herbs and spices." "We do chicken right." These are the slogans by which most of us know Kentucky Fried Chicken. Kentucky Fried Chicken is a national organization with franchises in almost every community. KFC began in 1956 as a creative idea developed by a retiree who received $105 a month from Social Security, and is now a dominant force in the fast food industry.

The idea for Kentucky Fried Chicken started when Harland Sanders was running a combination gas station/restaurant in Corbin, Kentucky. He sold meals to travelers who were tired of standard highway cooking. As the popularity of his restaurant spread, he opened a full-fledged restaurant and did away with the gas pumps. By the age of 66, his "original" chicken recipe was developed—including eleven secret herbs and spices cooked in a pressure cooker—and he believed he had an important product. When a new super-highway forced Sanders to sell the restaurant, he loaded up his 1946 Ford and began calling on restaurant owners. "Let me cook chicken for you and your staff," he told them. "If you like the way it tastes, I'll sell you my seasoning, teach you how to cook it, and you pay me a 4-cent royalty on every chicken you sell."

Many restaurant owners were impressed, and the franchise arrangement was based on a handshake. By 1960, Colonel Sanders' hard work paid off. He had over 400 franchises in the United States and Canada. The company continued to be his baby, and he ran it as a one-man show. The personal and informal process of establishing franchises enabled the Colonel and his wife to run the company. They did their own bookkeeping and paperwork, and his wife handled the mixing, packing, and shipping of the secret recipe.

In 1964, the Colonel Sanders' symbol was born when he appeared on a TV talk show in a white suit with a string tie—his only clean outfit at the moment. People made a connection between the white suit and the words "Kentucky Fried Chicken," and a symbol was born.

As the organization continued to grow, Sanders found himself employing seventeen people and housing them in an office behind his house. He joked that the organization was "almost getting out of hand." He did not have administrative interests or experience. The Colonel began to feel that "this danged business is beginning to run right over me."

To resolve this crisis, Colonel Sanders sold his company in 1964 to John Y. Brown, an aggressive lawyer and super-salesman, and Jack Massey, a million-aire businessman. Brown provided strong leadership and marketing skills. Kentucky Fried Chicken grew rapidly. Brown intended to make KFC the blue chip of the fast food industry. He promoted the Colonel as a living image, developed a unified advertising campaign for all franchises, and insisted upon a standard, free-standing structure for all new franchise units. Managers were excited by the fast growth. Brown and Massey spent over $7 million a year on advertising, and reaped $700 million in sales. They also worked 14 hours a day selling the concept.

Some problems began to appear as the growth slowed down and managers had to become concerned with internal efficiency. A few managers resigned, and Brown and Massey had a falling out. The business was sold to Heublein, Inc. in 1971. Heublein introduced new products, such as barbequed ribs, which boosted sales. They decentralized more control to the franchises, but the lack of control caused problems with appearance and uniform quality in stores. Heublein paid too much attention to marketing and long-range planning and not enough to store management. The organization seemed to be going several directions at once. The savior was Mike Miles, a senior vice president from Heublein. He took over Kentucky Fried Chicken, introducing internal control and tough standards for quality and appearance. Lower priority was given to rapid growth and marketing expertise. The organization is once again a solid performer and is experiencing growth and profits, although at a moderate pace. The crisis of red tape has not appeared yet, although Kentucky Fried Chicken may go through that as the next crisis as it develops into a mature organization.[38]

Kentucky Fried Chicken illustrates many of the life-cycle concepts. During the birth stage, KFC was run by one man, with Colonel Sanders holding all of the power. The colonel could not manage the organization as it grew larger. Brown took over, and the organization entered an explosive growth stage. Brown guided the organization through the youth stage. Transition into the midlife stage was associated with establishing formal procedures and control and the loss of some personnel. As the emphasis shifted from marketing to internal control, the organization stabilized and is again experiencing success as a company in the midlife stage of development.

SUMMARY

This chapter introduced the macro study of organizations as reflected in the field of organization theory. Because organizations are more than a collection of individuals, studying the macro approach is important for managers. Organizations are entities that have form, structure, and characteristics of their own. Organizations are an important feature on the social landscape, and the ability to understand them on the whole can make managers more effective.

Organizations are defined as social entities that are goal-directed, deliberately structured activity systems with an identifiable boundary. Structural and contextual dimensions, which can be used to analyze organizations, are defined. Contextual characteristics include size, technology, and environment. Structural characteristics include formalization, division of labor, hierarchy of authority, decentralization, complexity, professionalism, and personnel configuration.

Next we examined the bureaucratic model and the impact of size on bureaucracy. Bureaucracy is important because it provides a basis for designing a rational organization and provides managers with a structure for controlling large organizations. Without elements of bureaucracy, organizations could grow no larger than what a single manager could supervise. Large organization size tends to be associated with the characteristics of formalization, greater complexity, decentralization, larger support ratios and a smaller administrative component. Bureaucratic characteristics also tend to create conflict, since professional employees desire autonomy and self regulation.

Finally, we examined the concept of organizational life cycle, because organizations—like human beings—pass through different stages of development. We defined the four stages of birth, youth, midlife, and maturity. Each stage is associated with specific structural characteristics and internal priorities. Transition from one stage to the next is difficult and causes internal stress and crisis conditions. Leadership, control, and red-tape crises are associated with transition from one development stage to the next, and the turnaround crisis occurs during the mature stage of an organization's life.

KEY WORDS

administrative ratio
birth stage
bureaucracy
centralization
clerical ratio
contextual dimension
contingency
control crisis
decentralization
direct-to-indirect
   employee ratio
environment
formalization

geographical
   complexity
horizontal complexity
leadership crisis
life cycle
machine bureaucracy
maturity stage
midlife stage
personnel
   configuration
professional
   bureaucracy
professional staff ratio

professionalism
red-tape crisis
size
span of control
structural dimension
technology
turnaround crisis
vertical complexity
youth stage

DISCUSSION QUESTIONS

1. Why is the macro approach to organizations important for managers to understand? Would this perspective be more important for upper level or lower level managers? Discuss.
2. What is an organization? Briefly explain each part of the definition. What levels of analysis are typically studied in organizations?
3. Briefly explain the difference between formalization, complexity, and centralization. Would an organization that has a high level of one of these dimensions also have a high level of other characteristics? Discuss.
4. Why is greater bureaucracy required in organizations of large size? Would it be possible to design a large organization to be nonbureaucratic? Discuss.
5. The manager of a large oil-service firm once said, "We can't price our services as cheaply as small firms because they have lower overhead costs." Based upon the discussion in this chapter, would you agree with this manager? Why?
6. If you were an administrator in charge of a small medical practice, how might you structure the organization differently than if you were managing a small parcel delivery service? Explain.
7. Why do large organizations tend to have smaller top administrative ratios but larger clerical and professional staff ratios?
8. Compare the youth stage with the midlife stage of an organization's life cycle. What crisis is typically associated with the transition from youth to midlife?
9. What are the four crises typically associated with transitions through the life cycle? Why would transition be associated with a crisis rather than with gradual change? Discuss.

CASE 8.1:   Wang Laboratories, Inc.

Wang Labs' spectacular growth during the worldwide recession of the early 1980s has intrigued many observers. Why hasn't Wang suffered the reversals of other office automation manufacturers such as Xerox and Datapoint? What secret accounts for the company's glittering performance? And the most crucial question, how long will it last?

Not too much longer is the answer to the last question. Outside experts and inside executives agree that Wang's high-flying growth days are nearly over.

And, my, the growth was breathtaking while it lasted. In the five years prior to 1982, revenues soared 55% annually, and profits shot up at a 66% annual rate. Wang reported an unbroken string of 26 record growth quarters, and they are poised to join the $1 billion revenue club.

Despite the successes, internal problems are piling up that could deal a severe blow to Wang Labs. The company continues to operate as it did through its heyday of the 1970s, even though its work force increased sevenfold to 18,500 employees. Management has not kept pace with the company's growth. The company's extraordinary success was due to An Wang's uncanny timing in the marketplace and knowledgeable application of technology. But Wang, chairman and chief executive officer, admits that the company's internal organization is weaker than it should be. The company has grown so fast for so long that paperwork procedures and systems are behind.

Wang Labs faces an external problem also. They are in first place in sales of word processing equipment, but they have met with little competition. Now other giants like IBM and AT&T are positioning themselves to provide total integration of the office, which is the next step beyond word processing. Wang must not only get its management systems in order, but must launch a new series of products to stay ahead in office automation. Finding the right innovative product is getting harder as the company grows larger.

Management reform is essential. The company is trying to bring about change in three areas.

First, the company is putting in place a management team to replace An Wang's benevolent dictatorship. As a small, entrepreneurial company, Wang Labs flourished under his one-man management style. The centralized and highly personal management style was important to the company's success. That same style now exacerbates Wang Labs' problems with growing pains. One member of Wang's board of directors says, "the company took longer to go through adolescence because of the tight control at the top." Wang reserved final decision-making power for himself, and things like strategic planning and formal delegation of duties received little attention.

The new executive operating committee will now handle top management decision making. Wang has also turned over corporate development efforts to his son, Frederick Wang, who was promoted to senior vice president. The executive committee is made up of the top functional managers. The committee will make general strategic decisions and the functional departments will carry out the decisions. Decisions are now made through formal presentations to the committee that were once made during hallway conversations. To achieve greater coordination among the respective departments, Wang Labs is now institutionalizing processes that were once informal. An Wang will not be involved unless the committee cannot reach a decision.

Second, the research and development operation, which had become out of control, is now under the strict supervision of Fred Wang. In 1981, R&D accounted for a $64 million expenditure. For 1983, expenditures doubled to some $120 million. Many people have thought this is too much too soon. R&D at Wang exploded into pieces trying to cover all product bases. Rather than try to do everything simultaneously, R&D needs to be focused on selected product lines. The company is working to devise a process for allocating funds into selective, innovative products needed to hold its lead in office technology.

And third, the company is trying to clean up its balance-sheet problems. High fixed costs, combined with swollen inventories and accounts receivables, have increased the need for cash. Wang had to raise $465 million in public markets. The high-debt position means big interest payments, and these have drained earnings. Lax controls allowed the cash-flow problem to develop. Wang has had to institute new controls to bring receivables and inventories into line.

The balance-sheet problems were caused by Wang executives' lack of professional maturity in managing large groups of employees and in creating internal systems to manage growth. Operations such as manufacturing and product services have careened out of control. Until recently, Wang Labs had no system for tracking material used during production. There was little or no communication between functional groups; the engineers, for example, would never look into how much it would cost to manufacture or service a product they designed.

Wang's success at implementing these changes will be extremely important, or Wang could end up as an also-ran. "Wang watchers" believe the next two or three years will be the most critical in the company's history. They also worry whether it can undergo such extensive management change without losing the entrepreneurial spirit on which the company was built.

Other changes include pushing decision making further down into the organization, or decentralizing. The head of manufacturing set the tone for a change in management style by hiring a third tier of managers and delegating decisions to them. This has brought fresh management blood into Wang's inbred hierarchy. These new managers can install formal systems for things like materials planning and capital budgeting. A comptroller has been hired, and the day-to-day management of investor relations and marketing support have been turned over to newly hired professional employees. Product pricing and marketing plans, once settled over lunch, now are hammered out by committees.

The changes in research and development have also been dramatic. The new focus is on enhancing the current product line rather than on sheer innovation. Fred Wang wants R&D to carefully pick the products that will garner the most revenue. He also trimmed the staff by 10% and has created a dual career ladder for first-rate engineers, so they can be promoted upward and receive high salaries without going into management.

Wang managers believe they will get through the transition successfully because they have a two-year lead time on competitors for office systems. Wang has already penetrated about 75% of the nation's 1000 largest corporations. In late 1983, Wang unveiled fourteen new products to shore up some of its weaknesses. Other Wang products have had technical problems and failed to take off, such as a voice-mail system and Wangnet, a two-year-old proprietary local area network for linking office equipment. Wang products sell strongly in the traditional word-processing markets, and Wang is trying to break through in sales of large-scale office systems. Order rates are high, so the new products from big competitors like Digital and Data General have not yet seriously hurt Wang.

The critical question for the long run is whether Wang's new management committee can replace An Wang's entrepreneurial genius and his ability to inspire messianic zeal and loyalty among employees. He did so much right for so long that people believed in him. Life after An Wang may be difficult.[39]

CASE QUESTIONS

1. Identify the changes in organizations that are occurring at Wang. Why is this organization changing?
2. What crisis is driving these changes? What is likely to occur in the future?

NOTES

1. "A Slimmed-Down Brunswick is Proving Wall Street Wrong," *Business Week*, May 28, 1984, pp. 90–98; J. Bettner, "Bowling for Dollars: Wringing Out Salaries and Excess Operating Expense," *Forbes*, September 12, 1983, p. 138.
2. Arthur G. Bedeian, *Organizations: Theory and Analysis* (Hinsdale, IL: Dryden, 1980), p. 4; Aldrich, *Organizations and Environments*, pp. 4–6; Richard L. Daft, *Organization Theory and Design* (St. Paul, MN: West, 1983), p. 8.
3. Howard Aldrich, *Organizations and Environments* (Englewood Cliffs, NJ: Prentice-Hall, 1979), p. 3.
4. Henry Mintzberg, "Organization Design: Fashion or Fit?" *Harvard Business Review* (January –February, 1981): 103–116.
5. The definitions were heavily influenced by D. S. Pugh, "The Measurement of Organization Structures: Does Context Determine Form?" *Organizational Dynamics* 1 (Spring, 1973): 19–34; and D. S. Pugh, D. F. Hickson, C. R. Hinings, and C. Turner, "Dimensions of Organizational Structure," *Administrative Science Quarterly* 13 (1968): 65–91.
6. Charles Perrow, "A Framework for the Comparative Analysis of Organizations," *American Sociological Review* 32 (1967): 194–208.
7. Pugh, et al., "Dimensions of Organization Structure."
8. Richard H. Hall, J. Eugene Haas, and Norman J. Johnson, "Organizational Size, Complexity, and Formalization," *American Sociological Review* 32 (1967): 903–912; Richard H. Hall, *Organizations: Structure and Process*, 2d ed. (Englewood Cliffs, NJ: Prentice-Hall, 1977).
9. David D. Van Fleet, "Span of Management Research and Issues," *Academy of Management Journal* 26 (1983): 546–552; David D. Van Fleet and Arthur G. Bedeian, "A History of the Span of Management," *Academy of Management Review* 2 (1977): 356–372.
10. Ellen Wojahn, "Management by Walking Away," *Inc.*, October 1983, pp. 68–76.
11. Janet Guyon, "Food-Stamp Red Tape Raises Tension Level in Understaffed Offices," *The Wall Street Journal*, June 27, 1984, pp. 1–16.
12. A. Chandler, *Strategy and Structure: Chapters in the History of the American Industrial Enterprise* (Cambridge, MA: MIT Press, 1962), p. 21.
13. This discussion is based on Max Weber, *The Theory of Social and Economic Organizations*, translated by A. M. Henderson and T. Parson (New York: Free Press, 1947), pp. 328–340.
14. John Crewdson, "Corruption Viewed as Way of Life," *Bryan-College Station Eagle*, November 28, 1982, p. 13AA.
15. John R. Kimberly, "Organizational Size and the Structuralist Perspective: A Review, Critique, and Proposal," *Administrative Science Quarterly* 20 (1976): 571–597.
16. Robert Dewar and Jerald Hage, "Size, Technology, Complexity, and Structural Differentiation: Toward a Theoretical Synthesis," *Administrative Science Quarterly* 23 (1978): 111–136; Hall, Haas, and Johnson, "Organizational Size, Complexity, and Formalization."
17. Richard L. Daft and Patricia J. Bradshaw, "The Process of Horizontal Differentiation: Two Models," *Administrative Science Quarterly* 25 (1980): 441–456.
18. Bernard Reimann, "On the Dimensions of Bureaucratic Structure: An Empirical Reappraisal," *Administrative Science Quarterly* 18 (1973): 462–476; Peter M. Blau and Richard Schoenherr, *The Structure of Organizations* (New York: Basic Books, 1971); William A. Rushing, "Organiza-

tional Rules and Surveillance: A Proposition in Comparative Organizational Analysis," *Administrative Science Quarterly* 10 (1966): 423–443; D. S. Pugh, David J. Hickson, C. R. Hinings, and C. Turner, "The Context of Organization Structures," *Administrative Science Quarterly* 14 (1969): 91–114.

19. Roger Mansfield, "Bureaucracy and Centralization: An Examination of Organizational Structure," *Administrative Science Quarterly* 18 (1973): 477–488; Jerald Hage and Michael Aiken, "Relationship of Centralization to Other Structural Properties," *Administrative Science Quarterly* 12 (1967): 72–91.

20. Spyros K. Lioukas and Demitris A. Xerokostas, "Size and Administrative Intensity in Organizational Division," *Management Science* 28 (1982): 854–868; Frank J. Weed, "Patterns of Growth in Welfare Bureaucracies," *The Sociological Quarterly* 23 (1982): 391–401; A. Hawley, W. Boland, and M. Boland, "Population Size and Administration in Institutions of Higher Education," *American Sociological Review* 30 (1965): 252–255; John B. Kasarda, "The Structural Implications of Social System Size: A Three-Level Analysis," *American Sociological Review* 39 (1974): 19–28.

21. Richard L. Daft, "System Influence on Organization Decision Making: The Case of Resource Allocation," *Academy of Management Journal* 21 (1978): 6–22; James, "The Administrative Component in Complex Organizations"; John Child, "Parkinson's Progress: Accounting for the Number of Specialists in Organizations," *Administrative Science Quarterly* 18 (1973): 328–348; Blau and Schoenherr, *The Structure of Organizations.*

22. Richard L. Daft and Selwyn W. Becker, "Managerial, Institutional, and Technical Influences on Administration: A Longitudinal Analysis," *Social Forces* 59 (1980): 392–413.

23. Jeremy Main, "K-Mart's Plan to Be Born Again, Again," *Fortune*, September 21, 1981, pp. 74–85; Howard Rudnitsky, "How Sam Walton Does It," *Forbes*, August 16, 1982, pp. 42–44; Steve Weiner and Frank E. James, "Sears, A Power House in Many Fields Now, Looks Into New One," *The Wall Street Journal*, February 10, 1984, pp. 1–10; "How Sears Became a High Cost Operator," *Business Week*, February 16, 1981, pp. 52–57.

24. Hall, *Organizations: Structure and Process,* 2d ed.

25. Richard H. Hall, "Professionalization and Bureaucratization," *American Sociological Review* 33 (1968): 92–104.

26. Henry Mintzberg, *The Structuring of Organizations* (Englewood Cliffs, NJ: Prentice-Hall, 1979).

27. Arlyn J. Melcher, *Structure and Process of Organizations: A Systems Approach* (Englewood Cliffs, NJ: Prentice-Hall, 1976).

28. Robert K. Merton, "Bureaucratic Structure and Personality," *Social Forces* 18 (1940): 560–568.

29. Charles Perrow, *Complex Organizations: A Critical Essay* (Glenview, IL: Scott Foresman, 1979).

30. John Child, "Managerial and Organizational Factors Associated with Company Performance —Part II: A Contingency Analysis," *Journal of Management Studies* 12 (1975): 12–27; John Child, *Organizations* (New York: Harper & Row, 1977).

31. Daft and Becker, "Managerial, Institutional, and Technical Influences on Administration."

32. Steve Mufson, "Oil-Fields Highflier Signs Turbulent Skies in the Chip Business," *The Wall Street Journal*, August 26, 1983: 1–13.

33. Frederick C. Klein, "Some Firms Fight Ill of Bigness by Keeping Employees' Units Small," *The Wall Street Journal*, February 5, 1982, pp. 1–16.

34. George Getschow, "Loss of Expert Talent Impedes Oil Finding by New Tenneco Unit," *The Wall Street Journal*, February 9, 1982, pp. 1–23.

35. Robert E. Quinn and Kim Cameron, "Organizational Life Cycles and Shifting Criteria of Effectiveness: Some Preliminary Evidence," *Management Science* 29 (1983): 33–51.

36. Larry E. Greiner, "Evolution and Revolution as Organizations Grow," *Harvard Business Review* 50 (July–August, 1972): 37–46.

37. David A. Whetten, "Sources, Responses, and Effects of Organizational Decline," in John R. Kimberly and Robert H. Miles (eds.), *The Organizational Life Cycle* (San Francisco: Jossey-Bass, 1980): 342–374.

38. Based on Martha L. Elzen, Eric Klasson, Michele Mahan, and Sow-Mun Pang, "Kentucky Fried Chicken: Application in Organizational Theory and Design," unpublished manuscript, Texas A&M University, 1982; William Whitworth, "Profiles: Kentucky-Fried," *The New Yorker*, February 14, 1970; Robin Ashton, "The Spectacular KFC's Turnaround," *Institutions*, December 1, 1980, pp. 29–32; Robert Z. Chew, "KFC Finds a New Ad Niche: 'Its' Wholesome'," *Advertising*, March 27, 1978, pp. 1–98.
39. Based on "Wang Labs' Run For a Second Billion," *Business Week*, May 17, 1982, pp. 100–104; "Trouble in Paradise," *Datamation*, April 1983, pp. 42–44; and "The First Hint of Trouble at Wang," *Business Week*, October 17, 1983, pp. 45–46.

9 Organizational Technology

O ne of the important discoveries in the field of organization theory is the relationship between organization design and the nature of the organization's work. The sophisticated assembly process for Toshiba calculators places demands on organization structure different from the mechanical assembly processes used to produce ballpoint pens or washing machines. Craftspeople who design baccarat crystal are managed in a way different from employees who open envelopes for the Internal Revenue Service. When Iowa beef processors introduced a highly efficient mechanized workflow to the meat packing industry, a new management structure had to be adopted simultaneously. Firms unable to adapt their structures to the new technology were forced to get out of the industry.[1] Robotics is a third wave of technological development now entering the meat packing industry; this will require even newer forms of organization structure for efficient utilization.[2]

All organizations produce goods or services, and the purpose of this chapter is to explore how the nature of the production process influences design of organizations. We will examine variations in organizational technology and discuss what is known about the influence of technology on organization design. Research findings from the study of technology provide an explicit framework for diagnosing an organization's work process and for managing it correctly. We will also explore how to include human needs in organization decisions about technology and structural design.

RELEVANCE OF ORGANIZATIONAL TECHNOLOGY FOR MANAGERS

There are several reasons why technology is important for managers. First, the *organization's workflow has specific implications for the organization structure and management systems used to facilitate and control that workflow.* This relationship is illustrated in Exhibit 9.1. Without knowledge of technology, and

EXHIBIT 9.1
Technology and Organization Design

Technology	Organization Design
Routineness	Formalization
Manufacturing	Centralization
Service	Coordination
Interdependence	Employee needs

through trial and error, managers may design an incorrect organization structure. Understanding how management systems can be tailored to technology can directly increase a manager's effectiveness.

Second, *most increases in organizational efficiency and productivity come through changes in technology.* Robots are taking over work activities such as welding ships, painting refrigerators, die-casting, and packing cologne in gift wrapped containers.[3] Other high-technology areas such as fiber optics and gene splicing are revolutionizing production processes. New technology must be assimilated into organizations, and the new technology makes new demands on management. Understanding the structural requirements of a new workflow can smooth its implementation and the management of it.

The third reason is that *organizational technology influences job design.*[4] We discussed job design in Chapter 6, and saw that technology places constraints upon management's ability to vary job design. If machines or workflow are changed, then jobs are changed. For example, Paul Laincz works for AT&T as a telephone installer and repairperson.[5] Laincz used to go to work wearing jeans, with the tool belt around his waist. Now he is called a "systems technician," and he makes his calls wearing a suit and tie, carrying his tools in a briefcase. He drives a company car rather than a van. Instead of receiving job assignments from a supervisor, Laincz works exclusively with five corporate clients. He decides what needs doing and when. He can call in additional experts if needed. Paul Laincz's job has been caught up in the major technological change that has influenced the design of his task.

The final reason technology is relevant to managers is that *tasks influence human needs and satisfaction.* A fast-paced assembly line often creates small, routine jobs that are unsatisfying to employees and lead to negative attitudes and behavior. Managers have some say in the adoption and design of organizational technology, and this managerial discretion can be used to increase or decrease the satisfaction employees derive from jobs. The field of sociotechnical design has explored the relationship between the demands of technology and the social needs of employees. These findings provide ideas for designing organizational technology to be compatible with both human and organizational needs.

WHAT IS TECHNOLOGY?

A useful way to think about technology is as *workflow*. Workflow is the flow of raw material and the sequence of operations within the organization. Technology is a transformation process. Raw material inputs are brought into the organization from the external environment; they are transformed into useful outputs that are returned to the environment. Our definition of **technology** is the knowledge, tools, techniques and behaviors used to transform organizational inputs into organizational outputs.[6] Exhibit 9.2 illustrates how technology takes raw material inputs and transforms them into finished outputs using employee skills, machines, and tools organized into a work sequence. In a cotton mill, input is the bales of raw cotton purchased from farmers. The raw cotton is cleaned, formed into sheets, carded, spun, and then woven into sheets and pillowcases for distribution to wholesalers and retailers and finally sale to consumers. The tools, machines, and work activities used within the plant are the technology used to transform raw cotton into finished fabric.

EXHIBIT 9.2
Technology and Tasks for a Cotton Mill

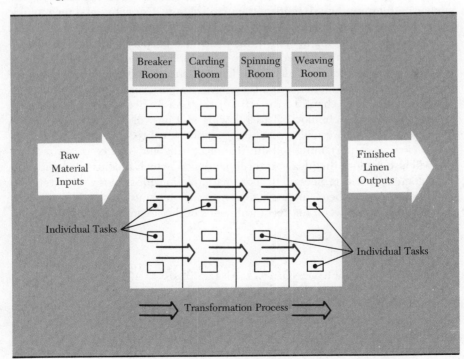

Technology is distinct from individual tasks, as Exhibit 9.2 illustrates. Technology is the aggregate of tasks within a specific department or for the organization as a whole. A **task** is a job performed by an individual employee. A task is an individual's part of the organization's transformation process.

The example in Exhibit 9.2 is just for manufacturing technology, but technology pertains to *all types of organizations.* Hospitals transform sick people into well people, a car wash transforms a dirty car into a clean car, and a television news crew transforms community events into news stories. Organizations are created to construct buildings, sell securities, provide legal advice, educate children, produce winning baseball teams, and fight wars. All forms of organizations require raw materials upon which action is taken that transforms them into the output of an organization.

Another distinction important to the analysis of technology is between department technology and organization-level technology.[7] Organizational technology is the transformation process that takes place within the technical core of the organization.[8] The **technical core** is used to produce the principal products or services of the organization. In manufacturing organizations, the technical core includes all shop work that transforms physical raw materials into products. Organizational-level technologies use processes in the technical core to transform crude oil into gasoline, raw cotton into finished linens, and iron ore into steel castings.

Today many organizations are large and complex, and different technologies appear in different departments of the organization. **Departmental technology** is the transformation process used in departments outside the technical core. Research and development transforms ideas into proposals for new products. Marketing transforms finished inventory into sales. The finance department transforms scattered bits of data into balance sheets and income statements. Each of these departments uses a technology to perform its own work.

Throughout this chapter, we will distinguish between department and organization-level technology. The following section will describe department technologies. Then we will turn to organization-level technologies, where we will review work pertaining to both manufacturing and service organizations. We will also explore the idea of interdependence, which is concerned with the management structure needed to coordinate relationships among departments. The final section of the chapter will deal with sociotechnical systems, discussing the relationship between the technical needs of the organization and the social needs of employees.

DEPARTMENTAL TECHNOLOGY AND STRUCTURE

Early researchers on organizations were puzzled by the observation that characteristics such as formalization and centralization were not the same throughout a given organization. This led to the discovery that variation of structure within organizations was based on task predictability in specific departments.[9] An extensive amount of subsequent research has shown that it is indeed possible to classify departments based on technology. Departments in hospitals, government agencies, and business organizations, for example, have been found to differ systematically based on technology.[10] One of the most useful frameworks for understanding these differences in departmental technologies was developed by Perrow.

Perrow's Model

Variety and Analyzability   Charles Perrow proposed that technology could be examined using two separate dimensions of work activities.[11] The first dimension is variety. **Variety** is the amount of variation and diversity in department work activities. In some departments, work activities are narrow and routine. Employees confront few problems, and the day-to-day job requirements are repetitious. Work on assembly lines and everyday clerical activities are examples of narrow, routine work. Other departments have work that is high in variety. The workflow contains many problems and unexpected demands. The work is unpredictable, and employees may not know what work is needed from one day to the next. Departments with high variety technologies often deal with the unknown, as in research and strategic planning departments, or they deal with constantly changing conditions, as in high-fashion apparel design.

The second dimension of technology is the analyzability of work activities within the department. **Analyzability** refers to a well-defined versus an ill-defined nature of activities. When the conversion process in a department is analyzable, the work can be reduced to explicit steps, and established techniques and programs are typically used to direct employee behavior. Analyzable activities are guided by standard procedures, instructions, or standard technical knowledge such as that available in a manual or handbook. Work that is not analyzable presents a different demand for employees. When problems arise, there are no obvious steps to follow to achieve a solution. Employees may use trial and error and rely on experience and intuition. An example of an unanalyzable task is when an instructor assigns a student group a term paper, but does not provide specific instructions. The students have to figure out how to accomplish this ill-defined task. Technologies in organizations that are not analyzable are those that require long experience to master, and perhaps special talent, such as the trades and crafts, glass blowing, weather forecasting, and artistic endeavors.

Four Technology Categories   The two dimensions of variety and analyzability are illustrated in Perrow's technology framework in Exhibit 9.3. The dimensions of variety and analyzability form the basis of four major categories of technology. **Routine technologies** are low in both variety and analyzability. A department with routine technology is characterized by standard procedures and few problems. **Craft technologies** are characterized by low variety in the work, but the conversion process is not analyzable or well-defined. Tasks may require training and experience, because employees deal with intangible factors. Wine tasters and perfume testers perform craft technologies. **Engi-**

EXHIBIT 9.3
Perrow's Technology Framework

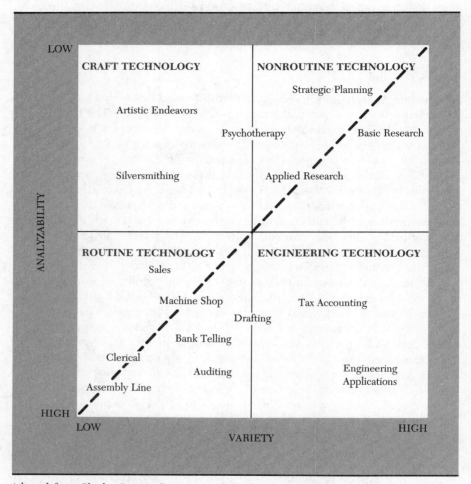

Adapted from Charles Perrow, "A Framework for the Comparative Analysis of Organizations," *American Sociological Review* 32 (1967): 194–208; and Richard L. Daft and Norman Macintosh, "A New Approach to Design and Use of Management Information," *California Management Review* 21 (1978): 82–92.

neering technologies are characterized by substantial variety in the tasks performed, including unpredictable problems. But the work activities are analyzable and can be accomplished using established procedures and techniques. Engineering and accounting departments fall into this category, because they have a well-developed body of data and procedures available to apply to problems. **Nonroutine technologies** are high in task variety but low in analyzability. This is the most difficult and complex form of department technology. New problems occur frequently, and the problems are not analyzable, so employees use trial-and-error procedures. Employees devote a great deal of effort to analyzing problems, and technical knowledge is combined with experience. Nonroutine technologies occur in many R&D or strategic planning departments.

Routine Versus Nonroutine   The dashed line in Figure 9.3 illustrates the pattern many technologies fall into along the routine-nonroutine diagonal. The dimension of analyzability and variety are interrelated in the real world. Technologies with high variety also tend to be low in analyzability. Technologies with low variety tend to be more analyzable.[12] The routine versus nonroutine concept combines both analyzability and variety; it is a useful shorthand device for analyzing departmental technologies. A few departments fit into the craft or engineering categories, but most departments can be categorized along the single dimension of routine versus nonroutine to diagnose basic structural and management requirements needed within the department.

A survey of fourteen manufacturing firms illustrated the way in which departments vary in technology.[13] Over 2600 managers were surveyed about the variability and analyzability of their jobs. When the data were analyzed for the extent of nonroutineness in the work, clear differences across departments were observed; Figure 9.4 illustrates these differences. Research and development departments represent nonroutine technologies within these organiza-

EXHIBIT 9.4
Percentage of Functional Groups Having Routine and Nonroutine Techologies

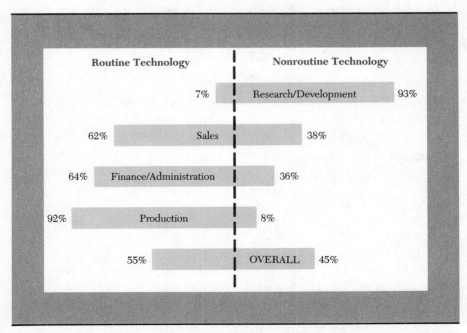

SOURCE: From *Organization Design, Development and Behavior* by Karl O. Magnusen, p. 19. Copyright 1977 Scott, Foresman and Company. Reprinted by permission.

tions, and production departments had the most routine technologies. Sales and finance were in-between, but they were categorized more often as routine rather than nonroutine technology. The evidence for technology differences among organizational departments is strong, and we will now examine the implications of these differences for organization structure and management practices.

Department Design

Department technology is associated with several structural and management characteristics, including formalization of activities, decision-making processes, communication, staff training, and goal orientation.[14] These characteristics are shown in Exhibit 9.5. The diagram shows how each characteristic relates to the four categories of technology defined by Perrow. Exhibit 9.5 can also be used to compare routine versus nonroutine technology, if that single dimension is used to analyze a department.

Formalization of activities is high for routine technology. The work is analyzable and contains little variety; rules, procedures, job descriptions, and formal documents prescribe work activities. Formalization is somewhat lower for craft and engineering technologies, because activities are less analyzable or variety is greater. Nonroutine technologies are characterized by low formalization. Activities are ill defined and variety is great; rules, procedures, and job descriptions are not appropriate. Employees figure out how to respond when problems arise, and they learn their activities through trial and error.

Decision making is centralized for routine technology and decentralized for nonroutine technology. When technology is routine, lower-level employees

EXHIBIT 9.5

Relationship Between Department Technology and Organization Structure and Process

DEPARTMENT TECHNOLOGY	Formalization of Structure	Decision Making	Communication
Routine	High	Centralized	Infrequent, Written
Craft	Moderate	Some Decentralization	Occasional, Verbal
Engineering	Moderate	Some Decentralization	Frequent, Written
Nonroutine	Low	Decentralized	Frequent, Written & Verbal

have little power and influence, because activities are well-defined. As jobs become more nonroutine, influence accrues to lower-level employees because they have knowledge and experience needed to diagnose activities and make decisions. Employees in nonroutine technologies thus have more discretion, and they are allowed to participate in management decision making or make the decisions themselves.

Communication patterns also are influenced by technology.[15] Since problems are less frequent in routine technologies, less communication is needed among employees to resolve issues. Written forms of communication are more prevalent than spoken interaction. As activities become more nonroutine, both communication frequency and spoken communication increase. More widespread discussion is needed to interpret and resolve issues, and to coordinate activities. Frequent face-to-face discussions are encouraged in nonroutine technologies, but they are not needed when activities are routine.

Professionalism of employees is also related to technology. Routine technologies require little training, because tasks are well-defined and activities are prescribed. Craft activities are intangible and difficult to analyze, so employees need on-the-job experience to learn this work. Engineering activities usually are complex and have a large body of knowledge; formal education outside the workplace, in technical schools or universities, is usually needed for engineering activities. Nonroutine technologies typically require large amounts of both formal education and on-the-job training.

The final department characteristic associated with departmental technology is *goal orientation*. The nature of the technology influences what managers try to accomplish. In routine technologies, work activities are easily measured and well defined, so managers stress efficiency; and they increase efficiency through

Staff Professionalism	Goal Orientation
Little	Production Efficiency
From Work Experience	Quality Output
From Formal Education	Reliability
From Education and Work Experience	Quality Output

measures of both inputs and outputs. Craft technologies are more difficult to measure, so the orientation is toward quality products and outputs. Engineering activities are measurable but very complex, so the emphasis is on the accomplishment of reliable outputs, such as computers, airplanes, and telephone systems. Nonroutine technologies are difficult to measure with respect to specific work procedures, so their goal is toward high-quality outputs. Managers evaluate performance by assessing output quality, rather than work inputs or procedures, because employees have the discretion and expertise to decide what procedures to follow.

The relationship between department technology and structure for a large computer manufacturer is illustrated by Up Close 9.1 on Datapoint Corporation. Departments at Datapoint make use of quite different technologies, and managers tailor structure and management processes to fit the technology.

UP CLOSE 9.1:   Datapoint Corporation

"You know, people worry about this mouse in the forest being trampled by a herd of elephants," mused Harold E. O'Kelley, chief executive of San Antonio-based Datapoint Corporation. "Well, I feel like we are fast enough on our feet to stay well out of the way." The elephants Datapoint must dodge are Xerox, IBM, Wang, and AT&T. The forest is the emerging market for the integrating electronic office.

In the race to create the electronic office, Datapoint is fast becoming one of the elephants. It had a modest beginning, with only 2 employees—founders Austin O. Roche and J. P. Ray. They developed the first solid-state communications terminal to replace the teletypewriter, a slow mechanical machine. The company came to life in July 1968, and, with one or two temporary setbacks, has grown rapidly. The company now emphasizes distributed data processing and the building-block concept, both of which it pioneered. Distributed data processing is a computer system made up of several small, inexpensive computers. Each can perform independently, yet all computers provide information to a central point. The building block concept involves the complete interchangeability of both hardware and software, with the capacity to add new equipment later. "It's the world's biggest Lego set," says Gerald L. Cullen, vice president:

This is a fast-moving and highly competitive industry, so research is Datapoint's number one priority. The vice president of research and development is considered an excellent manager. Clad in designer blue jeans, t-shirt, and sandals, he looks as if he might have belonged to a commune of the 1960s. According to the vice president, the people working in research and development are informal and have less bureaucracy than people in other departments. They have flexible working hours and no dress codes. A typical day for an R&D employee begins by a ride to work on a motorcycle and a walk in from the parking lot in running shoes. He might sit in his office working on a problem or go to the lab and start playing with the results of one of his creations.

Employees have few project specifications. They may simply investigate an idea to see how it might be applied to customers. One project is the task of coupling a terminal to a keyboard with infrared signals to eliminate the need for a big cable connected to the keyboard. The R&D department reports directly to the president, lifting the pressure from an authority chain for routinization or formalization. "Our job is to respond quickly to changes in the environment and company priorities, not to meet a dress code. We have free reign, but we also have a moral and professional obligation to respond to the company's needs," says the R&D vice president.

Things are somewhat more structured in the engineering department. The engineers are given product specifications. The researchers will have designed a product, and the engineers take over the development of that product. They encounter frequent difficulties, which they resolve through standard engineering principles. Engineers have to design products that are reliable and work correctly.

The production area includes both skilled and nonskilled work groups. Skilled employees are electronic technicians who diagnose electronic circuit boards and other computer parts to find out why they malfunction. This work takes experience and diagnostic ability. These employees have a degree in electronics technology. Other jobs are more routine. A large part of the production department is devoted to simple soldering and assembly work. The skills needed are manual dexterity and the ability to identify the right component. Task variety is small, and the work is prescribed as a series of explicit steps. Rules and procedures are fairly explicit. Employees have to be at work at a certain time, and do their work in a certain way. If they deviate too far, they have to be let go.[16] ■

Datapoint illustrates the nature of departmental technologies. The relationship between technology and structure has received a great deal of support from research on many organizations.[17] Research findings advocate that departmental managers design their department to be in tune with the requirements of technology. A study of R&D departments, for example, found that when the structure and communication characteristics were not consistent with the demands of the nonroutine technology, the departments tended to perform less effectively.[18] Managers who impose a tight, formalized, centralized structure on nonroutine activities are working against the requirements of technology. Likewise, imposing a loose, informal, decentralized structure for a routine technology tends to be inefficient. Upper-level managers should encourage different structures within different departments throughout their organization.

ORGANIZATIONAL TECHNOLOGY

Now we turn to technology at the organizational level. Organizational technology is the technology within the production subsystem or the technical core of the organization. Goods and services produced by the core technology represent the primary output of the organization. Organizations can be categorized according to whether they use manufacturing or service technologies. First we will discuss the nature of manufacturing technologies, and then we will examine the unique nature and structural characteristics of service organizations.

Manufacturing

The earliest and most influential typology of manufacturing technology was developed by Joan Woodward, a British industrial sociologist. She gathered data about organization structure and management relationships for 100 British manufacturing firms.[19] She gathered data to determine whether basic structural characteristics, such as administrative ratio, span of control, formalization, centralization, and number of hierarchical levels reflected similar management practices across organizations.

Woodward discovered that the patterns of organization structure only made sense when related to manufacturing technology. The organizations in her study were found to have three basic types of manufacturing technology.

I. *Small Batch and Unit Production.* Firms with this technology produce output in small amounts, and each product is typically designed to specific customer needs. The norm is custom work. This technology is also used to make large, one-of-a-kind outputs, such as specialized machines. Examples of small batch include custom clothing, special order manufactured products, custom electronic equipment, special order machine tools, and space capsules.

II. *Large Batch and Mass Production.* This technology is characterized by long production runs of standardized parts. The production is not designed for specific customer needs, so standardized products go into inventory for sale as customers order them. Examples of mass production include most assembly lines, such as those that produce textiles, tobacco products, television sets, and automobiles.

III. *Continuous Process Production.* The distinguishing feature of this technology is that the entire process is mechanized. The process runs continuously, so there is no starting and stopping. Production processes are uniform, and outputs are highly standardized. Illustrations of process production are petroleum products, nuclear power plants, chemical plants, liquor production, and some pharmaceuticals.

The distinguishing theme among the three manufacturing categories is **technical complexity.** Technical sophistication and difficulty increase from small batch, to mass production, to contiuous process technology. Machines are responsible for more of the work and employees for less of the work. Consequently predictability of the results is greater, and degree of machine control over the production process is greater for technologies of greater complexity. The first row in Exhibit 9.6 illustrates this.

Structure and Performance   Using the three classes of manufacturing technology, Woodward found distinct patterns of structural differences. A few of these

EXHIBIT 9.6
Woodward's Technology Framework and Organization Structure

	Manufacturing Technology		
	Small Batch	Mass Production	Continuous Production
TECHNOLOGY CHARACTERISTICS			
Technical Complexity	Low	Medium	High
Machine Control	Low	High	Very High
Predictability of Results	Low	High	Very High
STRUCTURAL CHARACTERISTICS			
Levels in Hierarchy	3	4	6
Direct/Indirect Labor Ratio	9:1	4:1	1:1
Administrative Ratio	Low	Medium	High
Supervisor Span of Control	23	48	15
Formalization	Low	Medium	High
Centralization	Low	Medium	High
Number Skilled Workers	High	Low	High
Communication—Written	Low	High	Low
Communication—Verbal	High	Low	High

differences are illustrated in the lower portion of Exhibit 9.6. Number of hierarchical levels, direct-to-indirect labor ratio, and the administrative ratio all show a positive relationship with increasing technical complexity. More hierarchical levels are required as technical complexity increases. The direct/indirect labor ratio changes because more indirect workers are required to support the complex mass production and continuous process technologies. A larger administrative ratio is also needed to manage more complex technologies.

The other structural characteristics in Figure 9.6 also show a relationship with the technology categories, but for these features the middle level of technical complexity—mass production—is distinct from the other two forms of technology. Supervisor span of control, for example, is very large for mass production, because the machines control the workflow. Unit production has a smaller span of control, because the work is more person intensive and needs greater supervision. Continuous process has a small span of control, because the process is so complex that it must be supervised closely. Worker skill is also higher for both unit production and continuous process, because the work is more difficult than for mass production. The mass production technologies also differ from the others because formalization and centralization are greater. The structural patterns discovered by Joan Woodward thus lead to the conclusion, "Different technologies impose different kinds of demands on individuals and organizations, and those demands have to be met through an appropriate structure."[20]

Another important finding of Woodward's study is that the relationship between structure and technology is directly related to company performance.

She evaluated commercial success as measured by profitability, market share, stock price, and reputation, and discovered that the more successful firms had structures that complemented technology. Most of the organization characteristics of the successful companies had characteristics very near to those in Exhibit 9.6, while poor performing firms had characteristics more typical of another technology type. Thus the appropriate organization structure seems to enable managers and employees to perform work effectively. This basic relationship between manufacturing technology and structure has been reinforced by other studies.[21] Although some of this research was conducted several years ago, the findings are still relevant to manufacturing firms today, as illustrated by the case of Witco Corporation.

UP CLOSE 9.2:   Pearsall Chemical Division

Mason Pearsall, Sr., founded Pearsall Chemical Company in 1954. He remained sole owner until 1975, when he sold his interest to Witco Chemical Corporation.

Pearsall got its start in the chemical industry by manufacturing anhydrous aluminum chloride, a catalyst used in many petrochemical processes. The demand for petrochemical process seemed to be increasing in the 1950s, so the future looked promising. Pearsall currently markets about 45 percent of all domestically produced aluminum chloride.

Pearsall employs only 126 employees. About thirty-five people are employed at the Brainards, NJ, plant, which is located on a 30-acre tract of land along the Delaware River in New Jersey. The plant encompasses 50,000 square feet of warehouse and office space. Pearsall produces aluminum chloride and chlorinated paraffins at this plant. Over twenty reactors are located here, and the majority are used for production of anhydrous aluminum chloride.

The aluminum chloride manufacturing process is relatively simple, as illustrated in Exhibit 9.7. Aluminum ingot or scrap is heated until it forms a molten pool of metal. Chlorine gas is then bubbled up through the molten aluminum. The reaction produces aluminum chloride gas, which is collected and condensed into a solid material. This reaction runs continuously while operators monitor the reaction rate and the equipment. The solidified aluminum chloride is ground into various sizes and stored in sealed containers.

Only a few employees are needed to run this process. The Brainards plant has three supervisors and five foremen. Eight operators monitor and run the equipment. They are supported by ten maintenance workers, drivers, and material handlers. Seven clerical employees also work at Pearsall's Brainard plant.

Pearsall is an informal company. They have only three formal documents. One describes personnel regulations for vacations, sick pay, and promotions. Another policy document contains technical specifications for production. The third contains the standardized MBO planning and accounting procedures.

EXHIBIT 9.7
Process for Producing Aluminum Chloride

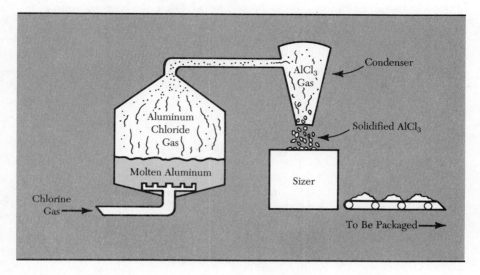

Structural characteristics at the Brainard's plant are as follows.

Number of management levels	*3*
Supervisor span of control	*4*
Direct/indirect labor ratio	*8:10*
Manager/total employees	*8:25*
Number skilled workers	*moderate*
Formalized procedures	*low*
Centralization	*low*
Verbal communication	*high*
Written communication	*high*

The technology at Pearsall is typical of continuous process. The structural characteristics are also consistent with this technology, except for written communication and number of management levels. This is because of the geographical separation from corporate headquarters that is resolved with written communications. The small number of management levels reflects small size. Only a few employees are needed to run a sophisticated mechanical operation, because the machinery does most of the work.[22]

Manufacturing Versus Service Technologies

Shortly after the publication of Woodward's findings about manufacturing technology, other research was undertaken to develop a classification that would incorporate technology in nonmanufacturing organizations. A definition that measures technology in all organizations had to be broadened to incorporate both manufacturing and service organizations.

Aston Studies   A research team from the University of Aston in England developed a scale for classifying a wide variety of organizational technologies. The scale had to be different from Woodward's notion of technical complexity, because many firms in the Aston research did not use the raw materials and machines typically associated with manufacturing technology. The result was a scale the Aston group called **workflow integration.** To determine the workflow integration of the organization's core technology, they evaluated three things: (1) **Automation of equipment,** which represents the amount of work activity performed by machines rather than by humans; (2) **Workflow rigidity,** which includes the extent to which people and equipment can only be used for a single purpose, and the degree to which the sequence of activities is tightly interconnected; and (3) **Specificity of evaluation,** which is the degree to which operational activities can be measured with precise, quantitative assessment.[23]

The Aston research covered fifty-two organizations; examples of workflow integration scores for a sample from their organizations is shown in Exhibit 9.8. A high workflow integration score in the chart means that the firm's technology is characterized by greater automation of equipment, greater rigidity of workflow, and more precise measurement of operations.

One obvious finding shown in Exhibit 9.8 is the difference between manufacturing and service firms. Almost all manufacturing firms have higher workflow integration scores, which means that manufacturing versus service firms also may have structural characteristics different from one another. The Aston findings, like the Woodward findings, suggested that structure was related to technology, but the relationships were not as strong. The Aston group found that as workflow integration increased, so did structural characteristics such as specialization, standardization, and formalization. The manufacturing firms were somewhat larger, somewhat more decentralized, and had a smaller administrative ratio than service firms. The Aston group introduced nonmanufacturing technology into their framework, and found that technology was related to selected characteristics of structure.

Service Organizations   More recent research into the nature of service technologies has provided a clearer definition of the way service differs from manufacturing. The two major differences are as follows:

1. **Intangibility.** The output of a service firm is intangible. It is often abstract, and cannot be stored in inventory. This is very different from manufacturing products, which are produced at one point in time and can be sold at another point in time because they are tangible and not perishable.
2. **Closeness to customer.** In service organizations, the customers are involved in the production process. The customer and the employee interact in order to deliver the service output. In service organizations, employees within the technical core have personal interactions with customers. Interaction between customers and technical core employees does not occur in manufacturing firms.[24]

EXHIBIT 9.8

Examples of Workflow Integration Scores for Manufacturing and Service Firms

Workflow Integration Score	Organization	Organization Type Service	Organization Type Manufacturing
17	Vehicle manufacturer		x
16	Brewery		x
15	Packaging manufacturer		x
14	Metal components manufacturer		x
13	Vehicle tire manufacturer		x
12	Glass components manufacturer		x
11	Printer		x
10	Local authority water department	x	
9	Nonferrous metal processor		x
8	Toy manufacturer		x
7	Local authority civil engineering department	x	
6	Insurance company	x	
5	Research division	x	
4	Savings bank	x	
3	Chain of shoe repair stores	x	
2	Department stores	x	
1	Chain of retail stores	x	

SOURCE: Based on David J. Hickson, D. S. Pugh, and D. C. Pheysey, "Operations Technology and Organization Structure: An Empirical Reappraisal," *Administrative Science Quarterly* 14 (1969): 385.

Other research has built on these ideas, suggesting that the single characteristic most important to the structure of service firms is the *amount of customer contact*.[25] Service firms vary in the amount that their employees within the core technology interact with customers, but most service firms require more direct interaction than manufacturing firms.

Exhibit 9.9 illustrates a continuum of service firms based upon the amount of customer contact with technical core employees. In **quasi-manufacturing** firms, technical core employees are buffered from the customer, either because little direct communication is required, or because service representatives handle the occasional interaction. Typical examples of quasi-manufacturing services are the Social Security Administration, mail-order firms, cable TV, and automated subway systems. In firms characterized as **mixed product and service,** there is some interaction with the customer, and the customer receives a tangible product as well as the intangible service. The tangible product delivered by the organization may be a manicure, an advertising campaign, an airplane seat, or a McDonald's hamburger, and these are provided by

EXHIBIT 9.9
Service Technology and Organization Structure

	Service Technology
	Quasi-Manufacturing
TECHNOLOGY CHARACTERISTIC	
Customer Involvement in Technical Core	Low
Examples	Insurance
	Mail Order
	Social Security
STRUCTURAL CHARACTERISTICS	
Formalization	High
Standardization	High
Training/Skills	Technical
Decision Making	Centralized
Structural Disaggregation	No
Buffer Roles	Yes

employees from the technical core who interact with the customer. In a **pure service** firm in Exhibit 9.9, an information or knowledge type of service is provided to the customer. This means that customer contact is high because the production process only takes place during interaction between customer and technical employee. The customer is heavily involved in the transformation process. Examples are lawyers' services, teaching, and consulting, where knowledge is exchanged during the customer transaction.

Providing a pure service through direct customer contact involves a technology different from a quasi-manufacturing firm. The customer contact has implications for structure and management characteristics. Exhibit 9.9 illustrates these characteristics as well. For example, frequent customer contact means that technical employees will experience more variety and problems, so standardization and formalization will be lower than for service firms that have less customer contact. Employee selection and training is also quite different. Social and interpersonal skills are important for customer involvement, while technical skills are the primary selection and training criteria in quasi-manufacturing technologies. Decision making tends to be decentralized in service firms, because the employee in direct contact with the customer must make decisions autonomously and often immediately to provide satifactory service. By contrast, a manufacturing technology produces standardized outputs, so centralized decision making is possible.

The last two structural characteristics in Exhibit 9.9 are *structural disaggregation* and *boundary roles*.[26] The service firm is often disaggregated into

Service Technology	
Mixed Product and Service	**Pure Service**
Medium	High
Cosmetics	Law Firm
Fast Foods	Teaching
Advertising Agency	Consulting
Medium	Low
Medium	Low
Technical & Interpersonal	Interpersonal
Some Centralized	Decentralized
Some	Yes
Some	No

small units that are located close to the customer. Consulting firms, fast-food franchises, brokerage firms, and medical practices are structured so that units are dispersed to facilitate interaction with customers. Manufacturing firms, by contrast, tend to aggregate operations in areas that have raw materials and an available workforce. The pure service firm does not have expensive machinery, long production runs, or tangible products, so it can easily be disaggregated into small, self-contained units that are located close to the customer. *Buffer roles* are positions established on the boundary between technical core employees and customers. Buffer roles are used in quasi-manufacturing service firms to handle customer requests and hence protect the technical core employees from disruptions. Workflow can be standardized in this manner, but pure service firms handle customer variety directly with technical employees.

Conclusion   Service firms tend to differ from manufacturing firms because the service output is intangible and the transformation process involves direct contact between the technical core and the customer. For these reasons, pure service organizations tend to be less formalized and centralized, and they require a different structure and set of employee skills than do manufacturing firms. Knowledge about the specific structure appropriate for different service firms is still rudimentary, but new research on service firms will provide better information with which to design these organizations. Hotels provide a mixed product and the following **Up Close** section illustrates how Marriott hotels are structured to meet customer needs.

Bill Marriott is risking $350 million on the most expensive hotel ever built. It is called the Marquis, is going up in Times Square, and is the beginning of an assault on the competitive downtown convention hotel business. In conjunction with this luxury market, Marriott is also moving into the huge moderate-price hotel market.

The building program reflects a simple strategy for Marriott Corporation: build new hotels where the customers are. This means building luxury hotels downtown and at airports, and developing locations in both suburbs and inner cities. Convention centers, like Atlantic City, are another target. Marriott will build 9000 new rooms next year, and these rooms will be scattered throughout the country.

In addition to locating close to the customer, Marriott tries to build in a sense of luxury. The Marquis in New York is lush—with a mammoth 48-story jungled atrium, in which glass elevators will move up and down between the lobby and the sky-view restaurant.

For the hotel's service, often employees are in contact with customers for only a few moments at the front desk. Many travelers check out automatically. Most of the hotel service is through the presentation of the room and other amenities, such as room service.

To make the right impression every time, Marriott uses a system of tightly centralized policies, procedures, and controls that regulate every operational detail. Every behind-the-scene job has a manual that breaks down the work into a number of steps. A hotel maid has 66 things to do in cleaning up a room, from dusting the tops of pictures (#7) to making sure the telephone books and bibles are in neat condition (#37). All 6000 recipes available to Marriott establishments have been tested and approved in central kitchens. Creative chefs are forewarned: "Deviations from the standard written specifications may not be made without prior approval and written consent of the vice president of food and beverages." The management of Marriott wants to be absolutely certain that the business travelers will receive the service they expect and deserve. Consistency is one of the best ways to assure this, they feel.[27]

The Marriott hotel service involves low to moderate customer contact between employees and customers. Jobs that do not require direct customer contact are formalized. Much of the service is through the physical structure and other products, such as food. In Marriott's case, their extensive rules, regulations, and bureaucracy seem to be a successful way to run their business. The organization is also desegregated, with hotels located wherever customers may need them.

TECHNOLOGICAL INTERDEPENDENCE

The last typology about organization-level technology we'll examine was proposed by James Thompson.[28] Thompson's typology incorporates both manufacturing and service organizations, but with an important difference. His research stresses interdependence among departments within the technical core as a major factor influencing organizational design. **Interdependence** is the extent to which departments depend on one another for the exchange of resources and information to accomplish their work.[29] Independent departments do their work autonomously, while departments that are interdependent must exchange resources and information to perform effectively.

The three categories of technology proposed by Thompson and the related interdependence are illustrated in Exhibit 9.10. These are: (1) mediating, (2) long-linked, and (3) intensive technologies. The three types of interdependence among departments are (1) pooled, (2) sequential, and (3) reciprocal. A **mediating technology** involves the mediation or linking of clients from the external environment. A commercial bank, for example, links depositors with borrowers. A real estate firm links people who wish to sell houses with people who wish to buy houses. Mediating technology is characterized by **pooled interdependence,** which means that each department works independently. Each department shares and contributes to a common resource pool, but the departments work on their own. In a commercial bank, the savings, investment, loan, and real estate departments are separate units that work independently of one another.

A **long-linked technology** refers to successive stages of production; each stage uses production of the preceding stage and in turn produces materials for the following stages of production.[30] Organizational activities occur in sequence, so that the output of department A becomes the input to department B, the output of department B becomes the input to department C, and so on. The most typical example of long-linked technology is the automobile assembly line. Long-linked technology is characterized by **sequential interdependence.** This is a higher level of interdependence than pooled interdependence, and it means that the organization has to coordinate the activities of departments to insure that the workflow moves efficiently through the organization. The demand on the organization structure for coordination and control will be greater here than for low-level pooled interdependence.

An **intensive technology** is characterized by a collection of specialized services designed to bring about change in a client. Each department possesses specialized skills, and skills from a number of departments are used to help clients. Hospitals are an excellent example of intensive technology because they have several specialties (X-ray, nursing, physical therapy, psychiatry, surgery), each of which provide services to the same client. The relationship among departments is characterized as **reciprocal interdependence.** Reciprocal is the highest level of interdependence, and it pertains to the mutual exchange

EXHIBIT 9.10
Thompson's Technology and Interdependence Framework

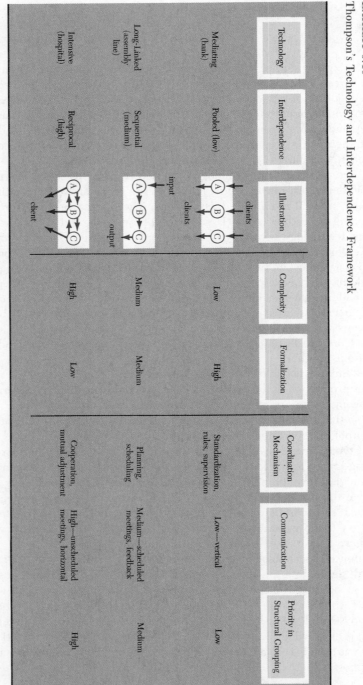

Technology	Interdependence	Illustration	Complexity	Formalization	Coordination Mechanism	Communication	Priority in Structural Grouping
Mediating (bank)	Pooled (low)		Low	High	Standardization, rules, supervision	Low—vertical	Low
Long-Linked (assembly line)	Sequential (medium)		Medium	Medium	Planning, scheduling	Medium—scheduled meetings, feedback	Medium
Intensive (hospital)	Reciprocal (high)		High	Low	Cooperation, mutual adjustment	High—unscheduled meetings, horizontal	High

of resources and information between departments. The output of department A is the input to department B, and the output of department B may become the input back again to department A. A hospital patient may move back and forth between X-ray, nursing, surgery, and physical therapy as needed to effect a cure. Reciprocal interdependence makes the greatest demands upon management structure, because continuous interaction and mutual adjustment among departments are required.

The structural characteristics associated with each technology are also illustrated in Exhibit 9.10.[31] As the technology shifts from low interdependence to high interdependence among departments, organization structure becomes more complex and less formalized. The complexity reflects more activities in the production process, and reduced formalization means less reliance on standardization, rules, and procedures to guide the workflow. Structural mechanisms are also needed to handle the coordination requirements of interdependence. For pooled interdependence, rules, procedures and supervisory control are sufficient to handle the few problems and exchanges that occur among departments. For sequential interdependence, plans and schedules are used as well as supervisory control, to ensure that the outputs of departments are sufficient to supply other departments in the sequence of operations. Under high levels of reciprocal independence, rules and schedules are insufficient. Coordination is through mutual adjustment, each department reacting to the needs of other departments continuously. Coordination needs are also reflected in communication. Low interdependence is characterized by simple vertical communication, while high levels of interdependence require frequent unscheduled meetings among department managers.

Finally, since interdependence influences the amount of managerial energy and structural effort involved in coordination, interdependence determines how departments should be physically *grouped* within the organization.[32] Departments that are reciprocally interdependent should be structured close to one another, to facilitate interaction and mutual adjustment. The first structural priority, then, is to locate reciprocal departments together under a common supervisor. Next in priority are departments that are sequentially interdependent. They will be grouped as close together as possible after the reciprocally interdependent departments have been located together. Pooled interdependent departments have the lowest priority in structural grouping. They do not need to be located near other departments because their work is independent. An occasional telephone call or memo is all that is required, and these communications can occur from any location.

Research into technology and the impact of departmental interdependence supports the types of structure and coordination mechanisms identified in Figure 9.10.[33] The three levels of interdependence can be seen in almost all organized activities, including athletic teams. The following **Up Close** illustrates how interdependence among players influences both the type of team structure and coaching needed to achieve success.

UP CLOSE 9.4:   Baseball, Football and Basketball Teams

Pete Rose said, "Baseball is a team game, but nine men who reach their individual goals make a nice team." Team members function autonomously in the sport of baseball, each taking a turn at bat and playing his own position. When interaction does occur it is usually only between two or three players, as in a double play. Players are widely dispersed, which makes coordination difficult. Coordination is achieved primarily through the structure of the game. Rules are defined for each activity. Each player must practice at his own specialty, take batting practice, and take responsibility for conditioning. The manager's job is to select members and develop skills consistent with a winning team. If the individual parts work successfully, the team will win.

Football differs from baseball in a number of ways. First, interdependence among players tends to be sequential. The line first performs blocks that enable the backs to run or pass. The flow of plays is also sequential from first down to fourth down. The players are physically located close together, which enables coordination. The basic unit is the group: offense, defense, and special teams. Each group must work together; coordination is important. The primary coordinating mechanism is planning and prescribed rules. Each player has an assignment that fits with other assignments, and management designs an extensive game plan to enable the coordination of activities sufficient to win games.

Basketball is free flowing. Division of labor is less precise than in football or baseball, because every player is involved in offense and defense, handles the ball, and attempts to score. Interdependence is reciprocal. The ball flows back

EXHIBIT 9.11
Interdependence and Structure in Three Sports

	Baseball	Football	Basketball
Interdependence	Pooled	Sequential	Reciprocal
Physical Density Among Elements	Low	Medium	High
Basic Unit	Individual	Group	Team
Coordinating Mechanism	Rules that govern the sport	Planning and prescribed roles	Responsibility sharing and mutual adjustment
Management Task	Select members and develop skills	Prepare, develop and execute game plan	Influence flow of game

SOURCE: Adapted from Robert W. Keidel, "Baseball, Football, and Basketball: Models for Business," *Organizational Dynamics* 1984 (Winter): 5–18.

and forth among players continuously. The basic unit is the team, and team members interact continuously to achieve success. Management skill required for success in basketball involves the ability to influence this dynamic process. Players must learn to go with the flow of the game and to adjust to one another as events unfold.

Interdependence is a primary reason for structure across the three sports. The differences are illustrated in Exhibit 9.11. Baseball is organized around an autonomous individual, football around groups on which the players are sequentially interdependent, and basketball around the free flow of reciprocal interdependence. The unfolding game reflects the interdependence built into the sport.[34] ■

SOCIOTECHNICAL SYSTEMS

So far in this chapter we have described models for analyzing departmental technology, manufacturing technology, service versus manufacturing technology, and interdependence among departments. We also discussed how organization structure, management systems, and employee selection and training should fit organizational technology. Senior management initially selects technology based upon organizational goals and efficiency requirements, and the organization is designed to be congruent with the technology.

Sociotechnical theory takes a somewhat different view. The needs of people and work groups are factored into the design equation. The "technical" portion of the theory refers to the tools, machines, skills, and knowledge used in the work process, which is similar to the definition of technology presented earlier in this chapter. The "socio" portion of the theory refers to the people who work in organizations and the relationships among them.[35] The goal of sociotechnical systems is **joint optimization,** which states that an organization will function optimally only if the social and technical systems of the organization are designed to fit the demands of one another.[36] This means that structural changes that meet human needs while ignoring the technical system, or changes that improve technology but ignore human needs, will not be effective in improving overall organization performance.

Sociotechnical principles are similar to the job design ideas covered in Chapter 6, with one notable difference. Job design concepts apply to the individual employee; the job is designed to provide greater motivation and satisfaction for the employee. Sociotechnical principles are more macro, applying to the department or organization levels; they assess the needs of major work groups in conjunction with overall technology.

Sociotechnical principles evolved from work by the Tavistock Institute, a research organization in England, during the 1950s and 1960s.[37] Researchers from the Tavistock Institute visited organizations, either because performance was low or because a new technology had been introduced. Through careful analysis, they aimed to find a fit between social and technical systems that would permit joint optimization. The researchers defined the needs of the organization with respect to efficient technology. They also defined the needs of the workforce to include a meaningful unit of work, autonomy, satisfactory interpersonal relationships within the group, and high skill level.

Over 130 examples of organizational changes using sociotechnical principles have been reported around the world.[38] These organizational changes have occurred in a railway maintenance depot, textile mills, auto manufacturing, and a pet food plant.[39] In the majority of these organizations, the changes brought about by sociotechnical researchers improved performance, safety, quality, absenteeism, and turnover by adjusting technology and workflow to fit human social needs. The positive results of added worker involvement and commitment to the organization more than made up for the deviations from the most efficient methods as based on mechanical principles.

One of the most famous applications of sociotechnical design was reported in a study of mechanization in British coal mines. A new mining technology destroyed working relationships among coal miners, and hence had a negative outcome on production. Adjusting the technology to accommodate social needs produced benefits to both the organization and employees.

UP CLOSE 9.5:   British Coal Mines

Prior to the 1950s, coal was mined by hand, and mining organizations sought mechanical methods that would improve productivity. One proposed new method was the "long-wall" method, which was to replace the "hand-got" method of mining coal used at that time.

Hand-got Method. *Conditions in the coal mines were dark, hazardous, and difficult. Coal miners worked in small groups, with each group assigned to a specific coal face, called a short wall. The group on a single shift consisted of two miners with one or two assistants. Each pair of miners had a full range of coal-face skills, that is, each could diagnose the vein, remove coal from the wall, and prepare it for transport. An important aspect of group design was that the work was accomplished over a three-shift cycle. Members of all three shifts were part of the same group. The day-shift members would take the cycle of activities as far as possible, and the work would be continued by the evening shift, as then by the night shift. The six miners perceived one another as a primary group, and they were paid the same wages based upon overall group productivity.*

Although working conditions were difficult, the coal miners had the social characteristics desired by sociotechnical theory. Workers could see the completion of their work. They had autonomy to set their own pace and take a break when needed. Miners had opportunites for satisfactory interpersonal relationships, and they were highly skilled because each person performed all tasks needed for mining the coal. Technology, however, was primitive and inefficient, so improved methods were needed to facilitate coal mining.

Long-Wall Method. *The new long-wall method used mechanical coal cutters and long-face conveyors. Previous teams, because of their small size, worked on short walls, but new mechanization gained greater efficiency by application to long walls. The new machines made extreme changes in the structure and social relationships among miners. The machines required large work groups and job specialization. As many as fifty miners might be deployed along a long coal face, each one performing only a single task, and receiving pay depending on the nature of that task. Employees had little opportunity for social interaction, and they did not identify with the work team. Work shifts began to compete with one another, leaving bad work for the next shift. Workers were unhappy with the new system, and the long-wall method failed to yield desired economic returns. Labor strife increased.*

Composite Long-Wall Method. *Researchers from the Tavistock Institute studied the problem, and learned that other mines had made adjustments to help increase social satisfaction among coal miners. The researchers were able to define a system that met the criteria of joint optimization. Approximately 40 miners were used as a work group operating over the three shifts. Group members had the freedom to select new employees for the group, and they performed all tasks required during their shift. Miners tended to specialize, but they had freedom to do different jobs. An incentive pay system was reinstalled to reward productivity. Each shift coordinated with following shifts so that total group performance was optimized.*

The composite long-wall method took advantage of the new technology, and allowed the work group members to satisfy social needs. Workers in the group were able to achieve closure by doing a meaningful unit of work. They had autonomy, good interpersonal relations, and a job that utilized their training and skills.

The joint optimization between social and technical systems had several advantages for the organization and the workers: members were more sensitive to one another and helped each other more; absenteeism dropped to roughly one-half the previous rate; productivity increased to an average rating of 95% compared to 78% in previous groups, and fewer conflicts and labor disputes were observed. The integration of both social and technical aspects of the job into the organization design was successful. This case became a forerunner for the development and further application of sociotechnical principles.[40] ▪

THE TECHNOLOGICAL IMPERATIVE

Early research results on the relationship of technology to organization structure were so promising that the concept called **technological imperative** developed. This concept means that organization structure and management processes *must* be congruent with the technology, or the organization will be inefficient. Technology was believed to be the most important determinant of organization structure. More recent views have begun to modify this approach.

Technology is considered an important variable, but within limits. Technology is not the sole cause of structure, and managers do not have to blindly accede to technology in every case, for the following reasons.

- *Senior managers have initial discretion for selecting and defining the core technology of the organization.* The technology used within the organization is the outcome of managerial choices about which products to produce and how to produce them. When organizations decide to move into education, aluminum chloride, automobiles, or travel, these choices select the technology that will be used. Within these basic choices, technology also can be adjusted. For example, Saab Scania redesigned its traditional assembly line for producing cars from semi-autonomous assembly work groups. Rather than accept the long assembly line as an imperative, managers defined technology so that groups could assemble selected portions at work stations.[41]

- *Technology has its greatest impact on organization structure located close to the workflow.* In small organizations where the entire structure is located close to the workflow, technology is a primary influence on structure. The same is true for small and medium-sized departments throughout the organization—structure within the department reflects the nature of the technology. In large, diverse organizations, however, several levels of structure may exist, and many employees are far removed from the workflow. Structure and management processes within these parts of the organization are heavily influenced by non-technology variables.[42]

- *Factors other than technology also influence organization structure.* We saw in the previous chapter that organization size imposes certain requirements for formalization, standardization, and centralization. Large organizations are structured differently from small organizations, so size must be considered in addition to technology as a factor in structure. The external environment also influences structure, which we will discuss in the next chapter.

The conclusion from current research is that technology does influence design, but it is not an absolute imperative for design. Managers should be aware of technology, especially in small organizations and at the department level, so that the structure fits the workflow. But the structural equation for organizations is complex, and design will also be influenced by management preferences, size, and other factors described through the remainder of this book.

SUMMARY

This chapter has explored the concept of organizational technology, which is an important concept for managers. Technology influences structure, and managers must understand technologies to adapt structure to them. Technology also influences job design and the opportunity for individuals to meet their social needs.

Technology exists at both organization and department levels. The important model for understanding department technology was developed by Perrow. Department technology is defined in terms of variety and analyzability. These two dimensions can be collapsed into a single dimension of routine-nonroutine department technology. Structure for nonroutine technologies typically differs from that of routine technologies because it has less formalization and centralization, more horizontal communication, more training and experience, and a different goal orientation.

Organizational technologies are classified as either manufacturing or service. The important framework for manufacturing technology was proposed by Woodward, and included small batch, mass production, and continuous process. The technical complexity inherent within these technologies influences organization structure. Service technologies are related to the amount of customer involvement in the production process. Services are more intangible than products, and high customer involvement means a less formal and more decentralized structure. Service firms often disaggregate to be close to the customer, and they have fewer buffers to protect the technical core from customer variations.

The concept of technological interdependence is also relevant to structure. Interdependence between departments can be pooled, sequential, or reciprocal. High levels of interdependence place demands upon structure. Reciprocal interdependence takes priority in departmental grouping, and is coordinated by mutual adjustment rather than by rules and procedures.

The sociotechnical framework explains how to tailor technology to the social needs of work groups. These concepts are consistent with the job design concepts in Chapter 6. Sociotechnical concepts are consistent with the conclusion that technology has influence on structure, but is not an imperative for structure. Managers have discretion to adjust technology as necessary to meet the needs of employees and to allow for organization size and environment.

KEY WORDS

analyzability
automation of
    equipment
closeness to customer
continuous process
craft technology
departmental
    technology
engineering technology
intangibility
intensive technology
interdependence
joint optimization
long-linked technology

mass production
mediating technology
mixed product and
    service
nonroutine technology
pooled
    interdependence
pure service
quasi-manufacturing
reciprocal
    interdependence
routine technology
sequential
    interdependence

service technology
small batch
sociotechnical theory
specificity of
    evaluation
technical complexity
technical core
technological
    imperative
technology
variety
workflow integration
workflow rigidity

DISCUSSION QUESTIONS

1. Why is the concept of technology important to managers?
2. Describe the concepts of variety and analyzability, and explain how they are associated with Perrow's technology categories of routine, craft, engineering, and nonroutine.
3. How would department structure and management processes be expected to differ for routine vs. nonroutine department technology?
4. In the Woodward framework, how do differences in small batch, mass production, and continuous process manufacturing technologies reflect differences in technical complexity? How do these differences influence organization structure?
5. Discuss the concept of workflow integration and why it will be different for service versus manufacturing firms.
6. What is a service technology? Are different types of service technologies associated with different structures? Explain.
7. Explain the typology of technology proposed by Thompson. How does interdependence between departments influence means of coordination?
8. What similarities exist among the technological frameworks developed by Woodward, Perrow, and Thompson? Can the frameworks be interchanged and lead to similar predictions about structure?
9. What is the major difference between sociotechnical systems theory and the other technology frameworks discussed in this chapter?
10. To what extent is technology an *imperative* for the design of organization structure?

CASE 9.1:   Acetate Department

The Acetate Department's product consisted of about twenty different kinds of viscous liquid acetate used by another department to manufacture transparent film to be left clear, or coated with photographic emulsion or iron oxide.

Before the change: The Department was located in an old four story building as in Exhibit A. The work flow was as follows:

1. Twenty kinds of powder arrived daily in 50 pound paper bags. In addition, storage tanks of liquid would be filled weekly from tank trucks.
2. Two or three Acetate Helpers would jointly unload pallets of bags into the storage area using a lift truck.
3. Several times a shift, the Helpers would bring the bagged material up the elevator to the third floor where it would be temporarily stored along the walls.
4. Mixing batches was under the direction of the Group Leader and was rather like baking a cake. Following a prescribed formula, the Group Leader, Mixers and Helpers operate valves to feed in the proper solvent and manually dump in the proper weight and mixture of solid material. The glob would be mixed by giant egg beaters and heated according to the recipe.
5. When the batch was completed, it was pumped to a finished product storage tank.
6. After completing each batch, the crew would thoroughly clean the work area of dust and empty bags because cleanliness was extremely important to the finished product.

To accomplish this work, the Department was structured as in Exhibit B.

EXHIBIT A

Elevation View of Acetate Department Before Change

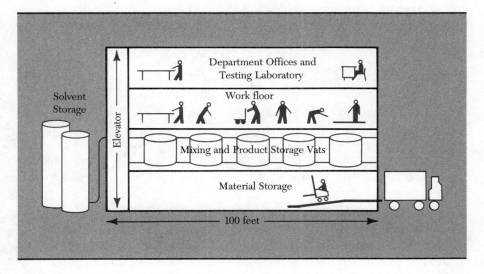

The Helpers were usually young men 18–25 years of age; the Mixers 25 to 40 and the Group Leaders and Foremen 40 to 60. Foremen were on salary. Group Leaders, Mixers and Helpers on hourly pay.

To produce 20,000,000 pounds of product per year, the Department operated 24 hours a day, 7 days a week. Four crews rotated shifts: for example, Shift Foremen A and his two Group Leaders and crews would work two weeks on the day shift 8:00 a.m. to 4:00 p.m., then two weeks on the evening shift 4:00 p.m. to midnight, then two weeks on the night shift midnight to 8:00 a.m. There were two days off between shift changes.

During a typical shift, a Group Leader and his crew would complete two or three batches. A batch would frequently be started on one shift and completed by the next shift crew. There was slightly less work on the evening and night shifts because no deliveries were made, but these crews engaged in a little more cleaning. The Shift Foreman would give instructions to the two Group Leaders at the beginning of each shift as to the status of batches in process, batches to be mixed, what deliveries were expected and what cleaning was to be done. Periodically throughout the shift, the Foreman would collect samples in small bottles which he would leave at the laboratory technicians' desk for testing.

The management and office staff (Department Head, Staff Engineer, Lab Technician, and Department Clerk) only worked on the day shift, although if an emergency arose on the other shifts, the Foreman might call.

All in all, the Department was a pleasant place in which to work. The work floor was a little warm, but well-lighted, quiet and clean. Substantial banter and horseplay occurred when the crew wasn't actually loading batches, particularly on the non-day shifts. The men had a dartboard in the work area and competition was fierce and loud. Frequently a crew would go bowling right after work, even at 1:00 a.m., for the community's alleys were open 24 hours a day. Department turnover and absenteeism were low. Most employees spent their entire career with the Company, many in one department. The corporation was large, paternalistic, well-paying, and offered attractive fringe benefits including large, virtually automatic bonuses for all. Then came the change. . . .

EXHIBIT B

Organization Chart of Acetate Department Before Change

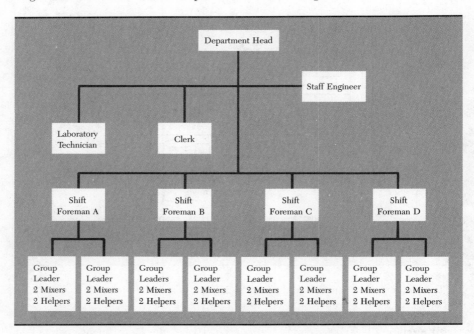

The new system: To improve productivity, the Acetate Department was completely redesigned, the technology changed from batches to continuous processing. The basic building was retained, but substantially modified as in Exhibit C. The modified work flow is as follows:

1. Most solid raw materials are delivered via trucks in large aluminum bins holding 500 pounds.

2. One Handler (formerly Helper) is on duty at all times in the first floor to receive raw materials and to dump the bins into the semiautomatic screw feeder.

3. The Head Operator (former Group Leader) directs the mixing operations from his control panel on the fourth floor located along one wall across from the Department Offices. The mixing is virtually an automatic operation once the solid material has been sent up the screw feed; a tape program opens and closes the necessary valves to add solvent, heat, mixing, etc. Sitting at a table before his panel, the Head Operator monitors the process to see that everything is operating within specified temperatures and pressures.

This technical change allowed the Department to greatly reduce its manpower. The new structure is illustrated in Exhibit D.

One new position was created, that of a pump operator who is located in a small separate shack about 300 feet from the main building. He operates pumps and valves that move the finished product among various storage tanks.

Under the new system, production capacity was increased to 25,000,000 pounds per year. All remaining employees received a 15 percent increase in pay. Former personnel not retained in the Dope Department were transferred to other departments in the company. No one was dismissed.

EXHIBIT C
Elevation View of Acetate Department After Change

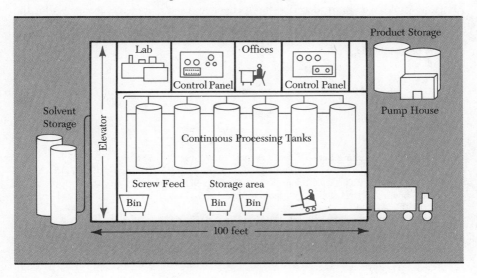

EXHIBIT D
Organization Chart of Acetate Department After Change

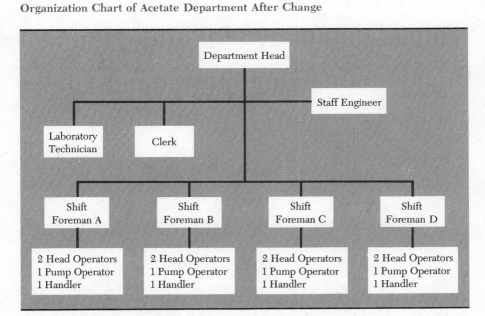

Unfortunately, actual output has lagged well below capacity in the several months since the construction work and technical training was completed. Actual production is virtually identical with that under the old technology. Absenteeism has increased markedly and several judgmental errors by operators have resulted in substantial losses.[43]

CASE QUESTIONS

1. How would Woodward describe the technology used before the change? After the change?
2. What is the source of the problem described in the Acetate Department? How might this be resolved?

NOTES

1. James Cook, "Nothing But the Best," *Forbes*, September 28, 1981, pp. 155–159.
2. "Field Report: Automated Beef Boning," *Food Engineering* 56 (February, 1984): 170.
3. Craig R. Waters, "There's a Robot in Your Future," *Inc.*, June 1982, pp. 64–74.
4. John Slocum and H. A. Sims, "A Typology of Technology and Job Redesign," *Human Relations* 33 (1980): 193–212.
5. Jeremy Main, "Work Won't be the Same Again," *Fortune*, June 28, 1982, pp. 58–65.
6. Charles Perrow, "A Framework for the Comparative Analysis of Organizations," *American Sociological Review* 32 (1967): 194–208; Denise M. Rosseau, "Assessment of Technology in Organizations: Closed versus Open Systems Approaches," *Academy of Management Review* 4 (1979): 531–542.
7. Donald Gerwin, "Relationships Between Structure and Technology," in Paul C. Nystrom and William H. Starbuck (eds.), *Handbook of Organization Design: Volume 2, Remodeling Organizations and Their Environments* (London: Oxford University Press, 1981), pp. 2–38.
8. James D. Thompson, *Organizations in Action* (New York: McGraw-Hill, 1967).
9. Richard H. Hall, "Intraorganizational Structural Variation: Application of the Bureaucratic Model," *Administrative Science Quarterly* 7 (1962): 295–308.
10. Peggy Leatt and Rodney Schneck, "Criteria for Grouping Nursing Subunits in Hospitals," *Academy of Management Journal*, 27 (1984): 150–165; Gerald D. Bell, "The Influence of Technological Components of Work Upon Management Control," *Academy of Management Journal* 8 (1965): 127–132; Andrew H. Van de Ven and Andre Delbecq, "A Task Contingent Model of Work Unit Structure," *Administrative Science Quarterly* 19 (1974): 183–197; Richard L. Daft and Norman B. Macintosh, "A Tentative Exploration into Amount and Equivocality of Information Processing in Organizational Work Units," *Administrative Science Quarterly* 26 (1981): 207–224; Lawrence G. Hrebiniak, "Job Technologies, Supervision and Work Group Structure," *Administrative Science Quarterly* 19 (1974): 395–410; A. J. Grimes and S. M. Kline, "The Technological Imperative: The Relative Impact of Task Unit, Modal Technology, and Hierarchy on Structure," *Academy of Management Journal* 16 (1973): 583–597; Michael Withey, Richard L. Daft, and William C. Cooper, "Measures of Perrow's Work Unit Technology: An Empirical Assessment and a New Scale," *Academy of Management Journal* 25 (1982): 45–63.
11. Perrow, "Framework for Comparative Analysis," pp. 194–208; Charles Perrow, *Organizational Analysis: A Sociological Approach* (Belmont, CA: Wadsworth, 1970).
12. Withey, Daft, and Cooper, "Measures of Perrow's Work Unit Technology," pp. 45–63; Andrew H. Van de Ven and Diane L. Ferry, *Measuring and Assessing Organizations* (New York: Wiley, 1980).
13. Karl O. Magnusen, *Organizational Design, Development, and Behavior* (Glenview, IL: Scott, Foresman and Company, 1977), p. 19.
14. W. Alan Randolph, "Matching Technology and the Design of Organization Units," *California Management Review*, Summer 1981, pp. 39–48; Jerald Hage and Michael Aiken, "Routine Technology, Social Structure and Organization Goals," *Administrative Science Quarterly* 14 (1969): 366–376; Charles A. Glisson, "Dependence of Technological Routinization on Structural

Variables in Human Service Organizations," *Administrative Science Quarterly* 23 (1978): 383–395; Bell, "The Influence of Technological Components," pp. 127–132; Michael L. Tushman, "Work Characteristics and Subunit Communications Structure: A Contingency Analysis," *Administrative Science Quarterly* 24 (1979): 92–98.

15. Richard L. Daft and Norman B. Macintosh, "A New Approach to Design and Use of Management Information," *California Management Review* 21 (Fall 1978): 82–92; A. Babelas, "Communication Patterns in Task-Oriented Groups," *Journal of the Acoustical Society of America* 22 (1950): 725–730.

16. Based on "Datapoint Corporation," by Richard Cone, Bruce Snow, and Ricky Waclawcayk, Texas A&M University, 1981; S. Chakravarty, "Elephant Walk," *Forbes*, October 12, 1981, pp. 188–192; and M. George, "The Data on Datapoint," *San Antonio Magazine.*

17. Randolph, "Matching Technology and the Design of Organization Units"; Daft and Macintosh, "Tentative Exploration into the Amount and Equivocality of Information Processing"; Hage and Aiken, "Routine Technology, Social Structure and Organizational Goals"; Glisson, "Dependence of Technological Routinization on Structural Variables in Human Service Organizations."

18. Michael L. Tushman, "Technological Communication in R&D Laboratories: The Impact of Project Work Characteristics," *Academy of Management Journal* 21 (1978): 624–625.

19. Joan Woodward, *Industrial Organization: Theory and Practice* (London: Oxford University Press, 1975); and *Management and Technology* (London: Her Majesty's Stationary Office, 1958).

20. Woodward, *Industrial Organizations*, p. vi.

21. Edward Harvey, "Technology and the Structure of Organizations," *American Sociological Review* 33 (1968): 241–259; William L. Zwerman, *New Perspectives on Organizational Theory* (Westport, CT: Greenwood Publishing Company, 1970); Pradip and Khandwalla, "Mass Output Orientation of Operations Technology and Organization Structure," *Administrative Science Quarterly* 19 (1974): 74–97.

22. Based on "Pearsall Chemical Division of Witco Chemical Corporation: Organizational History, Structure and Analysis," by Jack Calkins, Walter Hammond, and Glenn Telge, Texas A&M University, 1981; "The Witco Story," by William Wishnick; and "10-K Report," Pearsall Chemical Corporation, December 31, 1978.

23. Derek S. Pugh, David J. Hickson, Christopher R. Hinings, and Christopher Turner, "Dimensions of Organization Structure," *Administrative Science Quarterly* 13 (1968): 65–105; David J. Hickson, Derek S. Pugh, and Diana C. Pheysey, "Operations Technology and Organization Structure: An Empirical Reappraisal," *Administrative Science Quarterly* 14 (1969): 378–397.

24. Peter K. Mills and Newton Margulies, "Toward a Core Typology of Service Organizations," *Academy of Management Review* 5 (1980): 255–265; Peter K. Mills and Dennis J. Moberg, "Perspectives on the Technology of Service Operations," *Academy of Management Review* 7 (1982): 467–478; V. Fuchs, *The Service Economy* (New York: Columbia University Press, 1968).

25. Richard B. Chase and David A. Tansik, "The Customer Contact Model for Organization Design," *Management Science* 29 (1983): 1037–1050.

26. Chase and Tansik, "The Customer Contact Model for Organization Design."

27. Based on Thomas Moore, "Marriott Grabs for More Room," *Fortune*, October 31, 1983, pp. 107–122; and S. Riggs, "Marriott Moves to Centralize its System," *Restaurant Institution*, February 1, 1981, p. 26; "Marriott's New Deals Defy the Recession," *Business Week*, February 1, 1982; pp. 21–22.

28. Thompson, *Organizations in Action.*

29. Joseph E. McCann and Diane L. Ferry, "An Approach for Assessing and Managing Inter-unit Interdependence," *Academy of Management Review* (1979): 113–119.

30. Thompson, *Organizations in Action*, p. 40

31. Thomas A. Mahoney and Peter J. Frost, "The Role of Technology in Models of Organizational Effectiveness," *Organizational Behavior and Human Performance* 11 (1974): 122–138; R. Dennis Middlemist and Michael A. Hitt, "Technology as a Moderator of the Relationship Between Perceived Work Environment and Subunit Effectiveness," *Human Relations* 34 (1981): 517–532.

32. Thompson, *Organizations in Action.*
33. Andrew H. Van de Ven, Andre Delbecq, and Richard Koenig, "Determinants of Coordination of Modes Within Organizations," *American Sociological Review* 41 (1976): 322–338; Joseph L. Cheng, "Interdependence and Coordination in Organizations: A Role-System Analysis," *Academy of Management Journal* 26 (1983): 156–162; Moses N. Kiggundu, "Task Interdependence and the Theory of Job Design," *Academy of Management Review* 6 (1981): 499–508.
34. Robert W. Keidel, "Baseball, Football, and Basketball: Models for Business," *Organizational Dynamics* (Winter, 1984): 5–18.
35. William Pasmore, Carol E. Francis, and Jeffrey Haldeman, "Sociotechnical Systems: A North American Reflection on Empirical Studies of the 70s," *Human Relations* 35 (1982): 1179–1204.
36. F. Emery, "Characteristics of Sociotechnical Systems," Tavistock Institute of Human Relations, Document 527, 1959; Pasmore, Francis, and Haldeman, "Sociotechnical Systems."
37. Eric Trist and K. Banforth, "Some Social and Psychological Consequences of the Long Wall Method of Coal-Getting," *Human Relations* (1951): 3–38; Eric Trist, C. Higgin, H. Murray, and A. Pollock, *Organizational Choice* (London: Tavistock Publications, 1963).
38. Pasmore, Francis, and Haldeman, "Sociotechnical Systems."
39. Lyman, Ketchum, "Sociotechnical Design in a Third World Country: The Railway Maintenance Depot at Sennar in the Sudan," *Human Relations* 37 (1984): 135–154; A. K. Rice, *Productivity in Social Organization: The Ahmedabad Experiment* (London: Tavistock, 1958); J. P. Norstedt and S. R. Aguren, *The Sab-Scanie Report* (Stockholm: The Swedish Employers Confederation, 1973): 35–37; Richard E. Walton, "Using Social Psychology to Create a New Plant Culture," in Morton Deutsch and Harvey H. Hornstein, (eds.), *Applying Social Psychology: Implications for Research, Practice and Training* (Hillsdale, NJ: Lawrence Erlbaum Associates, 1975), pp. 139–156.
40. Trist and Bamforth, "Some Social and Psychological Consequences of Long Wall Method of Coal-Getting."
41. R. Katz and D. Kahn, *The Social Psychology of Organizations* (New York: Wiley, 1978), pp. 722–728; Randolph H. Bobbitt, Jr., and Jeffrey D. Ford, "Decision Maker Choice as a Determinant of Organization Structure," *Academy of Management Review* 5 (1980): 13–23.
42. Richard C. Reimann, "Organization Structure and Technology in Manufacturing: System Versus Workflow Level Perspectives," "*Academy of Management Journal* 23 (1980): 61–77; Hickson, Pugh, and Pheysey, "Operations Technology and Organization Structure."
43. From "Redesigning the Acetate Department," by David R. Hampton, Charles E. Summer, and Ross A. Webber, *Organizational Behavior and the Practice of Management* (Glenview, IL: Scott, Foresman and Company, 1982), pp. 751–755. Used with permission.

10 The External Environment

In previous chapters we examined both micro and macro building blocks of an organization, including individual differences, job design, group processes, and technology. Each of these topics pertains to the internal workings of the organization. The internal perspective is important, but it is not complete. Many issues relevant to managers of effective organizations originate in the environment. The environment encompasses the larger, or macro, forces and pressures to which organizations must respond and adapt in order to perform effectively. There are several dimensions to external environments of organizations.

The purpose of this chapter is to develop a way to think about and analyze external organization environments. We will define specific sectors of the environment and explore how these sectors create uncertainty for the organization. Research findings provide explicit frameworks that show how to design organizations to cope with environmental uncertainty, as well as how organizations can control key elements in the external environment. We will also examine new perspectives on organization-environment relations, such as the nature of interorganizational linkages and the population ecology model.

RELEVANCE OF EXTERNAL ENVIRONMENT FOR MANAGERS

The environment represents issues vital for several reasons to the success of the organization and its management. First, *organizations are open systems.*[1] As we discussed in Chapter 1, an organization system must import resources and export outputs to the environment. Organizations are open systems because they cannot close themselves off from the environment. To survive, organizations must interact with the environment. Organizations interact with the environment along a number of dimensions simultaneously. A court ruling may force the organization to provide more counseling and feedback before firing an employee; a reduced rate of inflation may alter the strategy of relying upon increased prices for the profit margin; minority interest groups may persuade the organization to include more of its members in important positions; an exotic technology such as molecule splicing or gene-splicing may drastically alter the way the organization does business; salary levels may be more influenced by salaries paid in the local community than by what managers wish to pay; and the availability of raw materials like electricity, fuel oil, and bank loans may determine whether the organization can expand or must decline. All organizations are open systems, and every manager must be aware of elements in the external environment.

Second, *the external environment is becoming more crowded with organizations.* Greater competition exists for limited resources, and the pace of external change is increasing.[2] Increasing complexity and rate of change can lead to environmental turbulence or even hyperturbulence.[3] Adaptive responses under increasing turbulence are difficult to formulate and implement. Overloaded environments have enormous implications for organizational survival, and these conditions will become more prevalent for managers in the future.

The third reason to study the environment is that *a number of structural features have been discovered to help organizations adapt to the environment.* In some environments the appropriate organization structure is flexible; in others the structure is more rigid. In some environments the organization may build linkages to other organizations; in other environments it may operate alone. Some organizations may need a large number of departments to cope with specific elements in the environment; others will have just a few departments. Organization structure can be tailored to the needs of the external environment, so an awareness of these options can increase managerial effectiveness.

The final reason is that *organizations sometimes have to reach out and control the external environment.* Organizations may have to do more than adapt to the external environment, they may have to control it. Techniques for external control include lobbying for favorable legislation, or engaging in a joint venture to explore oil in the North Sea to reduce individual risk. In a crowded organizational world where resources are scarce, effective organizations attempt to control those factors that cause the greatest uncertainty. Whether the organizations team up with others or go it alone, mechanisms for controlling the environment are important options for their managers to consider.

In the next section we will define and examine specific sectors in the organization's environment, and then we will discuss the dimensions of change, complexity, and resource dependence within each sector. Understanding these concepts enables us to then examine specific structural alternatives available for dealing with the environment. Then we will examine strategies organizations can use to control the external environment. We will conclude the chapter with a view of how organizations behave within a larger population of organizations.

TASK AND GENERAL ENVIRONMENTS

In one sense the environment of an organization is infinite and includes everything in the universe. However, it is immediately clear that only a subset of the universe has a bearing on the organization. Our definition of **organizational environment** is all elements existing outside the boundary of the organization that have the potential to affect the organization.[4] The environment includes the elements of competition, resources, technology, economic conditions, and other elements related in some way to the organization.

A further distinction can be made between task and general environments. **Task environment** refers to those parts of an organization's external environment that are directly relevant to goal setting and attainment.[5] The organization must respond to or interact with elements in the task environment to survive. These elements, which have direct impact on the organization, typically include such things as competitors in the same industry, customers, suppliers, and the work force. In contrast, the **general environment** refers to those parts of the external environment that affect the organization indirectly or infrequently. Elements in the general environment affect all organizations about equally, and include such things as economic conditions, the system of government, technology changes, and cultural factors. For example, an increase in the rate of inflation and a larger percentage of women in the work force are both part of an organization's general environment, because these factors affect all organizations about equally.

The concept of organizational domain overlaps the task and general environments. An organization's **domain** is the environmental field of action, the area in which it undertakes its activity. The domain is that set of environmental elements with which the organization seeks to interact. It includes decisions about markets to be served, products to be offered, supplies to be acquired, and what other organizations to interact with to accomplish goals. Environmental **sector** is a distinctive subdivision of the external environment that contains similar, or related, elements. One sector is technology, because technological developments are similar in their impact on the organization. Other sectors include economic conditions, customers, government, and suppliers.

The distinction between task and general environments, domain, and sector is not always clear and may differ across organizations. Exhibit 10.1 illustrates the task and general environments for one organization. Environmental elements are divided into ten sectors, with four in the task environment. However, for an organization in the electronics industry, technology might be part of the task environment instead of the general environment, because technological changes have frequent and immediate impact on organization goal attainment In a heavily regulated industry, the government might be defined as part of the task environment. Still, the sectors in Exhibit 10.1 are typical for many organizations in Canada and the United States. We will now examine specific sectors considered to be a part of the task and general environments of organizations.

Task Environment

Competitor Sector   Competitors are other organizations in the same industry or type of business that provide goods or services to similar customers. Apple and IBM are competitors in the computer hardware industry. The nature and extent of competition in this sector influences an organization's behavior. The recording industry is highly competitive with respect to signing recording stars

EXHIBIT 10.1
Task and General Environments in the Domain of an Organization

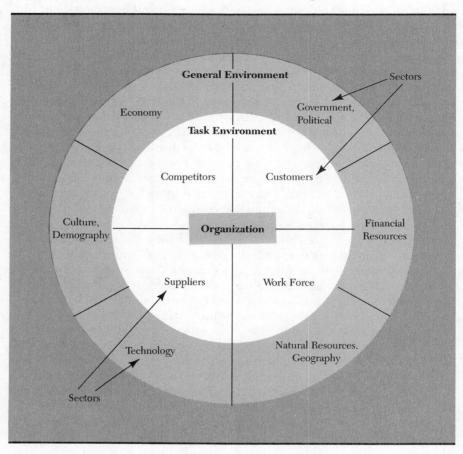

to contracts; a good deal of resources are allocated to this activity. In the pharmaceuticals industry, much effort is devoted to developing drugs and maintaining government regulation that reduces competition.[6] The extent of competition influences organization size, amount and type of advertising, number of customers, price, and profit margins.

Customer Sector   Customers represent the demand for goods and services in an organization's marketplace. All organizations try to satisfy customers, or users of organizational products and services. The market influences the organization through its demand for organizational products and services. If the number of customers is increasing, an organization has to expand in some way or lose business to other organizations. Customers are often considered to be the single most important element of the organizational environment.[7] Whether an organization sells 7-Up, Buicks, home computers, running shoes or health care, satisfied customers are associated with organization success.

Work-Force Sector   The work-force sector is made of immediate and potential employees. Organizations need a work force of trained, qualified personnel. Mary Kay Cosmetics depends heavily on adding to its work force to sell enough cosmetics in the home to maintain its growth rate. Because of more frequent employment outside the home in recent years, fewer women have been available to sell cosmetics, and fewer women are available to host Mary Kay parties. Mary Kay's rate of growth has dropped off because of a shrinking work force. Another element in the work-force sector is unions. Over 20 percent of all employees in North America are unionized, and a union can act as a counterforce to the organization. Employees, potential employees, employee organizations, and unions make up the work-force sector in the environment.

Supplier Sector   Organizations obtain raw materials from the supplier sector of the external environment. A university obtains paper and pencils, textbooks, desks, food for cafeterias, computers, maintenance trucks, fuel, electricity, and an almost endless list of other materials from suppliers. Other types of organizations may require supplies as diverse as coffee beans, coal, salt, and steel castings. These raw materials become the input to the technological transformation process described in Chapter 9. After input, the organization's technology produces outputs for consumption by the external environment.

General Environment

Technological Sector   This sector includes the level of scientific and technological advancement in the industry and society at large. New technological advancements can influence production processes across a number of industries. One recent area of technological advance is in the field of molecular engineering. Molecule-splicers can move atoms of a molecule around inside it, creating entirely new materials. Materials available for use in production technologies today that were completely unheard of in 1975 include a ceramic turbine engine, a composite "skin" used in the Boeing 767 airliner and the Beech Starship I, gallium arsenide lasers used in fiber optics, and the all-composite automobile body marketed by General Motors.[8]

Government-Political Sector   This sector includes the nature of the legal system, and specific laws concerning control, formation, and taxation of organizations. The political system, political parties, and the concentration of political power are also involved here. Most corporations are subjected to laws from the local community, county, state, and federal governments. A large number of agencies are devoted exclusively to regulating business and industry. The federal government controls organizations through occupational safety and health administration, fair trade practices, subsidies for certain products, product safety legislation, requirements for labor, and import-export restrictions. A recent court ruling overturning fair trade regulations in California has revolutionized competition in the liquor industry. Minimum liquor prices are illegal, and this has rippled through all large liquor markets. The organizations that make and sell liquor are now shaping up for a major price war and marketing battle.

Economic Sector   This sector pertains to the general economic health of the country or region where the organization operates. Unemployment rates, purchasing power, interest rates, inflation, and production possibilities are all part of the economic environment. The general economic system, (capitalism versus socialism, for example) the banking system, and fiscal policies influence the aggregate economy within which all organizations function.

Culture-Demographic Sector   This sector includes the number, geographical distribution, age, education, and sex of the population in society. Other dimensions include class structure, social roles, and the historical background, values, and norms of the society.[9]

Financial Resource Sector   Financial resources pertain to the availability of money. This sector includes stock and bond markets, insurance companies, venture capital, and banks. The easy access to financial resources encourages organizations to grow fast. If external financial resources are not available, organizational growth will be slower. Extensive borrowing may transfer some control of the company to lending organizations.

Natural Resources-Geography   This sector includes the type, quantity, and availability of natural resources such as oil, coal, and basic minerals. It also includes climactic and weather conditions. Geography pertains to location of cities, land formations such as mountains versus plains, and overall weather patterns. One reason agribusiness in the United States and Canada produces so much food is the industry's favorable climactic conditions here. Agricultural organizations in Northern Europe and Russia, by comparison, must attempt to grow grains during short growing seasons and bitter cold winters; this reduces productivity.

Summary   Each of the ten sectors in Exhibit 10.1 consists of external organizations and elements that have potential to influence the local organization. Those elements in an organization's task environment have direct impact on it specifically; the organization must deal with task elements directly. The general environment influences the organization less directly because the general environment sectors affect all organizations in the industry or community. Another point to consider is that sectors influence one another. Sectors are not independent. Economic conditions affect financial resources. Government policies can affect technology and industry. A number of sectors in the environment may influence one another and the organization at the same time. American Airlines, for example, faces a complicated and difficult environment, and it has learned to deal successfully with its environment, as illustrated in **Up Close 10.1.**

UP CLOSE 10.1:   American Airlines

The airline industry's financial storm still rages. Buffeted by deregulation since 1978, the airlines were facing red ink for three years prior to 1983. American Airlines now is flying high above the storm clouds. Practically alone among established airlines, it has figured out how to grow and prosper in the new world of deregulation.

American's current success has come at the end of a long battle. Just as the industry was coping with the confusing new environment of deregulation, American—and other airlines—got slugged from several other environmental sectors almost simultaneously. Fuel prices doubled in a year. The air traffic controllers went on strike and were fired by President Reagan, which decreased traffic at the busier airports. Then came the recession, which slashed passenger volume. Meanwhile, new airlines equipped with used aircraft were springing up, and fare wars began.

The environment of American Airlines is illustrated in Exhibit 10.2. This environment is extremely complex, and some sectors change rapidly. Most problems have originated in the task environment, although deregulation has affected all airlines and other industries previously controlled through government regulation. American has made major efforts toward cost cutting, including a cost-reduction pay structure that unions approved. The total work force was reduced by 7000 employees.

Industry competition has been fierce. Pan American made the competition's most recent move by introducing a $99 one-way fare for its entire system. American also was in head-to-head price-cutting competition with Braniff, which eventually went bankrupt. Commuter airlines and cut-rate carriers like People Express are also causing problems for many of the established carriers. The customer sector has become more favorable in recent months. With economic conditions improving, more people are signing up for business and vacation travel. American has adopted Super Saver fares and Airpass, and its frequent flyer discount program has been a big hit.

American was initially designed to fly under regulation, and it had too many big airplanes because the government dictated long hauls. With the acquisition of new aircraft, American now has a more flexible fleet. With new wage contracts, American is more cost efficient. American also adopted the hub-and-spoke route system, with Dallas as the hub. Its Saber computer reservation system dominates the travel agent business. American Airlines has confronted the environment and is ready for the decade ahead.[10]

EXHIBIT 10.2
Elements in the Domain of American Airlines

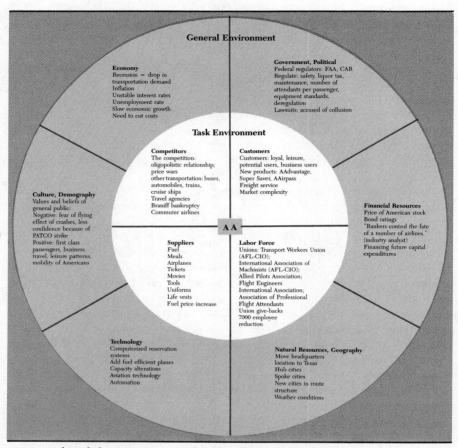

General Environment

Economy
Recession = drop in
transportation demand
Inflation
Unstable interest rates
Unemployment rate
Slow economic growth
Need to cut costs

Government, Political
Federal regulators: FAA, CAB
Regulate: safety, liquor tax,
maintenance, number of
attendants per passenger,
equipment standards,
deregulation
Lawsuits: accused of collusion

Task Environment

Competitors
The competition:
oligopolistic relationship;
price wars
other transportation: buses,
automobiles, trains,
cruise ships
Travel agencies
Braniff bankruptcy
Commuter airlines

Customers
Customers: loyal, leisure,
potential users, business users
New products: AAdvantage,
Super Saver, AAirpass
Freight service
Market complexity

Culture, Demography
Values and beliefs of
general public:
Negative: fear of flying
effect of crashes, less
confidence because of
PATCO strike
Positive: first class
passengers, business
travel, leisure patterns,
mobility of Americans

AA

Financial Resources
Price of American stock
Bond ratings
"Bankers control the fate
of a number of airlines."
(industry analyst)
Financing future capital
expenditures

Suppliers
Fuel
Meals
Airplanes
Tickets
Movies
Tools
Uniforms
Life vests
Fuel price increase

Labor Force
Unions: Transport Workers Union
(AFL-CIO);
International Association of
Machinists (AFL-CIO);
Allied Pilots Association;
Flight Engineers
International Association;
Association of Professional
Flight Attendants
Union give-backs
7000 employee
reduction

Technology
Computerized reservation
systems
Add fuel efficient planes
Capacity alterations
Aviation technology
Automation

Natural Resources, Geography
Move headquarters
location to Texas
Hub cities
Spoke cities
New cities in route
structure
Weather conditions

SOURCE: Adapted from Kim Penn and Rodney Slota, "Case Study of American Airlines."
Unpublished manuscript, Texas A & M University, 1982.

ENVIRONMENTAL UNCERTAINTY

American Airlines exists in a very complex environment. A large number of
elements are present in its domain, and the air carrier must be able to respond
and deal with those elements. Moreover, some elements change rapidly and
unpredictably. Changes cause problems for the organization. In this section we
are going to explore how elements in an organization's environment affect
organization structure and adaptability.

Environmental elements affect the organization through the amount of
uncertainty they create for organizational decision makers. **Uncertainty** is the
lack of information about environmental factors, activities, and future events.[11]

Uncertainty means that managers are unclear about what an event means, about why an event occurs, and about the probable success of a new course of action. Environmental uncertainty increases the risk of failure for the actions of organizations and makes it difficult to compute the costs and probable successes decision alternatives might provide.[12]

Uncertainty occurs through three characteristics of an organization's environment—change, complexity, and resource dependence.[13] Changes are reflected in the static-dynamic dimension of the environment, complexity is reflected in the simple-complex dimension, and resource dependence in the extent to which *other* organizations control the scarce resources needed by the organization.

Static-Dynamic Dimension

The **static-dynamic dimension** refers to whether elements in the environment change rapidly and unpredictably, or whether they tend to remain about the same from year to year. Under dynamic conditions, environmental elements may shift abruptly and surprise the organization. An aerospace firm that receives orders to build a satellite one year and an airplane the next would be in a dynamic environment. An auto parts company that makes spark plugs year after year exists in a static environment.

Some elements of the environment may be stable while others are dynamic. For General Motors, the market and customer sector has changed rapidly over the last several years. Government regulations have changed moderately, and natural resources and geography have changed hardly at all. The book publishing industry has recently undergone major changes in its market sector. Standard books on diet, sex, health and exercise, and pets have been selling much better than any other books. Novels and nonfiction are down, and bookstores have had to return large numbers of unsold books to the publishers. The industry has been groping to discover books and distribution systems that will allow them to better adapt to this changing market, which has been largely influenced by the easy accessibility of information through electronic media.[14]

Simple-Complex Dimension

Complexity refers to the number of external elements that are relevant to an organization's operations, and the extent of difference among those elements. In a simple environment, the organization must deal with only a few homogeneous elements. An organization may have a single supplier and sell to a single customer, such as a parts supplier for General Motors.

Organizations like Delta Airlines or the University of Michigan have complex environments. Hundreds of customers, suppliers, and other organizations are part of the environment. The University of Michigan contains a number of technologies, interacts with government regulatory and research granting agencies, affiliates with professional and scientific associations, alumni, parents, foundations, legislators, community residents, international agencies, donors, corporations, and athletic teams. When the organization's environment is very complex, the organization has to have a form and structure that enables it to deal with a large number of elements.

Change and Complexity Combined

The static-dynamic and simple-complex dimensions are combined into a framework in Exhibit 10.3. The diagram shows how increases in environmental change and increases in environmental complexity add to the amount of uncertainty for organizational decision makers.[15] The four levels of uncertainty are illustrated in the four quadrants in Exhibit 10.3.

In quadrant 1, the environment is stable and simple, so environmental uncertainty is low. Only a small number of environmental elements are relevant to the organization, and these elements change slowly and predicta-

EXHIBIT 10.3

Characteristics of Environment and Organization Uncertainty

	Simple	Complex

Stable	1. Low Uncertainty
	  a. Small number of external elements
	  b. Elements change slowly
	
	Examples: Soft drink bottlers, beer distributors, container manufacturer, local utility
		2. Moderately Low Uncertainty
		  a. Large number of dissimilar external elements
		  b. Elements change slowly
		
		Examples: University, hospital, insurance company, *Playboy*

Unstable	3. Moderately High Uncertainty
	  a. Small number of external elements
	  b. Elements change frequently and unpredictably
	
	Examples: Fashion clothing, music industry, Atari, toy manufacturers
		4. High Uncertainty
		  a. Large number of dissimilar external elements
		  b. Elements change frequently and unpredictably
		
		Examples: American Airlines, oil companies, electronic firms, aerospace firms

Environmental Change (vertical axis: Stable to Unstable)

Environmental Complexity (horizontal axis: Simple to Complex)

SOURCE: Adapted and reprinted from Robert B. Duncan, "Characteristics of Perceived Environments and Perceived Environmental Uncertainty," *Administrative Science Quarterly* 17, 3 (1972): 313–327 by permission of *The Administrative Science Quarterly*. Copyright 1972 by Cornell University.

bly. The organization can acquire good information and learn about those factors relevant to its operation. Organizations in low uncertain environments include distributors in the soft drink and beer industries, manufacturers of cardboard containers, and many small and medium-sized manufacturing companies that produce a single line of products.

The stable-complex environment in quadrant 2 represents a higher level of uncertainty for the organization. Elements are stable, but there are more elements to be scanned and analyzed in organizational decision making. Organizations in this quadrant include hospitals, insurance companies, and universities; the environments of these organizations change at a slow pace, but there are a large number of elements to be considered. The publishing division of *Playboy* magazine is in the category of low-moderate uncertainty. The division's environment has a relatively large number of factors, including local, state and federal courts, competitors such as *Penthouse*, the market for subscribers and over-the-counter sales, economic conditions, and cultural factors. *Playboy* has settled into a format acceptable to most people, so there is little turmoil associated with its publication. A large number of elements are involved, but they are not undergoing rapid change.[16]

The third quadrant in Exhibit 10.3 represents moderately high uncertainty for organizations, because a few elements change rapidly and unpredictably. This type of environment is typical for organizations in the fashion industry, such as Levi Strauss or Jordache, or the music industry. Manufacturers of children's toys and electronic games, such as Atari, are in this category because market tastes and competitive products change markedly from year to year.

Firms experiencing the highest uncertainty are in quadrant 4. These organizations have a large number of elements in their domains, and these elements change rapidly. They must continuously cope with the scanning, perception, and response to changes in a number of sectors. Examples of firms with high uncertainty are American Airlines and other commercial air carriers, computer manufacturers, aerospace firms and airplane manufacturers, firms in the oil industry, and other firms in industries that are undergoing change, such as electronics. In the **Up Close** discussion of American Airlines, not only did we see a large number of elements in American's domain, but many of these elements were behaving unpredictably. Changes in fuel prices, customers, airplane technology, union relationships, price wars, air traffic control, and federal regulation caused high uncertainty for management.

Resource Dependence

The third dimension of the external environment that adds to uncertainty is resource dependence.[17] All organizations must acquire and maintain needed external resources. The ability to acquire these resources depends on a *power relationship* among organizations. **Resource dependence** pertains to the relative power an organization has to obtain scarce resources from the environment. Organizations face uncertainty about acquiring valuable resources from the environment, and this uncertainty can be reduced by increasing organizational influence over elements that provide resources. Organizations work to reduce their vulnerability, and hence uncertainty, so they can be assured of having the resources they need for production and high performance.

Organizations attempt to reduce uncertainty by acquiring control over important resources or by reducing the control of other organizations over the resources. Social service agencies in local communities, for example, increase their independence from other organizations by generating alternative sources of funding and establishing numerous links with community leaders.[18] Airline companies banded together to control fuel supplies after fuel prices rose and shortages occurred. Some airlines even considered operating their own refineries but decided not to because the fuel crisis passed. Ever since cigarette commercials were banned from television in 1971, tobacco companies have purchased a disproportionate amount of print advertising. The tobacco industry ranks first in advertising expenditures for newspapers and second in magazines. Newspapers and magazines depend upon the tobacco industry for revenue, and they sometimes behave accordingly. A freelance writer's name was removed from the masthead of *Savvy* magazine for her review of a book entitled *The Ladykiller, Why Smoking is a Feminist Issue*. Some observers suggest that newspapers and magazines run few negative stories because they depend on the tobacco industry for resources. Anti-smoking groups claim numerous incidents in which the tobacco industry's powerful influence over publishing was reflected in decisions about publication content.[19]

In addition to the elements of change and complexity, resource scarcity creates uncertainty for organizations. Resource scarcity makes the organization dependent upon others, and this lack of influence means the organization is vulnerable to environmental whims and changes. Organizations typically respond by trying to reduce dependence in critical areas.[20] Other research has shown that scarcity in an organization's environment is associated with an increased number of *illegal* actions designed to procure needed resources.[21] Resource scarcity will cause organizations to move in a number of directions to reduce this uncertainty. Mattel, Inc. illustrates this.

UP CLOSE 10.2:   Mattel, Inc.

March 1, 1959 was an important date for the budgets of fathers of preteen girls. On that day, Mattel, Inc., a Hawthorne, California toymaker, began taking orders for its Barbie doll—a teenage doll that requires a dozen or two complete changes of costume to make her and her owner happy. After the introduction of Barbie and Chatty Cathy, Mattel rode the tide of their success to the top position in the toy industry by 1961.

Maintaining the number one position has not been easy. Mattel took advantage of Barbie's popularity by introducing companion dolls Ken, Midge, Allan, and Skipper, each with an array of outfits. Coloring books, doll houses, carrying cases, Barbie furniture and Barbie cosmetics soon followed. However, fads come and go in the toy business, and the owners worked hard to ease the *companies dependence on "hot flash" toys—toys that come and go in a single season. However, in 1972, Mattel stock plunged by 70 percent from the 1971 level. Sales dropped by $80 million. The new Hot Wheels line was not moving. Mattel also experienced a west coast dock strike which cut off shipments from plants in Hong Kong, Taiwan, and Japan. Top managers lacked the right information about the market, and suppliers did not always meet specifications. Stockholders sued Mattel, claiming managers deliberately mishandled finances. In 1977, a toy called "Slime" was introduced and sales took off. The recovery lasted into the 1980s, when new problems occurred with Intellivision. Sales for Intellivision started quickly, and then faded as the demand for electronic games dropped off.*[22] ■

Rapid change in the toy industry is characteristic of moderate-high uncertainty. Mattel also was dependent on cheap labor in the Far East and on the acceptance by distributors and customers of a small number of product lines. Mattel executives have since responded to uncertainty by redefining the environmental domain to include broader diversification, with toys amounting to only 50 percent of the product line. They also employed massive advertising to smooth demand.[23]

ORGANIZATIONAL RESPONSES TO THE ENVIRONMENT

How do organizations cope with environmental uncertainty? The structure, design and behavior of an organization will reflect the extent of environmental change, complexity, and resource dependency. Organizational responses are of two types. The first possible response is internal change. The organization can adapt its structure, work patterns, departments, or planning according to the nature of its environmental domain. The second alternative is an attempt to change or control elements in the external environment. The organization may establish linkages to other organizations, or it may realign elements in the external domain into a more favorable position. The discussion that follows examines concepts and frameworks with which to understand the nature of organizational responses to the environment. First we will look at internal structural responses to environmental uncertainty; then we will turn to techniques for establishing organizational control over the environment.

STRUCTURAL RESPONSES TO UNCERTAINTY

Organizations can make a variety of internal responses to environmental uncertainty. They can become more flexible, develop new departments, span the boundary to the environment, achieve better coordination among departments, or improve planning and forecasting. These types of organizational responses have been identified in some of the most important studies of organizational-environment relationships.

Organic-Mechanistic Structure   One of the first studies of organization-environment relationships was carried out by Burns and Stalker in Great Britain in 1961.[24] They examined twenty industrial firms, many in the electronics industry, to identify different managerial practices and environmental characteristics. The firms differed in uncertainty and rate of change in both the technology and market sectors. The research examined the effects of environmental change as it related to organization structure and management behavior.

Burns and Stalker found clear differences in the approaches to organization structure and management systems that were a function of change in the external environment. They specified two types of management systems, **mechanistic** and **organic,** which are described in Exhibit 10.4. The mechanistic organizations were characterized by centralization of control and authority, extensive task specialization and standardization, vertical lines of communication, and many rules and procedures. Organic systems, by contrast, displayed greater decentralization of control and authority, horizontal communications among people and departments at the same hierarchical level, few rules and procedures, and tasks that were not specialized or standardized. Mechanistic organizations were seen as relatively fixed and inflexible, while organic systems were seen as more flexible and adaptive.

The important point made from the Burns and Stalker research is that the rate of environmental change in key sectors has distinct impact on organization design. A stable environment, which produces little uncertainty for managers, is associated with mechanistic structural characteristics. The organization is more tightly managed and bureaucratic. In a rapidly changing environment, the organization must be loosely structured and informal. Because things change quickly, people figure out what to do as they go along. Rules and procedures that worked last year are no longer applicable. The organic structure is the appropriate structure for a rapidly changing environment if the organization is to adapt quickly to those changes.

An interesting sidelight from the research is that employees in the organically structured firms were sometimes uncomfortable with the lack of structure. They complained about having to "find out what they had to do," and about the unclear authority and resources they had to do their job. No one was sure about title, status, or even function. The frustration with lack of structure was offset by an understanding of common purpose among employees. They all knew what they were trying to do for the organization, and this common purpose helped bring out the cooperation necessary to deal with changing markets and technologies.[25]

Boundary Spanning   In an uncertain environment, the organization needs to establish contact with key external elements. **Boundary-spanning roles** link and coordinate the organization with other organizations. The person in a boundary role establishes a relationship with people and organizations in the environment. By carrying information back and forth between the environment and the organization, plans and activities can be coordinated and uncertainty

EXHIBIT 10.4

Comparison of Mechanistic and Organic Systems of Organization

Stable Environment	Dynamic Environment
Mechanistic	*Organic*
1. Tasks are highly fractionated and specialized; little regard paid to clarifying relationship between tasks and organizational objectives.	1. Tasks are more interdependent; emphasis on relevance of tasks and organizational objectives.
2. Tasks tend to remain rigidly defined unless altered formally by top management.	2. Tasks are continually adjusted and redefined through interaction of organizational members.
3. Specific role definition (rights, obligations, and technical methods prescribed for each member).	3. Generalized role definition (members accept general responsibility for task accomplishment beyond individual role definition).
4. Hierarchic structure of control, authority, and communication. Sanctions derive from employment contract between employee and organization.	4. Network structure of control, authority, and communication. Sanctions derive more from community of interest than from contractual relationship.
5. Communication is primarily vertical between superior and subordinate.	5. Communication is both vertical and horizontal, depending upon where needed information resides.
6. Communications primarily take form of instructions and decisions issued by superiors, of information and requests for decisions supplied by inferiors.	6. Communications primarily take form of information and advice.
7. Insistence on loyalty to organization and obedience to superiors.	7. Commitment to organization's tasks and goals more highly valued than loyalty or obedience.

SOURCE: Adapted from T. Burns and G. M. Stalker, *The Management of Innovations* (London: Tavistock Publications, Ltd., 1961), pp. 119–22.

reduced. Boundary-spanning roles serve a number of purposes. People in boundary-spanning roles:

- monitor the environment for information relevant to the organization
- represent the organization to the environment
- protect the organization from environmental threats
- serve as gatekeepers and provide information to relevant people within the organization
- negotiate with other organizations to acquire inputs and dispose of outputs
- coordinate activities between the organization and other organizations in the environment.[26]

EXHIBIT 10.5
Boundary Spanning Linkages Among Organizations

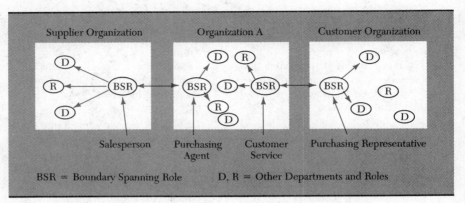

Exhibit 10.5 presents an illustration of boundary spanning. Boundary spanning activities help absorb uncertainty from the environment. A purchasing department provides a steady flow of materials to the production line. A customer service department handles inquiries and complaints so that demand for the company output remains high. A personnel department establishes contact with potential employees so they can be hired as needed. Market research monitors trends in consumer tastes. By identifying new developments, innovations, regulations, and other changes, boundary personnel supply information that keeps the organization in synchronization with environmental events.

The effect of environmental uncertainty on boundary spanning is to make the organization more complex. When the organization's environment includes a large number of important elements, then the organization will need a large number of departments and roles to monitor and interact with these external elements. In other words, a more complex organization structure is needed when the environment is complex. Since all organizations are open systems, all organizations will have boundary spanning activities.

Differentiation and Integration   The next study combined elements of both boundary spanning and the organic-mechanistic system. Lawrence and Lorsch from Harvard studied organization-environment relations by selecting six firms in divergent industries—plastics, packaged foods, and standardized containers.[27] These industries were selected because of variation in environmental uncertainty. The environment for firms in the plastics industry was characterized by a high degree of uncertainty and unpredictability. Technological innovation was rapid, and shifts in market demand were high, so firms had to change products and procedures on short notice. The container industry produced cardboard containers for a highly predictable environment. Competition centered around price and delivery instead of product change, and stable relationships with customers existed. The environment for packaged foods companies was in between the highly uncertain plastics industry and the very stable container industry. Food companies were characterized by a moderate amount of predictability and stability in environmental relations.

The issue concerning Lawrence and Lorsch was how organizations differed in successful performance across these diverse environments. One finding was differentiation, or the existence of structural variation from department to department within firms. **Differentiation** is "the differences in cognitive and emotional orientation among managers in different functional departments, and the difference in formal structure among these departments".[28] They found that members across major departments differed in terms of attitude, goals, and interpersonal orientation as well as in terms of formal management systems. The greater the variation in orientation and structure across managers in different departments, the greater the differentiation.

The differences Lawrence and Lorsch found to be associated with major departments were:

- Research and development was orientated toward the scientific-technological sector of the environment; and R&D employees displayed a goal of high quality, had a time horizon of up to five years in the future, were task oriented, and were part of an informal, organic management structure.
- Manufacturing was oriented toward the manufacturing-supplier sector of the external environment; and employees had a goal of efficient production, a short time horizon of only a few weeks, were task orientated, and had highly formalized management systems.
- The sales department was concerned with the customer sector of the environment, and their primary goal was customer satisfaction. Sales personnel displayed a short time horizon, a social rather than task orientation, and a relatively high degree of formal structure.

The implication of these differences is that coordination across departments is difficult. Lawrence and Lorsch found that when differentiation was great, more time and resources had to be devoted to achieving coordination so that the organization could perform as a unified whole. The needed coordination was called **integration,** which is defined as the quality of collaboration among departments to achieve organizational unity of effort.[29]

One of the major relationships drawn from this study is summarized in Exhibit 10.6. When environmental uncertainty is high, differentiation among departments is also high. Each department must be tailored to the demands of its specific environmental sector when change is rapid and uncertainty is high. In this way, each department reduces uncertainty for the organization. But high differentiation carries coordination costs. To achieve unified effort, greater energy must be devoted to achieving integration. The organization has to devote more time to developing plans and operating procedures, and to having managers meet with one another frequently to facilitate coordination. In the firms that were highly differentiated, as illustrated in Exhibit 10.6, about 22 percent of management personnel were assigned to integration activities, such as serving on task forces and committees or acting in liaison roles.[30] In

EXHIBIT 10.6

Environmental Uncertainty, Organizational Differentiation and Integration in
Three Industries

	Environmental Uncertainty	Departmental Differentiation	Percent Management in Integrating Roles
Plastics Firms	High	High	22%
Package Foods Firms	Moderate	Moderate	17%
Container Firms	Low	Low	0%

SOURCE: Based on Jay W. Lorsch and Paul R. Lawrence, "Environmental Factors and Organizational Integration," *Organization Planning: Cases and Concepts* (Homewood, IL: Irwin and Dorsey, 1972).

organizations with environments characterized by simple-stable environments, differentiation among departments was less, and almost no managers were assigned to integration roles. Seventeen percent of managers were in integrator roles in the moderately uncertain environment of the food industry.

Another major finding from Lawrence and Lorsch's research is that firms able to simultaneously achieve adequate levels of both differentiation and integration tend to be high performers. Organizations in an uncertain environment are expected to be highly differentiated and to then find mechanisms to integrate these differences. Firms that failed to differentiate in uncertain environments and hence required less integration, were less effective. High performers in a stable environment such as the container industry were not as differentiated but still maintained sufficient integration to enable unity of effort across departments. Therefore, in an uncertain environment, different goals, attitudes, and structures should be encouraged across departments, and management must devise integrating mechanisms to coordinate these differences.

Planning and Forecasting   The final internal organization characteristic is the extent to which the organization concentrates on long-range planning and forecasting. Information is harder to obtain when the environment is unstable. As a consequence, specific roles or departments devoted to developing plans and forecasts are created.[31] Forecasts can help managers anticipate external shifts and make necessary adjustments. Planning can soften the adverse impact of changes. Organizational planning can be extensive and may go beyond anticipating environmental changes to developing scenerios of organizational responses.

When the environment is stable and predictable, organizations are less likely to create a separate planning department. Managers already have current information on external events and will spend their time concentrating on operational problems and day-to-day efficiency. Because future environmental demands will be similar to what the organization faces today, long-range planning and forecasting do not have as much value.

Recent research also indicates that decision processes reflect environmental uncertainty. Managers can get good information about a stable environment, so they are free to choose a more logical procedure. When the environment is rapidly changing, information will not be comprehensive, even with a planning department. Managerial decisions will tend to be made through informal discussion and agreement. Quantitative decision procedures are impossible, because managers do not have sufficient facts. Formal, logical methods for making decisions about the environment are effective when environmental demands are clear and unchanging, and it is then that decision problems tend to be routine.[32]

INTERORGANIZATIONAL CONTROL OVER THE ENVIRONMENT

In addition to changes in internal organization arrangements designed to reduce uncertainty, organizations may reach out and create relationships with other organizations. These arrangements typically define some type of linkage to those sectors that are unpredictable or upon which the organization depends for scarce resources.

Contractual Arrangements   Organizations bargain and develop legal contracts to ensure the receipt of necessary resources. Contracts in this way reduce uncertainty for organizations. Typical contractual arrangements are union contracts that specify wages and wage increases for several years in the future. Contracts to purchase materials, such as fuel oil, assure a supply despite uncertainty about availability on the open market. A farmer may contract to sell next year's grain harvest on the futures market to reduce uncertainty about future grain prices. Through contractual arrangements, organizations can reduce uncertainty with respect to both inputs and outputs.

Cooptation   **Cooptation** means that organizations absorb individuals or organizations who disagree with or threaten the accomplishment of organizational goals. Leaders from important outside organizations or interest groups are brought into the organization. Cooptation occurs, for example, when business leaders are appointed to a hospital board of directors before a fund-raising campaign.[33] As board members the business leaders have a vested interest in seeing the hospital succeed. They will see and understand the needs of the hospital and help rather than thwart fund raising. Similarly, selecting an attorney as a director may help the hospital cope with regulation. Business corporations often follow a similar practice. Bringing key people under the influence of the organization reduces uncertainty about specific sectors in the environment and helps the organization achieve its goals.[34]

Advertising and Public Relations   Advertising is perhaps the most obvious way of influencing the external environment. Organizations spend large amounts of money to influence consumer tastes in favor of their products or services and consumer attitudes toward the organization. Public relations directors are responsible for obtaining favorable coverage in newspapers and magazines. During periods of high profits, oil companies spend large amounts of money to cultivate a positive public image. Advertising and public relations activities are mechanisms through which the organization can tell its story directly to important external groups.

Personnel Exchanges   The exchange of executives among organizations offers another method of establishing favorable linkages. Private industry that sells products to government makes frequent use of this linkage. The aerospace industry hires retired generals and other officers from the Defense Department. These officers have personal friends in the Defense Department, and this gives the aerospace organization a linkage that provides accurate and timely information about technical specifications, prices, and other needs. Defense contractors with favorable linkages are able to develop more effective proposals. Companies without these linkages may find it difficult to get a defense contract, not because of conscious discrimination against them, but because they do not have the best information with which to develop proposals.[35]

Executives are also exchanged informally among organizations. A study of senior executives found that in industries with relatively few firms, many executives had their last job within that industry, had undergone a number of job changes, and experienced relatively short tenure before becoming chief executives. This means that executives were moving informally among organizations; hence they would know one another and provide favorable organization linkages.[36]

Illegal Activities   Environmental pressures may encourage organization managers to undertake illegal activities. Low profits, pressure from senior managers, and scarce environmental resources unfortunately may lead organizations to paths other than those accepted by the courts. In the 1950s, executives from General Electric, Westinghouse, and several other large electrical equipment manufacturers met in secret and agreed to fix prices at a level that would allow each organization to win certain major contracts. The contracts won yielded very high profits. Price fixing also takes place when construction companies agree in advance on the bids to be submitted to state agencies for road and bridge construction. Aircraft manufacturers have allegedly provided kickbacks to members of foreign governments to secure aircraft sales. One study found that industries that experienced poor demand, shortages, and strikes were more likely to be convicted for illegal activities, implying that resource scarcity promotes greater frequency of illegal acts. The illegal acts included such things as price fixing, conspiracy, franchise violations, allocation of markets, bid-rigging, illegal entry barriers, refusal to bargain, reciprosity, and illegal mergers.[37]

Joint Ventures   A **joint venture** typically involves a mutual investment by two or more organizations that results in the creation of a new organization. Joint venture is a form of cooperation among organizations that are normally considered competitors. The newly created organization is often owned by organizations that compete in the market sector.[38] Oil companies and automobile manufacturers have commonly made joint ventures in recent years. Several oil companies have agreed through a joint venture to explore for oil on the continental shelf or in hard-to-reach regions of Alaska and Canada. The risk and expense of oil exploration is enormous, so organizations reduce the uncertainty through joint ventures and achieve what they could not achieve alone. U.S. auto manufacturers have gradually realized they are unable to be competitive with small cars. Thus Ford Motor Company has joined with Toyo Kogyo Co. to produce subcompacts in Mexico. American Motors Corporation produces the Alliance and Encore models, which are engineered through agreements with Renault. Chrysler Corporation concluded an agreement to jointly build subcompact cars with Mitsubishi Motors. All of these agreements allow the organizations to reduce uncertainty and achieve their goals without having to possess *all* necessary skills and resources.

Interlocking Directorates   *Interlocking directorates* pertains to the membership of boards of directors of corporations or community organizations. **Direct interlocks** means that two organizations have the same person on their boards. **Indirect interlocks** mean that two organizations each have a member on the board of directors of a third company.[39] For example, General Motors may have direct interlocks with as many as thirty firms and indirect interlocks with several hundred more firms. These mechanisms provide a way to establish horizontal coordination at the director level. Community structures often reflect the same interlock pattern. A few influential people may be on the boards of a school, hospital, theater, and United Way Agency. These people are in a position of decision-making influence, and they provide an informal way of coordinating activities among agencies.

Contracts, joint ventures, and interlocking directorates all provide mechanisms for organizations to reduce dependency on the environment. These mechanisms meet organizational needs for resources through interorganizational coordination and risk sharing. An organization may employ many linkages simultaneously, and many organizations may band together through interorganizational linkage. One example of many linkages occurs between the movie industry and the newly emerging home video industry, as illustrated in the following **Up Close.**

UP CLOSE 10.3:   The Home Entertainment Industry

Movie makers are suffering their own recession or worse. So they are busy working on ways to exploit cable television and other video programming for the home. But so far, the home video "revolution" has failed to deliver on its promise of a vast, rich market for the entertainment and information the moviemakers are capable of packaging. Although the market is growing, it isn't growing nearly as fast or so lushly as many people had expected. Uncertain of the shape the home TV market will take, even the richest companies are joining with others to try to guarantee a piece of the action and to spread their risks. Only one thing is certain: big money will be required to produce the programming demanded in the future.

The new alliances among film studios, television networks, and cable TV services could change the entertainment industry by blurring the distinction between makers and distributors of programs. They also could help smooth the

EXHIBIT 10.7
Interorganizational Linkages Among Moviemakers and Home Video Companies

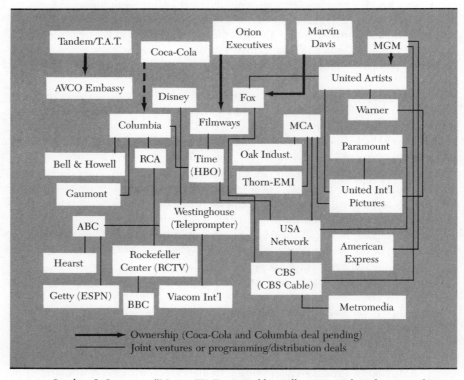

SOURCE: Stephen J. Sansweet, "Movie, TV Firms Building Alliances to Take Advantage of Home Video," *Wall Street Journal*, March 26, 1982, p. 23. Reprinted by permission of *The Wall Street Journal*, © Dow Jones & Company, Inc. 1982. All Rights Reserved.

industry's financial cycles with large alternate sources of revenue to counter two decades of stagnant box office ticket sales.

"The whole problem today is people trying to predict with certainty what can't be predicted," says Barry Dillard, chairman of Gulf and Western Industries, Inc.'s Paramount Pictures Corp. subsidiary. "There's so much technology and so little present application of it, it's absurd to try to guess which will turn into a national industry. We're in the dark." Paramount itself has quietly gone into home video distribution. It is manufacturing and marketing video cassettes of movies; and it has joined Time, Inc. and MCA, Inc. as partners in USA Network, an advertiser-supported cable channel that aims eventually at pay programming.

Columbia Pictures has organized ventures with four other companies. The most notable and controversial arrangement gives exclusive pay-TV rights on many Columbia films produced from January 1981 to mid-1984 to Home Box Office, the Time, Inc. subsidiary.

The myriad linkages among companies is sketched in Exhibit 10.7. Warner Communications Inc., has supplied home video to a joint venture with American Express Company. MCA, Inc.'s Universal Studios has arrangements with Oak Industries Inc., an operator of over-the-air pay-TV, and with the British entertainment company, Thorn EMI LTD. Even Walt Disney Productions has entered a joint venture, with The Western Electric Corp. subsidiary, to spend $100 million on producing programs for family entertainment channel over the next four years.

The television companies are just as busy making connections. American Broadcasting Co. has arrangements with Getty Oil's Entertainment and Sports Programming Network, Hurst Corp. and Westinghouse. RCA Corp., NBC's parent company, has deals with Columbia Pictures and Rockefeller Center Inc.'s new cable channel.

"Everyone wants to hedge his bets," says Dennis Forst, entertainment industry analyst for Bateman Eichler, Hill Richards Inc., the Los Angeles securities firm. "It isn't that they particularly love jumping into bed with each other, but all the alliances point out how expensive a proposition it's going to be to make it big in home video.[40] ■

Environmental Control Through Domain Management

Up Close 10.3 illustrates how organizations can band together to reduce uncertainty. Another form of organizational reaction is to control the external domain, that is, exert control over the sectors and organizations with which the organization must interact.

Political Activity Many organizations attempt to influence legislation or regulatory agencies in a direction favorable to themselves.[41] Legislation may provide favorable tax treatment for certain types of investments, thereby improving the financial resource sector. Other laws may restrict entry into the domain, which is the case when doctors or psychologists use licensing boards to restrict entry. For years the trucking and airline industries were very successful at restricting entry, thereby influencing their competition sector. In recent years, however, legislation has generated more airline and trucking competition. Other strategies include campaign contributions and contributions to political action committees that support certain legislation. Organizations may do other kinds of work, such as write position papers, make personal visits, publicize voting records, or use a letter campaign to stockholders and other constituents.[42]

Political activity can have enormous positive consequences for an organization. For example, Bethlehem Steel is trying to influence federal legislation to roll back foreign steel imports by 15 percent. Assuming that domestic consumption remains the same, increased domestic demand from the import rollback would have huge benefits for Bethlehem. The average price would increase by about $50 a ton, and the increase in tons for Bethlehem could mean a quarter of a billion dollars of new business, plus an additional half-billion dollars from higher prices on old volume. All totaled, the effect would amount to profits of over $9 per Bethlehem share of stock.

Trade Associations   Much of the work to influence the external domain is accomplished jointly with other organizations that have similar interests. The National Rifle Association has thousands of individual and corporate members who have similar interests concerning the freedom to use guns. Most manufacturing companies belong to the National Association of Manufacturers. By pooling resources, even small organizations can afford to lobby legislators, influence new regulations, develop public campaigns, and block new competition.[43]

Merger   A merger is when two or more organizations combine to become one, which typically occurs when one company acquires the assets of the other in exchange for stock or cash. A merger is perhaps the most direct way to alter an organization's domain. By acquiring another company, the organization immediately has access to different suppliers, markets, competitors, and government regulations.[44] Phillip Morris redefined its domain away from tobacco by acquiring other types of companies, including Seven-Up and Miller Brewing. Braniff tried to recover from its bankruptcy by merging with Pacific Southwest Airlines. The merger was to enable PSA to use 1500 Braniff personnel and Braniff airplanes on PSA routes. The plan would have been good for Braniff, but not very good for PSA, and the merger was never approved.

Many mergers involve domain management through vertical integration or diversification. **Vertical integration** involves the acquisition of companies that supply raw materials or that buy and distribute the company's products. Owning a company on the supply side reduces uncertainty with respect to inputs, and owning a company on the output side reduces uncertainty with respect to sales. **Diversification** takes place when the company acquires businesses that are unrelated to existing businesses. This reduces the firm's risk by spreading the product portfolio across a number of environmental domains. The following Up Close illustrates how Textron diversified to change its domain to reduce dependence on the textile industry.

UP CLOSE 10.4:   Textron

Textron was one of the first corporations to adopt the strategy of unrelated diversification. Textron began diversifying to break out of a low-return industry. The textile industry was overbuilt in the South, which created a lot of insecurity for everyone in the company.

Textron's first acquisition occurred in 1953, when management purchased Burkart Manufacturing Company. Burkart started out making horse blankets in St. Louis and graduated to auto upholstery stuffing. Two other companies, Dalemo Victor and MB Manufacturing, were acquired in 1954. This began the move outside the textile industry. In the late 1950s, Homelite Corporation was acquired. Then E-Z Go Golfcart Company in 1960. Bell Aircraft Corp. was acquired in 1960 to get into defense contracting. By 1967 Textron's total sales were $3 billion, a far cry from the struggling textile company of 1953. Diversification enabled Textron to change its domain and expand more rapidly than it could in the textile industry.

Textron's creator, Royal Little, believes diversifying is as desirable today as ever, but much harder. He claims that a well-run diversified company should not ever lose money. By covering several industries, he believes, a company can often outperform non-diversified companies.

Textron diversified into defense businesses. Other companies diversify away from defense when too much of their profit comes from defense contracts, which was the case with United Technologies. They depended on the Pentagon too heavily, and diversified into non-defense industries to reduce dependence on government contracts. A few top companies—IBM, Wang, Hewlett-Packard —have not diversified. They have excellent growth and return on capital and do not need to diversify.[45]   ■

Summary Model of Organization Responses

Three important themes in our discussion about organizational responses to the external environment emerge. Exhibit 10.8 summarizes these themes.

1. *Greater environmental change is associated with greater organization flexibility.* Change in key sectors means that the organization must act swiftly in response to unanticipated shifts in consumer demand, supplies,

EXHIBIT 10.8
Relationship Between Source of Environmental Uncertainty and Type of Organizational Response

Environment	Organization
Increase in external change	Structural and management flexibility and looseness. Less formalization, centralization, standardization.
Increase in external complexity	Structural complexity. More departments and boundary roles, greater differentiation. Additional integrator roles for coordination.
Increase in resource dependence	Additional interorganizational linkages, contracts, joint ventures. Redefine domain through vertical integration or diversification. Political activity.

or government regulation. An organic internal structure, with less formalization, less standardization and less centralization, is appropriate for a quick response. Employees are not constrained by a mechanistic structure and management system. On the other hand, if the environment is stable, then characteristics of a mechanistic structure, including formalization, centralization and standardization, are appropriate. These mechanistic structures were adopted to deal with past events, and in an environment of slow change the same structures will be appropriate for future events.

2. *Greater environmental complexity is associated with greater complexity within the organization.* When the environment is complex, the organization must respond to a large number of external elements. Boundary spanners are needed, and so is a greater division of labor, with specific positions and departments assigned to specific environmental sectors. The organization will have a larger number of departments, and these departments will be differentiated from one another. Even more positions are needed to achieve coordination within the organization. Integrator roles will help coordinate the differentiated structure so the organization can perform as a unified whole. When the external environment is simple, then the internal structure can be simple. Only a few departments are needed, and these departments will not be highly differentiated. Coordination and integration will be easier to achieve, typically through planning and meetings.

3. *Greater resource dependence is associated with organizational efforts to create interorganizational linkages or to control the environmental domain.* When the organization is vulnerable because of resource scarcity or because of dependence on other organizations, a typical response is to undertake some form of contractual arrangement, cooptation, joint venture, or exchange of key personnel. More extreme responses involve redefining the domain through mergers, vertical integration, or diversification. Over the long term, political activity and trade associations also help control the external domain. When the organization is successful and has adequate resources, new external linkages or control of the domain are not needed. The organization is a relatively autonomous unit and can concentrate on producing and selling goods without joint ventures, mergers, or political activity.

The **Up Close** discussions in this chapter illustrated these three patterns. American Airlines is in a complex environment, and it has a complex structure to deal with all of those elements. American's environment has also been undergoing rapid change, which requires flexibility and adaptability. This change brought about severe resource dependence, which American has countered with negotiation of new contracts with unions and suppliers. To this point, American has not participated in joint ventures or mergers to reduce dependence on the environment. Mattel experienced rapid change in its environment and had to adopt a flexible, organic structure in response. A substantial portion of Mattel's budget is devoted to development of new toys in an R&D atmosphere. The organization is also diversifying so it does not have to depend entirely on the volatile toy market. Mattel has also engaged in extensive advertising, market research, and other activities that have added to structural complexity but also have allowed the company to interpret and influence the external environment. Other organizations, like Textron, have achieved resource independence through acquisitions and diversification.

POPULATION ECOLOGY

The environmental frameworks discussed so far in this chapter pertain to established organizations. A recent perspective on organization-environment relations that is especially relevant to new businesses is called the population ecology model. This model is patterned a bit after natural selection, or the ecological perspective, in biology. Natural selection implies continuous variation in the creation of new organizations, but, as in living species, a limited number of new organizations will be selected by the environment. From the population perspective, the environment selects organizations for survival based on the fit between organization form and environmental characteristics.[46]

Organizational form is the configuration of technology, products, goals, structure and personnel of the organization. The environment will accept or reject a specific form. Each organization tries to find a niche sufficient to support it. New products and ideas are continuously proposed by entrepreneurial organizations. The challenge is to produce a product or service desired by the environment. The selection process that leads to acceptance or rejection of a new organization has three stages—variation, selection, and retention.

Variation   Variation pertains to the diversity of new organizational forms that appear. New organizational forms are initiated by entrepreneurs, established with venture capital, or set up by a government seeking to provide new services. A great number of new organizational variations continuously appear in a population of organizations.

Selection   Selection is the process through which certain organizations survive in the larger environment. A few variations will suit the needs of the external environment and be selected for survival, but most will fail. Organizations undergo a struggle for existence, and most are not suited to the environment. When demand for the product is insufficient or resources are not available, the organization will be selected out and perish.

Retention   Retention is the institutionalization of an organizational form that has survived and prospered in the environment. If an organizational form is valued by society, it may become a dominant part of the environment. Many organizations are currently institutionalized, such as the federal government, universities, churches, and the manufacturers of television sets and automobiles.

According to the population ecology model, managerial action has value in helping the organization find a correct niche, but other actions are less important.[47] Moreover, if the environment needs the contribution of a new organization, then the organization will probably survive regardless of other managerial decisions.

An example of organizational variation in the recent history of North America was the emergence of motels. Prior to the 1950s, hotels located in cities and towns were used by the traveling public. During the 1950s, motor hotels appeared along highways. This new organizational form met an environmental need and quickly found its niche. The best ones were filled each night. Then super highways began to crisscross the continent. New organizational forms kept emerging. The most important variation came from a group in Memphis, Tennessee, that developed a motel chain with standardized quality and a system of advance reservations, called Holiday Inn. Soon Holiday Inns stretched from coast to coast, and they were joined by other motel chains, such as Ramada Inn and Howard Johnson. The challenge to motel owners and managers is to find or keep a niche consistent with what the environment wants. If they cannot do this, they will fail, as did many of the older motels built beside the less traveled two-lane highways.

SUMMARY

In this chapter we have covered a number of ideas and concepts that can help managers understand the external environment. Organizations are open systems, so the external environment is crucial to survival and success. We began by defining ten sectors in the external environment of organizations, and we grouped these sectors according to task and general environments. The elements of the external environment include the domain within which the organization functions.

Then the concept of environmental uncertainty was introduced. Uncertainty is caused by environmental change, complexity, and resource dependency. As uncertainty increases, organizations develop mechanisms for responding. Responses to environmental change include a more flexible structure. Responses to environmental complexity include a more complex structure by using boundary spanning and additional departments. Responses to resource dependency include methods to control the external environment. Linkages to other organizations reduce uncertainty, and so does control of the environmental domain through political activity or diversification.

In the final section the population ecology model was introduced. This model argues that the needs of the overall environment are important for success and survival. In this view, the appropriate role of organization management is to find a niche so that the organization is providing products and services desired by the larger population.

KEY WORDS

boundary-spanning
  role
cooptation
differentiation
direct interlock
diversification
domain
general environment
indirect interlock
integration

joint venture
mechanistic structure
merger
organic structure
organizational
  environment
organizational form
population ecology
resource dependence

retention
sector
selection
simple-complex
static dynamic
  dimension
task environment
uncertainty
variation

DISCUSSION QUESTIONS

1. Define the concept of environment, and explain the differences among the concepts of task environment, general environment, sector, and domain.
2. What is environmental uncertainty? Would environmental complexity or environmental change have the greatest influence on uncertainty?

3. In what type of environment will differentiation and integration be greatest? Explain. In what type of environment would the percentage of managers devoted to integration be greatest? Explain.
4. Explain the relationship between organizational complexity and environmental complexity.
5. What types of responses do organizations make to resource dependency? Do these responses differ from responses to environmental change or complexity?
6. Why would a mechanistic organization structure be inappropriate in a dynamic environment?
7. Are planning and forecasting likely to be more important in a stable or dynamic environment? Explain.
8. What techniques can be used by organization managers to exert control over the external environment?
9. How does the population ecology perspective differ from the other concepts and models discussed in this chapter? Consider levels of analysis and type of organization in your answer.

CASE 10.1:   First National City Bank

The First National City Bank was founded in 1955 by William Jacks, who owned a controlling interest in the bank. His family had been in banking for many years, and he saw this as an opportunity to apply his banking and management experience to his own bank. The bank was located in a rapidly growing urban area in Arizona. During the initial years, First National City Bank concentrated on two goals: attracting and retaining depositors through personal service, and establishing a reputation as a safe and solid financial institution. The goals were successful, and the bank grew to $475 million in assets by 1974.

During the late 1970s, the bank's growth slowed, and Bill Jacks and the bank experienced some reversals. Two new branch locations were closed because they could not show a profit. One of the branches was located in a nearby city that had a large population of ethnic and minority people. The other branch had been located near a major university where most of the residents were college students. In both cases, the First National City branches seemed unable to attract depositors and borrowers from their local areas. The Bank did not have a positive reputation with those population segments, and did not seem to have the flexibility or types of service desired by potential customers.

By 1978, Bill Jacks began to replace some middle managers, hoping to bring in new energy and fresh ideas. Bill Jacks still believed that a bank succeeded because of its safety as a financial institution, and because it established personal relationships with middle class customers. He passed this philosophy and other management ideas on to the new managers. He stressed a traditional management structure, including centralized decision making and standardized procedures. All branch banks were encouraged to offer the same services, and many decisions were passed up the hierarchy to the top. Vertical communication and "following the rules" were deemed a safe and responsible management approach for a community bank.

As the new managers gained experience in the bank, they began to propose changes. One branch manager suggested that each of the branch locations establish an advisory board. The purpose of the advisory board would be to select people from the surrounding community to serve on a committee that would serve as a liaison between the community and First National City Bank and make recommendations to management. The advisory boards would be composed of the bank manager, Bill Jacks, and important people from the local area, such as business people, women, minority group members, or college students. The manager who proposed the idea argued that advisory board members could counsel prospective customers about bank services and in general provide good information to the bank manager and promote good will for the bank.

Another new manager proposed that the bank engage in more advertising and public relations. She argued that bank employees should become more involved in community groups, such as the Chamber of Commerce and United Way. She also argued that the bank should make a contribution to the State Association of Bankers to support lobbyists working at the state capitol to increase the interest rate ceilings, and to support lobbyists working in Washington to influence bank regulation.

As Bill Jacks considered these and other proposals, deregulation of banks became a hot topic in Washington. Deregulation had been successful in other industries, and President Carter signed into law the Depository Institutions Deregulation Act of 1980. President Reagan encouraged continued deregulation through the Depository Institutions Act of 1982. These changes dramatically affected the industry climate of banks. New powers were given to thrift institutions—credit unions, savings and loan associations—to compete directly with banks in business and consumer lending, retirement annuities, and other servies. Deregulation also gave banks the freedom to become financial supermarkets and provide services such as the sale of stocks and bonds, to offer high interest rates, and to charge for services. The new regulations seemed to favor large banks because interstate banking and bank holding companies were possible.

Bill Jacks and the other managers were very uncertain about the impact of deregulation on First National City Bank. A bank consultant was hired to assess the impact of deregulation on First National City's strategy. The consultant said that as deregulation was implemented over the next three years, the bank will need, "a strong commitment to the development and delivery of new products. Moreover, customer loyalty will fade and price competition combined with technological advances and internal efficiencies will be essential for maintaining and increasing a customer base."

A university professor conducted a survey of successful community banks to learn how they were coping with deregulation. The survey found that successful banks were making changes in four areas: (1) asset-liability management, (2) cost control, (3) marketing, (4) pricing and non-interest income. Better asset-liability management in many banks was accomplished through a new asset-liability committee that helped the bank make a transition to variable-rate loans, make loans according to profit margin, and explore new investment opportunities. Cost control was accomplished through technology and data processing, such as automated tellers and the automatic transfer of funds. New marketing techniques included market segmentation and the packaging of new products for each segment. Money market accounts, discount brokerage services, increased advertising, retirement accounts, and other marketing ideas were being adopted. Important new income was also being derived from non-interest sources for successful community banks. Seventy-five percent of the banks increased fees for returned checks, overdrafts and checking account services. Fees were also increased for routine balance inquiries and saving accounts.

In January of 1983, Bill Jacks felt overwhelmed, and wondered whether he was up to managing the bank. The bank had grown little over five years, and was losing market share to other, often recently established banks. Two of the newer managers quit out of frustration over not having impact on bank policy. The impact of bank deregulation was difficult to anticipate, and he was not sure how the bank should respond. Two of the brightest young managers in the bank had been to see him about a change in management structure and approach. They encouraged the creation of several internal committees to study the problems and to coordinate the needs of each department and branch. They also suggested the bank begin planning for the addition of new departments that would be responsible for new electronic technology, new services, and stronger advertising. "The banking industry is becoming more complex and its changing rapidly," one manager argued, "and if we don't adapt to it we will be left behind." Bill Jacks also thought back to earlier proposals, such as for advisory boards, on which he had not acted. Could the bank afford to invest in advertising, lobbying, new technology, and new departments? Would customers pay fees for services that had been provided free? Should the bank provide non-banking services? Could all of these activities be coordinated when things change so quickly? If he was unable to resolve these problems, Bill Jacks thought the best thing might be to retire and perhaps sell his interest in the bank to someone else.[48]

CASE QUESTIONS

1. Evaluate the complexity and rate of change in First National City Bank's environment? Which domains seem most imporant? Where would you place First National City Bank on the environmental uncertainty framework in Exhibit 10.2? Why?
2. Should the bank try to adapt to the external environment or try to exert greater control over the environment? Which of the proposals do you recommend the bank adopt? How should the bank change its structure in response to these proposals and to be congruent with the environment?

NOTES

1. James D. Thompson, *Organizations in Action* (New York: McGraw-Hill, 1967).
2. Alvin Toffler, *Future Shock* (Toronto: Bantom Books of Canada Ltd., 1971).
3. Joseph E. McCann and John Selsky, "Hyperturbulence and the Emergence of Type 5 Environments," *Academy of Management Review* 9 (1984): 460–470.
4. Richard L. Daft, *Organization Theory and Design* (St. Paul: West, 1983).
5. William R. Dill, "Environment as an Influence on Managerial Autonomy," *Administrative Science Quarterly* 2 (1958): 409–443.
6. Paul M. Hirsch, "Organizational Effectiveness and the Institutional Environment," *Administrative Science Quarterly* 20 (1975): 327–344.
7. Thomas J. Peters and Robert H. Waterman, Jr., *In Search of Excellence* (New York: Harper and Row, 1982).
8. Geoffrey Smith, "The New Alchemists," *Forbes*, April 9, 1984, pp. 101–104.
9. Fremont E. Kast and James E. Rosenzweig, *Organization and Management: A Systems and Contingency Approach*, 3rd ed. (New York: McGraw-Hill, 1979).
10. Based on Colin Lainster, "How American Mastered Deregulation," *Fortune*, June 11, 1984, pp. 38–50; Harlin S. Byrne, "Airline Industry Faces Another Big Loss, But Some Carriers are Weathering Storms," *The Wall Street Journal*, January 25, 1983, p. 52; Kim Penn and Rodney Slota, "Case Study of American Airlines," Unpublished paper, Texas A&M University, 1982.
11. Jay Galbraith, *Organization Design* (Reading, MA: Addison-Wesley, 1977).
12. Robert B. Duncan, "Characteristics of Organizational Environments and Perceived Environmental Uncertainty," *Administrative Science Quarterly* 17 (1972): 313–327.

13. Gregory G. Dess and Donald W. Beard, "Dimensions of Organizational Task Environments," *Administrative Science Quarterly* 29 (1984): 52–73; Howard E. Aldrich, *Organizations and Environments* (Englewood Cliffs, NJ: Prentice-Hall, 1979).
14. Raymond Sokolov, "Plagued by Rising Costs and Falling Sales, Book Publishers are in Throes of Change," *The Wall Street Journal*, July 2, 1982, p. 28.
15. Robert B. Duncan, "Characteristics of Organizational Environments and Perceived Environmental Uncertainty."
16. Kristen M. Dahlen, Sandra Hart, and Joanne Williams, "Breeding the Bunny: Playboy Enterprises Inc.," Unpublished case analysis, Texas A&M University, 1980.
17. Jeffrey Pfeffer and Gerald R. Salancik, *The External Controls of Organizations* (New York: Harper & Row, 1978); Jeffrey Pfeffer, *Power in Organizations* (Marshfield, MA: Pitman Publishing, 1981).
18. Jeffrey Pfeffer and A. Leong, "Resource Allocations in United Funds: An Examination of Power and Dependence," *Social Forces* 55 (1977): 775–790; Keith G. Provan, Janice M. Beyer, and C. Kruybtosch, "Environmental Linkages and Power in Resource Dependence Relations between Organizations," *Administrative Science Quarterly* 25 (1980): 200–225.
19. Janet Guyon, "Do Publications Avoid Anti-Cigarette Stories to Protect Ad Dollars?" *The Wall Street Journal*, November 22, 1982: 1–16.
20. David Ulrich and Jay B. Barney, "Perspectives in Organizations: Resource Dependence, Efficiency, and Population," *Academy of Management Review* 9 (1984): 471–481.
21. Barry M. Staw and Eugene Szwajkowski, "The Scarcity-Munificence Component of Organizational Environments and the Commission of Illegal Acts," *Administrative Science Quarterly* 20 (1975): 345–354.
22. Marc Conley, John Langford, Victoria Luquette, Shelby Willett, "Mattel, Inc.: A Case Study and Analysis," Unpublished manuscript, Texas A&M University, 1982; "Valley of the Dolls: How Mattel, Inc. Went From Thriving Concern to a Not-so-Thriving One," *Wall Street Journal*, June 20, 1973, p. 1; Stephen J. Sanswest, "Mattel Tries to Lure Skeptical Consumers by Selling Computers as High-Priced Fun," *Wall Street Journal*, March 14, 1980.
23. Marc Conley, et al., "Mattel, Inc.: A Case Study and Analysis."
24. Tom Burns and G. M. Stalker, *The Management of Innovation* (London: Tavistock, 1961).
25. Burns and Stalker, *The Management of Innovation*, p. 92–94.
26. David B. Jemison, "The Importance of Boundary Spanning Roles in Strategic Decision Making," *Journal of Management Studies* 21 (1984): 131–152; Robert Miles, *Macroorganizational Behavior* (Santa Monica, CA: Goodyear, 1980): Chapter 11; J. Stacy Adams, "The Structure and Dynamics of Behavior in Organization Boundary Roles," in M. D. Dunnette ed., *The Handbook of Industrial and Organizational Psychology* (Chicago: Rand McNally, 1976): 1175–1199; Howard Aldrich and Diane Herker, "Boundary Spanning Roles and Organization Structure," *Academy of Management Review* (1977): 217–239.
27. Paul R. Lawrence and Jay W. Lorsch, *Organization and Environment: Managing Differentiation and Integration* (Homewood, IL: Irwin, 1969).
28. Jay W. Lorsch, "Introduction to the Structural Design of Organizations," in Gene W. Dalton, Paul R. Lawrence and Jay W. Lorsch, eds., *Organization Structure and Design* (Homewood, IL: Irwin and Dorsey, 1970), p. 5.
29. Lorsch, "Introduction to Structural Design," p. 7.
30. Jay W. Lorsch and Paul R. Lawrence, "Environmental Factors and Organizational Integration," in Jay W. Lorsch and Paul R. Lawrence, eds., *Organizational Planning: Cases and Concepts* (Homewood, IL: Irwin and Dorsey, 1972), p. 45.
31. Rosalie L. Tung, "Dimensions of Organizational Environments: An Exploratory Study of Their Impact on Organization Structure," *Academy of Management Journal* 22 (1979): 672–693.
32. James W. Fredrickson and Terence E. Mitchell, "Strategic Decision Processes: Comprehensiveness and Performance in an Industry with an Unstable Environment," *Academy of Management Journal* 27 (1984): 399–423; Robert D. Duncan, "Multiple Decision-Making Structures in Adapting to Environmental Uncertainty: The Impact on Organizational Effectiveness," *Human Relations* 26 (1973): 273–291.
33. Jeffrey Pfeffer, "Size, Composition, and Function of Hospital Board of Directors: A Study of Organization-Environment Linkage," *Administrative Science Quarterly* 18 (1973): 349–364.

34. Phillip Selznick, *TVA and the Grass Roots: A Study in the Sociology of Formalization* (Berkeley: University of California Press, 1949).
35. Joseph McCann and Jay R. Galbraith, "Interdepartmental Relations," in Paul C. Nystrom and William H. Starbuck, eds., *Handbook of Organizational Design*, Vol. 2 (New York: Oxford University Press, 1981), pp. 60–84.
36. Jeffrey Pfeffer and Huseyin Leblebici, "Executive Recruitment and the Development of Interfirm Organizations," *Administrative Science Quarterly* 18 (1973): 449–461.
37. Barry M. Staw and Eugene Szwajkowski, "The Scarcity-Munificence Component of Organizational Environments and the Commission of Illegal Acts," *Administrative Science Quarterly* (1975): 345–354.
38. Jeffrey Pfeffer and Phillip Nowak, "Joint Ventures and Interorganizational Interdependence," *Administrative Science Quarterly* 21 (1976): 398–418.
39. F. David Schoorman, Max H. Bazerman, and Robert S. Atkin, "Interlocking Directorates: A Strategy for Reducing Environmental Uncertainty," *Academy of Management Review* 6 (1981): 243–251; Johannes M. Pennings, *Interlocking Directors: Origins and Consequences of Connections among Organization's Boards of Directors* (San Francisco: Jossey-Bass, 1980); Ronald S. Burt, *Toward a Structural Theory of Action* (New York: Academic Press, 1982).
40. Stephen J. Sansweet, "Movie, TV Firms Building Alliances to Take Advantage of Home Video," *The Wall Street Journal*, March 26, 1982: 23. Used with permission.
41. Jeffrey Pfeffer, "Beyond Management and the Worker: The Institutional Function of Management," *Academy of Management Review* 1 (April, 1976): 36–46; John P. Kotter, "Managing External Dependence," *Academy of Management Review* 4 (1979): 87–92.
42. John C. Aplin and W. Harvey Hagerty, "Political Influence: Strategy Used by Organizations to Impact Legislation in Business and Economic Matters," *Academy of Management Journal* 23 (1980): 438–450.
43. Pfeffer, "Beyond Management and the Worker."
44. Jeffrey Pfeffer, "Merger As a Response to Organizational Interdependence," *Administrative Science Quarterly* 17 (1972): 382–394.
45. Royal Little, "Conglomerates are Doing Better than You Think," *Fortune*, May 28, 1984: 50–60.
46. Michael T. Hannan and John Freeman, "The Population Ecology of Organizations," *American Journal of Sociology* 82 (1977): 929–964; Howard E. Aldrich and Jeffrey Pfeffer, "Environments of Organization," in A. Inkles, ed., *Annual Review of Sociology* (Vol. 4) (Palo Alto, CA: Annual Review, Inc., 1976): 79–105.
47. Howard Aldrich, Bill McKelvey and Dave Ulrich, "Design Strategy from the Population Perspective," *Journal of Management* 10 (1984): 67–86; Ulrich and Barney, "Perspective in Organizations."
48. This case was inspired and adapted from John F. Veiga and John N. Yanouzas, "The Constitution National Bank," *The Dynamics of Organization Theory: Gaining a Macroperspective* (St. Paul, MN: West, 1979): 139–140; Peter S. Rose, "What, How, Why and Whither of U.S. Bank Deregulation," *Canadian Banker*, 91, 1 (February 1984): 36–41; Judy Brown, "How High Performance Community Banks Cope with the Effects of Deregulation," *Journal of Retail Banking*, 5, 3 (Fall 1983): 17–24; and Richard C. Aspinwall, "Anticipating Banking Deregulation," *The Journal of Business Strategy*, Spring 1983: 84–86.

11 Goals and Effectiveness

A fter more than a decade of lackluster profits, Owens-Illinois Inc., is improving its financial performance. Improving financial performance is a new goal for Owens. "We were a volume-oriented company five years ago," says one marketing manager. Now, says the chairman, "We're more interested in profits than we are in market share." The change in goals has caused a major change in operations. A glass-container plant in Massachusetts was closed only six years after it opened. Owens also withdrew from the returnable-bottle market. These operations had helped maintain volume and market share, but did not add to profits, so they exist no more.[1]

The purpose of this chapter is to explore the topic of organizational goals and effectiveness. Goals represent the organization target toward which managers' strategies, objectives, and operations are directed. A change in goals reshapes internal activities, as happened at Owens-Illinois. Goals also represent the criterion of performance. The effectiveness of an organization is ultimately determined by its success at achieving specified goals. In this chapter we will carefully examine types of organizational goals, their function, and the processes by which organizations set goals and manage multiple goals simultaneously. We will also examine the topic of organizational effectiveness, and the criteria that can be used to assess effectiveness. The chapter will close with an examination of the reasons why organizations pursue certain goals and criteria for effectiveness rather than others.

RELEVANCE OF GOALS AND EFFECTIVENESS FOR MANAGERS

An organizational goal is a desired future state of affairs that the organization attempts to realize.[2] Goals pertain to the future, but they influence current activities. Goals are important because organizations are goal-attainment devices. Organizations exist for a purpose, and goals define and state that purpose.

The responsibility for defining and communicating goals rests with management. The presence of explicit goals provides several important benefits for the organization. Goals serve as guides to action, as a source of motivation, as a standard of performance, to legitimize the organization, and as a rationale for internal structure and decision processes.[3]

Guides to Action   Organizational goals provide a sense of direction for employees. Organizational goals focus attention on specific targets and provide a clear purpose for what the organization is trying to accomplish. By directing employee efforts toward certain outcomes, goals also tell employees which outcomes to avoid. Goals thus constrain behaviors not consistent with the accomplishment of preferred outcomes. At Owens-Illinois, for example, employees used to be directed toward maintaining a high volume of production. With the new goal of financial performance, employees are directed toward activities that add to profits and away from activities that just increase volume or market share.

Source of Motivation and Commitment   Goal statements describe the organization's mission to employees. Goals describe the purpose and nature of the organization, and they serve to facilitate employee identification with the organization. Goals also help motivate employees by reducing uncertainty and providing incentives. Goals reduce uncertainty by telling employees what they should accomplish. Goals provide incentives because rewards such as promotion and salary increases can be linked to the attainment of specific goals, which energize employees in the desired direction.

Standard of Performance   Since goals define outcomes for the organization, they also are the criteria of performance. Goals provide a standard of assessment. Following Owens-Illinois shift to profit goals, profit performance increased by 30%. This occurred during a period when two competitors reported earnings declines of 76% and 61%. Profit became the standard of performance, rather than volume or market share.[4] Goals can provide the standard of assessment throughout the organization. The board of directors can use goals to evaluate top management, top management to evaluate middle management, and so on. Organizations have goals at each level, and these goals provide multiple criteria of effectiveness.

Legitimacy   Goals inform people in the external environment of organizational mission and purpose. Goals justify and explain the organization's purpose to the public at large. This is important because an organization's success ultimately derives from its ability to survive in its environment. Goal statements symbolize and signal what the organization stands for. When the organization is perceived as illegitimate, its survival is threatened. Firms in the tobacco industry have continued to argue for the legitimacy of selling cigarettes, but declining cigarette sales suggest that these organizations may be gradually losing legitimacy. Cigarette manufacturers have acquired other types of businesses to be certain about the long-term survival of their firms.

Rationale for Organization Structure and Decision Processes   Goals help define the correct form and structure for the organization. In a rapidly changing environment, managers tend to adopt goals that can be met with a loose, flexible structure. At Owens-Illinois, when the profit goals were given priority over volume goals, organizational structure was altered by shutting down certain operating units. On the other hand, if Owens-Illinois had adopted goals of more volume or expansion, managers would add new departments and plants to the existing structure. Decision processes and guidelines are also influenced by goals. Through discussion and goal setting, managers become aware of what the organization is trying to accomplish; they will make their decisions so that internal policies, rules, performance, products, expenditures and structure are congruent with desired goals.

For each reason stated above, goals are an important component of manager activities and ultimately influence whether an organization is effective or ineffective. Goals should be congruent with other aspects of the organization, such as technology, environment, and human resource characteristics. The relationships among these elements and organizational effectiveness are illustrated in Exhibit 11.1. Organization, environment, employee characteristics, and goals taken together determine organizational effectiveness. Goals energize employees, provide guides to action, legitimize the organization to the public, and provide a rationale for structure and decisions. Goals play an important role in defining and communicating management policies within the organization.

TYPES OF GOALS

Organizations pursue several goals simultaneously. Different parts of the organization are responsible for attaining different goals. Official goals are the responsibility of top management. Operative goals are the responsibility of middle levels of the organization, and operational goals are the responsibility of individual supervisors and employees.

Official Goals

Official goals are the formally stated goals the organization says it is trying to achieve. Official goals are typically written down, and they specify what the organization is trying to accomplish, the reason it exists, and the values that underlie its existence.[5] Official goals may be written in an annual report, in a policy manual, or distributed to employees at hiring.

Official goals often appear abstract and general. They are not specific or measurable, because they pertain to the organization as a whole. For example, three official goals of a high school are:

1. "To develop in students a love of learning, intellectual curiosity, and skills in communications and basic subjects."
2. "To develop in students the ability to cope with problems and to seek solutions through effective use of knowledge, and the application of both logical and creative problem-solving techniques."

EXHIBIT 11.1
Major Influences on Organizational Effectiveness

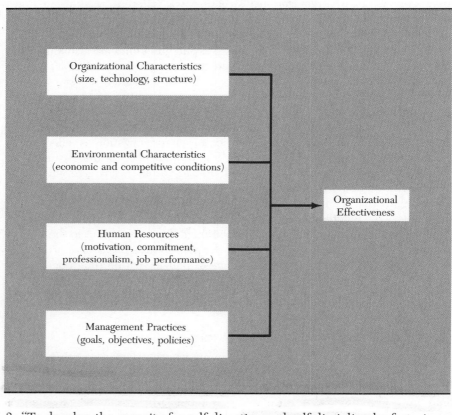

3. "To develop the capacity for self-direction and self-discipline by fostering a sense of self-worth and an awareness of one's ability to influence one's own destiny."[6]

Official goals for Hewlett-Packard include:

1. "To provide products and services of the greatest possible value to our customers, thereby gaining and holding their respect and loyalty."
2. "To honor our obligations to society by being an economic, intellectual, and social asset to each nation and each community in which we operate."
3. "To help our own people share in the company's success which they make possible: To provide job security based on their performance, to recognize their individual achievements, and to help them gain a sense of satisfaction and accomplishment from their work."[7]

Hewlett-Packard and the high school may have from seven to ten explicit official goals that define what the organization stands for and what it is trying to achieve. These goals serve the functions of establishing legitimacy in the external environment and engaging the commitment and identification of employees with the organization. Official goals are not specific enough to serve as guidelines for activities or as explicit standards of performance. However, organizations sometimes adopt highly visible behaviors to reinforce official goals. Jockey International Inc. shipped 16,800 undergarments to Poland with the request that the Roman Catholic Church distribute the garments to members of the Solidarity movement. Jockey also sent 15,576 T-shirts and knit sport shirts to Fort Wayne, Indiana in response to a desperate need for underwear and clothing after a major flood. These actions communicate that Jockey International stands for more than making a profit.[8]

Operative Goals

Operative goals are the outcomes that the organization actually seeks to accomplish through operating policies and activities.[9] Operative goals define what the organization is trying to do—what it has to do—to survive and be successful. Key departments must perform a number of different tasks for the organization to survive, and operative goals define the nature and desired outcomes of these tasks. Among the most frequently defined operative goals are the following.[10]

Market   **Market goals** define the market share or market standing desired by the firm. Market goals often are the responsibility of the marketing, sales, and advertising departments. Market goals may involve the introduction of new products or entry into new geographic regions. Market goals may describe sales volume, such as increasing units sold by 10 percent. Bausch & Lomb has an explicit market goal of capturing at least 50 percent of every segment of the contact lens market. Market share is a high priority goal at Bausch & Lomb because managers want to maintain market leadership in the industry.[11]

Resources   **Resource goals** pertain to the acquisition of needed physical and financial resources. Resource goals may specify the construction of new plants and facilities, frequency of inventory turnover, the hiring of employees of a certain caliber, the reduction of the collection period on accounts receivable, or finding new and less expensive sources for raw materials. Resource goals are typically executed by departments on the input side of the organizational transformation process. The personnel, finance, and purchasing departments help achieve these goals. Resource goals help maintain the organization system in a healthy state.

Innovation   **Innovation goals** pertain to the development of new services or products, and to the need for internal flexibility and readiness to adapt to changes in the environment. Innovation goals often are part of the mandate of R&D departments. R&D may be responsible for developing new products in time to beat competitors. Gillette has the innovation goal of introducing a new shaving system that will supercede the Atra razor system. Bausch & Lomb successfully attained an innovation goal of developing soft contact lenses to increase the number of consumers who would buy contact lenses.

Productivity **Productivity goals** pertain to the efficient utilization of re-sources. Productivity goals pertain to the number of inputs required to reach desired outputs. Organizations try to be efficient, and productivity goals are typically defined in terms of "units produced per day per employee," or "budgeted resources per employee."

Profitability **Profitability** reflects the overall performance of for-profit organizations. Profitability is a summary indicator of whether the organization is successful in balancing other goals—market, productivity, innovation, and resources. Profitability goals are typically defined in terms of net income, return on investment, or earnings-per-share. Not-for-profit organizations do not have profitability goals, but they do have goals that attempt to specify the delivery of service to the public within specified budget expense levels.

Employee Development **Employee development goals** pertain to human resource training, promotion, opportunity, and safety. Organizations try to develop employee potential and to encourage positive attitudes and satisfaction on the part of employees.

Operational Goals

Operational goals define specific behavior and performance objectives within the organization. Operational goals are more exact and measurable than operative goals. Operational goals often outline specific objectives for each department and each employee within the organization. Official goals tend to define the overall purpose and value of the organization for the public. Operative goals define the tasks that the major departments and functions of the organization try to accomplish. Operational goals pertain to lower hierarchical levels. They define specific activities that can be used to evaluate performance of managers, supervisors, and employees.

The three types of goals are interdependent. Official goals influence operative goals, and operative goals influence operational goals. Likewise, the accomplishment of operational goals enables the organization to meet its operative and official goals. How an airline's official goals are linked to operative market and productivity goals, and then to operational objectives, is illustrated in the following **Up-Close.**

UP CLOSE 11.1:   Airline Corporation

When asked about organizational goals, a senior executive for a major U.S. air carrier was quick to describe several goals. He indicated that his airline pursued official, operative, and operational goals, and they actually tried to evaluate performance on all of them.

This airline had three official goals, as indicated in Exhibit 11.2: (1) to return a profit adequate to finance future capital expenditures; (2) to provide high quality transportation services; (3) to be a good place to work for employees. In 1982, the company failed to attain two of the three official goals, in this executive's opinion. The airline industry is a capital intensity business, and without capital replacement the airline will eventually fail. The first official goal required a profit of 5% of sales. The company lost money in 1982 and made only 3% in the previous two years. Providing quality service was evaluated from ratings by the International Airline Passengers Association. The association rates airlines annually, and this carrier improved its rating from previous years, accomplishing this goal. As for being, "a good place to work," things have not gone well. During the recent period of industry decline, the airline had to lay off a number of employees. Employees felt a sense of insecurity. Moreover, as indicated by the productivity goals in Exhibit 11.2, the airline is trying to get additional productivity from employees. Managers have met with employees to reduce uncertainty associated with difficult times, but the goal has not been met.

A few of the airline's operative and operational goals are also illustrated in Exhibit 11.2. The operative goal of improved productivity is the reason for developing a more efficient fleet mix and increasing labor efficiency. These operative goals are to be attained through the operational goals or renegotiating with unions, limiting employee vacations, acquiring Boeing 767 jet aircraft, reconditioning current airplanes, and discontinuing the use of inefficient 707s.

An example of a resource goal is the desire to improve financial yields from existing flights, current investments, and aircraft purchases. Additional resources can be acquired through advanced purchase requirements, discount fares, and negotiating favorable rates for the Boeing 767 purchases.

Market goals are reflected in the airline's desire to expand both passenger and freighter service. The operational activities for passenger service include expanded operations at Dallas-Fort Worth, as well as new services to Mexican and South American locations. The freighter service goals can be met through an increased advertising program and adding to the size of the freight distribution fleet.

In the case of this air carrier, the operational goals describe the specific activities that will help the company achieve its operative goals. The operative goals apply to specific departments within the airline. Official goals, by contrast, pertain to the organization as a whole, although in this company the official goals are not as high-minded and abstract as those of other organiza-

EXHIBIT 11.2

Example of Selected Official, Operative and Operational Goals for an Airline

<table>
<tr><td colspan="2" align="center">Official Goals</td></tr>
<tr><td colspan="2">1. Provide high quality transportation services to customers.
2. Earn adequate profits to finance future capital expenditures.
3. Be a good place to work for employees.</td></tr>
</table>

Operative Goals	Operational Goals
Productivity 1. Develop more efficient fleet mix	a. Acquire 8 Boeing 767 twin-jet aircraft for medium-length flights b. Discontinue use of Boeing 707s c. Replace passenger seats with lighter and slimmer models d. Develop on-board computer programs to improve fuel utilization
Productivity 2. Improve labor productivity	a. Negotiate with unions for greater use of part-time employees b. Negotiate with unions to eliminate paid lunches c. Decrease size of flight attendant crew on selected flights d. Increase cockpit crew schedules by 5 hours/month
Resource 3. Improve yield through discounting and negotiation	a. Develop discount fares for price-conscious personal and vacation travelers b. Require advance ticket purchases and minimum stay requirements c. Negotiate favorable interest charges for 767 purchases
Market 4. Expand freighter service	a. Acquire 3 used 747s for a freight fleet of 6 aircraft b. Conflict other carriers to carry excess freight c. Initiate advertising campaign and discount fares to increase freight 15%

Market

5. Expand passenger service

    a. Initiate twice-a-day nonstop Hawaii service

    b. Expand Dallas-Fort Worth passenger terminal and parking area

    c. Explore New Mexico destinations and potential South American routes

    d. Maintain short-haul feeder lines to support long-haul routes

SOURCE: Adapted from Kim Penn and Rodney Slota, "Group Case Study of American Airlines," Texas A&M University, 1982.

---

tions. The official goal of being a good place to work is not being met during difficult economic times in order to achieve profit goals that will enable sufficient capital investment for long-run health and prosperity.[12] ■

GOAL CONGRUENCE

So far in this chapter, one point that should come through is that organizations pursue multiple goals. Each level in the organization pursues goals, and so does each major department. Often these goals are in conflict. A typical conflict is between the operative goals of market share and profit. At Owens-Illinois, the conflict was resolved by giving up some market share to maintain and meet profit goals. The airline in Up Close 11.1 had a conflict between the official goals of making sufficient profit for future investment and of being a good place to work. In any organization multiple goals have to be developed and pursued, but the goals also have to be coordinated so they reinforce each other rather than compete against one another. Coordination among goals is required in both vertical and horizontal directions.

Vertical Congruence

Vertical goal congruence means the linkage of goals up and down the hierarchy. Vertical congruence is attained through a means-ends chain. The **means-ends chain** refers to systematically linking the goals of each unit with the units immediately above and below it. The accomplishment of goals, or ends, at one level become the means for achieving goals at the next higher level. In this way goals at the top of the organization help define the subgoals to be accomplished at lower levels; and the goals at lower levels are the means for accomplishing higher level goals.

Vertical congruence existed in the airline **Up Close.** The purchase of three used 747s and increased advertising were the means for achieving the operative goal of expanded freighter service. The goal of expanded freighter service was the means to achieve the operative goal of profitability. Continental Illinois Bank's financial problems over the last few years are largely attributed to goals set at the top of the organization that rippled down through lower levels of the hierarchy. Top-level goals of short term high profits and rapid growth led to goals at lower levels of innovative loan packages, risky loans, and the acceptance of business that other banks turned down. Top management at Continental had the official goal of becoming one of the three biggest corporate lenders in the U.S. by 1985. It attained that goal four years early in 1981 through the use of aggressive marketing techniques. Lower-level employees went too far too fast, however, and the result was a bankrupt Continental Illinois.[13] Lower-level operational goals were influenced by high-level operative goals.

Horizontal Congruence

Horizontal congruence is the linkage of goals at the same level in the organization or the linkage of goals that may be competitive with one another. Each organization pursues several goals. Departments throughout organizations adopt distinct goal structures and performance criteria.[14] An example of multiple goals defined by business executives is given in the first column of Exhibit 11.3. A survey of executives found that several goals were important, which indicated that organizations try to attain all of them. In this survey, efficiency and productivity goals received highest priority, followed by profit maximization. Growth and leadership goals were next, followed by employee welfare, and finally social welfare. The processes within organizations that enable the accomplishment of multiple goals are as follows.

Priority setting means that management establishes explicit preferences about which goals are most important. In the case of Continental Illinois Bank, higher priority was given to rapid growth than to stability and safety. At Bausch & Lomb, the highest priority goal is to maintain market share rather than to earn high profits or ensure employee welfare. At Owens-Illinois, the first priority goes to profits, followed by market share, then employee welfare. Managers decide among multiple goals and set priorities that give direction to employees about the goal attainment expected. Exhibit 11.3 shows that managers tended to give priority to efficiency and productivity goals in many organizations.

Satisficing means that organizations accept satisfactory performance on several goals rather than maximum performance on any single goal.[15] This is a realistic approach to goal accomplishment. The organization cannot possibly maximize all goals simultaneously, so it accepts satisfactory levels of performance. Bausch & Lomb is satisfied with 50 percent market share; it does not try

EXHIBIT 11.3
Diversity of Organizational Goals Reported by Managers

Organizational Goal	Percent of Managers Rating High Performance
Organizational Efficiency	
1. Cost Efficiency	81%
2. High Productivity	80%
3. Profit Maximization	72%
Growth and Status	
4. Organizational Growth	60%
5. Industrial Leadership	58%
6. Organizational Stability	58%
Employee Development	
7. Employee Welfare	65%
Social Welfare	
8. Social Welfare	16%

SOURCE: Based on G. W. England, "Organizational Goals and Expected Behavior of American Managers," *Academy of Management Journal* 10 (1967): 108.

to maintain the 60 percent share it used to have, because this would require too much sacrifice in profit goals.

Goal succession means that goals are periodically evaluated and new goals adopted. If the environment changes dramatically, the organization has to adopt new goals to survive. New goals are adopted or old goals may receive higher priority. Many hospitals across the United States are currently undergoing major goal changes. Medicare has established new limits on hospital payments for most illnesses, which means that hospitals can no longer charge the government based on its own costs. Before the Medicare limits, hospital goals were to do as much business as possible and provide high quality care, relying on the government to pick up the tab. Now hospitals are adopting efficiency and productivity goals, because they must keep costs within the flat rate paid by the government or they will lose money.[16]

GOAL SETTING

An important task facing top- and middle-level managers is the actual setting of goals for the organization. Organizational goals can be very difficult to define. Goals are value judgments. Managers must decide among competing options and opportunities. Managers have the responsibility to define a set of goals that are appropriate for their organization at that time. These goals become the premise from which the lower levels of the organization set goals and perform tasks.

Top Management

Sometimes organizational goals are defined by a single, strong individual. This was the case with Eddie Rickenbacker when he ran Eastern Airlines from 1935 to 1959. Until he retired, he invoked the dominant goal of cost cutting, frugality and efficiency for Eastern. James S. McDonnell also ran McDonnell Douglas Corporation with an iron hand. He alone decided which goals were important. Single individuals also determine goals in many small and medium-sized organizations where the top manager is the owner. The owner/manager has strong ideas about what to accomplish with the organization and dominates the goal-setting process.

A more typical procedure in large organizations is defining goals through a dominant coalition.[17] A **coalition** is an informal alliance among senior managers who agree about organizational goals and values. Many uncertainties and options confront senior managers, and through discussion they are able to merge their perspectives and interests into a guiding set of goals for the organization. Not all managers will agree, but the dominant coalition is the majority of managers, so other managers go along. The process of building the coalition helps all managers understand the goals and to overcome inherent conflicts. The typically informal nature of coalitions encourages the establishment of goals for the organization and for major departments or functions.

Middle Management

Management by objectives, called MBO, was introduced in Chapter 4 on performance appraisal as a popular technique for implementing goals vertically down through middle and lower levels of the organization.[18] The purpose of MBO is to engage employees and supervisors in goal-setting discussions. These discussions in turn develop the objectives that are used for performance appraisal, as we discussed in Chapter 4. In the typical MBO process, preliminary goals are established at the top of the organization. These goals might specify the priority given to profits, market share, new products, and training and development. Using these overall goals as a guide, departmental managers and supervisors set goals for their units through meetings with their supervisors. In turn, all managers and supervisors have meetings with their subordinates to set objectives. Each supervisor and employee then meets on a one-to-one basis to set objectives that are consistent with departmental and organizational goals.

The value of this goal-setting process is that all employees are involved. Their specific goals emerge from joint discussions, so employees have a say in the goals they try to achieve. In this way all employees understand their own goals, they accept the goals because they participated in setting them, and they understand and acknowledge the goals of the organization. Employees throughout the organization are pursuing objectives that are congruent with the goals of the organization. In order for a goal-setting system like MBO to be effective, research suggests that certain characteristics should be present.

- *Specific objectives.* If objectives are vague and general, they have no motivating power for employees. When possible, goals should be expressed in quantitative terms, such as increase sales by 3 percent; decrease scrap by 1 percent; or increase the average teacher effectiveness rating from 3.7 to 3.9. Sometimes the nature of the goal is not quantifiable, so qualitative objectives may be used, but in a specific way. Examples of qualitative goals are "Develop a new job classification system for technical employees," or "Investigate opportunities for selling our product to wholesalers rather than to consumers."
- *Explicit deadlines.* All goals should be defined in terms of the date they will be accomplished. A goal for revising the job classification system should have a deadline, such as March 31, 1987. If the project involves a two-to-three year horizon, specific dates for when parts of the project will be completed can be specified. The deadline promotes an energizing effect for employees in accomplishing their goals on time.
- *Participation.* The objective-setting process is not effective without participation. If goals are prescribed in a unilateral, top-down fashion, employees will not accept the goals as their own. Superiors can act as counselors in the goal-setting meeting by helping subordinates sort out the various options, discussing whether the objectives are realistic and specific, and evaluating whether they are congruent with organizational goals. One-on-one discussion provides two-way communication from the organization to the employee and from the employee back to the organization.
- *Periodic reviews.* The MBO system needs to establish specific points during the year when progress toward goals will be monitored and discussed. Formal meetings are typically established once a year, at which time review and feedback discussions take place. Once every three or four months, an informal discussion about how employees are progressing toward their goals is also a good idea. Without periodic reviews, employees come to believe the goals are not important and will tend to give them less attention and be drawn into other activities.
- *Tie to reward systems.* The ultimate strength of a goal-setting system is that it influences pay as well as awards, promotions, and other rewards from the organization. People who succeed should receive positive rewards. Employees who consistently fail to attain goals will not be rewarded in the same way. Rewards should reflect both goal setting and goal attainment. Some goals may be more difficult to attain than others and managers will be in a position to evaluate the relative contributions of goals to the organization. When failure to attain goals results from factors outside the employee's control, a positive reward still may be appropriate, because the employee has accomplished partial goals under difficult circumstances.

Not-for-Profit Organizations

Major companies like Tenneco, General Foods, Black & Decker, and General Motors use formalized MBO systems. The value to these companies is that the formalized goal-setting system helps link the activities of each department and hierarchical level together. Goal congruence in both vertical and horizontal directions can be attained through the goal-setting process. Not-for-profit organizations, where goals often are more difficult to establish, also use objective-setting systems. Quantitative indicators of profit and market share typically are not available, so not-for-profit organizations receive even greater benefits from a formalized system that clarifies goals. The impact of an objective-setting system in a not-for-profit organization is illustrated in the Employment Development Department of the state of California.

UP CLOSE 11.2:   Employee Development Department of California

The official organizational goal for the Employee Development Department is to provide job placement to the unemployed and underemployed in the state of California. The department has over a hundred offices located in cities and towns throughout the state.

An operative goal is to place special emphasis on finding jobs for certain groups seeking employment, such as veterans, minorities, people receiving unemployment insurance benefits, and the handicapped. Top managers wish to give priority to placing individuals from these classifications.

The organization adopted specific operational goals by using a weighted average of the kinds of employment desired during a given period. A score was developed for the number of targeted and actual placements in each office. Heavier weights were assigned to placements from priority groups such as veterans, minorities, and the handicapped. This weighting system enabled the organization to develop placement targets and subsequent evaluations for every placement office and placement officer. Each level was assigned a target score that was referred to as the "balance placement formula," which became part of the MBO system for employees.

Relying exclusively on quantitative goals can sometimes distort the department's efforts away from qualitative targets. For example, a placement officer might score high by finding jobs for veterans and minorities, but if the jobs were poor, clients may only work a few weeks. To assess quality of employment, the department specified length of job placement as an indicator of quality. The placement scores of the offices and officers were adjusted as information that reflected job duration became available. Regular reports were sent from each office to senior managers at the Employment Development Department.[19]

The value of goal setting in the Employment Development Department is that offices that were previously finding jobs for applicants on an *ad hoc* basis moved to having clear goals and targets on which to focus. Consistent with a management-by-objectives system, the goals were specific; employees participated in setting goals that were appropriate for their region; the goals contained specific deadlines and reviews; and the goals were tied to the formal reward system. The objective-setting system provided clarity, direction, a basis of evaluation, and motivation for employees throughout the one hundred offices of the California Employment Development Department.

Summary of Goals   So far in this chapter we have discussed the topic of goals for organizations. We defined official, operative, and operational goals that exist within organizations. Managers are responsible for the goal-setting process, and sometimes they use formal systems such as management-by-objectives. Other times the goal setting process is less formal but may be just as effective as long as organizational goals are clearly defined and employees are encouraged to adopt congruent individual goals. Many organizations develop a goal setting-process that is successful for their unique circumstances. One such organization is Geico.

UP CLOSE 11.3:   Goal Setting at Geico

Geico is the tenth largest auto insurer in the U.S. Founded in 1936, it built a phenomenal success on a remarkably simple formula—selling low-cost auto insurance directly to safe drivers through the mail. Bypassing insurance agents saved commissions and allowed Geico to set tough underwriting standards. For years it sold exclusively to government employees. The drivers the company insured had fewer accidents and lower claims, so Geico was able to offer low prices and still make substantial profits. Since 1973, Geico has been buffeted by changing interest rates, price wars in the auto insurance industry, and the desire of its managers to expand the market. Through these changes, president Jack Byrne has held the company on its course with the help of the goal-setting process.

Byrne established an annual planning ritual that he says combines aspects of the Spanish Inquisition and a fraternity initiation. Each October, Byrne gathers together top managers, field managers, and other key executives. Prior to the meeting, every participant circulates copies of their proposed budget and goals for the next year. During the meeting, each manager in turn sits at the front of the room while the other managers try to rip his or her proposal to shreds. Any topic can be discussed, from Geico's corporate mission to the need to hire an extra person for the mailroom. The process lasts twelve to sixteen hours a day, five days a week, for three weeks.

At the end of the planning meeting, each exhausted executive has accepted personal responsibility for a one-year corporate operating plan detailed enough to fill 1400 pages. The pages define specific goals that each manager is expected to attain. Overcautious goals rarely survive the challenge session, so managers are encouraged to set realistic objectives. Byrne doesn't believe in giving any bonus to managers who don't meet their goals, so everyone has a strong incentive to attain their objectives.

Through these annual discussions, which resemble debates, the organization has decided that it will stick to auto insurance which is now 90 percent of its business, that it will earn a 5 percent pretax profit, and that it will be a low-cost operator in the insurance industry. With these goals in mind, employees are energized to be ruthless cost cutters. Geico's expense ratio dropped to 15 percent in 1982, compared to the industry average of 28 percent. The success of the management system has paid off for stockholders. The price of Geico stock, which was $2 in 1976, recently traded for $55, a spectacular profit for Geico's owners.[20]

Geico illustrates many of the concepts discussed in this chapter. Through discussion and debate, a coalition is formed among top managers to support company goals. Official goals of being a low-cost operator are translated into operative and operational goals that hold costs to a minimum. Through widespread participation in the goal-setting process, employees understand Geico's goals and set their own goals in alignment with the organization's goals. The goals are important for the organization through serving as guides to action, motivation, standards of performance, and providing a rationale for internal structure and decisions. The purpose of the organization is defined in the organizational goals, and operational goals are essential for helping the organization reach that purpose.

ORGANIZATIONAL EFFECTIVENESS

Now we turn to the concept of organizational effectiveness. Organizational effectiveness is related to the concept of organizational goals, because goals represent the purpose and mission of the organization. Effectiveness pertains to organization's performance at attaining those goals. In this section we will examine various approaches to evaluating organizational effectiveness and discuss how performance can be measured in organizations.

Effectiveness vs. Efficiency **Organizational effectiveness** is the degree to which an organization achieves its goals.[21] The definition of effectiveness pertains to operative goals, not official goals. Effectiveness is defined by what the organization is actually trying to do. Operative goals pertain to such things as profitability, productivity, employee welfare, and customer satisfaction. Moreover, organizations must achieve some success across multiple goals in order to perform well. An assessment of effectiveness must consider the diverse activities undertaken by an organization, including the acquisition of resources, sale of goods, profit making, and employee development. The diversity of organizational goals and activities means that the actual assessment of effectiveness can be a very complex problem.[22]

EXHIBIT 11.4

Employee Efficiency Ratios for Automobile Manufacturers.

Company	Number of Cars Produced	Number of Employees	Efficiency Ratio
British Leyland	500,000	130,000	4:1
General Motors	4,000,000	517,000	8:1
Volkswagen	1,600,000	150,000	11:1
Renault	1,700,000	100,000	17:1
Toyota	2,000,000	45,000	44:1

SOURCE: Based on Robert Ball, "Renault Takes Its Hit Show on the Road," *Fortune*, May 14, 1981, p. 284.

The concept of organizational efficiency pertains to the internal workings of the organization. Efficiency is the amount of resources used to produce a unit of output.[23] **Organizational efficiency** is the cost-benefit ratio incurred in the pursuit of organizational goals. Efficiency considers how much raw material, money, and people are necessary to attain a given volume of output. If two companies produce equal amounts of the same product, but one company uses fewer resources than the other, then the first company would be more efficient. Exhibit 11.4 gives an example of efficiency, showing the number of employees required to make automobiles in various companies. British Leyland produces only four cars per employee and is not considered efficient. Toyota produces forty-four cars per employee, and is highly efficient. The extensive use of robots and efficient production procedures enabled the Japanese manufacturers to attain extraordinary efficiencies.

Sometimes efficiency and effectiveness are related. Toyota has been both efficient and effective. Toyota has been effective because it attained its goals of increased market share and profits. The company also provides a positive environment for employees. Efficiency helps the organization attain its other goals, because a low price for a car of high quality enables the company to increase sales and make large profits. Ford Motor Company's decision to produce farm tractors is an example of efficiency not being related to effectiveness. Ford was able to build a versatile yet inexpensive tractor. The tractor was reasonably priced and produced by efficient methods. However, Ford failed to attain market and profit goals. The organization attempted to market the tractor through its existing automobile distribution channels. Automobile dealers, located in towns and cities, were not attuned to the needs of farmers, and they did not know how to reach the farming community. The tractor never reached the intended market, and sales were miserable. Ford realized the mistake and eventually developed a separate marketing and distribution system, but high levels of sales and profits were never achieved. Ford manufactured tractors efficiently, but the auto manufacturer's involvement with tractors has not been considered effective.[24]

FOUR EFFECTIVENESS APPROACHES

The problem of assessing organizational effectiveness is illustrated in Exhibit 11.5, which shows two lists: one list includes evaluation criteria typically used in studies of organizational effectiveness, and the other list includes important corporate goals reported from a survey of corporate executives. Both lists show how diverse goals and effectiveness criteria are in organizations. There is no simple solution to the problem of diverse goals and activities. Organizations are large, diverse, and fragmented. They perform many activities simultaneously. They generate many outcomes. What we understand about organizational effectiveness at this time suggests that the diverse activities of organizations can be consolidated into four approaches.[25]

Exhibit 11.6 illustrates the focus of each approach to organizational effectiveness. Consistent with the approach laid out in earlier chapters, the organization is viewed as a system that transformed inputs into outputs and interacts with the external environment. The **goal approach** is concerned with the output side of the transformation process and focuses on whether the organization achieves its goals in terms of the desired level, form, and return from output. The **internal process approach** looks at internal activities and assesses effectiveness

EXHIBIT 11.5
Organizational Goals and Effectiveness Criteria

Organizational Goals Reported by Corporate Executives	Evaluation Criteria in Studies of Organizational Effectiveness
Profitability	Adaptability-Flexibility
Growth	Productivity
Market Share	Satisfaction
Social Responsibility	Profitability
Employee Welfare	Resource Acquisition
Product Quality and Service	Absence of Strain
Research and Development	Control over Environment
Diversification	Development
Efficiency	Efficiency
Financial Stability	Employee Retention
Resource Conservation	Growth
Management Development	Integration
	Open Communications
	Survival

SOURCE: Adapted from Richard M. Steers, "Problems in the Measurement of Organizational Effectiveness," *Administrative Science Quarterly* 20 (1975): 546–558, and Y. K. Shetty, "New Look at Corporate Goals," *California Management Review* 22 (Winter 1979): 71–79.

EXHIBIT 11.6

The Focus of Four Approaches to the Measurement of Organizational Effectiveness

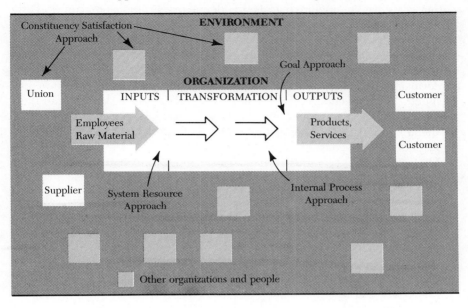

through indicators such as employee satisfaction and productivity. The **system resource approach** assesses effectiveness by observing the front end of the transformation process and determining whether the organization obtains the resources needed for high performance. The **constituency satisfaction approach** assesses organizational effectiveness by determining the satisfaction of each group that has a working relationship with the organization and a stake in the organization's performance. These four approaches to effectiveness are consistent with our earlier discussion of goals, because the operative goals we identified pertain to one or more of the activities associated with acquiring resources, managing internal processes, producing outputs, or maintaining constituent satisfaction.

THE GOAL APPROACH

The goal approach to effectiveness consists of identifying an organization's output goals and assessing how well it has attained those goals.[26] For business organizations, output is defined in terms of the operative goals of volume, sales, market share, and profits. This approach to effectiveness measures performance on the output side of the transformation process. In not-for-profit organizations, output goals are the operative goals that define organizational outcomes. For a hockey team, output goals would be the number of wins during the season. For a charity organization, output goals would be the number of clients helped and the quality of that help. In a study of youth-related welfare organizations, managers were surveyed to define the output goals along which they felt performance was evaluated. The operative output goals for a juvenile court included, "remove children from family situations that are damaging to their welfare," "protect the community from those youths who pose personal threats to the community," and "determine the best disposition for each child who appears before the court."[27]

The application of the goal approach to the assessment of organizations is constrained by two factors.

1. *Multiple outcomes.* As we have discussed, organizations pursue multiple goals and outcomes, and sometimes these goals are in conflict. Organizations may pursue five or six goals that pertain to output, with some of these goals requiring tradeoffs, such as a tradeoff between profit and market share. High achievement on one goal may mean low achievement on another goal. In order to assess output performance, several indicators need to be selected and combined. One example was seen in the Employment Development Department of the State of California discussed in **Up Close 11.2.** Output goals included the placement of veterans, minorities, handicapped, and other groups, so a weighted performance score that included placements in each area was calculated. Effectiveness should not be assessed on only one goal—this would oversimplify organizational activities and outcomes.

2. *Comparative basis.* The second problem with using the goal approach is the nature of performance comparisons. Hospitals pursue goals of patient rehabilitation, the Bank of America pursues goals of growth, market share, and profit, and hockey teams pursue goals of winning games. These outcomes are not directly comparable. The comparison base for a hospital is different from a bank, which is different from a hockey team.

To accurately assess performance using the goal approach, the frame of reference for comparison must include organizations or activities that are similar to the organization under consideration.

Comparisons across diverse organizations or industries can be misleading. For example, one study showed that the average rate of return for the recording industry was about 7 percent, while the average return on investment in the pharmaceutical industry was about 17 percent. The reasons were that pricing, distribution, and patent and copyright laws placed different constraints on firms in each industry.[28] A firm in the recording industry with a rate of return of 10 percent would be highly effective, while a firm attaining a return on investment of 10 percent in the pharmaceutical industry would be considered ineffective.

Most organizations assess output performance by comparing current goal attainment either to previous goal attainment or to goal *targets*. Targets are usually based on previous experience. Geico Insurance Company evaluates its output performance based on goals that grow out of previous performance. A growth rate of 10 percent is good, because in previous years growth rates averaged only 6 percent.

Internal Process Approach

The internal process approach is concerned with the operative goals of productivity and employee development. Effectiveness is evaluated in terms of internal operations and efficiency. The effective organization in this view has a smooth, well-oiled production process. Departmental activities are well coordinated. Employee needs are met, and employees contribute enthusiastically to the organization.

The internal process approach is not concerned with outputs or the external environment. The important goals pertain to what the organization does with the resources available to it, rather than with the acquisition of those resources for the attainment of output goals. The operational goals relevant to the internal process approach typically describe outcomes for employees, or internal efficiency standards. Employee goals and efficiency goals sometimes compete with one another, but proponents of the internal process approach argue that satisfied employees enable the organization to be more efficient.

The types of operational goals associated with employee development are as follows.[29]

- "Reward managers for performance, growth, and development of subordinates, and for creating an effective working group."
- "Encourage communication laterally and vertically for people to share relevant facts and feelings."
- "Have decisions made near the source of relevant information, regardless of where the sources are located on the organization chart."
- "Encourage departments to interact with each other. When conflicts occur, they should be resolved in the interest of the organization."

Operational goals that stress internal efficiency are less concerned with employee welfare and development and more concerned with financial efficiency. One method for developing goals for internal efficiency is to quantitatively measure resource inputs, the transformation of resources into outputs, and outputs from the organization.[30] Once the financial cost of inputs (I), transformation (T), and outputs (O) have been identified, then operational goals can be stated as ratios to provide the basis for assessing organizational performance. Two examples of operational goals are as follows.

1. *Improve O/I ratio by 3 percent.* This is the most popular assessment of efficiency. For business organizations, it is return on investment. For a hospital, it is the total number of patients treated within the annual budget. For a university, this ratio is the number of students graduated divided by resource inputs.

2. *Decrease T/O ratio by 5 percent over the next five years.* This ratio reflects the amount of transformation required to provide a given level of output. In a business firm, this might reflect the amount of R&D or capital investment divided by the volume of sales. In a hospital, the T/O ratio is the investment in medical technology divided by number of patients treated. Increasing investments in the transformation process lead to modernization and decreased labor costs.

Input, transformation, and output measures can be combined in different ratios to reflect different types of internal efficiency. If the organization is able to develop accurate financial measures of each variable, then the efficiency ratios provide insight into internal performance.

The internal process approach is valuable because it can be used to compare organizations whose goals are not the same. Internal efficiency or development of employees means that organizations are compared on a similar basis. Moreover, the efficient use of resources and harmonious internal relationships can be important aspects of organizational effectiveness.

The limitation of the internal process approach is that it represents a limited view of organizational effectiveness. An organization can be very efficient but still not attain its output goals or fail to attain needed resources. Organizations are created for purposes beyond being efficient, and these purposes, or goals, typically need to be evaluated to understand the complete picture of effectiveness. The internal process approach is a valuable perspective, but managers need to be aware of its limitations and know to evaluate effectiveness on other criteria as well.

System Resource Approach

The system resource approach is concerned with the operative goals of resource acquisition. The system resource approach focuses on the input side of the transformation process. Resources in the external environment are scarce and valued. Because many organizations seek to obtain resources, one aspect of effectiveness is whether an organization is successful at obtaining its share. Without inputs, the organization cannot achieve output goals. From this view, the definition of organizational effectiveness is, "the ability of the organization, in either absolute or relative terms, to exploit its environment in the acquisition of scarce and valued resources."[31]

In a narrow sense, effectiveness from this approach can be evaluated on the basis of the volume of resources acquired from the external environment. In a broader sense, the system resource approach encompasses the use of those resources and the overall exchange relationship the organization has with the environment. Examples of operative goals deriving from the system resource approach are as follows.

• "Improve the ability of the organization to respond to changes in resource supply."

- "Increase the organization's bargaining position with respect to the acquisition of scarce and valued resources from the environment."
- "Improve the ability of key managers to perceive and interpret the true properties of the external environment."
- "Increase the amount of financial and nonfinancial resources to encourage organizational growth."[32]

The system resource approach provides a perspective different from either the goal approach or internal process approach. One value of the system resource approach is that it acknowledges the organization's need to establish a good working relationship with its environment so that necessary resources can be obtained. The first step to effectiveness is survival. If the organization obtains sufficient resources to stay alive, one level of effectiveness has been achieved. Beyond survival, effectiveness can be assessed by the dollar value of needed resources obtained from the environment.

Establishing good relationships with suppliers can be important to output effectiveness. A critical shortage of semiconductors during 1983–1984 forced many producers of computers, videocassette recorders, and other electronic products to reduce their production. The explosive growth in the use of semiconductors outpaced the available supply. The only organizations to escape cutbacks were those that had developed strong relationships with suppliers who were able to give their orders priority and fill them on time.

Another value of the system resource approach is to provide a unique basis of comparison. Even if organizations are pursuing different goals, they have to acquire some of the same scarce resources. Evaluating the ability to acquire resources becomes the issue. A school district and a hospital pursue different goals and cannot be compared on the basis of outputs. But both the school and the hospital must obtain financial and human resources, office space, employees, and physical facilities. When organizations use different technologies to accomplish different goals, the ability to obtain common resources is a way to compare performance.

The major drawback of the system resource approach concerns the question, *resources for what?* Ultimately, the purpose of an organization is to accomplish certain outputs. If the organization is successful at acquiring inputs, but squanders them in meaningless ways, then the organization is not effective in an overall sense. A professional baseball team that acquires the best talent may be successful in the terms of the system resource approach, but if the team loses all of its games, it cannot be considered an effective organization. The system resource approach offers a useful perspective on effectiveness, but like the other perspectives, it is a limited view and needs to be used in conjunction with other measures.

Constituency Satisfaction

Constituency satisfaction is a broad-based approach that cuts across several operative goals. This approach pertains to employee development, customers, profits, and resource acquisition. A *constituency* is any group within or outside the organization that has a stake in the organization's performance. Stockholders, suppliers, employees, owners, and creditors are all constituencies. Effectiveness is assessed by determining how satisfied these groups are with the organization's activities.[33]

Each constituency will have a different criterion of effectiveness, because each constituency has a different interest in the organization. Creditors define effectiveness by how soon they get paid. Owners are concerned with productivity and financial returns. To apply this approach, managers must survey each constituency to learn whether the organization performs well from its point of view. Organizations have a large number of constituents, but a survey of ninety-seven small businesses in Texas found seven major groups that had a stake in each business.[34] The seven constituencies and the criteria of effectiveness for each are as follows.

Constituency	Effectiveness Criteria
1. Owners	Financial return, profits
2. Employees	Work satisfaction, supervision, pay
3. Customers	Quality of goods and services, price
4. Creditors	Credit worthiness, payment
5. Community	Financial and social contributions
6. Suppliers	Satisfactory transactions, payment
7. Government	Laws, regulations obeyed

The study of ninety-seven small businesses found that it was hard to satisfy the demands of all groups equally. One business might have high employee satisfaction, but it may fare less well in the eyes of the government or community. However, measuring all seven constituencies provided an accurate view of overall effectiveness. This approach has fewer limitations than the other approaches because it embraces multiple criteria. However, it is harder to use in practice because surveys of constituents are required.

The primary shortcoming of the constituency approach is that it does not set priorities across constituencies. It gives as much weight to creditors as it does to owners, yet the owners may have more power and influence over the organization and may have a larger stake in outcomes. Employees and customers are also important constituencies that should be given priority in evaluating effectiveness. Despite this shortcoming, the value of the constituency approach is that it combines elements of inputs, outputs, and transformation processes, as well as external groups not considered in other approaches. Thus it is the most comprehensive and broad-based measure of organizational effectiveness.

An illustration of why constituency satisfaction is important to managers is the appearance of special interest groups in recent years. The Natural Resources Defense Council has a $5-million annual budget to attack companies that unsafely dispose of hazardous wastes. The Center on Budget and Policy Priorities has emerged to fight certain cuts in social programs advocated by the Reagan administration. The Center for Auto Safety helps consumers fight car companies. Washington, D.C., is home to over a hundred well-organized public interest groups, and these groups have enough clout to make any company pay attention. The Center for Auto Safety helped force General Motors to recall 1.1 million X-body cars with faulty brakes. The Health Research Group contributed to Eli Lilly & Co.'s withdrawal of its potentially unsafe arthritis remedy, Oraflex.[35] Managers who ignore their organization's impact on constituencies may find themselves fighting legal battles and losing customers so that profit performance, resources, and internal efficiency will all suffer.

COMBINED APPROACH AND DOMAIN EMPHASIS

We have covered four approaches to the evaluation of organizational effectiveness. The goal, internal process, system resource, and constituency approaches all have something to offer. Each represents a certain aspect by which organizations may be considered effective. Each approach may tell us something about the overall effectiveness of an organization. For example, International Harvester was on the verge of bankruptcy for several years.[36] During this period, Harvester's poor performance was reflected in several ways: output or profit goals were not met at all; internal processes were in a shambles; the acquisition of resources was difficult because suppliers feared they would not be paid; and practically every constituency was dissatisfied about its relationships with the company. In this case any effectiveness approach by itself would tell only part of the Harvester story, but each one by itself also would detect poor performance. The need for a balanced view of effectiveness has led to two developments—the **combined approach** to effectiveness and the **domain emphasis approach,** which gives added weight to certain outcomes.

Combined Approach

Recent work on organizational effectiveness suggests that a combined approach is more accurate than single approaches in evaluating organizations. Organizations need to pursue goals and activities in areas covered by each effectiveness approach, so a logical step is to make an overall organizational assessment based on indicators of resources, output goals, internal processes, and constituencies.

The value of the combined approach is that the shortcomings of one performance indicator can be offset by measuring other performance characteristics. A balanced view of organizational effectiveness might include the assessment of resource inputs, the efficiency of the transformation process, the attainment of output goals, and the satisfaction of constituents. The point of the combined approach is to include measures from each perspective to provide managers with a comprehensive and balanced view of effectiveness. The following assessment of municipal fire departments is an example of the combined approach.

UP CLOSE 11.4:   Fire Department

Every community has a fire department, but how can its effectiveness be assessed? Evaluating the effectiveness of public sector organizations is difficult. Public sector services are not sold for a profit, so output goals are tricky to define and measure. However, fire departments do have the output goals of responding to fires and preventing fires within their communities, an evaluation of which represents the goal approach to organizational effectiveness. Fire departments also have to obtain adequate resources, as reflected in the system resource approach. Internal efficiency can be evaluated by examining the utilization of resources to reduce or prevent fire loss. The satisfaction of fire department constituencies can be evaluated with surveys of employees, municipal government officials, people who have experienced fire loss, and other community residents.

The specific measures to evaluate fire department effectiveness are as follows:

1. *Output goal: fire prevention*
     Measure: Number of fires per 1000 population
2. *Output goal: fire suppression*
     Measure: Dollars of fire property loss per 1000 population
3. *System resource: total revenue acquired*
        Measure: Annual fire department budget per capita; annual budget per employee
4. *Internal process: efficiency*
        Measure: Total cost (fire loss plus department budget) per capita
5. *Constituency: satisfaction with fire department*
      Measure: Reported satisfaction of employees, municipal officials, residents, fire loss victims, state fire marshall

A study of 324 municipalities evaluated the first four measures identified above; the statistical data did not include measures of constituent satisfaction.[37] The analysis suggested that effectiveness can indeed be measured by a combined approach. The research revealed that fire departments differ widely in their performance. Municipalities across the nation receive different levels of prevention, suppression, resources, and efficiency. Even more importantly, fire departments that scored high on one effectiveness variable did not necessarily score high on other effectiveness variables. Output goals, resource acquisition, and efficiency were not accomplished equally in the same department. Some fire departments, which had excellent records of fire suppression or fire prevention, may not have been efficient. Others, effective at obtaining resources, did not necessarily have a corresponding good performance on efficiency or output goals. Thus multiple criteria of efffectiveness afforded a better understanding of overall fire department performance. It also made clear that each community may place greater emphasis on one aspect of performance over another. By

*taking a combined view and evaluating the performance of organizations
across several criteria, a better view of effectiveness is obtained.* ■

Domain Emphasis

Another important question for organizational effectiveness is whether or how
to weigh success in given areas. We emphasized earlier in this chapter that
organizations cannot do everything well. Managers must set priorities. Certain
goals will receive more attention than others. Domain emphasis is one way to
answer the question of how and why organizations pursue and give greater
priority to goals in one area. Organizations do not ignore the lower priority
areas of activity, they just do not give them equal emphasis.

An important evaluation of effectiveness domains in universities was done by
Kim Cameron.[38] He found that universities seem to emphasize either the
teaching domain or research domain. Public universities in urban areas, which
among others attracted disadvantaged students, tended to expend resources to
train students who could move on to good jobs after graduation. As a result of
largely pursuing the teaching domain, performance in the research domain
suffered. Other universities, typically large, well-financed state institutions or
elite private universities, tended to emphasize the research domain. The
schools were making names for themselves in scientific research and gave little
emphasis to helping disadvantaged students get jobs. The important point this
work makes is that organizations consciously select domains within which to
excel, and the appropriate way to understand performance is to evaluate
organizations according to how they perform within their selected domain.
Organizations pursuing teaching excellence and student training should not be
evaluated on high standards for research because that would be an unfair
evaluation of what the organization was trying to do.

Organizational Dimensions   The areas of inputs, outputs, internal process,
and constituency satisfaction represent four domains along which organizations
can be evaluated. The framework in Exhibit 11.7 illustrates two dimensions of
organizations that influence domain emphasis. This framework, developed by
James Thompson, describes the clarity of desired outputs and clarity of internal
cause and effect relationships.[39] **Clarity of desired outputs** describes whether
clear standards exist for the definition and measurement of output goal
attainment. When desired outcomes are clear and measurable, the organization
can assess them accurately. If managers disagree or are unclear about desired
outputs, then the organization will consider alternative means to assess
effectiveness. **Clarity of cause-effect relationships** pertains to managers' understanding of the organization's internal transformation processes. When the
internal process is well defined, as is the process of an assembly line, then
managers know exactly what to do to achieve outcomes. In other types of
organizations, such as human service agencies, the internal technology is

nonroutine and intangible, and the organization has a difficult time defining exactly how to achieve desired outcomes.

Exhibit 11.7 shows how these two dimensions are related to four goal domains. In quadrant 1, managers have clearly defined outputs and good knowledge of internal processes, so they will normally select the efficiency domain to evaluate effectiveness. Managers will emphasize cost efficiency, which includes the acquisition of inputs and the precise calculation of the inputs needed to achieve output goals. Managers are concerned with acquiring and using resources efficiently; they would not want to attain goals that are inefficient. Most manufacturing organizations set goals and evaluate performance in this domain.

The output domain in quadrant 2 of Exhibit 11.6 comes into play when desired outputs are clear but knowledge about how to attain those outputs is vague. Managers cannot calculate internal efficiency in a precise manner, so the important goal becomes the attainment of outputs, regardless of cost. One example was seen at NASA, where putting an astronaut on the moon took precedence in the 1960s. Senior officials did not know how to do it, so internal efficiency was not an appropriate measure. Success was defined in terms of the goal of putting someone on the moon. Hospitals often stress the output domain of quality care over the goal of internal efficiency. College football and basketball teams also tend to use the output domain. The exact process needed to create a winning team is not at the fingertips of coaches and players. Coaches use different coaching techniques with different players, yet each may be able to achieve a winner. Schools often do not care what techniques a coach may use or how efficient those techniques are, as long as the coach produces a winning team. Because internal processes are hard to measure in most sports organizations, the output domain goal of winning games is emphasized.

The third quadrant in Exhibit 11.7 is the internal process domain. Organizations stress this domain when managers disagree about the exact outputs desired or when outputs cannot be measured. Organizations that face a long time horizon, for example, cannot measure outputs. The focus in research and development organizations is on internal process, because R&D outputs cannot be evaluated. If the organization is working smoothly, and employees are motivated and committed, then an organization in this category would be considered effective.

Quadrant 4, the social domain, encompasses organizations that do not know exactly what outcomes to achieve or how to achieve those outcomes. This may seem like an unusual situation, but in many types of organizations, particularly not-for-profit, both goals and processes are not well defined. Goals are qualitative rather than quantitative. In a welfare organization, for example, workers do not know exactly how to get people off welfare, which may be a goal. Moreover, managers may not agree upon precise goals, such as whether the organization should administer welfare benefits without question or try to break the welfare cycle. It becomes complicated because breaking the welfare cycle may be important to organizational survival. In this organizational setting, the social criterion comes to the forefront, because there are so many open

EXHIBIT 11.7
Relationship Between Organization Context
and Organizational Effectiveness Domain

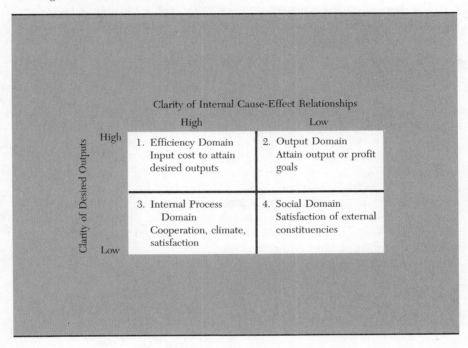

Clarity of Internal Cause-Effect Relationships

	High	Low
High	1. Efficiency Domain Input cost to attain desired outputs	2. Output Domain Attain output or profit goals
Low	3. Internal Process Domain Cooperation, climate, satisfaction	4. Social Domain Satisfaction of external constituencies

Clarity of Desired Outputs

SOURCE: Adapted from James Thompson, *Organizations in Action* (New York: McGraw-Hill, 1967), p.85.

questions. External constituencies become the source of effectiveness measurement. If people who have a stake in the organization, individuals external to the organization who benefit from its performance, are satisfied, this becomes the criterion of effectiveness. Managers in quadrant 4 organizations try to satisfy external constituencies rather than stress the attainment of output goals, which may be unspecific, or internal efficiencies.

Manager Priorities   Manager priorities can also determine which goal domain receives emphasis within the organization.[40] Especially when they are owners of the organization, managers may have strong feelings about the purpose and role of the organization, and what they want to accomplish within it. Frequently, the goal emphasis of owner/managers are consistent with the organizational dimensions described in Exhibit 11.7. Managers are more likely to adopt a goal emphasis of internal efficiency when both outputs and cause-effect processes are well defined and measurable. When outputs or cause-effect processes are not known or unclear, managers are more likely to adopt social criteria.

However, managers can impose their own values and deviate from expected patterns. Strong-minded managers rule the corporation with an iron hand. When an organization deviates from expected domain emphasis, the reason is typically because strong managers have other goals for the organization. Consider the impact of Gerald Roch on Hurco Manufacturing Company.

UP CLOSE 11.5:   Hurco Manufacturing Company

Hurco Manufacturing is a great success story. Year after year, Hurco sets an enviable record of growth and profits in the high-technology machine tool industry. From 1975 to 1980, Hurco's sales increased at an annual rate of 76 percent. Hurco now has almost 400 employees and over $30 million in sales.

How does Hurco do it? One answer is company goals. Management's goals are not just to increase sales and profits. On the contrary, the goals listed in an annual report pledged Hurco to "create products which contribute to the benefit of mankind; provide a stimulating, stable, and safe working environment which fairly rewards each employee in proportion to his or her contribution of talent and effort; be an example in a society which serves a living God, believes only in fair and ethical practices, and recognizes its responsibility to help preserve the free enterprise system."

These goals were defined by Gerald Roch, the company's founder and president, and are taken seriously at Hurco. Roch is interested in financial success, but is even more concerned about how Hurco achieves financial success.

Roch started Hurco in 1968 with a modest investment and a good idea—a new kind of control for press brakes. The idea was a good one and Hurco started to grow immediately. Hurco went public in 1971, and Roch's sales pitch to investors was enthusiastic, and filled with concern for potential buyers. He made clear that Hurco was a speculative venture and people should not invest money they were saving for their children's education. That same honesty, rooted in religious values, has created a bond with employees. Employees never doubt about where they stand with Jerry or where he is coming from.

With the influx of new employees, the personal, family, informal atmosphere began to evaporate. Gerald Roch's imprint was growing fainter as the company grew larger. Merit-based performance reviews were perceived by some employees as political. At one point a union vote was to be taken. Senior managers responded with detailed explanations of what the company stood for and the types of benefits available to employees. In comparisons with similar companies that were already unionized, employees discovered that they received more benefits and were treated better in almost every category at Hurco.

As the company continues to grow, Roch realizes that the managers have to be concerned with internal efficiency. Managers are implementing more formal policies and procedures, and greater emphasis is given to planning and rational goal setting. Managers are trying hard to attain a high level of internal efficiency.

However, Roch remains very conscious of the balance between profit motive and values. Profits and efficiency are important, but only because they make other things happen. Profits enable pay raises up and down the line, growth, new products, new buildings and community service. At Hurco, profits are only a means to an end.[41] ■

Hurco illustrates the impact of one manager's values. So long as Jerry Roch is president, there will always be a concern with human relations typical of the internal process domain. However, Hurco Manufacturing also gives emphasis to the efficiency domain. Hurco is moving toward greater concern for efficiency, which is typical of manufacturing organizations. The thing that distinguishes Hurco from other manufacturing firms is the equal emphasis on honesty and fair treatment of employees, which is the personal priority of president Gerald Roch.

SUMMARY

This chapter has been about organizational goals and effectiveness. Three types of organizational goals are official, operative, and operational. Goals are important because they state the purpose of the organization and define the activities and outcomes that are important to achieve. Moreover, goals set a standard of assessment for employees, provide motivation and incentives, serve as guides to action, and help legitimize the organization to the external environment. Goals do not just happen within organizations; they are set by managers. Goals typically reflect the values of the dominant coalition, and goals can be implemented throughout the organization by the use of a goal-setting process such as management by objectives.

Goals are related to effectiveness because goals provide the criteria for performance evaluation. The four approaches to evaluating organizational effectiveness are (1) the system resource approach, which is concerned with the acquisition of inputs; (2) the goal approach, which focuses on the accomplishment of desired outputs; (3) the internal process approach, which evaluates efficiency and employee development; and (4) the constituency satisfaction approach, which focuses on the satisfaction of groups that have a stake in the organization. The operative goals of organizations generally pertain to these four domains.

A combined approach that evaluates performance on several criteria provides a balanced view of organizational effectiveness. The concept of domain emphasis suggests that organizations typically give greater priority to one performance domain than to others, and this domain should receive greater emphasis in evaluations. The organizational characteristics of outcome clarity, clarity of internal cause-effect relations, and manager priorities influence whether the organization chooses to emphasize resource acquisition, outputs, internal process, or constituency satisfaction domains. By considering domain emphasis in the assessment of effectiveness, the organization will be evaluated on the goals it is trying to achieve and can be compared to other organizations that emphasize accomplishment in the same domain.

KEY WORDS

clarity of cause-effect
  relationships
clarity of desired
  outputs
coalition
combined approach
constituency
  satisfaction
  approach
domain emphasis
employee development
  goal
goal succession

horizontal congruence
innovation goal
management by
  objectives
market goal
means-end chain
official goal
operational goal
operative goal
organizational
  effectiveness
organizational
  efficiency

organizational goal
productivity goal
profitability goal
resource goal
satisficing
the goal approach
the internal process
  approach
the system resource
  approach
vertical congruence

DISCUSSION QUESTIONS

1. Why are goals important in organizations? Would an organization survive without goals? Discuss.
2. Compare and contrast official, operative, and operational goals. What function does each perform?
3. What are the major types of operative goals? Briefly explain each.
4. How do organizations handle multiple and competing goals simultaneously?
5. What characteristics should an MBO system have to be successful? Would these characteristics be different or more difficult in a not-for-profit organization?
6. A senior manager said, "The goal approach is ultimately the best way to evaluate organizational performance." Agree or disagree with that statement and explain why.
7. Compare the internal efficiency and constituency approaches to effectiveness. Analyze similarities and differences and explain when each approach might be preferred.
8. What is a major shortcoming of the system resource approach? Why is this a problem?
9. How does the concept of domain emphasis differ from the concept of a combined approach to organizational effectiveness? Explain.

CASE 11.1: Layoff at Old College.[42]

Memorandum: Office of the College President
To: College Budget Committee
Subject: Next Year's Budget Preparation

In my continuing effort to hold down the costs of running the college, I am ordering you to identify existing academic programs that will be subject to reduction or elimination. In order to support the academic programs that have proven to be effective and cost beneficial I am asking you to identify the five departments/programs/activities (D/P/A) of the lowest priority in the college. Elimination or reduction of these activities should result in a reduction of no less than 10% of your budget for this past year as a base. If the five D/P/A of the lowest priority do not amount to a 10% reduction in your budget, continue listing D/P/A until the 10% reduction is achieved.

The following criteria will be used in developing your reductions:

1. No across-the-board reduction (i.e., 10% from each D/P/A).
2. Assume that statutes and regulations can be changed to achieve the reduction (i.e., Faculty can be dismissed despite tenure status).
3. Identify exactly which D/P/As are to be reduced.
4. Identify the number of Faculty and Clerical/Technical (T/C) positions that would be eliminated/abolished.
5. Submit the information to my office immediately.

The proposed changes may result in radical changes in the character and objectives of the college. Consider carefully whether a program is absolutely essential for a well rounded college experience. Maintain the basic integrity of the college but at the same time carry out your duty. Whatever reductions you impose must be determined by a well-reasoned, thorough, and sensitive assessment of the potential implication of such reduction. There should be no illusion, however, that the required cuts can be accomplished in a painless or popular way.

Signed /S/ the College President
Attachment

REASON FOR THE BUDGET REDUCTION

The College President's memorandum ordering the reduction in personnel is a result of the tremendous recent and sustained drop in student enrollments, while at the same time the costs to maintain departments/programs/activities have substantially increased. The President has decided that not every college can be all things to all people and Old College simply can't provide every course or major that the faculty and students might like. There is a need to increase the efficiency of the college and now is the time to make the required reductions. It should be noted that personnel salaries compose over 80% of the total cost of running the college.

TIMEFRAME

The President will allow the reduction to be phased in over a three-year period if necessary to allow the laid-off people an opportunity to secure other employment. Also, each college job generates approximately a half position in the local community. The college is a major employer in the local geographical area. A phase-in over several years would also allow students in the affected areas to complete current graduation requirements. Appropriate admissions policies and criteria would be revised to limit access of new students to the threatened departments/programs/activities.

ORIGINAL MISSION OF THE COLLEGE

Upon its founding, Old College was expected to provide: (a) a general education for undergraduates, primarily in the first two years of college, (b) a wide range of academic majors and minors for students pursuing a baccalaureate degree, and (c) job-related education for potential teachers and other students seeking a variety of public and private employment. It was hoped that masters degrees might also be offered in a limited number of fields. The most prestigious occupational training programs such as dentistry, medicine, engineering, and law would never be attempted. Also, no programs in agriculture or natural resources, architecture and environmental design, or home economics would ever be offered.

At the founding ceremony, the trustees declared:

Students selecting Old College for their major educational experience will know and feel the spirit, imagination, and traumas of mankind, they should be able to understand and apply the method of scientific inquiry, they should know man as he is, and they should discover, develop, and practice their talents and interests through original expression. Thus, an array of offerings in Humanities, Physical and Life Sciences, Social Sciences, and Expressive Arts would be presented and retained for the enrichment of students at least for their first two years of college experience.

Job-related courses and programs should be offered to strengthen and extend the occupational opportunities of students in school-based services, client-oriented professions, management of public and private organizations, and quantitative data-processing occupations.

Upper division and graduate programs should be offered and sustained that will lead to an academic major or minor or to a master's degree, to prepare students for doctoral programs in other universities, proceed to teaching positions in secondary schools and community colleges, proceed to advanced occupational training programs in fields such as law, engineering, dentistry, and medicine elsewhere.

Specialized academic training is to be offered in ways that enrich the lives of the students and/or serve their communities.

LOCATION, HISTORY, AND PHYSICAL FACILITIES

Old College is located in a picturesque setting with rolling hills. Trees, grass, and flowering shrubs abound on the campus. The college strives to maintain a friendly atmosphere with close student-faculty relations, an emphasis on student self-government, and community involvement. The college has been in existence for 20 years. The peak enrollment occurred eight years ago and has since dropped 20%.

The physical facilities include large modern buildings for instruction, a bookstore, library, administration building, student health center, cafeteria, athletic stadium, theater and television facility a foreign language laboratory, a computer center, and an on-campus ecological field station.

The educational emphasis stresses small class size and easy student access to professors. The curriculum presents a balanced approach of liberal arts and applied degrees in undergraduate and graduate programs. There are extension and summer sessions, and late afternoon and evening classes. The college operates on the quarter system. The programs of the college are accredited by the appropriate associations.

CHARACTERISTICS OF THE STUDENTS

The total enrollment is 9,800 students—49% men and 51% women. Only about 1% of the students are from foreign countries. The undergraduates make up 70% of the students while the remaining 30% are graduate students. The average student age is 27 years. Undergraduate courses are 90% of the curriculum (many graduate students take undergraduate courses to meet the prerequisites for graduate study in a field other than that for which they hold an undergraduate degree). Fifty-five percent of the students carry 12 or more units per term, which is considered full time attendance. The ethnicity breakdown has been estimated at approximately: 72% Caucasian, 14% Black, 6% Oriental, 4% Chicano, 1% Filipino, 1% Central-Latin-South American, 1% Native American, 1% Other.

EXHIBIT 1
Staff Organization Chart for Old College

Area		Number of Positions
I.	Instructional Administration	36
	School (Administrative unit above the department level) Offices Clerical/Technical	
	Assistance to Administration	25
	Faculty Teaching Courses	403
	Clerical/Technical Assistance to Teaching Faculty	94
	Subtotal	558
II.	Academic Support	
	Library	63
	Audio-Visual	14
	Computer Center	33
	Subtotal	110
III.	Student Services	
	Social and Cultural Development	9
	Counseling	13
	Testing	3
	Placement	7
	Housing	2
	Disabled Students	2
	Equal Opportunity Program	15
	Financial Aids	13
	Health Services	21
	Subtotal	85
IV.	Institutional Support	
	Executive Management	26
	Financial Operations	35
	Personnel	7
	Logistical Services	
	Business Management	20
	Security	13
	Motor Pool	4
	Admissions and Records	48
	Plant Operations	165
	Community Relations	5
	Subtotal	323
	Total College Personnel	1,076

COMMENT: Approximately $30 million is required to meet this payroll. These salaries account for over 80% of the total cost of running the college for one year.

EXHIBIT 2

Relevant Statistics by Department

Department	A	B	C	D	E	F	G	H
Black Studies	1	1	0	4.4	2.0	.5	.0	1.56
English	18	0	.3	18.2	18.3	2.0	.0	4.15
Foreign Languages	19	1	0	13.7	20.0	1.75	1.0	3.50
History	21	0	0	17.2	21.0	2.0	.0	4.31
Philosophy	9	0	0	6.2	9.0	1.0	.0	1.45
Speech	9	0	1	9.5	10.0	3.0	.0	2.4
Biology	15	0	.7	16.1	15.7	3.0	5.5	4.11
Chemistry	11	0	.3	11.4	11.3	2.0	5.5	2.83
Geology	6	0	0	5.8	6.0	1.0	1.5	1.33
Health Sciences	1	0	0	1.3	1.0	0	0	.25
Mathematics	27	0	0	27.1	27.0	3.0	0	6.62
Nursing	4	3	.7	6.3	7.7	1.0	0	1.4
Physical Science	1	0	0	.5	1.0	0	0	.1
Physics	4	0	0	5.3	4.0	1.0	2.0	1.19
Statistics	8	2	.3	11.4	10.3	1.5	.5	2.78
Anthropology	8	0	.7	6.2	8.7	1.25	.25	1.76
Geography	7	0	.7	4.3	7.7	1.0	.5	1.25
Human Development	4	0	0	6.8	4.0	1.75	0	1.98
Mass Communication	3	0	.3	6.4	3.3	1.0	.75	1.61
Mexican-American Studies	1	0	0	.6	1.0	0	0	.13
Native-American Studies	0	1	0	.7	1.0	0	0	.15
Political Science	10	0	.7	7.9	10.7	1.75	0	1.98
Psychology	18	0	0	16.6	18.0	3.0	1.0	4.07
Sociology	13	0	0	16.0	13.0	2.5	.5	3.89
Art	15	0	0	11.6	15.0	2.0	4.5	3.02
Drama	3	0	.3	3.8	3.3	1.0	3.5	.83
Music	22	0	0	13.6	22.0	2.5	4.5	3.45
Accounting	11	0	.3	27.7	11.3	2.0	0	6.13
Management Sciences	14	4	0	28.5	18.0	1.5	0	6.31
Marketing	4	0	.3	6.3	4.3	0	0	1.19
Criminal Justice	1	0	1	4.9	2.0	0	0	.77
Economics	9	1	.7	17.5	10.7	1.0	0	3.88
Educational Psychology	20	0	0	15.0	20.0	3.0	0	3.67
Physical Education	21	0	.7	26.5	21.7	3.5	3.7	5.26
Public Administration	2	3	2	7.7	7.0	1.0	0	2.10
Recreation	1	1	0	3.1	2.0	1.5	0	.79
School Administration	5	0	0	2.0	5.0	.5	0	.59
Teacher Education	28	0	.7	19.0	28.7	4.0	.5	5.83
General Studies	0	0	0	2.5	0	0	0	.99
Women's Studies	0	0	0	.2	0	0	0	.05

Titles for Column Headings A to Q:

A. Number of tenured faculty in the department. Tenure is not permanent employment in a university. Tenure is only in a department or teaching service area. Professors have tenure only if there is work and they commit no illegal, immoral, or incompetent act. If the teaching service area or department is eliminated, faculty lose all job rights.

I	J	K	L	M	N	O	P	Q
130	0	14.0	0	0	211.4	113.7	21.5	18.6
312	46	18.8	0	1	202.2	115.3	16.3	18.0
155	10	11.5	9	0	198.4	135.2	12.8	12.8
.284	44	16.6	1	0	196.6	119.1	19.9	20.5
65	0	10.8	2	1	196.4	105.3	20.9	16.4
63	26	33.4	2	0	195.1	113.7	17.7	15.9
534	71	42.9	5	4	212.2	128.7	14.7	16.6
106	15	17.6	6	3	220.3	147.4	14.8	14.9
47	0	39.8	2	4	217.9	151.9	14.2	17.1
15	0	54.0	0	8	—	—	24.6	16.4
215	37	11.1	15	0	204.0	127.7	18.8	19.3
342	0	93.9	0	7	213.1	123.7	8.9	8.9
3	0	0	0	5	—	—	19.9	14.3
31	7	21.0	6	2	199.2	88.7	17.3	17.7
48	26	9.8	16	1	199.4	132.6	19.3	19.6
100	33	19.5	1	5	196.7	157.2	18.6	17.3
123	18	46.2	0	3	201.3	130.4	18.7	14.2
517	0	69.7	1	0	195.5	115.6	19.3	20.1
84	0	54.6	0	2	196.1	120.6	20.9	17.1
18	0	6.2	0	2	196.7	112.1	19.6	11.3
0	0	0	0	0	—	—	17.0	10.4
343	18	38.1	1	3	195.6	114.3	21.3	14.5
527	0	40.0	7	2	194.9	114.5	23.8	19.2
491	29	36.2	3	3	197.7	109.9	20.0	21.2
457	0	53.9	0	0	201.1	110.7	15.6	13.4
10	0	42.8	0	1	217.5	120.6	16.4	13.5
228	42	64.8	0	0	208.6	139.8	13.5	10.1
696	139	75.6	3	4	205.6	129.2	20.3	22.3
717	143	86.3	3	4	205.6	129.2	21.0	21.6
135	26	86.7	3	4	205.6	129.2	23.7	21.8
0	0	50.8	0	4	—	—	25.8	28.1
99	19	7.1	3	3	201.2	111.2	22.7	24.6
0	556	85.9	0	0	—	—	13.0	12.5
348	37	38.9	1	4	205.3	126.9	14.8	14.3
0	291	69.0	0	0	—	—	14.6	17.1
356	0	66.1	0	2	196.5	116.2	19.7	16.3
0	0	56.5	0	0	—	—	11.2	7.8
0	471	16.8	0	0	—	—	15.7	12.8
0	0	—	0	0	—	—	18.4	12.9
0	0	—	0	0	—	—	22.3	14.2

B. Number of faculty seeking tenure in the department. Typically a few members of the teaching faculty are new to the college and are seeking a tenured position. These faculty are evaluated for a period of up to seven years and are subject to yearly evaluation on their publications, teaching, committee work, and work in the community.

C. Number of temporary faculty who teach in the department (not tenure track). These are lecturers or temporary faculty who are usually Ph.D. candidates at other local universities.

D. Number of faculty positions that should exist in the department if all departments were held to a standard student-faculty ratio of 18:1. Since the college receives its money from the State Legislature on a ratio of one full-time faculty position for each 18 full-time equivalent students (usually expressed as 18:1) it could be a rough justice practice to require all departments to meet that ratio. Departments should use this ratio as a reference each year as they consider their teaching load. Classes that are small should be combined. A professor might even view his/her own contribution from this perspective. If one course has only 10 students, another class better have at least 26 to offset the smaller expensive offering. Any department that consistently falls below 18:1 is simply not paying its share.

E. Total number of faculty in the department (the sum of A, B, and C)—the total number of full-time teaching positions in the department now. No provision is made here to alert the reader of pending retirements or separations. These data are just as they appear on the course control computer printout.

F. Number of clerical positions in support of teaching faculty who work in the department. Clerical employees receive permanency after one year in their job. A clerical's permanency is to the whole college. Thus, if a particular clerical position is eliminated, the person would not necessarily separate from the university. Possibly that person would bump a person of less seniority in another part of the campus. Typing is the same anywhere on campus, thus the situation is not the same as with faculty. With faculty, a sociologist can't always teach biology or accounting. But clerical duties are essentially the same everywhere.

G. Number of technical positions working in the department. Technical support to faculty positions are glass blowers in chemistry, specimen preparers in biology, or piano tuners in music. Thus, while they have permanency rather than tenure, a highly skilled technician has fewer transferable skills to an entirely new area. We have no experience record to suggest what exactly will happen with the technical support positions in a layoff.

H. Percentage of courses taken by students in comparison to the college as a whole. This is a popularity ratio arrived at by counting the number of students taking a course in the department and expressing it as a ratio to the total enrollments in the college.

I. Number of undergraduate degrees awarded in the past five years. Self explanatory. What isn't here is whether this number is increasing, steady, or declining over the years.

J. Number of graduate degrees awarded in the past five years. Self explanatory. See I above.

K. Percentage of courses taken by students who major in the department. This is a concentration ratio that counts all students taking courses in a department and then checks their college major. A department with a low percentage is essentially a service department to other majors. To some extent, such service to others insures one's own survival. A high ratio shows that the majority of students taking courses there are their majors. A department with a high ratio could be eliminated without affecting many people other than those being eliminated.

L. Number of other departments that require students in their major to take courses in the department. Some departments offer courses highly regarded by the other departments. For example, a course in statistics is required by over a third of the departments on the campus, but no one but geographers are required to take a geography course. Obviously, any department with a zero in this column is more vulnerable to elimination than those with a higher number.

M. Number of other departments where a student in this major will have to take at least one course. This octopus variable shows how broad a background in other departments the major in this department is required to have for graduation. Health Sciences is well wired politically because it requires their students to have courses in eight other departments. These other departments are apt to come to their assistance if anyone would suggest they be eliminated.

N. Number of units a student in this major takes on the average before graduating (186 quarter units are required for graduation). Frequently students transfer from another college or change majors and so accumulate a larger number of units than needed before graduating.

O. Number of units a student takes here at Old College who majors in this department before graduating with an undergraduate degree (i.e., units not transfered in from another college). Self explanatory.

P. The average student-faculty ratio for this major at 18 comparable institutions. Self explanatory.

Q. The approximate student-faculty ratio for this department last academic year. These data were calculated for three regular academic quarters plus the summer session. No information is available on whether the ratio is raising, stable, or falling over the last five years.

CASE QUESTIONS

1. Distinguish between Old College's official, operative, and operational goals.
2. How should Old College's effectiveness be evaluated? Discuss.

NOTES

1. "Owens-Illinois: Giving Up Market Share to Improve Profits," *Business Week*, May 11, 1981, pp. 81–82.
2. Amitai Etzioni, *Modern Organizations* (Englewood Cliffs, NJ: Prentice-Hall, 1964), p. 6.
3. Herbert A. Simon, "On the Concept of Organizational Goals," *Administrative Science Quarterly* 9 (1964): 1–22; Donald N. Michael, *On Learning to Plan—and Planning to Learn* (San Francisco: Jossey-Bass, 1973), p. 149; Charles B. Saunders and Francis D. Tuggoe, "Corporate Goals," *Journal of General Management* 5, 2 (1979–80): 3–13.
4. "Giving Up Market Share to Improve Profits," *Business Week*.
5. Charles Perrow, "The Analysis of Goals in Complex Organizations," *American Sociological Review* 26 (1961): 854–866.

6. Richard L. Daft, *Organization Theory and Design* (St. Paul: West, 1983), p. 85.

7. Y. K. Shetty, "New Look at Corporate Goals," *California Management Review* 22 (Winter, 1979): 71–79.

8. Thomas J. Lueck, "One Last Worry for a Time of Crisis: Jockey Gives Underwear to Needy," *The Wall Street Journal*, April 27, 1982, p. 33.

9. Perrow, "Analysis of Goals."

10. A. Raia, *Managing by Objectives* (Glenview, IL: Scott Foresman, 1974), p. 38; Peter F. Drucker, *The Practice of Management* (New York: Harper & Brothers, 1954): 65–83.

11. "Bausch & Lomb: Hardball Pricing Helps It To Regain Its Grip in Contact Lenses," *Business Week*, July 16, 1984: 78–80.

12. Adapted from Kim Penn and Rodney Slota, "Group Case Study of American Airlines," unpublished paper, Texas A&M University, 1982.

13. "Continental Illinois' Most Embarrassing Year," *Business Week*, October 11, 1982: 82–93.

14. Michael A. Hitt, R. Duane Ireland, Barbara W. Keats, and Antonio Vianna, "Measuring Subunit Effectiveness," *Decision Sciences* 14 (1983): 87–102; Johannes U. Stoelwinder and Martin P. Charns, "The Task Field Model of Organization Analysis and Design," *Human Relations* 34 (1981): 743–762.

15. H. Simon, *Administrative Behavior: A Study of Decision Making Processes in Administrative Organizations,* 3rd ed. (New York: Free Press, 1976); James G. March and Herbert A. Simon, *Organizations* (New York: Wiley, 1958).

16. Carolyn Phillips, "Medicare's New Limits on Hospital Payments for Wide Cost Cuts," *The Wall Street Journal*, May 2, 1984, pp. 1, 19.

17. Richard M. Cyert and James G. March, *A Behavioral Theory of the Firm* (Englewood Cliffs, NJ: Prentice-Hall, 1963); James D. Thompson, *Organizations in Action* (New York: McGraw-Hill, 1967), pp. 83–98.

18. This discussion is based on Stephen J. Carroll and Henry L. Tosi, *Management by Objectives* (New York: MacMillan, 1973); Raia, *Managing by Objectives;* W. Giegold, *Volume II: Objective Setting and the MBO Process* (New York: McGraw-Hill, 1978); and J. Muczyk, "Dynamics and Hazards of MBO Applications," *The Personnel Administrator* 24, 5 (1979): 51–62.

19. Barry P. Keating, "Goal Setting and Efficiency in Social Service Agencies," *Long Range Planning* 14 (February 1981): 40–48.

20. Stratford P. Sherman, "Muddling to Victory at GEICO," *Fortune*, September 5, 1983, pp. 66–80; B. Brophy, "After the Fall and Rise," *Forbes*, February 2, 1981, pp. 86–87; G. Marciol, "Dull Companies Make GEICO's Portfolio Shine," *Business Week*, November 7, 1983, p. 109.

21. Etzioni, *Modern Organizations.*

22. Kim S. Cameron, "The Effectiveness of Ineffectiveness," in Barry M. Staw and L. L. Cummings, eds., *Research in Organizational Behavior* (Greenwich, CT: JAI Press, 1984), pp. 235–286.

23. Etzioni, *Modern Organizations;* Gary D. Sandefur, "Efficiency in Social Service Organizations," *Administration & Society* 14 (1983): 449–468.

24. Richard M. Steers, *Organizational Effectiveness: A Behavioral View* (Glenview, IL: Scott-Foresman, 1977).

25. Rosabeth Moss Kanter and Derick Brinkerhoff, "Organizational Performance: Recent Developments in Measurement," *Annual Review of Sociology* 7 (1981): 321–349; Kim Cameron, "Critical Questions in Assessing Organizational Effectiveness," *Organizational Dynamics* (Autumn 1980): 66–80.

26. James L. Price, "The Study of Organizational Effectiveness," *The Sociological Quarterly* 13 (1972): 3–15; Stephen Strasser, J. D. Eveland, Gaylord Cummins, O. Lynn Deniston, and John H. Romani, "Conceptualizing the Goal and System Models of Organizational Effectiveness —Implications for Comparative Evaluation Research," *Journal of Management Studies*, 18, 3 (1981): 321–340.

27. Richard H. Hall and John P. Clark, "An Ineffective Effectiveness Study and Some Suggestions for Future Research," *The Sociological Quarterly* 21 (1980): 119–134.

28. Paul M. Hirsch, "Organizational Effectiveness and the Institutional Environment," *Administrative Science Quarterly* 20 (1975): 327–344.

29. Richard Beckhart, *Organization Development: Strategies and Models* (Reading, MA: Addison-Wesley, 1969).

30. William M. Evan, "Organization Theory and Organizational Effectiveness: An Exploratory Analysis," *Organization and Administrative Sciences* 7 (1976): 15–28.

31. Ephraim Yuchtman and Stanley E. Seashore, "A System Resource Approach to Organizational Effectiveness," *Administrative Science Quarterly* 12 (1967): 377–395.

32. J. Barton Cunningham, "A System-Resource Approach for Evaluating Organizational Effectiveness," *Human Relations* 31 (1978): 631–656; Strausser, et. al., "Conceptualizing the Goal and System Models."

33. Terry Connolly, Edward J. Conlon, and Stuart Jay Deutsch, "Organizational Effectiveness: A Multiple-Constituency Approach," *Academy of Management Review* 5 (1980): 211–217; Michael Keely, "A Social-Justice Approach to Organizational Evaluation," *Administrative Science Quarterly* 23 (1978): 272–292.

34. Frank Friedlander and Hal Pickle, "Components of Effectiveness in Small Organizations," *Administrative Science Quarterly* 13 (1968): 289–304.

35. Burt Schorr and Christopher Conte, "Public-Interest Groups Achieve Higher Status and Some Permanence," *The Wall Street Journal*, August 27, 1984: 1, 8.

36. Geoffrey Colbin, "International Harvester's Last Chance," *Fortune*, April 19, 1982, p. 102—1??; Meg Cox, "Harvester's Woes Take a Heavy Toll on Those Serving Troubled Firm," *The Wall Street Journal*, May 21, 1982, pp. 1, 12.

37. Phillip B. Coulter, "Organizational Effectiveness in the Public Sector: the Example of Municipal Fire Protection," *Administrative Science Quarterly*, 24 (1979): 65–81.

38. Kim F. Cameron, "Domains of Organizational Effectiveness in Colleges and Universities," *Academy of Management Journal* 24 (1981): 25–47.

39. Thompson, *Organizations in Action*.

40. Cameron, "Critical Questions in Assessing Organizational Effectiveness."

41. John Halbrooks, "Making Money Isn't the Religion at Hurco," *INC.*, April 1981, pp. 104–110; "Hurco Starts Up 22,500 Square Foot Metal Cutting Tool Plant Addition," *American Machines*, August 1979, p. 41; "Hurco Will Buy Industrial Controls Division from Cross and Trecker," *American Materials Marketing*, June 11, 1984, p. 1.

42. Allen J. Schuh, "Layoff at Old College," used with permission.

12 Structural Design

During the 1930s, International Harvester's business was to produce farm machinery. Harvester was organized in a functional structure with decision making centralized at the top. By the 1970s, the company had expanded into trucking and construction and had moved into such diverse activities as IH Credit Corporation, insurance, and industrial hydraulics. Harvester had become a complex organization serving a complex and changing environment. Its functional structure was causing inefficiency. Finance, industrial relations, marketing, purchasing, and other departments were not able to coordinate quickly or effectively. Problems of size and diversification were overwhelming the company. Management decided to reorganize into a more decentralized product structure, with each product division becoming an autonomous and self-contained unit. The reorganization created the five divisions of trucks, farm machinery, construction equipment, turbo machinery, and components. By 1981, IH restructured back to a more centralized, consolidated structure. Duplication in departments, services, and facilities was removed by consolidating into just three divisions —manufacturing, trucks, equipment.[1]

The reorganizations at International Harvester illustrate the dilemma many organizations face. Through trial and error, firms try to find the structural design that will permit the efficiency of a functional structure, or the flexibility and autonomy of product divisions. The purpose of this chapter is to explore the structural alternatives available to organizations, and the appropriate situation in which to use each. We will examine the strengths and weaknesses of functional, product, hybrid, and matrix structural designs. In addition to finding the overall structure to best match their goals, organizations have to coordinate across departments and divisions. We also will examine structural mechanisms for achieving coordination.

DEFINITION OF STRUCTURE

When a company like International Harvester reorganizes, managers typically change reporting relationships and departmental groupings; this can be reflected on an organization chart. The organization chart summarizes a number of activities and relationships within organizations. Exhibit 12.1 gives an example of an organization chart for a medium-sized manufacturing firm. Defined on the chart are the primary organizational activities, such as controller, research, manufacturing, marketing, and industrial relations. The organization chart provides employees with information about their place in the organization, their tasks and responsibilities, and their formal reporting relationships. Based on these ideas, a formal definition of organization structure includes the following components.

- Organization structure describes the allocation of task responsibilities to individuals throughout the organization. The structure also denotes degree of specialization, the grouping together of individuals into departments, and the grouping of departments into the total organization.
- Organization structure designates formal reporting relationships, including lines of authority, decision responsibility, the number of levels in the hierarchy, and the span of control of managers and supervisors.
- Organization structure includes the design of systems and mechanisms that underlie the effective coordination of efforts among diverse individuals and departments. These systems provide for horizontal as well as vertical communication and coordination.[2]

The first two elements of the above definition—task allocation and reporting relationships—are readily visible on the chart in Exhibit 12.1. The third element, systems for coordination across departments, is not typically displayed on the organization chart. Coordination devices supplement the formal organization chart and include information systems, committees, planning meetings, and liaison positions.

RELEVANCE OF STRUCTURE FOR MANAGERS

The value of organization structure is that it defines the tasks, lines of authority, and groupings that the organization uses to perform effectively. Organization structure is the mechanism used to integrate organizational goals, size, technology, and environment. The correct organization structure will reflect these four factors as Exhibit 12.2 illustrates.[3] The four factors in Exhibit 12.2 show how the topics in the preceding four chapters jointly influence structure. A goal of product innovation requires a different structure than a goal of internal efficiency. Technological complexity will also influence structure, and the extent of technical interdependence among departments will influence departmental groupings. Large size makes demands on structure different from small size; large organizations have to consider whether to subdivide into autonomous divisions. Environmental change, complexity, and resource dependence influence the creation of departments, as well as the allocation of tasks, responsibilities, and extent of coordination within the organization. When a large corporation like International Harvester reorganizes, it is because managers are trying to find a better fit between the structural design and the demands of environment, size, technology, and goals. Structural reorganization is often caused by changes in these four factors.

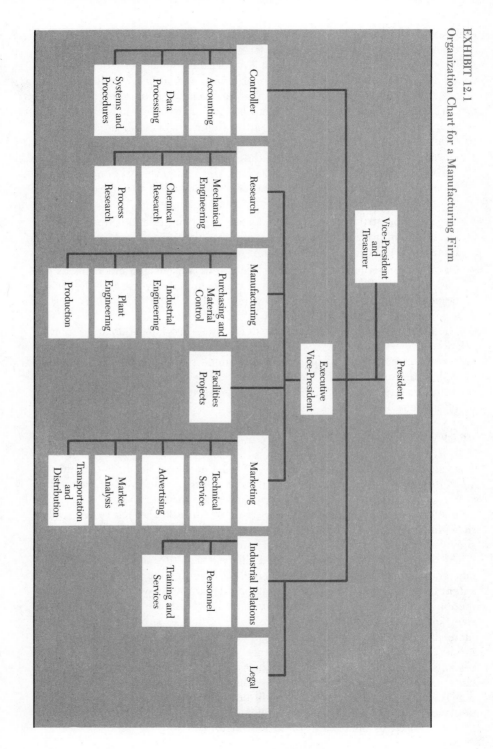

EXHIBIT 12.1
Organization Chart for a Manufacturing Firm

EXHIBIT 12.2
Factors that Influence the Design of Organization Structure

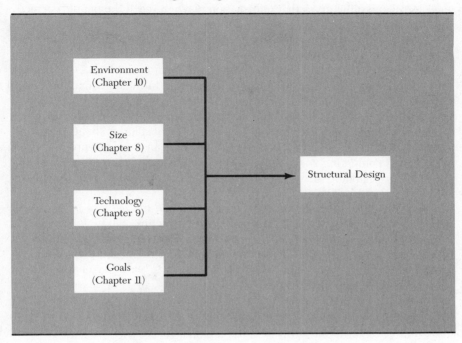

When organization structure is in alignment with the needs of the organization, it is hardly noticed. The division of labor, formal reporting relationships, grouping of departments, and systems for information and coordination help the organization achieve its performance objectives. The importance of organization structure is more visible when structure is incorrect. When the structure does not fit organizational goals, technology, size, or environment, certain types of problems begin to appear.[4]

When structure is incorrect, the organization does not respond quickly or innovatively to environmental changes. When an organization does not respond to environmental changes, the reason is either because managers are unaware of the change or unable to obtain cooperation for an organizational response. Organization structure should allocate resources to scan the environment and plan for anticipated changes. In addition, organizational response is slowed when employees focus only on needs and activities within their own departments, not allowing for coordination across departments. Organizational responsiveness requires that the organization react as a coordinated whole, and that departments cooperate with one another. For example, marketing must obtain cooperation from the R&D and production departments to implement product changes desired by customers.

When structure is incorrect, managerial decision making may be delayed or lack in quality. Improper structure may overload managers at the top of the organization with decisions, because the hierarchy funnels too many problems up to them. The structure may not delegate responsibility to the appropriate level. A related difficulty is that information may not reach the people correctly able to solve a problem. Necessary information may not be transmitted to the people in the best position to make the decision. The absence of information may reduce decision quality.

When structure is incorrect, too much conflict will be evident. Departments may be pursuing goals that are at cross purposes. Individuals may be under pressure to accomplish department goals and to avoid cooperation with others. When people meet at the interface between departments, or between headquarters and field offices, they may disagree constantly about priorities, procedures, and required tasks. Structural mechanisms may not provide a way to deal with conflicting goals and priorities within the organization. Organization structure can help direct organization departments toward a compatible set of objectives and priorities.

When structure is incorrect, the organization will not achieve performance goals. Performance deficiencies associated with structure will be felt in various ways within the organization: specific performance targets may not be met, or key managers simply may feel that the organization should be doing better in certain areas. Too much conflict, slow response to external changes, poor decision making, low morale, unclear responsibility, or poor resource utilization may cause a sense of performance deficiency. Any of these factors may have their roots in organization structure. Structural reorganization may be necessary to integrate the needs of goals, technology, size, and environment in a way that effects high performance.

Moreover, organization structure is under the control of management. The organization chart, lines of responsibility, and department groupings are all explicit, tangible organizational characteristics that managers can adjust to meet changing needs. Organization structure is an important tool through which managers can help their organizations become more efficient. How one manager, David Dawson of ESB Ray-O-Vac, used structure to overcome problems and improve performance illustrates how important structure can be.

UP CLOSE 12.1: ESB Ray-O-Vac

ESB Ray-O-Vac Corporation, the second largest battery manufacturer in the country, realized it was steadily losing market share. In the dry cell battery market, Union Carbide and Mallory had won market share at the expense of Ray-O-Vac. In the automotive battery business, the market share winners included Gould, Globe-Union, and General Battery.

ESB's new president, David Dawson, discovered that the important shortcoming at ESB was its inability to bring new products rapidly to market. The marketplace was changing, and ESB was not keeping up. The popular long-life alkaline dry cell batteries and maintenance-free automobile batteries were examples of the problem products. Both were introduced in the middle to late

1970s and were popular with customers. In each case, ESB was late into the market and fell behind its more aggressive competitors.

Dawson also discovered that in the case of alkaline dry cells and maintenance-free automobile batteries, ESB's scientists had mastered the new technology early enough for the company to be a market leader. But each time, the organization in effect smothered the opportunity for innovation. Vice presidents at the top of the hierarchy were overly cautious, and no manager felt responsible for a specific product or product line. The scientists could not obtain enough cooperation and favorable decisions to translate good ideas into marketable products quickly. In the high-profit product categories, where sales should be growing by 20 percent annually, ESB was losing market share —because the organization was structured to maintain the status quo.

Dawson's solution was to reorganize. He divided the organization into four clearly defined divisions, with a single division manager responsible for the operation of each. Responsibility for all decisions relevant to the product line was decentralized into the divisions. Ray-O-Vac division is responsible for dry cell batteries; Exide Co. for auto batteries; Systems and Electronics Co. for products such as pacemakers and emergency lighting systems; and Universal Electric Co. for small electric motors. Each company has its own research, product development, and market responsibility. Scientists now have fewer layers of management to contend with and can get a decision quickly. Scientists and marketers also share the joint interest of doing what is best for the success of their product line, so they cooperate readily. Dawson predicted that if the reorganization worked, ESB's profits would climb roughly 50 percent within three years.[5] ■

DEPARTMENTATION AND INTEGRATION

The design of an organization structure involves two basic choices: the choice about **departmentation** and the choice of **integration mechanisms.** The choice of departmentation comes first, and involves the decision of whether organization employees should be grouped on the basis of function, self-contained units, hybrid structure, or matrix structure. The departmentation decision is important because it not only defines tasks and reporting relationships, it defines the groups to which individuals belong and the boundaries between groups. The decision about departmentation is important because it has the following impact on employees and on organizational processes.[6]

Departmental grouping establishes a system of common supervision. A manager is named for primary units, and the department is perceived as a coherent whole. Employees share common goals and tasks, common values, and the department provides a source of identification. Employees may identify more strongly with the departmental unit than with the organization as a whole.

Departmental grouping typically involves the sharing of common resources and a common measure of performance. Departments share a budget, and they may share other resource inputs such as facilities and equipment. Employees are also responsible for the outputs of the department and for successful performance. Joint sharing of resource inputs and joint responsibility for departmental outputs enhances employee commitment to departmental outputs enhances employee commitment to departmental activities.

Departmental grouping encourages coordination and mutual adjustment within departments, but it may restrict cooperation between departments. Departmental employees report to a common supervisor, they share common facilities, and they have physical access to one another. Employees communicate informally within departments to accomplish their respective tasks. However, departmental boundaries inhibit communication and coordination for task accomplishment between departments. Employees identify with their own department and hence resist compromise, which is needed to accommodate the needs and goals of other departments.

The positive benefit of departmentation was illustrated in the ESB Ray-O-Vac case. Realigning structure so that research, marketing, and production departments were grouped together for each product line facilitated cooperation and decision making for new products. However, the identification, commitment, and shared responsibility within departments makes coordination across departments more difficult. This is similar to the phenomena of differentiation and integration discussed in Chapter 10.[7] At ESB Ray-O-Vac, the new structure may restrict coordination across product divisions. Organizations like ESB Ray-O-Vac are challenged to solve the problem of how to integrate differences across divisions.

After departmentation, the second major choice for organization design concerns integrating mechanisms. Integrating mechanisms are important because they build bridges between departments so the organization performs as a coherent whole. Integrating mechanisms are sometimes called *structural overlays*, because these devices overlay the formal departmental arrangement reflected on the organization chart. The overlays facilitate information sharing and coordination but in themselves have no formal authority.

This chapter will describe alternatives available to managers concerning the two basic choices of structure—departmentation and integrating mechanisms. First we will describe each alternative for structural departmentation and examine its strengths and weaknesses, and then we will examine integrating mechanisms that can be used to coordinate across departments.

FUNCTIONAL STRUCTURE

The most common type of departmentation is by **function,** which means that employees are grouped together according to similar tasks and resources. All employees who perform similar tasks are located in the same group, similar groups are located in the same department, and similar departments all report to the same senior manager. In a functional structure, functional similarity is the basis for grouping employees all the way to the top of the hierarchy.

The organization chart in Exhibit 12.1 (page 362) is an example of a functional structure. The primary functional departments are the controller, research, manufacturing, marketing, industrial relations, and legal. All tasks relevant to marketing are located in the marketing department. Within marketing, the technical service department provides advice to customers in the field; advertising is responsible for advertising media; market analysis is responsible for analyzing trends and making market forecasts; and transportation and distribution is responsible for the channels of distribution for products. Each of these departments performs activities relevant to marketing, and they all report to the marketing director. The same type of relationship occurs in the other functional areas. Task activities relevant to industrial relations all exist within that area, and the same is true for manufacturing and research.

The functional structure is sometimes called a centralized structure.[8] As defined in Chapter 8, *centralization* means that decisions are made at the top of the organization, while *decentralization* means that major decisions are pushed down to intermediate levels. The functional structure tends to centralize decision making, because the point at which the functions converge is the top of the organization. Decisions or problems that pertain to more than one function are funneled to top managers for resolution.

When to Use Functional Structure

As previously stated, organization structure is an outcome of size, technology, environment, and goals. The right organization structure is designed to fit the organization's context based on these factors.[9] The functional structure tends to work best in small- to medium-sized organizations. Smaller organizations tend to have only one or a few products, and they are not so large and complex that coordination across departments is difficult. The functional structure is also appropriate when technology tends to be routine, such as in manufacturing, and where the primary interdependencies are within functions. When mechanical engineering has to coordinate with electrical engineering and plant engineering, locating these departments together in an engineering department gives priority to communication and coordination among these groups. Functional structure also works best in a stable environment. Since activities are separated into functions, coordination across functions as required for a new product innovation or frequent adaptation is more difficult, and response time is slower. Finally, the functional structure works best when the organization's goals are internal efficiency, quality products, and technical specialization. The functional structure puts the emphasis on functional capabilities. The functional structure makes it possible to attain the efficient use of internal resources and also stresses specialization and technical quality in organizational outputs.

Strengths of Functional Structure

The functional form of organization structure offers a number of strengths.[10] These strengths are summarized in Exhibit 12.3.

EXHIBIT 12.3
Context, Strengths and Weaknesses for Functional Departmentation

---

When to Use
1. Stable, certain environment
2. Small-medium size
3. Routine technology, interdependence within functions
4. Goals of efficiency, technical quality

Strengths
1. Efficient use of resources
2. In-depth skill development
3. Career progress based on functional expertise
4. Central decisions and direction
5. Excellent coordination within functions

Weaknesses
1. Poor coordination across functions
2. Decisions pile on top
3. Slow response, little innovation
4. Responsibility for performance difficult to pinpoint
5. Limited general management training

SOURCE: Adapted from Robert Duncan, "What is the Right Organization Structure?: Decision Tree Analysis Provides the Answer," *Organizational Dynamics*, Winter, 1979 (New York: AMACOM, a division of American Management Association, 1979), p. 429.

---

1. Scarce resources are used efficiently. Common tasks are grouped together so that economies of scale are possible. Employees are pooled by skill, which can serve the rest of the organization efficiently. Because all experts are located in a single location, no duplication of personnel or resources occurs.
2. Skill development is in-depth. The functional structure simplifies training, because employees in a department perform similar tasks. Specialists have opportunities to deepen their experience and skill within the function, since they are readily exposed to all activities related to their expertise within their own department.
3. Career progress is based on functional expertise. Promotion is based on functional skills development. Functional skills (e.g. engineering, marketing) receive priority. Functional departments have status and are responsible for the primary activities of the organization. Employees identify with functional departments and try to excel at functional activities.
4. Decisions and directions are centralized. Strategic decisions are made at the top, which provides unity of direction for the organization. The functional structure funnels major decisions to top managers, who provide central coordination and control for organizational goals and strategy.
5. Excellent coordination occurs within functions. Primary communication and coordination occur among those departments within the same general

function. They share physical facilities, have similar training and experience, identify with functional goals, and typically exchange information as necessary to accomplish functional tasks.

Weaknesses of Functional Structure

The functional structure also has several weaknesses that make it inappropriate in many situations.[11]

1. Coordination across functions is poor. In a functional structure, employees typically identify with their own department and sometimes are reluctant to compromise with other departments to achieve organizational goals. Organizations with a functional structure often have to use extensive integration mechanisms, such as task forces and committees, to achieve coordination across departments.
2. Decisions pile on top. This may cause overload for senior managers. Important issues that affect more than one department are funneled to the top as the source of authority over all departments. Managers may be overloaded, and this may cause slow decisions or poor decisions.
3. Slow response and little innovation. The functional structure focuses employees on functional goals and activity. Responses to the external environment require new ways of doing things within functions, compromise with other departments, and coordination for changes such as new products. Organization-wide changes are difficult to implement in a functional structure, and hence innovations tend to occur less frequently and response time is slower.
4. Responsibility for performance is difficult to pinpoint. Organizational performance is made up of activities in research, engineering, finance, production, and marketing. When the organization succeeds or fails, the contribution of each department may not be identified correctly. The question of whether product failure was due to poor market information, poor design, or inefficient production cannot always be answered.
5. General management training is limited. Most employees move up the organization hierarchy through functional departments, and hence their experience is limited to specialized activities such as finance, personnel, or engineering. General management responsibility, in contrast, requires managers who have an understanding of several functions and who can integrate differences rather than advance the cause of a single function. Functional organization structures tend to produce fewer managers with general management skills.

SELF-CONTAINED UNIT STRUCTURE

A **self-contained unit structure** means that all functions needed to produce a given product or service are grouped together into an autonomous department or division. In the functional structure, departmentation is by common resource or task. In the self-contained unit structure, departmentation is by output. Functional activities needed to produce a given output are assigned to a single division. The difference between a functional and self-contained unit structure is illustrated in Exhibit 12.4. In Exhibit 12.4a, research, manufacturing, accounting, and marketing activities for all three product lines are performed within each function. Exhibit 12.4b shows the same organization reorganized into self-contained units. The functions are separated and allocated to divisions that work on a specific product.[12]

Most large corporations adopt some form of self-contained units.[13] General Motors has separate divisions for Chevrolet, Pontiac, Oldsmobile, Buick, and Cadillac. General Motors is now considering reorganizing into two product groups, one for large and one for small cars. Westinghouse, DuPont, and other Fortune 500 firms use the product structure, generally because the functional structure becomes unworkable in large firms. Large firms are very complex, with hundreds of functional departments, and coordination across functions is difficult. The management problem is simplified by reorganizing into self-contained units.

The self-contained unit structure is sometimes called a decentralized structure. Responsibility for strategic decisions is pushed down at least one level in the organization, as we saw in ESB Ray-O-Vac (**Up Close 12.1**). One purpose of this structure is to simply the hierarchy and push decision making to lower levels for faster decisions and improved coordination among functions. Another example of a medium-sized company that used a functional structure but was considering a product structure is Bonanza International. The functional structure is illustrated in Exhibit 12.5a. Bonanza sold franchises for restaurants to independent business operators but kept the real estate on which those restaurants were built. Bonanza provided other services to franchisers, including marketing, finance, and operational advice. As Bonanza grew larger and as the environment changed, Bonanza gradually developed three product lines: (1) the traditional Bonanza restaurants; (2) refurbished Bonanza restaurants called the B-80, which had waiters and waitresses, a salad bar, and a redesigned eating area; and (3) People's, which was an experimental restaurant based on a family dining concept with the addition of a bar.

Problems occurred when owners of each type of restaurant did not feel they were getting adequate attention from headquarters. Most people at headquarters were trained in the traditional Bonanza concept, but People's, for example, required different real estate, marketing, and operational skills. Locations, advertising campaigns, and store atmosphere were distinct for each product line. The proposed solution was to reorganize into three product groups, as illustrated in Exhibit 12.5b. Headquarters personnel could be assigned to specific product lines, where they would specialize in the skills needed to serve that type of restaurant. This would enhance coordination among marketing, operations, finance, and real estate, because all employees are located in the same physical area and identify with the same product. This structure would provide a clear focus of responsibility for each product line, and would generate greater client satisfaction, because each franchisee would know whom to

EXHIBIT 12.4
Functional Versus Self-Contained Unit Structure

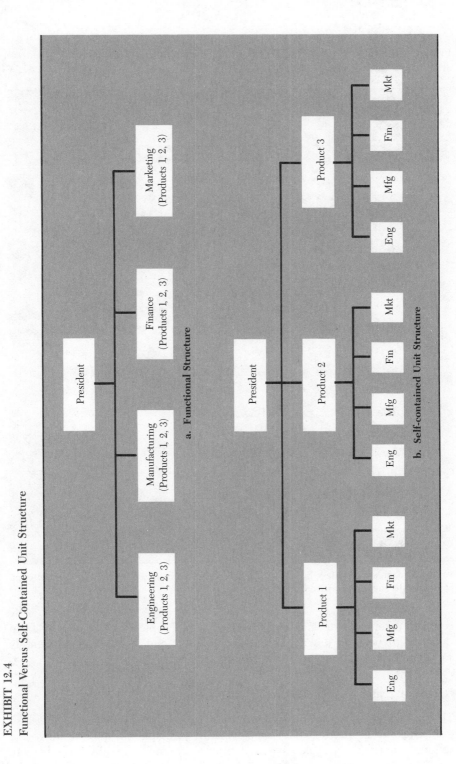

a. Functional Structure

b. Self-contained Unit Structure

EXHIBIT 12.5
Proposed Reorganization from Product to Self-Contained Unit Structure
at Bonanza International

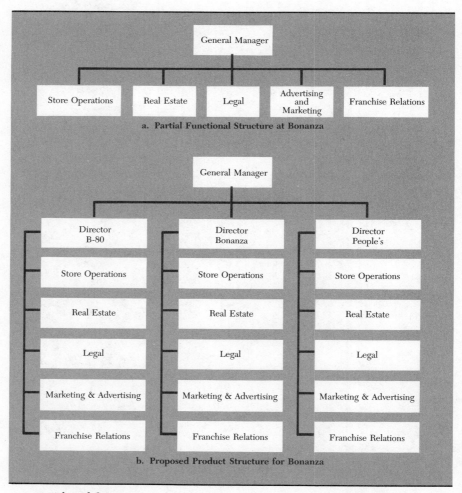

a. Partial Functional Structure at Bonanza

b. Proposed Product Structure for Bonanza

SOURCE: Adapted from Mary S. McCarthy, "Bonanza International." Unpublished manuscript, Southern Methodist University, 1981.

contact. After considering this structure, the People's line broke off from Bonanza to become a separate business entity, and it has been extremely successful operating as a self-contained unit.[14]

Geographic and Customer-Based Departmentation

The use of self-contained units is frequently called a product structure because groupings are by product line, as at Bonanza and General Motors. However, self-contained units may be formed on other criteria. Geography is the basis of one common variation. Large retail store chains, for example, often structure the organization by region. The manager in charge of the Ontario region would be responsible for warehousing, merchandising, advertising, personnel, finance, and other functional activities within that region. A retail chain may divide into five to seven geographical areas, with each area being a self-contained unit.

Departmentation by market or customer is another form of self-contained unit. A supplier may create a self-contained unit specifically to meet the needs of a very large client, such as the U.S. government. All resources and functions needed to produce the output for the client would be assigned to an autonomous division. In some cases the need to service a group of similar customers may lead to departmentation by market. A company such as MacMillan, which produces textbooks, divides itself into self-contained units for the grade-school market, the high-school market, and the college market. There are several customers and products within each market, but they are similar to one another and therefore the products can be produced and marketed through a self-contained division.

When to Use Self-Contained Unit Structure

The product structure tends to be preferred in situations not appropriate for functional structure.[15] When an organization is large and complex, and can be subdivided into coherent divisions with responsibility for specific products, markets, or geographical areas, the product structure is used. Large organizations have resources sufficient to assign to several self-contained units. The product structure is more amenable to change, because all functions involved in a new product are located within a product division. Thus the product structure is appropriate when environmental uncertainty is moderate to high and requires frequent adaptation and innovation. Self-contained units are appropriate when technological interdependencies fall across functions; that is, when marketing, accounting, production, and engineering depend on one another to perform their organizational tasks. Finally, the product structure is consistent with goals that emphasize product specialization rather than functional specialization. The product structure allows the organization to excel at serving a specific market segment, at satisfying clients who desire specific products, and at providing coordinated action to accomplish needed changes in the product line.

Strengths of a Self-Contained Unit Structure

A self-contained structure has several strengths.

1. It is suited to fast change in an unstable environment, because each division is fairly small. Divisions are flexible, because employees have easy access to one another across functions, and divisions are independent of one another.
2. The product structure is also effective for producing high client satisfaction. Each self-contained division is designed to specialize in a specific product,

customer, or geographical region, therefore the outputs are tailored to customers. In addition, when an organization has multiple products, customers know exactly which division to contact to resolve product problems.

3. Another strength is high coordination across functions. Employees within each department tend to identify with the entire unit, and they will compromise and collaborate with other functions in that division so that conflict is reduced.

4. The self-contained unit is suited to the control of several product lines. It provides a mechanism for internal control, because each division can be a profit center, and top managers can pinpoint success or failure for a product to the division level.

5. Another strength is the ability to train general managers. Managers whose careers are developed within self-contained units are trained in an environment that emphasizes coordination across functions rather than specialization within functions.

6. Finally, product goals receive priority under this organization structure, because employees see the product line as the primary purpose of the organization. Product goals and client satisfaction take priority over functional goals.[16]

Weaknesses of Self-Contained Unit Structure

A self-contained unit structure has several weaknesses.

1. The major weakness tends to be duplication of resources. Instead of fifty mechanical engineers sharing a common laboratory and physical facility in a functional structure, ten engineers may be assigned to each of five product divisions or geographical areas. Five mechanical engineering facilities are required and each may not be fully utilized.

2. Self-contained units do not provide in-depth technical training and specialization. The size of the technical specialist pool is smaller, and people are less concerned with technical specialization than with the general skills needed to deliver a product. Thus the overall functional competence within the organization is less.

3. Organizations using a self-contained unit structure experience difficulty coordinating across product lines. Each division may operate on its own without regard for the activities of other divisions. In fact, they may enter into direct competition with one another, attempting to win customers away from other divisions. Interdivisional coordination has been a problem with divisional structures at Xerox and IBM, and these companies have had to consider ways of reorganizing to overcome these differences.

4. Finally, since the organization is somewhat decentralized, top managers may feel they are losing control. Central management may act as a holding company for ownership of several divisions, with each division acting on its own, since divisions have profit responsibility. Coordination across divisions to achieve the goals of the overall corporation may be difficult.[17] The appropriate context for self-contained unit structure as well as a list of strengths and weaknesses appear in Exhibit 12.6.

EXHIBIT 12.6
Context, Strengths and Weaknesses for Self-Contained Unit Structure

When to Use
1. Unstable, uncertain environment
2. Large size
3. Technological interdependencies between functions
4. Goals of product specialization, innovation

Strengths
1. Fast change in an unstable environment
2. Client focus and satisfaction
3. High coordination between functions
4. Responsibility and control for multiple products
5. Develops general managers
6. Product goal emphasis

Weaknesses
1. Duplication of resources
2. Less technical specialization and expertise
3. Poor coordination across product lines
4. Less top management control

SOURCE: Adapted from Robert Duncan, "What Is the Right Organization Structure?: Decision Tree Analysis Provides the Answer," *Organizational Dynamics*, Winter, 1979 (New York: AMACOM, a division of American Management Associations, 1979), p. 431.

UP CLOSE 12.2:   Western Electric

Western Electric is the world's largest maker of telecommunications equipment. For decades it had been a captive supplier to its owner, AT&T, but deregulation has changed all that. Beginning in January, 1984 AT&T was ordered by government decree to divest its telephone companies. AT&T still owns Western Electric, but Western Electric is free from the government limitation that it design products only for the Bell system. Now it can adapt telephone networks to diverse markets, and will be expected to produce products not included in its standard catalog.

The change may be hard for Western. During recent years it has experienced declining competitiveness. Even with direct sales access to the Bell system, employment and income has dropped, and the company is running at 60 percent of capacity. Now it has to cope with toe-to-toe competition with veteran telecommunications manufacturers such as Northern Telecom and ITT to get telephone company business. As part of the AT&T family, Western was a monopoly immune to market forces. The shift to direct competition will be difficult—and it requires a change in structure.

Western's functional structure was replaced by a structure more suited to the competitive market. In May of 1983, Western Electric reorganized itself into four divisions, each specializing in a product line. The network systems division sells switches and transmission products to telephone companies. The other divisions include a components division for technology systems, a division for computer systems, and a government division. The bigger divisions have their own staffs for product development, marketing, and other basic corporate functions. The challenge to Western's management is to get departments within these divisions working together so that products can be priced according to the competition, and so that innovations hit the market soon enough to meet customer changes.

Years may pass before the sweeping reorganization proves its worth. The market-oriented divisions are worlds apart from the old functional arrangement. Decisions on new products used to be made by a top executive group at AT&T. These decisions now must be made in each division, which is three or four levels down the hierarchy. Instructions and orders used to come from AT&T, and each function at Western did as it was told. Now the divisions figure out for themselves what to do, and what they decide is tested in the marketplace. The functional structure was suited to the stable environment, moderate innovation, and technical efficiency that were expected when Western was shielded from market competition. Western is now in a free market that requires rapid innovation and customer satisfaction. The divisional structure, it is projected, will enable Western to compete. Divisional managers are anxious to learn and willing to change, so the new structure may facilitate Western Electric's hoped-for emergence as a powerhouse in the telecommunications industry.[18] ■

HYBRID STRUCTURE

Many corporations are not organized into either a pure functional structure or a pure product structure. When an organization grows large, it typically reorganizes into self-contained units of some type. Functions that are important to each product division are decentralized and located in the self-contained units. However, one or more functional departments may also be centralized and located at company headquarters. Thus each division may not have employees from that functional specialization; or each division may have only a few employees, with the rest of the employees located in a central functional department. The **hybrid** structure contains elements of both functional and self-contained unit structures. The organization has self-contained divisions, but a few functions are maintained as centralized functional departments.

An example of a hybrid structure for a greeting card company is in Exhibit 12.7. This company has five product divisions: greeting cards, gallery figurines, stationery, bath line, and candles. Each of these product divisions has its own functional departments of accounting, finance, advertising, creative develop-

EXHIBIT 12.7
Hybrid Structure for a Greeting Card Company

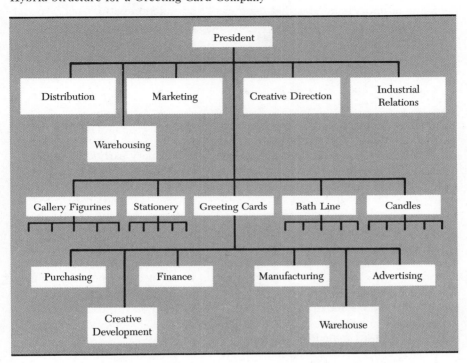

ment, purchasing, manufacturing, and warehousing. These functions are central to the timely development of each product line. Each product line operates as an autonomous unit with respect to product creation, manufacturing, and storage.

The greeting card company in Exhibit 12.7 also has centralized functional departments. These departments include marketing, distribution, warehousing, employee relations, and a creative director. Marketing is centralized because of economies of scale. Most of the divisions sell to similar outlets such as specialty shops, so a centralized marketing division can sell all products simultaneously through a single sales force. The distribution function is relevant to all divisions, because all products share a distribution and transportation system. The company owns a truck fleet, and it achieves economies by delivering products from several product lines simultaneously. Employee relations and the creative director provide in-depth specialization and expertise that would not be possible with small departments in each division. The creative director has a staff of "idea" people who provide advice and assistance to all product lines. Employee relations is responsible for employees throughout the organization. The single department prevents wide differences from developing across divisions in benefits, pension plans, and union contracts.

The greeting card company strikes a balance between the need for functional structure and the need for self-contained units by incorporating elements of both. Functions that need close coordination within each product line are deployed to each product division. The company also has central departments for those activities that require greater specialization, training, and standardization, or that have to be jointly shared by all product divisions to achieve economies of scale.

When to Use Hybrid Structure

The hybrid structure typically is used in situations similar to a product structure, because product divisions make up the primary part of the organization. Hybrid structures tend to be adopted in organizations that have moderate to high change in the external environment, especially in the task environments sectors of customers and competitors. Large organizations use hybrid structures more than small organizations. This structure is able to help achieve goals that strike a balance between client satisfaction, innovation, and functional efficiency. Client satisfaction and adaptation are met through the product divisions, and efficiency is met in the centralized functional departments. The hybrid structure also allows the organization to meet two types of technical interdependencies. Interdependency within the product line can be met by grouping functions into the decentralized, self-contained units. Interdependency within functions is coordinated by centralizing all activities relevant to each function into a single department.

Strengths of Hybrid Structure

The hybrid structure has the following strengths:

1. Perhaps the biggest advantage of the hybrid structure is that it provides for simultaneous coordination within product divisions and between product divisions. Those functions within each division are coordinated, because they are located together and share a common purpose. Product divisions are coordinated with each other through the activities of centralized functions, which work with all product divisions to achieve a common outcome.
2. Another advantage is the alignment between corporate goals and divisional goals. Divisions are able to pursue their own goals, but they are not so autonomous that overall corporate goals are ignored. The corporation is visible and involved in product division activities through the activities of centralized departments.
3. Finally, the product structure helps the organization attain the dual goals of adaptability and efficiency. The organization can attain economies of scale in some functions by centralizing them. This often happens in R&D because facilities are too expensive to duplicate for each division. The creation of a

EXHIBIT 12.8
Context, Strengths and Weaknesses for Hybrid Structures

When to Use
1. Unstable environment, especially in customer/competitor sectors
2. Large size
3. Technological interdependencies with both functions and product lines
4. Goals of product specialization and adaptation, plus efficiency in some functions

---

Strengths
1. Provides coordination within and between product divisions
2. Alignment between corporate and division goals
3. Helps organization attain adaptability in some departments and efficiency in others

---

Weaknesses
1. Conflict between corporation and divisions
2. Administrative overhead

---

central function can serve all divisions equally. Functions that are subdivided and assigned to divisions enable effective coordination and rapid innovation to respond to changes in the external environment.

Weaknesses of Hybrid Structure

Hybrid structure usually is associated with two major disadvantages.

1. One weakness is conflict between headquarters and the divisions. Headquarter functions typically do not have line authority over divisional activities, yet they attempt to coordinate and influence divisional activities. Division managers often come to resent headquarter's intrusions, and headquarter's managers resent the efforts on the part of divisions to go their own way. Headquarter's executives may not understand the unique circumstances of each division, and they may treat divisions alike even if they are trying to satisfy different markets and customers.
2. The other weakness is administrative overhead. Hybrid structures often are responsible for the buildup of large corporate staffs to oversee divisions and to provide functional coordination across divisions. Often some functions are duplicated, with experts working in both the divisions and at the home office. Administrative overhead can be costly in terms of personnel, and, if the headquarters staff grows large through well-intentioned efforts to provide greater control over product divisions, the organization may begin to take on characteristics of a functional structure. Decisions may be centralized and delayed, because people at headquarters have to approve everything within the division. Quick response and adaptation within the product divisions can be lost.

MATRIX STRUCTURE

The matrix organization is a unique form of structure used as an alternative to the other forms of structure. If an organization finds that neither functional, product, nor hybrid structures work, then it may try reorganizing into matrix relationships. The unique aspect of **matrix** structure is that both product and functional structures are implemented simultaneously, as illustrated in Exhibit 12.9. Rather than have the separate functional and product structures of the hybrid organization, a dual hierarchy is created that affects each department within the organization. Product managers and functional managers have equal authority within the organization, and many employees report to both managers simultaneously.

The matrix structure typically is placed at the top of the organization, and below the matrix a single line of authority exists.[19] Exhibit 12.9 illustrates the three levels of managers who actually work in the dual-authority matrix structure. The *top leader* is responsible for both sides of the matrix. The top leader oversees both the product and functional authority structures, and his or

EXHIBIT 12.9
Example of Matrix Structure

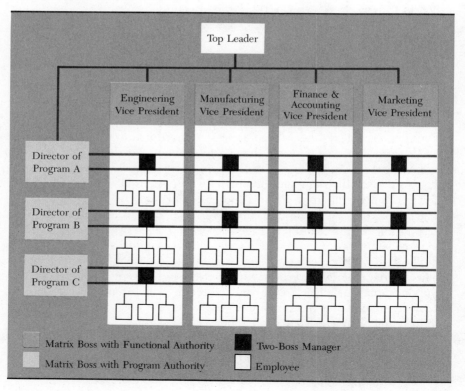

her responsibility is to maintain a power balance between the two sides of the organization. The *matrix boss* is a product or functional boss who is responsible for one side of the matrix. A functional manager's responsibility is to ensure that functional expertise, rules, and standards apply to all members within that function. The business or product-line boss is responsible for coordinating across all functions to meet the profit goals and schedules for the product line. The *two-boss managers* are at the center of the matrix and report to two supervisors simultaneously. They often receive conflicting demands from the matrix bosses and must resolve them. The two-boss manager must be willing to confront senior managers and reach joint decisions. Two-boss managers need a dual loyalty to both function and product, as well as human relations skills to integrate diverse interests.

The matrix form of structure is quite unusual; it tends to exist under three conditions:

1. When there is strong outside pressure for a dual organizational focus
2. When managers need to process large amounts of information for coordination
3. When organization experiences pressure to achieve economies of scale and efficiency in the use of resources.[20]

The pressure for dual focus means that the organization has to pursue more than one goal, such as emphasis on both products and functions, in order to be effective. A high-technology manufacturing organization may have to have strong scientific and technical expertise, and at the same time it must respond quickly to market changes. The need to process large amounts of information usually means that the organization is experiencing high uncertainty in several environmental sectors. Things change quickly, requiring enormous amounts of information processing and coordination within the organization. The pressure for shared resources indicates that the organization is not large enough nor rich enough to provide separate facilities and personnel to each product or market division, and so facilities must be shared by several product lines.[21]

Under these conditions, neither functional, product, nor hybrid structure is sufficient, because each tends to give priority to a single goal, and each requires separate facilities and personnel on a divisional basis or economies of scale in each function. The solution is to provide both vertical and horizontal lines of authority simultaneously. In this way equal recognition is given to the functional and product structures within the same organization. A dual-authority structure is created that provides a balance of power. This structure facilitates information processing for coordination, enables both product and functional goals to be pursued simultaneously, and each product division shares resources made available by the functional departments.

The organization chart for the aerospace firm in Exhibit 12.10 illustrates dual lines of authority. This company has four major programs underway: the F-15, the F-16, the antitank laser guided bomb, and the radar-guided

EXHIBIT 12.10
Matrix Structure for Aerospace Corporation

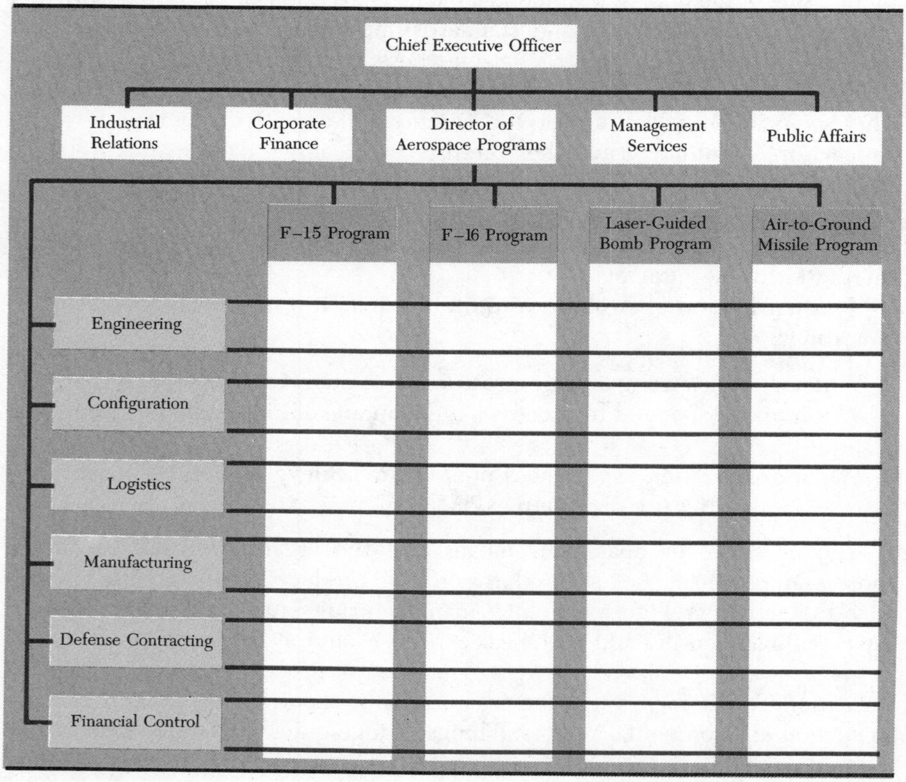

air-to-ground missile system. The managers for each program have authority over functional personnel assigned to that program. This system enables program managers to achieve coordination necessary to complete program requirements on time. On the other hand, managers of the respective functions such as engineering, manufacturing, program control, and design also have authority over personnel. This authority ensures that personnel are up to date with recent technological developments and company specifications, and it provides a home base for training and reassignment to other programs. The flexible and shared use of organizational resources is accomplished.

The matrix structure engenders a certain amount of conflict, because some employees have two bosses. The employees who report to both a program and a functional manager may receive contradictory advice or instructions. Consequently they have to meet with their bosses to resolve conflicts. An engineering supervisor meets with other engineers to achieve coordination in engineering procedures and specifications. Engineers also meet with specialists from other functions to make engineering decisions congruent with design, logistics, manufacturing, and control. Each person who reports to two bosses is caught in a conflict, and by resolving these conflicts the diverse interests of the organization are integrated. The matrix design facilitates discussion and coordination in both vertical and horizontal directions to resolve issues that pertain to both products and functions.

When to Use Matrix Structure

With respect to the contextual variables of environment, size, technology, and goals, the matrix structure is best used in a situation different from other structural forms discussed in this chapter.[22] The matrix is appropriate in an environment that is highly uncertain and changes frequently, and that requires two types of organizational expertise. Dual expertise is reflected in organizational goals, such as simultaneously providing in-depth technical expertise and rapid product innovation. A matrix structure usually appears in organizations of medium size with a moderate number of products. In a very large organization the dual lines of authority are difficult to maintain, and in a small organization informal communications allow sufficient coordination. The technology of an organization that adopts a matrix structure is nonroutine and relatively sophisticated, and interdependence is high both within and across functions. The dual authority structure provides a way to coordinate these dual interdependencies. The context as well as strengths and weaknesses are summarized in Exhibit 12.11.

EXHIBIT 12.11
Context, Strengths and Weaknesses of Matrix Structure

When to Use
1. Very uncertain, shifting environment
2. Medium-large size
3. Nonroutine technology, high interdependence
4. Dual goals of product and functional specialization

Strengths
1. Can manage dual demands from environment
2. Flexible, efficient use of scarce resources
3. Adaptation and innovation
4. Development of functional and general management skills

Weaknesses
1. Dual authority cause frustration and confusion
2. High conflict
3. Time consuming
4. Special training required
5. Difficult to maintain power balance

SOURCE: Adapted from Robert Duncan, "What is the Right Organization Structure?: Decision Tree Analysis Provides the Answer," *Organizational Dynamics*, Winter, 1979 (New York: AMACOM, a division of American Management Associations, 1979), p. 429.

Strengths of Matrix Structure

The matrix structure has characteristics that make it the best structure for certain organizations at certain times.

1. One of the greatest strengths of the matrix structure is that it enables an organization to meet demands from more than one more sector of the environment simultaneously.
2. The matrix also provides for the flexible use of a limited number of functional specialists, because these resources can be allocated across several product lines.
3. The matrix is also suited to adapting to frequent changes from the environment. It can adapt to changing workloads by reallocating people internally, and it can contribute to frequent innovation by having separate product lines.
4. With respect to training and skill development, the matrix structure provides opportunities for both functional specialization and for the development of general management skills. Matrix bosses and two-boss managers are forced to see the big picture and to integrate across functional areas. It also provides a home base for functional specialists where training can be provided between projects.[23]

Weaknesses of Matrix Structure

The weaknesses of the matrix typically are associated with the dual-authority structure.

1. The major problem is that the dual authority structure can be frustrating and confusing for both bosses and subordinates. The two-boss manager is frequently faced with conflicting demands from matrix bosses. The matrix bosses are able to exert authority over only "half an employee," who they share with another matrix boss.
2. The dual lines of authority also lead to interpersonal conflict, which, while helpful for coordinating, calls for excellent interpersonal skills for participants. The implementation of a matrix structure typically requires human relations training so people learn to confront one another and handle conflict.
3. The matrix is also time consuming, because frequent meetings are needed to coordinate all of the activities associated with each product line and to resolve conflicts.
4. The matrix will not work unless participants understand it. They must see the big picture of the organization and not think in terms of narrow personal interests. If major power struggles occur between project and functional bosses, then the cooperative, teamwork attitude is absent and the matrix will not be successful.
5. Finally, if the matrix is implemented when the organization is not experiencing a genuine dual pressure from the environment, it probably will not

succeed, because the side of the matrix most closely aligned with meeting organizational objectives will gradually become dominant.[24]

Dow-Corning Corporation was formed in 1943 as a joint venture of the Dow Chemical Company and Corning Glass Works to develop and market a new class of materials called silicones. Over the years, the company changed little. It grew larger and more complex, but most sales remained in silicones and the company operated in a simple functional structure. By the early 1960s, a large number of silicone products were produced, and some products were tailor-made for individual applications. The diversity of markets and products put a great strain on the functional structure. Coordination across functions became a problem that needed a solution.

In 1962, Dow-Corning moved to a hybrid organization structure, which is illustrated in Exhibit 12.12. Each operating division had responsibility for both short-term profitability and long-term growth of the product line. Manufacturing, marketing, and product development all reported to divisional managers. A few staff functions such as basic research, industrial relations, and finance remained centralized at the corporate level, although these functions had relatively few people compared to the operating divisions.

By 1967, the divisional structure was no longer appropriate for Dow-Corning. Coordination between functions within each division was good, but coordination between divisions and with the corporate staff groups deteriorated. This was a serious problem, because the divisions used similar technologies and it was not efficient to have a separate basic research department in each division. The divisions also could share some common manufacturing facilities. Likewise, there were some opportunities for sharing marketing and distribution capabilities.

The organization structure adopted by Dow-Corning to accommodate the needs for improved coordination and dual lines of authority was a product-functional matrix illustrated in Exhibit 12.13. This structure was instituted in 1968. The product groups are called businesses, and are similar to the former divisions. The business manager has profit responsibility for the product lines. The functional managers are responsible for professionalism and efficiency.

The internal structure of each function is designed to accommodate the product line. For example, within the marketing function a separate department manager is assigned the responsibility of marketing the product for one business. The marketing managers have dual reporting relationships, to the director of the marketing function and to the business manager for that product line. This structure provides a way for Dow-Corning to allocate functional resources across multiple product lines, achieve coordination across functions and product lines, and to achieve the dual needs for technical specialization and for tailoring products to customer needs.[25] ■

EXHIBIT 12.12
Partial Chart of Dow Corning's Product Division Structure

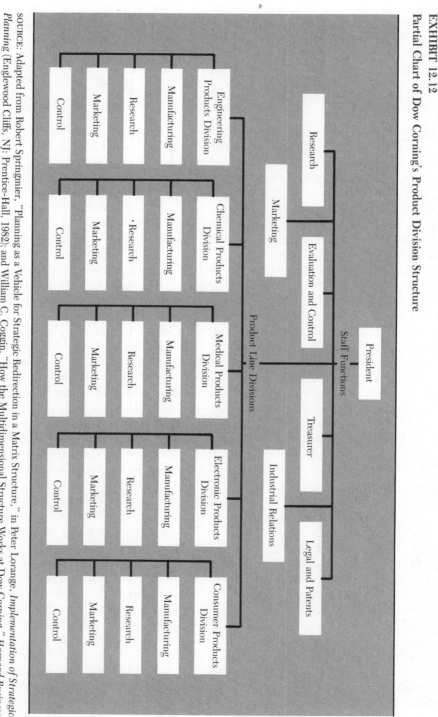

SOURCE: Adapted from Robert Springmier, "Planning as a Vehicle for Strategic Redirection in a Matrix Structure," in Peter Lorange, *Implementation of Strategic Planning* (Englewood Cliffs, NJ: Prentice-Hall, 1982); and William C. Coggin, "How the Multidimensional Structure Works at Dow Corning," *Harvard Business Review*, January-February, 1974: 54-65.

INTEGRATING MECHANISMS

At the beginning of this chapter, organization structure was defined as the allocation of tasks, the designation of formal reporting relationships and lines of authority, and the grouping together of individuals into departments and the total organization. Organizational managers can choose among the four types of departmentation—functional, self-contained units, hybrid, matrix—for the overall structure of the organization.

Our definition of structure also includes the design of systems to ensure effective communication and coordination of effort in both vertical and horizontal directions, so the organization can perform as an integrated whole. Whatever form of departmentation the organization selects facilitates communication and coordination within groups, but it hinders communication and coordination across groups. Moreover, in large organizations the communication and coordination between top and bottom levels may be difficult. To overcome these coordination difficulties, managers can implement a number of systems and mechanisms to enhance coordination across departmental bound-

EXHIBIT 12.13
Partial Chart of Dow Corning's Matrix Structure

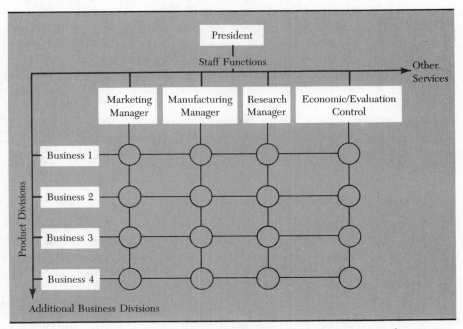

SOURCE: Adapted from Robert Springmier, "Planning as a Vehicle for Strategic Redirection in a Matrix Structure," in Peter Lorange, *Implementation of Strategic Planning* (Englewood Cliffs, NJ: Prentice-Hall, 1982); and Allen J. Sanger, *Matrix Organization of Complex Businesses* (New York: The Conference Board).

aries. Coordination mechanisms frequently are not revealed on the organization chart because they do not follow formal lines of authority. Sometimes dashed lines are used to indicate a special information-sharing relationship, but most coordination mechanisms are separate from the organization chart and are designed to complement the organization chart. These mechanisms are sometimes called **structural overlays** because the systems and information flow overlay the formal lines of authority and responsibility. The integrating mechanisms that overlay the organization chart range from simple sharing of information through paperwork and information systems to formalized liaison roles, teams, and integrators.[26]

Information Systems

Information systems are the written documentation processed among employees within the organization. Information systems include simple memos and bulletins routed to managers in different departments to inform them about activities in which they are not directly involved. By making other departments aware of activities and decisions, some aspects of coordination can be accomplished. The use of computers in organizations has greatly extended the power and scope of formal information systems. Information systems can make data available up and down the hierarchy and across several departments to inform managers of diverse activities. These systems have the capacity to summarize data on, for example, scrap levels, volume produced, inventory levels, machine breakdowns, average interest rate earned, and anticipated profit levels. Information systems can help managers extend their reach in an organization. A consumer finance company in Canada uses daily computer reports from each office to make decisions about allocating resources among branches. Airline managers use computer-based information to make decisions about the allocation of airplanes, air crews, maintenance, and food service. These decisions involve coordination among major departments. Written information, whether a copy of a memo or an on-line computer-based system handling millions of pieces of data, represents an important subsystem that facilitates coordination of effort within organizations.

Planning and Scheduling

Plans represent organizational and departmental targets for future performance, and **schedules** represent the defined sequence of activities needed to accomplish those targets. The budget is one widely used plan in organizations. Plans are also created for specific projects which must be accomplished by certain deadlines. Carefully designed plans and schedules are powerful coordination devices, because they inform all participants of what is expected. The development of a new product for pipeline flow control may require coordination among the departments of process research, mechanical engineering, and electrical engineering. By jointly establishing a plan and then adhering to specific schedules, the need for day-to-day discussions and coordination is reduced—each department knows which tasks are to be finished by which dates. Plans and schedules link managers to one another.

Liaison Roles

A **liaison** role is taken by a person in one department who has formal responsibility to act as coordinator with another department. The liaison role facilitates the flow of information between two or more departments by designating a person to act as coordinator. In manufacturing organizations, an engineering department often has a person assigned as liaison to the production department. This person coordinates activities and builds a positive relationship between departments so that engineers are able to pilot test the production of a new product or the modification of a machine. Staff departments frequently have a liaison person to coordinate with departments that use their services. The computer department may assign a liaison to work exclusively with the marketing department to help design computer systems to fit marketing needs. The personnel department may assign a liaison person to work with supervisors in the manufacturing department on employee relations and the legal and regulatory basis for responding to employee complaints. In a hybrid structure, liaison roles are frequently assigned at headquarters to provide a coordination relationship with product divisions. General Mills has set up several liaison positions to keep information flowing freely between corporate headquarters and its five industry groups.[27]

Exhibit 12.14 illustrates a liaison role for a manufacturing company between the home office and the manufacturing plant. The quality control and machine maintenance supervisors within the plant report directly to the plant manager, but they also work with the quality control and maintenance people from the home office. The home office expert acts as a liaison, visiting the plants periodically to ensure that they are operating under home office procedures and standards. Liaison roles are sometimes drawn as dotted-line relationships, because the liaison person is responsible for coordination and information sharing but does not have direct authority over others.

Task Forces

A **task force** is a temporary committee composed of representatives from several departments. Task force members represent their departments, and they carry information back to their departments from committee deliberations. A task force provides a way to link several departments to solve a specific problem. Colleges of Business create a task force every few years to evaluate their undergraduate and graduate curricula. The group will have a member from each department within the college and perhaps a member or two from outside the college. The task force brings together diverse opinions about changes in their respective fields and the nature of proposed new courses. After each meeting, task force members learn whether their department's interests are being served when they receive feedback from their departments. Departmental viewpoints can then be exchanged at the next task force meeting. Task forces may last from a few weeks to a year or more, but they are temporary and will be disbanded after the assignment has been completed. A task force could be used in a business firm to study the possibility of acquiring a subsidiary, for

EXHIBIT 12.14
Liaison Roles in a Manufacturing Firm

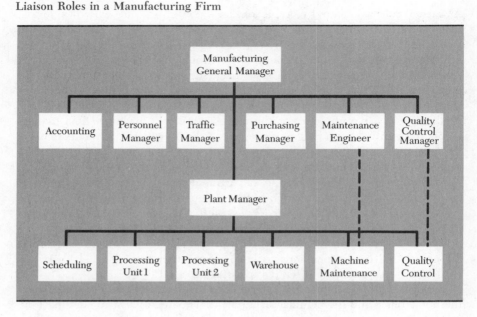

example; the task force also could be used to integrate the subsidiary into the corporation after it is purchased. Task forces are used in book publishing companies to coordinate the editing, production, and marketing of a special book. Task forces are widely used to solve temporary problems that require coordination across several departments within organizations.

Teams

Teams are permanent task forces and are used when several departments need to be coordinated on a continuous basis. When a new product is being introduced in an organization with a functional structure, a project team will often be created to coordinate the diverse inputs required to develop, produce, and market the product. The team may be in existence for several years and may also be charged with additional new products that come into existence. In the aerospace industry, employees from industrial engineering, manufacturing, design engineering, and production control are frequently assigned to work on the development of a single innovation, such as a guidance system. The teams provide the coordination necessary to integrate the ideas and resources from each department into the design of the guidance system.

The Inland division of General Motors uses teams to help the division respond quickly to annual model changes. Inland supplies equipment such as steering wheels and padded dashboards for GM cars. Teams of twenty-five to seventy-five members are created to be responsible for one or more of Inland's product lines. The team's chief position is rotated among managers from manufacturing, product engineering and production engineering so that team chiefs get broad general management experience. The teams are used to coordinate across the functional structure, which proved itself inadequate for quick response time. The first step toward creating teams at Inland was to bring together managers from engineering and manufacturing. The teams were later expanded to include managers from purchasing, finance, and sales. Prior to the teams, managers identified closely with their own departments. Quality control inspectors were not concerned about production problems, and engineering managers were oblivious to manufacturing difficulties. Now everyone sees things as part of Inland's overall problems and works to resolve any difficulty associated with the product line.[28]

Integrator Role

An **integrator role** is the creation of a full-time position or department for the purpose of integrating the activities of other departments.[29] The integrator role is different from a liaison role, because the integrator is not a member of one of the departments being coordinated. Integrators have formal positions outside the departments they are responsible to coordinate. Integrator roles often have titles such as product manager, project manager, program manager, or brand manager. The integrator is assigned to coordinate departments on a full-time basis to achieve desired product or project outcomes for the organization.

General Mills uses integrators within its food division to coordinate each of its twenty-five products. The integrators, called product managers, are assigned to Wheaties, Bisquick, Hamburger Helper, and Gold Medal Flour. The product manager's responsibility is to set annual marketing goals, develop strategies to achieve those goals, and obtain cooperation from advertising, production, marketing, and any other department needed to implement product strategy. The brand manager may also coordinate with procurement, the controller, and the research lab at some point. Decisions for a new package, a new recipe, or a new TV commercial are all coordinated by the product manager.[30]

An unusual nomenclature for the integrator role was developed at Florida Power & Light Company to facilitate the construction of a nuclear power plant. To keep the plant on schedule, a squadron of managers were assigned to give motherly care to critical parts of the construction project. They were nicknamed "Mothers." Fifteen mothers were assigned to handle fifteen specific problems. The philosophy of the man in charge, Bill Derrickson, was, "if you want something to happen, it has to have a mother." The mother may have an assigned team that could comprise a full department if the responsibility was large enough. One mother had a computerized list of 20,000 tasks to be completed on tight deadlines. He met with supervisors constantly to make sure they were on schedule. Those who didn't have answers or who fell behind were replaced. Although the supervisors did not report directly to the mother, the mother had a great deal of responsibility, which encouraged departmental managers to listen and cooperate.[31]

UP CLOSE 12.4:   Hewlett-Packard

Hewlett-Packard, the high-technology company that produces electronic instruments and computers, has experienced enormous growth and success over the past ten years. Earnings have increased tenfold, and the annual rate of growth has averaged 24 percent. The company began as a manufacturer of test and measurement instruments, and in the last few years it has scored another success in the booming market for small computers, where it now ranks number three. Computer sales are now larger than those of instruments, and total H-P sales are over $4 billion.

The decentralized product structure that has been successful for H-P in the past is now causing problems. The structure assigns the design and manufacturing to small divisions, giving responsibility for sales to separate marketing groups. The result is overlapping markets and lagging development of new technology. Customer needs often involve product combinations, but H-P has been coming across to customers as separate divisions that don't talk to each other. For example, H-P sold a new printer that had graphics capability to a company in Boise, Idaho. The buyer quickly discovered that the printer was not compatible with the graphics software made by another H-P division. The user was frustrated and blamed it on the divisional structure.

The challenge facing John Young, president of Hewlett-Packard, is to provide the cement to hold the divisions together while keeping divisions small and entrepreneurial. To achieve this end, he has launched several initiatives that include broad participation in planning, the development of task forces, and the use of program managers to coordinate product development with marketing. Outsiders agree that a coordinated approach is becoming more important to success than sheer engineering skill. A huge company needs more than engineering skills to survive.

The coordination problem is large, but not insurmountable. Twenty-two divisions work on some aspect of information processing. Young set up a computer strategy council to improve coordination across computer divisions. The council coordinates product introductions and establishes data communication standards so that divisional equipment is compatible. Another step was to name a program manager with broad powers to tap H-P divisions for necessary components and software. The program manager concept is also being introduced to coordinate three computer divisions that are separately responsible for personal computers, computer terminals, and technical computers for engineers. The three divisions previously had not worked together, and their pricing and marketing strategies were unrelated. For example, to improve communication and develop a coordinated strategy, a program manager for personal computers was created. The initial outcome of this position was the announcement of two new personal computers—one from the terminal group and one from the technical computer group—which looked alike and used the same software and peripheral products.

The next challenge is to achieve greater coordination across marketing divisions, although that may become less of a problem as the design and manufacturing of products are better coordinated. Marketing divisions then will no longer be pushing products that are not compatible with each other.[32] ■

Hewlett-Packard illustrates many of the topics discussed in this chapter. The product structure is appropriate, because the company is large and must respond quickly to a changing environment. Each division is kept small to be creative and entrepreneurial in response to technology and market changes. However, coordination across product divisions is a problem. Divisions have gradually become separate entities, developing incompatible products that are marketed in competition with each other. The computer strategy council and the use of program managers to coordinate across divisions make use of task force and integrator roles. The improved coordination will help Hewlett-Packard continue its outstanding growth and profitability in the future.

SUMMARY

This chapter has explored the topic of organization structure and design. Organization structure consists of two sets of choices for managers—choice of departmentation and choice of integrating mechanisms to coordinate across departments. The selection of departmentation and integrating mechanisms enables the organization to operate as an integrated whole.

Four types of departmentation were discussed—functional, self-contained units, hybrid, and matrix. The functional structure involves grouping by common task and is suitable for small organizations in stable environments. Self-contained units involve departmentation by organizational output, and functions are decentralized into divisions based on product, market, customer, or geographical area. The product structure is appropriate for large organizations that have sufficient resources for several divisions, and for an environment that requires innovation and rapid change. The hybrid structure contains elements of both functional and self-contained unit structures. Some functions are centralized at headquarters and serve the entire organization, while other functions are decentralized to product groups. The matrix structure involves organization participants in both a functional and product structure simultaneously. The organization has two lines of authority with equal responsibility given to product and functional managers. The matrix structure is appropriate when the environment changes rapidly, when resources must be shared among several product lines, and when the organization must succeed on a functional as well as a product-line basis. The matrix structure is used only in unique organizational circumstances. Hybrid, functional, and self-contained unit structures are used more frequently in business and government organizations.

Once the form of departmentation has been established, integrating mechanisms are used to achieve coordination across departments and to improve communication up and down the hierarchy. These mechanisms are sometimes called structural overlays because they are used in addition to the formal lines of authority. Integrating mechanisms include formal information systems and techniques for planning and scheduling, both of which convey information about diverse activities among department or division managers. Integrating mechanisms that can be formalized as organizational positions are liaison roles, task forces, teams, and integrator roles. Depending on the needs of the organization, such as whether coordination is required among two departments or several departments, whether coordination is temporary or permanent, or whether coordination is needed part time or full time, senior managers can implement integrating mechanisms to achieve horizontal coordination. Integrating mechanisms overcome departmental differences and achieve unity of effort for the organization as a whole.

KEY WORDS

centralization	integrator role	self-contained unit
decentralization	liaison role	structural overlays
departmentation	matrix boss	task force
functional structure	matrix organization	team
geographic structure	plans	top leader
hybrid structure	product structure	two-boss manager
information systems	schedules	
integrating		
mechanisms		

DISCUSSION QUESTIONS

1. Define organization structure. To what extent does an organization's structure appear on the organization chart? Explain.
2. Organization structure may be a problem when the organization does not respond quickly to environmental changes. Discuss the type of organization structure most likely to cause this problem and the alternative structures that might be more appropriate.
3. Discuss the statement, "Departmentation sews the seeds for conflict between departments in organizations."
4. When is a functional structure preferable to a product structure? Many large corporations tend to use hybrid structures. Explain the rationale for this.
5. What is the difference between a liaison role and an integrating role? Between a task force and a team? Which of these mechanisms provides the greatest amount of coordination?
6. How do managerial requirements differ for a matrix organization than for either functional or product structures?
7. Explain the strengths and weaknesses of a hybrid structure. Does the hybrid structure offer any advantages compared to the functional or product structure? Explain.
8. A management consultant said, "The matrix structure should be used only as a last resort. The disadvantages usually outweigh the advantages." Do you agree with the

consultant? Discuss. Under what conditions do you think a matrix would be appropriate?

9. Chapter 8 described the relationship between organization size and bureaucratic characteristics. To what extent would reorganizing into self-contained units help solve the problem of bureaucracy for a large corporation? Explain.

CASE 12.1   C & C Grocery Stores, Inc.

The first C & C grocery store was started in 1947 by Doug Cummins and his brother Bob. Both were veterans who wanted to run their own business, so they used their savings to start the small grocery store in Charlotte, North Carolina. The store was immediately successful. The location was good, and Doug Cummins had a winning personality. Store employees adopted Doug's informal style and "serve the customer" attitude. C & C's increasing circle of customers enjoyed an abundance of good meats and produce.

As business grew, Doug used the store's profits to open two additional stores in the Charlotte area. Over a period of twenty years the C & C chain expanded up the East coast and through the southeastern United States. Growth was at a moderate rate, because Dough did not want to overextend the chain's resources or take chances. Giving customers good service and value were more important than rapid growth. During the 1970s new stores were opened in the South and reached as far west as Texas.

By 1984, C & C had over 200 stores. A standard physical layout was used for new stores. Company headquarters moved from Charlotte to Atlanta in 1975. The organization chart for C & C is shown in Exhibit 1. The central offices in Atlanta handled personnel, merchandising, financial, purchasing, real estate, and legal affairs for the entire chain. For management of individual stores, the organization was divided by regions. The southern, southeastern, and northeastern regions each had about seventy stores. Each region was divided into five districts of ten to fifteen stores each. A district director was responsible for supervision and coordination of activities for the ten to fifteen district stores.

Each district was divided into four lines of authority based upon functional specialty. Three of these lines reached into the stores. The produce department manager within each store reported directly to the produce specialist for the division, and the same was true for the meat department manager, who reported directly to the district meat specialist. The meat and produce managers were responsible for all activities associated with the acquisition and sale of perishable products. The store manager's responsibility included the grocery line, front-end departments, and store operations. The store manager was responsible for appearance of personnel, cleanliness, adequate check-out service, and price accuracy. A grocery manager reported to the store manager and maintained inventories and restocked shelves for grocery items. The district merchandising office was responsible for promotional campaigns, advertising circulars, district advertising, and for attracting customers into the stores. The grocery merchandisers were expected to coordinate their activities with each store in the district.

During the recession in 1980–81, business for the C & C chain dropped off in all regions and did not increase with improved economic times in 1983–84. This caused concern among senior executives. They also were aware that other supermarket chains were adopting a trend toward one-stop shopping, which meant the emergence of super stores that included a pharmacy, dry goods, and groceries—almost like a department store. Executives wondered whether C & C should move in this direction and how such

EXHIBIT 1
Organization Structure for C & C Grocery Stores, Inc.

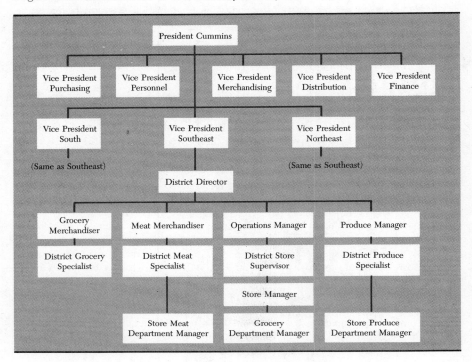

changes could be assimilated into the current store organization. However, the most pressing problem was how to improve business with the grocery stores they now had. A consulting team from a major university was hired to investigate store structure and operations.

The consultants visited several stores in each region, talking to about fifty managers and employees. The consultants wrote a report that pinpointed four problem areas to be addressed by store executives.

1. The chain is slow to adapt to change. Store layout and structure were the same as had been designed fifteen years ago. Each store did things the same way even though some stores were in low-income areas and other stores in suburban areas. A new grocery management system for ordering and stocking had been developed, but after two years was only partially implemented in the stores.

2. Roles of the district store supervisor and the store manager were causing dissatisfaction. The store managers wanted to learn general management skills for potential promotion into district or regional management positions. However, their jobs restricted them to operational activities and they learned little about merchandising, meat, and produce. Moreover, district store supervisors used store visits to inspect for cleanliness and adherence to operating standards rather than to train the store manager and help coordinate operations with perishable departments. Close supervision on the operational details had become the focus of operations management rather than development, training, and coordination.

3. Cooperation within stores was low and morale was poor. The informal, friendly atmosphere originally created by Doug Cummins was gone. One example of this problem occurred when the grocery merchandiser and store manager in a Louisiana store decided to promote Coke and Diet Coke as a loss leader. Thousands of cartons of Coke were brought in for the sale, but the stockroom was not prepared and did not have room. The store manager wanted to use floor area in the meat and produce sections to display Coke cartons, but those managers refused. The produce department manager said that Diet Coke did not help his sales and it was okay with him if there was no promotion at all.

4. Long-term growth and development of the stores chain would probably require reevaluation of long-term strategy. The percent of market share going to traditional grocery stores was declining nationwide due to competition from large super stores and convenience stores. In the future, C & C might need to introduce non-food items into the stores for one-stop shopping, and add specialty sections within stores. Some stores could be limited to grocery items, but store location and marketing techniques should take advantage of the grocery emphasis.

To solve the first three problems, the consultants recommended reorganizing the district and the store structure as illustrated in Exhibit 2. Under this reorganization, the meat, grocery, and produce department managers would all report to the store manager. The store manager would have complete store control and would be responsible for coordination of all store activities. The district supervisor's role would be changed from supervision to training and development. The district supervisor would

EXHIBIT 2
Proposed Reorganization of C & C Grocery Stores, Inc.

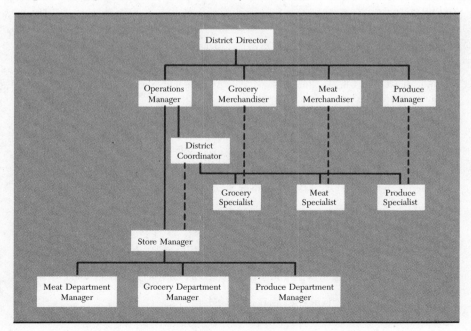

head a team that included himself and several meat, produce, and merchandise specialists who would visit area stores as a team to provide advice and help for the store managers and other employees. The team would act in a liaison capacity between district specialists and the stores.

The consultants were enthusiastic about the proposed structure. By removing one level of district operational supervision, store managers would have more freedom and responsibility. The district liaison team would establish a cooperative team approach to management that could be adopted within stores. The focus of store responsibility on a single manager would encourage coordination within stores, adaptation to local conditions, and provide a focus of responsibility for store-wide administrative changes.

The consultants also believe that the proposed structure could be expanded to accommodate non-grocery lines if enlarged stores were to be developed in the future. Within each store, a new department manager could be added for pharmacy, dry goods, or other major departments. The district team could be expanded to include specialists in these departments who would act as liaison for stores in the district.[33]

CASE QUESTIONS

1. Use the concepts of functional, self-contained units, and hybrid structures to describe the structure at C&C grocery stores both for the current structure and the proposed structure.
2. What integrating devices are currently used to achieve coordination at C&C grocery stores? How have these coordinating devices changed under the new structure? Will the new coordinating devices be more effective?
3. Evaluate the proposed organization structure. Does this meet the needs for both departmentation and coordination at C&C grocery stores? Do you foresee any problems? Would you recommend any modifications of the proposed structure?

NOTES

1. Norman Peagan, "Harvester Trims 5 Divisions to 3 in Restructuring," "The Wall Street Journal, September 10, 1981, p. 2; "International Harvester: Axing the Fat Off a Company Gone Flabby," Business Week, June 26, 1978, pp. 66–71; Melynda Cloud, Art Drummond, Cheryl Host, and Cathy Ullrich, "International Harvester," unpublished manuscript, Texas A&M University, 1982.
2. John Child, Organization (New York: Harper & Row, 1977): p. 10.
3. W. Alan Randolph and Gregory G. Dess, "The Congruence Perspective of Organization Design: A Conceptual and Multivariate Research Approach," Academy of Management Review 9 (1984): 114–127; Jay R. Galbraith, Organization Design (Reading, MA: Addison-Wesley, 1977).
4. This discussion is based upon Child, Organizations; Galbraith, Organization Design; Robert Duncan, "What is the Right Organization Structure?" Organizational Dynamics, (Winter 1979): 59–80.
5. "ESB Ray-O-Vac: Decentralizing to Recharge Its Innovative Spirit," Business Week, March 12, 1979: 116–117; Charles Davies, "Batteries Not Included," Canadian Business, May 1982: 59–63.
6. Henry Mintzberg, The Structuring of Organizations (Englewood Cliffs, NJ: Prentice-Hall, 1979).
7. Paul R. Lawrence and Jay W. Lorsch, Organizations and Environment (Homewood, IL: Irwin, 1969).
8. Duncan, "What Is the Right Organization Structure?"

9. This discussion is based on Duncan, "What Is the Right Organization Structure?," and Galbraith, *Organizational Design,* Chapter 1.

10. Duncan, "What Is the Right"; and Galbraith, *Organization Design.*

11. Duncan, "What Is the Right"; and Galbraith; *Organization Design.*

12. Duncan, "What Is the Right"; and Galbraith, *Organization Design.*

13. Richard P. Rumelt, *Strategy, Structure, and Economic Performance* (Cambridge, MA: Harvard University Press, 1974).

14. Mary S. McCarthy, "Bonanza International," unpublished manuscript, Southern Methodist University, 1981; Bruce B. Bakke, "People's Restaurants Are Expanding at Fast Clip," *Houston Chronicle,* October 17, 1982, Section 4, p. 18.

15. This discussion is based on Duncan, "What Is the Right Organization Structure?"

16. Duncan, "What Is the Right".

17. Duncan, "What Is the Right".

18. Bro Uttal, "Western Electric's Cold New World," *Fortune,* June 27, 1983, pp. 81–84; "Western Electric Prepares Sales and Marketing Strategies for 1984 When Ties to AT&T Break," *Fortune,* February 7, 1983, p. 8.

19. Davis and Lawrence, *Matrix,* p. 24.

20. Stanley M. Davis and Paul R. Lawrence, *Matrix,* (Reading, MA: Addison-Wesley, 1977): 11–24.

21. Harvey F. Koladny, "Managing in a Matrix," *Business Horizons,* 24 (March/April 1981): 17–24.

22. This discussion is based on Duncan, "What Is the Right Organization Structure?"; and Jay R. Galbraith, "Matrix Organization Designs: How To Combine Functional and Project Forms," *Business Horizons* 14 (1971): 29–40.

23. Duncan, "What Is the Right"; and Galbraith, "Matrix Organization Designs."

24. Duncan, "What Is the Right"; and Galbraith, "Matrix Organization Designs."

25. Robert Springmier, "Planning as a Vehicle for Strategic Redirection in a Matrix Structure," in Peter Lorange, *Implementation of Strategic Planning* (Englewood Cliffs, NJ: Prentice-Hall, 1982), pp. 194–205; Allen R. Janger, *Matrix Organization of Complex Businesses* (New York: The Conference Board); William C. Coggin, "How the Multidimensional Structure Works at Dow-Corning," *Harvard Business Review* (January-February, 1974), pp. 54–65.

26. The discussion of integrating mechanisms is based on Jay R. Galbraith, *Designing Complex Organizations* (Reading, MA: Addison-Wesley, 1973), and *Organization Design* (Reading, MA: Addison-Wesley, 1977).

27. "How to Manage Entrepreneurs," *Business Week,* September 7, 1981, pp. 66–69.

28. "GM's Test of Participation," *Business Week,* February 23, 1976, pp. 88–90.

29. Paul R. Lawrence and Jay W. Lorsch, "New Managerial Job: The Integrator," *Harvard Business Review* (November-December, 1967): 142–151.

30. Ann M. Morrison. "The General Mills Brand of Managers," *Fortune,* January 12, 1981, pp. 99–107.

31. Ron Winslow, "Utility Cuts Red Tape, Builds Nuclear Plant Almost on Schedule," *The Wall Street Journal,* February 22, 1984, pp. 1–18.

32. "Can John Young Redesign Hewlett-Packard?," *Business Week,* December 6, 1982, pp. 72–78; Bill Saporito, "Hewlett-Packard Discovers Marketing," *Fortune,* October 1, 1984, pp. 51–56.

33. This case is based on Robert A. Luke, Jr., Peter Block, Jack M. Davey, and Vernon R. Averch, "A Structural Approach to Organizational Change," *The Journal of Applied Behavioral Science* 9 (1973): 611–635; Ross A. Webber, "Sherman and Jackson Stores, Inc.," *Management* (Homewood, IL: Richard D. Irwin, 1979); John Merwin, "A Piece of the Action," *Forbes,* September 24, 1984, pp. 146–156.

PART

IV

Organizational Processes: A Synthesis of Micro and Macro Perspectives

T he micro and macro building blocks from the organization sciences are now in place. In this section, we turn to the study of organizational processes that are a critical part of the dynamic model described in Chapter 1. The material in the following chapters pertains to the day-to-day operating processes within organizations. These processes are the essence of management and the mechanisms through which the ideas and frameworks presented in the previous chapters are implemented and used in organizations. Our examination of key processes begins in the next chapter with leadership. From there we'll move to decision making, power and politics, conflict, communication, control and organizational innovation. These topics embrace both micro and macro issues, and each chapter will describe the concepts from both perspectives.

13 Leadership

Steven J. Ross built Warner Communications with a hands-off approach to management. Ross believes that running a division is up to the division chief. Internal growth in the company has been fueled by this philosophy, and Ross is not about to change—despite recent problems with the Atari division and some belief by outsiders that the company is not under control.[1] Ross B. Kenzie, in contrast, pushes change from the top at Buffalo Savings Bank. Kenzie left Merrill Lynch & Co. to become chairman of Buffalo Savings, and his presence has been felt there. The new chairman fired 15 percent of the managers, and he has pushed relentlessly for growth. The bank has quadrupled in size by acquiring financially weak thrift institutions with the help of the Federal Deposit Insurance Corporation. Kenzie initiated the construction of a new headquarters building and has imposed a philosophy of testing people by shifting them from job to job. People who don't perform well in new jobs are shifted out of the company.[2]

Steven Ross and Ross Kenzie represent two different styles of leadership. This chapter will explore the nature of leadership styles in organizations and examine when specific styles tend to be most effective. We will examine leadership from both a micro and a macro perspective. The micro approach describes the relationship between leaders and their immediate subordinates; the micro approach has special relevance for managers at lower and middle levels of the organization. The macro approach pertains to leadership for the organization as a whole; the macro approach has special application to the middle and upper levels of the organization. Taking the micro approach, we will define basic leadership concepts, such as the leader's orientation toward people and toward tasks, and then we will examine those situations when each leader orientation is effective. Taking the macro approach, we will examine leadership as the broader task of top-level management, and we will examine how leaders influence the strategy and culture of an entire organization.

DEFINITION OF LEADERSHIP

Leadership can mean many things. Leadership is associated with motivation, influence, providing a good example, and giving direction. Leadership can be seen as an attribute of an organizational position, such as "vice president" of a corporation. Leadership can be a characteristic of a person—a person having leadership is someone who enthusiastically gives directions and other people follow along. Leadership can be viewed as the attainment of goals, and the necessary communication to direct people toward those goals.

Within all of the images associated with leadership, three stand out —*people, influence,* and *goals.* Leadership pertains to people. It occurs between people. Leadership is distinct from the concept of management, which embraces the activities of control, organizing, decision making and administration that are not directly related to people. Leadership involves the use of power or influence. Influence means that the relationship between people is not passive. Leadership also is proposive and designed to achieve some end or goal. People and influence are used to accomplish goals desired by the leader. With these three elements in mind, our formal definition of leadership is as follows:

> *Leadership is a behavioral process in which one person attempts to influence other people's behavior toward the accomplishment of goals.*[3]

This definition captures the idea that a leader is involved with other people and uses influence to reach goals. The term *behavioral process* indicates that leadership is an ongoing activity.

Goals and *influence* depend upon the leader and the people who are led. Some leaders, such as corporate managers, may use the formal authority provided by the organization, while others, such as a Winston Churchill or Martin Luther King, exerted influence through personal eloquence and charisma. The impact of leadership on people can range from grudging compliance to voluntary and enthusiastic acceptance of direction based on faith and identification with the leader. The effect can also extend from immediate subordinates within one's small work group to a social movement that spans an entire country.

RELEVANCE OF LEADERSHIP FOR MANAGERS

Leadership has been a phenomenon studied with interest in both psychology and sociology, because leaders arise wherever human groups exist. Psychologists focus on characteristics of the leader, sociologists on characteristics of the larger group. Regardless of perspective, leadership is important for managers because the ability to lead can have substantial impact on group performance and satisfaction. Leadership has a special relationship to management and is important to study for two major reasons.

Leadership is where the practice of management is implemented. Leadership is where the action is. Leadership translates plans and ideas into people motivated to accomplish those plans and ideas. Leadership is where the topics we have been studying in this book come together. Leadership draws upon motivation, individual differences, group behavior, goals, organization structure, and organizational effectiveness. Leadership is the critical process that translates these concepts into activities that accomplish organizational goals.

Don Lennox, who was asked to save International Harvester from bankruptcy, is a leader. International Harvester was in deep trouble, and he provided the direction, the focus, the goals, the enthusiasm, and the agreement to implement a turnaround at Harvester. He invoked harsh actions to save Harvester, including cutbacks in the work force, the elimination of nonperforming assets, and a redirection of the style of other managers from record keepers to record setters.[4] Ruth Love, Chicago's former superintendent of schools, is also a leader. She persuaded the first black astronaut to address 10,000 public high-school children on the importance of learning science and math. Her "Adopt-A-School" program became a model for attracting funds from corporations. Love also was a budget cutter and hard-line bargainer in attempts to bring expenses in line with tax revenues.[5] Don Lennox and Ruth Love are leaders because they have drawn upon skill and knowledge of organizations to influence people and implement courses of action to attain important goals.

Informal leaders can be as important as formal leaders. Most discussions of leadership pertain to leaders in organizational positions, yet much leadership occurs outside formal work organizations. Family, church, volunteer organizations, athletic teams, social groups, and sororities and fraternities all have a need and opportunity for exercising leadership. People not in formal leadership positions still provide leadership. Martin Luther King led an entire social movement without a formal position, and so did Ghandi and Lenin. Coaches of athletic teams often call certain players team leaders even though the players are not in official leadership positions. Pete Rose was always a natural leader in baseball, and Dick Butkus had a great career as a leader on the football field for the Chicago Bears. Whenever a peer group gathers at work, in church, at a community activity, or on a social occasion, some people exert more influence than others. The point is that leadership opportunities are available to everyone.

Moreover, sometimes formal leadership fails. Don Lennox, Ruth Love, and Ross Kenzie were made leaders because previous leaders failed. In many settings, informal leaders rise to fill the leadership void. The following explanation of leadership, for example, applies as much to informal leaders as to leaders who have formal designation.

Leadership is the ability to persuade others to seek defined objectives enthusiastically. It is the human factor which binds a group together and motivates it toward goals. Management activities such as planning, organizing, and decision making are dormant cocoons until the leader triggers the power of motivation in people and guides them toward their goals.[6]

LEVELS OF LEADERSHIP

Leadership is important at all levels in the organization, but leadership activities and functions change with hierarchical level. The leader plays a different role and needs different skills at lower levels than at higher levels. The micro perspective on leadership applies to leading immediate subordinates, while the macro perspective relates to the organization as a whole.

Leadership requirements at top, middle, and lower organization levels are summarized in Exhibit 13.1. Leadership requirements are classified by whether they pertain to the cognitive or affective dimension of organizations.[7] The **cognitive dimension** is the thinking, conceptual, planning, task accomplishment, and decision-making aspect of leadership. The **affective dimension** is the emotional, social, and human relations aspect of leadership. Both functions are needed at each hierarchical level.

Top-echelon executives are concerned with administering the organization as a whole. Their responsibility is to make decisions about the overall goals of the organization and to define strategies for achieving those goals. Cognitive skills pertain to planning and the analysis of events and trends for the long term. Top managers must work out the relationship of the organization with the external environment in terms of products and markets. As far as affective skills, top managers are responsible for the organization's human resource climate and internal culture. Top leaders cannot interact with every employee personally, so they symbolize the values and internal culture that is integrated with organizational goals and strategy.

Middle-level leaders are concerned with decision making at the department level. Their cognitive requirements are to define operative goals for their

EXHIBIT 13.1
Leadership Requirements at Each Level in the Organizational Hierarchy

Leadership Ability and Skill	Organization Level		
	Top	Middle	Lower
Cognitive	Analyze events and trends, define strategy and structure, plan, deal with environment. Adopt long time horizon.	Define operative goals, rules, department structure, coordinate with other departments. Adopt medium time horizon.	Provide technical knowledge of tasks, apply rules and procedures, achieve efficient production, targets and efficiencies. Adopt short time horizon.
Affective	Define human relations climate and practices, create positive internal culture, values, and symbols.	Establish relations with peers, subordinates, and other departments. Motivate employees, enhance teamwork, resolve conflicts.	Motivate subordinates, administer rewards and sanctions, be sensitive to needs of immediate group.

departments; they also define any structure and direction that has not been provided from the top. At this level managers are concerned with the department's place and stature within the organization. Managing relationships across departments is another major issue. Time perspective is medium term. Human relations skills are important at the middle level for dealing with peers and with subordinates. Affective skills include the ability to manage the conflicting demands from within the department, encourage teamwork, set the correct tone for the department, and encourage subordinates to work toward the goals of the department.

Lower-echelon supervisors are responsible for day-to-day operations in a single work group. At this level technical knowledge is more important than administrative knowledge and ability. Cognitive skills require knowledge of organization procedures and the specialized techniques used by subordinates, such as market research, accounting, or machine work. The time horizon at this level is short, and leaders are concerned with efficient production and accomplishment of group goals. The affective skills are concerned with rewards and sanctions to encourage high employee performance. Employee participation and managers' sensitivity to the attitudes, feelings, and needs of subordinates can also be important.

In the next part of the chapter we will define more explicitly the behaviors required of leaders at the micro level, and we will develop the concepts of task versus human skills in detail. Then we will shift to the organizational level and examine the role of top leaders for establishing strategies and for defining human resource values for the organization as a whole.

LEADERSHIP BEHAVIOR

The earliest work on leadership in the field, dating back hundreds of years, tried to explain the emergence of great leaders. This research was called "the great man" approach to leadership, and it concluded that great leaders had special inborn characteristics that destined them to attain positions of influence. As we entered the twentieth century, the focus of leadership investigation shifted from explaining the emergence of a few great leaders to identifying leadership traits in organizational situations. By the twentieth century, the emergence of large business and government organizations called for redefining leadership, since so many people were finding themselves in leadership positions. Understanding the traits associated with leadership success became the goal of new research.

Leader Traits

Between 1904 and 1948, a total of 124 studies of leader traits were reported. These studies were reviewed by Ralph Stogdill, who found that they suggested a number of traits which could predict the difference between leaders and nonleaders.[8] Successful leaders tended to exhibit the following characteristics:

EXHIBIT 13.2

Traits and Skills Found to be Characteristic of Successful Leaders

Traits	Skills
Adaptable to situations	Clever (intelligent)
Alert to social environment	Conceptually skilled
Ambitious and achievement-oriented	Creative
Assertive	Diplomatic and tactful
Cooperative	Fluent in speaking
Decisive	Knowledgeable about group task
Dependable	Organized (administrative ability)
Dominant (desire to influence others)	Persuasive
Energetic (high activity level)	Socially skilled
Persistent	
Self-confident	
Tolerant of stress	
Willing to assume responsibility	

SOURCE: Gary A. Yukl, *Leadership in Organizations* (Englewood Ciffs, NJ: Prentice-Hall, 1981), p. 70. Used with permission.

- *Intelligence:* leaders tended to be rated higher on intelligence tests, were more fluent, and displayed greater overall knowledge and originality than nonleaders.
- *Physical stature:* leaders tended to be taller than followers, to be older and to have a good physical appearance.
- *Personality:* leaders showed self confidence, independence, initiative, persistence, and a need to achieve.

In 1974, Stogdill reported a review of 163 additional trait studies conducted from 1949 to 1970.[9] The more recent research used a greater variety of measures and better methods than earlier studies. However, the leader characteristics identified were similar to previous research. The traits and skills associated with successful leadership according to Stogdill's review are in Exhibit 13.2.

From all the research into traits of successful leaders, the most promising conclusion Stogdill reached was that many characteristics could be associated with successful leadership. The profile of leader characteristics varied from situation to situation. In one case the successful leader may be assertive, decisive, and self confident. In another case the leader may be cooperative, fluent, and creative. As a consequence of the conclusion that a wide variety of leader traits could be effective depending on the situation, research began to examine how leaders interacted with groups under various conditions. This research began to look at the actual behavior of leaders to understand their impact on those led.

Leader Behavior

The shift in focus from leader traits to leader behavior was significant, because successful behaviors could be adopted by anyone who wants to be an effective leader. Research at the University of Michigan and at Ohio State University during the 1940s and 1950s was devoted to identifying behavioral characteristics and consolidating them into a minimum number of fundamental behaviors associated with leader success.

Work at the University of Michigan's Survey Research Center developed two dimensions of leadership behavior. Researchers discovered that supervisors tended to be either employee-centered or job-centered.[10] **Employee-centered leaders** are concerned with the personal needs of subordinates. Employee-centered leaders stress positive interpersonal relationships, are willing to adapt to differences among employees, and are friendly and approachable. **Job-centered leaders** tend to emphasize completion of the task. They are concerned with production efficiency and attaining production targets, even if employees are unhappy as a result. These leaders are concerned with getting work accomplished.

The general conclusion from the research was that leaders who were employee-centered tend to have higher productivity and subordinates are more satisfied. The job-centered leaders, although primarily focused on accomplishing the work, tend to have groups that are less satisfied and less productive.[11]

At about the same time, researchers at Ohio State University were investigating leader dimensions to identify fundamental clusters of behavior associated with leader success. They began with hundreds of dimensions of leader behavior, and surveyed thousands of leaders and subordinates. Through this research, they discovered two basic leader behaviors called initiating structure and consideration.[12]

Initiating structure is the extent to which leaders define and direct subordinate work activities toward goal attainment. Leaders with this style typically have high standards of performance, emphasize deadlines, give directions, schedule group activities, and emphasize planning and target setting. They tend to be concerned with getting a task accomplished by organizing and directing group members.

Consideration is the extent to which leaders emphasize respect for subordinates, listen to their ideas, have regard for their feelings, and establish mutual trust with them. Leaders high on consideration take time to listen to subordinates, are friendly, and are concerned with the personal welfare of group members.

The Ohio State characteristics of consideration and initiating structure are very similar to the University of Michigan characteristics of employee-centered and job-centered leadership. The one difference is that the University of Michigan tended to assume that leaders were either job-centered or employee-centered, but not both. The Ohio State research suggested that leaders might display behaviors that include either, both, or neither consideration or initiating structure.

Exhibit 13.3 illustrates the two dimensions of leader behavior. Leaders can fit anywhere within the four quadrants depending on the behaviors they display. Research into the Ohio State dimensions suggests that leaders high in both initiating structure and consideration tended to achieve higher performance and satisfaction in their groups than leaders rated in the other quadrants of Exhibit 13.2. Absenteeism, turnover, and grievance rates were lower for leaders characterized as "high-high."[13] However, exceptions to this pattern were found. In some situations effective leaders tended to be high on employee-oriented behavior but low on initiating structure. In other situations initiating structure seemed to be more important. Thus while the high-high style was often effective, other leadership styles could work as well, depending on the situation.

A third line of research also produced a two-dimensional view of leadership behavior. Blake and Mouton of the University of Texas proposed a grid figure, called "The New Managerial Grid," which categorized leadership behavior based on "concern for production" and "concern for people." The two dimensions presented by these researchers are similar to the Ohio State and Michigan dimensions of leader behavior in Exhibit 13.3. Research findings by Blake and Mouton suggested that managers perform best when they use a leadership style characterized as high in concern for both people and production.[14]

Exhibit 13.3 is an interpretation of all three streams of research on leader behavior. The significance of the research is that each stream discovered the same two fundamental dimensions of leadership style. The behaviors associated with task versus people orientations can be used to characterize leader

EXHIBIT 13.3
Dimensions of Leadership Behavior

Consideration	High	1. High Consideration 2. Low Initiating Structure	1. High Consideration 2. High Initiating Structure
		1. Low Consideration 2. Low Initiating Structure	1. Low Consideration 2. High Initiating Structure
	Low	Low	High

Initiating Structure

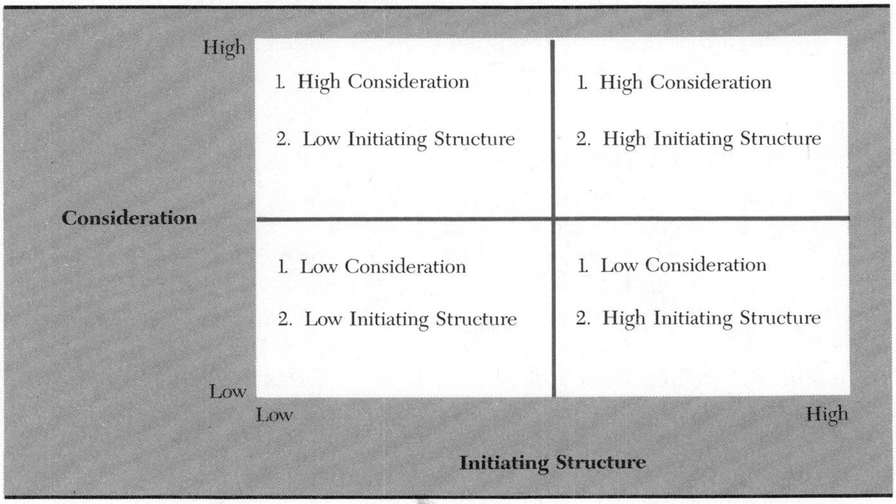

differences. This finding suggests that organizational work groups have two basic needs—the social needs of employees and the production needs of the organization. Effective leaders play a part in meeting either or both of these needs within their departments. In the following **Up Close,** both leader styles are used, and they seem appropriate to the situation.

UP CLOSE 13.1:   Simon & Schuster Inc.

Richard Snyder, president of Simon & Schuster of New York, makes intense demands for high performance. His demands make the organization into what's typically called a pressure cooker. Employees act as if he is aware of every detail, which generates both excitement and anxiety. His demands for performance, however, produce results within the organization. When the book Mayor *by New York City Mayor Ed Koch got good reviews, the head of production set up a cot next to the printing press to make sure the book was off press in time to be distributed to stores within seventy-two hours. The typical time frame for distribution is two weeks.*

Snyder expects people to do well every time. He has a quick, flaring temper that has driven employees from the company. Snyder admits that he yells at people, and that it's not always the correct thing to do, but he believes it is harder to confront people and win respect than to be nice. His job as leader is to drive the company to high performance, and it works. This summer Simon & Schuster had eleven books on the best seller list, far more than any of its competitors.[15]

Contrast Snyder's leadership style with that of Skip Griggs. When Griggs worked for a well-known manufacturer of household appliances, he supervised assembly lines that produced knives and electric toothbrushes. Each day the people who worked on the assembly line were given half an hour for lunch and two eight-minute breaks. The company would not allow the workers to use the nearby cafeteria for their breaks, so workers took breaks in the restrooms instead.

Management was afraid that if workers were allowed in the cafeteria, employees might decide to take off for the restrooms just before the lines started up again, costing the company a couple of minutes. Management did not believe that attention to employee needs could produce results. Griggs couldn't stand this treatment; he wanted to do more things for his people. Griggs opened the cafeteria on his own. The employees cheered, but management chewed him out. Working in the company was frustrating, he found, because people received so little consideration. Griggs eventually left the company. He came away with his strong belief still intact—the belief that managers can get the most out of employees by trusting them and meeting their social needs. Griggs went on to apply this belief successfully as a division president at Kollmorgen Corporation.[16] ■

Richard Snyder and Skip Griggs illustrate different leadership styles. Snyder is directive and would be considered high on initiating structure. Griggs is concerned for people and would rate high on consideration. Both managers eventually found success. The hard-driving, high-expectation style of Snyder has made Simon & Schuster the best-performing trade book publisher in the industry. Griggs' employee-oriented approach proved successful in his next job, where his skills enabled him to become a division president at Kollmorgen Corporation.

The concepts of people orientation and task orientation provide the basis for more sophisticated contingency theories of leadership. In the next section we will consider two contingency theories that have received major attention: 1) Fiedler's contingency theory, and 2) House's path-goal theory. These theories provide a more detailed statement about leader behaviors, suggesting when they should be adopted, depending on the organizational situation or the leader's relationship with subordinates.

FIEDLER'S CONTINGENCY MODEL

Fred Fiedler developed the first and perhaps best-known contingency model of leadership.[17] The model represented an advancement over the behavioral models of leadership by specifying that a group's performance depends upon both leadership style and the nature of the leadership situation.

Leadership Style

Fiedler measured leadership style by evaluating people's orientation toward **least-preferred co-workers** (called LPC). Fiedler used a questionnaire that contained sixteen scales anchored by positive and negative adjectives. Each leader was instructed to think of the person with whom he or she worked least well, and to rate that person on each of the sixteen scales. Three sample scales are below:[18]

Boring	—	—	—	—	—	—	—	—	Interesting
Quarrelsome	—	—	—	—	—	—	—	—	Harmonious
Gloomy	—	—	—	—	—	—	—	—	Cheerful

Leaders tended to follow distinct patterns in their evaluation of least-preferred co-workers. Some leaders saw least-preferred co-workers in quite positive terms, and a favorable description suggested a leader who was people- or relationships-oriented. Respondents who reported an unfavorable description of least-preferred co-workers tended to be task-oriented. Simply by asking leaders to evaluate someone they typically did not like to work with, Fiedler was able to assess whether they were people-oriented or task-oriented. Low-LPC leaders gained satisfaction and self-esteem through achieving task-related goals. High-LPC leaders gained satisfaction and self-esteem through positive relationships with others and a positive group atmosphere.

Situational Factors

The next aspect of Fiedler's model defined the situation in which the leader functions. Whether the situation is favorable or unfavorable to the leader is the issue. In other words, does the situation lend itself to making the leader's role easy or difficult. Fiedler defined and measured the situation along three dimensions.[19]

1. *Leader-member relations.* This refers to the group's attitude toward and acceptance of the leader. When the group atmosphere is good, and group members have confidence, trust, and respect for the leader, then the situation is favorable. If members do not accept the leader, get along poorly with the leader, or do not trust the leader, then the group atmosphere would be unfavorable to the leader.
2. *Task structure.* This refers to the extent that tasks are well defined, with explicit goals and work procedures. When tasks are routine and well defined (e.g., an assembly line worker) employees know exactly what to do, and the situation is more favorable to the leader. When tasks are nonroutine, ambiguous, and goals are unclear (e.g., strategic planner), the situation is less favorable to the leader. The more task structure, the easier it is for the leader to tell group members what to do.
3. *Position power.* This refers to the extent to which a leader possesses a strong and legitimate power base over subordinates. Can the leader effectively reward or punish subordinates, and do subordinates accept the authority of the leader? If so, the leader is in a strong power position, which is favorable. If the leader is in a weak power position, or if the power is equal between leader and subordinates or in dispute, then the situation is unfavorable to the leader.

EXHIBIT 13.4
Fiedler's Classification of Situation Favorableness

Leader-member relations	Good	Good	Good	Good	Poor	Poor	Poor	Poor
Task structure	High		Low		High		Low	
Leader position power	Strong	Weak	Strong	Weak	Strong	Weak	Strong	Weak
Situations	I	II	III	IV	V	VI	VII	VIII

Very favorable ◄──────────────► Very unfavorable

SOURCE: Fred E. Fiedler, "The Effects of Leadership Training and Experience: A Contingency Model Interpretation," *Administrative Science Quarterly* 17 (1972): 455. Used with permission.

Work situations can be evaluated by whether they are rated high or low with respect to each of the three dimensions. Combining the three dimensions leads to a list of eight leadership situations, called octants, which are illustrated in Exhibit 13.4. Leader-member relations can be rated as either good (octants 1–4) or bad (octants 5–8), task structure can be rated high (octants 1, 2, 5, and 6) or low (octants 3, 4, 7, and 8), and leader position power can be rated as strong (octants 1, 3, 5, and 7) or weak (octants 2, 4, 6, and 8).

Using these three dimensions to evaluate work situations, overall favorableness to the leader can be evaluated. Situation favorableness to the leader is highest in octant 1, where leader-member relations are good, task structure is high, and position power is strong. Situational favorableness is lowest in octant 8, where leader-member relations are poor, task structure is low, and position power is weak. All other octants present degrees of intermediate favorableness to the leader; the general pattern in Exhibit 13.4 is that the situation becomes less favorable to the leader as it shifts from octant 1 to octant 8.

Leader Effectiveness

An important outcome of Fiedler's research was that he correlated leadership style with actual group performance. He did the research on a number of groups where performance measures could be obtained. The initial research groups included bomber crews, artillery crews, ROTC cadets, supervisors of a steel plant, and athletic teams. In each case Fiedler obtained a measure of group performance, a measure of whether the leader was high LPC (relationship-oriented) or low LPC (task-oriented), and ratings of leader-member relations, task structure, and position power.[20]

Fiedler's approach to analysis and the pattern of findings from his research are illustrated in Exhibit 13.5. Fiedler was able to identify work situations that fit into each of the eight octants. He then examined the statistical correlation between the leaders' LPC scores and group performance for each situation. A strong positive correlation meant that a high LPC score (relationship-oriented leader) was associated with high group performance. A negative statistical correlation meant that a low LPC score (task-oriented leader) was associated with high performance. The extent to which these correlations were positive or negative indicated which type of leadership was associated with performance in each situation.

In Exhibit 13.5, negative correlations emerge at both ends of the situational favorableness continuum. This means that if the situation is either highly unfavorable or highly favorable, a low LPC (task-oriented leader) is more effective in securing group performance. The interesting point of this finding is that task-oriented leaders tend to excel in opposite situations. When the situation is highly favorable, everyone gets along, the task is clear, and the leader has power. All that is needed is for someone to take charge and provide some direction, and employees will do the rest. Similarly, if the situation is highly unfavorable to the leader, a great deal of structure and task orientation is

EXHIBIT 13.5
Findings from Contingency Theory Research

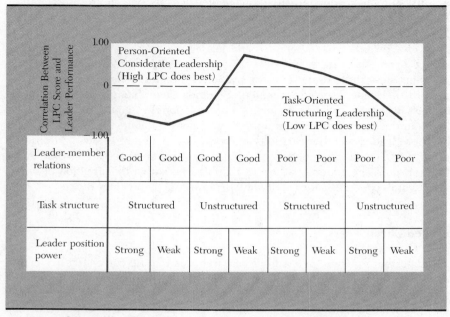

SOURCE: Fred E. Fiedler, "The Effects of Leadership Training and Experience: A Contingency Model Interpretation," *Administrative Science Quarterly* 17 (1972): 455. Used with permission.

needed. A strong leader is needed to create structure for ambiguous tasks and to establish authority over group members. Since leader-member relations are poor, the task orientation does not run the risk of making the leader unpopular.

In the middle of the situational continuum in Exhibit 13.5, positive correlations between LPC and group performance were found. These situations were intermediately favorable to the leader, because some factors were favorable and others were unfavorable. Fiedler concluded that the high LPC (relationship-oriented) leader was more effective in these cases, because human relations skills were important for facilitating group performance. In these situations the leaders were moderately well liked, had some power, or supervised jobs that contained some ambiguity. A leader with good interpersonal skills could create a positive group atmosphere that could improve leader-member relations, clarify task structure, and establish position power. Thus when the situation was clearly favorable or clearly unfavorable to the leader, a task orientation worked best. But when the situation was intermediately favorable, greater interpersonal skills were needed to cope with ambiguity, sort things out, and attain high performance.

Follow-up research into the relationships discovered by Fiedler have tended to show similar findings and to validate the model.[21] Despite the research findings, the model has been criticized. Critics argue that the LPC scale is an indirect measure of leader orientation and may lack validity. Critics also argue that the classification of work situations is too simplistic, and that additional factors should be included.[22] These criticisms are justified, but they do not diminish the usefulness of the model. This research helped demonstrate that the fit between leader and situation, not leadership behavior alone, makes the leader effective. Fiedler went on to propose that leaders be selected to fit the situation. In cases where leaders could not be changed, then situations should be changed to fit the leaders.

The following **Up Close** gives an example of how Fiedler's contingency model applies to real situations. The difficult situation facing Gordon McGovern at Campbell Soup illustrates how a strong, task oriented leadership-style is needed when the situation is unfavorable.

UP CLOSE 13.2:   Campbell Soup

To overhaul their organizations, top managers sometimes must create a difficult management situation from the top. An organization in the throes of change can be difficult to lead. Hierarchical relationships begin to break down, and people are uncertain and insecure about what they should be trying to accomplish. The leader in this situation needs to be strong and to have courage. Gordon McGovern used a strong, task-oriented approach at Campbell Soup. Campbell's performance was moderately successful in the early 1980s, but not good enough. McGovern instituted swift and sweeping changes. He reshuffled top management and divided the company into about fifty business units. Things are in constant motion for middle managers. During informal conversations in the halls or in the cafeteria, McGovern will sometimes criticize one manager's product to another manager, expecting word to get back to the one with the problem. McGovern believes that the indirect criticism will motivate people to prove him wrong. McGovern also short circuits the chain of command if it will get the job done. He will bypass the marketing vice president and talk directly to the soup marketing manager to get an answer. This may ruffle the bypassed manager's feelings, but accomplishing the task counts most. The ground rules are not well defined under McGovern, and this fits his directive style. For example, McGovern learned that the non-spicy form of V-8 vegetable juice was often used in Bloody Marys. McGovern was instrumental in getting Campbell to break tradition and plan its first advertisement for Playboy magazine, whose readers include a high percentage of Bloody Mary drinkers.[23] ▪

McGovern's style fits the Campbell Soup situation, which would be considered unfavorable to the leader. In this case, McGovern actually helped create the conditions of uncertainty that fit his high-powered, directive style. Leadership effectiveness is contingent on fitting style with the organizational setting. Now we will turn to another contingency theory, which provides further ideas for tailoring leadership behavior to the organizational setting.

THE PATH-GOAL MODEL

The path-goal situational theory of leadership was developed from the work of Evans and House.[24] The model is based on the expectancy theory of motivation discussed in Chapter 4. It suggests that leaders are effective when they increase employees' motivation. The leader increases the motivation of subordinates by either 1) clarifying the path to the rewards that are available, or by 2) increasing the rewards that are valued and desired by subordinates. Path clarification means the leader will work with subordinates to help them learn the behaviors that will lead to successful task accomplishment and rewards. Increasing rewards means that the leader must talk with subordinates to learn which rewards are important to them, and whether they are intrinsic rewards from the work itself or extrinsic rewards such as raises or promotions. To be effective, the leader is responsible for:

> . . . *increasing the number and kinds of personal payoffs to the subordinates for work-goal attainment and making paths to these payoffs easier to travel by clarifying the paths, reducing roadblocks and pitfalls, and increasing the opportunities for personal satisfaction en route.*[25]

Leader Behavior

The leader's responsibility is to clarify paths to rewards or increase rewards. To do this, the path-goal theory identifies four kinds of leader behavior.[26]

- *Supportive leadership:* Show concern for the well-being and personal needs of subordinates, be friendly and approachable, be considerate, create a friendly climate, and treat subordinates as equals. This style is similar to consideration leadership behavior.
- *Directive leadership:* Tell subordinates what they are expected to do, give guidance and direction, provide standards and schedules, set performance targets, and ask subordinates to follow rules and regulations. This style is similar to initiating structure.
- *Participative leadership:* Consult with subordinates about job activities, schedules, and targets, ask for opinions and suggestions, allow for participation in decision making, and take subordinates' views into account.
- *Achievement-oriented leadership:* Set challenging goals, seek improvement in performance, emphasize excellence in performance, and show expectation and confidence that subordinates have ability to attain high standards.

An important aspect of this model is that the leader is expected to adopt any of the four styles, depending on the situation. The styles are not treated as personality traits, but as consciously selected leadership strategies tailored to the needs of subordinates and the availability of rewards. A number of situational factors can influence which leadership style will have the greatest impact on the performance of subordinates.

Situational Factors

Two situational factors considered important to leadership style in the path-goal model are *subordinate characteristics* and *work environment characteristics*. Subordinates may differ in their confidence in their own ability, in locus of control, and in their needs for esteem, affiliation, autonomy, or responsibility. If people lack confidence in their ability, they may need a supportive leader who is understanding and sympathetic. If they have high confidence, they may prefer a directive leader who would simply point out the path to the goal. Locus of control refers to whether or not people see themselves in control of events. People who believe that external forces determine what happens may prefer a directive leader. If people have an internal locus of control and believe what happens is a function of their own effort, they may prefer a participative leader so they can influence their own course of action. Subordinates with a high need for esteem and for affiliation may prefer supportive leaders who are concerned for meeting these needs. Subordinates with needs for autonomy and responsibility may prefer directive or achievement-oriented leaders.

Characteristics of the work environment include the extent to which tasks are structured or mechanized, and the degree of formalization imposed by the organization in terms of rules, procedures and job descriptions. When task structure is high, directive leadership has little to offer, because employees already have directions and know what to do. The same is true of the formal authority system. The higher the formality, the less directive leadership is needed. Participative or supportive leaders who can meet the social needs of subordinates will play a greater role when task structure is high. Relationships among subordinates within the work group are also important situational factors. When group members have positive relationships and the group is cohesive, then a supportive leader is less important because human needs are already met within the group. A directive leader or achievement-oriented leader would induce higher levels of performance. If interpersonal relationships within the group are poor, a supportive leader will be important, because the leader will be the main source of social need fulfillment.

Leader Impact

According to the path-goal model, the challenge for leaders is to analyze their situation. What are the personalities, motivations, and goals of subordinates? Are tasks well defined? Are rewards sufficient? Is the work group cohesive and friendly? Leaders must talk to subordinates, learn about their needs, analyze the work environment, and then use the appropriate style to either increase the amount of reward value to subordinates or show subordinates the path through which rewards are available. Depending on the nature of the situation, any of the four leadership styles identified in the path-goal theory may be effective, as Exhibit 13.6 illustrates. Supportive and directive leadership styles are used most often, but some occasions may warrant participative and achievement-oriented leaders.

EXHIBIT 13.6
Path-Goal Leader Situations and Behaviors

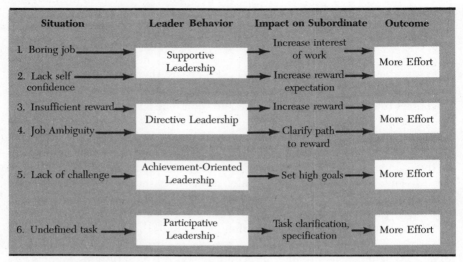

SOURCE: Adapted from Gary A. Yukl, *Leadership in Organizations* (Englewood Cliffs, NJ: Prentice-Hall, 1981), pp. 146–152.

In situations 1 and 2 of Exhibit 13.6, subordinates may have a boring, routine job, or they may lack self confidence. These situations call for a supportive leadership style. Social support will increase the value of the work itself, which will be rewarding to employees. Increased self confidence will encourage subordinates to move down the path toward greater rewards. The outcome in both cases is greater effort on the part of subordinates. In situations 3 and 4 of Exhibit 13.6, the task roles are ambiguous or the magnitude of rewards is too small, so employees are not performing effectively. In these cases directive leadership is important for reducing role ambiguity by giving directions to employees, or for unilaterally increasing rewards for tasks well done. In both cases the paths to rewards are clarified, and this will increase effort. In situation 5, subordinates are unchallenged by the task, and an achievement-oriented supervisor will set high goals. This clarifies the path to reward and increases employee effort. Finally, situation 6 is characterized by an unstructured task, and the participative leadership style can be effective. Through involvement in decision making, subordinates obtain knowledge about their jobs and clarification of ambiguities, making the path to rewards clearer so effort is increased.

In each of the diagrams in Exhibit 13.6, the leader is expected to adopt the leader style appropriate to the situation. The leader adapts to the situation that exists at that time, and he or she can be supportive, directive, achievement oriented or participative as needed to increase rewards or clarify the path to rewards for subordinates. Like all theories, the path-goal theory has been criticized for being incomplete or for not describing all situations. However, research backs up the assertion that the ideas contained in the path-goal theory are associated with effective leadership styles.[27] Leaders are able to motivate employees to perform well by analyzing the situation and working to increase rewards or clarify the path to rewards.

One example of a leader who uses a combination of participative and directive leadership styles is Jack Byrne at Geico. We discussed Geico's goal setting process briefly in Chapter 11 (**Up Close** 11.2). Here we will see that Byrne uses more than one leader style to motivate employees toward high performance.

UP CLOSE 13.3:   GEICO Corporation

John Byrne, chairman of Geico, sums up his management style as "muddling through." He has built a foundation of consensus management combined with inflexible operating rules. Geico, formerly Government Employees Insurance Company, insured drivers who had fewer accidents than most and was able to offer low prices. Before Byrne took over, the company had just experienced a period of reckless growth, but then the emphasis shifted toward internal cost reduction as a source of income gains. Byrne believes that moderate growth is now needed, but he wants to move ahead only by consensus. He does not make major decisions by himself. Before any major issue comes up for group discussion, Byrne goes from office to office, listening and explaining.

The ultimate participation is realized at the annual planning meeting. Managers from the twenty-eight major centers come together to have challenge sessions concerning proposed budget and goals for the next year. Managers debate their goals until unrealistic ones are gone, and managers agree on what is left. Goals are set through widespread participation so that Byrne's subordinates know exactly what they are to attain for the next year.

Once the goals are set through participation, Byrne is inflexible about implementation and rewards. He doesn't give even token bonuses to managers who don't meet their goals. Many goals pertain to cost reduction, and Geico's managers have become born-again cost cutters. Since Byrne gives the rewards to the people who attain their goals, managers have a strong incentive to perform well. Byrne insists that performance is the only thing that counts. He cares for substance more than form. As long as an employee gets results, he says, "I don't care if he shines his shoes with a brick."[28]

Byrne uses a combination of participative and directive leadership styles at Geico. Participation helps clarify goals and objectives for the coming year. Employees have learned to participate, which gives them a strong sense of ownership of their objectives. Byrne is directive in that he insists on high performance, and he withholds rewards until performance is achieved. The combination of participative and directive styles is just right for the senior management team at Geico.

SUBSTITUTES FOR LEADERSHIP

The two leadership styles most important to situational models are the people (or relationships) orientation and the task (or initiating structure) orientation. The value of the situational models is that they show how each leadership style tends to be effective in certain settings. The situational models recognize that group characteristics, work tasks, and formal organization all influence leader behavior and impact. Recent work by Kerr and Jermier systematically identified situational factors that may substitute for leadership impact.[29] This approach is significant, because it outlines those situations in which a specific leadership style is not important or needed. Some situations may be almost self-contained in the sense that situational factors may replace the need for leadership involvement. Other situations need task- and people-oriented leaders to help the group perform effectively.

Kerr and Jermier distinguished between situations that substitute for or neutralize leadership style. **Substitutes** for leadership make leader behavior unnecessary and redundant. Substitutes provide either the personal relationships or the task structure subordinates need so that leaders do not have to perform this function. An assembly line creates highly structured tasks, so the leader need not initiate structure for subordinates. **Neutralizers** are situational characteristics that prevent the leader from implementing the leadership function. If the leader is physically set apart too far from subordinates, for example, or if subordinates are uninterested in available rewards, then the impact of leader behavior is neutralized.

Exhibit 13.7 shows the situational variables that tend to substitute for or neutralize relationship- and task-oriented leadership. Based on their research into leader behaviors, Kerr and Jermier argued that the fourteen characteristics in the diagram reduce leadership impact.

- *Subordinate.* When subordinates have ability, experience, training, independence, and a professional orientation, then leadership functions are less important. High-quality employees do not need as much task direction or as much consideration and concern. Employees' indifference toward organizational rewards also tends to neutralize leader behavior, because subordinates do not respond to leader influence.
- *Task.* Tasks that are unambiguous, routine, and repetitious, and provide feedback directly to the employee tend to substitute for task-oriented leadership style. The task provides all the direction that it needed, so leader direction is redundant. Tasks that are intrinsically satisfying tend to substitute for people-centered leadership.
- *Organization.* Extensive plans, procedures, formalization, and organizational inflexibility tend to offset task-centered leadership. Closely knit, cohesive work groups substitute for both relationship- and task-oriented leaders. When the leader does not have power or control over organizational rewards, or when there is substantial distance between superiors and subordinates, then the leader is neutralized with respect to both relationship and task functions.

EXHIBIT 13.7
Substitutes for Leadership

Characteristic	Substitutes for Leadership Will Tend to Offset	
	Relationship-oriented, People-centered, Consideration Leadership	Task-oriented, Instrumental Job-centered, Initiating Structure Leadership
Of the Subordinate		
1. Ability, experience, training, knowledge		S
2. Need for independence	S	S
3. "Professional" orientation	S	S
4. Indifference toward organizational rewards	N	N
Of the Task		
5. Unambiguous and routine		S
6. Methodologically invariant		S
7. Provides its own feedback concerning accomplishment		S
8. Intrinsically satisfying	S	
Of the Organization		
9. Formatization (explicit plans, goals, and areas of responsibility		S
10. Inflexibility (rigid, unbending rules and procedures)		N
11. Highly specified and active advisory and staff functions		S
12. Closely knit, cohesive work groups	S	S
13. Organizational rewards not within the leader's control	N	N
14. Spatial distance betweens superior and subordinates	N	N

S = substitute, leader behavior is unnecessary and redundant

N = neutralizer, prevents or counteracts leader behavior

SOURCE: S. Kerr and J. Jermier, "Substitutes for Leadership: Their Meaning and Measurement," *Organizational Behavior and Human Performance*, 1978, 22, p. 378. Used with permission.

The leadership models discussed so far in this chapter are consistent with the situational substitutes and neutralizers in Exhibit 13.7. Leader impact is not equal in every situation. Subordinate, task, and organizational factors may replace the need for leader involvement. Just as important, there are many situations not listed in Exhibit 13.7 in which leader impact is vital. When subordinates lack experience and professionalism, when tasks are nonroutine, and when the organization lacks plans and procedures, leader involvement is crucial. For the organization to be effective, the task and people needs must be met through leadership.

ORGANIZATIONAL LEADERSHIP

What do top leaders in organizations do? As discussed in Chapter 1 and earlier in this chapter, the view from the top is quite different from the views of lower and middle managers, because top leaders are responsible for the organization as a whole. Top leadership is a macro perspective, and the functions and responsibilities of top leaders are different from the functions and responsibilities of lower-level leaders. In his study of chief executive behavior, Henry Mintzberg answered the question of what top managers do. His research and follow-up work produced a number of interesting findings about top leaders.[30]

Top leaders perform much work at an unrelenting pace. Top leaders work hard and there is little break in the pace of activity. They have an average of eight meetings per day and process thirty-six pieces of mail. Coffee and lunchtime are devoted to meetings, and so a true break seldom occurs. Many top managers take work home four nights out of five. One reason managers adopt such an extraordinary pace and workload is the open-ended nature of the job. The top manager is responsible for the success of the organization, and there are no tangible indicators that say the task is complete.

Top leader activity is characterized by brevity, variety, and fragmentation. Managers have little time to concentrate. Something new happens every nine minutes on the average. Managers may be involved in hundreds of transactions each day. Even when secretaries and assistants are assigned to help top leaders, they receive an extraordinary number of interruptions.

The top leader sits between the organization and a network of contacts.[31] The top leader is an information processor. Top leaders exchange information with peers, with people outside the organization, with immediate subordinates, and with others throughout the organization. Top managers develop personal relationships that produce useful information, including gossip, advice, and ideas. Through these contacts the leader receives current, vital data about the state of affairs both inside and outside the organization.

A fast pace and continuous communication draw the leader into diverse activities. Mintzberg discovered that top leaders play at least ten roles during the course of their activities.[32] These roles include the development of interpersonal relationships, information processing, and decision making. Exhibit 13.8 illustrates the ten roles top managers play. The **interpersonal**

EXHIBIT 13.8
Ten Roles of Top Leaders

Interpersonal Roles	Informational Roles	Decisional Roles
1. Figurehead	4. Monitor	7. Entrepreneur
2. Leader	5. Disseminator	8. Disturbance Handler
3. Liaison	6. Spokesman	9. Resource Allocator
		10. Negotiator

SOURCE: Henry Mintzberg, *The Nature of Managerial Work* (New York: Harper & Row, 1973), Chapter 4.

roles pertain to relationships among people. The *figurehead* role takes on ceremonial activities of a routine nature. The *leader* role encompasses relations with subordinates, and the *liaison* role develops outside contacts and relations with peers. The **information roles** describe the activities needed to maintain and develop an information network. The *monitor* scans data from numerous sources. The *disseminator* forwards information to others throughout the organization. The *spokesman* role makes the official statements to outsiders on behalf of the organization. The **decisional roles** are also important, and through these roles the manager explicitly controls the organization. The *entrepreneurial* role is the way to initiate change, the *disturbance handler* role allows the resolution of conflict, the *resource allocator* role involves the distribution of resources to achieve desired outcomes, and the *negotiator* role is the bargaining to achieve resources and goals.

This view of top leaders proposed by Mintzberg and others is intriguing. Top leaders are extraordinarily busy, well-informed, and make important decisions. But to what end? These activities, information, and the decisions must achieve some purpose. Top managers are so busy and their work so fragmented that it is easy to lose track of their basic purpose in the organization. Mintzberg learned that top leaders were trying to accomplish specific outcomes, but they were unable to achieve the outcomes through long periods of concentrated effort. Rather, they used specific episodes and fragments to nudge the organization toward each purpose in an incremental manner. The hard work and fragmented activities are not random. These activities are designed to accomplish two overall functions similar to the leadership functions discussed previously in this chapter—initiating structure and consideration. The two major functions of top leaders are as follows.[33]

The top leader must determine the organization's goals and strategy, and therein adapt the organization to a changing environment. By defining strategy and goals, the top leader initiates structure and gives direction to the organization. The appropriate strategy is often a response to threats and opportunities in the external environment. The monitor and disseminator roles serve as an informational link between the organization and environment. The decisional roles of entrepreneur and resource allocator are means to implement the strategy deemed important to organizational success. The liaison role helps link up important constituents both inside and outside the organization.

The top leader must influence the cultural values within the organization, and therein maintain the stability and integrity of organizational operations. By influencing corporate culture, top leaders can establish the tone and values important to the "people needs" within the organization. The top leader sets an example for cooperation, relationships, and values that encourages employee commitment to the organization. The top leader articulates and implements the values that enable the organization to function as a cohesive unit through the roles of leader, figurehead, spokesman, and disturbance handler.

It is important to understand that the formulation of organizational goals and strategy is analogous to the dimension of initiating structure described in our earlier leadership models, only now the leader is concerned with the entire organization. Influencing internal culture so the organization will operate as a cohesive unit is analogous to the dimension of consideration. Strategy and culture are basic responsibilities of top leaders. Because these two functions are important to the organization, we will briefly discuss each and explain how it relates to organizational success.

Organizational Strategy

Organizational strategy is the set of plans, decisions, and objectives an organization adopts to achieve its goals.[34] Recall from Chapter 11 that goals pertain to the desired future state of the organization. Strategy is oriented toward the future and toward the external environment. Strategy is designed to help the organization identify a path through the environment that will accomplish future goals. *Strategy formulation* is the process of choosing a strategy, formulating policies and objectives, and defining the organization's mission. *Strategy implementation* is the use of organization structure, resource allocation, and control systems appropriate to achieve the strategy.[35] Strategy formulation is outward looking and seeks a fit between organizational goals and environmental opportunities and threats. Strategy implementation is inward looking and concerned with the structure, work activities, and resource allocation that will ensure the strategy is followed.

Strategy is important because it determines success or failure of the firm. Strategy provides direction to all other employees within the organization. The wrong strategy in market identification or product development can cause the organization to fail. The right strategy can mean enormous success.

One classic example of how strategies can lead to success or failure occurred in the retail industry shortly after World War II.[36] Sears Roebuck and Montgomery Ward were similar in size and were engaged in direct competition. Top managers at Sears perceived the environmental characteristics of growing economic prosperity and population migration to the suburbs. Top leaders at Sears decided to undertake aggressive expansion and move the stores from urban to suburban locations. Sears borrowed heavily and built large stores in major shopping centers throughout the country.

Top managers at Montgomery Ward adopted a different strategy. Sewell Avery, the chief executive, believed a severe depression would follow the war. Wards decided not to build new stores. They adopted a cost-cutting strategy to save cash to make investments during the coming business downturn. Wards' strategy turned out to be a mistake. They misdiagnosed the external environment. Wards fell way behind Sears and would forever be smaller. Wards was never again a well-matched competitor in the retail industry. Sears is now four times the size of Wards and continues to grow.

Business strategies can be classified according to whether they are prospectors, defenders, or analyzers.[37] The **prospector** strategy is characterized by aggressiveness and expansion. Top leaders anticipate a dynamic, growing demand from the environment. The market is believed to be increasing in size. The strategy is to seek new market opportunities and invest in new products and extensive advertising. The strategy is implemented through the creation of a diverse internal structure that is flexible and loosely controlled to encourage growth and change. Top leaders at Sears adopted a prospector strategy after World War II. Top leaders at Goodyear recently adopted a prospector strategy in the tire industry.[38] They are investing several hundred million dollars in new tire plants, anticipating that consumer driving will increase rather than decrease despite threatened shortages of gasoline.

The **defender** strategy is at the opposite extreme. This strategy is characterized by stability and retrenchment. Top leaders perceive that environmental demand is not growing. The market is stable or declining. The strategy is to protect market share and the customer base the business has. Top managers strive for efficient internal production and tight control as a source of profit. The strategy adopted by top leaders at Wards after World War II is an example of a defender strategy. Firestone has also adopted a defender strategy in the 1980s. Firestone's managers closed five domestic plants and plan no new factories. They are expecting the demand for tires to decline, and do not want to be caught with excess capacity.

The **analyzer** strategy is intermediate between the prospector and defender. The environment is changing at a moderate rate. Top leaders want to maintain the stable business while gradually innovating in selected product lines. Top leaders work to protect the customer base they have, but also devote some attention to locating new opportunities. This strategy is implemented with a structure that provides tight control over existing activities but looser control for growing product lines and new activities.

Strategy formulation is one of the most difficult tasks within organizations, because decision making is so uncertain. Leaders try to analyze the environment and internal factors, but the decisions often represent an educated guess, and many strategies turn out to be wrong. Once top management decides on a strategy, it is important that they adopt a strong "initiating structure" posture toward the rest of the organization so the strategy gets a fair chance. The importance of sticking to the strategy is illustrated by the successful tenure of

Robert Townsend as the top leader at Avis Corporation. Avis grew rapidly because Robert Townsend kept everyone focused on the key objectives Avis was pursuing. In Townsend's own words:

> One of the important functions of a leader is to make the organization concentrate on its objectives. In the case of Avis, it took us six months to define one objective—which turned out to be: "We want to become the fastest-growing company with the highest profit margins in the business of renting and leasing vehicles without drivers."
>
> That objective was simple enough so that we didn't have to write it down. We could put it in every speech and talk about it wherever we went. And it had some social significance, because up to that time Hertz had a crushingly large share of the market and was thinking and acting like General Motors.
>
> It also included a definition of our business: "renting and leasing vehicles without drivers." This let us put the blinders on ourselves and stop considering the acquisition of related businesses like motels, hotels, airlines, and travel agencies. It also showed us that we had to get rid of some limousine and sightseeing companies that we already owned.
>
> Once these objectives are agreed on, the leader must be merciless on himself and on his people. If an idea that pops into his head or out of their mouths is outside the objectives of the company, he kills it without a trial.[39]

Organizational Culture

Top leaders influence the people needs of the organization through culture. **Culture** is the shared values, beliefs, language, and symbols of employees within an organization. Culture represents the organization's unwritten rules and values. Culture provides employees with a sense of what they ought to do and how they ought to behave. Culture pertains to the feeling, emotional part of the organization. It enables the employees to identify with something larger than themselves. Culture also enhances social system stability and serves to guide and shape employee behavior.[40] J. C. Penney has a dominant value in its culture of taking care of employees and customers. Customers are expected to receive fair value. One store manager was reprimanded by the president for making too much profit, which was unfair to customers. Customers are encouraged to return merchandise with no questions asked. Employees are encouraged to participate in the decision making process, and layoffs are avoided. Employees who fail in one job are transferred to a new job rather than fired. Employees know they are valued by the Penney's organization.[41]

How do managers influence cultural values within organizations? Culture tends to have a life of its own, and it changes slowly. But top managers are prominent and visible, and more than anyone they can influence the direction and nature of internal culture.

The most powerful tool of cultural influence is symbolic management. Top executives do not drive trucks or run machines. They deal in symbols.[42] Top managers signal values and goals to organizational participants through their public statements, activities, and ceremonies. Employees watch top executives to learn what counts in the organization. Top managers also use conventional means of influencing cultures, such as the training and socialization of new employees, and communicating management philosophy and values in both written and spoken forms. Written memos and reports have some influence, but the top manager's strongest weapon for influencing culture is the use of symbols. The two types of symbols most frequently used by top managers are 1) language and 2) activity, ritual, and ceremony.[43]

Language   *Language* includes the use of public statements and metaphors to communicate to a large number of employees. Managers can consciously select words and phrases that capture the essence of organizational culture. At J. C. Penney, the founder laid down seven guiding principles, called the "Penney Idea," that brought forth tremendous loyalty from staff and customers. T. J. Watson, Jr. used the metaphor "wild ducks" to describe the type of employee needed by IBM.[44] Wild ducks symbolized the atmosphere of freedom and opportunity that must be prevalent to keep creative employees at IBM. Tom Clausen, CEO at Bank of America, always talked about "laying pipe." This is shorthand for the need for two-way communication among bank departments and between Clausen's office and others. Effective communication enables the bank to anticipate events and ready a response. "Laying pipe" communicates the need for a cooperative atmosphere.[45]

Other values that have been communicated through the use of language to organizational employees are the following.

People are our most important resource and asset; therefore, we will never have a layoff.

Ideas can come from anywhere in this organization so we must maintain a climate of total openness.

The only way to manage a growing business is to hire good people, give them clear responsibility, and leave them alone.

The customer is the key to our success, so we must be totally dedicated to total customer service.[46]

Top leaders in organizations can influence the internal culture by taking advantage of every opportunity to transmit their ideas and values to employees. The effective use of language can communicate an essential value throughout a vast corporation. Effective top leaders are aware of their impact and use language to ensure the culture is consistent with the "people needs" as well as the strategy of the organization.

Activity, Ritual, and Ceremony   *Rituals* and *ceremonies* are periodic rites that communicate important values to employees. *Activities* represent the day-to-day work involvement of top managers, which signals those things managers consider important. An example of ritual is an annual Christmas party through which certain awards or bonuses may be made. Every Christmas at one major Midwestern firm, the chairman of the board would come down from his office on the top floor to walk through every department, shaking hands with each employee. This was the only time he would be seen by many, and this ritual served as a symbol of concern for his "family."[47]

Watson at IBM used elaborate rituals to instill the appropriate company spirit. The Hundred Percent Club rewarded sales representatives who had succeeded in fulfilling their quota. Special conventions were held and awards were passed out to Club members. Through the use of ritual and ceremony, attaining one hundred percent of quota became the dominant value in the IBM culture.[48]

One example of how chief executive activities can communicate values occurred when Roy Ash took over at Addressograph-Multigraph. Rather than write his ideas and distribute them through memos, Ash demonstrated them. Employees did not communicate with one another face-to-face, so Ash left his office door open, answered his own telephone, and sought out people in person to help break down the bureaucracy. He had several copying machines removed to stop breeding paperwork. He became aware of a complaint from an important customer in Minneapolis, so Ash personally visited the customer to resolve it. This action demonstrated that employees must work to satisfy customers. His most dramatic move was to relocate company headquarters to Los Angeles. Ash justified the move as necessary to provide a new setting to give employees a different idea of the company's future. For much the same reason, he also changed the corporation's name to A-M Corporation, which symbolizes the lean, responsive company of the future.[49]

Top leaders are concerned with the organization as a whole. Chief executives perform the functions of *initiating structure* and *consideration*, just as lower-level leaders do. Strategy is the mechanism through which top managers initiate structure for the organization, and culture is the mechanism through which they are considerate of the social needs of employees. A manager who understands and takes advantage of the symbolic role of the top leader to influence both strategy and culture is Jim Treybig of Tandem Computers. He helped the company evolve an internal culture and a strategy that are just right for it.

UP CLOSE 13.4:   Tandem Computers

At four o'clock every Friday afternoon, the employee beer bust is in full swing at Tandem Computers' offices around the country. Every week 60 percent of the company drops in at the beer bust for an hour, joined by visiting customers and suppliers. President Jim Treybig does not confine the fun to Fridays. Last year they had a Halloween costume party. Another big event was the "incredible hunk" contest sponsored by the company female employees.

Is this company for real? After only seven and a half years, Tandem is selling over $300 million a year and is on Fortune's second 500 list. Despite all the fun, *success has not been an accident. Treybig picked the right strategy and developed an internal culture to enhance it. The strategy is to build foolproof computers for a precise market niche: on-line computer operations, like bank transactions or hotel bookings, where it is critical that a system never garble the data. Tandem accomplishes this by providing two computers, working in tandem, that split the workload evenly. If one half has a problem, the entire burden shifts to the other half to guard the data from contamination. Treybig reinforces his strategy by giving stock options to every employee in the company. He also makes sure employees understand the consequence of mistakes. He explains the business and the five-year plan, and shows them how a little oversight, such as shipping several computers late, can drop profits, which in turn leaves less money for research and employee incentives.*

Treybig is even more serious about his five cardinal points for running a company, which define the Tandem culture.

1. *All people are good.*
2. *People, workers, management, and company are all the same thing.*
3. *Every single person in a company must understand the essence of the business.*
4. *Every employee must benefit from the company's success.*
5. *You must create an environment where all of the above can happen.*

Employees are soaked in an endless stream of company information urging loyalty, hard work, and respect for co-workers. New employees go to orientation lectures and breakfasts, receive newsletters and glossy magazines, and study the mandatory volume entitled, Understanding Our Philosophy, *which is the core of a two-day course.*

Everyone learns that employee welfare is taken very, very seriously at Tandem. For example, Understanding Our Philosophy *says "You never have the right at Tandem to screw a person or to mistreat them. It's not allowed . . ." After reading these kinds of statements in the handbook, any employee will be quick to complain if mistreated, and there are many managers who will listen.*

One reason the culture works is that Tandem is able to select compatible people. One stock clerk came for four interviews, taking about four hours. A potential middle manager can expect twenty grueling hours of interviews, both with top-level managers and prospective peers.

Treybig is a symbol, almost a hero. He symbolizes single-minded hard work and concern for people. Without question the system works. Tandem's productivity figures are among the highest in the industry. And the employees love it. They say the culture helps them grow. The rich opportunities for promotion, learning, and initiative are great for the self-image of employees, and lets them move toward achieving their goals of self realization.

The morale is fantastic and Treybig is convinced continued growth is inevitable. He recently announced plans to expand the $300 million company of 3000 employees into a $1 billion company of 11,000 employees over the next three years. Most people think he can do it.[50] ■

The language of the company's five cardinal rules and its book of philosophy, combined with the ceremonial Friday beer bust and other parties, is an effective way of communicating corporate culture. But Treybig also gives strategic direction to the firm, and the strategy is to increase the market share in the area of fail-safe computers. The combination of strategy and structure is why Treybig has had enormous impact on the growth and success of Tandem Computers.

SUMMARY

This chapter has been about organizational leadership. Leadership is defined as the process through which one person influences other people's behavior toward the accomplishment of a goal. Leadership involves people, influence, and goal accomplishment. Leadership is important because through leaders the practice of management is implemented in organizations. Each topic studied in this book is implemented through the ability of leaders to influence people to accomplish organizational and group goals.

Consideration and initiating structure are fundamental leader attributes discovered from leadership research. These behavioral attributes sometimes go by different names, such as people orientation and task orientation, but the terms all represent the people versus task dimensions of organizations. These two concepts are relevant to leadership at all levels in the organization, although leadership requirements change with hierarchical level. Lower levels are concerned with technical knowledge of tasks, the efficient production of goods, and rewards and sanctions for employees. Top levels are concerned with the overall strategy and planning for the organization's relationship with the environment, and for the internal cultural values of the organization.

Two contingency theories of leadership were discussed. The Fiedler model relates leadership style to the situational factors of leader-member relations, task structures, and position power. Task-oriented leaders tend to perform best in situations highly favorable or unfavorable to the leader, while people-oriented leaders do best in situations of intermediate favorability. The path-goal model defines the role of leaders as helping subordinates identify the path to the goal or to increase rewards for achieving the goal. The path-goal model suggests that directive, supportive, achievement-oriented, or participative leadership styles may be appropriate, depending on the situation.

Finally, the functions of top leaders in organizations were discussed. Research into top manager behavior indicates that these managers perform a great deal of work at a fast pace and spend most of their time processing information and building a communication network both inside and outside the organization. The fast pace and diverse activities are the ways top managers perform their basic functions—taking charge of the organization's strategy-making machinery and influencing the internal culture. Organizational strategy is essential to organizational success, and the manager must formulate and implement strategy congruent with organizational goals and environmental changes. Internal culture represents the internal values and beliefs shared by employees. Top managers influence internal culture through symbols such as language, ceremony, and ritual.

KEY WORDS

achievement-oriented leadership	informational roles	position
affective dimension	initiating structure	prospector
analyzer	interpersonal roles	situation favorableness
cognitive dimension	job-centered leaders	substitutes for leadership
consideration	leadership	top leader roles
culture	least-preferred coworker	
decisional roles	neutralizers	
defender	organizational strategy	
employee-centered leaders	participative leadership	
	path-goal theory	

DISCUSSION QUESTIONS

1. What is leadership? Why is it important?
2. What behavioral characteristics of leaders are most important? What conclusion can be drawn about the relationship between these characteristics and leader effectiveness?
3. What is the basic finding of Fiedler's contingency theory of leadership? Can you identify situational factors not in the model that may influence leader performance? Discuss.
4. What is the path-goal theory of leadership? What is different about this model compared to other leadership theories?
5. What is meant by substitutes for leadership? What is meant by neutralizers? Do these factors mean leaders are not needed? Explain.
6. Discuss the concept of organizational strategy. How does it relate to the concepts of initiating structure for consideration?
7. What is organizational culture? Describe the tools managers can use to influence internal culture?
8. To what extent does the content of top leaders' jobs differ from the jobs of lower-level leaders? Why?

CASE 13.1:   Budget Motors, Inc.

Plant Y was the largest and oldest of six assembly plants of Econocar division, a subsidiary of Budget Motors, Inc. It had close to 10,000 employees and was managed by Mr. Wickstrom. During the last few years, it fell behind all the others in performance. Not unexpectedly, headquarter management (HQM) started showing some uneasiness as there were signs that things would not improve in the foreseeable future. In its attempt to straighten things out, it has exerted steady pressure and issued specific directions for local plant management to follow.

Wickstrom was a respected and competent manager. He was not new to the responsibility of running a large plant. After all, he came up the hard way through the ranks, and was well known for his ambition, technical competence, human-relations skills, and hard work. Moreover, he was a no-nonsense manager, well liked by his subordinates. Under his leadership, plant Y had performed adequately until the energy and environmental crises teamed up to hit the auto industry really hard in the early 1970s. At that time, in all six plants, there was a hysteria to fill the demand for little compacts that are economically cheap to run and environmentally safe to use. The speed of the lines was stepped up, three-shift operations were begun, workers (mostly immigrants) were hired, and a large number of managers had to be placed in new jobs.

Although all the plants of the Econocars division had their share of the stress and strain inherent in the sudden changeover from bigger to smaller cars, the managers of these plants adapted themselves differently to this new development in the market situation. Instead of comparing Wickstrom's adaptive behavior with that of his counterparts in other plants, we would rather concentrate on contrasting his style with that of Mr. Rhenman, his successor in the same plant. Following are some examples that illustrate how Wickstrom tried to cope with this crisis atmosphere:

- One day, while doing his regular plant tour, he personally ordered the foreman of a given section to change the sequence of assembling the instrument panels. He thought this change would speed up the operation. When his production manager, Mr. Aberg, found out about the new system, he got upset because it disturbed the schedule. He went to see Wickstrom in his office and to make a new suggestion about the sequencing—one that coordinated Wickstrom's plan with his own. Much to Aberg's surprise, Wickstrom reacted in a rude manner and told Aberg that things would remain the way he had ordered.

- When Wickstrom read the weekly performance record of the body assembly line, he flew into a terrific temper and called in the foreman of this line, Jorgen, to his office and threatened to fire him if the production was not speeded up. This tactic shook up Jorgen who instantly thought of the incident two weeks before when his colleague, Ulf, had indeed been fired. He tried to justify the slowness of production by complaining that he was operating against overwhelming handicaps: antiquated and rundown equipment, inexperienced workforce, and uninteresting and noninvolving job structure. Unfortunately, nobody cared to listen to him.

- One day the supply of electric power for the plant was reduced and the next day it was shut off completely. This was due to a breakdown in the power station outside the plant. It was not Wickstrom's policy to run the plant by committee meetings, but faced with this crisis at hand, he summoned a meeting of the production managers and the foremen. It was clear the electric company would need at least a week to repair its network. The upshot of the meeting was a decision to shut down production and to seek union's support for half pay for the workers in exchange for two days of paid holidays. Upon submitting the minutes of this meeting to the HQM, his decisions were vetoed immediately. The HQM argued that since economical compacts sell almost as fast as they can be rolled off lines, production should not stop and that a mobile auxiliary power unit be brought in, no matter what its cost would be. This proved to be a very expensive proposition and it also meant a lot of trouble for workers and managers alike. For no sooner had Wickstrom called his second meeting to give his top aides the feedback he received from the HQM, when some of his managers angrily protested this high-handed interference in their "domestic affairs." Here again, they said, is one more example of "the H.Q. boys telling us how to run our show." Other plant managers, equally concerned, blamed their boss, Wickstrom, for his inability to stand by his guns, fight with the HQM and challenge its excessive domination, as other plant managers did. They felt they were put at the order-receiving side, which had no real feeling for what was going on in the plant.

Some plant managers further complained that carrying out daily instructions from HQM had become Wickstrom's chief preoccupation. Managers in such staff services as accounting, quality control, material control, and personnel also complained that they themselves were receiving too many specific orders from HQM. Like their line counterparts, they generally resented this controlling behavior on the part of the HQM. They complained that they were no longer allowed to run their own departments or stations, or to manage within their sphere of competence. This, in turn, left them no choice but to withdraw legitimate authority from their immediate subordinates and interfere in the handling of the subordinates' affairs, thereby compounding the problem through the hierarchy.

In responding to the voices from below, HQM argued that the trouble with plant Y lay in Wickstrom's lack of control rather than in bad equipment, boring jobs, and inexperienced personnel.

With the intensification of the energy crisis caused by the sudden outbreak of the Mideast War of October 1973, the demand for little cars far outstripped the available supply. Being dissatisfied with plant Y's performance, HQM decided to replace Wickstrom with Rhenman. The latter accepted the job on condition that he should have "carte blanche" in running his own show for a reasonable period of time. This he got from HQM, which also assured him that there would be no interference and that he was free to proceed in any manner he saw fit.

At the outset, Rhenman indicated that although HQM thought the dead wood should be removed from the staff, he disagreed and would give everyone ample opportunity to prove their worth. (It developed, in fact, that only a handful of people in an organization of 10,000 were dismissed during his regime.) He asked for money from HQM to modernize the plant, starting first with the cafeteria and washrooms used by blue-collar workers. Rhenman also went to the cafeteria during lunch hours, mingled with workers, foremen, and the lower-level managers. He not only listened to their complaints, he also secured their cooperation and suggestions. He encouraged groups to meet regularly to solve common problems and, more importantly, to engage his long-range planning and consultation to prevent daily crises. His foremen often met informally, thereby increasing lateral communication. He structured an ongoing problem-solving dialogue between his staff and line personnel. Through this dialogue, staff personnel had learned how irrelevant or self-defensive their services had been in the line. He inspired confidence and loyalty and erased the fear-and-crisis syndrome that had prevailed. He did not change the formal organization structure of the plant. He expected his managers to set goals for their units and be responsible for their achievements. He delegated to them the requisite authority and left them alone to perform their jobs.

Now, after about six months in his job, plant Y has started heading toward a rebound. Its performance record shows marked improvements. Rhenman was promoted to a top executive job at the HQ. Interestingly enough, plant Y is performing well without him. On the other hand, Wickstrom was given an early retirement.[51]

CASE QUESTIONS

1. Using the material from the book dealing with Fiedler's description of leadership, describe Wickstrom's situation and leadership style.

2. How would the path-goal model describe the situation and what leadership style would be predicted to be effective? What style did Rhenman use?
3. How would you describe the organization culture under Wickstrom? How did Rhenman change the culture?

NOTES

1. "How Steve Ross's Hands-Off Approach is Backfiring at Warner," *Business Week*, August 8, 1983, pp. 70–71.
2. Julie Salamon, "Acquisitive Chief of Buffalo Savings Buys Time, Cleans House—and Makes Big Splash," *The Wall Street Journal*, April 23, 1982, pp. 33–36.
3. R. Tannenbaum, I. R. Weschler, and F. Massarik, *Leadership and Organization* (New York: McGraw-Hill, 1961), p. 24.
4. "Can Don Lennox Save Harvester?", *Business Week*, August 15, 1983, pp. 80–84.
5. Robert Johnson and Frederick C. Klein, "School Superintendent in Chicago Generates Change, Controversy," *The Wall Street Journal*, April 4, 1984, pp. 1–20.
6. Keith Davis, *Human Relations at Work: The Dynamics of Organizational Behavior*, 3rd ed. (New York: McGraw-Hill, 1967), p. 96.
7. D. Katz and R. Kahn, *The Social Psychology of Organizations*, 2d ed. (New York: Wiley, 1978).
8. R. M. Stogdill, "Personal Factors Associated with Leadership: A Survey of the Literature," Journal of Psychology 25 (1948): 35–71.
9. R. M. Stogdill, *Handbook of Leadership: A Survey of Theory and Research* (New York: Free Press, 1974).
10. Francis Likert, *New Patterns of Management* (New York: McGraw-Hill, 1961); Francis Likert, *The Human Organization* (New York: McGraw-Hill, 1967); D. Katz, N. Maccoby, and N. Morse, *Productivity, Supervision, and Morale in an Office Situation* (Ann Arbor, MI: Institute for Social Research, 1950).
11. Likert, *New Patterns of Management*, and *The Human Organization*.
12. Ralph M. Stogdill and A. E. Coons (eds.), *Leader Behavior: Its Description and Measurement*, Research monograph no. 88 (Columbus, OH: Bureau of Business Research, Ohio State University, 1957); S. Kerr, C. Schriesheim, C. Murphy, and R. Stogdill, "Toward a Contingency Theory of Leadership Based Upon the Consideration and Initiating Structure Literature," *Organizational Behavior and Human Performance* 12 (1974): 62–82.
13. Gary A. Yukl, *Leadership in Organizations* (Englewood Cliffs, NJ: Prentice-Hall, 1981), pp. 108–113.
14. Robert R. Blake and Jane S. Mouton, *The Managerial Grid* (Houston: Gulf Publishing Co., 1964).
15. Steven Flax, "The Toughest Bosses in America," *Fortune*, August 6, 1984, pp. 18–23.
16. Lucian Rhodes, "The Passion of Robert Swiggett," *Inc.*, April, 1984, pp. 121–139.
17. Fred E. Fiedler, *A Theory of Leadership Effectiveness* (New York: McGraw-Hill, 1967).
18. Fielder, *A Theory of Leadership Effectiveness*.
19. Fielder, *A Theory of Leadership Effectiveness*.
20. Fielder, *A Theory of Leadership Effectiveness;* Fred E. Fiedler and M. M. Chamers, *Leadership and Effective Management* (Glenview, IL: Scott, Foresman, 1974).
21. Yukl, *Leadership in Organizations*.
22. Yukl, *Leadership in Organizations;* Chester A. Schriesheim, B. D. Bannister and W. H. Money, "Psychometric Properties of the LPC Scale: An Extension of Rice's Review," *Academy of Management Review* 4 (1979): 287–294.
23. Damon Darlin, "Road Can Be Bumpy When New Chief Acts to Enliven His Firm," *The Wall Street Journal*, September 17, 1984, pp. 1–22.
24. Martin G. Evans, "The Effects of Supervisory Behavior on the Path-Goal Relationship," *Organizational Behavior and Human Performance* (1970): 277–98; Robert J. House, "A

Path-Goal Theory of Leader Effectiveness," *Administrative Science Quarterly* 16, (1971): 321–332.

25. Robert J. House and Terence R. Mitchell, "Path-Goal Theory of Leadership," *Journal of Contemporary Business*, Autumn 1974, p. 86.

26. House and Mitchell, "Path-Goal Theory of Leadership."

27. Yukl, *Leadership in Organizations*, pp. 151–153.

28. Stratford, P. Sherman, "Muddling To Victory at Geico," *Fortune*, September 5, 1983, pp. 66–80.

29. S. Kerr, and J. Jermier, "Substitutes for Leadership: Their Meaning and Measurement," *Organizational Behavior and Human Performance* 22 (1978): 375–403.

30. Henry Mintzberg, *The Nature of Managerial Work* (New York: Harper & Row, 1973); Henry Mintzberg, "Managerial Work: Analysis from Observation," *Management Science* 18 (1971): B97–B110; Lance B. Kurke, "Mintzberg Was Right!: A Replication and Extension of *The Nature of Managerial Work*," *Management Science* 29 (1983): 975–984.

31. Robert E. Kaplan, "Trade Routes: The Manager's Network of Relationships," *Organizational Dynamics* (Spring 1984): 37–52.

32. Mintzberg, *The Nature of Managerial Work*, Chapter 4.

33. John P. Kotter, "What Effective General Managers Really Do," *Harvard Business Review* (November–December, 1982): 156–167; Mintzberg, *The Nature of Managerial Work.*

34. Henry Mintzberg, "Patterns in Strategy Formulation," *Management Science* 24 (1978): 934–938; Lloyd L. Byars, *Strategic Management* (New York: Harper & Row, 1984).

35. Byars, *Strategic Management.*

36. Milton Leontiades, *Strategies for Diversification and Change* (Boston: Little, Brown) 1980, p. 63.

37. Raymond E. Miles and Charles C. Snow, *Organizational Strategy, Structure, and Process* (New York: McGraw-Hill, 1978).

38. Ralph E. Winter, "Goodyear, Firestone Split on Future Demand for Tires," *The Wall Street Journal*, February 13, 1981, p. 21; Ralph E. Winter and Paul Ingrassia, "Chief's Style and Ideas Help to Keep Goodyear No. 1 in the Radial Age," *The Wall Street Journal*, January 18, 1983, pp. 1–20.

39. Robert Townsend, *Up the Organization* (New York: Alfred A. Knopf, 1974), pp. 129–130. Used with permission.

40. Linda Smircich, "Concepts of Culture and Organizational Analysis," *Administrative Science Quarterly* 28, 1983, pp. 339–358.

41. "Corporate Culture: The Hard-to-Change Values that Spell Success or Failure," *Business Week*, October 27, 1980, pp. 148–160.

42. Thomas J. Peters, "Symbols, Patterns, and Settings: An Optimistic Case for Getting Things Done," *Organizational Dynamics* (Autumn 1978): 2–23.

43. Vijay Sathe, "Implications of Corporate Culture: A Manager's Guide to Action," *Organizational Dynamics* (Autumn 1983): 5–23.

44. Richard Ott, "Are Wild Ducks Really Wild: Symbolism and Behavior in the Corporate Environment," paper presented at the Northeastern Anthropological Association, March, 1979.

45. Thomas J. Peters, "Management Systems: The Language of Organizational Character and Competence," *Organizational Dynamics* (Summer 1980): 3–26.

46. Edgar H. Schein, "The Role of the Founder in the Creation of Organizational Culture," technical report, ONR 12, Sloan School of Management, Massachusetts Institute of Technology, March 1983.

47. Thomas C. Dandridge, "Symbols at Work," working paper, School of Business, State University of New York at Albany, 1978.

48. Ott, "Are Wild Ducks Really Wild."

49. L. Kraar, "Roy Ash is Having Fun at Addressogrief-Multigrief," *Fortune*, February 27, 1978, pp. 46–52.

50. Myron Magnet, "Managing by Mystique at Tandem Computers," *Fortune*, June 28, 1982, pp. 84–91; T. E. Deal and A. A. Kennedy, *Corporate Cultures: The Rites and Rituals of Corporate Life* (Reading, MA: Addison-Wesley, 1982), pp. 3–19.

51. Sami Kassem, University of Toledo, Toledo, Ohio. Used with permission.

14 Decision Making

T op management at Fiat, Italy's largest private company, blundered in 1974. Under pressure from labor unions and the government to pay high wages and witnessing quadrupled oil prices, management decided there was little future in the automobile. Income was invested in other industries, new models were delayed, and Fiat lost market share at home and abroad. By 1979, Fiat was weaker than ever before in its history, so management started on a new course. Billions of dollars were invested to develop a new generation of light, highly electronic, fuel-efficient cars. Robots and other forms of automation were used to increase productivity. International joint ventures with companies like France's Peugeot led to new opportunities for the development of engines and trucks. By 1984, the decisions proved successful. Fiat's new car lines are selling rapidly, and productivity is so good the company will continue to increase profits even if sales remain stable. Fiat's auto operations will earn the highest profits in the company's history.[1]

In 1974, Fiat's management moved the company away from the auto business with disastrous results. In 1979 management reversed itself and invested heavily again in the auto business, taking the chance that this would lead to better profits. These moves are examples of organizational decision making, and the purpose of this chapter is to explore how decisions are made within organizations. Managers make decisions to solve problems and to take advantage of opportunities. A few decisions are made by solitary individuals working alone within the company. Other decisions are made through wide-spread participation and may affect the company as a whole. Many decisions are straightforward and easy, other decisions are complex and difficult. In this chapter we will define decision making and examine the types of decisions made in organizations. The micro perspective on decision making includes decisions made by individual managers and by leaders of work groups. The macro perspective pertains to organizational-level decisions, which involve managers representing several departments. After examining decision making at both the individual and organizational levels of analysis, we will discuss decision shortcomings in organizations and review techniques for improving the quality of decision making.

RELEVANCE OF DECISION MAKING FOR MANAGERS

Many people refer to managers as "decision makers." Managers perform a number of roles in organizations, as discussed in the previous chapter, and one of the most important roles is decision making. Decision making takes place constantly within organizations. Every organizational action is preceded by a decision. Analyzing and understanding the process by which organizational decisions are made can make managers more effective, for several reasons.

Decision making is one of management's primary responsibilities. If leadership can be called the heart and soul of an organization, then decision making is the brain and nervous system of the organization. Decision making involves the acquisition of information about the organization and the external environment, the detection of shortcomings or discrepancies in expected behavior and performance, analysis of events and alternatives, and the implementation of new courses of action. The decision at Fiat to reinvest billions of dollars in auto making was no accident; rather it was the outcome of an explicit process. Decision making is a conscious activity that may involve allocating scarce resources, hiring employees, investing capital, or introducing new products. Managers spend a large portion of their time processing information, and this information is used to make decisions. If they are to perform effectively, managers need to be aware of the basic processes by which decisions are made.

Decision making may involve the participation of subordinates. One of the most difficult questions facing managers is when to involve subordinates in the decision-making process. Managers know that participation is a way to motivate employees. Yet in some cases employees have little knowledge, experience, or information relevant to decision outcomes. In other cases employees may have more knowledge and experience than the manager. Employee participation may also make implementation of the decision easier. When subordinates understand the decision rationale, they willingly undertake new activities. Since everyone cannot be involved in every decision, the decision-making process provides guidelines for when to involve subordinates or other managers in the decision-making process and when it is appropriate to make decisions alone.

Decision making helps the organization learn. As we discussed in Chapter 10 on the environment, organizations operate in a world of uncertainty. When external conditions change, managers are not certain how to achieve organizational goals. Under conditions of uncertainty, many decisions just don't work out. Decisions produce errors. Yet it is through occasional mistakes that the organization learns to succeed. Managers who are afraid to make a decision because it may be wrong prevent the organization from learning. When Fiat decided to invest in non-automobile businesses, it learned that the automobile business was more important to its long-run success than managers previously realized. Decision making is a trial-and-error process. Organizations move ahead gradually, undertaking new activities based on manager decisions.

Decisions that fail can be as important as decisions that succeed. Of course managers should use all available information to make the best decisions possible. But the organization learns by trying things even if some don't work. New decisions can minimize the mistakes and increase the chances for a successful outcome.

DEFINITION OF DECISION MAKING

Decision making is the process of finding and solving organizational problems. A *problem* exists when managers detect a gap between existing and desired levels of performance. Problems can arise in organizations because of a performance deficiency, because of a crisis, or because an opportunity increases the desired level of performance. Problem formulation and problem solution are two distinct aspects of the decision process, as Exhibit 14.1 indicates. Based on formal plans and managerial experience, managers have implicit models about appropriate organizational behavior and performance.[2] Managers monitor information that tells them whether activities match desired performance. **Problem formulation** involves the development of a desired model of performance, acquisition of information, and diagnosis of systems and triggering events that lead to problem detection. Once the problem and its causes have been defined, the problem-solving stage can unfold. **Problem solution** is the search for alternative answers or courses of action, appraising the feasibility of these alternatives, and choosing and implementing a potential solution.[3] Implementation may involve changes in organizational behavior and activities. After implementation, managers again monitor organizational activities to learn whether the problem has been solved or whether it is necessary to repeat the problem formulation stage.

Types of Decisions

The process of making decisions is affected by whether the decision is programmed or nonprogrammed.[4] **Programmed decisions** are made in response to problems that are repetitive and well defined. Many small problems occur repeatedly in organizations. These problems are common, and managers have well-defined performance criteria, clear information, and decision alternatives. The programmed decision process is characterized by high levels of certainty for both problem formulation and problem solution. Rules and procedures define exactly how to respond. Examples of programmed decisions include whether to admit an applicant to college, when to reimburse managers for travel expenses, the decision rule for replacing office equipment, and the response to an employee who misses a day of work without an excuse.

Nonprogrammed decisions are made in response to problems that are novel and poorly defined. Managers have not encountered the problem before, are not certain of desired performance levels, and wrestle with ambiguous, unclear information. The solution has to be creative and customized for the specific

EXHIBIT 14.1
The Problem Formulation and Solution Steps in Decision Making

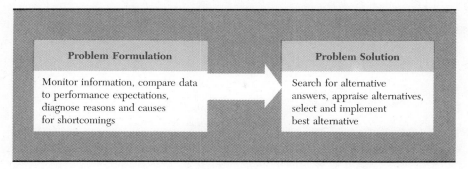

problem. The decision process is characterized by uncertainty. No rules or procedures tell managers how to proceed. Nonprogrammed problems include the General Motors' decision to reorganize because it was responding too slowly to environmental changes, the decision by Gulf & Western to undertake a joint venture with AT&T to foster innovations in information processing, and Levi Strauss's decision to construct a new headquarters building in San Francisco. These decisions are novel, enormously complex, and made in stages.

Hierarchical Level

Managers at all organizational levels make decisions, but there is a distinct relationship between hierarchical level and the extent to which decisions are programmed or nonprogrammed. As we discussed in Chapters 8 and 9, supervisors work within the technical core of the organization. Operations tend to be routinized. Bureaucratic rules and procedures tend to define the appropriate decision response when problems occur. Lower-level managers are concerned with a larger proportion of operational problems than are managers at middle and higher levels, as Exhibit 14.2 illustrates.

Top management decision making, by contrast, is characterized by nonprogrammed decisions. As we discussed in Chapter 13 on leadership, managers at this level are concerned with strategic issues pertaining to the relationship between the organization and the environment. Major decisions may be infrequent, but when a problem arises it is typically novel and complex. Top managers will not have clear information, and they may have to undertake an extensive search to understand and diagnose the causes of problems. The solution will be customized, and top managers may have little assurance that the solution will work. Top managers at Volkswagen, for example, have become increasingly aware of a major problem—decreasing sales in the United States. Top managers have focused a great deal of search and analysis on the decision to move into new models, such as the Golf and the redesigned Jetta, which they hope will regain some of the ground lost to the small cars built by Japanese and American competitors.[5]

EXHIBIT 14.2
Relationships of Decision Type to Management Level in Organizations

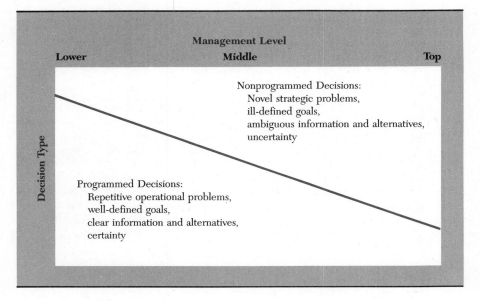

Middle-level management is responsible for both programmed and nonprogrammed decision making. Nonroutine problems from lower levels of the organization may be passed to middle levels for resolution. Middle-level managers also are concerned with coordination with other departments, structural design, and responses to the environment, all of which contain elements of uncertainty. The Dean at a business school may find that budget allocation is a programmed decision, based on a regular 3 percent increase allocated to each academic department over the previous year. An unexpected budget decrease of 15 percent, however, is a nonprogrammed problem, and the Dean will work with department heads to formulate a solution. Solutions could be a raise in auxiliary funds from outside the college or a reduction in expenses internally to minimize the damage from decreased resources. In the next section we will examine the micro perspective, looking at how individual managers make programmed and nonprogrammed decisions.

MANAGER DECISION MAKING

The Rational Model

A 1955 article in *Fortune* magazine pointed out that chief executives from some of the most important companies did not use a systematic process to arrive at their decisions.[6] This was a provocative observation, because it raised the question of whether business decision making might be closer to an intuitive art rather than a conscious, rational process. In contrast, Peter Drucker wrote that managers could lessen the burden of decision making if they would adopt a rational and systematic process that included a defined sequence of steps. Drucker defined the process as "defining the problem, defining expectations, developing alternative solutions, and knowing what to do after the decision was reached."[7]

The notion that decision making could be a rational, systematic process took hold, and a number of writers developed models of an ideal decision process. The rational model assumes that decisions maximize goal achievement and that people strive to be economically rational. Economic rationality means that people attempt to objectively maximize their advantage or outcome, such as money or the amount of goods produced. People try to identify and then select a course of action that has the greatest advantage or payoff. The rational model has sometimes been referred to as the "economic man" model of decision making.[8] An example of the rational decision process is shown in Exhibit 14.3. The model consists of six steps, three of which pertain to problem formulation and three to problem solution.[9]

1. *Monitor the decision environment.* This is an intelligence-gathering activity. Managers monitor internal and external information which would indicate the need for a decision, because of deviations from planned or acceptable behavior or because of a new opportunity.
2. *Define the problem.* The manager responds to a potential deviation by identifying whether a problem exists. The manager clarifies the criteria for successful performance and defines the performance gap.
3. *Diagnose the problem.* In this stage, the manager digs below the surface to analyze causes of the problem. Understanding the underlying cause enables the manager to begin the search for solutions.
4. *Develop and evaluate alternative solutions.* The manager may rely on previous experience, refer to standard rules and procedures, or seek ideas from other people. The manager assesses the merits of each alternative as well as the probability that each may solve the problem.
5. *Choose the desired alternative.* Analysis may indicate which alternative has the best chance of success. The appropriate alternative may be defined in the standard rules of the organization or the manager may choose it based on his or her judgment and experience.
6. *Implement the chosen alternative.* Decision makers use managerial, administrative, and persuasive abilities to give directions and ensure that the decision is implemented and carried out. Once implemented, the monitoring activity that assesses whether the problem has been solved will begin again.

The rational model provides a series of steps that can lead to a more effective decision. The rational model is an *ideal* pattern of decision making. It describes how managers should make decisions rather than how they actually make decisions. The model is applicable to programmed decisions in which the goal and problem are well defined and information on alternatives is available. The model also assumes that managers are motivated to make the best decision

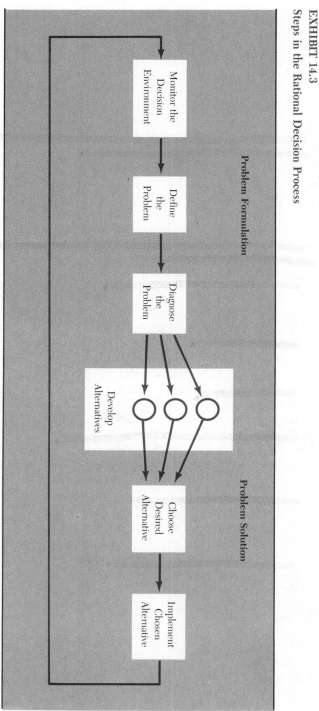

EXHIBIT 14.3
Steps in the Rational Decision Process

Problem Formulation

- Monitor the Decision Environment
- Define the Problem
- Diagnose the Problem
- Develop Alternatives

Problem Solution

- Choose Desired Alternative
- Implement Chosen Alternative

possible, and that they will spend time and effort to define goals, clarify information, diagnose problems and develop alternatives. The organizational world is often complex and disorderly, so the rational model often is not used, especially for nonprogrammed decisions. The bounded rationality model of organizational decision making explains how managers *actually* make decisions under complex organizational circumstances.

Bounded Rationality Model

As discussed in the last chapter, managers are extremely busy. They operate under the pressure of time and frequent interruptions. The organizational world can raise incredibly complex problems for managers, and the concept of bounded rationality describes how managers muddle through. It is not logical or practical for managers to spend a large amount of time defining and diagnosing problems, doing a comprehensive analysis of alternatives, and calculating the alternative with the highest probability. Simon introduced the concept of bounded rationality to explain how managers realistically cope with baffling complexity.[10] People have limits, or a boundary, on how rational they can be. People necessarily simplify problem situations. A hurried executive may have a choice among a hundred ties on a rack but will grab the first one that matches his suit. He doesn't carefully, logically examine every tie. The first tie that solves the problem to a satisfactory extent is selected, and the manager moves on to the next activity.

The bounded rationality model assumes that managers are deliberately rational, which means they try to make good decisions. However the ideal rational model can be realistically applied only for well-defined, programmed decision processes, and even then short cuts may be needed. Strategic and other nonprogrammed problems are not amenable to comprehensive analysis. The bounded rationality model rests on certain assumptions that deviate from the ideal model of decision making.[11]

- Because nonprogrammed problems are complex, only small parts of them can be dealt with at one time. Organizations typically divide problems into parts that can be handled in succession or divided among departments. In this way, adequate information and analysis can be accomplished for smaller problems without great cost.

- The search for solutions causes managers to search for alternatives where they have had success before. Managers will seek a solution similar to those previously used to solve similar problems. This is sometimes called the use of heuristics, a process which guides the search for alternatives into areas that have high probability for yielding satisfactory solutions. Managers seek to find an answer quickly rather than evaluate all possible alternatives.

- Managers settle for a satisfactory rather than an optimal solution; this is called *satisficing*, which was discussed briefly in Chapter 11. Managers look for alternatives until they get one which in their experience will produce a reasonable result. At that point the search stops and the solution is tried to see if it is satisfactory. If not, the problem will reoccur and a new search process will take place.

An example of a bounded rationality approach to decisions is illustrated in job interviews for graduating college students. Students seeking jobs may have access to as many as a hundred companies that visit campus. Graduating students usually search for a job until they have two or more acceptable offers, at which point their search activity often rapidly drops off. Two offers give the student two alternatives, but is far short of the maximum number of alternatives possible. The complexity of the search process combined with limited time and resources simply do not enable a comprehensive search. Once a student has a satisfactory offer, the interest in further search wanes. The student accepts the satisfactory job and can turn attention to other problems.[12]

Intuition   The complex and ill-defined nature of nonprogrammed decisions is associated with what has been called intuitive decision processes. The problem formulation and problem solution stages involve ambiguous, ill-defined, and incomplete information. Bits and scraps of unrelated information from informal sources may form a pattern in the manager's mind. The manager cannot prove a problem exists but may feel that a certain area needs attention. Intuitive processes are also used in the problem solution stage. Managers frequently make decisions without explicit reference to the impact on profits or other measurable outcomes. However, this does not mean that the person makes the decisions in a random or irrational fashion. Intuitive processes reflect previous trial-and-error experience. Past experience with intangible elements provide the manager with a "gut feeling" or "hunch," which actually may be more accurate than analytical procedures for nonprogrammed problems.[13] Managers should use data and systematic analysis when available, and the best solution to many problems will combine both hard data and intuition. Intuition has produced startling successes that could not be achieved by rational analysis alone.

Confronted in 1960 with what his lawyer called a bad deal—$2.7 million for the McDonald name—Ray Kroc says, "I closed my office door, cursed up and down, threw things out of the window, called my lawyer back and said: 'take it!' I felt in my funny bone it was a sure thing." System-wide sales of Kroc's hamburgers have exceeded $5 billion.[14]

In the late 1960s, Donald G. Fisher, who was then in the real estate business in San Francisco, bought a pair of Levi Strauss & Co. cords at a trade show. When he got them home and found that they didn't fit, he asked his wife to look in local stores for the same style in his size. When she came up empty-handed, Mr. Fisher decided to open a store that carried every size and every style that Levi made. The idea has led to the Gap Stores, Inc., which in 1983 sold $481 million worth of pants and other sportswear.[15]

Victor K. Kiam tried an electric razor and was so taken with it that he bought the company that made it, Remington Products, Inc., in 1979. Mr. Kiam, who appears in Remington's ads, thinks his total belief in the product's quality has helped turn the company into a fast growing, highly profitable concern. "Chief executives are supposed to be analytical and bland," Mr. Kiam says. "I think there's too much detachment and too much analysis of numbers, rather than the ingredients that go into the business."[16]

Intuitive decisions are made under conditions of bounded rationality. Intuitive decisions may lead to a satisfactory solution in a situation characterized by ill-defined goals, unclear information, time pressures, and experience. Huge decisions, such as the introduction of a new automobile, may involve combinations of rational and intuitive decision making. The organization may try to be scientific where it can, but the ultimate decision will rest on the gut feeling of senior executives. The introduction of the Tempo by Ford illustrates how a complex decision is made.

UP CLOSE 14.1:   Ford Motor Company

On May 26, 1983, Ford Motor Company launched its new compact car. Ford had been at work for more than four years on the new model, to be sold as Ford Tempo and Mercury Topaz. The undertaking involved thousands of people and an investment of more than $1 billion.

During those four years, Ford engineers, designers, and marketing experts made countless decisions about what consumers will want in a compact car for the next ten years. Ford executives did everything they could to minimize the risk of failure. They analyzed sales statistics to see what features were popular, and they tore apart competitors' cars to see what worked. They talked to consumers, and used market-research surveys and panels. Executives also were forced to trust their instincts, and sometimes reversed subordinates' decisions based on intuition.

Ford's top managers gave the company's designers authority to break new ground with the Tempo by using aerodynamics as the basis for styling. The staff argued this was the wave of the future, even if it meant that Ford differed from competitors, perhaps by too much. Selecting radical new styles was a non-programmed decision, because the designers wanted a design that would receive a favorable response but not outrun the market.

Market research had impact on many decisions. Designers first wanted to create a deep trunk by mounting the spare tire vertically behind the back seat. Consumer testing showed that women thought they wouldn't be able to get the spare tire out, so the trunk was redesigned with the well in the floor so the spare tire would lay flat. The redesign had to leave the trunk deep enough so that sacks of groceries could stand upright.

Senior management overrode designers on several details. In an early version of the Tempo, the parking lamps were designed to curve gracefully downward, as they wrapped around the front fender. Top managers thought the design gave the car a sad look, and they ordered the curve reversed, to project a smiling appearance. Moreover, several engineers argued for a stiff suspension so the Tempo would provide better handling and make the car fun to drive. Marketing managers overruled this approach, and insisted from their experience that the marshmallow soft ride is what most Americans want.[17]   ▩

The decision-making process for Ford Tempo illustrates that organizations use both rational and intuitive approaches to make decisions. The approach worked at Ford, because the Tempo is selling very well. Rational processes work best for the analyzable, programmable aspects of problems. Intuitive processes, because of bounded rationality, are used for the nonprogrammable decisions and include elements of the problem that cannot be quantified. In the next section we turn to group decision-making processes. For many problems, people make decisions jointly through work group participation.

GROUP DECISION MAKING

One issue facing decision makers is whether to involve group members or other managers in the decision-making process. Managers often have the option of making a decision by themselves, but just as many have the notion of including subordinates or peers in the decisions. Making the decision as a group has both advantages and disadvantages compared to making the decision as an individual, as Exhibit 14.4 illustrates.

Advantages   Involving other people in problem formulation and problem solution provides a broader perspective. The diagnosis and understanding of problems can be enriched, and more knowledge and facts can be brought to bear on identifying potential solutions and producing more alternatives. People who participate in decisions are more satisfied with the decision and are more likely to support it, thereby increasing the probability of successful implementation. Group decision processes also serve as an important communication function because they allow people to know about problems and solutions facing the department. Most importantly, the group decision-making process has the potential to lead to better decisions because of greater knowledge and broader perspective. However, certain disadvantages may prevent this from happening.[18]

Disadvantages   Group decisions tend to be slower. It takes time to consult everyone and to jointly diagnose problems and discuss solutions. Compromise also may occur because of differing views, and this may mean that a less satisfactory alternative is chosen. Effectiveness in group decision making also can be reduced when a high-status individual or clique dominate the discussion processes so that the breadth of perspective is not realized. Group decision processes also prevent management from acting decisively in crisis situations. Finally, in many work groups, norms evolve to reduce dissent and conflict within a group. The group may feel a need to provide a strong front and to protect its own existence, and so the diverse perspectives and internal conflicts that lead to better decision may be missing.[19]

EXHIBIT 14.4
Advantages and Disadvantages of Group Decision Making

Advantages	Disadvantages
1. Broader perspective for problem analysis	1. Slow decision process
2. More knowledge, facts, and alternatives	2. Compromise decisions may be suboptimal
3. Facilitates communication among members	3. Group may be dominated by individual or clique
4. Participation provides member satisfaction and support for decision	4. Group norms may reduce dissent and opinion diversity

Groupthink   A major threat that affects decision making in some groups is called *groupthink*. Groupthink emerges when group members are highly cohesive, somewhat isolated from events, and pressure to maintain consistent thinking patterns builds within the group. Irving Janis discovered groupthink in his research into government policy-level decision making.[20] Janis analyzed several decision fiascos, such as the failure prior to World War II to adequately protect Pearl Harbor, the Bay of Pigs invasion in the early 1960s, and the Watergate cover-up. Janis defined **groupthink** as "a mode of thinking that people engage in when they are deeply involved in a cohesive in-group, when the members' strivings for a unanimity override their motivation to realistically appraise alternative courses of action."[21] Janis found that groupthink caused "a deterioration of mental efficiency, reality testing, and moral judgment . . . ."[22]

The events leading to the American invasion of Cuba at the Bay of Pigs provided a graphic example of groupthink. Janis' research revealed that President Kennedy's closest advisors failed to voice their objections to the plan because they incorrectly perceived that everyone else was in favor of the invasion.[23] Group pressures for conformity were strong enough that no individual wanted to be a lone dissenter. The Central Intelligence Agency planners also dismissed correct information and persisted in their misperceptions, which were consistent with group thinking patterns. Group members who were capable and even brilliant allowed their critical powers to be blunted by the desire to maintain solidarity with the group. One advisor to President Kennedy, Arthur Schlesinger, Jr., said,

> In the months after the Bay of Pigs I bitterly reproached myself for having kept so silent during those crucial discussions in the Cabinet Room, although my feelings of guilt were tempered by the knowledge that a course of objection would have accomplished little save to gain me a name as a nuisance. I can only explain my failure to do more than raise a few timid questions by reporting that one's impulse to blow the whistle on this nonsense was simply undone by the circumstances of the discussion.[24]

EXHIBIT 14.5
Eight Warning Signals of Groupthink

Symptom	Description
1. Illusion of Morality	Believe group's position is inherently ethical and moral compared to other views.
2. Negative Stereotyping	View opposing groups as the enemy, as too different to negotiate with.
3. Illusion of Invulnerability	Overly optimistic, take extreme risks, oversimplify potential failure.
4. Rationalizations	Discredit or explain away warning signals and negative feedback.
5. Self-censorship of Dissenting Views	Keep doubts and conflicting ideas to oneself. Minimize doubts.
6. Mindguards	Protect group from negative information that could cause conflict or threaten group cohesion.
7. Strong Conformity Pressure	Dissenting views seen as disloyal, members pressured to agree.
8. Illusion of Unanimity	Assume everyone believes in the group's judgment.

SOURCE: Based on Irving L. Janis, *Victims of Groupthink: A Psychological Study of Foreign-Policy Decisions and Fiascos* (Boston: Houghton Mifflin, 1972).

Janis defined eight symptoms of groupthink, which are shown in Exhibit 14.5. The isolation of a group from real events may provide an illusion of invulnerability; members believe their position is ethical and moral; and opposing views are stereotyped as negative. Group members actually believe they are doing the right thing. They share a common set of values and ideology. Members withhold dissenting ideas to preserve the illusion of unanimity, and people will even work to protect the group from hearing information counter to group beliefs. Groupthink can be destructive to the organization, and to members who fight against it. Consider the example of Citibank.

UP CLOSE 14.2:   Citibank

For two years David Edwards went to his boss and his boss's boss with a story of tax evasion and currency trading violations in his department. Edwards, in charge of foreign exchange traders in Paris, warned bank officers that big trouble was brewing. He discovered the practice of "parking"—the bogus transfer of foreign exchange deposits to shift bank profits to countries with low tax rates. Parking helped CitiCorp minimize its worldwide taxes, but Edwards pestered his superiors to stop it. He also discovered kickback schemes associated with illegal money transfers.

International banking regulations are ambiguous. The line between legal and illegal activities is hazy. Bank officers cannot define correct behavior on most transactions. Managers who were involved did not see parking and other schemes in the same negative terms as did Edwards, and they resisted his efforts to change bank practices. Edwards told his bosses, "It's bad business. We risk being tossed out of some of these countries."

When the word finally got out to regulators, the reality of the shady practices came through to bank officials. France, West Germany, and Switzerland hit the bank for back taxes and fines for the questionable activities. The U.S. Comptroller of the Currency said the bank operations were inconsistent with sound banking principles. The Enforcement Division of the SEC recommended civic action against Citicorp but did not prosecute. The bank eventually changed its ways. In the meantime, Edwards was fired.[25] ■

Organizations can guard against groupthink by encouraging diversity and nonconformity during group decision making, and by listening to dissidents such as David Edwards. Group leaders can encourage members to critically evaluate proposals. Perhaps more importantly, leaders can promote open inquiry among members by refraining from stating their own position up front. Another technique is to invite experts from outside the group to challenge members' views. Scheduling a second-chance meeting a week or two after the preliminary decision has been made is another good technique. This allows group members to rethink the issue and express doubts.[26]

Leader Determination of Group Participation

Managers often face a dilemma about when to encourage work group participation in decision making. Participation can be a good thing because it increases both knowledge and acceptance, but group decisions also take more time and may not produce a favorable outcome. Vroom and Yetton developed a theory of leadership that prescribes the correct amount of participation for decisions. This model is similar to the contingency theories of leadership discussed in Chapter 13; it describes contingencies that lead to more or less group participation. The leader is assumed to be able to form relationships with subordinates ranging from autocratic to consultative and to use the style appropriate to the decision situation. The Vroom-Yetton model includes three parts: the definition of decision styles, the definition of decision quality, and the definition of decision rules that guide the amount of participation in decisions.[27]

Leader Decision-Making Styles Vroom and Yetton identified five styles of leadership, ranging from highly autocratic to highly participative. The highly autocratic style means that the decision maker makes the decision alone. Highly participative style means that group members participate in the decision and may even be allowed to make the decision on their own without the leader.

The five leader styles are shown in Exhibit 14.6. Autocratic leadership styles are represented by A, consultative style by C, and a group decision by G. The

EXHIBIT 14.6
Five Decision Styles

Decision Style	Description
A1	You solve the problem or make the decision yourself using information available to you at that time.
A11	You obtain the necessary information from your subordinates, then decide on the solution to the problem yourself.
C1	You share the problem with relevant subordinates individually, getting their ideas and suggestions without bringing them together as a group. Then you make the decision.
C11	You share the problem with your subordinates as a group, collectively obtaining their ideas and suggestions. Then you make the decision.
G11	You share a problem with your subordinates as a group. Your role is much like that of chairman. You do not try to influence the group to adopt "your" solution, and you are willing to accept and implement any solution that has the support of the entire group.

Note: A = autocratic;   C = consultative;   G = group

SOURCE: Reprinted, by permission of the publisher, from "A New Look at Managerial Decision-Making," by Victor H. Vroom, *Organizational Dynamics*, Spring 1973, pp. 67, 70. © 1973 AMACOM, a division of American Management Associations, New York. All rights reserved.

five styles fit along a continuum, and the manager should use any of the five styles depending upon the particular situation. In one situation the manager may make the decision alone (AI), in other situations adopt a consultative decision style (CI), or in others let the group make the decision on its own (GII).

Decision Effectiveness   An important factor influencing the correct decision style is decision effectiveness. Vroom and Yetton define decision effectiveness as consisting of three factors. *Decision quality* refers to how important decisions are for group performance. For example, a decision on where to place a water cooler or when to take a vacation has little impact on group performance, so there is not a high need for decision quality. Decisions on strategy, goals, or work requirements bear directly on group performance, so the need for decision quality is high. *Decision acceptance* refers to how important it is for group members to accept the decision in order for it to be implemented successfully. Some decisions do not require group acceptance (what color to paint the walls in the restrooms), while other decisions must be accepted if they are to be realistically implemented (setting performance goals for sales people). *Time required to reach decisions* is the third factor. Some decisions must be made in a timely fashion, while others can be made slowly. The model suggests that a decision is effective to the extent that it satisfactorily accommodates these factors—quality, acceptance, and timeliness.

Decision Rules   To select the appropriate decision strategies, the Vroom-Yetton model specifies seven decision rules in the form of questions managers can use to diagnose the situation. These rules help the manager interpret the need for decision effectiveness and the best way to reach that level of effectiveness. The questions guide managers in diagnosing each situation quickly and accurately.

A. Does the problem possess a decision requirement for high quality? Such a requirement may mean that the leader has to be actively involved.
B. Do I have enough information to make a high-quality decision? If the leader does not have sufficient information or expertise, some subordinate involvement will be required.
C. Is the decision problem well structured? If the problem is ambiguous and poorly structured, the leader will need to interact with subordinates to clarify the problem and possible solutions.
D. Is acceptance of the decision by subordinates important for effective implementation? If acceptance of the decision is crucial, then leaders should involve subordinates in the decision process.
E. If I were to make the decision by myself, is it reasonably certain that it would be accepted by my subordinates? If subordinates typically go along with the leader's decision, subordinate involvement in the process is less important.
F. Do subordinates share the organizational goals to be attained in solving this problem? If subordinates do not share the goals of the organization, then the leader should not allow the group to make the decision alone.
G. Is conflict among subordinates likely over preferred solutions? Conflict is typically resolved by allowing participation and interchange by group members.

Although the questions may seem detailed, they have considerable value to managers. The questions serve to quickly narrow the options available to managers and point to the appropriate level of group participation in decision making.

Combining Leadership Style and Situational Factors   Use of the Vroom-Yetton model is simplified by the use of what is known as the decision tree, shown in Exhibit 14.7. Vroom and Yetton developed the decision tree to allow leaders to select a strategy by answering the questions in sequence. The leader begins at the left side of the chart in Exhibit 14.7 with question A: Does the problem possess a quality requirement? If the answer is yes, the manager then proceeds to question B. If the answer to question A is no, the manager proceeds to question D, since questions B and C are irrelevant if quality is not a requirement. By working across the flow chart, the manager quickly arrives at the decision-making style most appropriate to that decision problem. Many situations offer a choice of decision styles that are equally acceptable. When that happens, Vroom and Yetton recommended using most autocratic style, since this saves time without reducing decision quality or acceptance.

EXHIBIT 14.7
Decision Tree for Determining Group Participation in Decision Making

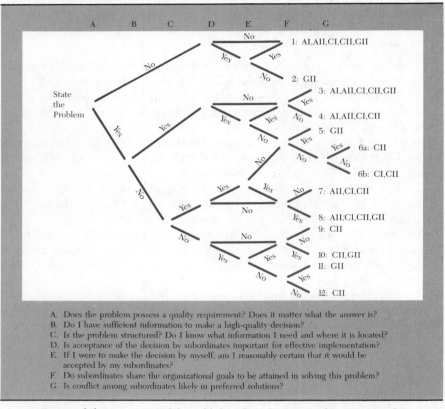

A. Does the problem possess a quality requirement? Does it matter what the answer is?
B. Do I have sufficient information to make a high-quality decision?
C. Is the problem structured? Do I know what information I need and where it is located?
D. Is acceptance of the decision by subordinates important for effective implementation?
E. If I were to make the decision by myself, am I reasonably certain that it would be accepted by my subordinates?
F. Do subordinates share the organizational goals to be attained in solving this problem?
G. Is conflict among subordinates likely in preferred solutions?

An example of using the Vroom and Yetton model is as follows:

Consider yourself the supervisor of a group of twelve engineers. Their formal training and work experience are similar, permitting you to use them interchangeably on projects. Today you were informed that an overseas affiliate had requested that four of your engineers be sent abroad for a period of from 6 to 8 months. Your supervisor concurred with this request, even though such overseas assignments are not generally regarded as desirable by company engineers. Your job is to select the four persons who will go. All of your people are capable of handling the assignment and there is no reason why any particular engineer should be retained over the others.[28]

If you were supervisor of these engineers, the model in Exhibit 14.7 can help you determine whether the leadership style should be autocratic, consultative, or group. The answer to question A concerning the quality requirement is no, because any engineer could serve equally well. The next question is D, and the answer is yes because subordinate acceptance is critical to the effective implementation of the decision. Question E asks whether acceptance is likely without participation, and the answer is no. According to the decision tree in Exhibit 14.7, the appropriate decision procedure is GII. The group decision is appropriate, because there is no specific quality requirement and the engineers will be much more accepting about who goes if they make the decision themselves.

Preliminary research into the model suggests that using it to predict decision style is effective. In situations in which leader behavior agreed with the defined set of acceptable decision styles, 68 percent were judged to have been successful. When leader behavior violated the defined set of acceptable decision styles, only 22 percent of the decision styles were judged successful.[29] Other research has looked at various aspects of the model, such as the extent to which managers enjoy participating and the relative degree to which managers at different hierarchical levels participated.[30] The findings are quite promising, suggesting that the model is significant for providing guidelines and for training managers to use participation to reach high-quality decisions in a timely fashion.

Barouh-Eaton Allen Corporation is run by a manager who believes in subordinate involvement in important decisions. His style, which fits the Vroom-Yetton model, helps explain why his company has been so successful.

UP CLOSE 14.3:   Barouh-Eaton Allen Corporation

Victor Barouh is founder, chairman, and majority shareholder of Barouh-Eaton Allen Corporation, a growing company with international sales of more than $50 million. The company is sometimes called Ko-Rec-Type, after its best-known consumer product. Ko-Rec-Type is the company's largest independent manufacturer of ink ribbons for typewriters, printers, and bar-code markers. The company has plants on both coasts and in Puerto Rico, Canada, and Ireland. Its principal competitor is IBM, which almost put Barouh out of business a few years ago.

The company started prospering when Vic Barouh invented the product that provided his company's early growth. A typist kept a piece of white chalk by her machine. To erase an error, she would lightly rub over the error with the chalk. It took several times, but the correction was neat. One of Barouh's products was carbon paper, and one day he got an idea. He rubbed chalk on one side of a sheet of paper, put the paper between the error and the typewriter, and struck the key. Most of the error disappeared under a thin coating of chalk dust. That is how Ko-Rec-Type was developed. Demand for the product was enormous, and the company prospered.

Then IBM invented the self-correcting typewriter. On a Saturday IBM announced that it had come out with a new typewriter that could lift off errors. By Monday morning about forty people told Barouh the company was in trouble because nobody was going to buy Ko-Rec-Type any more. "We immediately went down to the IBM showroom, and when the salesman was demonstrating the machine he looked at me and said, 'If you buy one of these machines, you'll never have to buy Ko-Rec-Type again.'"

Barouh bought a machine, took it to the plant, called everybody together and told them what they had to do. To survive, the company had to learn to make this ribbon. They also had to learn to make the cartridge that held the ribbon because cartridges were not available on the market. They had to learn to make the spools that held the tape. They had to learn to make the ink, the machine that puts ink on film, injection-molding to make the spools, and so on. It was an enormous challenge. Barouh got everyone involved regardless of position or education.

Within six months, Ko-Rec-Type produced its first self-correcting ribbon. It was the only company in the entire world to produce that product. Later they found out IBM invested six years in the product. With the new product, sales remained high and Barouh-Eaton Allen avoided disaster.[31] ■

Barouh-Eaton Allen's invention of the process to make the self-correcting typewriter ribbon is an example of the advantages of group decision making. By pooling everybody's knowledge and ideas, Ko-Rec-Type was able to come up with far better decisions than if Barouh or any other employee tried to do the job alone. Barouh's decision style was congruent with the Vroom-Yetton model. Decision quality was critical, Barouh had little expertise or information, and the problem was unstructured, so the correct approach was to involve subordinates.

ORGANIZATIONAL DECISION MAKING

Organizations are composed of managers and work groups who usually make decisions according to the concepts presented so far in this chapter. Now we turn to the macro approach to decision making, which pertains to upper-management decisions for the organization as a whole. This decision process is different from individual decision making or group decision making. For one thing, most decisions are nonprogrammed. These decisions pertain to strategy, structure, or environmental issues that are difficult to interpret and analyze. Moreover, most decisions involve multiple managers. Both problem formulation and problem solution may entail several departments and multiple

EXHIBIT 14.8
Steps in Organizational-Level (Macro) Decision Making

Problem Formulation	Problem Solution
Build a coalition by:	Muddle through implementation by:
1. Identifying key groups	4. Searching for or designing solution increments
2. Defining special problems and goals of key groups	5. Selecting and authorizing solution
3. Diagnosing cause of shared problem	6. Implementing solution by trial and error

viewpoints. Decisions are large and complex, and the outcomes affect many employees. In addition, big organization decisions are typically composed of subdecisions. Large problems are solved through a series of small, incremental decisions rather than by a single major choice. Thus both problem formulation and problem solution represent somewhat different processes at the organizational level, as Exhibit 14.8 illustrates.

Problem Formulation   The important activity during problem formulation is coalition building. Early research into organizational decision making at Carnegie-Mellon University revealed that many managers are involved in organizational decisions.[32] Managers form a coalition that includes people from line departments, staff specialists, or even external groups such as important customers, bankers, or labor unions. A coalition can work well because decisions are nonprogrammed and because decisions affect many people and departments. Overall organization goals sometimes are ambiguous, and operative departmental goals may be in conflict. Because managers disagree about problem priorities, problem formulation is difficult. Managers bargain about problems and build a coalition around problem priorities. **Coalition building** is important, because it ensures that key managers and groups are represented and agree with the problem to be solved. Without a coalition, influential people can derail the decision process later on. Managers making decisions on the organization level should identify key groups and lower-level managers who have a stake in the decision, learn about their problems and priorities, and jointly define the scope of the problem to be resolved.

The failure to build a coalition often can be seen in the administration of public schools and hospitals that serve diverse constituencies. One school superintendent ultimately lost his job because of his desire to build a new 7000-seat football stadium and cover the field with "astro-turf." The school's athletic teams were excellent, and the new facilities could enhance school visibility and serve as a magnet to professional families who would move into the area. However, the teachers were angry about the proposal because they wanted the money to be spent on salary increases. Many residents were upset because they perceived that tax rates would increase. Parental groups disagreed with the superintendent because they felt that special programs for handicapped children were more important than a new football stadium. The school board was also divided about whether a stadium and "astro turf" were needed. The superintendent had not built a coalition who agreed with him that the school district had a problem with respect to the stadium. Other groups felt other problems were more important, and failure to agree upon problem formulation caused the proposal to fail.[33]

Problem Solution   At the organizational level, problem solution is often accomplished through incrementalism, or "muddling through."[34] Even when defined, problems are not clear or easy to solve. Under conditions of uncertainty, big decisions are unwise because a failure could have drastic consequences. Thus the organization moves incrementally, attempting one small solution, then another. If the increment works, the organization can make additional increments in the same direction. If one fails, it can avoid that path and try something else. The incremental approach is exploratory and relies on trial and error rather than rational analysis. Organizations sometimes have clearly defined goals and use rational analysis in the incremental process; this is called "logical incrementalism."[35] The appropriate role for managers working with incrementalism is to search for the small decision steps that will potentially alleviate problems. Managers can add additional increments as needed. Mistakes are not penalized. Managers ultimately are expected to make correct decisions, but the organization only learns by trying. Some alternatives will not work, but they still provide valuable information to decision makers.

The odyssey of Levi Strauss moving into their new San Francisco headquarters building is an example of incremental decision making. Managers used analysis and research to plan a building, and upon moving in found that the layout was not consistent with their internal culture. Levi employees preferred an informal atmosphere and easy access to one another. Levi learned from this bad experience, and top managers promptly ordered the design of yet another building that would be compatible with employee needs. Several small intermediate decisions about design, real estate acquisition, and rising construction costs had to be made during this process. Top managers learned from each attempt. The new building was nearly perfect. Although it took Levi Strauss several years to get into the right building, the incremental decision process produced the correct design and layout.[36]

Organizational Decision Process Model

Twenty-five nonprogrammed decisions made by senior managers were studied by Henry Mintzberg and his associates at McGill University.[37] They traced the events associated with each decision from beginning to end. The decisions were strategic in nature and included the choice of which jet aircraft to acquire for a regional airline, identifying a new market for a deodorant, installing a

EXHIBIT 14.9
The Organizational Decision Process Model

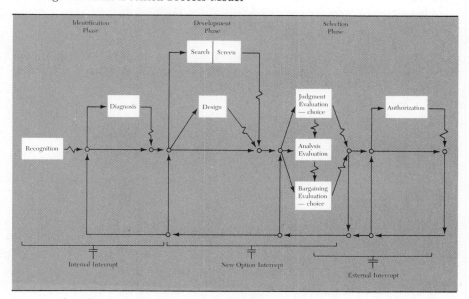

SOURCE: Adapted and reprinted from Henry Mintzberg, Duru Raisinghani, and Andre Theoret, "The Structure of Unstructured Decision Processes," *Administrative Science Quarterly* 21, 2 (1976): 266, by permission of *The Administrative Science Quarterly*.

controversial medical treatment at a hospital, developing a new supper club, developing a new container terminal in a harbor, and the decision to fire a star radio announcer.[38]

For most decisions, the complete process from problem formulation through problem solution took from one to three years. The researchers found that these major decisions were a series of small choices that added up to produce the major decision. The organizations progressed through incremental stages, and they often hit barriers, which were termed "decision interrupts." An interruption means that the organization has to recycle back through a previous decision and change direction. Decision loops and cycles are the way the organization learns which alternatives work.

The decision model that evolved from Mintzberg's study of top manager decisions is shown in Exhibit 14.9. The decisions evolved through three major phases: the identification phase, the development phase, and the selection phase.

Identification Phase   The identification phase begins with problem recognition. *Recognition* is usually stimulated by managers' awareness of a problem or an opportunity. The second step is *diagnosis*, in which additional information is gathered to define the problem. Identifying key groups and building a coalition about goals and problem priorities begins during the identification phase.

Diagnosis may include systematic analysis in some cases, although many severe problems are poorly defined and require an immediate response, and so recognition and diagnosis are done informally through management discussions.

Development Phase   The development phase is the shaping of a response to resolve the problem defined in the identification phase. Organizations may do a quick search to see whether any standard solutions or alternatives within the organization would be appropriate. *Search* includes relying on managers' own experiences, talking to other managers, or examining the formal policies and procedures of the organization. If a standard solution is not available, which is often the case, the organization has to *design* a custom solution. Mintzberg found that in these cases decision makers have only a vague idea of the ideal solution. They work through a series of trials to test the feasibility of alternative solutions. Gradually, through trial and error, a custom solution emerges. The solution evolves from an incremental procedure rather than from careful analysis and one big decision.

Selection Phase   The selection phase is where the solution is chosen. At this point the choice is not necessarily among several alternatives. In the case of custom-made solutions, this phase is simply an evaluation and acceptance of the single alternative that seems feasible. Mintzberg observed three types of selection. *Judgment* occurs when the choice involves experience rather than logical analysis. *Analysis* occurs when alternatives are evaluated on a more systematic, quantitative basis. *Bargaining* occurs when managers disagree about the solution and must discuss and bargain until a coalition is formed which agrees with the solution. *Authorization* occurs when the decision is formally accepted by the organization.

Interrupts   The lower part of Exhibit 14.9 shows a line running back toward the beginning stages of the decision process. Problems frequently arise that force the organization to look back to an earlier stage. If a custom solution is not perceived as satisfactory or if it is tried and fails, the organization may have to go back to the very beginning and reconsider whether a problem truly exists. Feedback loops can be caused by problems of timing, politics, disagreement among managers, turnover of managers, or the sudden appearance of a new alternative. For example, when a regional airline made the decision to acquire jet aircraft, the board authorized the decision to purchase new airplanes. But shortly thereafter a new chief executive was brought in and he cancelled the contract. The organization had to loop back to the beginning. He then accepted the diagnosis of the need for new aircraft, but insisted upon a search for alternatives. At about that time, a foreign airline went out of business and used aircraft became available at a bargain price. This unexpected option seemed to fit the problem, so the chief executive used his own judgment to authorize the purchase of the aircraft.[39]

Organizational decision making is a dynamic process that may require a number of cycles and may extend over a long period of time before a problem is solved. An example of the dynamic process is illustrated in **Up Close 14.4** about the decision to build a new plant for a manufacturing company. What started out as a straightforward decision evolved into a number of small decisions made in response to several interrupts. The period from problem formulation to problem solution for the new plant took four years to complete.

UP CLOSE 14.4:   Manufacturing Plant

A small manufacturing firm was faced with a series of pressures that indicated its plant was obsolete. A proposal to sell the building was developed (design), and a real-estate agent contacted (search), but no buyers were found. It was then realized that the city might expropriate the land (interrupt), and an agent was hired to negotiate a good price should that occur. Meanwhile, a neighboring firm moved out, and their adjoining parking lot was acquired to provide a room for expansion or to increase the expropriation value of the property (evaluation-choice). At the same time, the firm employed architects to investigate two alternatives, but rejected both proposals as too expensive (evaluation-choice), and attention was then focused on moving. Three alternative sites were found (search), and employees were polled and road networks investigated (evaluation). One area proved to be the most desirable, and when an existing facility was found there at a good price (search), it was identified as a favorite candidate and purchased (evaluation-choice). The company planned the modification of the building (design) and commenced the alteration. Two months later, however, the provincial government gave the firm a short time to vacate (interrupt). Now the firm faced a crisis. It did, however, have a considerable source of funds from the expropriation and could consider buying land and building a new plant. Only one area was investigated, and a suitable site was located (search). The firm obtained re-zoning sanctions from the municipal government, a mortgage from the bank (design), and the assurance that this property would not be expropriated (authorization). The site was purchased (evaluation-choice), and the engineering department, in consultation with the architect, prepared building plans (design); the plans were quickly finalized (evaluation-choice).[40]   ▄▄▄

ESCALATING COMMITMENT TO A DECISION

Organizational decision making is not without puzzling aspects; one of these is the tendency for organizations to continue along a major course of action despite repeated failures. It is appropriate for an organization to recycle as small problems occur, but research indicates that on some occasions organizations persist in investing time and money despite repeated failures and strong evidence that additional investment is not warranted. Not only do top managers remain committed to a decision, but the concept of escalating commitment implies they continue to throw good money after bad even after they begin to suspect that the general strategy is incorrect. Consider the following example.

> *The epic blunder by the Washington Public Power Supply System (WPPSS— now commonly called Whoops) caused a $2.3 billion municipal bond default in 1983. WPPSS began construction of nuclear power plants to meet the increasing power needs of the Northwest in 1972. The original estimated cost for three power plants was $3.1 billion. By 1974, cost overruns on plant construction had already amounted to nearly $1 billion, and managers saw that construction delays could lead to further escalations in costs. Moreover, managers saw evidence that the expected increases in power consumption were not going to materialize. However, WPPSS financial statements disclosed little negative information, and money was raised through bond issues to continue building the power plants. Indeed, plans for two additional nuclear power plants—for a total of 5—were started and funds were raised.*
>
> *The bandwagon rolled on for several years. As late as 1981, Whoops raised another $200 billion in bonds for plants four and five. Then came the shocker—the cost of the entire project had soared to $23.8 billion from the estimated $8.9 billion, and analysis of power demand showed that all the plants were not needed. Ten years after the project began, and only with enormous negative public exposure and default on bonds, was the project brought to a halt.*[41]

Why do organizations pursue a course of action even after managers receive information that the decision was a mistake? In order to explain such behavior, Barry Staw undertook a line of research to see whether escalating commitment would occur in a laboratory.[42] Staw hypothesized that social psychological processes might be at work so that individuals bias their own attitudes and perceptions to justify their previous behavior. When people are personally responsible for a decision and its negative consequences, they may block or distort negative information, while at the same time investing more time and resources in the project to make it succeed to justify their previous action.

Staw and his colleagues carried out a series of experiments focusing on how willing people would be to commit valued resources to a course of action after they received information that the original decision had been in error.[43] Decision makers in these experiments allocated more money to company divisions that were showing poor results than to those showing good results. Also, decision makers allocated more money to divisions when they personally, rather than someone else, had been responsible for the original decision to back the division. In brief, decision makers were most likely to spend money on projects for which they were responsible, even if the projects produced negative consequences.

EXHIBIT 14.10
Reasons for Commitment to a Course of Action

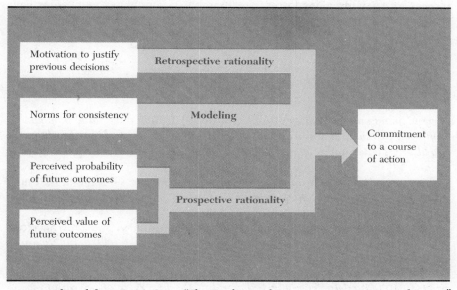

SOURCE: Adapted from B. M. Staw, "The Escalation of Commitment to a Course of Action," *Academy of Management Review* 6 (1981): 582.

The explanation for escalating commitment is summarized in Exhibit 14.10. This model suggests determinants of commitment to a course of action. First, managers have motivation to justify previous decisions. To demonstrate their own competence, managers rationalize the decision as correct and stick to it in hopes of turning the situation around. This is called **retrospective rationality.** The decision maker wants to appear competent in previous decisions by continuing the course of action.

Second, **norms of consistency** influence commitment. In contemporary society, consistency is valued, and consistent managers are considered better leaders than those who switch from one course of action to another. Norms for consistency are based on activities of managers who model their behavior after people they see as successful because of commitment to a course of action.

Third, other factors—the probability of future outcomes and the value of future outcomes—jointly influence what is called prospective rationality. **Prospective rationality** is a decision maker's belief that future courses of action are rational, correct, and will solve the problem. After committing the organization to a course of action, managers are more likely to perceive information that reinforces positive outcomes from this action if successful. Perceived positive outcomes also intensify because the successful outcome can also cover past losses.

In summary, the incremental decision process is necessary and appropriate in organizations, but organizations may continue on a major course of action that is failing, and managers are reluctant to change. Pressure builds to succeed to justify previous decisions, to appear consistent, and to attain the benefits of success to cover previous losses. For example, a number of companies have spent too much money on the teletex concept, as illustrated in the following **Up Close.**

UP CLOSE 14.5:   Videotex Services, Inc.

"If you spend enough money," Nobel physicist I.I. Rabi once said, "you can do anything, provided it doesn't violate the laws of physics." Rabi obviously never heard of videotex and teletext, where $1 billion has already been spent to little effect.

Time Inc. has been in and out of the teletext business—sending data and information over home video screens—at a loss put by some analysts in the neighborhood of $30 million.

Not everyone is giving up. Times Mirror's subsidiary, Videotex Services, Inc., has invested about $10 million in a venture that will bring two-way "interactive" services like home banking, home shipping, and electronic mail to Orange County and Los Angeles beginning in September. "We think we can get 5,000 to 10,000 customers before the end of the first year of operation," says Videotex Services President James Holly, optimistically.

There are problems in Times Mirror's effort. It ran a nine-month test of the service on 350 Los Angeles and Orange County homes. Half the test group decided to give up the service midway through the experiment—at the point when they would have had to start paying for it. But hope springs eternal in Videotex. Says Holly: "If the jet set likes it, it will go on. If not, it will go the other way."

Why do companies seemingly keep throwing good money after bad? In the beginning, particularly for communications companies, it was because of fear. If this is the newspaper of the future, the reasoning went, a publisher ought to be in videotex. Says Albert J. Gillen, president of Knight-Ridder's videotex subsidiary, Viewdata Corp. of America, Inc.: "We thought it could be a breakthrough medium just as television was in 1946."

Will the Times Mirror service be different? If it fails to make a profit, as all others have so far, there are additional contenders in the wings. CBS, for example, is developing a videotex service called Trintex in a joint venture with IBM and Sears, Roebuck.

Videotex is an idea that has everything going for it. Except for one thing: a market.[44] ▪

The teletext business is an example of commitment to a course of action. Companies stay in it beyond the point where investment is no longer sensible. This may be because of norms for consistency or motivation to justify previous decisions. Additional factors are competitive pressure and fear that other companies will get an advantage. Prospective rationality is high in terms of perceived payoff, which may explain why new companies are waiting in the wings. Companies want to pursue this course of action despite previous failures.

TECHNIQUES FOR IMPROVING DECISION MAKING

Managers readily learn the rational method for making programmed decisions, as described earlier in this chapter. Costly mistakes are rare with the rational method. Nonprogrammed decisions, however, are made under uncertainty. They are characterized by trial and error, and mistakes are more frequent. A number of techniques have evolved to help managers resolve difficult decisions that confront both work groups and the organization as a whole. These techniques can be adopted to help managers with either the problem formulation or problem solution stage of decision making.

Improving Problem Formulation

Problem formulation includes analysis of the causes of unsatisfactory behavior or performance. Group processes, which reduce conflict and lead to group-think, often hinder the formulation of unstructured problems. Members of a group or coalition may share a common frame of reference and may not question whether a problem truly needs solving. Escalating commitment is an example of continuing to try to solve these problems beyond the point when managers should recognize that a course of action is nonproductive.

Techniques for improving problem formulation involve structured debate.[45] **Structured debate** surfaces unstated assumptions and alternative points of view during early stages of the decision process. Three techniques that prevent premature closure during problem formulation are the *devil's advocate, multiple advocacy,* and *dialectical inquiry.* Exhibit 14.11 summarizes these techniques.

EXHIBIT 14.11
Techniques for Improving Decision Making in Organizations

Problem Formulation	Problem Solution
Structured Debate:	*Creativity Stimulants:*
1. Devil's Advocate	1. Brainstorming
2. Multiple Advocacy	2. Nominal Group Technique
3. Dialectical Inquiry	3. Delphi Technique

SOURCE: Based on Charles Schwenk and Howard Thomas, "Formulating the Mess: The Role of Decision Aids in Problem Formulation," *Omega* 11 (1983): 239-252.

Devil's Advocate   A devil's advocate is given the assignment of disagreeing with the group. This device helps prevent the group from reaching premature consensus about problem identification. The devil's advocate should be given a clearly defined assignment to present arguments as cleverly and forcefully as possible. The person employing this technique should actively collect information opposing the proposed policy and incorporate unpopular views. The devil's advocate can challenge the assumptions underlying the group's reason for trying to solve a problem or for escalating commitment to a problem.[46]

Multiple Advocacy   Multiple advocacy is similar to a devil's advocate except that more advocates and points of view are presented. Representatives of minority opinions and unpopular views are presented to decision makers. The advocates are viewed as custodians of unpopular views and are expected to present them forcefully to the decision-making group.[47] The proponents of unpopular views must be given adequate time and resources, and they must have enough influence and persuasion skills to represent their cases with force equal to the popular view. Decision makers should not be involved in the debate, and time should be allowed for give and take over key issues and assumptions.

Dialectical Inquiry   Dialectical inquiry is another device for structuring debate and conflict among decision makers. Groups or individuals are assigned to challenge the underlying assumptions associated with problem formulation. Dialectical inquiry typically begins by identifying the prevailing view of the problem and its associated assumptions. Next an individual or a group is asked to test these assumptions by developing a counter problem that is credible but rests on different premises. An informal debate is conducted that brings out different interpretations of the same information. By using the same information to develop different problems and potential solutions, the decision makers are able to understand and evaluate the assumptions underlying the original problem. Once assumptions have been understood and perhaps changed, the decision makers come away with a better understanding of ill-structured problems. Dialectical inquiry, like the devil's advocate and multiple advocacy methods, helps groups break away from traditional thinking and avoid the problems of groupthink and escalating commitment. Decision makers are assigned to challenge current thinking and orient themselves toward reanalysis of their positions.[48]

Improving Problem Solution

Problem solution involves the development and evaluation of alternative courses of action, as well as the selection and implementation of the preferred alternative. Whether decision makers actually have the time or opportunities to examine multiple or creative alternatives is perhaps the major shortcoming of problem solution. Decision making may be enhanced by providing expanded search processes at low cost. The easiest and most practical techniques managers have to use for generating additional alternatives are *brainstorming*, the *nominal group technique*, and the *Delphi technique*. These techniques are called **creativity stimulants,** because they provide a focused approach for developing additional and novel alternatives for problem solution.

Brainstorming   Brainstorming is used with a face-to-face, interactive group to encourage the free flow of ideas. One individual defines a specific problem for the group, and members are encouraged to "throw out," or "brainstorm," possible solutions aloud. One member can record the ideas on a blackboard or flip chart while other members toss out ideas. Criticism of ideas is ruled out, and freewheeling is welcomed. The more novel and unusual the idea, the better. The group should strive for quantity and not worry about quality. Once the group has exhausted all possible ideas for solutions, they turn to a more systematic analysis of each idea. The ideas that have potential value are kept and analyzed for possible implementation. Brainstorming allows the group to come up with a great number and variety of possible solutions in a short time, and group members find the process stimulating and enjoyable.[49]

Nominal Group Technique   This technique, often called NGT, differs from brainstorming because members do not share ideas aloud. Members meet as a group but begin by silently and independently generating ideas in writing for the specific problem. The silent period encourages maximum differences in opinion among members, because they are not distracted by ideas suggested by other members. The next step is a round-robin procedure in which every group member presents one idea from their list to the group. No discussion of the idea is allowed, and each idea is recorded on a blackboard or flip chart. After all ideas are presented and recorded, each idea is discussed for the purpose of clarification and evaluation. After discussion is complete, the final step is for group members to silently and independently rank order the ideas as a possible solution to the problem. The rank ordering is recorded, and the solutions with the best ranking from the group will be candidates for possible implementation. This technique is called *nominal* group technique because members do not engage in discussion and interaction typical of a real group. The advantage of this procedure is that each member generates and rates solutions without influence from other group members.[50]

Delphi Technique   The delphi is similar to NGT, but group members do not meet face to face. A specific problem is identified, and group members are asked to provide written answers on a carefully designed questionnaire. The answers are completed independently; members remain physically located in their own offices. Each member's written answers are then circulated to all other group members. After reviewing all answers, members are again requested to formulate a written answer, but this time with the benefit of other people's ideas. This process can continue through several repetitions until group members' opinions begin to show a consensus on a prospective solution.[51] The delphi technique is effective when the problem is very difficult to solve and creativity and deep thinking are required. Separate, written answers enable each participant to develop thoughtful solutions to a difficult problem. Sharing these answers enables participants to take advantage of the creativity of other members and gradually reach a consensus about a solution.

SUMMARY

This chapter explored the topic of decision making within organizations. Decision making is defined as the process of problem formulation and problem solution. Organizations make decisions concerning both programmed and nonprogrammed problems, and at different levels within the hierarchy. Macro-level decisions pertain to the organization as a whole and tend to be nonprogrammed, while micro-level decisions made by lower-level managers often tend to be programmed.

The rational model of decision making is an effective way for individual managers to resolve programmed problems. For nonprogrammed problems, bounded rationality means that managers may take shortcuts by engaging in limited search and by accepting a satisfactory rather than optimal solution. Managers often rely on experience and intuition for resolving complex issues in a short time.

The advantages and disadvantages of group decision making were discussed. Group participation provides broad knowledge and facilitates communication and implementation. But the disadvantages of group decisions are the suppression of conflict, time, and compromise on a less than satisfactory solution. The Vroom-Yetton model provides an explicit technique for defining how much group participation to use in decision making. Managers can evaluate such things as the quality requirement, amount of information available, and importance of subordinate acceptance to select the amount of subordinate participation in decision making.

For organization level decision making, many managers have a stake in the decision, so the decision may have to accommodate the goals and perspectives of various departments or even constituents outside the organization. Problem formulation thus includes a coalition-building process wherein key constituents are brought into agreement about priorities of problems. Problem solution at the organization level often is an incremental process. Through trial and error, the organization finds a solution that resolves the nonprogrammed problem. The organizational model of decision making illustrates that many interrupts and recycles may be required before the problem is finally solved. One difficulty of decision making at the organizational level is escalating commitment. Norms of consistency and a desire to show that the original course of action was correct often cause managers to throw good money after bad.

Finally, we examined processes for improving decision making. The formulation of nonprogrammed problems can be enhanced through structured debate. Specific techniques are devil's advocate, multiple advocacy, and dialectical inquiry, each of which provide a forum for minority viewpoints, which help decision makers challenge problem assumptions. Problem solution is enhanced through creativity stimulants that expand the range and creativity of activities. Brainstorming, nominal group technique, and delphi technique help increase both the range and creativity of solutions available to decision makers.

KEY WORDS

bounded rationality model	escalating commitment	problem formulation
	groupthink	problem solution
brainstorming	multiple advocacy	programmed decisions
coalition building	nominal group	prospective rationality
creativity stimulants	technique	rational model
decision making	nonprogrammed	retrospective
decision process model	decisions	rationality
delphi technique	norms of consistency	structured debate
devil's advocate	participative decisions	
dialectical inquiry	styles	

DISCUSSION QUESTIONS

1. Describe the six steps in the rational model of decision making.
2. Think of a nonprogrammed decision you have made. Did you follow the steps in the rational model, or did you rely on intuition?
3. Discuss the advantages and disadvantages of group decision making compared to individual decision making.
4. What is groupthink? Can you give an example from your experience where disagreement was suppressed to maintain group solidarity?
5. When is it appropriate for a manager to be more participative in decision making?
6. When and why is coalition building important for organizational decision making?
7. Describe the three major phases in the organizational decision process model. How do these phases compare to the rational model of decision making?
8. Why do organizations sometimes stay committed to a decision even when it is not working?
9. What advantage does structured debate have for preventing groupthink or escalating commitment to a decision?

CASE 14.1:   The New Library

Jefferson University is a sizable and complex institution with an enrollment of over 10,000 students in a number of undergraduate, graduate, and professional programs. The formal organization of the senior administration is shown in Exhibit 1.

Ralph White, the executive vice-president, had called the meeting. "I've asked each of you to look at the proposal for the new library for our health sciences campus from

EXHIBIT 1
Administrative Organization Chart for Jefferson University

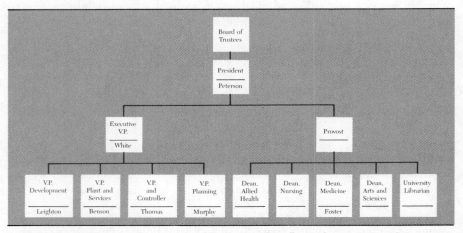

SOURCE: John A. Dunn, Jr., "Organizational Decision Making," in Walter C. Swap and Associates, eds., *Group Decision Making* (Beverly Hills, CA: Sage, 1984), p. 282. Used with Permission.

your own points of view," he said. "I have to make my recommendation to the president and the board tomorrow. What position should we take?" Having posed the question, he sat back and listened.

When the vice-president for Development came in, the rest of the group was sitting around the big table on the fourth floor of Jefferson Hall. "Evelyn," said Al Benson, the vice-president for Plant and Services, "we've already set your target for you." Evelyn grinned; somehow, lately, all the big decisions seemed to rest on the ability of her shop to find new money. This time, however, she wasn't sure she could deliver.

The problem was the size of the project. Conversations about the need for a major library/learning resources center on the health sciences campus had been going on for years. A fund-raising campaign had been started four years before but, aside from about $3,000,000 in major gifts, had not produced anything like the funds to cover the project. Changes in the medical school's leadership and in faculty ideas about the sort of facility needed had muddied the water.

During those four years, a good deal of money had been spent on the project. An architectural programmer had been hired to work with faculty members and administrators in clarifying specifically what the building should consist of. Schematic designs had been prepared. Fund-raising staff had been hired and paid; lots of proposals had been written, brochures prepared, prospects identified and solicited, trips made. The net result was that the expenses of the campaign had eaten up a great deal of what had been raised; about a million was still due to be collected in the future.

Mike Thomas, vice-president and controller, did not let Evelyn forget the cash-flow problem either. The bills had to be paid as they were incurred; much of the fund-raising progress was in pledges; payments were dribbling in over a number of years. That meant that Mike had to use other money to pay the bills, to be refunded when and if the pledges were paid. The payment record was good; these were major donors, who honored their commitments. Mike could be pretty sure of his repayments. There remained a related problem, however. Time was going by, and inflation was a major factor. He was paying bills in current dollars; the pledges, when they were paid, would be worth less, but the costs of the building would be going up—potentially leaving a gap in the financing.

There didn't seem to be much doubt about the need for the building. The present library conditions were less than marginal. The accreditation team for the American Medical Association gave the school its accreditation, to be sure, but only on the clear understanding that the new facility would be complete by time of their next visit. The accreditation teams for the nursing and allied health schools had also criticized the inadequacy of the facility and scope of the collection. Working with expert consultants, the university librarian had developed a detailed program for the needed facility.

The medical school also had an image problem. The allied health school had its own new building, constructed about ten years ago. The nursing school was building superb new facilities. The medical school, the "flagship" of the complex, had never in its eighty years of existence had a new building. It was housed in converted manufacturing buildings. These made good laboratories, because they were constructed to support sizable machinery; but the close columns and relatively low ceilings made for terrible classrooms. The recent advent of the nursing school had required shoehorning additional faculty members into already crowded quarters. In an era when all three schools were trying to increase research activity, there was a critical shortage of research lab space. Some of the functions that could be moved from present quarters into the new building would free space that could be converted to lab use (at additional capital cost, of course).

So the needs were clear, but the financing wasn't. Early cost estimates ranged from $9,000,000 to $15,000,000, depending on the size of the building and the mix of components proposed for it. A site was acquired in a good central location. Cost estimates kept rising as people got more and more enthusiastic about the possibilities, and as construction costs rose with inflation. Evelyn Leighton took over the development division after the campaign had started, reviewed the discouraging progress to date, changed the fund-raising staff, and set to work. Not much happened. There was an acting dean of the medical school at the time who, despite his best efforts, could not be as effective as a permanent dean could be; and there was still some general skepticism about the university's ability to raise that kind of money. Some of the alumni remembered the strenuous efforts that had been made to raise funds for the new allied health tower, and the disappointment when the campaign fell far short. The building plans had to be cut back; and for years the allied health students have had to carry an extra $800 per student per year on their tuition to pay the mortgages on the building.

This year, Dr. Peter Q. Foster was appointed dean of the medical school. He had been the director of a major medically oriented foundation. A nationally known researcher, he also brought strong administrative skills and high aspirations to the city campus. He quickly realized the need for the new facility, but added an even more urgent dimension to its importance. He and many of his health science colleagues realized that the ways in which future health practitioners and others needed to have access to information was radically different from the past. They should not be looking through card indices or thumbing through past issues of periodicals; they should be inquiring directly from data bases by computer. Nothing of that sort existed at the university, though there were of course computer terminals in the library for accessing Medlines and other search services.

For the health schools, such developments had particular urgency. Each of the schools is linked for educational purposes with many associated institutions. The medical school has over a dozen major teaching hospitals and an additional thirty hospitals with specialized programs. The health sciences schools could and should provide core information access services to all these institutions, tying them together into an even more effective teaching patient care network. The development of the new library would provide that possibility. Unfortunately, however, money doesn't come just because you need it.

Dr. Foster promptly undertook a series study of the possibilities. An outside consulting group worked with a core group of medical school and central administration people in a financial feasibility study. Cost estimates for various building sizes and configurations were prepared, starting at about $20,000,000 and going on up to $35,000,000. Estimates of the incremental costs of operating the building were worked out; the added costs would raise the tuitions of all three of the health sciences schools from $800 to $1300 per student per year. The consultant, acknowledging the importance of the project, recommended down-sizing the building as much as possible, so as to bring it within the capacity of Jefferson University to afford.

Then came an almost incredible break. President Peterson and Evelyn Leighton had over the course of two years been working quietly in Mexico with an elderly, very wealthy medical school alumna. And indeed, with long and patient work, she was persuaded to grant the school a total of $15,000,000 through a private foundation. Suddenly, everyone's mood brightened.

It was now clearly possible to build the building. The question of total size remained. The huge grant was not enough. Would $23,000,000 be adequate? $25,000,000? $30,000,000? How much more could the university raise? What would the operating costs be, and who was going to pay them?

"Damn it, Evelyn, I think we ought to be going," said Al, after reviewing the fact sheets White had distributed. "The old gal gave us enough to get started; but we have to go through a formal application process to her foundation, and the deadline for that is a month from now. It will take my people that long to get the application done, once we've made our decision to go ahead. Our present estimate is $23,000,000. There's some room for slack in that, because we can always leave a couple of administrative office floors unfinished if we have to, and we can save the cost of the furnishings on those floors. Can't we raise the $8,000,000?"

"What about the operating costs of the new building?" asked Ralph White.

"They are going to be high," said Jerry Murphy, the vice president for Planning. "That building will add about $1,500,000 to the budgets of the schools every year. With 600 medical students, 600 allied health students, and 200 nursing students; that means over $1000 per student per year. Maybe the medical students can stand it. The tuition is very high there, but there are still a lot of people who want to get into medical school; and the earning potential of the graduates is high. But interest in allied health is slowing down, and their earnings aren't as high; I don't want to see us sock another $1000 on top of the $800 they are already paying for their own building. And as for the nursing school, those tuitions are already incredibly high; I'd hate to see us load anything more there. It's going to be hard enough to get the nursing school onto a balanced budget under the best of circumstances."

Mike Thomas took out his calculator. "Since we can only count on about 5 percent or 6 percent as a long-run payout rate on endowment, it would take an endowment of $30,000,000 to generate that $1,500,000 annual income, if the students aren't going to pay for it. Can you raise $38,000,000, Evelyn?"

"Come on, you guys," replied Leighton. "We got you the $15,000,000. Give us a little time and I think we can probably raise at least enough to cover the balance of the cost of the building. Psychologically, having the grant money in hand helps us, because it gives a sense of reality to the whole project. This is the biggest project we're going to have on the health sciences campus for many years. We can do it. It may take some time, that's all."

"Let me add one complexity," said Murphy. "If all we were doing was to build a conventional library building, we'd know how to do it. The building itself will not be complicated; Al and his crew have a good handle on those costs. What about the new technology? We're going to try communications and computer linkages that haven't been tried anywhere else. That means that there's going to be added systems development expense, and some rather unusual equipment costs, right? And we can pretty well bet that there are going to be some mistakes made; we're not perfect; we don't have all the answers going in. My own guess is that we could easily add $1,000,000 to $1,500,000 in unanticipated systems development costs to the project. When can we have any better handle on those costs?"

"Dr. Foster has several committees working on the program right now," said Al. "The problem is that they may take some months thinking through all the pieces of this puzzle, and we have to make a decision very quickly. I can pretty well specify the cash payment schedule for the building right now, though. Figure about $100,000 per month starting in April when the project gets board approval, and then after a year, figure $1,000,000 per month for the twenty-three months of construction."

Evelyn piped in: "Some of my staff has been working with the National Library of Medicine to see if we can get systems development support. They don't have any money right now, but it's possible that something may come through on that in the future. We may also be able to get some support from computer manufacturers who'd like to be involved in the development so they could use the technology elsewhere."

"Evelyn let's come back to the fund raising for a minute," said White. "How sure are you?"

"My best guess is as follows: I can be 90 percent sure of raising $4,000,000; for $6,000,000, I guess about 70 percent sure; for $8,000,000, about 50 percent sure. I think there is a chance we can go even higher—maybe $10,000,000, but that's very risky. We should be able to get pledges in the next three years; most of those pledges will be payable over three years. And just to anticipate Mike's next question, you should deduct about 8 percent to 15 percent from the total for fund-raising costs."

"You guys are all forgetting the problem of how we get from here to there," added Mike. "Al, you're going to be spending money on the building design and then on the construction. We can draw down on the foundation grant pretty quickly, but what do we do for the rest of the money? Evelyn can't guarantee that she can raise it. And even if she does, you heard how long it's going to take. That means I may not get some of my cash for six or seven years. We're awfully tight for working capital now. We financed the classroom renovation project out of working capital, and the hockey rink as well. And we haven't yet raised the funds to pay for those. There's just so far I can stretch. I can borrow some from the banks, of course, but that will cost us at least one point over prime. Who's going to be paying those interest charges? They should be charged to the project, but that just raises the total cost; the medical school operating budget is already tight and probably can't afford to absorb them."

"Look, we're not getting anywhere," said Murphy. "Al, you want to build the building, and you've got time constraints. We need a decision now. Mike, you've got real cash flow problems, and you're worried about whether or not we'll ever raise the construction money. I'm concerned about the operating costs and the unknowns in the systems development. Evelyn's a born optimist, but even she can't guarantee how much she and the president and Dr. Foster can raise, or when."

Al boomed in: "Come on. I say we go ask the board for approval of the $23,000,000 project. That's what Dr. Foster wants. We've got some flexibility within that total to cut back if we need to—maybe $2,000,000. That gives Evelyn her fund-raising target. And it gets us the building we've all been talking about, the best thing that's happened to this place in years."

"Okay," said Ralph White. "You've brought out the important factors. I think we've chewed on this enough. I understand the various concerns around the table. Now here's what I think I'll recommend to the president and the board: can you all support a recommendation to. . . ."[52]

CASE QUESTIONS

1. What problems are faced by the planning group? In attempting to come to agreement on a solution has the group faced decision interrupts?
2. What decision making style would the Vroom-Yetton model predict would be useful? Do you agree?
3. The chapter describes techniques available for improving decision making. Which, if any, would be useful for this group?

NOTES

1. "Fiat: The Uno Car Is Helping to Make It No. 1," *Business Week,* January 23, 1984, pp. 79–82; "Fiat: Going Back to the Basics to Make It Through the 1980s," *Business Week,* January 12, 1981, pp. 46–48.
2. Charles Schwenk and Howard Thomas, "Formulating the Mess: The Role of Decision Aides In Problem Formulation," *Omega* 11 (1983): 239–252; W. F. Pounds, "The Process of Problem Finding," *Industrial Management Review* 11 (Fall 1969): 19.
3. K. MacCrimmon and R. Taylor, "Decision Making and Problem Solving," in M. D. Dunnett (ed.), *Handbook of Industrial and Organizational Psychology.* (Chicago: Rand McNally, 1976): 1397–1453.
4. Herbert A. Simon, *The New Science of Management Decision,* rev. ed. (Englewood Cliffs, NJ: Prentice-Hall, 1977).
5. "Can VW Regain Its Magic Touch?" *Business Week,* August 6, 1984, pp. 50–58.
6. Earnest R. Archer, "How to Make a Business Decision: An Analysis of Theory and Practice," *Management Review* 69 (February 1980): 54–61.
7. Archer, "How to Make a Business Decision."
8. Herbert A. Simon, *Administrative Behavior,* 2d ed. (New York: The Free Press, 1957).
9. Archer, "How to Make a Business Decision"; D. Miller and M. Starr, *The Structure of Human Decisions* (Englewood Cliffs, NJ: Prentice-Hall, 1967).
10. James G. March and Herbert A. Simon, *Organizations* (New York, Wiley, 1958).
11. Jorge Stein, "Strategic Decisions Methods," *Human Relations* 34 (1981): 917–933.
12. Per O. Solberg, "Unprogrammed Decision Making," *Industrial Management Review* 8 (1967): 19–29.

13. Thomas S. Issack, "Intuition: An Ignored Dimension of Management," *Academy of Management Review* 3 (1978): 917–922.

14. Roy Rowan, "Those Business Hunches Are More Than Blind Faith," *Fortune*, April 23, 1979, p. 112.

15. Trish H. Hall, "For a Company Chief, Where There's a Whim There's Often a Way," *The Wall Street Journal*, October 1, 1981, pp. 1, 18.

16. Hall, "For a Company Chief."

17. Douglas R. Sease, "Ford Awaits the Payoff on Its 4-Year Gamble on New Compact Car," *The Wall Street Journal*, May 4, 1983, pp. 1, 22; "Adopts Radical Styling and New Labor Policies Under Chairman P. Caldwell," *New York Times*, September 11, 1983, p. F1.

18. Norman P. R. Maier, "Assets and Liabilities in Group Problem Solving: The Need For An Integrative Function," *Psychological Review* 47 (1967): 239–249; Linda N. Jewell and H. Joseph Reitz, *Group Effectiveness in Organizations* (Glenview, Ill: Scott, Foresman, 1981).

19. Walter C. Swap, "Destructive Effects of Groups on Individuals," in Walter C. Swap and Associates (eds.), *Group Decision Making* (Beverly Hills, Ca: Sage, 1984); Janice M. Byer, "Ideologies, Values, and Decision Making in Organizations," in Paul C. Nystrom and William H. Starbuck (eds.) *Handbook of Organizational Design*, Vol. 2 (London: Oxford University Press, 1981).

20. Irving L. Janis, *Victims of Groupthink: A Psychological Study of Foreign-Policy Decisions and Fiascos* (Boston: Houghton Mifflin, 1972).

21. Irving L. Janis, *Groupthink*, 2d ed. (Boston: Houghton Mifflin, 1982), p. 9.

22. Janis, *Groupthink*, p. 9.

23. Janis, *Victims of Groupthink.*

24. Janis, *Groupthink*, p. 39.

25. Roy Rowan, "The Maverick Who Yelled Foul at Citibank," *Fortune*, January 10, 1983, pp. 46–56; "Close Encounters: Was Law Firm's Study of Citibank's Dealings Abroad A Whitewash?" *Wall Street Journal*, September 14, 1982, p. 1.

26. Irving L. Janis, "Groupthink," *Psychology Today*, November 1971.

27. This discussion is based on Victor H. Vroom and Phillip H. Yetton, *Leadership and Decision-Making* (Pittsburgh, PA: University of Pittsburgh Press, 1973); and Victor H. Vroom, "A New Look at Managerial Decision Making," *Organizational Dynamics*, (Spring 1973):

28. Adapted from Vroom and Yetton, *Leadership and Decision-Making.*

29. Vroom and Yetton, *Leadership and Decision-Making.*

30. Arthur G. Jaygo, "An Assessment of the Deemed Appropriateness of Participative Decision Making for High and Low Hierarchical Levels," *Human Relations* 34 (1981): 379–396; Arthur G. Jaygo and Victor H. Vroom, "Predicting Leader Behavior From a Measure of Behavioral Intent," *Academy of Management Journal* 21 (1978): 715–721.

31. Tom Richman, "One Man's Family," *Inc.*, November 1983, pp. 151–156.

32. Richard M. Cyert and James G. March, *A Behavioral Theory of the Firm* (Englewood Cliffs, NJ: Prentice-Hall, 1963); and James G. March and Herbert A. Simon, *Organizations* (New York, Wiley, 1958).

33. Douglas R. Sease, "School Superintendent, Once Pillar of Society Now is Often a Target," *The Wall Street Journal*, June 2, 1981, pp. 1, 18; and "Fort Jackson High School District," in Richard L. Daft, *Organization Theory and Design* (St. Paul, MN: West, 1983), pp. 375–376.

34. Charles Lindblom, "The Science of 'Muddling Through,'" *Public Administration Review* 19 (1954): 79–88.

35. J. B. Quinn, "Strategic Change: 'Logical Incrementalism,'" *Sloan Management Review* (Fall 1978): 7–21.

36. Journey Breckenfeld, "The Odyssey of Levi Strauss," *Fortune*, March 22, 1982, pp. 110–124.

37. Henry Mintzberg, Duru Raisinghani, and Andre Theoret, "The Structure of 'Unstructured' Decision Processes," *Administrative Science Quarterly* 21 (1976): 246–275.

38. Mintzberg, Raisinghani, and Theoret, "The Structure."

39. Mintzberg, Raisinghani, and Theoret, "The Structure," p. 270.

40. Mintzberg, Raisinghani, and Theoret, "The Structure," p. 273.

41. "Whoops: How It Happened," *Dun's Business Month*, October 1983, pp. 48–57.
42. Barry M. Staw, "The Escalation of Commitment to a Course of Action," *Academy of Management Review* 6 (1981): 577–587; and Barry M. Staw, "Knee-deep in the Big Muddy: A Study of Escalating Commitment to a Chosen Course of Action," *Organizational Behavior and Human Performance* 16 (1976): 27–45.
43. Barry M. Staw and F. V. Fox, "Escalation: The Determinants of Commitment to a Chosen Course of Action," *Human Relations* 30 (1977): 431–450; and Barry M. Staw and J. Ross, "Commitment to a Policy Decision: A Multitheoretical Perspective," *Administrative Science Quarterly* 23 (1978): 40–64.
44. Ellen Benoit and Stephen Kindel, "Hope Springs Eternal," *Forbes*, August 13, 1984, p. 34. Used with permission.
45. Charles Schwenk and Howard Thomas, "Formulating the Mess."
46. Charles R. Schwenk, "Devil's Advocacy in Managerial Decision-Making," *Journal of Management Studies* 21 (1984): 153–168.
47. A. George, "The Case for Multiple Advocacy in Making Foreign Policy," *The American Political Science Review* 66 (1972): 751–785.
48. Richard O. Mason and Ian I. Mitroff, *Challenging Strategic Assumptions* (New York: Wiley, 1981); Richard O. Mason, "A Dialectical Approach to Strategic Planning," *Management Science* 15 (1969): B403–B414.
49. A. Osborn, *Applied Imagination* (New York: Charles Scribner's Sons, 1953).
50. A. Delbecq, A. Van de Ven, and D. Gustafson, *Group Techniques for Program Planning* (Glenview, IL: Scott, Foresman, 1975); L. Richard Hoffman, "Improving the Problem-Solving Process in Managerial Groups," in Richard A. Guzzo (ed.), *Improving Group Decision Making in Organizations* (New York: Academic Press, 1982), pp. 95–126.
51. N. Delkey, *The Delphi Method: An Experimental Study of Group Opinion* (Santa Monica, CA: The Rand Corporation, 1969).
52. From John A. Dunn, Jr., "Organizational Decision Making," in Walter C. Swap and Associates (eds.), *Group Decision Making* (Beverly Hills, CA: Sage, 1984), pp. 280–310.

15 Power and Politics

H arry Gray, chairman and chief executive officer of United Technologies, has never believed in grooming successors. The four men who might have succeeded the 64-year-old Gray have either quit or been forced out.

While Harry Gray didn't found United Technologies, in the past thirteen years he has refashioned it so completely (even down to its name) that it has become his own creation. Now he is in the position of others who founded or transformed companies and found that turning over their power to others was almost unbearable. This difficulty isn't hard to understand. As one observer notes, "For people who have been attuned to power, there is an awful fear of giving it up."

During his tenure, Gray ran United Technologies with an iron hand. As he neared retirement age, members of the Board of Directors became increasingly uneasy about his use of power to thwart the succession process. The stock market also reflected this uneasiness. In the end, the board suggested a compromise and established a committee to "work with Gray" to find a successor. When the committee and board found their candidate, they went to great lengths to avoid formally naming the successor. Instead they announced that, with Gray's help, they had developed "an outstanding succession plan." It did not mention who would succeed Gray.[1]

Power and political processes in organizations, such as those happening at United Technologies, are of central importance in the study of organizations. Along with other group processes such as communication and decision making, power and politics influence both the behavior and the attitudes of employees at all levels of the organization. These processes also influence the extent to which various units within the organization secure the resources needed to accomplish tasks and achieve ultimate organizational effectiveness.

Power is very much a part of group functioning. Within work groups, power relationships determine group structure and reinforce role relationships and norms. Communication patterns and the actual messages themselves are often influenced by power distributions. Decision making, too, is constrained and guided by who has power over whom. In short, power and the political process are facts of organizational life, and managers must be equipped to deal with them.

RELEVANCE OF POWER AND POLITICS FOR MANAGERS

Organizations are comprised of alliances and coalitions between various parties and factions who compete with one another for scarce and valued resources. A major influence on how a decision is reached is the group or groups in support of each decision alternative. Power distributions throughout an organization can have serious repercussions on many aspects of organizational life, including work attitudes, motivation, communication, and retention. Hence an awareness of power dynamics at work is important for managers.

Since power is closely related to both leadership and authority, managers must understand when one method of influence stops and another begins. There is often a fine line between the exercise of legitimate authority by a manager and the use of unauthorized power. Awareness of power tactics commonly employed in organizations can help managers respond appropriately to threats. Not all attempts to exercise power against someone succeed. A major determinant of success or failure is the extent to which the object of the powerplay understands what is going on and responds appropriately.

For these reasons, contemporary managers must understand how power and politics work on both a micro level—power between individuals or groups —and a macro level—power in the larger organizational or transorganizational setting.

DEFINITION OF POWER

One of the earliest definitions of power was suggested by Weber, who defined it as "the probability that one actor within a social relationship will be in a position to carry out his own will despite resistance."[2] Emerson notes, "The power of actor A over actor B is the amount of resistance on the part of B which can be potentially overcome by A."[3]

We shall define **power** as an interpersonal (or intergroup) relationship in which one individual (or group) can cause another individual (or group) to take an action that it would not otherwise take. In other words, power involves one person changing the behavior of another. In most situations we are talking about *implied* force to comply, not *actual* force. That is, person A has power over person B if person B believes that person A can force B to comply with A's wishes.

For example, Harry Gray held considerable power primarily because the board and company felt he was indispensable to corporate success. He had a proven track record and they needed him. On several occasions, Gray responded to board opposition by threatening to resign. Such moves reminded board members how much they needed him.

DYNAMICS OF POWER AND INFLUENCE: A MICRO PERSPECTIVE

Clearly power is related closely to authority and leadership; this relationship is shown in Exhibit 15.1. In fact, power has been referred to by some as "informal

EXHIBIT 15.1
Three Types of Influence in Organizations

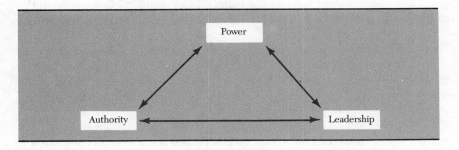

authority,"[4] while authority has been called "legitimate power."[5] However, important differences exist between these three concepts.

Power is the ability of one person or group to secure compliance from another person or group. In contrast, **authority** is the *right* to seek compliance by others. In other words, authority is backed by legitimacy. A manager who instructs a secretary to type certain letters presumably has the authority to make such a request. However, if the same manager asked the secretary to run personal errands, this would not be a legitimate exercise of authority. While the secretary might act on this request, her compliance would be based on power or influence considerations, not authority.

Thus, authority is based on group acceptance of one's right to exercise legitimate control. As Grimes notes, "What legitimizes authority is the promotion or pursuit of collective goals that are associated with group consensus. The polar opposite, power, is the pursuit of individual particularistic goals associated with group compliance."[6]

Finally, **leadership** is the ability of one individual to exercise influence over and above required or mechanical compliance. This *voluntary* aspect of leadership sets it apart from power and authority. A distinction is often made between *headship* and *leadership*. A department head has the right to require certain actions, but a leader has the ability to inspire certain actions. Although both roles may be played by the same individual, such is not always the case. In fact, a major lesson from the literature on group dynamics is that many organizations develop leadership patterns that do not include the supervisor or department head.

Five Bases of Power

At least two efforts have been made to identify the **bases of power.** The first model, proposed by Etzioni, identifies three types of power and argues that organizations can be classified according to which of the three types of power is most prevalent.[7] **Coercive power** involves forcing someone to comply with one's wishes. For example, a prison organization is a coercive organization. **Utilitarian power** is based on performance-reward contingencies; that is, a person will comply with his or her supervisor to receive a pay raise of promotion. Business organizations are essentially utilitarian organizations. Finally, **normative power** rests on the beliefs of the members in the right of the organization to govern their behavior. An example here would be a religious or fraternal organization.

While useful for comparative analysis of divergent organizations, this model may have limited applicability since most business and public organizations rest largely on utilitarian power. A model developed by French and Raven of the **bases of power** may be more helpful.[8] French and Raven identified five primary ways power can be exerted in social situations.

Reward Power   **Reward power** exists when person A has power over person B because A controls rewards B wants. These rewards can cover a wide array of possibilities, including pay raises, promotions, desirable job assignments, more responsibility, new equipment, and so forth. Research indicates that reward power often leads to increased job performance as employees see a strong performance-reward contingency (see Chapter 5).[9] However, supervisors and managers often do not control many rewards. For example, raises and promotions for most blue-collar workers are based on labor contracts, not performance appraisals or merit.

Coercive Power   This power is based primarily on fear. Person A has power over person B because A can administer some form of punishment to B. Thus, this kind of power is also referred to as punishment power. As Kipnis points out, coercive power need not rest on the threat of violence: "Individuals exercise coercive power through a reliance upon physical strength, verbal facility, or the ability to grant or withhold emotional support from others. These bases provide the individual with the means to physically harm, bully, humiliate, or deny love to others."[10] Examples of coercive power in organizations include the ability to fire or demote someone, transfer someone to an undesirable job or location, or strip them of perquisites. A good deal of organizational behavior—such as prompt attendance, looking busy, avoiding whistle-blowing—can be attributed to fear of coercive power. As Kipnis explains, "Of all the bases of power available to man, the power to hurt others is possibly the most often used, most often condemned, and most difficult to control."[11]

Legitimate Power   **Legitimate power** exists when person B submits to person A because B feels that A has a right to exert power in a certain domain. Legitimate power is really another name for authority. A supervisor has a right, for instance, to assign work. It differs from reward and coercive power in that it depends on the official position a person holds, not on his or her relationship with other individuals.

Legitimate power derives from three sources. First, prevailing cultural values can assign power to some group. In Japan, for instance, older employees derive power because of their age. Second, legitimate power can be attained as a result of the accepted social structure. For example, some countries have royal families that serve as cornerstones to their societies. Third, legitimate power may be designated, as when a board of directors chooses a new company president or an executive promotes a subordinate into a managerial position. Whatever the reason, people exercise legitimate power because subordinates assume they have a right to exercise it. A principal reason for the downfall of the Shah of Iran is that the people came to question and then reject his legitimate power.

Referent Power   Sometimes person B admires person A and, as a result, follows A because of A's personal qualities or other characteristics. In this case, A has **referent power** to influence B. Referent power has also been called *charismatic power* because allegiance is based on the interpersonal attraction of one individual for another. Referent power can be seen in advertisements in which companies use celebrities to recommend their products in the hope that the appeal of the person will rub off on the products. In work environments, junior managers often emulate senior managers and develop subservient roles based more on admiration and respect than on formal authority.

Expert Power   **Expert power** is demonstrated when person A gains power because he or she has knowledge or expertise useful to B. For instance, professors presumably have power in the classroom because of their mastery of a particular subject. Other users of expert power are staff specialists in organizations (e.g., accountants, labor relations managers, management consultants, and corporate attorneys). In each case, the individual has credibility in a particular area as a result of experience and expertise, and this credibility gives the individual power in that domain, and not in others.

In summary, at least five bases of power can be identified. In each case, the power of the individual rests on a particular attribute of the powerholder, the follower, or both. In some cases (e.g., reward power) power rests with the superior; in others (e.g., referent power) it is given to the superior by the subordinate. In all cases the exercise of power involves delicate and sometimes threatening interpersonal consequences for the parties involved, as can be seen in the following example.

UP CLOSE 15.1:   The French Civil Service

The importance of the bases of power in organizations can be seen in a classic study of bureaucracy by Michael Crozier, a French sociologist who examined patterns of influence between groups of production workers and maintenance workers on a shop floor.[12] The two groups had dramatically different backgrounds. Production workers were recruited from among people legally entitled to government employment under French law. This included war widows, orphans, disabled veterans, and ex-military personnel. They enjoyed considerable job security through civil service, were protected against unfair disciplinary action, and could not be replaced or transferred arbitrarily. However, while secure, these people were less skilled and more heterogeneous than the maintenance workers, who were highly skilled technicians recruited through difficult competitive examinations. They tended to have similar backgrounds and shared similar values.

An additional difference between the two groups was the reward systems in use. Production workers used a piece-rate incentive plan, so their wages increased with their production. In contrast, maintenance workers were salaried and governed by strict seniority.

As might be expected from the above details, Crozier found that the Achilles' heel in terms of power was the control the maintenance workers had over machine stoppages and "repairs". In this otherwise highly predictable, highly routine factory, machine stoppages were the only major events that could not be predicted or programmed. Thus, production workers were clearly dependent on maintenance workers, who were not dependent on production workers. Maintenance workers had a form of expert power (that is, they knew how to fix and maintain the machines) over the production workers and they took advantage of this power.

To maintain their position, maintenance workers "built a fence" around their jobs. They adhered to a guild apprenticeship system to restrict entry, disregarded blueprints and maintenance directions, used ambiguous machine settings, and generally kept their skills at a rule-of-thumb level. Not even supervisors had enough expertise or knowledge to check their work. As a result, they succeeded in protecting their base of power in the factory and could successfully bargain with the production workers for whatever they wanted. ■

Power Dependencies in Organizations

In situations involving power, at least two persons (or groups) can be identified: the person attempting to influence others (using various bases of power) and the target or targets of that influence. Until recently, attention focused almost exclusively on how people tried to influence others. Only recently has equal attention been paid to how people respond to influence attempts. The extent to which influence attempts are successful is now recognized to be determined in large part by the **power dependencies** of those on the receiving end of the influence attempts. Not all people are subject to (or dependent on) the same bases of power. At least three factors have been identified in people's vulnerability to influence attempts, as shown in Exhibit 15.2.[13]

Subordinates' Values   Person B's values can affect his or her susceptibility to influence attempts. For example, if the outcomes A can influence are important to B, then B is more likely to be open to influence attempts than if the outcomes are unimportant. Hence, if an employee places a high value on money and believes a supervisor actually controls pay raises, that employee should be

EXHIBIT 15.2
Relationship Between One Person's Bases of Power and Another Person's Power
Dependencies

Person A's *Bases of Power*	Person B's *Power Dependencies*
A's reward power ———————→	
A's coercive power ——————→ ←————— B's values and goals	
A's legitimate power —————→ ←————— B's relationship with A	
A's referent power —————————→ ←————— Extent of B's counterpower	
A's expert power ———————————→	

highly susceptible to the supervisor's influence. Comments that young people
don't want to work hard may reflect the perception that some young people
don't place a high value on traditional rewards like money. In other words, the
complaints may really be that young people are more difficult to influence than
they were in the past.

The Nature of Relationships   The nature of relationship between A and B can
be a factor in power dependence. Are A and B peers, or a superior and a
subordinate? Is the job permanent or temporary? A person on a temporary job,
for example, may feel less need to acquiesce since he or she won't be holding
the position for long. Moreover, if A and B were peers or good friends, the
influence process would likely be more delicate than if they were superior and
subordinate.

Counterpower   A third factor to consider in power dependencies is **counterpower.** The concept of counterpower focuses on the extent to which B has other
sources of power to buffer the effects of A's power. For example, if B belongs to
a union, the union's power may negate A's influence attempts. The use of
counterpower can be clearly seen in a variety of situations in which various
coalitions attempt to bargain with each other and check the power of their
opponents.

UP CLOSE 15.2:   Women in Management

*The traditional problems of women in management illustrate how formal and
informal practices often combine to cause powerlessness. Historically, women
in management have filled the more routine, low-profile staff positions, where
they support generally male line managers but have little real power.*[14]
    *One reason for this powerlessness arises from the behavior of male managers
toward their female counterparts. For instance, male managers can make a*

woman powerless by patronizing her. That is, when one is put into a "safe" job, not exposed to high risk, not given visible assignments, or not given enough to do to prove one's ability, one has little opportunity to demonstrate responsibility and earn respect—and power—for making substantive contributions to the organization. In addition, women can be rendered powerless when other managers show obvious signs of a lack of managerial support. For example, allowing someone supposedly in authority to be easily bypassed means that no one need take that person seriously.

Since power is closely related to the nature of interpersonal relationships, women can lose it by being excluded from the social life of the organization. A woman who is consistently not invited to management parties or social occasions loses opportunities to develop close social ties with other managers. Finally, even when women acquire some power, they are often unable to translate it into an organizational power base. Power bases typically develop when the powerholder can pass on or share power with subordinates through a mentoring system. Women are generally the recipients of such sponsorship, not the sponsors. Thus, they have little opportunity to develop a power network in which they are the central figures.

When mechanisms such as these are in place, it becomes relatively easy to impede the ability of anyone—man or woman—to acquire or use power in an organizational setting. Whether this situation will change dramatically in the near future depends on women's continued drive to acquire a greater power base and men's willingness to provide a more supportive environment in which power accrues according to ability, not gender. ■

Symbols of Managerial Power in Organizations

How do we know when a manager has power in an organization? Kanter had identified several common symbols of managerial power.[15] For example, managers have power to the extent that they can intercede favorably on behalf of someone in trouble with the organization. They also have power when they can get a desirable placement for a talented subordinate or obtain approval for expenditures beyond their budget. Other manifestations of power include the ability to secure above-average salary increases for subordinates and the ability to get items on the agenda at policy meetings and conferences.

In addition, someone who can gain quick access to top decision-makers or get early information about decisions and policy shifts has power. Finally, power is evident when a manager's opinions on important questions are sought by top decision-makers. Through such actions, the organization sends clear signals concerning who does and who does not have power. In this way, the organization condones the existing power structure.

POLITICS AND POLITICAL PROCESSES

Related to the topic of power is the equally important topic of politics. In any discussion of the exercise of power, particularly in intergroup situations, a knowledge of basic political processes is essential. The following discussion, then, will subsequently enable us to consider political strategies for acquiring and maintaining power.

One of the earliest definitions of politics was offered by Lasswell, who described it as who gets what, when, and how.[16] Even this simple definition demonstrates that politics involves the resolution of differing preferences about the allocation of scarce and valued resources. Politics is one mechanism for resolving allocation problems when other mechanisms, such as the introduction of new information or the use of majority rule, fail to apply. We shall adopt Pfeffer's definition of **politics** as "those activities taken within organizations to acquire, develop, and use power and other resources to obtain one's preferred outcomes in a situation in which there is uncertainty to dissensus about choices."[17] In comparing the concepts of politics and power, Pfeffer goes on:

> *If power is a force, a store of potential influence through which events can be affected, politics involves those activities or behaviors through which power is developed and used in organizational settings. Power is a property of the system at rest; politics is the study of power in action. An individual, subunit or department may have power within an organizational context at some period of time; politics involves the exercise of power to get something accomplished, as well as those activities which are undertaken to expand the power already possessed or the scope over which it can be exercised.*

Pfeffer's definition makes clear that political behavior is activity that is initiated to overcome opposition. In the absence of opposition, there is no need for political activity. Moreover, political activity need not be suboptimal for organizationwide effectiveness. Many managers believe that their political actions on behalf of their departments are in the best interests of their organizations as a whole. Finally, politics, like power, is not inherently bad. The survival of the organization often depends on a department or coalition of departments successfully challenging a traditional but outdated policy or objective. That is why an understanding of organizational politics as well as power is essential for managers today.

Political vs. Rational Behavior in Organizations

Modern organizations are highly political. Indeed, much of the goal-related effort produced by organizations is directly attributable to political processes. In the realm of interpersonal and intergroup behavior, Miles observes, "conditions that threaten the status of the power or encourage the efforts of those wishing to increase their power base will stimulate the intensity of organizational politics and increase the proportion of decision making behavior that can be classified as political as opposed to rational."[18]

There are five major reasons why behavior in organizations is often more political than rational:

1. *Scarcity of resources.* Politics typically emerge when scarce resources must be allocated. If resources are ample, there is no need to use politics to claim one's share.

2. *Nonprogrammed decisions.* With **nonprogrammed decisions** (those not predetermined by policy guidelines), conditions surrounding the decision problem and process are usually ambiguous, leaving room for political maneuvering. Programmed decisions, on the other hand, are typically specified in such detail that little room for maneuvering exists. Hence, political behavior commonly involves major questions, such as long-range strategic planning decisions.

3. *Ambiguous goals.* When the goals of a department or organization are ambiguous, more room is available for politics.

4. *Technology and environment.* Political behavior often increases when the internal technology is nonroutine and the external environment is dynamic and complex.

5. *Organizational change.* Periods of organizational change also present opportunities for political behavior. Efforts to restructure a particular department, open a new division, introduce a new product line, and so forth, are invitations to join the political process as different factions and coalitions fight over territory.[19]

UP CLOSE 15.3:   Mary Cunningham

A classic example of a structural change in an organization leading to the exercise of political behavior can be seen in the case of Mary Cunningham.[20] Cunningham joined Bendix Corporation at the age of twenty-eight after graduating from Harvard Business School. She was hired by the president, William Agee, after a three-hour interview in New York at the Waldorf Astoria. Cunningham described the interview as "a meeting of kindred spirits." Her position was executive assistant to the president.

Cunningham took to her job with enthusiasm and, by most accounts, competence. Soon she began screening Agee's calls and mail, writing his speeches, and, as other executives at Bendix saw it, building a very substantial power base. No one could see Agee without going through Cunningham.

In addition, many at Bendix observed that Agee and Cunningham were inseparable after as well as during work. Rumors about the couple began to spread. These rumors increased when Agee's divorce from his wife of twenty-three years was announced. Meanwhile, Cunningham was promoted to vice president for corporate and public affairs. Her power base continued to grow. Three months later she was promoted to vice president for strategic planning (at age twenty-nine).

By this time resentment was building. Questions were raised by other executives and board members about Cunningham's experience and competence for such a high-level position. Innuendos concerning the personal relationship between the two grew so blatant that Agee called a public meeting of Bendix employees to deny there was any affair. For her part, Cunningham pointed out that if she had been a man, she would have been hailed as a "whiz kid."

Finally the board of directors, responding to all the negative publicity in the media about Agee and Cunningham, decided she should resign. Cunningham did resign, received a severance check for $120,000, and immediately took a job at Seagram's as vice president for strategic planning.

The case of Mary Cunningham provides a good example of political behavior in organizations. Cunningham began her eighteen-month career at Bendix near the top of the hierarchy and was promoted rapidly. She was young and female and had no time to establish solid bases of power in the organizations. Her only source of support—Agee—proved incapable of stemming the tide of resentment and jealousy that emerged. (Agee himself was subsequently forced out of Bendix in another conflict.)

In essence, Agee had made a major structural change in the managerial hierarchy—placing Cunningham in the center of decision making—and had attempted to shift the power balance within the organization. The other executives responded to this threatened loss of power (and to the bad publicity the company was receiving) by working to remove the source of the problem. They succeeded. ■

Given that most contemporary organizations have scarce resources, ambiguous goals, increasingly complex technologies, and more sophisticated and unstable external environments, it seems reasonable to conclude that many contemporary organizations are highly political. As a result, contemporary managers must be sensitive to political processes as they relate to the acquisition and maintenance of power in work organizations.

Policy guidelines and standard operating procedures (SOPs) have been developed by organizations to reduce the extent to which politics influence decisions. The desire to encourage more rational decisions in organizations motivated Weber's development of the bureaucratic model. Thus, increases in the specification of policy statements often are inversely related to political efforts, because such actions reduce the uncertainties surrounding a decision and hence the opportunity for political efforts to be made.

POWER IN ORGANIZATIONS: A MACRO PERSPECTIVE

To this point, we have discussed the concepts of power and politics and presented a simple model of the way power is exercised in interpersonal relations. Shifting our focus from the individual or interpersonal to the organizational level of analysis complicates the picture. In explaining how political strategies are used to attain and maintain power in intergroup or organization-wide relations, we shall highlight two issues. The first is the relationship between power and the control of critical resources; the second is the relationship between power and the control of strategic contingencies. Both illustrate how subunit control can lead to the acquisition of power in organizational settings.

Controlling Scarce Resources

When one subunit of an organization controls a scarce resource that is needed by another subunit, the first subunit has power because it can bargain for the resources it needs from the organization. Hence, while all subunits may contribute something to the organization as a whole, power allocation within the organization is influenced by the relative importance of the resources each contributes. Salancik and Pfeffer explain:

> Subunit power accrues to those departments that are most instrumental in bringing or in providing resources which are highly valued by the total organization. In turn, this power enables these subunits to obtain more of those scarce and critical resources allocated within the organization. Stated succinctly, power derived from acquiring resources is used to obtain more resources, which in turn can be employed to produce more power—"the rich get richer."[21]

UP CLOSE 15.4:   University of Illinois

Salancik and Pfeffer examined the relationship between control of resources and subsequent power and favorability of decision outcomes among various academic departments of a major state university.[22] Their aim was to test the hypothesis that departments that controlled critical resources had more power and could secure more favorable decision outcomes.

In the study, power was measured by having department heads rate the amount of influence each department had over decisions and by examining departmental representation on important university-wide committees. The key resources needed by the university were adequate numbers of students, prestigious departments, outside grant support, visible department activities, administrative and service contributions by departments to the university, and professional and business contacts outside the university.

The investigation found that the best predictors of the extent of departmental power were the department's ability to provide outside funds to the university in the form of contracts and grants, the size of the department's graduate student body, and the national prestige of the department, particularly the first. In addition, the study examined how three common resource allocation decisions were made. The three resources were the amount of funds to support graduate student fellowships, faculty research grants, and summer faculty fellowships. It was found that the more scarce the resource, the more political (as opposed to rational) the decision-making process. Moreover, the amount of departmental power was found to be related to the allocation decisions on these three resources.

In summary, Salancik and Pfeffer concluded that departments or subunits that had more power found it easier to secure a greater share of the scarce resources available and that these resources reinforced their power. Hence, a continual cycle was established whereby power led to increased resources, which led to continued power, and so forth. ■

Controlling of Strategic Contingencies

In addition to controlling scarce resources, groups can attain power by controlling **strategic contingencies**. A *contingency* is defined by Miles as "a requirement of the activities of one subunit that is affected by the activities of other subunits."[23] For example, the business office of most universities represents a strategic contingency for the various colleges within the university because it can approve or veto financial expenditures of the schools. Since its approval is far from certain, it is a source of uncertainty in the decision-making process. A contingency becomes strategic when it can alter the balance of interunit or interdepartmental power so that units' interdependencies are changed.[24]

One way to illustrate this is to consider power distribution in organizations as they attempt to deal with a major source of uncertainty—the external environment. In a classic study by Lawrence and Lorsch, influence patterns were examined in companies in three industries: container manufacturing, food processing, and plastics.[25] For *successful* firms, power distribution conformed to the firms' strategic contingencies. For example, in the container-manufacturing companies, where the critical contingencies were customer delivery and product quality, the major share of power in decision making resided in the sales and production staffs. In contrast, in the food-processing firms, where the strategic contingencies focused on expertise in marketing and food sciences, major power rested in the sales and research units. In other words, those who held power in the successful organizations were in areas that were of central concern to the firm. The functional areas that were most important for organizational success were under the control of the key decision makers. For less successful firms, this congruence was not present.

The evolving nature of strategic contingencies can be seen in the evolution of power distribution in major public utilities. Many years ago, when electric companies were developing, most senior officers were engineers and technical development was the central issue. Today, however, as utilities face more litigation, government regulation, and controversies over nuclear power, lawyers predominate in the leadership of most companies. This reflects Miles' point that "subunits could inherit and lose power, not necessarily by their own actions, but by the shifting contingencies in the environment confronting the organization."[26]

UP CLOSE 15.5:   Apollo and Sabre

Strategic contingencies in action are clearly seen in computerized airline reservation systems. Seventy percent of all reservations in this country are made through two computer systems: American Airlines' Apollo system and United Airlines' Sabre system. Each travel agency contracts with one of these systems and all airline reservations made by the agency go through that system.[27]

Each system is supposed to list all flights and all cost information for all airlines in an equitable way. Information is supposed to be updated daily. Hence, in theory, travel agents can easily find the best connections and the lowest fares for their customers. However, many smaller carriers claim that American and United list their own flights first, fail to list some competing flights, and delay updating competitors' flight or price changes as long as possible.

The end result? The travel agent is guided by the computer system to select American or United. In short, the information provided travel agents is owned and controlled by companies that have a vested interest in the choices travel agents make. As a result, American and United control a central strategic contingency that can make the difference between success and failure for the other carriers. While many solutions to this apparent conflict of interest have been proposed (including legislative controls and legally mandated divestiture of the computer systems by the airlines), no resolution is in sight. ■

POWER TACTICS IN ORGANIZATIONS

The two bases of intergroup power—control of critical resources and control of strategic contingencies—imply various tactics that can be employed to gain power. We are now in a position to review several power tactics that can be found in organizational settings.[28]

- *Controlling access to information or individuals.* Most decisions rest on the availability of relevant information, so persons controlling access to information play a major role in decisions made. A good example of this is the common corporate practice of pay secrecy. Only the personnel department and senior managers typically have salary information—and power—for personnel decisions. A related power tactic is the practice of controlling access to persons. A well-known factor contributing to former President Nixon's downfall was his isolation from others; his two senior advisors had complete control over who saw him.

- *Selective use of objective criteria.* Very few organizational questions have one correct answer; instead, an appropriate decision is made that best fits the established criteria. Those who selectively use objective criteria that can lead to a decision favorable to themselves have significant power. According to Herbert Simon, if an individual is permitted to select decision criteria, he or she needn't care who actually makes the decision. Attempts to control objective decision criteria can be seen in faculty debates over who gets hired or promoted. One group may emphasize teaching and tries to set criteria based on teacher competence, knowledge of subject area, interpersonal relations, and so on. Another group may emphasize research and argues for criteria related to number of publications, reputation in the field, and so forth.

- *Controlling the agenda.* One easy way to influence a decision is to ensure that it never comes up for consideration in the first place. There are several strategies for controlling the agenda. Efforts may be made to order the topics at a meeting in such a way that the undesired topic is last on the list. Failing this, opponents may raise a number of objections or points of information concerning the topic that cannot be easily answered, thereby tabling the topic until another day.

- *Using outside experts.* Another way to gain an advantage is by using outside experts. The group wishing to exercise power may take the initiative and bring in experts from the field or experts sympathetic to their cause. Hence, if a dispute arises between spending more money on research or on actual production, outside research and production consultants would likely produce different answers. Most consultants have had clients feed them information and biases they hoped the consultants would repeat in a meeting.

- *Bureaucratic gamesmanship.* Sometimes the organization's own policies and procedures provide ammunition for power plays, or bureaucratic gamesmanship. For instance, a group may drag its feet on making changes by staging a red-tape work slowdown, or by *working to rule*. In this way, the members let it be known that the work flow will continue to slow down until they get their way.

- *Using coalitions and alliances.* One group can effectively increase its power by forming an alliance with other groups that have similar interests. This technique is often used when multiple labor unions in the same corporation join forces to gain contract concessions for their workers. It can also be seen in the tendency of corporations within an industry to form trade associations to lobby for their position. While the members of a coalition need not agree on everything—and may be competitors—agreement on the problem under consideration is necessary as a basis for action.

UP CLOSE 15.6:   The Keidanren

The use of coalitions in power dynamics can be seen in the role of the Japanese Keidanren *in international trade and economic development. This example carries our macro analysis to the broader perspective of the power relationships between nations.*[29]

As the U.S. struggles to improve its balance of trade, controversy increases over its sizable trade deficit with Japan. As the size of the deficit increases, many sectors in the U.S. (e.g., the American automobile manufacturers) have intensified their efforts to achieve greater protection from high-quality, low-price Japanese goods. In the face of this movement, the Japanese have sought politically acceptable means of redressing the imbalance. One such mechanism is "reverse investment."

Reverse investment is the process by which one country's firms (in this case Japan) build manufacturing plants in another country (the U.S.), thus creating jobs in the second country while making their products close to their ultimate markets. Many Japanese firms have initiated such moves, including Sony, Nissan, Honda, Fujitsu, and others.

In April 1984, the Keidanren, a powerful economic development organization made up of Japan's leading executives, sent teams of executives to various states in the U.S. The teams had two primary goals: to seek possible new plant sites for further Japanese expansion and to spread the word that future development was tied to repeal of the unitary tax, a corporate income tax states levy in which worldwide corporate income (instead of state or U.S. income) forms the basis for tax calculations. Japan argues that the tax is unfair and requires submission of confidential corporate income data. As a result, the companies represented in the Keidanren have banded together to change state income tax laws.

The strategy is paying off. Shortly after the Keidanren visits, the governor of Oregon called the legislature into special session and repealed the unitary tax. Several Japanese firms promptly announced plans to build plants in Oregon. Florida, Indiana, and California have similarly begun looking into repeal of the tax. The message is clear for states interested in attracting Japanese firms as part of their economic development programs: in exchange for their investment of foreign capital (and jobs), the Japanese want what they consider more equitable tax treatment in the U.S. ■

While additional power tactics could be discussed, these examples illustrate the diverse techniques available to those interested in acquiring and exercising power in organizational situations. In reviewing the major research carried out on the topic of power, Pfeffer states:

> *If there is one concluding message, it is that it is probably effective and it is certainly normal that these managers do behave as politicians. It is even better that some of them are quite effective at it. In situations in which technologies are uncertain, preferences are conflicting, perceptions are selective and biased, and information processing capacities are constrained, the model of an effective politician may be an appropriate one for both the individual and for the organization in the long run.*[30]

SUMMARY

This chapter examined the related topics of power and politics. Power is an interpersonal or intergroup relationship in which one party can cause another party to take an action the second party would not have taken otherwise. This definition presupposes implied force, not actual force. Five bases of power include reward power, coercive power, legitimate power, referent power, and expert power. The concept of power dependency, or the ability of the recipient of a power attempt to neutralize that power attempt, was also examined.

Politics includes all activities initiated to acquire, develop, and use power and other resources to obtain one's preferred outcomes in situations of uncertainty. Among the reasons why behavior in organizations is often more political than rational are scarcity of resources, the ambiguity associated with non-programmed decisions, the consequences of ambiguous goals, changing technology and environments, and changes in organization design.

Two approaches to implementing power and politics in organizations are the control of scarce resources and the control of strategic contingencies. Through such controls, one party hopes to influence or control another. Finally, several specific power tactics commonly found in organizations include: 1) controlling access to information or individuals; 2) the selective use of objective criteria; 3) controlling the agenda; 4) the use of outside experts; 5) bureaucratic gamesmanship; and 6) the use of coalitions and alliances.

KEY WORDS

authority	legitimate power	power dependencies
bases of power	nonprogrammed	referent power
coercive power	decisions	reward power
counterpower	normative power	strategic contingencies
expert power	politics	utilitarian power
leadership	power	

DISCUSSION QUESTIONS

1. What is the difference between power and politics? Provide examples of each to illustrate your answer.
2. Of the five bases of power, which should be most influential in a large retail organization? A high-technology firm? A military organization? A public governmental organization? Explain.
3. Explain how power dependencies work and provide an example.
4. Why, if organizations are rational entities, is so much political behavior observed in business organizations?
5. Describe how the strategic contingencies model works as an exercise in power. Provide an example from your own experience.
6. At the end of the chapter, several power tactics were identified. As a manager in a large organization, how might you go about resisting or nullifying each tactic? Be specific.
7. Overall, how important do you feel power and politics are in everyday life in organizations? Do you approve of this state of affairs? Why?

It was a shocking experience for me "upstairs." After eight years of running car divisions, I suddenly found myself in the fall of 1972 with no direct operating responsibilities and a non-job as a group executive. I had no business to manage directly. Where I had been a quarterback for eight years, I now was watching the game from the sidelines. I still wanted to play in the games. On the field. These feelings of occupational emptiness were complicated by personalities.[31]

At the time in my career when I was just one of the corporate boys spending my working and non-working hours with General Motors people or the company suppliers, I had a tightly knit group of corporate friends, and I obeyed the corporate dictates in behavior and dress. But as I grew it dawned on me that all of us were becoming too inbred. We were losing contact with America. With our customers. In addition, while I enjoyed work, I've always placed enjoying life high on my list of priorities. So I made a habit of widening my circle of friends and broadening my tastes. This awareness precipitated a seemingly endless chain of personality conflicts, the most difficult of which was with Roger M. Kyes, who was my boss while I was running the Pontiac and Chevrolet divisions. He made life unbearable for me, and he was dedicated to getting me fired; he told me so, many times. Fortunately, I had the protection of my ability as I ran those two divisions to fend off Kyes. But I remember vividly my conflicts with him, especially when he was irritated by my style of dress. The corporate rule was dark suits, light shirts and muted ties. I followed the rule to the letter, only I wore stylish Italian-cut suits, wide-collared off-white shirts and wide ties.

"Goddamnit, John," he'd yell. "Can't you dress like a businessman? And get your hair cut, too."

My hair was ear length with sideburns. I felt both my clothes and hair style were contemporary but not radical. . . .

The fact that I had been divorced, was a health nut and dated generally younger actresses and models didn't set well with the corporate executives or their wives either. And neither did my general disappearance from the corporate social scene. . . .

I thought all of this was an improper intrusion into my personal life, but I didn't pay much attention to it, which I guess perpetuated the problem. I figured I was loyal and dedicated to GM. I did my job and did it well. The company had a right to know how I was spending my business life; but it had no right to know how I was spending my private and non-business life.

Nevertheless, my clothing and lifestyle were increasingly rattling the cages of my superiors, as was the amount of publicity my personal and business lives were generating. I was being resented because my style of living violated an unwritten but widely revered precept that said no personality could outshine General Motors. The executives were supposed to be just as gray and almost as lifeless as the corporate image.

The resentments toward me festered and grew to great proportions without my knowledge: I knew some people disliked me. But since I didn't play the corporate political game, I was not wired into the underground flow of information which would have given me better knowledge about those who viewed themselves as my corporate enemies. . . .

It bothered me when Tom Murphy, my boss during my term at Chevrolet, many times said to me, "You know, John, everybody said I was going to have a helluva lot of trouble with you. But I would really have to say that this is untrue. As far as I am concerned you do the best job of running your division of anyone. You keep me informed of the important things. I know what you are doing. Far and away I have less trouble with you than anybody in the divisions."

Those were kind words from Murphy, the only top manager with whom I felt I had a good rapport. However, the warnings he was getting from other members of management that I was "trouble" indicated to me now that my papers were being graded "upstairs" by something other than my test scores. But my support from Murphy suddenly ended. It was a sinister occurrence which terminated it.

In November 1972, the corporation was staging a massive management meeting of the top 700 GM executives in Greenbrier, West Virginia. These were infrequent gatherings, at least three years apart, which were designed to discuss in total all of the corporation's problems and exchange ideas on how to solve them. Many of The Fourteenth Floor executives were given broad subjects on which to address the conference. As a group executive, I was given the topic of "Product Quality." I prepared a tough talk which in essence said the only way we can remain a success and grow is to deliver real value to the customer. I said that I felt the emphasis at General Motors had switched from this goal to one of taking the last nickel out of every part to improve profits in the short run. I singled out specific products and programs for criticism. The talk was both critical and constructive. It was the kind of talk that was for corporate ears and none other.

As is the required practice, we submitted early drafts of our talks to top management through the public relations department. Management then made corrections and generally edited the draft along the lines it felt was proper. In the process, an executive could wind up writing a speech four or five times or more. After each new draft was prepared, all the copies of the previous version were destroyed. My final draft was toned by management and edited to complement the speeches of the other executives.

Just prior to the conference, my Greenbrier talk turned up in the hands of Bob Irvin, automotive writer for the *Detroit News*. And he printed it. It was not the final version which he wrote about. It was one of the earlier drafts. The only people who had copies of that version were me, the public relations staff and top management. I hadn't leaked it. Nothing in the world could do me more harm personally and internally than to leak this type of a speech. My job was to sell our cars, not criticize them publicly. I was trying, with the talk, to impress people in the corporation with the need for drastic improvement in product quality to counter the growing wave of consumer unrest, fulfill our responsibility to our customers and restore our tarnished image.

The leak destroyed the Greenbrier conference for me and was probably the single thing that hurt me most in the corporation. I could tell that my solid image in Murphy's eyes began to diminish from the day the newspaper story appeared. I was shocked and sick. So was my staff. It was obvious that someone who wanted to give me a good shot to the gut, did.

A short time later, a friend of mine lunching in a downtown Detroit restaurant ran across a private investigator who knew GM's operations and who told him that the speech was leaked by a man on the GM public relations staff.

If I was having my doubts about staying with the corporation, and I was, it was now quite obvious that some people in the corporation were taking steps to see that I couldn't stay. . . .

I balked at becoming a group executive when the job was first offered to me in September. . . . Nevertheless, after two weeks of ceaseless pressure from my bosses, I relented and went upstairs. A non-Chevrolet man was named to the post I was departing. It was not very long before I realized I had made a horrible mistake. On my second day on the new job my boss, Richard Terrell, who succeeded Kyes as executive vice-president for Car and Truck, Body and Assembly, called me into his office. I had heard very little from him when I was running Chevrolet. Not once did we get into a serious discussion about the division's business. I suspect this was his choice since, until he succeeded Kyes, Terrell's entire 36-year GM career was spent in nonautomotive businesses, first with the Electromotive Division and then the Frigidaire Division. He, therefore, knew little directly about GM's automotive operations. This was my first meeting with Terrell in my new capacity. He is moderately tall, with thin gray hair, steel-rimmed glasses, a perpetual smile that looks more like a smirk and a manner that often gives a false sense of authority to what he says.

I walked into his office and sat down in front of his desk. Terrell pushed a button under the cabinet behind his desk which closed the office door, leaned forward in his chair, looked sternly across his desk and said to me in steely tones, "I want you to disappear into the wallpaper up here. I don't want to see you in the newspaper."

Those were not his exact words. He couched his message in terms of "team play," "good of the corporation," and how "no man is above the corporation." But the point of Terrell's message was as obvious to me as the dark suit and white shirt he wore.

"DeLorean, disappear into the boondocks."

I was shocked. And I knew that, while I hadn't heard from Terrell when I was running Chevrolet, I was going to be hearing a lot from him in the secretive quarters of The Fourteenth Floor because I was not protected by my ability and performance as I had been when I ran the car divisions. Up here I had nothing to operate to show that ability. I thought to myself: "Dealing with Terrell is going to be the Kyes situation all over again."

About a week or so later, I was in the office of Elliott M. (Pete) Estes, who was executive vice-president of operations. I was talking to him about some of my doubts about the business in general and life upstairs, and he said, "I've always told them that it's good for GM to have someone like you in the ranks. It shows how democratic we are."

I am sure Pete didn't realize the impact on me of his comment. He didn't say anything about how well I'd managed my business, the people I had developed, or what I'd contributed to the corporation in terms of quality products and substantial profit. All he said was I was sort of a weirdo. Until then, I guess I had deluded myself into thinking I was held in high esteem by my superiors, even if they didn't like me personally, because I was a business success. I had risen faster in the corporation than any of them, and I thought for that reason that I at least had their professional respect.

So I was tragically shocked to realize that this was not the case. Just as the corporation at the time had token blacks, token women and token Chicanos, I was viewed as their token hippie. I just didn't fit in. When I thought over the meetings with Terrell and Estes, I began to realize once again that I could no longer stay with General Motors. I agonized over the prospect of leaving.

The Greenbrier incident made it obvious that someone in the corporation was making an effort to hurt my business reputation. . . . I then began a campaign to leave the corporation which was going to culminate tomorrow morning when I officially resigned. Late Sunday night, I went to sleep.

. . . At about 9:30 A.M., I arrived at the General Motors Building at 59th Street and Fifth Avenue. A minute or so later I walked into the office of Chairman Richard D. Gerstenberg on the twenty-fourth floor. In the room were Gerstenberg, Murphy, by now the vice-chairman, and Kenneth C. MacDonald, who was secretary of the board's bonus and salary committee. . . .

The atmosphere in Gerstenberg's office was neither friendly nor bitter. It was strictly businesslike. The meeting lasted less than 20 minutes. I signed the document of resignation, effective May 31, 1973, which was prepared by the corporation. We all shook hands, and I left the room and headed for the bank of elevators.

Once on the main floor, I walked out into Fifth Avenue. For the first time in a quarter of a century I was out of work in the auto industry. There was a slight feeling of relief because the struggle was over. Bill Finelli took me back to LaGuardia and a flight to Detroit.

The board met that afternoon and approved my resignation. The public relations department prepared a news release—which was made public later in the month—announcing my resignation in which Gerstenberg praised my contributions to General Motors and wished me well in my new ventures. Once back in Detroit I drove home.

As I ate dinner quietly at home that night with my wife, Cristina, and my son, Zachary, I fully realized I had done what few top executives have ever done in the automobile industry. I had quit General Motors.

CASE QUESTIONS

1. DeLorean discusses several power relationships in this excerpt. What bases of power are being used by the various people mentioned?
2. How is the concept of power dependency illustrated in this case?
3. Some would explain DeLorean's leaving as a result of politics. What is meant by this explanation?

NOTES

1. Geoffrey Colvin, "Why Harry Gray Can't Let Go," *Fortune*, November 12, 1984, pp. 16–21.
2. A. M. Henderson and T. Parsons, *Max Weber: The Theory of Social and Economic Organization* (New York: The Free Press, 1947), p. 152.
3. R. Emerson, "Power-Dependence Relations," *American Sociological Review* 27 (1962):32.
4. Chester Barnard, *The Functions of the Executive* (Cambridge, MA: Harvard University Press, 1938).
5. A. Grimes, "Authority, Power, Influence, and Social Control: A Theoretical Synthesis," *Academy of Management Review* 3 (1978):725.
6. Grimes, "Authority, Power, Influence," p. 726.
7. Amitai Etzioni, *A Comparative Analysis of Complex Organizations* (New York: The Free Press, 1975).
8. J. R. French and B. Raven, "The Bases of Social Power," in D. Cartwright and A. Zender (eds.), *Group Dynamics* (New York: Harper & Row, 1968).
9. Y. Shetty, "Managerial Power and Organizational Effectiveness: A Contingency Analysis," *Journal of Management Studies* 15 (1978):178–81.
10. D. Kipnis, *The Powerholders* (Chicago: University of Chicago Press, 1976).
11. Kipnis, *The Powerholders.*
12. Michael Crozier, *The Bureaucratic Phenomenon* (Chicago: University of Chicago Press, 1964).
13. Terrence Mitchell, *People in Organizations* (New York: McGraw-Hill, 1978).
14. R. M. Kanter, "Power Failure in Management Circuits," *Harvard Business Review*, July–August, 1979, pp. 65–75.
15. Kanter, "Power Failure."
16. H. D. Lasswell, *Politics: Who Gets What, When, How* (New York: McGraw-Hill, 1936).
17. Jeffrey Pfeffer, *Power in Organizations* (Marshfield, MA: Pitman, 1981), p. 7.
18. Robert Miles, *Macro Organizational Behavior* (Glenview, IL: Scott, Foresman, 1980), p. 182.
19. Miles, *Macro Organizational Behavior.*

20. P. W. Bernstein, "Things the B-School Never Taught," *Fortune*, November 3, 1980, pp. 53–54; Mary Cunningham, *Powerplay* (New York: Simon & Schuster, 1984).
21. G. Salancik and J. Pfeffer, "The Bases and Uses of Power in Organizational Decision Making," *Administrative Science Quarterly* 19(1974):470.
22. G. Salancik and J. Pfeffer, "The Bases and Uses of Power."
23. Miles, *Macro Organizational Behavior*, p. 170.
24. Miles, *Macro Organizational Behavior.*
25. Paul Lawrence and Joy Lorsch, *Organization and Environment* (Boston: Division of Research, Graduate School of Business Administration, Harvard University, 1967).
26. Miles, *Macro Organizational Behavior,* p. 169.
27. Craig Carter, "A Different Air War," *Fortune*, February 18, 1985, p. 120.
28. Pfeffer, *Power in Organizations.*
29. Steven Carter, "Sony Leader Expects More U.S. Plants," *The Oregonian*, November 4, 1984, p. D6.
30. Pfeffer, *Power in Organizations*, p. 370.
31. J. Patrick Wright, *On a Clear Day You Can See General Motors* (New York: Avon Books, 1980), pp. 9–17.

16 Intergroup Relations and Conflict

C oordinating interdivisional relations in a major corporation like Hewlett-Packard is no easy task. Consider the example of HP's Computer Peripheral Group, which was marketing a new printer with extensive graphics capabilities. When HP users rushed out to buy the printer, they found that the operating software for their computers, which was made by another HP division, wouldn't allow them to use it for graphics. As one observer noted, "If anything is frustrating for the [computer] user, it's that divisional structure." At the heart of this problem was a collision within HP between its unique entrepreneurial culture and the increasing need for controls in the fast-growing computer industry.

The decentralized management style that HP forged over the years, which assigns the design and manufacture of products to individual divisions and gives sales responsibility to separate marketing groups, has resulted in overlapping products, lagging development of new technology, and a piecemeal approach to new markets. Indeed, HP is sometimes described as "three or four companies that don't seem to talk to each other."[1] To resolve these conflicts, HP's CEO, John Young, has initiated several programs to improve planning, coordinate marketing, and strengthen HP's computer-related research and development. In doing so, he walks a thin line. While organizational reform may be in order, Young doesn't want to damage the entrepreneurial and individualistic spirit that has largely been responsible for HP's growth to date.

The above example shows how intergroup relations affect organizational effectiveness. In this chapter we shall address the issues of intergroup behavior and conflict. When conflict between groups is minimized, greater resources and energy can be focused on corporate objectives.

RELEVANCE OF INTERGROUP RELATIONS AND CONFLICT FOR MANAGERS

An organization is a collection of individuals and groups. If the organization is to succeed, a way must be found to harness the energies of these sectors and interest groups for the overall good of the organization. After all, the well-being of employees rests on the success of the organization.

EXHIBIT 16.1
Determinants of Intergroup Performance

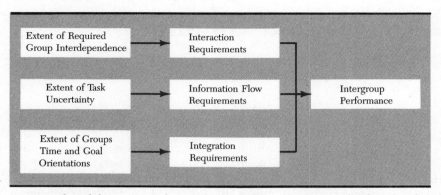

SOURCE: Adapted from A.D. Szilagyi and M.J. Wallace, *Organizational Behavior and Performance*, 3rd ed. (Glenview, IL: Scott, Foresman, 1983), p. 213.

Conflict often permeates an organization. Some conflict is inevitable. Simply making a decision to do A instead of B often alienates the supporters of B, despite the soundness of the reasons behind the decision. Conflict can have many causes. Whatever the nature of the conflict, its existence must be recognized and dealt with by managers. Hence, a knowledge of the causes of a conflict can help in identifying possible remedies. The consequences of conflict can be costly to an organization, as can be seen in labor disputes, as well as in conflicts between departments in the same organization. In an era of increasing competition both from abroad and at home, reducing wasteful conflict is important.

For these reasons, contemporary managers need a firm grasp of how intergroup relations and conflict work.

A MODEL OF INTERGROUP PERFORMANCE

To understand how groups interact with each other, we must identify the primary variables that characterize intergroup behavior. We can do this by using the model of intergroup performance suggested by Szilagyi and Wallace.[2] A version of this model is shown in Exhibit 16.1. Intergroup performance is largely influenced by three intervening variables—requirements for interaction, information flow, and integration. Each requirement, in turn, is influenced by the extent of required group interdependence, task uncertainty, and group time and goal orientations.

Interaction Requirements

Interaction requirements refer to the frequency and quality of interaction between groups required for successful task accomplishment. To be successful, organizations must achieve enough intergroup interaction to coordinate resource allocation and utilization to achieve corporate objectives. The amount of required interaction is determined by the extent of *interdependence* between the groups.

As noted in Chapter 9 on organizational technology, group interdependence takes three primary forms:

1. **Pooled interdependence** occurs when various groups are largely independent of each other, even though each contributes to and is supported by the larger organization. For example, while the physics and music departments may not interact frequently, both contribute to the larger goals of the university and both make use of university resources.
2. **Sequential interdependence** exists when the outputs of one unit or group become the inputs for another. For example, the shipping department is clearly dependent on manufacturing for the success of its own operation, while the manufacturing department is much less dependent on shipping.
3. **Reciprocal interdependence** occurs when two or more groups depend on each other for inputs. For example, without product engineering, the marketing department would have nothing to sell. On the other hand, without consumer information from marketing, product engineering might not know what to manufacture. Both units are highly dependent on each other, thereby requiring a high degree of interaction.

In summary, the type of interdependence determines in large part the degree of dependence of one group on another (Exhibit 16.2), which in turn

EXHIBIT 16.2
Three Types of Group Interdependence

Type of Interdependence	Degree of Dependence and Required Interaction	Description
Pooled	Low	Groups relatively independent of each other, although each contributes to over all goals of organization.
Sequential	Medium	One group's output becomes another group's input.
Reciprocal	High	Some of each group's outputs become inputs for the other.

determines the extent of required interaction. High dependence typically requires high intergroup interaction, while low dependence typically requires relatively low intergroup interaction.

UP CLOSE 16.1:   Summer Camp

The impact of intergroup dependence can be seen in a classic study by Muzafer Sherif[3] which sought to examine how groups learned to cooperate—or compete—with each other in the performance of their tasks. The study was carried out among boys attending a summer camp.

Sherif created two cohesive groups and, over time, put them through a series of competitive exercises (win-lose situations) in which both group identity and intergroup conflict and hostility increased. Resentment between groups surfaced, and each group adopted critical attitudes toward members of the other group. The emergence of extreme hostility led Sherif to conclude early in the experiment that when two groups are placed in a situation in which only one group can win, the competition engenders hostility between the groups and facilitates solidarity within the groups.

Sherif tried several conflict resolution strategies, including dispensing accurate favorable information about the opposing group, appealing to moral values and brotherhood, and introducing a common enemy to both groups, but each failed. In the end, Sherif placed the groups in a situation in which each needed the other to solve shared problems (a pooled interdependence situation). Problems included finding a broken waterpipe serving the camp, choosing a motion picture to be shown, and fixing the camp truck so groceries could be secured. The cumulative effect of having the groups pursue superordinate goals gradually reduced the hostility between them. The development of procedures for cooperating in specific activities had transfer value to new situations, thus promoting intergroup cooperation. As the experiment drew to a close, members of previously opposing groups became good friends. ■

Information Flow Requirements

The second requirement for successful intergroup performance is an optimal **information flow system.** (See Chapter 17 for a detailed description.) To be successful, groups need the appropriate amount and quality of information. Information flow is influenced to a large degree by the extent of **task uncertainty** (See Exhibit 16.3). When groups are working on highly uncertain tasks (e.g., a new product, an experiment, or an old product in a new environment), the need for communication increases. Where task uncertainty is low, less information is typically needed.

Task uncertainty, in turn, is influenced by two factors, as shown in Exhibit 16.3. The first, **task clarity**, is the extent to which the requirements and responsibilities of the group are clearly understood by the group. The standard

EXHIBIT 16.3
Relationship Between Task Uncertainty and Information Flow

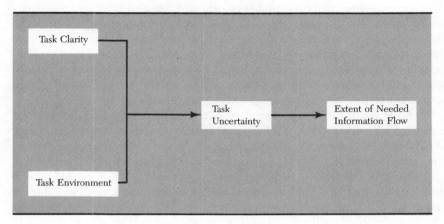

operating procedures often used in organizations are an example of a group requirement. They specify how operating procedures and routine decisions are to be made.

The **task environment**—those factors inside and outside the organization that can affect the group's performance—must also be considered. Two aspects define the task environment: the number of groups that must be dealt with, and the extent to which the environment is stable or dynamic. Obviously, the more groups that must be interacted with and the more dynamic the environment, the greater the task uncertainty. In a dynamic environment, groups tend to expand their information-gathering efforts to detect and hopefully cope with environmental changes. Hence, the greater the task uncertainty, the greater the need for comprehensive information flow systems.

Integration Requirements

The final requirement for successful intergroup cooperation and performance is **integration**. Integration requirements focus on the extent of collaboration, cooperation, or structural relationships between groups needed to ensure success. Chapter 9 on organization design demonstrated that different units within an organization have different goals and time orientations. A technical research department, for example, often sees its goals in scientific terms and has a long-term time perspective. The marketing department in the same company, on the other hand, focuses its goals on market considerations and typically has a short-term time orientation. The production department is often concerned with technical goals and attempts to maintain a moderate time orientation to take advantage of the economies of scale associated with longer production runs.

A successful organization finds ways to integrate these various groups so they coordinate their efforts on behalf of corporate objectives. The trick is achieving some commonly acceptable coordinating mechanism, not achieving a state in which all units have the same goals and time orientations. The latter state would prove disastrous as the research unit looked for short-term results or the marketing department ignored short-term shifts in the marketplace. Through integration, various units learn to accommodate each other's needs while maintaining their individuality. In this way, the strengths of all groups are brought to bear on organizational problems.

When we put these various requirements and their antecedents together, we can see why achieving intergroup coordination and performance is no easy task. Exhibit 16.4 shows the defining characteristics of four typical units of an organization: research, development, sales, and manufacturing. The interdependence, task uncertainty, and time and goal orientation of each unit are shown. In view of this exhibit, consider the complexities managers face in attempting to lead an organization efficiently and effectively. Indeed, business magazines are filled with examples of corporate failures that can be traced to management's failure to coordinate such units. These examples point to an endless array of potential sources of conflict, which reduces the capacity of a company to compete successfully in an ever-changing environment.

EXHIBIT 16.4

Intergroup Characteristics in Four Units of One Company

Group	Interdependence Examples	Task Uncertainty	Time and Goal Orientation
Research	*Reciprocal* with development *Sequential* with market research *Pooled* with shipping	High	*Time:* Long term *Goal:* Science
Development	*Reciprocal* with market research *Sequential* with manufacturing *Pooled* with shipping	Moderate to High	*Time:* Long term *Goal:* Science and Techno-economic
Sales	*Reciprocal* with market research *Sequential* with manufacturing *Pooled* with personnel	Moderate	*Time:* Moderate term *Goal:* Market
Manufacturing	*Reciprocal* with accounting *Sequential* with shipping *Pooled* with research	Low	*Time:* Short term *Goal:* Techno-economic

SOURCE: A. Szilagyi and M. Wallace, *Organizational Behavior and Performance*, 3rd ed.: (Glenview, IL: Scott, Foresman, 1983), p. 212.

UP CLOSE 16.2: Plant Inventories

Unlike the Japanese, who put a premium on cooperation, many U.S. manufac-turing managers have often been their own worst enemies. The guesswork involved in purchasing inventories often causes factory managers problems with both line and financial departments. Haggling among plant managers becomes common.

For example, a marketing manager might promise quick delivery of a product to an important customer, then order the plant manager to pull out all the stops to meet the production deadline. Unsure of his inventory, the plant manager nonetheless agrees to deliver. He delivers, but at the cost of late delivery on three previously scheduled orders, since he was forced to pull components from them to complete the new order. His reward: three dissatis-fied customers and an angry marketing manager. In turn, the plant manager resents the marketing manager for putting him in an untenable position. Meanwhile, corporate financial people blame the plant manager for allowing a buildup of inventory—the remaining parts for the three unfinished jobs.

As one observer notes, "The average manufacturing company is a madhouse of finger-pointing. We've lost sight of the goal, and the competition has become the other department, not the competitors."[4] Help may be on the way, however, in the form of more sophisticated information control systems to help factory managers control inventories, schedule production, and plan how to deploy limited resources. When properly used, such systems can help reduce conflict and foster a new sense of teamwork that boosts productivity and morale. The computer provides a mechanism for increasing information flow and integration, thereby enhancing intergroup performance. ▄

INTERGROUP CONFLICT

As we have seen, the need for intergroup cooperation brings with it the probability of intergroup conflict. Whenever divergent groups must coordinate their activities for the greater good, one or more will likely feel that its interests have been shortchanged.

Definition of Conflict

There are many ways to define conflict as it relates to work situations. Pondy suggests four approaches, each dealing with one aspect of the conflict process:

> *(1) Antecedent conditions* (e.g., scarcity of resources, policy differences) of conflictful behavior; *(2) affective states* (e.g., stress, tension, hostility, anxiety); *(3) cognitive states* of individuals (i.e., their perception or aware-ness of conflictful situations); and *(4) conflictful behavior*, ranging from passive resistance to overt aggression.[5]

The term "conflict" may be used to refer to the entire process, including antecedent conditions, affective states, cognitive states, and actual conflictful behaviors. This approach yields the following insight into conflict: "Conflict is the process which begins when one party perceives that the other has frustrated, or is about to frustrate, some concern of his."[6] In other words, **conflict** involves situations in which the expectations or actual goal-directed behavior of one person or groups is blocked—or about to be blocked—by another person or group. Hence, if a sales representative cannot secure enough funds to mount what he or she considers an effective sales campaign, conflict can ensue. Similarly, if A gets promoted and B doesn't, conflict can emerge. Finally, if a company finds it necessary to lay off valued employees because of difficult financial conditions, conflict can occur. Many examples can be presented in which someone or some group cannot do what it wants to do and experiences frustration as a result.

Nature of Conflict

Conflict includes four types:

1. **Goal conflict** occurs when one group desires a different outcome than another. This is simply a clash over whose goals are to be pursued.
2. **Cognitive conflict** results when one group holds opinions that are inconsistent with those of another group. This type of conflict is evident in political debates.
3. **Affective conflict** emerges when one group's feelings or attitudes are incompatible with those of another group.
4. **Behavioral conflict** occurs when one group does something that is unacceptable to another group. If the manufacturing department were chronically late in delivering its products to shipping, conflict would be likely, particularly if the shipping department was punished for tardiness.

Functions and Dysfunctions of Conflict

Not *all* conflict is bad; under some circumstances a moderate amount of conflict can be helpful. For instance, conflict can lead to a search for new ways to solve organizational problems. It can also motivate employees to excel, to push themselves to meet performance objectives.

Conflict can help individuals and group members grow. Coser explains:

Conflict, which aims at a resolution of tension between antagonists, is likely to have stabilizing and integrative functions for the relationship. By permitting immediate and direct expression of rival claims, such social systems are able to readjust their structures by eliminating their sources of dissatisfaction. The multiple conflicts which they experience may serve to eliminate the causes for dissociation and to reestablish unity. These systems avail themselves, through the toleration and institutionalization of conflict, of an important stabilizing mechanism.[7]

Yet conflict can also have serious negative consequences for both individuals and organizations when people divert energies from performance and goal attainment while attempting to resolve the conflict. Continued conflict can take a heavy toll on psychological well-being. As we shall see in the next chapter, conflict is an important factor in the creation of stress and its psychophysical consequences. Finally, continued conflict can inhibit group cohesiveness.

Thus, conflict can be either functional or dysfunctional in work situations, depending on its nature, intensity, and duration. The issue for management, therefore, is not how to eliminate conflict, but how to manage and resolve it when it occurs in such a way that damage to groups and individuals is minimized and payoff to the firm is maximized.

Reasons for Intergroup Conflict

Several factors can cause one group to experience conflict with another group:[8]

Task Interdependencies   As noted above, the greater the interdependence between individuals or groups (that is, the more they must work together to accomplish a goal), the more likely conflict is. This is so in part because high task interdependency heightens the intensity of relationships. Hence, a small disagreement can very quickly get blown up into a major issue.

Differences in Performance Criteria and Reward Systems   Such differences often provide potential for organizational conflict. In a single organization, different groups are evaluated and rewarded by varying criteria. For example, production personnel are often rewarded for their efficiency, which is facilitated by the long-term production of a few products. Sales departments, on the other hand, are rewarded for their short-term response to market changes, often at the expense of long-term production efficiency. In such situations, conflict arises as each unit attempts to meet its own performance criteria.

Status Inconsistencies   Differences in status between individuals or groups can also promote conflict. For example, managers can often take time off during the day to run errands, while nonmanagerial personnel cannot. This can have negative effects on the nonmanagers' view of organizational policies and fairness.

Jurisdictional Ambiguities   Conflict can also emerge when it is unclear exactly where responsibility for something lies. For example, many organizations use an employee selection procedure in which applicants are evaluated both by the personnel department and by the department in which the applicant would actually work. Since both departments are involved in the hiring process, what happens when one department wants to hire an individual but the other department does not?

Scarce Resources   Another factor that can contribute to conflict is dependence on common resource pools. Whenever several departments must compete for scarce resources, conflict is almost inevitable. When resources are limited, someone wins and someone else usually loses.

Poor Communication   Finally, when one group misunderstands a message, conflict can occur. Conflict can also occur when a group intentionally withholds information from another group for its own benefit. Such a practice jeopardizes trust between groups, which can have long-lasting repercussions.

UP CLOSE 16.3:   Johns-Manville

Ironically, the reward for a chief executive officer who takes a dying company and makes it profitable can be termination. Consider the case of W. Richard Goodwin, ex-president of Johns-Manville Corporation. Goodwin was hired by the board of directors in 1969 to turn the building materials company around. He immediately began to reorganize the company, emphasizing long-range planning and return on investment. He got rid of much deadwood and brought in young, aggressive managers. As a result, sales rose 91 percent over the next five years, while profits rose 115 percent.

As he flew to a board of directors meeting in 1976, Goodwin looked forward to reporting that the first half of that year had set a company record for earnings. Instead, as he was about to enter the board meeting, he was summarily fired. Why? As one observer said, "The spectacular rise and fall of Dick Goodwin is a story of one man's style and personality—and how some of the very qualities that brought him so much success finally brought him down."[9] In essence, Goodwin thought the company's impressive performance record gave him much more power and authority than the rather staid and conservative directors were willing to yield. One senior company executive suggested that Goodwin "just didn't accept the fact that they (the board of directors) were the bosses."

Goodwin's "crimes", and the actions that created so much conflict, involved two proposals that directly opposed the interests of board members. First, he proposed that an upcoming stock offering be handled by several investment houses, instead of just one. This alienated a board member who was vice-chairman of the investment house that heretofore had exclusive rights to J-M stock offerings. In addition, Goodwin proposed that the board be expanded from twelve to fifteen members, and eventually to twenty. One can only guess how the original twelve felt about diluting their power. What is clear is that, in spite of an enviable track record, the board decided it was time for new leadership and Goodwin was "not the right man to steer J-M through the next phase of its history."

The case of Richard Goodwin illustrates how various factors (e.g., relative power distribution, jurisdictional ambiguities, and poor communication) can combine to lead to conflict. Goodwin took a lackluster company and made it shine. In the process, however, he created severe conflicts with the one entity that could resolve the conflict in its favor—the board of directors. ■

CONSEQUENCES OF INTERGROUP CONFLICT

When conflict occurs, several changes often occur within and between the groups. At the very least, two types of changes are likely.[10]

Changes Within Groups

Within groups that are experiencing conflict, three changes are common.

Increased Group Cohesiveness   External threats to the group can cause members to become more cohesive. The group thereby becomes more attractive and more important to the members, individual differences of opinion become less important, and group loyalty ("Are you with us or against us?") emerges as a defining characteristic.

Increased Focus on Task   Increased efforts are directed toward meeting the challenge. Less time is spent idly. The emphasis is on achieving the group's activities and defeating the "enemy". A sense of urgency emerges.

Rise of Autocratic Leadership   Where intergroup conflict is severe, a more autocratic form of leadership often arises. A strong, decisive leader may be thought better able to carry the group through the difficult situation, and a more participative approach may be considered weak or unable to respond quickly to external threats.

The major goals of these group changes are to ensure member support, marshall member efforts, and ensure centralized leadership during the conflict. In this way, the group hopes to respond more rapidly, push harder, and capture the initiative in conflict resolution.

Changes Between Groups

While the above activities are occurring, several changes may also be happening *between* groups.

Negative Attitudes   A primary characteristic of a conflict situation is hostility. The rival group is seen as the enemy and reasons are found for disliking that group. Unfortunately, these negative attitudes often linger long after the conflict is over, as can be seen in the long aftermaths of many labor disputes.

Distorted Perceptions   Accompanying the negative attitudes can be distorted perceptions. Negative stereotyping often occurs, in which one group overemphasizes its own contribution to the organization and deemphasizes the other group's. Union members who choose to join a strike are all seen as greedy, while managers are seen as inhumane or anti-union.

Decreased Communication   Partly because of the negative attitudes and distorted perceptions, communications between the two groups tend to decrease. The feeling is often, "There's no reason to talk to those bums." Unfortunately, this attitude only heightens the conflict and makes resolution more difficult.

Increased Surveillance   In situations of conflict, one group often tries to increase the amount of information it has about the other. Why do they feel that way? Who are their allies? What is their next move? Do they have a weak point? Monitoring the other group's activities is felt essential to staying ahead of the other side and winning the conflict.

Activities such as these are common manifestations of the conflict process. The challenge for management is to find ways to minimize such actions and thus create a more open climate for conflict resolution. The first step involves understanding how the conflict emerged.

A MODEL OF INTERGROUP CONFLICT AND CONFLICT RESOLUTION

A Model of the Conflict Process

A model recently proposed by Kenneth Thomas attempts to describe how conflict comes about in organizations by diagramming the basic conflict process. The model, shown in Exhibit 16.5, consists of four stages: frustration; conceptualization; behavior; and outcome.[11]

As explained earlier, conflict originates when an individual or group feels *frustration* in the pursuit of important goals. This frustration may be caused by a wide variety of factors, including performance goals, promotion, pay raises, power, scarce economic resources, rules, and values. As Thomas notes, conflict can be traced to the frustration of anything a group or individual cares about.[12]

In stage 2, *conceptualization*, parties to the conflict attempt to understand the problem, their goals, their opponents' goals, and various strategies each side might use to resolve the conflict. This is the problem-solving and strategy phase. For instance, when management and union negotiate a labor contract, both sides attempt to decide what is most important and what can be bargained away in exchange for high-priority needs.

A major part of the conceptualization stage consists of deciding how each party will attempt to resolve the conflict. Thomas identifies five modes for conflict resolution, as shown in Exhibit 16.6: competing, collaborating, compromising, avoiding, and accommodating. Also shown in the exhibit are situations that seem most appropriate for each strategy.[13]

The appropriateness of a conflict resolution mode depends to a great extent on the situation and the goals of the parties. This is shown in Exhibit 16.7. Depending on the relative importance of one's own concerns, as opposed to the other party's, the appropriate mode that a group or individual selects can vary

EXHIBIT 16.5
A Process Model of Conflict Episodes

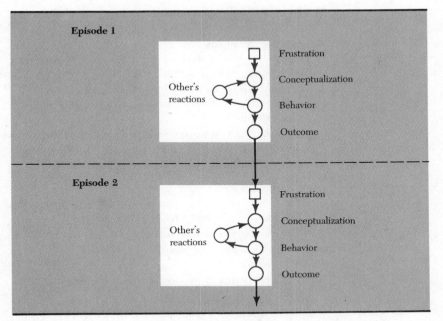

SOURCE: Kenneth Thomas, "Conflict and Conflict Management," in M.D. Dunnette, ed., *Handbook of Industrial and Organizational Behavior* (New York: John Wiley & Sons, 1976), p. 895.

significantly. Hence, if union negotiators feel confident they can win on an issue that is of primary concern to union members (e.g., wages), they may choose a direct competition mode. On the other hand, for issues on which the union is either indifferent or supports management's concerns (e.g., plant safety), one would expect an accommodating mode.

What is interesting in this process is the assumptions groups make about their modes compared to their opponents'. In one study, executives typically described themselves as using collaboration or compromise to resolve conflict, while they described their opponents as using a competitive mode almost exclusively.[14] In other words, the executives underestimated their opponents' concern for satisfying both sides. They saw their opponents as uncompromising and may have exaggerated their own willingness to satisfy both sides in a dispute.

The third stage in Thomas' model is actual *behavior*. As a result of the conceptualization process, both parties attempt to implement their resolution modes by competing or accommodating. Finally, both sides determine the extent to which a satisfactory *outcome* of the conflict can be achieved. When one party to the conflict feels dissatisfied or only partially satisfied, the seeds of discontent are sown for later conflict, as shown in Exhibit 16.5. One unresolved

EXHIBIT 16.6
Five Modes of Resolving Conflict

Conflict-Handling Modes	Appropriate Situations
Competing	1. When quick, decisive action is vital—e.g., emergencies.
	2. On important issues where unpopular actions need implementing—e.g., cost cutting, enforcing unpopular rules, discipline.
	3. On issues vital to company welfare when you know you're right.
	4. Against people who take advantage of noncompetitive behavior.
Collaborating	1. To find an integrative solution when both sets of concerns are too important to be compromised.
	2. When your objective is to learn.
	3. To merge insights from people with different perspectives.
	4. To gain commitment by incorporating concerns into a consensus.
	5. To work through feelings which have interfered with a relationship.
Compromising	1. When goals are important, but not worth the effort or potential disruption of more assertive modes.
	2. When opponents with equal power are committed to mutually exclusive goals.
	3. To achieve temporary settlements to complex issues.
	4. To arrive at expedient solutions under time pressure.
	5. As a backup when collaboration or competition is unsuccessful.
Avoiding	1. When an issue is trivial, or more important issues are pressing.
	2. When you perceive no chance of satisfying your concerns.
	3. When potential disruption outweighs the benefits of resolution.
	4. To let people cool down and regain perspective.
	5. When gathering information supersedes immediate decision.
	6. When others can resolve the conflict more effectively.
	7. When issues seem tangential or symptomatic of other issues.

Accomodating	1. When you find you are wrong—to allow a better positon to be heard, to learn, and to show your reasonableness.
	2. When issues are more important to others than yourself—to satisfy others and maintain cooperation.
	3. To build social credits for later issues.
	4. To minimize loss when you are outmatched and losing.
	5. When harmony and stability are especially important.
	6. To allow subordinates to develop by learning from mistakes.

SOURCE: K. W. Thomas, "Toward Multidimensional Values in Teaching: The Example of Conflict Behaviors," Academy of Management Review, 2, (1977): 487.

conflict episode can easily set the stage for a second episode. Managerial action to achieve a quick and satisfactory resolution is vital. Failure leaves the probability that new conflicts will soon emerge.

SPECIFIC STRATEGIES FOR RESOLVING CONFLICT

As noted above, conflict pervades all organizations and some conflict can be good for organizations. People can learn from conflict as long as it is not dysfunctional. The challenge for managers is to select a resolution strategy appropriate to the situation and individuals involved. A review of past management practice in this regard reveals that managers often make poor strategy choices. That is, they often select repressive or ineffective conflict resolution strategies.

Ineffective Conflict Resolution Strategies

At least five *ineffective* conflict resolution techniques can be identified.[15] Perhaps the most common managerial response to conflict is *nonaction* —ignoring the problem in the hope that it will go away. Unfortunately, ignoring the problem may only increase the frustration of the parties involved.

In other situations, managers acknowledge that a problem exists but take little serious action. Instead, they continually report the problem is "under study" or "more information is needed." Telling a person who is experiencing a serious conflict that "these things take time" hardly relieves his or her anxiety or solves any problems. This ineffective strategy for resolving conflict is termed **administrative orbiting.**

EXHIBIT 16.7
A Two-Dimensional Model of Conflict Behavior

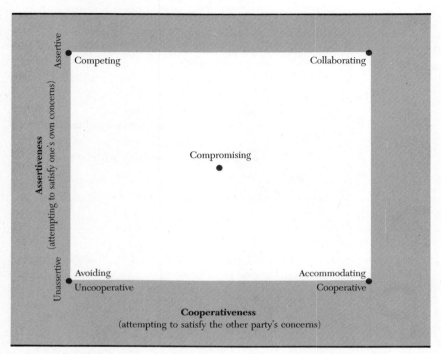

SOURCE: Adapted from Kenneth Thomas, "Conflict and Conflict Management," in M.D. Dunnette, ed., *Handbook of Industrial and Organizational Behavior*, (New York: John Wiley & Sons, 1976), p. 900.

Another common approach is to set up a procedure for redressing grievances that is long, complicated, costly, and perhaps even risky. The **due process nonaction** strategy is to wear down the dissatisfied employee while claiming that resolution procedures are open and available. This technique is often used in conflicts involving race and sex discrimination.

Sometimes managers attempt to reduce conflict through *secrecy*. They feel that, by taking secretive actions, they can make controversial decisions with a minimum of resistance. One argument for pay secrecy is that it reduces the likelihood employees will feel inequitably treated. Essentially, this is a "what they don't know won't hurt them" strategy. A major problem with this approach is that it leads to distrust of management. When managerial credibility is needed for other issues, it may be lacking.

The fifth resolution technique that typically fails to work is *character assassination.* The person with a conflict, perhaps a woman claiming sex discrimination, is labeled a "troublemaker." Attempts are made to discredit her and distance her from others in the group. The implicit strategy here is that if the person can be isolated and stigmatized, he or she will either be silenced by negative group pressures or leave. In either case, the problem is supposedly "solved."

Strategies for Preventing Conflict

On the more positive side, there are many things managers can do to reduce conflict. These solutions fall into two categories: actions directed at conflict *prevention* and *reduction*. We shall start by examining conflict prevention techniques, since preventing conflict is often easier than reducing it once it begins.[16] These include:

- *Emphasizing organization-wide goals and effectiveness.* To the extent that employees focus on organization-wide goals and objectives and are committed to facilitating effective operations, goal conflict should be reduced. Employees are more likely to see the "big picture" and work together to achieve corporate goals.
- *Providing stable, well-structured tasks.* To the extent that work activities are clearly defined, understood, and accepted by employees, conflict should be less. Conflict is most likely to occur when task uncertainty is high. Specifying or structuring jobs minimizes ambiguity.
- *Facilitating intergroup communication.* Misperceptions about the abilities, goals, and motivations of others often leads to conflict, so efforts to increase the dialogue between groups and to share information should help reduce conflict. As groups come to know more about each other, suspicions often diminish and greater intergroup teamwork becomes possible.
- *Avoiding win-lose situations.* To the extent that win-lose situations can be avoided, less potential exists for conflict. When resources are scarce, management can seek some form of resource sharing to achieve organizational effectiveness. Moreover, rewards can be given for contribution to overall corporate objectives, thus fostering a climate in which groups seek solutions acceptable to all.

The above points bear a close resemblance to descriptions of the so-called Japanese management style. Considerable effort is invested in Japanese firms in preventing conflict. In this way, more energy is available for constructive efforts toward task accomplishment and competition in the marketplace.

UP CLOSE 16.4: American Can Company

Perhaps one of the best ways for preventing conflict before it starts is to ensure that all parties to a potential conflict keep in touch with each other. Open and continuous communication between groups allows problems to be dealt with before they become major crises and before each side becomes wedded to a particular resolution mode.

This increased emphasis on communication can be seen in fundamental changes that are occurring in collective bargaining efforts across North America. Some have described this occurrence as a "quiet revolution" in the way workers and managers reach contract agreements. Consider the case of American Can Company. Until recently, operating schedules at American Can were discussed only at contract time. Now they are discussed and dealt with throughout the year. Said one corporate executive, "We've gone to year-round collective bargaining. Changes are occurring too rapidly to wait three years."[17]

As a result, potential conflicts and problems are dealt with when they arise and both sides have a better chance to find a remedy before resentment sets in and opposing positions harden. At American Can, this year-round approach to bargaining and labor relations seems to have reduced conflict in this area. ▪

Strategies for Reducing Conflict

If conflict already exists, clearly something must be done. Two general approaches are possible: Managers may attempt to change *attitudes* or change *behavior*.[18] If they change behavior, open conflict is often reduced but groups often still dislike each other. The conflict may simply become less visible as the groups are separated from each other. Changing attitudes, on the other hand, often leads to fundamental changes in the way groups get along. Attitude change can improve the ongoing relationships between groups. It also takes considerably longer than behavior change in that it requires a fundamental change in social perceptions, as described in Chapter 3.

Nine conflict resolution strategies are shown in Exhibit 16.8. The techniques near the top of the scale focus on changing behaviors, while those near the bottom focus on changing attitudes.

Physical Separation   The quickest and easiest solution to conflict is physical separation. Separation is useful when conflicting groups are not working on a joint task or do not need a high degree of interaction. While this approach does not encourage members to change their attitudes, it does provide time to seek a better accommodation.

Use of Rules and Regulations   Conflict can also be reduced through the increasing specification of rules, regulations, and procedures. This approach, also known as the bureaucratic method, imposes solutions on groups from above. Again, however, basic attitudes are not modified.

Limiting Intergroup Interaction   Another approach to reducing conflict is to limit intergroup interaction to issues involving common goals. Where groups agree on a goal, cooperation becomes easier. An example of this can be seen in recent efforts by U.S. and Canadian firms to "meet the Japanese challenge."

Use of Integrators   Integrators are individuals who are assigned a boundary-spanning role between two groups or departments. To be trusted, integrators

EXHIBIT 16.8
Strategies for Reducing Intergroup Conflict

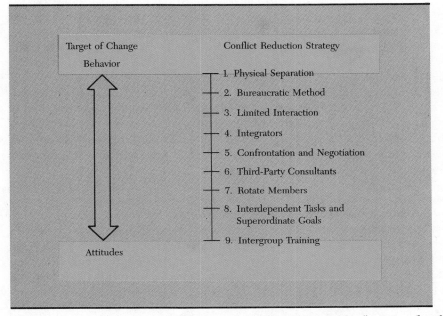

Target of Change

Behavior

Conflict Reduction Strategy

1. Physical Separation
2. Bureaucratic Method
3. Limited Interaction
4. Integrators
5. Confrontation and Negotiation
6. Third-Party Consultants
7. Rotate Members
8. Interdependent Tasks and Superordinate Goals
9. Intergroup Training

Attitudes

SOURCE: Adapted from E.H. Neilsen, "Understanding and Managing Conflict," in J. Lorsch and P. Lawrence, eds., *Managing Group and Intergroup Relations* (Homewood, IL: Richard D. Irwin), pp. 329-343.

must be seen by both groups as having legitimacy and expertise. The integrator often takes the "shuttle diplomacy" approach, moving from one group to another, identifying areas of agreement and attempting to find areas of future cooperation.

Confrontation and Negotiation In this approach, competing parties are brought together face to face to discuss the basic areas of disagreement. The hope is that, through open discussion and negotiation, means can be found to work out problems. Contract negotiations between union and management represent one such example. To the extent that a "win-win" solution can be identified through these negotiations, the chances of an acceptable resolution of the conflict increase.

Third-party Consultation In some cases, it is helpful to bring in outside consultants who understand human behavior and can facilitate a resolution. An outside consultant not only serves as a go-between, but can speak more directly or bluntly to the issues in some cases because he or she is not a member of either group.

Rotation of Members   By rotating from one group to another, individuals come to understand the frame of reference, values, and attitudes of other members. Communication is also increased. To the extent that those rotated are accepted by the receiving groups, attitude as well as behavioral change becomes possible. This approach is clearly a long-term technique, as it takes time to develop good interpersonal relations and understanding between group members.

Identification of Interdependent Tasks and Superordinate Goals   A further strategy for management is to establish goals that require groups to work together to achieve overall success, as when company survival is threatened. The threat of a shutdown often causes long-standing opponents to come together to achieve a common objective (in this case, keeping the company going).

Use of Intergroup Training   The final technique on the continuum is intergroup training. Outside training experts are retained on a long-term basis to help groups develop relatively permanent mechanisms for working together. Structured workshops and training programs can help forge more favorable intergroup attitudes and, as a result, more constructive intergroup behavior.

UP CLOSE 16.5:   General Electric

At General Electric, considerable emphasis is placed on preventing conflict. General Electric does this in a variety of ways, including launching extensive employee education efforts prior to a conflict-threatening major organizational change. When a decision is made by management that might adversely affect employees, managers go to work well in advance to cushion the impact on employees. Employee input is solicited as early as possible and efforts are made to avoid a "crisis environment."[19]

An example can be seen in the three-year reorganization of GE's Lighting Business Group, which produces incandescent, fluorescent, and quartz lamps. To cope with slower market growth in the lamp business, GE decided to close ten of its forty-two lamp plants and consolidate operations. The company announced the decision in June 1983, nearly a year before the first plant was due to close, to give employees time to adjust to the change.

GE produced a twenty-minute videotape to explain the reasons behind the action. Moreover, each manager was expected to conduct a continuing education program through newsletters and monthly meetings with employees. GE also hired outplacement counselors to help laid-off workers find new jobs.

While no retrenchment is easy, General Electric's efforts have been well received, particularly in view of the circumstances. As one union official noted, "We're unhappy about any close-down at any time. But under the circumstances, I think GE has handled it very well." Or, as one laid-off worker commented,

"We are saddened but not really angry. The company went out of its way to explain it to us, and they have always been honest."

Efforts such as these can go a long way toward avoiding conflicts in difficult situations. In the case of GE, the problem was indeed severe (the need for plant closures), but the actions taken by the company were not unduly expensive. Moreover, a potential conflict of sizable proportions was averted. ■

SUMMARY

This chapter's examination of intergroup relations and conflict began with a consideration of a model of intergroup performance that recognized requirements for interaction, information flow, and integration. These three factors combine to determine the quality of performance between groups.

When various groups must coordinate their efforts for task accomplishment, significant opportunities exist for conflict. The topic of conflict is a central concept in organizational dynamics. Conflict can be either functional or dysfunctional. Moreover, the reasons for the prevalence of intergroup conflict include the nature of task interdependencies, differences in performance criteria and reward systems, status inconsistencies, jurisdictional ambiguities, scarce resources, and poor communication.

The consequences of intergroup conflict as they relate to changes within and between groups were also examined. Potential changes within the group include increased group cohesiveness, increased focus on task, and the rise of autocratic leadership. In addition, relations between groups also experience changes, such as more negative intergroup attitudes, members' distorted perceptions of each other, decreased communication, and increased surveillance.

A four-part model of intergroup conflict and conflict resolution was presented. Conflict originates when an individual or group experiences frustration in the pursuit of important goals. In stage two, the individual or group attempts to understand or conceptualize the nature of the problem and its causes. In stage three, efforts are made to change behavioral patterns in such a way that the desired outcome, or stage four, is achieved.

Finally, a series of possible strategies for resolving conflicts are divided into conflict prevention strategies and conflict resolution strategies. Conflict prevention strategies include: 1) placing an emphasis on organization-wide goals; 2) providing stable, well-structured tasks; 3) facilitating intergroup communication; and 4) avoiding win-lose situations. Conflict resolution strategies include: 1) physical separation of parties to the conflict; 2) the use of rules and regulations; 3) limiting intergroup interaction; 4) the use of third-party integrators; 5) confrontation and negotiation; 6) third-party consultation; 7) rotation of members; 8) identification of interdependent tasks and superordinate goals; and 9) the use of intergroup training. To the extent possible, efforts should be made to prevent conflicts before they occur, rather than trying to resolve them after they appear.

KEY WORDS

administrative orbiting	information flow	reciprocal
affective conflict	system	interdependence
behavioral conflict	integration	sequential
cognitive conflict	interaction	interdependence
conflict	requirements	task clarity
due process nonaction	pooled	task environment
goal conflict	interdependence	task uncertainty

DISCUSSION QUESTIONS

1. Evaluate the utility of the intergroup performance model from the standpoint of managers. How might managers make use of this model to better understand possible problems between groups?
2. What would you do as a manager to facilitate better intergroup cooperation on tasks within an organization? Explain.
3. Identify the types of conflict commonly found in organizations and provide examples of each.
4. How can conflict be good for an organization?
5. Identify some reasons for the prevalence of intergroup conflict in organizations.
6. How does intergroup conflict affect behavior within a work group? Behavior between two or more work groups?
7. Review the intergroup conflict model. What lessons for management follow from this model?
8. Of the various strategies for resolving and preventing conflict that are presented in this chapter, which ones do you feel will generally be most effective? Least effective? Why?

CASE 16.1:   Scott Trucks, Ltd.

"Mr. McGowan will see you now, Mr. Sullivan," said the secretary. "Go right in."

Sullivan looked tired and tense as he opened the door and entered McGowan's office. He had prepared himself for a confrontation and was ready to take a firm approach. McGowan listened as Sullivan spoke of the problems and complaints in his department. He spoke of the recent resignation of Tobin and the difficult time he had in attracting and keeping engineers. McGowan questioned Sullivan as to the quality of his supervision and direction, emphasizing the need to monitor the work and control the men.

"You have got to let them know who is boss and keep tabs on them at all times," said McGowan.

"But Mr. McGowan, that is precisely the point; my engineers resent surveillance tactics. They are well-educated, self-motivated people. They don't want to be treated like soldiers at an army camp."

The discussion was beginning to heat up. McGowan's fist hit the table. "Listen Sullivan, I brought you in here as a department manager reporting to me. I don't need your fancy textbook ideas about leading men. I have 10 years as a military officer, and I have run this plant from its inception. If you can't produce the kind of work I want and control your men, then I will find someone who can. I don't have complaints and holdups from my other managers. We have systems and procedures to be followed, and so they shall or I will know the reason they aren't."

"But that is just the point," continued Sullivan, "my men do good work and contribute good ideas and, in the face of job pressures, perform quite well. They don't need constant supervision and direction and least of all the numerous and unnecessary interruptions in their work."

"What do you mean by that?" asked McGowan.

"Well both Tobin and Michaels have stated openly and candidly that they like their work but find your frequent visits to the department very disconcerting. My engineers need only a minimal amount of control, and our department has these controls already established. We have weekly group meetings to discuss projects and routine work. This provides the kind of feedback that is meaningful to them. They don't need frequent interruptions and abrasive comments about their work and the need to follow procedures."

"This is my plant and I will run it the way I see fit," screamed McGowan. "No department manager or engineer is going to tell me otherwise. Now I suggest, Mr. Sullivan, that you go back to your department, have a meeting with your men, and spell out my expectations."

By this time Sullivan was intimidated and very frustrated. He left the office hastily and visibly upset. McGowan's domineering style had prevailed, and the meeting had been quite futile. No amount of pleading or confrontation would change McGowan's attitude.

Sullivan returned to his department and sat at his desk quite disillusioned with the predicament. His frustration was difficult to control and he was plagued with self-doubt. He was astonished at McGowan's intractable position and stubbornness.

He posted a notice for a meeting that would be held the next day with his department. He outlined an agenda and included in it mention of resignation. He left the plant early, worrying about the direction he should take.

BACKGROUND

Scott Trucks is housed in an old aircraft hangar in the Debert Industrial Park, near Truro, Nova Scotia. The government of Nova Scotia sold the building for a modest sum as it no longer had use for the hangar after the armed forces had abandoned it. The facility, together with the financial arrangements organized by Mr. McGowan, the president of Scott, made the enterprise feasible.

Inside the building, renovations have provided for an office area, a production operation, and an engineering department. The main offices are located at the front of the building, housing the sales team and the office clerks. The sales manager, Mike McDonald (see Exhibit 1), and two assistants make up the sales team at the Debert location of Scott Trucks. Three or four field representatives work in southern Ontario and the United States.

EXHIBIT 1
Organizational Chart, Scott Truck

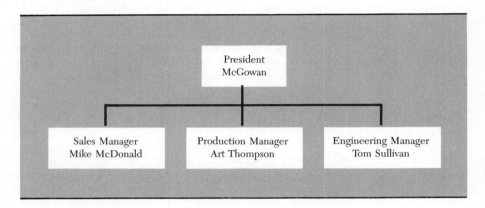

Mike is considered a good salesman and often assumes a role much broader than sales. Customer complaints, ordering, and replacement parts also fall into his domain. The production manager frequently makes reference to Mike's ability to talk on two phones at the same time!

Art Thompson has been production manager at Scott Trucks for eight years. The area he manages is behind the sales office and takes up most of the space in the building. The engineering department, comprising small offices, is located behind the production department which is divided into two areas by a long, narrow corridor. The shop floor is divided into basic sections of assembly with a paint, a welding, and a cab section as well as other areas used to assemble the large Scott trucks.

Owing to the limited capacity of the plant, only two or three truck units are in production at any one time. Another constraint on capacity is the nature of the system used to produce the trucks. There are no pulleys, belts, or assembly lines used in the system; rather the production takes place in large bays where sections of the trucks are individually completed in preparation for the final assembly.

The truck units are used for a variety of functions, particularly where a heavy truck requirement is in demand. Fire trucks, highway maintenance trucks, and long-distance hauling trucks are some of the units produced by Scott. To some extent the trucks are custom-made, as each purchaser will request changes on the basic design. The engineers also adapt the trucks to meet the various standards and specifications of the Canadian government and the vigorous Canadian climate.

Tom Sullivan, who is a recent graduate of Nova Scotia Technical Institute with a degree in engineering, is the newest of the managers at Scott. He shows good promise as an engineer but, as with his predecessor, is having adjustment problems as a manager. Tom received an M.B.A. from Dalhousie University and majored in management science and organizational behavior. He completed project work in participative management styles under the direction of a specialist in this area. He tries to practice this approach in his new position and enjoys the ideas and flow of discussion at the department meetings. Tom works in a department with men much his senior and is the youngest of the department managers at Scott Truck. He works hard and is well liked by his subordinates. Personal satisfaction, though infrequent, comes as a direct result of the open and participative management style he uses.

THE ENGINEERS

The composition of the group of engineers at Scott is unusual. One of the group is not an engineer by qualification but had many years of practical experience. He moved from Detroit to Truro, having worked with Ford Trucks for 15 years. Since his recruitment by McGowan he has worked with Scott for eight years. Retirement for this man is not far off, a fact he frequently makes known to the group. His work is good, and he seems to have many answers to difficult problems—a redeeming factor in the absence of an engineering degree. Don Jones, another member of the group, is a good engineer. His workday is solid. However, most evenings are spent at a local tavern. His wife was killed recently, and he does not seem to care any more. The remainder of the group are a combination of senior and junior men who have been with the company for a number of years. Two engineers had just left the group for better jobs and for a "less confining" atmosphere, as they put it. Tom Sullivan's effort to lead the group is proving to be a difficult task.

THE PRODUCTION WORKERS

Work for the men in the production plant is reasonably stable. A good-paying job in production in Truro is difficult to find, a situation of which the men are fully aware; many of them have experienced the monotony of unemployment and job hunting before this opening presented itself.

With the exception of a few French-Canadian welders, the workers are Maritimers whose experience and skills range from those of a skilled tradesman to those of a casual laborer. The local trades school in Truro has provided the organization with a number of good machinists, welders, and painters that the foreman hired and began to develop.

The morale on the plant floor has been very good, particularly since the company has improved its sales position. The once-frequent layoffs that were due to work shortage have ceased in the presence of higher demand for the trucks. The new field sales group contributes significantly to the situation with their efforts in southern Ontario and the northern United States. The pay scale is above average for the area and there is a good rapport between the production manager and the workers.

ADMINISTRATIVE CONTROL

Administrative control in the plant has been accomplished by two methods; one in terms of the quality of the product and the other in terms of its cost. Attention has been paid to the quality control function through a quality control supervisor whose task it is to examine the end product in a thorough manner using rigorous criteria. The other method of control is that implemented by the accounting office. Through the adoption of a standard cost program, material labor, and overhead variances are accumulated and presented on data report sheets.

The production manager, Art Thompson, is responsible for collecting cost data and for sending it to the office on a weekly basis. Art is not an easygoing person; he frequently gets upset when problems occur on the shop floor. He is closely watched by Mr. McGowan, the president. Consequently, to Art the monthly meetings of the managers are a real ordeal, since McGowan, as owner, tries to watch the costs very carefully and to make sure the plant is running as efficiently as possible.

McGowan uses three approaches to managing the operation at Scott Trucks. The first is a monthly meeting with the three managers. The second technique is a series of interdepartmental memos that interpret the results of cost figures presented to him throughout the month. The third method is by frequent plant visits and observations.

None of these controls is favorably received by the managers, as they feel they are being watched too carefully. Interdepartmental memos may read as follows:

May 12, 19—
To: Mr. Art Thompson, production manager
From: Mr. McGowan, president, Scott Trucks
Re: Materials quantity variance

I noticed a considerable amount of material quantity variance in your production reports for last week. The standard cost system has been implemented for six weeks now, and it no longer suffices to say that you are still "working the bugs out of the system." It is time you paid closer attention to the amount of materials going into the production process and to avoiding any spoilage.

Another example of an interdepartmental memo reads as follows:

May 20, 19—
To: Mr. Art Thompson, production manager
From: Mr. McGowan, president, Scott Trucks
Re: Inaccurate recording of time, and use of time cards

I noticed last week on your labor cost submissions that a number of employees have been neglecting to punch time cards. Please see that this system is properly followed.

Art Thompson's reaction to these memos has been one of apprehension and concern. It is the practice of the foreman and himself to try to resolve the problems as quickly as possible, and together they have been able to rectify these difficulties quite rapidly as the men are eager to cooperate.

The plant visits to the production area made by Mr. McGowan are frequent and effective. He has been known to come out in shirt-sleeves and literally assume the workman's job for a period of time. This is particularly true of a new worker or a young worker, where he will dig in and instruct the individual on how he should be doing his job. On such occasions he will give specific instructions as to how he wants things done and how things should be done.

It makes McGowan feel right at home when he is involved with the workers. He spent 15 years as a navy commander, and he often used to remark that there was only one way to deal with his subordinates. The reaction of the workers to this approach is mixed. Some of the production people dislike this "peering over the shoulders"; others do not seem to mind and appreciate McGowan's concern for a "job well done." The workers grumble at McGowan's approach but feel most of his criticisms to be constructive.

McGowan's management approach in the monthly meetings is not considerably different from that with the production workers. McGowan assumes a very authoritarian style in dealing with his managers.

The monthly meetings are an integrative effort among engineering, sales and production, with the purpose of ironing out difficulties both on a personality basis and on a work basis. The workload in the engineering department has been growing for the last six months at a considerable rate. This reflects the increase in production and the need for people in the area of engineering and design to provide a high quality of technical expertise.

The number of engineers currently working at Scott is eight. Relations between the engineering department and other departments have been less than satisfactory, and a good deal of conflict has occurred over a number of issues. For example the reports from quality control at Scott have been poor from time to time, and increasingly the problem has been traced to unclear engineering specifications. Upset about these conditions, McGowan has expressed strong disapproval in his memos to the department.

Lately the engineers have been bombarded with McGowan's memos, the results of more frequent complaints about the engineering department from the quality control manager and the production manager. Along with other factors, they have provided the ammunition McGowan needed to confront the engineering department. The engineers, however, have resisted, refusing to accept these memos in the same way that the production people have. As a result of these memos, complaints and misunderstandings have arisen. The engineers have responded by suggesting that the production people cannot interpret the blueprints and that they never bother to question them when a change is not understood or clear.

Disturbed by this situation, McGowan has made it a point to visit the engineering section at regular intervals, and his tactics have been much the same as with the production people. Unfortunately the engineering manager, Tom Sullivan, was feeling the pressure and could not seem to keep his department running smoothly. Being new to the job, he did not know how to handle McGowan. The two engineers had quit recently and left the company, not explaining their discontent but only referring to better jobs elsewhere.

Tom Sullivan had reacted poorly to this situation and had been in a somber mood for about two months. His work and his adjustment had not been successful. The veterans in the department, though understanding his frustration, could not help Sullivan, who felt he was better off trying to accommodate McGowan than resisting him. To make matters worse the two engineers who had recently quit had left a large backlog of work incomplete, and efforts to recruit new engineers had been a strain on Sullivan. The marketplace quickly absorbed all the engineers graduating from Nova Scotia Tech, and Debert, Nova Scotia, had few attractions available to enable it to compete with larger centers.

Tom did get a big break, however, in his recruiting drive when he discovered through a contact in Montreal two engineers who were wishing to return to the Maritimes. Both men were young and had experience and good training in engineering. In their interview they discussed their experiences and their ability to work independently. Moreover both were looking for a quieter environment. Sullivan liked their credentials and hired the two men.

McGowan had been on vacation at the time and had not met the new engineers until a month after they had been on the job. His first encounter, however, was a cordial meeting with the two engineers and, although the climate in the department was always unpredictable and changing, activities and relations were smooth for a month or two much to the relief of Sullivan. McGowan maintained his surveillance of the plant, including the engineers. Tim Michaels and Bill Tobin, the new engineers, felt uncomfortable with McGowan around but just proceeded with their work and ignored the long stares and the continued presence of the "boss."

One Friday afternoon McGowan walked into the engineering section with a smug look on his face. It was near the end of the month, just prior to the monthly meeting. Sullivan looked up immediately as McGowan moved towards Tobin's drafting table. McGowan was irate. He began talking to Tobin in a loud voice. Shaking his fist, he threw down a report on a change proposed by Tobin for the interior of the cabs made at Scott.

"What gives you the right to implement such a change without first going to Sullivan, then to me?" screamed McGowan. "You have only been with this company for two and a half months and already you feel you can ignore the 'system.'"

"Well, Mr. McGowan, I thought it was a good idea, and I have seen it work before," responded Tobin, flustered by McGowan's attack.

In the meantime Sullivan came out from his office to see what the problem was about. McGowan turned to him and asked him why he couldn't control his men, adding that the changes were totally unauthorized and unnecessary. Sullivan glanced at the blueprint and was taken by surprise when he examined it more carefully. In the meantime McGowan raved on about Tobin's actions.

"Oh, um, ah, yes, Mr. McGowan, you're right; this should have been cleared between, uh, you and me before production got it; but, ah, I will see that it doesn't happen again."

McGowan stormed out, leaving Tobin and Sullivan standing by the desk. Tobin was upset by "this display of rudeness," as he put it.

"Tom," he went on, "this was a damn good idea and you know it."

Sullivan shook his head. "Yes, you're right. I don't know how to deal with McGowan; he wears me down sometimes. But also Bill, you have to channel your changes through the system."

Tobin turned back to his table and resumed his afternoon work.

For the next six weeks the plant operated smoothly as production picked up and more people were hired. Work in the engineering department increased correspondingly as people wanted new and better parts on their trucks. New engine and cab designs were arriving and put an increased burden on the engineering department. In fact it fell well behind in its efforts to change and adapt the truck specifications to meet the Canadian environment. The lengthy review process required to implement change also put an added burden on the operation at Scott.

These difficulties were compounded further by the fact that engineers were hard to find, and at Scott they were also hard to keep. Moreover summer was approaching, which meant decreased manpower owing to the holidays.

McGowan's frequent visits added to the difficult situation in the engineering department. Sullivan had taken to group meetings once a week with the engineers in an attempt to solve engineering problems and personal conflicts. At each meeting Tobin and Michaels discussed their work with the group and showed signs of real progress and development. They were adjusting well and contributing above expectations. At these meetings, however, they both spoke openly and frankly about McGowan's frequent visits and his abrasive style. A month had passed since they first suggested to Sullivan that he talk to McGowan about the problems he presented to the engineers by his visits to the department. At first the rest of the group agreed passively to the idea that Sullivan confront McGowan on this issue, but by the fourth week the group was being very firm with Sullivan on this issue, insisting he talk with McGowan.

Tom Sullivan knew the time had come and that he would have to face McGowan. That very morning he had received a call from a local company about Mr. Tobin and the quality of his work. Presumably Tobin had been looking for work elsewhere. This was the last straw. Sullivan picked up the phone and asked the secretary for an appointment with Mr. McGowan.

He wondered as he hung up the phone how he would deal with the problems he faced in his department and with Mr. McGowan.[20]

CASE QUESTIONS

1. Describe the basic nature of the conflict in this case.
2. What do you feel has caused this conflict? In your analysis, make use of the conflict model outlined in the chapter.
3. As a manager, what would you do to resolve the conflict?

NOTES

1. "Can John Young Redesign Hewlett-Packard?" *Business Week*, December 6, 1982, pp. 72–73.
2. Andrew D. Szilagyi, Jr., and Marc J. Wallace, Jr., *Organizational Behavior and Performance*, 3rd ed. (Glenview, IL: Scott, Foresman, 1983), pp. 206–230.
3. M. Sherif, *In Common Predicament: Social Psychology of Intergroup Conflict and Cooperation* (Boston: Houghton Mifflin, 1966).
4. "Production Problems Become More Manageable," *Business Week*, April 25, 1983, pp. 70–71.
5. Louis Pondy, "Organizational Conflict: Concepts and Models," *Administrative Science Quarterly* 12 (1967): 299.
6. Kenneth Thomas, "Conflict and Conflict Management," in M. D. Dunnette (ed.), *Handbook of Industrial and Organizational Psychology* (Chicago: Rand McNally, 1976), p. 891.
7. L. Coser, *The Functions of Social Conflict* (New York: The Free Press, 1956), p. 154.
8. Robert Miles, *Macro Organizational Behavior* (Glenview, IL: Scott, Foresman, 1980).
9. Herbert E. Meyer, "Shootout at the Johns-Manville Corral," *Fortune*, October 1976, p. 150.
10. James L. Gibson, John M. Ivancevich, and James H. Donnelly, Jr., *Organizations: Behavior, Structure, and Processes* (Dallas: BPI, 1982), pp. 214–216.
11. Thomas, "Conflict and Conflict Management."
12. Thomas, "Conflict and Conflict Management."
13. Kenneth Thomas, "Toward Multi-dimensional Values in Teaching: The Example of Conflict Behaviors," *Academy of Management Review* 2 (1977): 484–490.
14. Kenneth Thomas and Louis Pondy, "Toward an Intent Model of Conflict Management Among Principal Parties," *Human Relations* 30 (1977): 1089–1102.
15. Miles, *Macro Organizational Behavior*.
16. Robert R. Blake, Herbert A. Shepard, and Jane S. Mouton, *Managing Intergroup Conflict in Industry* (Houston: Gulf Publishing Co., 1964).
17. Carey English, "Unions, Employers Try New Paths to Labor Peace," *U.S. News & World*

Report, March 12, 1984, p. 74.
18. Eric H. Neilsen, "Understanding and Managing Conflict," in J. Lorsch and P. Lawrence (eds.), *Managing Group and Intergroup Relations* (Homewood, IL: Irwin, 1972), pp. 329–343; and Richard Daft, *Organizational Theory and Design* (St. Paul: West, 1983), pp. 438–442.
19. "How Companies Are Getting Their Message Across to Labor," *Business Week,* September 24, 1984, p. 58.
20. Cohen, Gadon, Fink, and Willits, *Effective Behavior in Organizations* (Homewood, IL: Richard D. Irwin, 1984).

17 Communication and Control

S ecretaries at Xerox Corporation use electronic mail computers to swap and file memos from their bosses, reducing to a minute's time a task that previously required typing letters and mailing them coast-to-coast. Executives at Control Data Corporation hold televised conference meetings. When one person writes on the electronic "blackboard," the information automatically appears on a terminal screen for other participants in other cities. Atlantic Richfield Company is designing a teleconferencing network so that employees worldwide can confer with one another visually through a satellite hookup and wall-high projection screens. In many large corporations, chief executives communicate with employees through closed-circuit television, or by videotaping their remarks for later presentation at divisional meetings.[1]

The purpose of this chapter is to explore the topic of organizational communication and control. Teleconferencing, electronic mail, and closed-circuit television are new techniques that help organizations communicate faster and more efficiently. In this chapter we will examine the ways managers communicate to one another both as individuals and in groups; this type of communication represents the micro aspects of communication. Then we will turn to the macro perspective, which is organizational-level communication. Communication at the organizational level is heavily oriented toward control in the organization. We will explore how management information systems and other devices enable managers to monitor and control the work of thousands of employees. We will also examine common barriers to communication and control in organizations and discuss techniques for overcoming these barriers.

RELEVANCE OF COMMUNICATION AND CONTROL FOR MANAGERS

The development of sophisticated devices to speed organizational communication recognizes the primary place of communication within organizations. Devices that make the communication of information more efficient will ultimately make organizations more efficient. Understanding communication and control processes within organizations can directly influence a manager's skill and effectiveness for two reasons.

Communication is the process through which manager functions are carried out. Motivating, learning, leading, organizing, decision making, intergroup relations, power, politics, and managing the environment all require communication. Communication is so important that managers spend approximately 80 percent of their time communicating.[2] Several of the managerial roles described in Chapter 13 pertain to information processing. Managers make personal contacts with peers, subordinates, and people outside the organization. Managers act as figureheads, monitors, spokespersons, and disseminators of information. Communication is such a constant part of the manager's job that managers sometimes take it for granted. But the skill with which the managers perform is directly related to the quality, accuracy, and timeliness of their communications.

Information is the lifeblood of organizations. At the macro level, communication processes enable the organization to scan and interpret the external environment, coordinate activities across departments, establish goals and target, disseminate rules and instructions, and provide for the assessment of performance through reports, financial statements, and statistical data. Communication processes allow the organization to make decisions, identify and respond to problems, and monitor performance. Without communication, the organization would not function. Communication processes provide information to all parts of the organization for coordination and task accomplishment.

The next section will discuss managerial communication and focuses on communication between individuals. Subsequent sections of this chapter discuss communication processes for workgroups and for organizations as a whole. By the end of the chapter we will have examined how managers can be efficient communicators and how organizations can be designed to facilitate communication and control.

MANAGERIAL COMMUNICATION

Communication is the transmission of messages between people. Messages may be communicated by speaking, writing, symbolic gestures, or direct observation. Successful communication occurs when the message is received and conveys the exact meaning the sender intended. When the communication is unsuccessful, the underlying meaning is not conveyed. A basic model of the typical communication process between people is shown in Exhibit 17.1. The model illustrates the basic components of managerial communication, including the sender and receiver, meaning, encoding and decoding, the medium, feedback, and noise.[3]

Sender and Receiver

Communication requires two or more people. The sender and receiver are the communicators. The sender is anyone who wishes to convey a message to influence others, to ask for information, or to express an idea or emotion. The

EXHIBIT 17.1
Basic Model of Communication

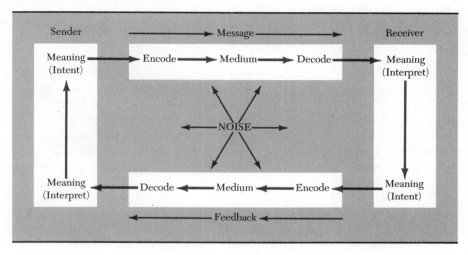

receiver is the person to whom the message is sent. Within organizations, managers communicate frequently with other managers, customers, supervisors, and people outside the organization. Managers take the role of either sender or receiver many times daily during organizational transactions.

Meaning, Message, and Medium

Meaning is a concept, thought, feeling, image, fact, or idea. Meaning that is to be conveyed to someone else exists within a sender's mind. The **message** is the tangible formulation of the concept or thought that is actually sent to the receiver. The message may be sent in the form of a letter, spoken words, or telephone conversation. A message can be a simple statement like, "Let's go get a Coke," or a memo such as, "Nancy: If you are unable to resolve the continuing disagreement between your people and the sales staff, we may have to let you go." The **medium** is the carrier or channel through which the message is sent. The medium can be a computer printout, formal report, telephone call, or face-to-face meeting.

Encoding and Decoding

Encoding is the translation of meaning into specific symbols such as words or behavior. Encoding is the expression of an idea, concept, or fact in symbolic form. The symbols used for encoding depend upon the person's experience and background. Encoding is typically language based, and it reflects the sender's culture and training. Mathematicians may use symbols and jargon to encode messages that non-mathematicians have difficulty interpreting. **Decoding** is the translation of a symbolic message into meaning. The symbols are deciphered into a mental image, idea, or fact. The receiver's experience is important because people interpret messages based upon their own background, vocabulary, and understanding.

Feedback

Feedback is the receiver's response to the sender after receiving the message. When no feedback exists one-way communication occurs. Two-way communication occurs with feedback. Feedback is a powerful aid to communication because it enables the sender to determine whether the receiver interpreted the message correctly. Without feedback, the sender does not know whether the message has been received and understood. For complicated or difficult messages, feedback is important so the sender can try again if the message was not received correctly.

Noise

Noise is any element that can distort the communication. Noise can occur at any point in the communication process. If a manager is distracted while writing a letter, the encoding of the idea into a message may not be clear. Static on a telephone line, or other people talking in the room may interfere with sending or receiving a message. The medium itself may be poor, such as when the teacher uses an overhead projector that does not focus correctly. Or the message simply may not be effective for conveying meaning, because the manager was too brief, or because the experience, background and vocabulary of sender and receiver are different. Because feedback provides a check on whether the message was received accurately, the feedback process is especially important when communication must cope with noise.

Types of Communication

Communication between managers may use several media. Managers may use a public address system, a newsletter, the telephone, paging devices, or face-to-face meetings. The array of communication methods available to managers can be organized into three categories.[4]

Oral Communication   This consists of all forms of spoken information and is by far the most prevalent type of communication managers use. Managers prefer face-to-face and telephone communication to written communication and spend most of their time sharing information this way.[5] New technologies are being developed to take advantage of the popularity of face-to-face communication. Teleconferencing enables managers to interact face-to-face over long distances. Picture phones enable people to see one another during the telephone conversation. Many communication seminars teach managers how to speak fluently and listen carefully, because these skills are related to effective performance.

Written Communication   Written communications include letters, memos, policy manuals, reports, forms, job descriptions, and other documentation used to share information in the organization. The development of word processors, personal computers, and electronic mail improve speed and efficiency of written communications. Managers use written communication less often than oral communication, but there are many occasions when written documentation is important. Writing down the message and sending it as a letter or memo enables a precise statement to be made, provides a reference for later use, and can serve as an official document for the organization. Written messages also can be disseminated to many members of the organization at the same time in the form of newsletters, flyers, or memos.

Nonverbal Communication   Nonverbal communication includes all messages that are not encoded with words.[6] The most common form of nonverbal communication is body language. Posture, dress, hair length, facial expressions, and eye contact communicate impressions to others. Posture may indicate the extent to which the person is open and friendly, self confident, or shy, timid, and reclusive. Physical symbols are the other form of nonverbal communication. The type of car we drive tells other people about our social class and values. An office arrangement can indicate a warm, approachable occupant or a cold, aloof occupant. Some managers use arrangements of furniture to invoke dominance over visitors. When chair height is uneven, for example, the visitor, while seated, has to look up to the manager and the manager looks down on the visitor. Or a large, imposing-looking desk can act as a barrier between manager and visitor.

Information Richness

Recent research has attempted to explain why managers seem to prefer face-to-face communication.[7] The concept of information richness describes why certain channels tend to be efficient for messages. **Information richness** is the amount of learning that can be conveyed during a communication episode. Rich information promotes more understanding than information low in richness. Exhibit 17.2 illustrates that oral and written messages can be divided into four types: face-to-face, telephone, addressed documents (letters, memos), and unaddressed documents (flyers, bulletins). In terms of the basic model of communication described in Exhibit 17.1, the media differ with respect to feedback and the number of channels or cues utilized during a communication transaction. The better the feedback and the more channels and cues in operation, the richer the information sent through the medium. Face-to-face and the telephone communication provide immediate feedback, memos and letters have slow feedback, and unaddressed messages typically have no feedback. With respect to channels and cues, face-to-face communication utilizes several channels simultaneously, including voice, facial expression, and body language. Telephone provides no nonverbal cues other than voice inflection. Notes and memos are limited to the words written on the paper, and the same is true for the unaddressed written communication.

EXHIBIT 17.2

Hierarchy of Media Richness for Managerial Communications

Media		Characteristics			Best for Communications that are:
		Feedback	Cues & Channels	Media Richness	
Face-to-Face	Oral	Immediate	Audio & Visual	High	Ambiguous, emotional, divergent backgrounds
Telephone		Rapid	Audio		
Addressed Documents	Written	Slow	Limited Visual		
Unaddressed Documents		Slowest	Limited Visual	Low	Clear, rational, official, similar backgrounds

SOURCE: Adapted from Richard L. Daft and Robert H. Lengel, "Information Richness: A New Approach to Managerial Information Processing and Organization Design," in Barry Staw and Larry L. Cummings, *Research in Organizational Behavior*, Volume 6 (Greenwich, CT: JAI Press, 1984), pp. 191–233.

Research among managers indicates that they select the medium based upon the nature of the message to be communicated.[8] When the message is difficult or ambiguous, or when differences in background or opinions exist between sender and receiver, then face-to-face is preferred because greater learning is needed. Multiple channels combined with immediate feedback enable managers to communicate back and forth rapidly until disagreements are overcome and a common understanding is reached. Examples of communications for which managers prefer rich media are, "To work out a personality problem that has affected the working relationship between you and your boss," and "To persuade one of your peers to stay with your firm and turn down an attractive offer with another firm."[9]

Managers prefer written media when the message is clear and well defined, and when they have a similar background and understanding about the issue. For routine issues, a simple memo or bulletin is sufficient to communicate the message efficiently because learning needs are minimal. Examples of communications for which managers prefer less rich media are, "To remind a superior that she is scheduled to attend a meeting with your work group on Friday," and "To give your subordinate a cost figure he requested."[10]

Communication difficulties occur when managers use the wrong medium for the message. Using a memo or flyer for a complex topic about which different perspectives exist, leads to unsuccessful communication. An unaddressed document, a medium low in richness, does not provide sufficient cues or opportunities for feedback to resolve differences. Managers sometimes prefer rich media for simple messages, even when multiple cues and feedback are not necessary. Misunderstanding can occur when nonverbal cues like facial expression disagree with the verbal statement. The routine message may be confounded by the noise from excess cues.

Many managers try to balance the written and oral communication they receive to construct a more complete and accurate picture of the organization. Senior managers can become isolated from lower-level employees out in the field if they rely only on written reports to evaluate activities. Written reports do not provide sufficient richness about problems people encounter, how employees feel, or about morale and attitudes within the organization. To learn about these factors, managers have to leave the office and talk to employees face-to-face. One manager who makes use of rich media to complement written communications is Patrick Foley, President of Hyatt Hotels.

UP CLOSE 17.1:   Hyatt Hotels Corporation

Patrick Foley is President of Hyatt Hotels Corporation. Like most chief executives, he receives abundant written information—memos, special reports, and financial figures. These data provide a good view about how each hotel is performing and help him identify trends and problems in the corporation. But these data don't inform Foley about other areas he considers important, such as employee morale and the frustrations felt by people doing their work at lower levels of the corporation.

To understand climate and morale, Foley instituted employee gripe sessions. Once or twice a month, Foley goes to one of the hotels to meet with employees. At one recent session, fourteen of 1000 employees from a Chicago hotel met with him over lunch. It takes a while for employees to warm up to talking to the president. The sessions last from two to three hours, typically starting with work-related gripes. In one session, employees began by expressing concern about items on the menu, having to change lightbulbs, and style of uniforms. But by the end of the session, employees were talking about issues Foley wanted to hear, such as coping with supervisors who are not cooperative, low morale, and poor opportunities for career advancement. These kinds of problems can't be identified or solved through the formal reporting system. As employees learn to trust Foley, they become honest and direct with their feelings about the company.

The sessions have some disadvantages. Supervisors get nervous about employees reporting on them in an unfair manner. The sessions take a lot of time, and employees who are not invited sometimes feel left out. Discussions are also dominated by problems rather than by good things about working for the organization, although Foley learns about some good things as well.

Despite the disadvantages, Foley will continue these sessions to learn as much as he can about problems of employee morale and internal climate. He states, "It's as good a communication tool as we found. I think it really makes them feel part of the company."[11] ▪

The employee gripe sessions did cause some problems, but at bottom line the sessions enabled Foley to learn much about morale, lack of cooperation, and other problems faced by workers. Foley used rich, face-to-face communication to stay in touch on an informal basis with members of the Hyatt organization.

GROUP COMMUNICATION

Now we turn to communication processes within groups. The same ideas from the basic model of communication apply to communications at all levels in organizations. However, communication within work groups differs from managerial communication because group structure and tasks can influence communication requirements.

Group Structure

Research into work group communication has focused on two characteristics. The first is the communication network, which is the extent to which group communications are centralized.[12] The network defines the set of communication channels available to members. Examples of communication networks called the chain, wheel, circle, and all channels are shown in Exhibit 17.3. In a *centralized network* group members are forced to communicate

EXHIBIT 17.3
Characteristics of Group Communication Networks

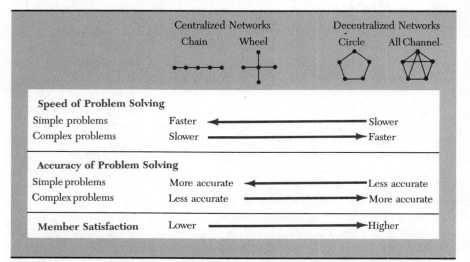

SOURCE: Adapted from A. Bavelas and D. Barrett, "An Experimental Approach to Organization Communication," *Personnel* 1951; M.E. Shaw, *Group Dynamics: The Psychology of Small Group Behavior* (New York: McGraw-Hill, 1976); and E.M. Rogers and R.A. Rogers, *Communication in Organizations* (New York: The Free Press, 1976).

through one central individual in the group problem-solving or decision-making process. This is typical of communication in the chain or wheel, because the centrally located person is the focus of all communications and tends to be the leader and decision maker. In a *decentralized network,* individuals can communicate with several people within the group, and any individual is equally likely to be a leader. Members process information equally among themselves until all members agree on a decision.

The other characteristic of group communication is the nature of the task, whether it is simple or complex. Simple problems are clear and straightforward, while complex problems tend to be ambiguous in both problem formulation and solution. Simple versus complex problems are analogous to programmed versus nonprogrammed decisions, as described in Chapter 4.

Laboratory research has provided valuable information on the extent to which network centralization influences group effectiveness in problem solving.[13] Groups were given problems to solve, but the communication channels among group members were restricted to the chain, wheel, circle, or all channels as illustrated in Exhibit 17.3. Some groups were given simple tasks, such as identifying which symbol was common to a set of printed cards distributed to each group member. Other groups were given complex tasks, such as solving arithmetic or word problems. Groups were given problems one at a time. Researchers evaluated how long it took the group to solve the problems and how many errors were made. After the experiment, members were asked to complete questionnaires describing how satisfied they were with the group activity.

Exhibit 17.3 shows the findings from this research. The speed of problem solving was related to the nature of the problem. The centralized networks were faster for simple problems, because members could pass the relevant information to the central person, who made the decision or solved the problem almost immediately. The decentralized networks were slow, because information was passed around almost randomly until finally one individual put it together and solved the problem. For complex problems, however, the decentralized network was faster. A single individual did not have all the information needed, and pooling of information around the circle or through the all channel network provided greater input. The central person could not solve the complex problem alone, so the centralized network had a difficult time combining everyone's ideas in an equal manner.

In much the same way, the accuracy of communication and decision making was related to simple versus complex problems. The centralized networks made fewer errors on simple problems but more errors for complex problems. The reverse was true for decentralized networks, which were less accurate for simple problems but more accurate for complex problems.

Group members' perceived level of the job satisfaction was also related to network centralization. In general, because member involvement was so small, centralized networks did not provide positive satisfaction to members. Rather than actively participating in decision making, members simply passed a message to the leader and then learned of the outcome. In contrast, members

EXHIBIT 17.4
Summary of Relationships Between Department Tasks and Communication Processes

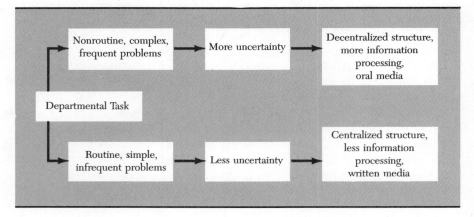

of decentralized networks were highly satisfied. All members participated about equally in problem solving and decision making, and they enjoyed the satisfaction of their achievements.[14]

Department Technology

Another line of research has investigated the relationship between information processing and departmental tasks within ongoing organizations. This research as applied to department technology was described in Chapter 9. It consisted of a survey of a number of organizational groups, including project groups in research and development, accounting auditors, bank clerks, production engineers, sales personnel, and machine operators.[15] The basic finding about communication is similar to that of laboratory research on group networks. As the complexity or frequency of problems increases, the group has to process more information. This leads to decentralized communication processes in which all members of the group communicate with one another as needed to gather information and solve the problem. Departments having nonroutine, complex technologies, such as research and development or strategic planning departments, have to allow for decentralized information processing among employees. If employees are restricted from gathering information and solving problems jointly, group effectiveness diminishes. Employees working on routine technologies, such as assembly-line workers or bank tellers, do not need as much information processing. Communication can be centralized, because problems are simpler and a single individual can make decisions and communicate the results.[16]

The overall pattern of findings for group and departmental communication is summarized in Exhibit 17.4. As the frequency or complexity of problems facing a work group increase, greater information processing is needed. Frequent, complex problems create uncertainty for managers and employees, and to resolve these problems information must be obtained and discussed. Uncertainty also is related to the media used within the group. When problems are frequent and complex, face-to-face discussion is needed to enable rapid feedback and the resolution of differences. When problems are simple and infrequent, written media often will suffice for communicating basic data or the outcome of a decision made by a single manager.

The implications of the relationships shown in Exhibit 17.4 are important for the structure and design of work groups. Groups that deal with complex problems need a free flow of communication and a decentralized structure. Members can be encouraged to discuss problems with one another, and a large percentage of group time will be devoted to information processing. When groups are engaged in routine activities, a larger percentage of the time will be spent directly on the task, and the structure can be centralized so that information is channeled efficiently and quickly to a central source for a decision.

ORGANIZATIONAL COMMUNICATION AND CONTROL

At the organization level of analysis, communication systems pertain to the organization as a whole. Organizational communications typically flow in three directions—downward, upward, and horizontally. Downward and upward communication follow the vertical lines on the organization chart. Horizontal communication involves individuals in different departments and divisions. Horizontal communication does not follow formal lines of authority, and enables managers to coordinate across departmental boundaries.

Downward Communication

Downward communication is used primarily by management to direct and influence personnel at lower levels in the organization. Downward communication usually pertains to one of the following five topics, which are summarized in Exhibit 17.5.[17]

1. *Goals, strategies, and objectives for the organization and its departments.* Communicating goals and strategies provides information about specific targets to managers; it gives direction and reduces uncertainty for lower levels of the organization.
2. *Job instruction and rationale.* Communications about job instruction and rationale explain the nature of specific tasks and why the task is important in relationship to other tasks in the organization.
3. *Policy, procedures, and structural arrangements.* Statements of policy, procedures, and structural arrangements define the formal characteristics of the organization; they may include policy manuals, personnel manuals, job descriptions, and organization charts.

EXHIBIT 17.5
Downward, Upward, and Horizontal Communication in Organizations

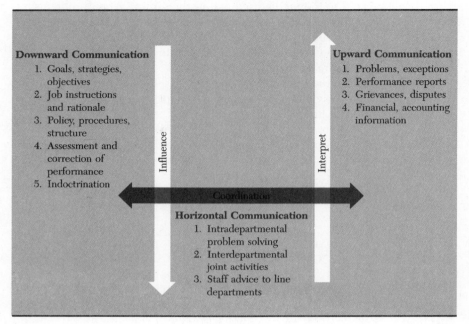

4. *Assessment and correction of performance.* Communications that provide for assessment and correction of performance give feedback to individuals and departments from higher management about the accuracy and quality of how tasks are performed.
5. *Indoctrination.* These communications tell, or indoctrinate, employees about cultural values, important symbols, special ceremonies and other events the company thinks are important, such as picnics, United Way campaigns, or timely news about organizational activities or successes.

Downward communication may follow a number of channels. Oral media include speeches by executives, public address systems, and formal conferences and supervisor meetings. Written media include policy and procedure manuals, letters and memoranda, newsletters and magazines, and bulletin boards and posters. These media are in effect channels that can be used to communicate goals, instructions, rules, and other information that affects employees.

Downward communication is not always successful in large organizations with several levels of hierarchy, because messages can be distorted and misinterpreted. Communication passed down from level to level is not always understood or transmitted correctly. A study of a hundred organizations reported substantial loss of information with each level in the hierarchy, as Exhibit 17.6 illustrates. A 34 percent loss of understanding was experienced just from top management to the vice presidential level. An 80 percent loss occurred by the time information reached the production worker.[18] For effective downward communication, top managers must continue to repeat important themes and use multiple channels. A single communication is likely to be lost and have only modest impact.

Upward Communication

Upward communication typically provides data to upper-level management about activities and performance throughout the organization. Upward communication helps managers interpret organizational activities, and the messages

EXHIBIT 17.6
Percentage of Information that Reaches Lower Levels During Downward Communication

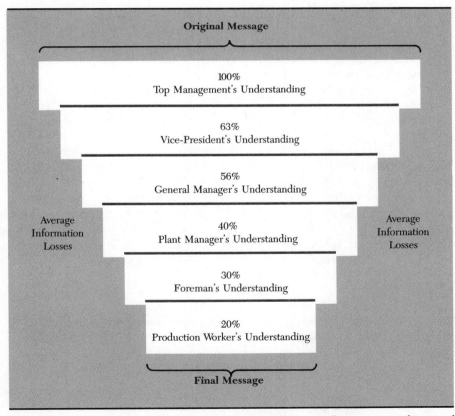

SOURCE: Adapted from Ralph G. Nichols, "Listening is Good Business," *Management of Personnel Quarterly* 1,2 (1962): 4; and E. Scannell, *Communication for Leadership* (New York: McGraw-Hill, 1970), p. 5.

typically are about organizational performance. The four major types of information communicated upward are summarized in Exhibit 17.5 and include the following:[19]

1. *Problems and exceptions.* Exceptions to routine performance and serious problems that cannot be handléd at lower levels are communicated upward so senior managers are aware of difficulties and can have a say in resolving them.
2. *Performance reports.* These reports include both computer-based and written reports of a periodic nature (weekly, monthly) that inform management about how departments are performing.
3. *Grievances and disputes.* Employee grievances are pushed up the hierarchy for resolutions, as are disputes between departments.
4. *Financial and accounting information.* Information pertaining to costs, accounts receivable, sales volume, anticipated profits and return on investment are of interest to senior managers and are part of the upward flow of data; information from the accounting department is most typical.

Top managers use multiple sources of upward communications to learn about and interpret organizational activities and performance. Oral media include the open-door policy, through which managers can hear directly from employees at all levels, supervisory meetings, conferences, and the telephone. Written media include employee surveys, special reports prepared by staff members, management information systems that provide daily, weekly or monthly data on operations, and formal memos and suggestion boxes.

Although multiple channels exist for upward communication, problems with accuracy still appear. The content of upward communication is often influenced by degree of trust and by what subordinates think their boss wants to hear. Ambitious subordinates who want to succeed are likely to distort communications to present a positive image of themselves.[20] Junior managers tend to filter upward communication so positive messages are highlighted or exaggerated and negative messages are downplayed or omitted. As trust toward superiors increases, the accuracy of upward communication also increases. When trust is low, or when employees feel their superior has substantial influence over promotions and rewards, upward messages are often distorted.[21]

Horizontal Communication

Horizontal communications are the lateral information flows that occur both within and between departments. The purpose of horizontal communication is coordination. Coordination is the process by which people and departments work together to accomplish the overall goals of the organization. Horizontal communication typically falls into three types.[22]

1. *Intradepartmental problem solving.* These communications take place between members of the same department and pertain to coordination and accomplishment of tasks within the department.

2. *Interdepartmental activities.* Interdepartmental communications facilitate the accomplishments of projects or tasks that require joint activities, such as when engineering helps production develop specifications for a new machine tool.
3. *Staff advice to line departments.* Specialists from operations research, finance, or other staff departments may undertake specific projects that result in written reports for line departments. Staff specialists also may consult with line managers on a face-to-face basis to solve task problems.

Some communications across departments involve written media such as formal reports, memoranda, and schedules. Most horizontal communication across departments consists of oral media, such as face-to-face meetings and telephone calls. Techniques for attaining horizontal coordination, which were described in Chapter 12, include direct contact among managers, liaison roles, task forces, teams, and integrators.[23] Horizontal communication within departments is typically face-to-face and occurs spontaneously and informally as needed to accomplish a task.[24]

Horizontal communication across departments can present difficulties. As described in the chapter on organization structure, Chapter 12, departmental boundaries are barriers to communication. Employees identify with the goals of their own department, but they may feel competitive toward other departments. Employees can be reluctant to share information openly and spontaneously outside of their departments. However, horizontal communication is essential if the organization's activities are to be coordinated, especially when rapid responses are needed that cannot be processed up and down the hierarchy. Most organizations acknowledge the right of individuals to cross departmental boundaries to provide or obtain information relevant to task accomplishment.

Informal Communication

The upward, downward, and horizontal communications described so far are part of formal communication channels used to accomplish the work of the organization. But in addition to formal channels, organizations have informal channels of communication. Informal communications consist of the **grapevine,** which is actually an important source of information for managers and employees at all levels. The grapevine conveys information in all directions, information which is not commonly available through formal channels. Research on the grapevine phenomena discovered that it is extremely fast and quite accurate. Information can travel widely through a company on the grapevine in one or two days, and this information is 75 to 95 percent accurate.[25] Because of its relative efficiency, managers can use the grapevine as a supplement to formal channels.

The grapevine is valuable simply because it allows employees to learn what is happening in the organization. It facilitates social interaction, and employees who act as linking pins get recognition from others. Problems with the grapevine include the obvious spreading of false rumors. At times of change within an organization, when employees experience anxiety or uncertainty (such as when a company is about to be taken over or a plant closed) rumors will often spring up as an attempt to reduce uncertainty. Rumors are often based on scraps of information that are not necessarily accurate. Managers can combat the negative effects of the grapevine by acting to reduce uncertainty by releasing information through formal channels. Management should not try to eliminate the grapevine but rather use it to complement official information and "get the word out" to employees.[26]

Managing upward, downward, horizontal, and informal communications is a challenge for top management. The right communication flow can mean success, as illustrated by the Boddie Nowell chain of Hardee's restaurants.

UP CLOSE 17.2:   Boddie Nowell Enterprises Inc.

Nick and Mayo Boddie run a small empire of 208 Hardee's restaurants in five states, grossing more than $210 million a year. Ten franchises is often the size at which franchise companies plateau, because the managers cannot personally supervise a larger number. Additional growth requires communication systems that enable the owners to extend beyond this limit.

Brothers Nick and Mayo found the right formula for vertical communication. Downward communication is largely face-to-face. They give direction when a restaurant is opened to start it running properly. They visit restaurants frequently, talk to employees, and make suggestions and corrections on the spot. They've been known to fire managers immediately if they discover long customer lines and litter on the floor. They have staff assistants who provide written procedures, but their personal communications to restaurants are frequent.

Upward communication is highly automated. BNEI's management information system is detailed and fast. A headquarters computer is tied to a computer in each restaurant and to every cash register. Top management can learn what is happening in any unit at any time. The upward flow of information includes data on which restaurant did the best job of the day on suggestive selling, how many coupons were collected, how many customers were served, which restaurant was over payroll, and the amount of drive-in window business. The information is so detailed that top managers can learn in an instant how much it costs to put ketchup on a single burger, how many gallons of water a unit uses, non-food sales, net sales, paid insurance, total cash, eat-in, eat-out, drive through, cash short, sales tax, and almost every other action in a restaurant's life.

Horizontal communication within restaurants is excellent. The Boddie brothers promote a family atmosphere, and employees work together to coordinate unit activities. Communication between restaurants is virtually non-existent. It just isn't needed. Each restaurant is a stand-alone unit

EXHIBIT 17.7
Basic Model of Organizational Control

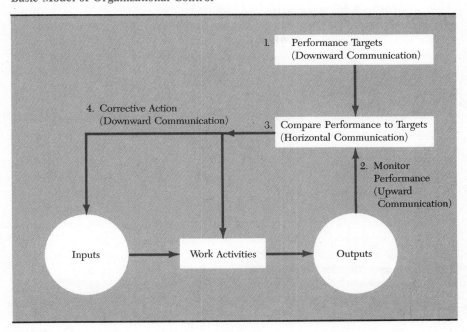

connected to the central office. The primary communication flows are vertical between headquarters and the restaurants and horizontal within restaurants. There is a need for information to be shared in this manner, and the communication system fulfills that need. The company is successful as a result. The 208 restaurants run by Nick and Mayo Boddie outperform other franchises in the Hardee's system. The brothers' average sales per store was $979,000 in 1983, as opposed to an average of $700,000 for other stores in Hardee's operations.[27] ▪

A BASIC MODEL OF ORGANIZATIONAL CONTROL

A large part of vertical communication, both upward and downward, typically is associated with organizational control. **Organizational control** is the regulation of organizational activities to attain organizational goals. It is an ongoing process that includes the definition of goals, identification of paths toward those goals, and procedures for limiting organizational activities to be congruent with achieving goals. This control process consists of four interrelated steps, which Exhibit 17.7 shows.[28]

1. *Performance targets.* Managers define operative goals in specific, operational terms that become the standard for organizational activities. As described

in Chapter 11, standards should be explicit and attainable. Examples of standards include "achieve a six percent return on investment," "reduce scrap costs by $100,000 a year," or "hire seven new people in the Accounting Department." Once the standards are established, downward communication channels are used to communicate them to the people in the organization who need to know. Downward communication is often written in the form of policies, regulations, and management by objectives. Written communication may be augmented with spoken statements and supervisory meetings.

2. *Monitor performance.* Performance is monitored by the measurement of organizational work activities and its communication to management. Quantitative measurements can be accumulated on a daily or monthly basis and communicated upward through the computer-based information system. Boddie Nowell Enterprises used computer information to monitor the activity of Hardee's Restaurants in **Up Close 17.2.** Monitoring follows upward channels in organizations, and it is often part of the formal management control systems. Managers often supplement these data with tours and face-to-face discussions with lower-level employees to learn first-hand how things are going.

3. *Compare performance to the targets.* The third stage in the control process is the explicit comparison between monitored performance and performance targets. This assessment may involve some horizontal communication, because managers may discuss with one another how to interpret the data. Managers may decide that everything is alright because activities are on target; or they may respond to deviations by discussing whether new targets or corrective action are needed to improve performance.

4. *Corrective action.* Corrective action includes the steps managers take to make changes in organizational work activities. Managers may encourage employees to work harder, they may decide to redesign the production process, or they may fire some employees and hire new ones. Corrective action utilizes the downward communication channel and is often performed face-to-face.[29] Corrective action is often complicated, and managers need to consider the specific circumstances associated with the problem. Thus they often meet face-to-face with subordinates to interpret the causes of shortcomings, and to propose corrections. In well-defined situations, managers propose corrective action through written directives.

An organization is composed of a series of control loops similar to the one in Exhibit 17.7. Top-level managers monitor the inputs, outputs, and performance of the entire organization. Mid-level managers establish a control loop for major departments and divisions. Supervisors control their own work group through the process of setting standards, monitoring performance, and taking corrective action.

Most organizations impose control procedures in areas considered vital to the organization's success. One example is the customer service department at American Express.[30] From an analysis of customer complaints, American Express determined that timeliness, accuracy, and responsiveness were the important outputs to be achieved. Management set targets with respect to getting bills out on time and responding to customer complaints within a limited number of days. Managers eventually identified 180 standards, each of which measured a different aspect of service quality provided to customers. American Express managers also developed monitoring devices to evaluate the speed with which complaints were answered, timeliness of billing, and the approval of new applications. The company estimated that it earned thirty-three cents of extra sales each day earlier a card is in the hands of a customer. The outcome of this control system proved extremely successful. The time required to process credit card applications fell from thirty-five days to fifteen days. Cards are replaced in two days, compared to a previous fifteen. Response to customer inquiries has been reduced from sixteen to ten days.

TYPES OF ORGANIZATIONAL CONTROL

Managers at the top and middle levels of the organization have three basic strategies they can choose for organizational control. William Ouchi identified these three types of control: bureaucratic control, market control, and clan control.[31] Each type uses different information for monitoring and corrective action, and each type tends to be suited to specific situations. All three types of control are frequently used in organizations, but the emphasis given to each type may vary. The typical situation and information requirements associated with each type of control are illustrated in Exhibit 17.8.

Bureaucratic Control

Bureaucratic control is the use of rules, regulations, the hierarchy of authority, and other bureaucratic mechanisms to direct behavior and assess performance. This type of control uses bureaucratic characteristics described in Chapter 8. Within a large organization, thousands of behaviors and information exchanges take place every day. Rules and policies based on organizational goals evolve to regulate these behaviors. Bureaucratic control mechanisms are general in nature; they do not attempt to measure or control every specific behavior or transaction. The organization establishes a division of labor, assigns tasks,

EXHIBIT 17.8
Types of Organizational Control

Type	Information and Control Source
Bureacracy	Rules, standards, goals, authority structure, policies
Market	Prices, competition, costs
Clan	Shared values, trust, common tradition and beliefs

specifies targets, and provides rules and regulations that give direction to employees and standardize behavior. Bureaucratic control mechanisms are supplemented by supervision. The division of labor enables supervisors to monitor employee behavior and determine whether it is congruent with organizational policies.

Virtually every organization uses bureaucratic control. Rules, goals, and directives supply information about appropriate behavior through downward communications.

Market Control

Market control is the use of prices and competition to monitor and evaluate the output and productivity of an organization. Market control is an economic concept.[32] Outputs are priced in dollar terms and sold to other organizations or other divisions. The price mechanism is an efficient form of control information because managers can compare prices and profits to evaluate the efficiency of the corporation. Top managers use market control to evaluate total corporate performance as reflected in the profit and loss statement; they can compare this information to that of previous years or to other corporations. The profit and loss statement provides market information about how the organization is doing in a competitive environment.

Market control can also be used within organizations to control major departments or divisions, which are called profit centers. Profit centers are self-contained business units, as described in Chapter 12. Each division is responsible for all costs associated with producing a product. Each division in a corporation can be evaluated on the basis of profit or loss compared to other divisions. S.I. Newhouse and Sons is a large newspaper chain, and managers use market control to evaluate each newspaper business in the chain.[33] The newspaper in each city is an autonomous business unit. Top managers at Newhouse monitor performance through the use of monthly, quarterly, and annual cost figures and profit statements. If the financial information for each newspaper is not consistent with planned targets, then changes to improve performance can be made. Market control is efficient here, because little surveillance is required in the form of direct supervision, and few rules and procedures are needed. Supervisors within a division are free to do as they please and to establish their own rules, as long as the outputs are congruent with expected targets.

Market control is not useful in organizations where outputs cannot be priced and sold, or when there is no price competition. It is not appropriate in not-for-profit organizations simply because their services are not priced and sold. Not-for-profit organizations are not in competition with one another, and if prices were devised for services provided to clients, the price might not reflect the true cost and hence be a poor assessment of internal performance.

Market control also is not efficient for the exchange of services among functional departments within a single organization. If the research and development or personnel departments were forced to sell their services to production and marketing, this use of market control would probably fail. In a true market, prices are arrived at through competitive bidding. There is no way to establish competition or to set accurate prices for personnel or R&D services. Moreover, production and marketing departments might decide not to use the services if payment is required, which would not be consistent with the goals of top management to have strong R&D and personnel departments.

Clan Control

Clan control is the use of social characteristics such as values, traditions, shared beliefs, and employee commitment to control behavior. It requires extensive trust, involvement, and shared values among employees. Clan control uses norms and values rather than market or bureaucratic mechanisms to set targets and monitor behavior. Under clan control, the information that pertains to the values, traditions, and goals desired by the group is most important. Members work toward these goals because they share the same values with each other. Employees think of themselves as a large family, or clan, and the satisfaction of membership is sufficient to regulate behavior. Clan control relies on the unwritten and unmeasurable norms and values to regulate behavior.

This type of control is often used in small, informal organizations because personal involvement and direct commitment to the purpose and activities of the organization is possible. People may be hired under clan control because they are committed to the organization's purpose, which happens in a religious organization. Many small companies employ clan control by hiring family members to occupy key positions. As part of a true family, members trust one another, and less surveillance, fewer rules, and fewer market indicators are needed to monitor and influence behavior.

Mixed Control

Overall control strategies differ substantially from organization to organization. Most organizations use some bureaucratic control, and many organizations also use clan control and market control. Bureaucratic control is important when organizations are large, and when the environment and technology are certain, stable, and routine.

Clan control is prominent when organizations are small, or when the environment and technology are uncertain and unstable, making trust, tradition, and shared values important. Clan control is used in selected areas throughout large organizations. In an R&D department, for example, technology is uncertain and conditions are changing, so clan control may emerge among research scientists even though bureaucratic control is prominent in other departments. Clan control also appears in the inner circle of managers. Top managers work under high uncertainty and rely on the trust and shared traditions and values of the top management team.[34]

Market control has somewhat more limited application. Market mechanisms are used when organizational costs and outputs can be priced, and when a market is available for price competition and comparison. Market control is appropriate for self-contained units in a business corporation because each division is a profit center. Market control also can be used in the acquisition of raw materials and human resources. The organization can specify acceptable prices and quality of goods to be purchased and then let market forces work to provide resources that meet those specifications. Market control can be used whenever goods can be priced and sold under competition.[35]

UP CLOSE 17.3:   Manchester State College

Senior officials at Manchester decided to organize the business school, engineering school, school of arts and science college, and graduate school into profit centers. Each school would receive the tuition income from students and pay the cost for providing education. The university imposed overall tuition guidelines and academic standards and then gave each school substantial freedom. The professional schools, such as business and engineering, experienced a greater demand from students, so students were charged a tuition premium. These schools also paid higher salaries to professors, who were in short supply. Each school could not offer every course needed for a degree, so transfer payments were made between schools for teaching courses to students enrolled in other schools. An overhead payment was made to the university each semester for the use of centralized services such as the library, buildings, maintenance, and utilities. Each school had to keep salaries and tuition rates at reasonable levels because other universities in the area competed for students.

After a trial period of two years, the profit center plan worked well, and top administrators considered extending it to the computer center. Each user of computer services could be given a code that indicated the school to be billed, and all transactions could be automatically recorded by the computer. The university president decided to make the computer center a profit center. It was to become self-sufficient by selling its services to other schools in the university.

Within three years after making the computer center a profit center, the schools were in an uproar. The computer center had steadily increased the price of computer services. The teaching and research budgets of the schools were being drained. More and more money had to be allocated to cover the cost of computer services for teaching and research. The colleges joined forces and insisted that the computer center be brought back under the control of central administration.

A university committee met to analyze the computer situation and make a recommendation. They discovered that users of the computer center were being charged a price nearly three times the actual cost to the computer center. Computer center managers used the revenue to hire additional staff and to finance their own research. They were able to increase the price because no competitive computer services were available. Each school had to buy services from the computer center or use no service at all. The price did not reflect the true value of computer services.

The university committee recommended that the computer department once again be made a part of administration and that services be provided free of charge. The schools were in unanimous agreement. They even offered to increase the overhead payment to the university administration to cover computer costs.[36] ▪

Manchester State shifted from bureaucratic to market control. Market control was effective for each college because the tuition price was an accurate reflection of the market and performance. But the decision by administrators to use market control for the computer department did not work because competition did not exist. The prices for computer services reflected what the computer department wanted to charge, which made computer service less attractive to other departments. Senior officials at Manchester reverted back to bureaucratic control for the computer department by establishing goals and procedures to regulate computer services.

MANAGEMENT INFORMATION AND CONTROL SYSTEMS

Organizations can use overall strategies of bureaucratic, market, or clan control. Within the organization, managers at the middle level use management information and control systems to keep informed about departmental activities. **Management control systems** are the formal planning, data gathering, and transmission systems that provide middle management with information about organizational activities.[37] Management control systems provide formal upward and downward communications via operating budget, cost control systems, and operational reports. Management control systems are a subset of the *bureaucratic control* processes in the organization. They provide the day-to-day data to supplement formal bureaucratic structure and division of labor.

Control System Components

A survey of managers of eighty-six departments in twenty companies asked managers which control systems they used to evaluate and influence departmental performance. Four management control systems were identified as an important part of the management control process.[38]

1. *Operating budget.* The operating budget consists of formal statements of estimated expenses, assets, and related financial figures for the coming year. Operational expenses are normally budgeted in three categories: personnel salaries, equipment, and other operating expenses (e.g., travel, paper and pencils). Budgets are projected annually, and monthly budget reports are typically issued that compare budget expenditures with targets. Budget reports are usually developed for every cost center, including small departments.

2. *Periodic statistical reports.* Statistical data, such as the number of personnel hours worked, number of new customer contracts, delinquent account ratios, volume of orders received, scrap rate, and other statistics relevant to the department comprise these reports. Three to six statistical reports might be used to manage departments. Most statistical reports contain non-financial data and are issued weekly, monthly, or quarterly.

3. *Performance appraisal system.* This system is the formal method of evaluating and recording the performance of managers and employees. It frequently includes standardized forms and rating scales for performance evaluation, as described in Chapter 5. The performance appraisal system also includes objective setting (management by objectives) in many organizations. Annual meetings between managers and subordinates are used to define future objectives and to evaluate performance to date.

4. *Standard operating procedures.* Standard operating procedures (SOPs) include the policies, rules, and procedures for the department. Many organizations make available to department managers manuals that put in writing policy guidelines, as well as specifying rules and procedures to guide particular activities, such as dismissing an employee or handling a grievance. These materials also include job descriptions and other specifications to direct work activities.

Other types of management control systems also exist in organizations, such as capital budgets and human resource reports. However, the four control systems of budget, statistical reports, performance appraisal, and SOPs are the major systems managers use to monitor and control departmental activities.

Control System Focus

Management control systems focus on specific parts of the work process. Recall from Chapter 9 on technology that each department can be characterized as a transformation process. Inputs come into the department, are transformed through work activity, and become outputs that leave the department. These three aspects of the transformation process are the focus of management control systems, as illustrated in Exhibit 17.9.

Input Control   Input control focuses on the resources flowing into the department. It is sometimes called feedforward control or steering control because it begins before the primary transformation process.[39] Input control is designed to make sure that the appropriate amount of human resources, materials, and finances are available for the department or division to do its task. Input control tries to anticipate the needs of the department and meet them in advance.

Process Control   Process control focuses on ongoing work activities within the organization. It includes direct supervision by managers, as well as the use of rules and procedures to direct and monitor activities. Process control is designed to make sure that work activities are meeting expectations.

EXHIBIT 17.9
Focus of Management Control Systems

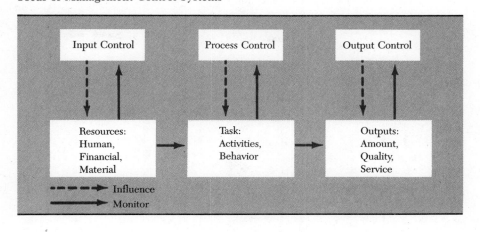

Output Control Output control focuses on the end result or output of the department or division. Outputs are the department's finished products or services. Output control is sometimes called feedback control because it occurs after the production process.[40] Information feeds back into the input and process control mechanisms to enable corrective action early in the transformation process. Output control is concerned more with past activities than future events.

Management Control System Package The four elements of management control systems focus on different aspects of the transformation process, as illustrated in Exhibit 17.10. They complement one another by focusing on different aspects of departmental activities. The elements of management control systems form an overall package that provides managers with information about inputs, process, and outputs.[41]

The budget is primarily an input control device. Managers use the budget for planning the future and for reducing uncertainty about human and raw material resources needed to perform necessary tasks. Statistical and operational reports, by contrast, provide a control function over outputs. These reports apply to volume, quality control, and other output indicators that provide feedback to management about departmental results. The performance appraisal system and policies and procedures are directed at process control. Formal performance appraisals are designed to evaluate and correct employee work activities. Standard operating procedures provide explicit directions for behavior needed to attain outcomes. Managers can use direct supervision in conjunction with the performance appraisal and SOPs to keep departmental work activities within desired limits.

Each management control subsystem is associated with the cycle of specific targets, monitoring of behavior, and corrective action. Thus on a month-to-

EXHIBIT 17.10
Four Management Control Subsystems and the Focus of Control

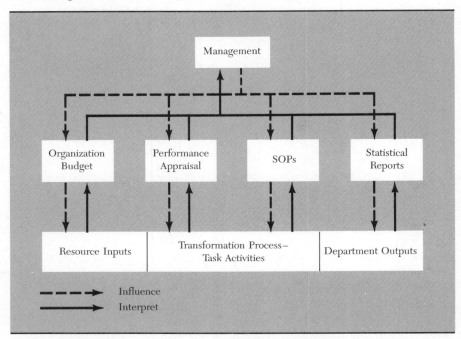

SOURCE: Based on Richard L. Daft and Norman B. Macintosh, "The Nature and Use of Formal Control Systems for Management Control and Strategy Implementation," *Journal of Management* 10 (1984): 43–66.

month basis, budget expenditures are monitored to ensure they are on target. The same is true for the performance appraisal system and the statistical reports. Each management control subsystem works independently to control selected activities. The four subsystems combine into a larger control loop for middle and upper management. Budgets provide resource inputs for departments, and statistical reports provide feedback about results. The performance appraisal and SOPs provide additional mechanisms for taking corrective action if statistical reports indicate that problems exist. Taken together, the four control subsystems provide one management control system for the target setting, monitoring, and corrective action needed to influence organizational performance.

The implementation and use of effective control systems does not just happen. Managers must design systems and put them into effect to meet the need for information and control. When control systems are not in place, when both planning and feedback are nonexistent, organizations can experience disaster. This happened at Singer.

UP CLOSE 17.4: The Singer Company

The mid-1970s was the beginning of a difficult period for Singer. Joseph Flavin was hired to run a company that seemed out of control. Under Flavin's leadership, the company soon took a $411 million write-off. Singer's managers and most outsiders believed that the Singer business was basically sound. But several months later Singer wrote off another $130 million, and the presence of deep problems became obvious.

Singer executives had completely missed the drop in demand for sewing machines. Executives were aware of a drop in sales, but they didn't understand the extent of the drop and the underlying reasons. Singer had never collected market information nor polled its customers. The company was late in understanding changing trends in demand for its products. They finally discovered that only about 18 percent of females in the 16–24 age group would probably own sewing machines in 1985, compared to 46% in 1970. The drop was shown as even more dramatic among older women. More women work outside the home, so they have more money to buy clothes and alternative ways to use their leisure time.

They did perceive that by 1979 the market for consumer sewing machines was dropping dramatically, and along with it Singer's sales volume. That was the first year Singer lost money. The demand for sewing machines had been cut in half since 1972.

Compounding the problem of poor information about output demands was the continued use of inefficient plants. The Clydebank plant in Glasgow, Scotland was ninety-three years old in 1979. A machine that cost $123 to make at Clydebank could be produced by competitors for $65. Internal management control systems were not providing the information about plant inefficiency to senior managers.

Singer executives acted for years prior to this time as if the sewing business could run without a coherent business plan, without effective budgeting, without efficient plants, and without good reports about operations and marketing. Managers were given extreme latitude, and they built small empires and did not communicate with one another. As the managers slowly woke up, they realized they had to close the Clydebank plant, leaving 3000 workers unemployed.

Looking back, a disappointed Singer executive summarized his view: "What happened was not at all mysterious. We had no control systems. It's a classic case that will be studied for a long time to come."[42] ■

Singer lacked internal control and managers also lacked information about the environment. Information systems and management control systems are typically designed to provide information for use in planning and goal setting. Without the appropriate information and control systems, Singer did not realize what was happening and was unable to reduce budgets and increase efficiency for the coming decrease in unit sales.

SUPERVISORY CONTROL

The types of control and management control systems we have discussed pertain to middle and upper levels of the organization. At these levels, managers are concerned with resource inputs and departmental outputs. At lower management levels in organizations, supervisors are concerned with performance of individual employees. Supervisors are not in charge of entire departments, but are responsible for evaluating and providing feedback to a few employees. The two types of control mechanisms typically used by managers to control immediate subordinates are output control and behavior control.[43]

Output control is based on written records that measure employee outputs and productivity. It is effective when outputs of individual workers can be measured easily. An example is a piece-rate job where the number of units produced per hour by each employee is easily calculated. Sales jobs can be controlled with output control because measurement of performance is reflected in number of sales or in commissions earned. Output information is typically reported and communicated through written records.

The effectiveness of advertising agency designers and copywriters is normally evaluated by output control. The process of how to create an exciting new campaign and how to write good ad copy is not well understood. So the test of effective performance lies with whether the advertising campaign increases the client's sales. In this sense employees can behave however they believe necessary as long as they produce the desired output, an effective ad.

Behavior control is based upon personal observation of employees. The foundation of it is supervisor surveillance of the procedures and work behaviors of subordinates. Behavior control is often used when outputs are not easily measured or evaluated. The outputs of college teaching are how much the student learns and how well students apply learning in their careers. These outputs are nearly impossible to measure, so teachers are evaluated on how they behave in teaching or the procedures they use. Student evaluations provide information about a teacher's classroom behavior, which is fed back to both the teachers and department heads. In some schools department heads, deans, or senior teachers visit the classroom to directly observe teacher performance.

The choice of output versus behavior control partly depends upon the ability to measure day-to-day behavior versus finished outputs. In many jobs, both behavior and outputs can be evaluated. Supervisors can use both types of control or emphasize one or the other depending upon the goals of the organization. Some retail department stores encourage the use of output measures, evaluating sales personnel strictly on total sales.[44] Sales people thus concentrate on increasing sales without regard to following specific procedures. In other department stores, output control does not achieve the goals desired by management. In stores that have a wealthy clientele, output control may cause sales personnel to use hard sell techniques that might offend customers. These stores emphasize behavior control and reward employees for doing things consistent with the store's image, such as using a soft sell with customers, providing services that do not yield immediate sales but build good will, and cleaning and straightening displays. Many stores use a balance of both output and behavior control to provide a broad perspective on employee performance.

IMPROVING ORGANIZATIONAL COMMUNICATION AND CONTROL PROCESSES

This chapter has covered several concepts and models about communication and control. A number of problems were discussed that hinder the effectiveness of communication and control. These problems include distortion of messages or reports, failure to have messages passed down the hierarchy, and lack of information sharing across departments. Several techniques exist to improve organizational communication and control. These techniques can be used for upward, downward, and horizontal communications, and they are summarized in Exhibit 17.11.[45]

Improving Downward Communications

As shown in Exhibit 17.11, important techniques for improving communications with subordinates involve clarifying the nature of the job or task. Employees should be helped to understand organizational goals and strategies, including what each person is expected to do and why. In addition to clarifying job instructions and rationale, managers can provide more feedback to help employees work toward organizational targets. Managers can use multiple communication channels, including both written and verbal media to send messages down the hierarchy. Sometimes managers may bypass formal communication channels and go directly to the intended receiver with the message. This type of direct contact will avoid noise and distortion during transmission.

Improving Upward Communication

Management control system reports and meetings with subordinates can create a problem in upward communication—information overload. Overload can be reduced by information screening, or transmitting only the important aspects of a message up through the hierarchy and omitting unnecessary details. An important way to screen information is called *management by exception*. In this procedure, routine information is not provided to managers. Control systems only send reports about exceptions, deviations, and emergencies. Another way to improve upward communication is to foster an organizational climate of trust so subordinates do not fear negative outcomes from delivering bad news. Managers need negative information more than positive information, but in an atmosphere of retribution and negative consequences employees will distort this information. Another strategy is reliance on written records and management control system reports because they are more objective and less

EXHIBIT 17.11

Techniques for Improving Organizational Communications and Control Process

---

Downward Communications

1. Job instructions and rationale can be presented clearly to employees so they understand more precisely what is expected and why.
2. Managers can stress goals and objectives so employees know the target to be attained.
3. Management can provide greater feedback concerning the nature and quality of performance, thereby keeping employees "on target."
4. Multiple communication channels—written and face-to-face—can be used to increase the chances that the message is properly received. Important messages can be repeated.
5. In some cases, it is desirable to bypass formal communication channels and go directly to the intended receiver with the message.

Upward Communications

1. Upward messages can be screened so only the relevant aspects are received by top management.
2. Mangers can attempt to create a climate of trust and openness so subordinates feel free to transmit negative as well as positive messages without fear of retribution.
3. Managers can sensitize themselves and obtain information from multiple sources so they are better able to detect bias, distorted messages, and inaccurate reports.
4. Managers can try to use "distortion-proof" messages, such as management control systems requiring quantified or standardized data.

Horizontal Communications

1. Efforts can be made to develop interpersonal skills between group members and departments so greater openness and trust exist.
2. Reward systems can be utilized that reward interdepartmental cooperation.
3. Interdepartmental meetings can be used to share information concerning what other departments are doing.
4. In some cases, the structure of the organization can be changed to provide greater interdepartmental contacts (e.g., adopting teams, task forces, liaison personal or matrix organization design).

SOURCE: Adapted from R. M. Steers, *Organizational Effectiveness: A Behavioral View* (Glenview, IL: Scott, Foresman and Company), 1977, p. 151.

---

amenable to distortion.[46] Standard forms and reports reduce the potential for bias in reporting.

Improving Horizontal Communication   Accurate horizontal communication can spell the difference between success and failure when a rapid response is needed or when an emergency exists. Managers can facilitate horizontal communication between departments by supporting interpersonal trust and openness between departments. Cooperation between departments, rather than competition, can be rewarded. A manager's bonus may be contingent upon the performance of all departments jointly rather than on his or her department's performance alone. Rewards can be adjusted to reflect how much a manager helps other departments reach their goals. Other techniques are frequent interdepartmental meetings with members of other departments invited to share information, problems, and solutions. Specific structural mechanisms such as task forces, project managers, teams, or even a matrix organization (as described in Chapter 12) can accomplish improved horizontal communication and coordination. These mechanisms assign official responsibility to people for processing accurate communication between departments.

One example of overcoming communication barriers was Sperry Corporation's active listening program. The program involved all 90,000 employees in an attempt to improve upward, downward, and horizontal communication. The listening program consisted of a seven-hour seminar. The managers and employees learned specific listening skills, with successful results. People became conscious of listening and trying to understand without distortion. A major trend in the results suggested that many people felt Sperry was different from other companies because employees listened—to customers and to each other.[47]

SUMMARY

This chapter examined several aspects of organizational communication and control. Communication can be examined from the point of view of the manager, the work group, or the total organization. Managers spend 80 percent of their time communicating. A basic model of communication was proposed, showing the necessary steps in effective communication and where noise can occur. The concept of media richness was also discussed. Managers select oral versus written media, depending on the nature of the message and the difficulty of transmission. Group communication is influenced by the complexity of the task. Complex tasks create uncertainty for members and require greater amounts of information processing. Simple tasks enable employees to spend less time communicating and more time in direct task activities.

Organizational communication can be characterized as upward, downward, or horizontal. A variety of media can be used in organizational communications. Most communications at the organization level of analysis are designed for control. Three strategies of control are bureaucratic, market, and clan. Each uses different types of information and is suited for specific organizational situations. Management control systems are also an important aspect of organizational communication and control. Four components of management control subsystems are budget, performance appraisal system, standard operating procedures, and statistical reports. The budget focuses control on resource inputs, the performance appraisal system and SOPs focus control on work activities, and statistical reports focus control on finished outputs. The four management control systems complement one another to provide overall control of major organizational departments and divisions. Several strategies for improving upward, downward, and horizontal communications and control processes were discussed.

KEY WORDS

behavior control
bureaucratic control
centralized network
clan control
communication
decoding
downward
   communication
encoding
feedback
grapevine

horizontal
   communication
information richness
management control
   systems
market control
meaning
medium
message
noise
operating budget

organizational control
output control
performance appraisal
   system
periodic statistical
   reports
standard operating
   procedures
upward
   communication

DISCUSSION QUESTIONS

1. What is the importance of communication in organizations?
2. Identify several sources of noise in a communication transaction. Which part of the communication model is affected by the noise?
3. What is the relationship between communication networks and communication? Does this relationship also apply to departmental communications? Explain.
4. Many managers believe they need to receive information that is independent of the written memos and reports. Agree or disagree with this point of view and explain why.
5. Discuss the differences between upward, downward, and horizontal communications. Are different problems associated with effective communication in each direction?
6. Explain the control cycle and how it works in organizations.
7. Government organizations tend to rely heavily on bureaucratic control, while business organizations make greater use of market control. Explain why this occurs.
8. How does the management control system package help managers control inputs, production process, and outputs?
9. If managers are receiving poor information about organizational activities, what suggestions would you make?

CASE 17.1   Southern Bank

Southern Bank, established shortly after the Civil War, had developed a distinguished record for prudent, conservative financial service. An independent, single-location bank situated in a medium-sized city, it now (1985) employs some 750 persons and is one of the largest institutions of its kind in the area.

The bank is organized into eight divisions: General Administrative; Banking; Investment; Trust Administration; Business Development; Management Consulting; Marketing; and Legal. In addition, there are three service groups: Planning and Personnel, Building and Office Services, and the Controller's Group. There are six levels of management in the bank: President; Division; Group; Department; Section; and Unit.

About a hundred of the bank's employees are officers, of whom six are women; another hundred employees are men in various stages of professional banking careers. The remaining 350 employees are women, about fifty of whom are highly trained career specialists. Approximately one half of the female employees are young, unmarried high-school graduates. These women typically work for the bank for two or three years.

Since the inauguration of a new president in 1979 and the subsequent employment of a number of "bright young men," the bank has aggressively been exploring new ways of rendering financial services to its customers. This combination of aggressiveness and innovation has proved to be highly successful in promoting the growth and profitability of the bank. The Management Consulting Division, for example, has become a profitable new service and has also served to bring valued new accounts to the bank.

The top management people in Southern Bank believe that if the institution is to continue to grow through aggressiveness and innovation, the ideas and cooperation of all employees at all levels should be solicited and encouraged. Excellent communication is considered by top management to be vital to the successful operation of this dynamic organization. To this end, Mr. Harold Walsh of the Personnel office was designated in 1983 as the coordinator of communications and training. Also to this end, a variety of communication techniques, channels, and devices, described on the following pages, have been adopted.

OFFICERS' MEETINGS

The president meets formally with the board of directors once each month. A day or two after this meeting, the president holds his regular monthly meeting for the bank's officers. In this meeting, the president reports on selected topics from the board meeting and reviews the monthly financial statements. At the end of this presentation, which usually lasts about fifteen minutes, the president asks for and responds to questions from the officers in attendance.

Each officer is free to decide which of the nonconfidential topics covered in the officers' meetings, if any, will be reported back to his subordinates. Officers typically do not hold group meetings for this purpose.

The officers' meetings are the only regularly scheduled meetings in the bank designed for the purpose of routinely disseminating information.

COMCOM

"COMCOM" (a popular abbreviation for "Communications Committee") was the brainchild of Alice Davey, an officer in the bank, who suggested her idea to President Libbert at a cocktail party one evening in 1983. Mrs. Davey felt that something was needed to bolster communication to and from the lower levels of the organization. The stated objective of COMCOM was to "promote internal understanding of all matters of common concern at all levels throughout the organization."

President Libbert accepted Mrs. Davey's suggestion and announced the establishment of COMCOM in a memo dated October 2, 1983.

ALL BANK MEMO/October 2, 1983

For an extended period of time, I have personally felt that a committee should be established to serve as an organized pipeline for the flow of information throughout the organization. We all like to know "what's going on when it's going on," and I believe that the *Communications Committee* can provide this type of information for all of us. I have appointed the following to serve on this committee:

> George Storm—Co-Chairman
> Alice Davey—Co-Chairman
> Ronald Brooks
> John Cassidy
> Norman Euler
> Ruth Hobgood
> Roy Munford
> Elmer Nagel
> Jack Phillips
> Ed Ralston
> George Robinson

The committee is currently in the organizational stage, and when its program for effective internal communications has been established, it will be announced.

Frederick E. Libbert

Each of the eleven members of COMCOM is an officer in the bank; all eight divisions are represented on the committee. George Storm and Alice Davey are the co-chairmen. Each COMCOM member is expected to solicit questions from employees at all levels in his division for submission to President Libbert for discussion at the monthly officers' meetings. Questions on any topic except grievances and personalities are welcomed.

"COMCOM" members report that they devote perhaps two hours each month to the task of gathering questions. These questions are reviewed at a regular monthly "COMCOM" meeting held one week prior to the officers' meeting. Suitable questions are agreed upon and an average of four questions per month are forwarded to the President in advance of the officers' meeting. Most of these questions originate with the "COMCOM" members themselves or from persons in the top three levels of the organization.

The President feels that "COMCOM" is working well; the "COMCOM" co-chairmen feel that the committee is reasonably successful in reaching its objectives; the Personnel Manager feels that "COMCOM" is failing to attain its objectives and wonders how it might be made more effective.

SOUTHERN MESSENGER

The *Southern Messenger*, the bank's unusual house organ, originated in 1946 through spontaneous employee interest. A few employees volunteered to produce the publication on their own time if the bank would provide the necessary supplies and equipment.

Southern Messenger is now published bi-monthly entirely on company time and entirely at company expense. The present editor spends about 40 percent of her time at the editor's job; the remainder of her time is spent at a clerical job in the bank. Nine hundred fifty copies of each issue are printed.

The editor has twenty people (including three officers), scattered throughout the bank who serve as informal reporters. These reporters serve on a voluntary basis and tend to obtain and report news items on an opportunistic, rather than a systematic, basis.

According to the editor, *Southern Messenger* space allocations run about as follows:

1/3	News about company plans and activities
1/6	Information regarding company policy
1/6	"Profiles of New Employees"
1/12	Gossip and personal items
rest	Crossword and scientific puzzles

The puzzles have proved to be highly popular with the employees, partly because of their intrinsic appeal and partly because of the prizes offered for the best solutions. The winner for each puzzle receives a pair of theater tickets. The crossword puzzles often contain words related to business and banking.

TASK FORCE

The Communications Task Force was established in February, 1985, at the suggestion of John Templeton, Vice President and Personnel Manager for the bank. Templeton felt that the Task Force might be more successful than "COMCOM" had been in improving communication to and from personnel in the lower echelons of the bank. The Task Force consists of five nonofficer employees nominated for the part-time assignment by their respective Division heads. Task Force members were notified of their appointments by interoffice memorandum from Mr. Templeton.

The Task Force's basic assignment, as seen by the chairman, Stuart Seaton, is to circulate among and talk with lower level employees to discover questions, problems, and suggestions from the ranks. These items are then cleared by "COMCOM" which may modify but not block them, after which they are passed on to the Management Committee, which consists of the President and four Vice Presidents. The Personnel Manager's memo directing the establishment of the task force is below.

INTEROFFICE MEMORANDUM/February 1, 1985

To: Stuart Seaton
cc: June Hugger   Louis Newton
     Benjamin Allen   Byron Edwards

The Management Committee of Southern Bank is interested in the effectiveness of communications within the company, especially as it affects the ability of supervisors and officers to apply and to interpret to others the policies and procedures of the Company, and to supply information about new developments that should be of interest to all employees.

The Committee requested nominations from Division Heads and selected you to organize and direct the project. You will be assisted in this task force study by the persons listed above as recipients of copies of this memo.

For purposes of this project, "communications" refers to formal and informal exchange and diffusion of information about such matters as:

a. Responsibilities and authorities.

b. Policies governing personnel administration.

c. Applications of various procedures, such as performance review, purchase requisitions, expense approvals, etc.

d. Information about significant new developments, new personnel, changes in benefit programs.

e. Problems in supervision and administration which require the attention of higher levels of management.

To carry out this project, the task force will be expected to:

a. Determine the best way to assess communications; e.g., by interviews, questionnaires to supervisors, etc.

b. Consult with the Chairmen of the Communications Committee, with personnel officers, and with the Supervisory Development Groups, to establish the kinds of possible communications problems that may exist.

c. With the Chairmen of the Communications Committee, meet with the Management Committee to discuss findings.

I shall be available to assist in whatever way seems appropriate to the task force.

John Templeton

The Task Force, which has now been in existence for five months, had a flurry of meetings immediately following its establishment but has had only one meeting during the past two months because of vacations and the demands of other work. To date, the Task Force has made six suggestions to the Management Committee via "COMCOM."

The Communications Task Force is only one of several task forces presently operating in the bank. Others include the Training, New Services (Marketing), and Trust Administration task forces. Conceptually, each task force is assembled to accomplish a specific, well-defined job, and upon completion of that job the task force is to be disbanded.

Chairman Seaton indicated that Communications Task Force members spend perhaps one hour per week on this assignment, and that most of the group's suggestions to date have originated from among its members.

When asked what caused him to believe there was a need for a Communications Task Force, the Personnel Manager replied, "There's no feedback around here, particularly from the lower levels. An order, report, or policy change is sent down the line and we wait for questions, or complaints, or some kind of response. What we get back is silence. Absolutely nothing. We find it very difficult to measure the impact of, say, a policy change. It's like shouting down a well and getting no echo. It's eerie."

Asked whether employees complain about poor communication in the bank, the Personnel Manager replied, "No. Oh, there is an occasional comment in the lunch room, but these are not specific and are mentioned in a very casual way. No one appears to be disturbed about it."

The chairman of the Communications Task Force, when.asked about the condition of the bank's grapevine, replied, "Healthy."

PERFORMANCE REVIEW

Top management at Southern Bank believes that the bank's system of regular performance review provides an excellent opportunity to foster communication between each supervisor, at whatever level, and his subordinates. The private performance review sessions, which deal primarily with the employee's job performance, also provide an opportunity for the employee to talk and for superior and subordinate to plan together the employee's future growth and progress.

Performance reviews are held after 90 days for new employees, then annually on the employee's anniversary date. The reviews, which are keyed to the employee's job description, average perhaps thirty minutes in length. The same basic system is used for all employees—from clerks to vice presidents.

Supervisors use a checklist form in rating their subordinates and use this form as a basis for the performance review discussion. Items on the checklist include such things as job knowledge, quality of work, effort, dependability, teamwork, communication, and profit-mindedness. The applicability of each item on the form with respect to the employee's particular job is recorded. The supervisor then checks whether the employee's performance "exceeds," "meets," or "falls short" of standard on each item. The resulting profile provides the core of the review discussion.

The supervisor retains the checklist rating form and notifies the personnel office regarding the result of the review in a separate summary report. Most employees receive a pay increase following their annual performance review. The amount of this increase, which usually ranges between 5 percent and 10 percent of present rate, depends upon the supervisor's evaluation of the employee's performance. The typical supervisor in the bank has from eight to ten subordinates to review during the course of a year.

The Personnel Manager believes that many of the performance reviews are too superficial, but wonders how much time and effort a supervisor should spend in reviewing a young clerk who may leave the bank next month. He also is concerned about what he believes to be inadequate training in interviewing techniques on the part of some supervisors in the bank. (Supervisors receive nine hours of in-bank training on the performance review system, of which one hour is devoted to interviewing techniques.)

When asked how the nonmanagement people feel about the performance review system, the Personnel Manager said, "We really don't know. There is very little feedback. Occasionally, in an exit interview, a terminating employee will say that his supervisor had not kept him informed as to the adequacy of his performance or about his future potential with the bank."

ALLBANK MEMO

When information on matters of bank-wide interest is to be disseminated, an "AllBank Memo" is used. Each employee receives a personal copy. An average of two AllBank Memos per month are issued. AllBank Memos may deal with such matters as holiday announcements, changing hours of work, etc. Occasionally an AllBank Memo deals with a policy change. In such cases, supervisors sometimes call their subordinates together to discuss the change and to answer pertinent questions.[48]

CASE QUESTIONS

1. What are the methods of communication used within Southern Bank? What are the objectives of each method?
2. Why do people disagree on the effectiveness of the media?
3. What problems do you see in the methods currently being used? How could these media be used differently?

NOTES

1. "Now the Office of Tomorrow," *Time,* November 17, 1980, p. 80.
2. Henry Mintzberg, *The Nature of Managerial Work* (New York: Harper & Row, 1973).
3. This discussion is adapted from C. Shannon and W. Weaver, *The Mathematical Theory of Communication* (Urbana: University of Illinois Press, 1948).
4. A. Uris, *The Executive Desk Book* (New York: Van Nostrand Reinholt Company, 1970); Michael McCaskey, "The Hidden Messages Managers Sent," *Harvard Business Review* 57 (Nov.–Dec. 1979): 146–147.
5. Mintzberg, *The Nature of Managerial Work.*
6. A. Meherabian, *Silent Messages* (Belmont, CA: Wadsworth, 1971); R. Harrison, *Beyond Words: An Introduction to Nonverbal Communication* (Englewood Cliffs, NJ: Prentice-Hall, 1974).
7. Richard L. Daft and Robert H. Lengel, "Information Richness: A New Approach to Managerial Behavior and Organization Design," in Barry Staw and Larry L. Cummings (eds.), *Research in Organizational Behavior* 6 (Greenwich, CT: JAI Press, 1984): 191–233; W. D. Bodensteiner, *Information Channel Utilization Under Varying Research and Development Project Conditions: An Aspect of Inter-organizational Communication Channel Usages.* Ph.D. Dissertation, University of Texas, 1970.
8. Robert H. Lengel and Richard L. Daft, "An Exploratory Analysis of the Relationship Between Media Richness and Managerial Information Processing," Unpublished manuscript, Texas A&M University, 1984.
9. Lengel and Daft, "An Exploratory Analysis."
10. Lengel and Daft, "An Exploratory Analysis."
11. Adapted from Lawrence Rout, "Hyatt Hotels' Gripe Sessions Help Chief Maintain Communications With Workers," *The Wall Street Journal,* July 16, 1981, p. 27, 33.
12. A. Bavelas and D. Barrett, "An Experimental Approach to Organization Communication," *Personnel* 27 (1951): 366–371; E. M. Rogers and R. A. Rogers, *Communication in Organizations* (New York: The Free Press, 1976).
13. Bavelas and Barrett, "An Experimental Approach"; M. E. Shaw, *Group Dynamics: The Psychology of Small Group Behavior* (New York: McGraw-Hill, 1976).
14. Bavelas and Barrett, "An Experimental Approach"; Shaw, *Group Dynamics.*
15. W. A. Randolph, "Organization Technology and the Media and Purpose Dimensions of Organization Communications," *Journal of Business Research* 6 (1978): 237–259; Richard L. Daft and Norman B. Macintosh, "A Tentative Exploration into the Amount and Equivocality of Information Processing in Organizational Work Units," *Administrative Science Quarterly* 26 (1981): 207–224.
16. Michael L. Tushman, "Technical Communication in Research and Development Laboratory: The Impact of Task Characteristics," *Academy of Management Journal* 21 (1978): 624–645.
17. B. Katz and R. Kahn, *The Social Psychology of Organizations* 2d ed., (New York: John Wiley & Sons, 1978).
18. Ralph G. Nichols, "Listening is Good Business," *Management of Personnel Quarterly* 1, 2 (1962): 2–10; E. Scannell, *Communication for Leadership* (New York: McGraw-Hill, 1970).
19. W. H. Read, "Upward Communication in Industrial Hierarchies," *Human Relations* 15 (February 1962): 3–15.

20. Michelle J. Glauser, "Factors Which Facilitate or Impede Upward Communication in Organizations," paper presented at the Academy of Management Meetings, New York, August, 1982; W. Read, "Upward Communication in Industrial Hierarchies."

21. W. Read, "Upward Communication in Industrial Hierarchies."

22. Rogers and Rogers, *Communication in Organizations.*

23. Jay Galbraith, *Strategies of Organization Design* (Reading, MA: Addison-Wesley, 1973); Daft and Lengel, "Information Richness: A New Approach to Managerial Behavior and Organization Design."

24. Lyman W. Porter, "Communication: Structure and Process," in H. L. Fromkin and J. L. Sherwood (eds.), *Integrating the Organization* (New York: Free Press, 1974), pp. 216–246.

25. Keith Davis, "Business Communication and the Grapevine," *Harvard Business Review* 31 (1953): 43–49; "The Care and Cultivation of the Corporate Grapevine," *Dun's Review* 102, (1973): 44–47.

26. Davis, "Business Communication and the Grapevine"; "The Care and Cultivation."

27. Adapted from Craig R. Waters, "Franchise Capital of America," *Inc.*, September 1984; pp. 99–108.

28. Paul J. Stonich, "The Performance Measurement and Reward System: Critical to Strategic Management," *Organizational Dynamics* (Winter 1984): 45–57; Kenneth A. Merchant, "The Control Function of Management," *Sloan Management Review* 23 (Summer 1982): 43–55.

29. Richard L. Daft and Norman B. Macintosh, "The Nature and Use of Formal Control Systems for Management Control and Strategy Implementation," *Journal of Management* 10 (1984): 43–66.

30. "How American Express Measures Quality of Its Customer Service," *Management Review* (March 1982): 29–31.

31. William G. Ouchi, "Markets, Bureaucracies, and Clans," *Administrative Science Quarterly* 25 (1980): 129–141, and "A Conceptual Framework for the Design of Organizational Control Mechanisms," *Management Science* 25 (1979): 833–848.

32. Oliver A. Williamson, *Markets and Hierarchies: Analyses and Antitrust Implications* (New York: Free Press, 1975).

33. Daniel Machalaba, "Newhouse Chain Stays with Founder's Way and with His Heirs," *The Wall Street Journal*, February 12, 1982, p. 1, 15.

34. Rosabeth Moss Kanter, *Men and Women of the Corporation* (New York: Basic Books, 1977).

35. William G. Ouchi, "A Conceptual Framework for the Design of Organizational Control Mechanisms."

36. Richard L. Daft, *Organization Theory and Design* (St. Paul, MN: West, 1983): 313–314.

37. Richard L. Daft and Norman B. Macintosh, "The Nature and Use of Formal Control Systems for Management Control and Strategy Implementation," *Journal of Management* 10 (1984): 43–66; D. T. Otley and A. J. Berry, "Control, Organization and Accounting," *Accounting, Organization and Society* 5 (1980): 231–244.

38. Daft and Macintosh, "The Nature and Use of Formal Control Systems."

39. Harold Koontz and Robert Bradspies, "Managing Through Feedforward Control," *Business Horizons* 15 (June, 1972): 25–36.

40. James H. Donnelly, Jr., James L. Gibson, and John M. Ivancevich, *Fundamentals of Management*, 5th ed. (Dallas, TX: Business Publications, Inc., 1984), pp. 221–222.

41. Daft and Macintosh, "The Nature and Use of Formal Control Systems"; R. N. Anthony and J. Dearden, *Management Control Systems* (Homewood, IL: Irwin, 1980).

42. Thomas O'Hanlon, "Behind the Snafu at Singer," *Fortune*, November 5, 1979, pp. 76–79.

43. William G. Ouchi and Mary Ann McGuire, "Organizational Control: Two Functions," *Administrative Science Quarterly* 20 (1975): 559–569.

44. Ouchi and McGuire, "Organizational Control: Two Functions."

45. Richard M. Steers, *Organizational Effectiveness: A Behavioral View* (Glenview, IL: Scott, Foresman & Co., 1977), p. 151.

46. Steers, *Organizational Effectiveness;* A. Downs, *Inside Bureaucracy* (Boston: Little, Brown, 1967).

47. J. L. DiGhetani, "The Sperry Corporation and Listening: An Interview," *Business Horizons* 25 (March-April, 1982): 34–39.

48. Jack L. Rettig, School of Business Administration, Oregon State University. Used with permission.

18 Innovation and Change

Facit Corporation manufactured mechanical calculators, typewriters, and office furnishings. Facit had fifty years of continuous success selling these products. Senior managers believed that no other company could produce such high-quality calculators at a comparable low cost. When the "electronic revolution" began in the late 1960s, a few Facit engineers and managers saw the potential for new forms of calculators and typewriters. But because the company had already invested in new plants to make mechanical calculators, top managers and the board decided against the production of electronic calculators. Based on industry tradition, the board believed customers would not switch rapidly to electronic devices. By 1970, however, Facit's sales plummeted. The board continued to concentrate on manufacturing mechanical calculators, and losses mounted. The electronic revolution bewildered and terrified top management. As the company moved toward bankruptcy, it was acquired by another company, which promptly fired all of Facit's top managers. [1]

The purpose of this chapter is to explore how organizations adapt, or fail to adapt, to the environment through innovation and change. Organizations are creatures of habit, and Facit Corporation failed because it trusted to habit. Organization rules, structure, and technology lead toward predictable, patterned behavior that can slow the company's response to environmental change. Yet many organizations welcome change and seek out opportunities for innovation and reorganization. These innovative companies solve the adaption problem at both the micro and macro levels. Micro level change is concerned with harnessing the creativity of the organization's employees, as well as overcoming resistance to the implementation of new techniques. Macro level change is concerned with the introduction of change on a larger scale. Macro change includes major changes in technological processes, organization structure, or the behavior and skills of all employees. Facit Corporation failed because top managers did not recognize the need for change, and they were unable to respond with the creation and implementation of new technology. The concepts presented in this chapter provide guidelines for an organization's management of change to adapt to internal problems or to the external environment.

RELEVANCE OF INNOVATION AND CHANGE FOR MANAGERS

Change is in. Marketable new ideas, new technology, improvements in productivity, and innovative methods for conserving energy are high on the agenda of most organizations. Two popular books, *Future Shock* and the more recent *Megatrends*, expressed the reason change is important. [2] According to *Future Shock*, change in the environment is becoming so rapid that it threatens to overwhelm individuals, to overpower their ability to adapt. *Megatrends* identified important trends characterizing the environment of the 1980s, including a shift from industrialization to an information-based service economy, more emphasis on high-technology action, integration of North America into a global structure, pressure for decentralization in both government and business organizations, and a shift in industry, business, residency from the north to the south in the United States. The turbulence of the external environment is the reason change is an important factor for managers to understand and control.

Change is a fact of life for organizations. Organizations are open systems. Organizations cannot buffer themselves from the turbulence and trends in the external environment. Organizations must respond to both internal and external pressures. The continued knowledge explosion, changes in production processes, new values toward work and social responsibility, government legislation, increasing scarcity of resources, heightened competition among organizations, and the natural forces of growth and change over the organization's life cycle all push managers for new designs, new behaviors, new organizational habits. Managers can work through these aspects to help their organizations succeed at innovation and change and hence make a difference to overall success. To survive, organizations must renew themselves.

Organizational renewal is accomplished through the methods and concepts described in this book. Organizational change is the final chapter because it cuts across and brings together the other topics in this book. Forces for change come from the environment and from new technology. The implementation of change may require knowledge of job design, new organization structure, improved leadership skills, sophisticated approaches to organizational communication and control, an understanding of group behavior, new methods for motivation and performance evaluation, or the resolution of internal conflict. No management function is immune to change.

Facit Corporation was unable to change because its managers did not see a need, or did not have the management skills, to respond to a new technology. Yet other organizations have responded to technological change with anticipation and delight. The Warren Featherbone Company is preparing for its centennial celebration despite the demise of the original Featherbone, (a popular replacement for whalebone) after the turn of the century. Threatened by the introduction of plastics, Warren managers shifted to plastics, and now the company produces six million pair of baby pants a year. [3] Genesco has reached out to the special needs of working women with new designs for footwear. Within two years, Genesco's Career Collection was a shining success.[4] When Hewlett-Packard introduced its first mass-produced calculator, the managers of Keuffel & Esser Co. knew the slide rule was about to become obsolete. The top management group went to Texas Instruments and negotiated to distribute calculators. Four years later, the production of slide rules ended, and Keuffel & Esser gave its production equipment to a museum. Fortunately, they had already shifted to other businesses.[5] Sara Lee got hit with the trend toward fresh baked goods, which cut into its market for packaged sweets. The company responded with a move into new frozen baked goods that could compete with freshly baked products.[6]

These organizations and hundreds of others are successfully adapting to change because managers understand that the organization must move with change rather than remain stable. The concepts in this book are directed at the process of improving organizations, renewing organizations, and helping organizations adapt to the problems and crises that arise. The purpose of the concepts in this book is to help managers implement learning and change in organizations.

MODEL OF THE CHANGE PROCESS

Organizational change is the adoption of an idea, technique, or behavior that is new to the organization.[7] **Organizational innovation** is the adoption of an idea, technique, or behavior that is new to an industry or larger set of organizations.[8] An innovating organization is typically an early adopter, or a leader in the industry, with respect to new products, production processes, or structural arrangements. A changing organization would incorporate techniques new to itself, but it would not be the first user compared to other organizations. The difference between innovation and change is whether the idea is new to the organization or new to the industry. From within organizations, however, the process of both innovation and change is nearly identical. The process has to start with a need and end with the implementation of a new idea. Since the process is so similar within organizations, the concepts of innovation and change will be used interchangeably throughout this chapter. Exhibit 18.1 illustrates the steps in the process of innovation and change as they occur within organizations.[9]

Most forces for change originate in the external environment. Organizations monitor the external environment to detect both threats and opportunities. Since the environment continuously changes, the organization must maintain congruence with these changes. When McDonald's discovered that customers were tired of eating hamburgers in their cars, top managers decided to incorporate sit-down facilities in McDonald's restaurants, a decision made in response to a change in the external environment. The environment is also a source of new ideas and techniques. Innovations created elsewhere represent positive opportunities for the organization. When Texas Instruments saw the

EXHIBIT 18.1
Model of Managed Organization Change

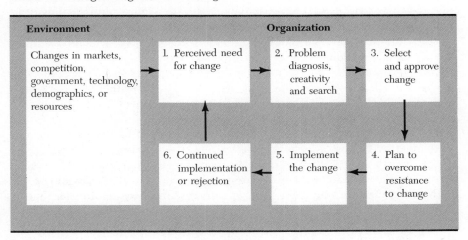

potential in the calculator created by Hewlett-Packard, TI's top managers quickly seized an opportunity and began adopting this new technology for a variety of products including wristwatches and home computers. Forces for change can arise from any of the environmental sectors described in Chapter 10. Changes in customer tastes, market conditions, competitor strategies, technology, human resources, or economic conditions can all generate either threats or opportunities to which an organization will respond.

The first step in the internal change process is the perceived need for change. This is similar to the performance gap described in Chapter 14 on decision making. The perceived need for change occurs when managers detect a problem or lower-than-acceptable performance. The perceived need activates the subsequent stages of the change process, which help the organization respond to the environment. The extensive competition in the soft drink industry has motivated Royal Crown to try a number of innovations. Royal Crown has lost market share to the industry leaders of Coca-Cola, Pepsi, Dr. Pepper, and Seven-Up. In response, RC introduced the first decaffeinated cola in 1980. It was first to successfully market soft drinks in cans. RC was the first to sell soda in 16-ounce bottles, and RC was the first to introduce diet cola. Unfortunately, these innovations have not helped RC increase market share. The other soft drink makers have quickly copied the ideas all along and kept the market share from RC.[10]

The second step is to carefully diagnose both the problem and potential change. If the organization is experiencing a problem, such as declining sales, then careful diagnosis of the problem and a search for solutions within the organization is appropriate. The organization may wish to create an innovation to resolve the problem. If the problem was caused by the appearance of a new product in the environment, then diagnosis and creativity will be used to adjust and modify the technology for adoption by the organization. Genesco, for example, had a problem with lackluster sales in their line of women's shoes; which were either too sexy or too informal for a day at the office. Careful diagnosis yielded lots of information about the shoe lines sold by competitors and the needs of working women. Genesco created a separate marketing group to study the problem and to develop the new line of shoes, which they called the Career Collection. It has been a success.[11]

The third management step is to select and adopt the specific change. This pertains to the formal assessment of the proposed innovation and the formal authorization to proceed. Top management is usually involved at this point. A division or department head may approve small changes. Major changes, such as the product innovations developed by Royal Crown or the new shoe line developed by Genesco, have to be approved by corporate presidents.

The fourth step is to systematically plan the implementation of change. Every change will require new techniques, task designs, or behaviors on the part of organization members. Appropriate resources to acquire machinery, provide training programs, facilitate communication and in other ways smooth implementation are identified at this point. Extensive planning is required for the efficient implementation of major changes.

The fifth step is to implement the change. This is the major action step in the innovation process. Materials are purchased, products are produced, workers are trained, and any other steps necessary to actually bring about the change are accomplished. At Sara Lee the decision to move into new frozen baked goods meant closing one production line for frozen sweet goods. Consultants were hired, employees were trained, and the new products were developed to implement the production of quality frozen baked goods that could compete with freshly baked products.

The final step in the change process is the continued implementation, modification, or rejection of the change. Continued implementation means that the innovation is succeeding and resolving the performance gap for which it was adopted. Sometimes changes don't work, and the organization must be prepared to modify or reject the change. For example, Genesco's first Career Collection did not sell up to expectations. The shoes were not stylish enough; executives erred on the conservative side. But the concept was right, and the line was redesigned the second year to be more stylish without being too casual for the work place.

Each of the six steps in the Exhibit 18.1 cycle is essential for successful innovation and change. Without a perceived need, organization members will not take action and change attempts will not get off the ground. Even a great new innovation will not be adopted unless managers and employees perceive that it meets a serious need. Careful diagnosis, search, and adaptation of ideas are important for the innovation to fit the unique characteristics of the adopting organization. Authorization by top management is essential to give legitimacy and provide the support needed for implementation. Thoughtful plans for implementing the change, including involvement of users and explanation of benefits, will smooth the change process. Actual implementation is another point at which the change process can break down. The employees must be able to make things happen. They must bring together the resources, people, skills, and materials to implement the innovation. Finally, the organization must be quick to modify and reject changes that don't work.

Facit Corporation, described at the beginning of this chapter, failed because managers were locked into old habits and could not complete the steps for managed organizational change in Exhibit 18.1. The inability to manage change led to Facit's impending bankruptcy. An organization may be experiencing several, perhaps hundreds, of changes simultaneously. Each part of the organization may be responding to overcome perceived problems posed by the environment. These changes may be small, such as the acquisition of a new copying machine, or large, such as a major restructuring of a company's product line. No matter what the change, the six steps in Exhibit 18.1 must be accomplished for it to be implemented successfully. Consider, for example, the revamped purchasing program undertaken at International Harvester.

UP CLOSE 18.1:   International Harvester

International Harvester has had its share of changes over the last few years as it has attempted to become more efficient and to overcome the decline in demand for farm implements. One extremely successful change was the maintenance, repair, and operating (MRO) buying program. Signals from both the environment and within IH suggested that purchasing was inefficient. Buyers were buried under an avalanche of 14,000 requisitions per year, inventory turnover was slow, too many suppliers were competing for routine parts orders, purchasing controls deteriorated and costs were driven up, and there was insufficient coordination between purchasing and warehousing. Managers in the Construction Equipment Group manufacturing plant in Melrose Park, Illinois saw a need for change. They decided to design a new MRO program that would reduce paperwork, lower inventory, reduce costs of supplies, reduce the number of suppliers, and free buyers from repetitive, routine orders.

Managers had heard about the concept of systems contracting used in other organizations but had been unable to try it at International Harvester because purchasing was highly centralized. However, James Hall proposed a plan that received an enthusiastic response from plant management. Hall proposed a redesigned requisition process, added a computerized inventory control system in the plant, and developed a procedure for analyzing vendor capability for negotiating new agreements. Top Harvester officials decided to accept the proposal upon the recommendation of Pierre Bodeau, the buyer who headed MRO purchasing at the Melrose plant.

A carefully devised plan of implementation involved several steps: a survey of 120 industrial suppliers, a request for quotes pertaining to system purchases that Harvester required, on-site evaluations of supplier capabilities, and internal training to acquaint employees with new procedures. The change was *implemented when Harvester picked a small set of suppliers who would be the only ones used to meet Harvester's system requirements. Regularly needed supplies would be purchased under an umbrella contract to save routine purchasing activity and keep Harvester inventories low. The program was launched in June, and by April of the next year only 10 percent of the purchases were not covered under the umbrella contracts with system suppliers. After two years, huge savings justified continued implementation. The supplier list was trimmed and single sources for additional products were developed with lower cost per-part. The umbrella contract included buy-back arrangements so that vendors had to take back excess Harvester stock. Cost savings through price reductions amounted to $78,000 in the first year. MRO inventories dropped $1 million in eight months.*[12]   ∎

The change at Harvester is an example of successful planned change, following the steps outlined in Exhibit 18.1. Responding to a perceived need, managers used adequate diagnosis and plans to implement change, enabling the MRO program to produce major cost savings and competitive benefits.

CHANGE AT THE MICRO LEVEL

All changes take place through people. Each step in the change process is enacted by individuals. The micro perspective on change focuses on the characteristics of individuals who facilitate the change process. The micro approach also pertains to context of the group, which creates a climate that can either facilitate or inhibit change.

The role of individuals in micro-level change can be divided into two parts: initiation and implementation. Initiation is the awareness of problems and the development and proposal of solutions. The organizational challenge here is to harness employees' creativity and energy in the development of new ideas. Implementation is the process of overcoming resistance to change among employees. The challenge of implementation is to understand why individuals are reluctant to adopt new procedures and to develop techniques for educating and overcoming resistance.

Initiation of Change

The initiation of change is typically associated with two phenomena: creativity and idea champions. **Creativity** is the development of novel solutions.[13] Creative individuals develop ideas that solve organizational problems or provide new opportunities. An **idea champion** pushes a new idea through to acceptance.[14] Sometimes the idea champion is the same person who created the idea. Other times an idea champion is someone who believes intensely in the value of an idea and pushes hard to gain acceptance and approval for it within the organization.

EXHIBIT 18.2
Characteristics of Creative People and Departments

The Creative Individual	The Creative Department
1. Originality	1. Assigns non-specialists to problems Allows eccentricity
2. Conceptual fluency	2. Open channels of communication Contact with outside sources Overlapping territories Suggestion systems, brainstorming, nominal group techniques
3. Less authoritarian; Independent	3. Decentralized; loosely defined positions Resource slack to absorb errors Risk-taking norms
4. Persistent; Commitment; Highly focused	4. Resources allocated to creative personnel and projects without immediate payoff Reward system encourages innovation and challenges Absolved of peripheral responsibilities
5. Playful, undisciplined exploration	5. Allows freedom to choose and pursue problems Not run as tight ship Freedom to discuss ideas

SOURCE: Adapted from Gary A. Steiner (ed.), *The Creative Organization* (Chicago: The University of Chicago Press, 1965): 16-18, and Rosabeth Moss Kanter, "The Middle Manager as Innovator," *Harvard Business Review* (July-August 1982): 104-105.

Creativity   Individual creativity has been the focus of study in psychology for a number of years. People differ widely in their capacity for creativity. Creative people within organizations have been characterized as having an intense interest in problem solving; an open-minded willingness to pursue leads in any direction; a relaxed attitude; a somewhat disorganized, undisciplined approach; conceptual fluency and originality with respect to possible solutions; persistence in analysis; and they are open to ideas from outside.[15]

Selected characteristics of creative individuals are listed in Exhibit 18.2. Research into group characteristics suggest that creative departments are quite distinct from departments oriented toward efficiency and productivity.[16] Creative departments tend to be organic and loosely structured. Channels of communication are open and information is exchanged freely, both within and outside the group. The department is likely to be heterogeneous, with diverse skills, and with non-specialists assigned to problems. The creative department encourages experimentation and basic learning and research processes. The creative department also has sufficient resources to absorb the time and mistakes associated with truly original thinking. Creative people are backed up by the department's resources, and the reward system emphasizes investment in both people and projects rather than immediate payoffs. Employees are given substantial freedom to choose and promote their solutions.

The conditions given in Exhibit 18.2 enable organizations to harness the spontaneous creativity of individuals and encourage that ideas be continually generated. At General Mills, brand manager Cal Blodgett observed huge, 6×300-foot sheets of Granola rolling out of an oven to be crumbled into cereal bits. He thought, "Let's cut that into bars." Nature Valley Granola Bars were born through this idea. In another part of the organization, months of research were spent developing a new snack food only to have the bits stick together when they got moist. As frustration mounted, Craig Nalen had an idea to turn the problem into a product: "Why not peddle the snack food as a toy?" With that idea Likity Stick was born and General Mills entered the toy market.[17] The same type of creative people and departments enabled 3M to become one of the most innovative companies in the world. Company scientist Spencer Silver tried to develop a super strong adhesive but instead came up with one that didn't stick very well. A few years later, Arthur Fry put some of the weak glue on a piece of paper that marked his place in a church hymnal. At that instant, Post-it Notes, the stick-on note pads, were born. ScotchGuard fabric protector was formed when a chemist spilled some liquid on her tennis shoes. Curious as to its affect, she experimented and found that the treated sneakers repelled water and dirt.[18]

General Mills and 3M have made a conscious effort to harness the creative potential of employees and to have departments where creativity is supported. Both companies as a result have developed a string of new products that help them grow and prosper despite heavy competition and rapidly changing external environments.

Idea Champion   The other important role in the initiation of organizational change is that of the idea champion. Change does not happen by itself. Research has discovered that a focus of organizational energy and effort is required to successfully promote a new idea.[19] A good idea is not automatically welcomed and accepted. Idea champions often have to fight to convince others of the merit of a new idea or a new line of research. Idea champions may be called advocates, change agents, or entrepreneurs. Whatever an idea champion is called, he or she is an individual who strongly believes in a particular concept. Sometimes the idea champion is a middle manager who did not create the idea but who sees its value and acts to sponsor it. The sponsor assigns the finances and resources needed to successfully carry the idea through to implementation. For example, a senior sales manager may sponsor an idea from engineering, helping the engineer to work with field sales personnel to fine tune and successfully complete the innovation.

Idea champions are found in every type of organizational change. Operations research and management science techniques are more successful when advocates support these techniques.[20] Structural changes in the form of new departments have been associated with a strong push provided by idea champions.[21] Idea champions frequently appear in engineering or R&D departments; they take the responsibility for the development and promotion of new products.[22] New classes and educational programs in high schools are initiated in a climate that encourages teachers to act as idea champions to promote ideas they believe valuable.[23] Idea champions make things happen. Without them, organizational change would be diffuse and inefficient.

Implementation of Change

The implementation of a new technique sometimes encounters road blocks. People do not agree with the change, or they fight against the new idea. There are important reasons why resistance may occur. Managers need to understand these reasons in order to overcome resistance to change. We will first discuss some basic reasons for resistance to change, and then explain techniques for planning change implementation to avoid resistance.

Reasons for Resistance   Idea champions, managers, and others who support a change are often frustrated and concerned by the lack of interest and response from people within the organization. Many times employees seem to prefer the status quo. Employees often attempt to keep work relationships as they are. Figure 18.3 summarizes the major reasons that have been identified to explain employee resistance to new behaviors.

EXHIBIT 18.3
Sources of Resistance to Change

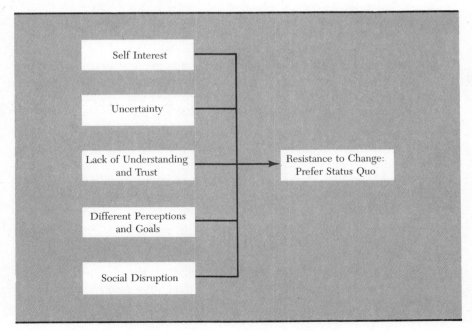

- *Self interest.* Employees typically behave in ways that help them achieve personal and work-group goals. A proposed change in structure or technology may threaten their own interests. The change could conceivably result in economic loss, such as a reduction in the number of employees. Power, status, or prestige for the individual or department may be lost in a proposed reorganization. A change may benefit the organization as a whole, but at a loss to selected individuals and departments. Managers and employees tend to resist changes that work against the attainment of their own goals and interests.[24]

- *Uncertainty.* The prospect of change often creates uncertainty. Uncertainty represents a fear of the unknown, and employees may be anxious or nervous because they don't know how the change will affect them. Because they don't understand the consequences of change, they may assume the worst and fight against implementation. Most employees are dependent upon the organization for economic and social outcomes, and uncertainty about whether those outcomes will continue (indeed whether their jobs may continue) causes a preference for the status quo. Employees also may worry about whether they will be able to meet the demands of new procedures or technologies.[25]

- *Lack of understanding and trust.* Many times employees simply don't understand the intended purpose of the change. They may not trust the source of change because working relationships might have been negative in the past. In one study, engineers seemed unable to gain the cooperation of line employees for testing new production techniques. In the past, the engineers had exploited the workers and not given them credit for their role in successful production changes. Those production employees resisted every change proposed from that engineering group. Another engineering group in the same company had exactly the opposite results. They had been friendly and helpful with production employees. Based on the trusting relationship the engineers had established, they were able to explain their procedure so production workers understood what was happening. Production workers also received credit for later successes. Understanding and trust smoothed the path of successful implementation.[26]

- *Different perceptions and goals.* Employees often have legitimate disagreements about the outcomes of change. Goals, values, and task orientation differ among people in finance, R&D, marketing, production, and engineering. Employees in each department may have different perceptions about the costs and benefits of an innovation. They may legitimately disagree about whether adoption and implementation is needed, simply because the change may be appropriate for one department but less appropriate for another. The accomplishment of R&D goals for a new product may thwart production's goals for low-cost manufacturing. Thus resistance in many cases has a legitimate base, and managers who are promoting the change should take the time to assess these differences in developing their plan for implementation.[27]

- *Social disruption.* Social disruption is an intangible yet very powerful cause of resistance. Idea champions may be unaware of the patterns of communication, social status, and working relationships in a department. Social patterns permit friendships to develop and provide a source of satisfaction. Group norms regulate behavior in predictable ways that employees find satisfying. Idea champions should be especially careful to assess the impact of change on social relationships, otherwise resistance will surface that may seem irrational. Social needs are important to employees, and change will be resisted if social patterns are disrupted.[28]

Overcoming Resistance to Change

Resistance to change can be managed. Most resistance has a logical cause, and understanding the cause enables managers and idea champions to work with employees to accomplish implementation. Strategies for overcoming resistance include educating employees, encouraging them to participate in the change, negotiating the change, or simply forcing the change on employees using the formal power structure of the organization. Kotter and Schlesinger have studied the methods for dealing with resistance to change, which include six specific strategies. Exhibit 18.4 summarizes the advantages and disadvantages of each strategy.[29]

- *Education and communication.* This strategy can be used to overcome either a lack of information or inaccurate perceptions about the change. Education helps employees see the need for change and understand the reasons for it.

- *Participation and involvement.* With this strategy people affected by the change are involved in its development. In the design of management information systems, for example, managers are more likely to use the new reports and computer printouts if they have some say in their design. Participation helps ensure that the change meets the needs of people affected by it.[30]

- *Facilitation and support.* Facilitation means providing additional support to people affected by the change. This may involve new training programs to enable them to take other jobs, additional training to cope with a new technology, or simply listening to and helping employees overcome fears about what lies ahead. This technique is especially appropriate when employees are having personal problems associated with the change.

- *Negotiation and agreement.* Negotiation means the use of formal bargaining to win acceptance and approval of a desired change. A powerful department may fear losing something with the change, and negotiations can modify the change in a way that agreement among departments is reached.

- *Manipulation and cooptation.* This is a more covert tactic. Managers may selectively use information or try to win over key individuals in order to smooth the implementation process without widespread participation or education.

EXHIBIT 18.4
Methods for Dealing with Resistance to Change

Approach	Commonly used in situations	Advantages	Drawbacks
Education + communication	Where there is a lack of information or inaccurate information and analysis.	Once persuaded, people will often help with the implementation of the change.	Can be very time consuming if lots of people are involved.
Participation + involvement	Where the initiators do not have all the information they need to design the change, and where others have considerable power to resist.	People who participate will be committed to implementing change, and any relevant information they have will be integrated into the change plan.	Can be very time consuming if participators design an inappropriate change.
Facilitation + support	Where people are resisting because of adjustment problems.	No other approach works as well with adjustment problems.	Can be time consuming, expensive, and still fail.
Negotiation + agreement	Where someone or some group will clearly lose out in a change, and where that group has considerable power to resist.	Sometimes it is a relatively easy way to avoid major resistance.	Can be too expensive in many cases if it alerts others to negotiate for compliance.
Manipulation + co-optation	Where other tactics will not work, or are too expensive.	It can be a relatively quick and inexpensive solution to resistance problems.	Can lead to future problems if people feel manipulated.
Explicit + implicit coercion	Where speed is essential, and the change initiators possess considerable power.	It is speedy, and can overcome any kind of resistance.	Can be risky if it leaves people mad at the initiators.

SOURCE: Reprinted by permission of the *Harvard Business Review.* An exhibit from "Choosing Strategies for Change" by John P. Kotter and Leonard A. Schlesinger (March/April 1979). Copyright ©1979 by the President and Fellows of Harvard College; all rights reserved.

- *Explicit and implicit coercion.* This technique involves the use of formal and informal power within the organization. Employees are told to accept the change or be threatened with a loss of rewards and valued resources. To use this technique, the people responsible for change need to be in a powerful position. It can be used in crisis situations when the organization is under pressure for a rapid response. Employees are forced to go along whether or not they like it.

Summary of the Micro Perspective on Change

Individual employees play an important role in the micro-level change process. Change takes place through employees. Individuals are responsible for creating change, and they provide the thrust and focus to accomplish change by acting as idea champions. Employees often throw up resistance to change as well. People not involved in the development of change may greet it with uncertainty, different perceptions, or a belief that it will harm their self interest. Managers can develop techniques for overcoming change with a conscious implementation strategy. Methods of implementation include education, negotiation, manipulation, participation, and coercion.

Dun & Bradstreet Corporation is an example of an organization that has learned to make use of the creativity of its members and at the same time overcome resistance to change. Although a huge organization, D&B continues to grow and prosper from innovative new products.

UP CLOSE 18.2:   Dun & Bradstreet Corporation

Dun & Bradstreet Corporation has been an innovative company. For years it did just fine with a stable portfolio of products, experiencing steady growth as its markets grew. Yet Harrington Drake, D&B's chief executive officer, is determined to wipe out the status quo. He insists that D&B's goal is to be in a state of continuous transition.

Drake's strategy to encourage creativity includes rotating managers to other divisions to cut emotional ties to a single product line. He brings managers together in meetings to develop interdisciplinary cooperation that may lead to new products. He also provides consultants and trainers to help staff learn about new equipment that may be useful to D&B products.

Another strategy used at D&B to facilitate innovation is mixing people from various parts of the organization. Divisions once exclusively populated with sales people and operating specialists now include computer experts and market researchers. Financial officers, data processing managers, and other functional specialists are pooling ideas at joint meetings. Work boundaries are becoming fuzzier as employees join together to create new products.

Managers are also learning how to communicate. D&B has hired a staff of consultants to offer courses in the art of listening. Listening helps managers bridge interpersonal and interdepartmental barriers to understanding.

The company's reward system has also been changed to foster cooperation. Drake insists that he will not dictate operations. Managers at the lower levels need freedom to pursue ideas. Drake sees his job as ensuring that a manager's contribution to a new idea doesn't count against him. If sharing a new development with another division interferes with a manager achieving his or her objectives, D&B will compute what the manager would have accomplished independently. The bonus will be based on anticipated performance so managers are not penalized for trying novel ideas.

By 1985, virtually every divisional executive has worked in at least one other area and knows people throughout the company. People have developed a good working knowledge of their counterparts' abilities and they all have old friends to turn to in other divisions.

The result of this creativity has been impressive. At least 150 new ideas have been adopted in just a few years. Dun's "Financial Profile" provides detailed financial data on 800,000 companies; it cost only $200,000 to develop, yet brings in about $5 million in revenue. Salesnet, another new product, is a marketing system that gives telephone salespeople access to computer terminals that furnish a prospect's name, telephone number, and a preprogrammed sales script.

Although top management wants D&B to be innovative, they will not stand for change just for the sake of change. One rule is that no product is worth creating unless the need has been established. Innovation in response to a true need from the environment is so important that people have been assigned to debrief salespeople about customer problems. The focus on needs combined with the decentralized, creative climate yields a high success rate—and helps explain why a financial services company that most observers would expect to be stodgy and traditional is the innovator in the industry.[31] ■

At Dun & Bradstreet, the initiation and implementation of change are intermingled. The breaking down of barriers that facilitates creativity also provides the education and involvement that facilitates implementation. Dun & Bradstreet has gained the best of employee creativity by increasing the rate of initiation and decreasing resistance to implementation.

CHANGE AT THE MACRO LEVEL

Now we shift perspective from the individual and group to look at the types of change that affect the organization as a whole. Macro change can take place within and affect three components of the organization: the technological component, the administrative component, and the human component.[32] The changes associated with each of the three components are illustrated in Exhibit 18.5.

Technological Component   Technology involves the production process of the organization or of major departments. Changes in technology pertain to innovations in the production process or new products and services. Changes in

EXHIBIT 18.5
Types of Changes in Each Organizational Component

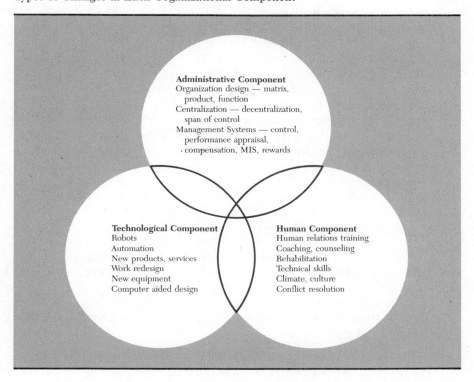

Administrative Component
Organization design — matrix,
    product, function
Centralization — decentralization,
    span of control
Management Systems — control,
    performance appraisal,
    · compensation, MIS, rewards

Technological Component
Robots
Automation
New products, services
Work redesign
New equipment
Computer aided design

Human Component
Human relations training
Coaching, counseling
Rehabilitation
Technical skills
Climate, culture
Conflict resolution

technology represent such things as the adoption of new equipment, robots, computers, automation, products, or redesigned work. Changes improve the efficiency of the production process or change products in accordance with market demands.

Administrative Component   Changes in the administrative component pertain to the structure and design of the organizational hierarchy, coordination mechanisms, and the administrative systems used to manage and control the organization. Changes in organization structure include changes in the organization chart, such as movement toward a matrix, product, or functional structure. Changes in centralization-decentralization, span of control, task forces, brand managers, new departments, and liaison roles are in the administrative subsystem. Changes in management tools used for control, performance appraisal, compensation, and management information are also considered part of the administrative component of the organization.

Human Component   The human component is concerned with behavioral changes. These changes involve the attitudes, values, human relations skills, and technical qualifications of employees. Behavioral changes are typically targeted at characteristics of employees. Behavioral changes are frequently accomplished through intensive training and organizational development programs, including career planning, sensitivity training, counseling, and technical training of various types.

Examples of change in each component are illustrated in Exhibit 18.5. The three components are interrelated. Changes in technology sometimes require modifications in structure or human behavior. Changes in administration or changes in behavior may require associated changes in the other areas. Managers must be prepared for a change to ripple through other components, especially if the planned change is large scale.

Virtually every organization undergoes changes in all three components. At Adolph Coors Company, for example, changes in technology include the two-piece aluminum can, press-tab cans, and changes in the brewing process to increase brewing capacity from 15 million to 25 million barrels per year while reducing brewing time. Administrative changes include the creation of two new positions of division president, one for sales and marketing and one for production. Other administrative changes include a new employee benefit package, modification of goals, and an equal opportunity program. Behavioral changes at Coors are concerned with training people to acquire supervisory skills. Other training has been undertaken to provide equal opportunity for all employees, and to improve attitudes and reduce conflicts between unionized employees and management.[33]

Change in each subsystem is essential to organizational survival. We will now discuss strategies for promoting change in each of the three major subsystems of the organization.

Technology Change

The dilemma facing organizations wishing to promote technical change is how to achieve the right balance between creativity and routinization. As we discussed earlier in this chapter, decentralized, organic conditions help facilitate creativity. However, centralized, mechanistic organizational conditions may be more appropriate for implementing change and for attaining efficient production. One answer to this dilemma is the ambidextrous approach to technological change.[34] **Ambidextrous** means that organizations must have structures that are appropriate to both initiation and implementation of change. An organic structure is appropriate for initiation and a mechanistic structure is better for implementation. There are three ways organizations can achieve technological innovation through the ambidextrous approach.

Switching Structures   Switching structures means that a department or organization will switch between organic and mechanistic structures depending on innovation needs. For example, one manufacturing plant faced severe financial losses. Management closed down production for two days and asked employees to meet in small groups to discuss ideas for improving performance and increasing efficiency. The two-day meeting was the start of an organic structure that enabled employees to define problems and create solutions. At the end of the two days, task forces were created to analyze ideas and implement promising changes. The plant was restarted the third day, and over the next two or three months several new ideas were implemented and the plant gradually improved its performance. The switch to an organic structure for idea generation proved to be very effective, and the plant switched back to a mechanistic structure for routine operations and change implementation.

Separate Departments   In many organizations, some departments are assigned the responsibility of creating and initiating change and thus are structured for creativity. Research and development departments, for example, typically fit the characteristics of creative departments described in Exhibit 18.2. Engineering, operations research, and project management departments may initiate changes for adoption in other departments. Creative departments are organically structured to facilitate the generation of new ideas and techniques. Departments that typically adopt these innovations tend to be efficiency oriented and mechanistically structured. Adoptors are usually line production and marketing departments, whose working through of these ideas is the implementation of new products and production processes. In order for one department to initiate change and other departments to implement change, effective coordination is needed. The organization must have coordination mechanisms such as task forces, face-to-face discussions, and other means to create a positive working relationship among departments responsible for change initiation and change implementation.[35]

In high-tech companies, for example, the critical linkage is between marketing and R&D. Marketers need to know what research and development is doing—what is on the horizon—so they can realistically plan future marketing efforts. R&D participates actively in the market planning process so they are aware of customer needs—so they know what to develop. Face-to-face, in-person interaction and frequent meetings must be deliberately structured. At Micom, a microcomputer company formed in 1980, marketing and R&D people are assigned to periodic meetings according to specific product lines so that coordination and joint agreements are reached.[36]

Temporary Teams   A more recent technique for fostering creativity is the use of venture teams or venture departments. Venture teams may be separated completely from the company and given a separate location and facilities. At Convergent Technologies Inc., venture teams are called strike forces, and one was created to develop a new personal computer. The venture group was literally formed as a company-within-a-company. It was financed by the parent company but left on its own until it came up with the right product idea. Venture teams are kept small so they have autonomy and can react better to changes in technology.[37] A temporary department or division can be created to foster innovation with respect to almost any product or production problem facing the organization. At 3M ideas are often developed within small groups, which eventually grow to become separate divisions if the idea is successful. The creators of the idea run the division and share in the profits of their efforts. The venture management concept is especially important in large companies that run the risk of becoming dominated by a production mentality and bureaucratic procedures. A giant corporation like IBM has found the use of separate departments, which they call business units, to be the source of its most promising innovations.

UP CLOSE 18.3: IBM

Since 1981, IBM has started fourteen independent business units to explore innovative opportunities outside its main lines of business. These tiny businesses have led IBM into the areas of robots, customized software, and electrocardiographs. The small groups bring back the entrepreneurial spirit that centralized organization structures prevent. A large company like IBM can have trouble allowing good ideas to surface and be developed for the marketplace. One executive says that the rationale for these little units is straightforward compared to the traditional development of large mainframe computers: "To manage new ventures with the same controls and procedures used for a new mainframe would inhibit them." Each business unit is free to manage its own finances, manufacturing, and marketing, while developing and proving their innovations.

IBM executives realize that not every new venture will succeed, but a few of these successes have been stunning. IBM's Personal Computer was built by a business unit and is practically walking off the shelves. In the field of computer-aided design equipment, another business unit's product is running second to the industry leader.

IBM also seeks innovations in new and emerging markets. One business unit is called the information network, representing IBM's entry into computing services. The new unit collected $40 million in revenues in 1980, and is growing at the annual rate of 70 percent. With these kinds of successes, IBM and other companies will continue to use venture teams to create innovations that can then be assimilated back into the main organization for large-scale production and marketing.[38]

IBM, Apple, Convergent Technologies, and many other companies use temporary business units to foster innovation. The small, innovative divisions allow creativity and idea champions to flourish. They work with new technology and develop new products that fuel growth and encourage industry leadership.

Administrative Change

Administrative change pertains to the hierarchy of authority, goals, policies, reward systems, coordination, and control.[39] Administrative change is important because some organizations must adopt structural rather than technology changes to survive. Many organizations operate in a relatively stable environment in those sectors that affect the technical core, but they experience uncertainty in sectors that impinge upon the administrative part of the organization. Environmental elements affecting administration include changes in government regulation, legislation, financial resources, or human resource administration. An organization that experiences change in these sectors must be organized to innovate primarily in the area of structure and administration rather than technology. Types of organizations who must do this include city governments, federal agencies, fire departments, and other organizations which have routine technologies. Organizations operating under conditions of crisis also may have to make substantial changes in the structural domain.

A framework for understanding administrative innovation is the dual core model. The **dual-core model** proposes that the need for organic versus mechanistic structure partly depends upon the need for administrative versus technological change.[40] Many organizations—schools, hospitals, welfare agencies, and many business firms—have dual cores, a technical core and an administrative core. When environmental uncertainty influences the administrative core, then the appropriate organizational arrangement will be to have an organic administrative core and a mechanistic technical core. The organic administrative core enables managers to create and develop administrative changes necessary to adapt to the external environment. These changes are usually implemented in a top-down fashion. Creative personnel and idea champions are administrators rather than technical specialists.

When the dominant issue facing the organization pertains to technological change, then a horizontal or bottom-up innovation process occurs. The initiation and implementation of change occurs within the technical departments, and the administrative core is only involved with respect to approving change. The overall thrust of change is in a bottom-up direction. Exhibit 18.6 illustrates the type and direction of administrative and technology change.

One finding from research into administrative innovation is that organization structures that facilitate technology changes tend to inhibit administrative change, and vice versa.[41] Because power is decentralized, an organic technical core may make it difficult for administrators to impose administrative change downward. Of course an organic technical core is associated with environmental change in technology areas, so decentralization is needed. Likewise, when the administrative core is organic and the technical core mechanistic, administrative change is facilitated and technical change is inhibited. The appropriate structure for the administrative and technical subsystems will be determined by the organizational needs for administrative versus technology innovations. Many government organizations have routine technologies but must adapt frequently to changes in administration. For these organizations, a top-down innovation process illustrated in Exhibit 18.6 is appropriate.

Behavioral Change

Behavioral change is change in the human component of the organization. Behavioral change pertains to the attitudes, values, skills, and behavioral patterns of employees. Behavioral change tends to have impact on either the cognitive or emotional aspects of people, as illustrated in Exhibit 18.7.[42] Some

EXHIBIT 18.6
Top-Down Versus Bottom-Up Patterns of Organizational Change

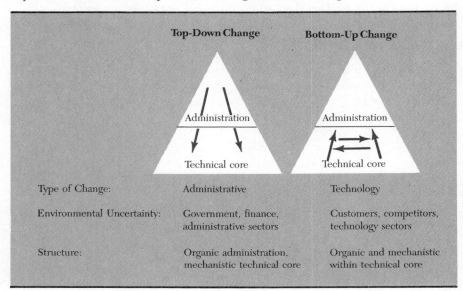

changes simply apply to employee roles and patterns of interaction, and this is the smallest and easiest type of behavioral change to implement. Next is change in technical skills, a somewhat deeper change which is still primarily cognitive. Next is human relations skills, or how people relate to one another. This change pertains to the social skill of relating with others well. The deepest change applies to basic attitudes, values, and motivations, and it is almost exclusively in the domain of emotional rather than cognitive change.

All four types of behavioral change are classified in Exhibit 18.7 by their cognitive or emotional aspects. Interaction patterns and technical skills can be altered through specific training programs. Human relations skills can be altered through what is known as organizational development training. Organizational development also can be used to influence basic values and attitudes underlying organizational climate and the involvement of employees in the organization.

Training Departments   Cognitive change is brought about in most organizations through training programs. Many organizations establish training groups within the personnel department as a mechanism for both initiating and implementing cognitive change. Training departments can be used to socialize new employees into their jobs' best interaction patterns and role requirements. Training departments also focus on specific skills, both technical and managerial, that employees need to advance to higher-level jobs. Formal training can be accomplished through a variety of techniques, including case studies, business simulations or games, films, videotapes, and lectures. Many organizations send employees to training programs in their areas of expertise. An employee who has been assigned to the budget department may attend a budgeting course offered by the American Management Association. Educational organizations specialize in offering a variety of supervisory and management training courses, including communication, bargaining, time management, and leadership. Formal training is a powerful way to instruct employees in the role requirements and technical skills associated with their jobs.

Exhibit 18.8 is an example of how a coordinated training program can influence the entire organization.[43] Musashi Semiconductor Works in Japan used formal training to introduce a new system for quality control. Corporate personnel taught most sessions. The entire training program took over three years to complete. The first training sessions were with senior management, and subsequent sessions worked down through the hierarchy to acquaint all employees with the necessary skills for the program.

Organizational Development Organizational development, often called OD, refers to planned organizational changes that focus on the quality of human relationships. **Organizational development** utilizes behavioral science approaches to create a more open and honest atmosphere in organizations to

EXHIBIT 18.7
Cognitive Change Versus Emotional Change and Type of Behavioral Change

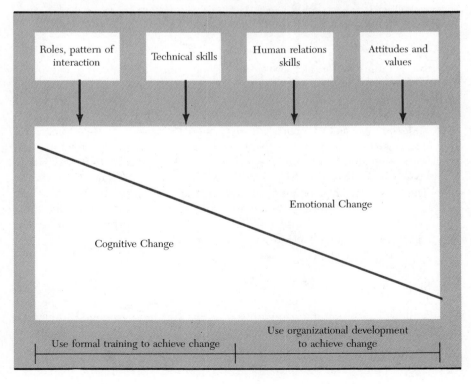

EXHIBIT 18.8
Training Programs for Small Group Systems Implementation

Position in Plant Hierarchy:		
General Managers	**Top Management Course (O)** Motivation seminar Leadership seminar	
	Small Group Course (O) Group structures seminar	
Department Heads		**Management Course (O)**
	Small Group Course (H) Planning methods seminar	
Section Heads		**Middle Management Course (O)**
	Small Group Seminar (H) Statistical analysis technique seminar	
Senior Supervisors (Engineers and Subsection Managers)	**Small Group Course (H)** Group management training seminar Auditing seminar	
Foremen		**Lower Management Course (P)**
Workers		**Orientation (P)**

Key:
(O) = Course held outside the company
(H) = Held at parent headquarters
(P) = Held at plant

Time

SOURCE: William Davidson, "Small Group Activity at Musashi Semiconductor Works," *Sloan Management Review* 23 (Spring, 1982): 5. Used with permission.

improve communication and problem solving among individuals and groups. OD is frequently a large-scale activity that involves the entire organization. The goal is to improve organizational performance by creating an improved organizational climate and employee functioning and well being. The values that underlie typical OD efforts are described in Exhibit 18.9. A successful organizational development intervention leads to greater use of human resources by engaging employees as much as possible in organizational activities. Employees will become active problem solvers and contribute fully to the organization rather than being treated as just another part of the production process doing routine work.[44] People are given an opportunity to develop their human potential, their work is made more challenging, and people are given the opportunity to influence the work environment.

OD Steps   Organizational development is a difficult type of change that usually requires help from outside experts. OD specialists diagnose problems within the organization and provide the intensive training needed to change basic attitudes and values. Three major steps in organizational development are initial diagnosis, data collection, and intervention.[45]

EXHIBIT 18.9
Basic Values Implemented Through Organizational Development

- Development of Human Potential
- Appreciation for Unique and Complex Needs of Employees
- Emphasis on Collaboration Rather than Competition
- Provide Challenging Work, Opportunity to Influence Organization
- Develop Climate of Trust, Authentic Behavior, Expression of Feelings

---

SOURCE: Adapted from Anthony P. Raia and Newton Margulies, "Organizational Change and Development," in Steven Kerr (ed.) *Organizational Behavior* (Columbus, OH: Grid Publishing, 1979): 355-378, and Robert Tannenbaum and Sheldon A. Davis, "Values, Man, and Organizations," *Industrial Management Review* (Winter 1969): 67-86.

The first step of diagnosis occurs when the OD consultant works with managers to determine why productivity is low or why employees are unsatisfied. Discussions with senior managers and interviews with middle-level managers help define the current state of the organization. Once the organizational development consultant identifies the general type of problem, then a more formal data collection process can be designed.

The formal data collection step often involves questionnaire surveys and group discussions. These surveys encompass specific organizational characteristics, such as job satisfaction, leadership style, climate, decentralization, and employee participation in decision making. Group discussions can also be part of the formal data collection phase. Data are analyzed and specific conclusions are derived based upon comparison with organizational norms. Problem areas in specific departments may be identified. Data collection and analysis are used to guide the formal OD intervention.

The intervention step involves the training to overcome the problems that the consultants identified. The intervention may include a three-to-five day retreat for employees to discuss how to develop a better climate. The intervention may involve feedback to a particular department concerning job satisfaction, or it may involve specific training in areas of leadership motivation that were identified as problems. Intervention also includes the maintenance of desired new behaviors, which can be done by establishing an internal task force to monitor organizational performance and conduct follow-up surveys. Additional interventions can be undertaken as needed to maintain job satisfaction and a sense of challenging work and involvement for employees.

OD Techniques Organizational development consultants and researchers have developed a number of behavioral science techniques for diagnosing problems and bringing about behavioral changes in organizations. Three of the most important techniques are survey feedback, team building, and quality circles.

Survey feedback. **Survey feedback** begins with a questionnaire given to employees about values, climate, participation, and innovation within the organization.[46] Typical questions that appear on the employee questionnaire are as follows.

	Never true	Sometimes true	Always true
1. Employees at different levels (supervisors, subordinates) treat one another as equals here.			
2. Supervision is very good in my department.			
3. There are many close friendships among employees in this organization.			
4. There is very little conflict among employees in my department.			

The distinguishing feature of the survey feedback technique is that answers are tabulated for each group, department, division, and for the organization as a whole, and then they are fed back to employees. The OD consultant meets with each group and explains what the results mean. The participants see where they stand in relation to other departments and can use the feedback to discuss problem areas and issues that have been troubling them. The survey feedback technique is quite powerful because it helps employees and managers confront problems of leadership, conflict, and job satisfaction. Follow up action by the OD consultant involves training programs to improve communication, leadership, participation, or other areas identified by the questionnaire as needing improvement. Each department may have different problems, so the intervention can be tailored to suit department or work-group needs.

Team building. **Team building** involves a series of exercises to help employees who work together learn to act and function as a team.[47] Most team development activities focus on the members of a work group or department who work together on a day-to-day basis. Team building activities can also be used to assist the functioning of temporary teams, such as a task force formed with members from different departments. A change agent works with group members to increase communication skills, facilitate their ability to confront one another in problem areas, and to become a cohesive unit. One form of team building has evolved from Blake and Mouton's work on the Managerial Grid, which was discussed briefly in Chapter 13.[48] Team members learn to define their values with respect to concern for people versus concern for production. Members are able to confront these values and decide which are best for the team's situation. Training based on the managerial grid system helps groups attain high levels on both the production and people dimensions. Barriers that would thwart team development are identified and overcome during the training process.

Quality circles. **Quality circles** are voluntary groups of employees who work on a similar task or share similar responsibility. The concept of quality circles has evolved in recent years as a way to improve the quality of work life for lower-level employees. Employees agree to meet on a regular basis and try to solve problems related to their work efficiency. Because people are brought together for the purpose of attaining organizational objectives, these meetings are sometimes called conference groups. The meetings are not intended to air personal gripes or to examine interpersonal relationships. Members are encouraged to meet regularly, perhaps once a week. They select a problem area for analysis and attempt to develop a list of potential solutions. The recommended solution is made available to management, and if acceptable, it is implemented immediately. Many large companies have introduced quality circles, with promising results. The U.S. Postal Service uses what it calls the conference method to bring about planned change in the fifty largest post offices. Lower-level employees and supervisors begin by identifying problems and are encouraged to initiate changes on their own to improve organizational effectiveness. Quality circles do seem to help increase employee involvement, and they allow employees to take more pride in their work. The result is improved quality and efficiency.[49]

Summary. The organizational development process can be effective for changing the values and quality of work life within organizations. However, techniques such as quality circles, team building, and survey feedback require the help of experts. Many organizations acquire this expertise through a consulting relationship. Outside experts have experience with the formal process of problem diagnosis, data collection, and intervention. Other organizations hire full-time experts to act as internal change agents. Ebasco Services, for example, uses internal change agents to manage the behavioral changes their organization needed due to problems with a matrix structure.

UP CLOSE 18.4:   Ebasco Services Inc.

Ebasco provides engineering and consulting services to the utilities industry. A few years ago, a matrix management structure was installed similar to the matrix described in Chapter 12. The structural innovation created dual reporting relationships so engineers had to satisfy two or more bosses. The matrix structure worked well enough, but over time it caused friction and confusion among employees. Problems appeared most often at the sites for construction of nuclear power plants. Because these projects take more than a decade to complete, and changes in government regulations and technology are apt to throw schedules off at any time, some problems are expected. In addition, reporting relationships change as a project moves from one stage to another.

Multiple pressures make cooperation essential, but employees still tend to be protective of their speciality and resentful of employees with different priori-

ties. Andrew Manzini, vice president for human resources, developed an organizational development staff to diffuse the emotional side of these conflicts.

The OD programs have been diverse because they were developed to solve specific problems. Over one hundred formal seminars have been scheduled to help employees learn the appropriate matrix behaviors. A forty-five hour supervisory development course has been credited with smoothing relations among personnel. For example, the project manager for a nuclear power plant in Louisiana lost his construction manager to another company. The project manager moved on-site, and construction people saw his presence as a threat. He explained the problem to Manzini, who developed a two-day team-building session for the fifteen top people at the site. Manzini was able to create a positive, nonthreatening atmosphere where both construction personnel and project personnel could exorcise their resentments and fears. The result made the on-site presence of the project manager more comfortable for everyone. The availability of OD experts means that whenever a division or site has problems someone can be called in. OD people are often used to run important meetings. When there is friction, the participants can get angry at the facilitator rather than at each other.

OD facilitators have been so successful that the top echelon at Ebasco has started to use a team-building approach. They established a two-day meeting of twelve senior corporate staff members to discuss long-range planning and other strategic areas as a team. Next they will look at matters of motivation and internal conflict.

The organizational development training has not removed all problems. Technical employees still feel the technical job is most important, and engineers feel they are spending too much time reporting, planning, scheduling, and budgeting. Still, follow-up surveys of employee attitudes and performance show that emotional tensions at project sites have been reduced dramatically through OD diagnosis and intervention.[50]

Ebasco illustrates how organizational development can be used to change basic attitudes and resolve emotional conflicts among employees. The matrix was a structural change, which was originally implemented in a top-down fashion. But the new reporting relationships and behavioral patterns caused problems with people that required OD training to resolve. Ebasco illustrates how change in the administrative component of the organization can create a need for change in the human component as well.

SUMMARY

The purpose of this chapter has been to explore the process of organizational change. Innovation and change is important to managers, because change is an ongoing fact of life in organizations. Organizations are open systems that must adapt to the external environment. Understanding change processes within organizations enables managers to apply the methods and concepts studied in this book to solve organizational problems.

A model of the change process identified the stages that must be present for change to be successful. These steps include a perceived need for change, problem analysis and search, selection and approval of a specific change, a plan to overcome resistance, implementing the change, and continued implementation or rejection of the change.

Next we examined change at the micro level. The initiation of change should harness the creativity of employees. Factors associated with creative individuals and with creative departments were identified. The idea champion has an important role in pushing a change to gain acceptance. Implementation of change often is associated with resistance. Reasons for resistance were identified, and techniques for overcoming resistance to change were defined.

Change at the macro level is concerned with overall strategies for change in the technological, administrative, and human components of the organization. Technological change is accomplished through the ambidextrous model, which says the organization must establish conditions for both the initiation and implementation of change. Administrative change occurs when an organization experiences changes in environmental sectors relevant to administration. Frequent administrative changes are created in an organic administrative core and implemented downward to a mechanistically structured technical core. Behavioral change that involves cognitive skills can be accomplished through training procedures. Organizational development techniques can be used with the help of outside experts to initiate and implement changes in employee attitudes, values, and work climate.

KEY WORDS

administrative change	human change	steps of change
ambidextrous model	idea champion	process
behavioral change	innovation	survey feedback
change	OD steps	switching structures
coercion	organizational	team building
creativity	development	technological change
creative department	quality circles	temporary teams
dual core model	social disruption	

DISCUSSION QUESTIONS

1. Why do individuals resist change in organizations? What strategy would you use to overcome each cause of resistance?

2. Carefully planned change is assumed to be more effective than change that is not planned. Do you agree, or should organizational change be allowed to follow its own course? Discuss.

3. What are the characteristics of a creative department? How do these relate to creative individuals?
4. Which role is more critical to successful organizational change on a continuous basis, the creator of change or the idea champion? Explain.
5. Explain the ambidextrous model. How is it applied in organizations?
6. How does organization structure differ to facilitate administrative change versus technology change? Do the same organizations typically have to adopt both administrative and technical changes?
7. What values underlie organizational development? How do these values differ from the values that seem to underlie administrative or technical change? Discuss.
8. One management consultant said, "Every organization should experience survey feedback every five years. It's beneficial for every department and employee." Discuss whether you agree with this statement and why.
9. Many organizations create a separate staff department to deal with problems that arise. Is this a logical approach based on concepts in this chapter? Explain.
10. In the Ebasco **Up Close,** behavioral change followed the implementation of structural change. Discuss the extent to which this relationship between structure and behavioral change might exist for many reorganizations.

CASE 18.1. Sunflower Incorporated

Sunflower Incorporated is a large distribution company with over 5000 employees and gross sales of over $400 million (1981). The company purchases and distributes salty snack foods and liquor to independent retail stores throughout the United States and Canada. Salty snack foods include corn chips, potato chips, cheese curls, tortilla chips, and peanuts. The U.S. and Canada are divided into twenty-two regions, each with its own central warehouse, salespeople, finance department, and purchasing department. The company distributes national as well as local brands and packages some items under private labels. The head office encourages each region to be autonomous because of local tastes and practices. The northeastern U.S., for example, consumes a greater percentage of Canadian whiskey and American bourbon, while the West consumes more light liquors such as vodka, gin, and rum. Snack foods in the Southwest are often seasoned to reflect Mexican tastes.

Early in 1980, Sunflower began using a financial reporting system that compared sales, costs, and profits across regions. Management was surprised to learn that profits varied widely. By 1982, the differences were so great that management decided some standarization was necessary. They believed that highly profitable regions were sometimes using lower quality items, even seconds, to boost profit margins. This practice could hurt Sunflower's image. Other regions were facing intense price competition in order to hold market share. National distributors were pushing hard to increase their market share. Frito-Lay, Borden, Nabisco, Procter & Gamble (Pringles), and Standard Brands (Planter's) were pushing hard to increase market share by cutting prices and launching new products.

As these problems accumulated, Mr. Jack Steelman, president of Sunflower, decided to create a new position to monitor pricing and purchasing practices. Mrs. Agnes Archer was hired from the finance department of a competing organization. Her new title was director of pricing and purchasing, and she reported to the vice president of finance,

Mr. Mason. Steelman and Mason gave Archer great latitude in organizing her job and encouraged her to establish whatever rules and procedures were necessary. She was also encouraged to gather information from each region. Each region was notified of her appointment by an official memo sent to the regional managers. A copy of the memo was posted on each warehouse bulletin board. The announcement was also made in the company newspaper.

After three weeks on the job, Archer decided that pricing and purchasing decisions should be standarized across regions. As a first step, she wanted the financial executive in each region to notify her of any change in local prices of more than 3 percent. She also decided that all new contracts for local purchases of more than $5000 should be cleared through her office. (Approximately 60 percent of items distributed in the regions was purchased in large quantities and supplied from the home office. The other 40 percent was purchased and distributed within the region.) Archer believed that the only way to standardize operations was for each region to notify the home office in advance of any change in prices or purchases. Archer discussed the proposed policy with Mason. He agreed, so they submitted a formal proposal to the president and board of directors, who approved the plan. Sunflower was moving into the peak holiday season, so Archer wanted to implement the new procedures right away. She decided to send a telex to the financial and purchasing executives in each region notifying them of the new procedures. The change would be inserted in all policy and procedure manuals throughout Sunflower within four months.

Archer showed a draft of the telex to Mason and invited his comments. Mobley said the telex was an excellent idea but wondered if it was sufficient. The regions handled hundreds of items, and managers were used to decentralized decision making. Mason suggested that Archer visit the regions and discuss purchasing and pricing policies with the executives. Archer refused, saying that the trips would be expensive and time-consuming. She had so many things to do at headquarters that the trips were impossible. Mason also suggested waiting to implement the procedures until after the annual company meeting in three months. Archer said this would take too long, because the procedures would not take effect until after the peak sales season. She believed the procedures were needed now. The telexes went out the next day.

During the next few days, replies came in from most of the regions. The executives were in agreement with the telex, and said they would be happy to cooperate.

Eight weeks later, Mrs. Archer had not received notices from any regions about local price or purchase changes. Other executives who had visited regional warehouses indicated to her that the regions were busy as usual. Regional executives seemed to be following usual procedures for that time of year.[51]

CASE QUESTIONS

1. Using the model of managed organization change (Exhibit 18.1), describe the incident in the case.
2. What type of change is being proposed? According to the chapter, what type of structure is necessary for this change?
3. Do you believe the innovation has been successful? If not, what should have been done?

NOTES

1. William H. Starbuck, "Organization as Action Generators," *American Sociological Review* 48 (1983): 91–102; and Paul C. Nystrom and William H. Starbuck, "To Avoid Organizational Crises, Unlearned," *Organizational Dynamics* (Spring 1984): 53–65.
2. Alvin Toffler, *Future Shock* (New York: Random House, 1970); J. Naisbett, *Megatrends* (New York: Warner Books, 1982).
3. Eric Morgenthaler, "Featherbone Maker Prospers by Adapting as Product Dies," *The Wall Street Journal*, October 11, 1982, p. 21.
4. "Success is a Shoe-in for Genesco's New Venture Marketing Division," *Nashville!* (April 1982): 76–78.
5. "Sliding Toward Oblivion," *Newsweek*, July 23, 1984, p. 11A.
6. "Here Comes the 'Intrapreneur'," *Business Week*, July 18, 1983, pp. 188–190.
7. John L. Pierce and Andre L. Delbecq, "Organization Structure, Individual Attitudes and Innovation," *Academy of Management Review* 2 (1977): 27–37; Michael Aiken and Jerald Hage, "The Organic Organization and Innovation," *Sociology* 5 (1971): 63–82.
8. Pierce and Delbecq, "Organizational Structure"; Aiken and Hage, "The Organic Organization and Innovation."
9. This model is based on G. Zaltman, R. Duncan, and J. Holbeck, *Innovations and Organizations* (New York: John Wiley & Sons, 1973) and Richard L. Daft and Selwyn Becker, *Innovation in Organizations: Innovation Adoption in School Organizations* (New York: Elsevier, 1978), Chapter 6.
10. Margaret Loeb, "Royal Crown Shakes Soft-Drink Business with Changes but Never Quite Gets Ahead," *The Wall Street Journal*, May 24, 1982, p. 21.
11. "Success is a Shoe-in for Genesco's New Venture Marketing Division," *Nashville!* (April 1982): 76–78.
12. Jabby Lowe, Greg Millsap, and Bill Breedlove, "International Harvester," Unpublished manuscript, Texas A&M University, 1982; "Harvester Revamps MRO Buying with Big Results," *Purchasing*, October 8, 1981, p. 19, 23.
13. Charles Pearlman, "A Theoretical Model for Creativity," *Education* 103 (1983): 294–305; Gary A. Steiner (ed.), *The Creative Organization* (Chicago: University of Chicago Press, 1965), p. 4.
14. Alok K. Chakrabrati, "The Role of Champion in Product Innovation," *California Management Review* 17 (1974): 58–62.
15. Pearlman, "A Theoretical Model for Creativity"; Steiner, *The Creative Organization*; Gordon Vessels, "The Creative Process: An Open-Systems Conceptualization," *The Journal of Creative Behavior* 16 (1982): 185–196.
16. Augustus Abbey and John W. Dickson, "R & D Work Climate and Innovation in Semiconductors," *Academy of Management Journal*, 26 (1983): 362–368; Rosabeth Moss Kanter, "The Middle Manager as Innovator," *Harvard Business Review* (July-August 1982): 95–105; Donald C. Pelz and Frank M. Andrews, *Scientists in Organizations: Productive Climates for Research and Development* (Ann Arbor, MI: Institute for Social Research, 1976); Victor A. Thompson, *Bureaucracy and Innovation* (University, AL: University of Alabama Press, 1969).
17. Paula Doody, Pat Hall, and Mike Nelson, "General Mills," Unpublished paper, Texas A&M University, 1983; "Look Who's Playing with Toys!" *Forbes*, December 15, 1971, p. 22.
18. "The 'Blunders' Making Millions for 3M," *Business Week*, July 16, 1984, p. 118.
19. Jay R. Galbraith, "Designing the Innovating Organization," *Organizational Dynamics* (Winter 1982): 5–25.
20. Michael W. Lawless, Abe Feinberg, Alan Glassman, and William C. Bengtson, "Enhancing the Chances of Successful OR/MS Implementation: The Role of the Advocate," *Omega* 10 (1982): 107–114.
21. Richard L. Daft and Patricia J. Bradshaw, "The Process of Horizontal Differentiation: Two Models," *Administrative Science Quarterly* 25 (1980): 441–456.
22. Galbraith, "Designing the Innovating Organization"; Chakrabrati, "The Role of Champion in Product Innovation."

23. Daft and Becker, *Innovation in Organizations*.
24. Rino J. Patti, "Organizational Resistance and Change: The View From Below," *Social Service Review* 48 (1974): 371–372.
25. G. Zaltman and R. Duncan, *Strategies for Planned Change* (New York: Wiley Interscience, 1977).
26. Paul R. Lawrence, "How to Deal with Resistance to Change," in G. W. Dalton, R. P. Lawrence, and L. E. Greiner, *Organizational Change and Development* (Homewood, IL: Irwin and Dorsey, 1970), pp. 181–197.
27. Daft and Becker, *Innovation in Organizations*.
28. Zaltman and Duncan, *Strategies for Planned Change;* H. R. Knudson, R. T. Woodworth, and C. H. Bell, *Management: An Experiential Approach* (New York: McGraw-Hill, 1979), Chapter 7.
29. John P. Kotter and Leonard A. Schlesinger, "Choosing Strategies for Change," *Harvard Business Review* 57 (March–April, 1979): 106–114.
30. William R. King and Jaime I. Rodriguez, "Participative Design of Strategic Decision Support Systems: An Empirical Assessment," *Management Science* 27 (1981): 717–726.
31. "How D&B Organizes for a New-Product Blitz," *Business Week*, November 16, 1981, pp. 87–90; and "Dun & Bradstreet Forms a New Business, Plans to Close Old One," *The Wall Street Journal*, September 18, 1981, p. 38.
32. Anthony P. Aria and Newton Margulies, "Organizational Change and Development," in Steven Kerr (ed.), *Organizational Behavior* (Columbus, OH: Grid Publishing Inc., 1979), pp. 355–378.
33. Bill Tidwell, John Van Dyke, Lisa Rotter, and Tommy Parker, "The Adolph Coors Story," Unpublished manuscript, Texas A&M University, 1982.
34. Robert B. Duncan, "The Ambidextrous Organization: Designing Dual Structures for Innovation," in Ralph H. Killman, Louis R. Pondy and Dennis Slevin (eds.), *The Management of Organization*, Volume 1 (New York: North-Holland, 1976), pp. 167–188.
35. Rolph P. Lynton, "Linking an Innovative Subsystem into the System," *Administrative Science Quarterly* 14 (1969): 398–414.
36. William P. Shanklin and John K. Ryans, Jr., "Organizing for High-Tech Marketing," *Harvard Business Review* (November–December, 1984): 164–171.
37. Erik Larson and Carrie Dolan, "Large Computer Firms Sprout Little Divisions for Good, Fast Work," *The Wall Street Journal*, August 19, 1983, pp. 1–11.
38. Peter D. Petre, "Meet the Lean, Mean, New IBM," *Fortune*, June 13, 1983, pp. 69–82; "How the PC Project Changed the Way IBM Thinks," *Business Week*, October 3, 1983, pp. 86–90.
39. F. Damenpour and W. M. Evan, "Organizational Innovation and Performance: The Problem of 'Organizational Lag'," *Administrative Science Quarterly* 29 (1984): 392–409.
40. Richard L. Daft, "A Dual-Core Model of Organizational Innovation," *Academy of Management Journal* 21 (1978): 193–210; Richard L. Daft, "Bureaucratic vs. Nonbureaucratic Structure in the Process of Innovation and Change," in Samuel B. Bacharach, (ed.), *Perspectives in Organizational Sociology: Theory and Research* (Greenwich, CT: JAI Press, 1982), pp. 129–166.
41. Daft, "A Dual-Core Model of Organizational Innovation"; G. H. Gaertner, K. N. Gaertner, and David M. Akinnusi, "Environment, Strategy and the Implementation of Administrative Change: The Case of Civil Service Reform," *Academy of Management Journal* 27 (1984): 525–543.
42. Paul R. Lawrence and Jay W. Lorsch, *Developing Organizations: Diagnosis and Actions* (Reading, MA: Addison-Wesley, 1969).
43. William H. Davidson, "Small Group Activity at Musashi Semiconductor Works," *Sloan Management Review* 23 (Spring, 1982): 3–14.
44. Raia and Margulies, "Organizational Change and Development."
45. Michael Beer, *Organizational Change and Development: A Systems View* (Santa Monica, CA: Goodyear, 1980).
46. David A. Nadler, *Feedback and Organization Development: Using Data-Based Method* (Reading, MA: Addison-Wesley, 1977).

47. W. G. Dyer, *Team Building: Issues and Alternatives* (Reading, MA: Addison-Wesley, 1977).

48. Robert R. Blake and Jane S. Mouton, *The Managerial Grid* (Houston, TX: Gulf Publishing, 1964).

49. B. A. Scott, *Quality Circles: An Employee Participation Program that Works.* President's Papers, Fall 1980 OD Network Conference, San Francisco, California, October, 1980.

50. "How Ebasco Makes the Matrix Method Work," *Business Week,* June 15, 1981, pp. 126–131.

51. From Richard L. Daft, *Organization Theory and Design* (St. Paul: West, 1983), pp. 334–336. This case was inspired by "Frito-Lay May Find Itself in a Competition Crunch," *Business Week,* July 19, 1982, p. 186, and "Dashman Company," in Paul R. Lawrence and John A. Seiler, *Organizational Behavior and Administration: Cases, Concepts, and Research Findings* (Homewood, IL: Irwin and Dorsey, 1965), pp. 16–17.

ACKNOWLEDGMENTS

22 Reprinted with permission, INC. magazine, (June, 1982). Copyright © 1982 by INC. Publishing Company, 38 Commercial Wharf, Boston, MA 02110.

45 From *Explorations in Personality*, edited by Henry A. Murray. Copyright 1938 by Oxford University Press, Inc. Renewed 1966 by Henry A. Murray. Reprinted by permission of the publisher.

55–60 Reprinted by permission of the Harvard Business Review. "Case of the Plateaued Performer" by E. K. Warren, T. P. Ference, and James A. F. Stoner (January/February 1975). Copyright © 1975 by the President and Fellows of Harvard College; all rights reserved.

72, 109, 111, 161, 163, 165 From *Introduction to Organizational Behavior*, second edition, by Richard M. Steers. Copyright © 1984 by Scott, Foresman and Company.

97 From *Psychology of Work Behavior*, third edition, by Frank J. Landy. Copyright © 1980 by Richard D. Irwin, Inc. Reprinted by permission.

104 From *Managerial Attitudes and Performance* by Lyman W. Porter and Edward E. Lawler III. Copyright © 1968 by Richard D. Irwin, Inc. Reprinted by permission.

119–122 From *False Promises* by Stanley Aronowitz. Copyright © 1973 by McGraw-Hill Book Company. Reprinted by permission.

126 From "Performance Appraisal—A Survey of Current Practices" by Alan H. Locher and Kenneth S. Teel in *Personnel Journal*, May 1977. Copyright © 1977 by Personnel Journal, Costa Mesa, California. Reprinted by permission. All rights reserved.

131 From *Increasing Productivity Through Performance Appraisal* by Gary P. Latham and Kenneth N. Wexley. Copyright © 1981 by Addison-Wesley Publishing Company. Reprinted by permission.

132 From *Personnel: A Diagnostic Approach*, third edition, by William F. Glueck. Copyright © 1982 by Business Publications, Inc. Reprinted by permission.

133 Appendix A from "The Assessment Center as Aid in Management Development" by William C. Byham, *Training and Development Journal*, December 1971. Copyright © 1971 by the American Society for Training and Development, Inc. Reprinted by permission. All rights reserved.

170 From "Motivation Through the Design of Work: Text of a Theory" in *Organizational Behavior and Human Performance* by J. R. Hackman and G. R. Oldham. Copyright © 1976 by Academic Press, Inc. Reprinted by permission.

179–183 From *Managing Organizations: Readings and Cases* by David A. Nadler, Michael L. Tushman and Nina G. Hatvany, pp. 492–496. Copyright © 1982 by David A. Nadler, Michael L. Tushman and Nina G. Hatvany. Reprinted by permission of Little, Brown and Company.

182 From "Development of the Job Diagnostic Survey" by J. Richard Hackman and Greg R. Oldham in *Journal of Applied Psychology* 60:159–170. Reprinted by permission.

193 From *The Social Psychology of Organizations*, second edition, by Daniel Katz and Robert L. Kahn. Copyright © 1978 by John Wiley & Sons, Inc. Reprinted by permission.

196 Adaptation of figure on page 92 from *Group Dynamics: Research and Theory*, Third Edition, by Dorwin Cartwright and Alvin Zander. Copyright 1953, © 1960 by Harper & Row, Publishers, Inc. Copyright © 1968 by Dorwin Cartwright and Alvin Zander. Reprinted by permission of Harper & Row, Publishers, Inc.

255 From *Organization Design, Development and Behavior,* Karl O. Magnusen (Glenview, IL: Scott, Foresman, 1977), p. 19.

278–281 From *Organizational Behavior and the Practice of Management*, David R. Hampton, Charles E. Summer, and Ross A. Webber (Glenview, IL: Scott, Foresman, 1982), pp. 751–755.

350–357   From "Layoff at Old College," Allen J. Schuh. Reprinted by permission of the author.

407, 418   Gary A. Ukl, *Leadership in Organizations*, © 1981, p. 70. Reprinted by permission of Prentice-Hall, Inc., Englewood Cliffs, New Jersey.

426   "Up the Organization," Robert Townsend. © 1974 Alfred A. Knopf, Inc. Reprinted with permission.

431–434   "Budget Motors, Inc.," M. Sami Kassem, University of Toledo. Reprinted by permission of the author.

460   "Whoops: How it Happened," Reprinted with the permission of *Dun's Business Month*, October 1983, Copyright 1983, Dun & Bradstreet Publications Corporation.

462   "Hope Springs Eternal," Ellen Benoit and Stephen Kindel, *Forbes*, August 13, 1984, p. 34. Reprinted with permission.

467–472   From John A. Dunn, Jr., "Organizational Decision Making," in Walter C. Swap and Associates (eds.), *Group Decision Making* (Beverly Hills, CA: SAGE, 1984): 280–310. Reprinted with permission.

492–495   J. Patrick Wright, "Why I Quit General Motors," Chapter One from *On a Clear Day You Can See General Motors*. Copyright © 1979 by J. Patrick Wright. Reprinted with permission from Multimedia Product Development, Inc.

498, 502   From *Organizational Behavior and Performance*, third edition, by Andrew D. Szilagy and Marc J. Wallace. Copyright © 1983 by Scott, Foresman and Company.

515   From *Managing Group and Intergroup Relations*, edited by Jay W. Lorsch and Paul R. Lawrence. Copyright © 1972 Richard D. Irwin, Inc. Reprinted by permission of Richard D. Irwin, Inc. and the authors.

518–525   This case study was prepared by Professor Peter McGrady of Lakehead University School of Business as a basis for class discussion rather than to illustrate either effective or ineffective handling of an administrative situation. Copyright © 1982 by Lakehead University, Thunder Bay, Ontario. Reprinted by permission of the author.

510–511   From "Toward Multidimensional Values in Teaching: The Example of Conflict Behaviors" by Kenneth W. Thomas in *Academy of Management Review*, July 1977. Copyright © 1977 by the Academy of management. Reprinted by permission.

512   Kenneth Thomas, "Conflict and Conflict Management" in M. D. Dunnette, ed., *Handbook of Industrial and Organizational Behavior*. Copyright © 1976 by John Wiley & Sons, Inc. Reprinted by permission.

558–563   "Southern Bank," Jack L. Rettig, Oregon State University. Reprinted with permission.

594–595   From *Organization Theory and Design*, Richard L. Daft. © 1983 by West Publishing Company. All rights reserved. pp. 334–336. Reprinted with permission.